HING
AT ITS BEST

TEACHING AT ITS BEST

A Research-Based Resource for College Instructors

Fourth Edition

Linda B. Nilson

JOSSEY-BASS
A Wiley Imprint
www.josseybass.com

Published by Jossey-Bass
A Wiley Brand
One Montgomery Street, Suite 1000, San Francisco, CA 94104-4594—www.josseybass.com

Jossey-Bass books and products are available through most bookstores. To contact Jossey-Bass directly call our Customer Care Department within the U.S. at 800-956-7739, outside the U.S. at 317-572-3986, or fax 317-572-4002.

Wiley publishes in a variety of print and electronic formats and by print-on-demand. Some material included with standard print versions of this book may not be included in e-books or in print-on-demand. If this book refers to media such as a CD or DVD that is not included in the version you purchased, you may download this material at http://booksupport.wiley.com. For more information about Wiley products, visit www.wiley.com.

Library of Congress Cataloging-in-Publication Data

Names: Nilson, Linda Burzotta, author.
Title: Teaching at its best : a research-based resource for college
   instructors / Linda B. Nilson.
Other titles: Jossey-Bass higher and adult education series.
Description: Fourth edition. | San Francisco, CA : Jossey-Bass, 2016. |
   Series: Jossey-bass higher and adult education series
Identifiers: LCCN 2016015848 (print) | LCCN 2016020998 (ebook) | ISBN
   9781119096320 (pbk.) | ISBN 9781119107804 (ePDF) | ISBN 9781119107798
   (ePub) | ISBN 9781119107804 (pdf) | ISBN 9781119107798 (epub)
Subjects: LCSH: College teaching. | Effective teaching.
Classification: LCC LB2331 .N55 2016 (print) | LCC LB2331 (ebook) | DDC
   378.1/7—dc23
LC record available at https://lccn.loc.gov/2016015848

Cover design: Wiley
Cover image: © aon168/iStockphoto

Printed in the United States of America
FOURTH EDITION
PB Printing 10 9 8 7 6 5 4 3 2

The Jossey-Bass
Higher and Adult Education Series

CONTENTS

Part 4
INQUIRY-BASED METHODS
FOR SOLVING REAL-WORLD
PROBLEMS   191

Part 5
TOOLS AND TECHNIQUES
TO FACILITATE LEARNING   223

To all North American faculty
committed to teaching at its best

Linda B. Nilson is the founding director of Clemson University's Office of Teaching Effectiveness and Innovation. Her career as a full-time faculty development director spans over 25 years. Along with four editions of *Teaching at Its Best: A Research-Based Resource for College Instructors* (1998, 2003, 2010, 2016), she has authored three other books: *The Graphic Syllabus and the Outcomes Map: Communicating Your Course* (Jossey-Bass, 2007); *Creating Self-Regulated Learners: Strategies to Strengthen Students' Self-Awareness and Learning Skills* (Stylus, 2013); and *Specifications Grading: Restoring Rigor, Motivating Students, and Saving Faculty Time* (Stylus, 2015). Her current book project is *Online Teaching at Its Best* with coauthor Ludwika A. Goodson.

She has also coedited several books: *Enhancing Learning with Laptops in the Classroom* (with Barbara E. Weaver, Jossey-Bass, 2005) and volumes 25 through 28 of *To Improve the Academy: Resources for Faculty, Instructional, and Organizational Development* (with Douglas Reimondo Robertson, Anker, 2007, 2008; with Judith E. Miller, Jossey-Bass, 2009, 2010). *To Improve the Academy* is the major publication of the Professional and Organizational Development (POD) Network in Higher Education.

Her other publications include articles and book chapters on a range of topics: validity problems with student ratings, ways to measure learning in a course, the instability of faculty development careers, teaching with learning objects and mind maps, designing a graphic syllabus, improving student-peer feedback, teaching large classes, fostering critical thinking, and graduate student professional development.

Dr. Nilson has given well over 450 webinars, keynotes, and live workshops at conferences, colleges, and universities nationally and internationally on dozens of topics related to college teaching and academic career success. Her repertoire of speaking topics spans every chapter in this book, as well as early faculty career management and scholarly writing and publishing.

Before coming to Clemson in 1998, she directed the Center for Teaching at Vanderbilt University and the Teaching Assistant Development Program at the University of California, Riverside. At the latter institution, she developed the disciplinary cluster approach to training teaching assistants (TAs), a cost-effective way for a centralized unit to provide disciplinary-relevant instructional training. Her entrée into educational development came in the late 1970s while she was on the sociology faculty at UCLA. After distinguishing herself as an excellent instructor, her department selected her to establish and supervise its Teaching Assistant Training Program. As a sociologist, she conducted research in the areas of occupations and work, social stratification, political sociology, and disaster behavior. Her career also included a few years in the business world as a technical and commercial writer, a training workshop facilitator, and the business editor of a regional magazine.

Dr. Nilson is a member of the POD Network, which honored her work with the 2000 Innovation (Bright Idea) Award, and the Canada-based Society for Teaching and Learning in Higher Education. She has held leadership positions in the POD Network, the Southern Regional Faculty and Instructional Development Consortium, the Society for the Study of Social Problems, Toastmasters International, and Mensa.

A native of Chicago, Dr. Nilson was a National Science Foundation fellow at the University of Wisconsin, Madison, where she received her Ph.D. and M.S. degrees in sociology. She completed her undergraduate work in three years at the University of California, Berkeley, where she was elected to Phi Beta Kappa.

Back in 1997 when I was writing the first edition of *Teaching at Its Best*, I never dreamed I'd be revising and updating it for the third time 18 years later. It's a tremendous honor to be able to write the fourth edition of *any* book, but especially this one. Previous editions have inspired many unsolicited e-mails from faculty thanking me for helping them survive and thrive in their early years of teaching. I have saved and still treasure every e-mail. Each one motivates me to keep writing.

This edition, like the previous ones, is meant for a broad audience of new and experienced faculty who teach undergraduates at all types of postsecondary institutions. It is especially useful for those teaching relatively young students in a traditional classroom or hybrid environment. Some of the strategies explored in this book transfer smoothly to online courses, but that is more by happy accident than design. At this point, most undergraduate instruction is still based in classrooms and will continue to be this way for the foreseeable future.

One thing that all faculty share is a lack of discretionary time, and their professional development is among the first luxuries to be eliminated. So once again I wrote this new edition for people who don't have time to read a book—like you. The writing style is concise and informal, the paragraphs fairly short, the 28 chapters generously sectioned, and the table of contents detailed with chapter section headings. In addition, the six major parts are sequenced according to your likely chronological need for the material. Still, you can read the chapters in any order, and the text often cross-references other chapters that elaborate on a given subject. You can casually browse or quickly locate specific topics, skipping over tools you're already familiar with. I hope my preference for writing in the second person and the first-person plural personalizes the writing, eases reading, and simplifies the presentation of the instructions and challenges of various methods—all to facilitate your use of a new tool right away.

The research on college-level teaching, called the scholarship of teaching and learning (SoTL), provides the foundation and inspiration for this book. This fertile body of literature has expanded the toolbox for both classroom and technology-enhanced instruction. As with physical tools, you have to find the right tool for the job, but you can choose from among several right tools for any given teaching job. This book offers plenty of alternatives for facilitating student learning, enhancing instructor-student rapport, managing the classroom, and assessing student achievement. And it avoids playing champion for certain methods over others and for the latest innovations over the well-proven ones.

You will find the how-to's and why-do's for many teaching tools, along with their trade-offs, just as the research reports them. This is what you need to make your own choices and execute them with confidence.

Because quite a few colleges and universities use this book in extended new-faculty orientations and college teaching courses, a few colleagues have suggested publishing an accompanying instructor's manual with discussion questions. After considerable thought, I have decided instead to offer these general discussion and reflection questions, which will fit just about every chapter:

1. What common problems faced by faculty does the chapter try to prevent or solve? How well do the recommendations in the chapter prevent or solve these problems?
2. What practices explained in the chapter do you already implement? What have your results been?
3. What new practices explained in the chapter do you want to try? What reservations, if any, do you have?
4. What practices explained in the chapter do you think wouldn't work well for you, and why? Would this be due to your students' expectations, values, knowledge or skill background, or level of maturity; or your class sizes, time pressures, or teaching style; or some other reason? Can you think of any ways around these roadblocks?

These questions direct readers to the main purpose of this book: practical ways to maximize student learning, promote productive instructor-student relationships, and make the life of faculty easier and more rewarding. These three goals represent my personal job description as a faculty developer.

While preserving the most appreciated features of the third edition, this fourth edition has deleted a few less important chapters to make room for new material: seven new or mostly new chapters (3, 4, 7, 20, 22, 24, and 28); extensive evidence-based updates on major topics; and line-by-line editing to further improve the writing and eliminate nonessential words. Here is a synopsis of the book, along with the major changes in this edition.

Part 1, "Preparation for Teaching" guides you through the decisions you have to make and the tasks you have to complete before the term begins. Because understanding your students and how they learn anchors all your plans, this topic is featured in the first chapter. The section on how people learn brings in more principles and findings from cognitive and educational psychology, as well as more concrete implications for teaching. Chapter 2 on course design adds Wiggins and McTighe's (2005) six "facets of understanding," which blend cognitive with affective and social outcomes, and Hansen's (2011) approach to limiting outcomes to the "big ideas" and "enduring understandings" that your subject matter offers. The chapter also presents a simpler slant on the next steps in course development. The totally new third chapter gives you strategies for incorporating critical thinking into your course. Most importantly, it clears the fog around critical thinking, a teaching topic that has been clouded by a polyglot of competing schools of thought that rarely, if ever, cross-reference each other. Unlike any other published work, this chapter identifies common ground among them, presents lists of critical thinking outcomes suitable to various disciplinary groups, and lays out concrete questions and tasks from the different schools that engage students in critical thinking. Since instructional technology changes so quickly, chapter 4 treats many new teaching options that barely existed when the third edition came out: the flipped classroom, social media, mobile learning, e-textbooks, computer games, and MOOCs. It also summarizes research on how faculty and students view technology. Chapter 5, on the syllabus, explores the latest trend in downplaying course policies and rules and focusing on creating an encouraging learning environment, elucidating the relevance of the course material, and explaining the alignment among the outcomes, learning experiences, and assessments. The chapter also examines the backlash against the increasing length of the document and different approaches to trimming it. Finally, chapter 6 translates copyright guidelines into plain language; mercifully, the law hasn't changed much lately.

Part 2, "Human Factors," deals with ways to bring out the best in your students. It opens with a large new chapter on creating and maintaining a warm and welcoming classroom climate, which includes first-day social and content-related activities, proven ways to learn students' names, and guidelines for ensuring an inclusive learning environment. Chapter 8 on motivating students features a new section on how students' values about college affect their motivation and two additional theories of motivation—self-determination and social belonging—for a total of six. These six theories in turn generate 55 strategies for motivating students, many of which didn't appear in the third edition. Chapter 9 updates approaches for preventing and responding wisely to classroom incivility and features a new, comprehensive section on why students occasionally behave with apparent disrespect and indifference. The last chapter in part 2, chapter 10, gives the latest facts and figures on the prevalence of cheating, the students most likely to do it, and the reasons that they do it, including the very different view that international students have of plagiarism. It also suggests some new ways to prevent cheating among the 42 ways listed.

Part 3 "Tried-and-True Teaching Methods," opens with a chapter's worth of advice on selecting the teaching formats, methods, and moves that, according to the research, best help students achieve specific cognitive outcomes. Chapter 11 also provides a new graphical view of course and curriculum alignment and two new tools: Davis and Arend's (2013) model of learning outcomes, ways of learning, and teaching methods and Fink and Fink's (2009) three-column planning grid for developing a well-aligned course. The rest of the part 3 describes instructional methods that have proven their worth over many decades when implemented and managed properly: lecture, discussion (including questioning techniques), experiential learning, and group work.

Chapters 12 through 15, which cover these methods, contain a considerable amount of new material: statistics on student boredom during lecture; the "seventh-inning stretch" lecture break; the latest research on laptop versus long-hand note taking; more resources on simulations and games; statistics on the prevalence of service-learning courses; more resources about service-learning and a new topic, civic engagement; a section on maximizing the value of experiential learning with metacognitive and meta-emotional reflection assignments; additional caveats about group learning; a section on managing and troubleshooting in-class ad hoc groups; and a much expanded section on team-based learning.

Part 4, "Inquiry-Based Methods for Solving Real-World Problems," examines some old and some new teaching methods that focus on problem solving—solving, in particular, the kinds of multidisciplinary, open-ended, ill-defined problems that are hanging over our world. The most daunting ones are termed *wicked problems* because their conditions or constraints are incomplete, contradictory, or changing and often difficult to identify. In fact, solving one facet of such a problem may uncover or cause other problems. The strategies to teach students how to tackle such challenges fall in the category of inquiry-guided learning, which is the focus of chapter 16, which opens in this part. These strategies include the case method (chapter 17), problem-based learning (chapter 18), and challenging scientific activities that demand more than simple knowledge and comprehension (chapter 19). The new material in these chapters includes these added features: three examples of brief cases; two examples of problem-based learning (PBL) problems; updated online sources of well-designed cases, PBL problems, and STEM labs and problems; the latest research on PBL's effectiveness; updates on STEM education research; a section on modest, learning-enhancing changes faculty can make in STEM courses within a lecture format; and another section on how to make STEM problems more challenging and realistic, as well as where to find examples of such problems.

Part 5, "Tools and Techniques to Facilitate Learning," explains ways that you can help your students learn more efficiently and effectively, whatever the material or the discipline. It features two new chapters: chapter 20 about teaching students self-regulated learning and chapter 24 on improving student learning with feedback. Beginning with the major mental processes involved in learning and memory, chapter 20 makes the case that learning is something that learners ultimately do to themselves and presents questions that self-aware, self-regulated learners ask themselves as they study or do an assignment. After presenting evidence that self-regulated learning greatly increases student achievement, it describes almost 30 short assignments and activities that will acquaint your students with their learning process, enhance their learning, and demonstrate the benefits of self-regulated learning, while adding little or nothing to your grading workload. The scope of chapter 21 encompasses student compliance and comprehension of videos and podcasts, as well as readings to accommodate the conditions of the flipped classroom and online courses. In view of recent research discrediting learning styles, chapter 22 now focuses on the more evidence-based multimodal learning framework and provides guidance on teaching in each mode. However, it does recognize the value of two learning style models that are at least partially backed by neurological or psychological findings. Chapter 23 gives extensive attention to teaching in the especially powerful visual mode. After summarizing in depth why our feedback to students can fail, chapter 24 examines ways to make it succeed in a variety of contexts: student peer, self-assessment, student portfolios, and our own formative and summative feedback to students. It also considers classroom assessment techniques, which give fast feedback to both us and our students, and various forms of formative feedback on our teaching that we can solicit from our students and use for our own improvement.

Finally, part 6, "Assessments and Grading," first showcases best practices in preparing students for exams (chapter 25), constructing exams and assignments (chapter 26), and grading these assessments instruments (chapter 27). This last chapter contains a section explaining a new grading system, specifications (*specs*) grading, that has gained currency because of its advantages over our current system. For instance, research suggests that it raises academic standards, motivates students to do higher-quality work, increases their sense of responsibility for their grades, and reduces faculty grading time. Another new section in chapter 27 highlights self-regulated learning "exam wrappers" that help students learn by their mistakes. The holistic grading section in the same chapter displays an alternative version of a rubric that allows for more flexibility.

Chapter 28, the final one of the book, focuses how you are assessed as an instructor—specifically, what teaching effectiveness means, how institutions evaluate it, and how to document yours for review purposes. I have revised this chapter heavily in view of new research that undermines the validity of student ratings (aka student evaluations) as measures of teaching effectiveness. They are in fact unrelated to learning (they used to be related), more biased than in the past, and factually inaccurate much of the time. Unfortunately, almost all institutions use them to evaluate faculty teaching. As a result, they have created an unsustainably disjointed state of affairs: prioritizing and measuring student learning for accrediting agencies but rewarding and sanctioning faculty primarily on student satisfaction.

This book aims to enhance student *learning* and its covariants, such as motivation, self-efficacy, and self-regulation. As faculty, we regard helping students learn as our calling, the reason we do what do and the primary source of our career satisfaction. But because many of us depend on high ratings to stay employed, chapter 28 has a section on what you can (and cannot) do to improve your ratings. Fortunately, some of the instructor behaviors that raise ratings also promote learning. In addition, this chapter suggests a wide range of ways that you can document student learning in your courses, the criterion on which institutions *should* assess faculty to be consistent with how accrediting agencies assess institutions, colleges, and programs.

Topics not addressed in this book include most of the "high-impact practices" that Kuh (2008) recommends, such as first-year seminars and experiences, common core curricula, learning communities, diversity and global learning, internships, capstone courses, and undergraduate research. These are wonderful practices that encourage student persistence and retention, but they tend to grow out of institutional, departmental, and program decisions and initiatives. This book focuses on what *you*, the individual faculty member, can do, so it covers just a few high-impact student experiences like service-learning and collaborative assignments and projects. Another topic not dealt with here is how to conduct research on teaching and contribute to SoTL. The well-established literature on this topic does a far better job than I could in a page or two of this book.

Some colleagues may fault me for using the term *teaching* where others might prefer the phrase *teaching and learning*. To my mind, *teaching*, not *teaching and learning*, best describes what we faculty *do*, and this book is all about what we *do*. We intend the *effect* to be student learning, which is quite different from our behavior. I also choose to use the terms *faculty*, *instructors*, and occasionally *professors* to refer to those who teach at the postsecondary level; I reserve the word *teachers* for those at the K–12 level. Only in the past 10 years has the term *teacher* been attached to college and university faculty.

My gratitude for the support and help given me while writing the book extends to so many people, literally tens of thousands whom I will acknowledge first.

Thank you, all of you college and university faculty who are dedicated to teaching at its best. Not just because you may buy this book, but because you are working—tirelessly and devotedly for endless hours, despite modest recognition and remuneration—to improve the fates of multiple generations and ultimately the entire world. Such is the power of education. In my mind, I'm not exaggerating in the least, and this is why I dedicate this edition to you.

Thank you, Wiley and Jossey-Bass, for the opportunity to write this fourth edition. Thank you, Lesley Iura, vice president and publisher (education) at Wiley, and Alison Knowles, assistant editor at Jossey-Bass, for your sound business and book-writing advice and your reassurance that despite all the reorganization that Wiley underwent, you really wanted this book and believed in me as an author.

Thank you, members of the five writing groups I led for Clemson faculty and graduate students while working on this book—those of the summer and fall of 2014 and the spring, summer, and fall of 2015. I am indebted to you for holding me accountable for writing, revising, and editing every paragraph, section, and chapter and making it all come together. You pushed my progress along at an excellent pace.

Thank you, my beloved husband, Greg Bauernfeind, for encouraging my efforts, celebrating my progress, tolerating endless hours alone while I wrote, and taking care of business on the home front. Without you, I certainly would not have written all that I have over the past 15 years. You have helped me realize my potential and my dreams.

Linda B. Nilson
Clemson, South Carolina
April 2016

PART 1

PREPARATION FOR TEACHING

CHAPTER 1

Understanding Your Students and How They Learn

Whenever we prepare an oral presentation, a publication, or even a letter, the first issue we consider is our audience. Whoever that is influences our content, format, organization, sentence structure, and word choice. The same holds true in teaching. The nature of our students—their academic preparation, aspirations, and cognitive development—affects our choices of what and how to teach. We need to think of our job not as teaching art, biology, English, history, math, psychology, and so on but as teaching *students*.

For teaching, another critical consideration is how the human mind learns. Some ways of receiving and processing new knowledge are easier for people to attend to, grasp, and remember. Yet in spite of the fact that we are all responsible for encouraging human minds to learn, too few of us know how the human mind works.

Knowing both who your students are and how their minds learn is the starting point for teaching at its best.

■ YOUR STUDENT BODY PROFILE

If you're not already familiar with your student audience or your experience tells you that its composition has changed, your institution's admissions or student affairs office can provide the student data you need. At a minimum, you should find out the distributions and percentages on these variables: age, marital and family status, socioeconomic background, race and ethnicity, full-time and part-time employed, campus residents versus commuters, native versus international, geographical mix, and special admissions.

If your students are older, research suggests that they share certain characteristics. Most want to talk about and apply their work and life experience in class, discussion forums, assignments, and group work, so do draw on and refer to it whenever you can. Because they know the world to be complex, they expect to learn multiple ways of solving problems and to have discretion in applying the material. Adult learners need the opportunity for reflection after trying out a new application or method; rote learning doesn't work well with them. In addition, they want the material to have immediate practical utility and relevance (Aslanian, 2001; Vella, 1994; Wlodkowski, 1993). But they are not difficult learners. In fact, they are often highly motivated, eagerly participatory, and well prepared for class.

You also need to know your students' level of academic preparation and achievement. You can assess your institution's selectivity by comparing the number of applicants each year with the number of those accepted (a two-to-one ratio or above is highly selective). For each entering class, you can find out about its average scholastic test scores (SATs, ACTs), the percentage ranked at varying percentiles of their high school graduating classes, the percentage of National Merit and National Achievement Finalists (over 5 percent is high), and the percentage that qualified for Advanced Placement credit (over a third is high). For several hundred American colleges and universities, almost all of this information is published every summer in the "America's Best Colleges" issue of *U.S. News and World Report*.

Another question you might want to answer is where your students are headed in life. Your institution's career center should have on file the percentage of students planning on different types of graduate and professional educations, as well as the immediate employment plans of the next graduating class. Often departments and colleges collect follow-up data on what their students are doing a few years after graduation. Adult learners are usually seeking a promotion or a new career.

■ HOW PEOPLE LEARN

Whatever your student body profile, certain well-researched principles about how people learn will apply. Those that follow don't represent every learning principle ever discovered. In fact, the next section, "How Structure Increases Learning," addresses an interrelated set of learning principles. In addition, you'll find a few more principles in chapter 23 that explain how visual representations contribute to learning. Nevertheless, the following list provides a broad range of robust findings about learning.

1. People are born learners with an insatiable curiosity. They absorb and remember untold billions of details about their language, other people, objects, and things they know how to do (Bransford, Brown, & Cocking, 1999; Spence, 2001). They most readily learn what they regard as relevant to their lives (Ambrose, Bridges, DiPietro, Lovett, & Norman, 2010; Bransford et al., 1999; Persellin & Daniels, 2014; Svinicki, 2004; Winne & Nesbit, 2010).

2. People learn through elaborative rehearsal, which means thinking about the meaning of the new knowledge and connecting it to what they already know and believe (Bransford et al., 1999; Tigner, 1999).

3. People learn new knowledge most easily if it fits in with their prior knowledge (Ambrose et al., 2010; Bransford et al., 1999; Zull, 2002).

4. People learn only when they concentrate on the material and the learning process (see chapter 4).

5. People learn in interaction with others when they are constructing knowledge together (Stage, Kinzie, Muller, & Simmons, 1999), but in most contexts, learning is an internal, individual activity (Nilson, 2013a; Spence, 2001; see principle 8).

6. People learn more when they are motivated to do so by the inspiration and enthusiasm of their instructors or other people in their lives (Hobson, 2002; Sass, 1989).

7. People learn better when they are actively engaged in an activity than when they passively listen to an instructor talk. The human brain can't focus for long when it is in a passive state (Bligh, 2000; Bonwell & Eison, 1991; Hake, 1998; Jones-Wilson, 2005; McKeachie, 2002; Spence, 2001; Svinicki, 2004). Group work generally increases engagement (Persellin & Daniels, 2014).

8. People learn new material best when they actively monitor their learning and reflect on their performance, a mental operation called *metacognition* or *self-regulated learning* (Ambrose et al., 2010; Bransford et al., 1999; Hattie, 2009; Nilson, 2013a; Winne & Nesbit, 2010; Zimmerman, Moylan, Hudesman, White, & Flugman, 2011).

9. People learn procedures and processes best when they learn the steps in the same order that they will perform them (Feldon, 2010).

10. People learn most easily when the instruction is designed to minimize cognitive load—that is, to reduce the effortful demands placed on working memory (Feldon, 2010; Winne & Nesbit, 2010).

11. People learn best when they receive the new material multiple times but in different ways— that is, through multiple senses and modes that use different parts of their brain (Doyle & Zakrajsek, 2013; Hattie, 2009; Kress, Jewitt, Ogborn, & Charalampos, 2006; Tulving, 1985; Vekiri, 2002; Winne & Nesbit, 2010; Zull, 2002).

12. People learn better then they review or practice new material at multiple, intervallic times than when they review it all at one time (Brown, Roediger, & McDaniel, 2014; Butler, Marsh, Slavinsky, & Baraniuk, 2014; Cepeda, Pashler, Vul, Wixted, & Rohrer, 2006; Dunlosky, Rawson, Marsh, Nathan, & Willingham, 2013; Hattie, 2009; Rohrer & Pashler, 2010; Winne & Nesbit, 2010). This schedule of practice is called *spaced* or *distributive*, and it can take the form of being tested or self-testing (see principle 14).

13. Relatedly, people learn better when that practice is *interleaved* than when it is *blocked*. In other words, they benefit when they occasionally review old material as they are learning new material (Butler et al., 2014; Dunlosky et al., 2013; Rohrer & Pashler, 2010).

14. People learn more from being tested or testing themselves on material than they do from rereading or reviewing it, as the former involves more effortful cognitive processing (see principle 18) and retrieval practice (Brown et al., 2014; Dempster, 1996, 1997; Dunlosky et al., 2013; Karpicke & Blunt, 2011; Roediger & Karpicke, 2006; Rohrer & Pashler, 2010; Winne & Nesbit, 2010).

15. In fact, people learn more after being pretested on material before they even start learning it (Carey, 2014).

16. People learn from practice only when they receive targeted feedback that they can use to improve their performance in more practice (Ambrose et al., 2010).

17. People learn more from making and correcting mistakes than from being correct in the first place, and research on mice reveals a biological base: when an organism gets an error signal, its brain releases calcium, which enhances the brain's ability to learn, that is, its *neuroplasticity* (Najafi, Giovannucci, Wang, & Medina, 2014).

18. People can remember what they have learned longer when they have to work harder to learn it—that is, when they have to overcome what are called *desirable difficulties* (Bjork, 1994; Bjork & Bjork, 2011; Brown et al., 2014; McDaniel & Butler, 2010).

19. People learn better when the material evokes emotional and not just intellectual or physical involvement. In other words, a lasting learning experience must be moving enough to make the material memorable or to motivate people to want to learn it. This principle mirrors the biological base of learning, which is the close communication between the frontal lobes of the brain and the limbic system. From a biological point of view, learning entails a change in the brain in which new or fragile synapses are formed or strengthened (Leamnson, 1999, 2000; Mangurian, 2005, Zull, 2002, 2011).

20. People learn best when they get enough sleep and exercise and feel they are in a safe, fairly stress-free environment (Doyle & Zakrajsek, 2013).

These key learning principles extrapolate to complementary teaching principles, and they echo through the rest of this book:

1. Explain to your students the relevance of your material to their current and future careers, consumer decisions, civic lives, and personal lives as well as real-world problems. Use examples and analogies out of their lives and generational experiences. Also ask them how they can apply the material.

2. Ask students to connect new knowledge to what they already know and believe either in class or in a brief writing assignment such as a self-regulated learning exercise (see chapter 20).

3. Start where your students are. Find out your students' mental models and convince them that your discipline's models better explain phenomena than their faulty models (see the next section).

4. Minimize student distractions in class, the most tempting of which are technological (see chapter 4).

5. Allow students to work in groups some of the time, especially on the most challenging tasks, but also inform them that learning is ultimately an inside job—that is, it requires them to focus their mind on the material and their progress in comprehending and recalling it (see chapters 15 and 20).

6. Express your enthusiasm and passion for your material, your teaching it, and your students (see chapter 9).

7. Engage students in active and experiential learning techniques (see parts 3 and 4 in this book), and when you do lecture, do so interactively, with frequent breaks for student activities (see chapter 12).

8. Teach your students how to learn your material, and build in self-regulated learning activities and assignments that make them observe, analyze, and assess how well they are learning (see chapter 20).

9. Teach procedures and processes in the same order that students will perform them.

10. Minimize cognitive load by (1) eliminating information that doesn't contribute to students' understanding or problem-solving facility (e.g. reading text aloud that students can read themselves); (2) integrating explanatory text into visual materials; (3) scaffolding new material— for example, modeling and providing explicit instructions, step-by-step procedures, and partially worked examples) (Feldon, 2010; Kirschner, Sweller, & Clark, 2006; Mayer, 2009; Mayer & Moreno, 2003); and (4) helping students identify patterns and similarities and thereby *chunk* material into categories, concepts, and the like (Gobet et al., 2001).

11. Teach in multiple modalities. Give students the opportunities to read, hear, talk, write, see, draw, think, act, and feel new material into their system. In other words, involve as many senses and parts of the brain as possible in their learning. If, as is commonplace, students first read or listen to the material, have them take notes on it, discuss it, concept-map it, free-write about it, solve problems with it, or take a quiz on it (see chapters 22 and 23).

12. Build in activities and assignments that have students review and practice retrieving the same material at spaced intervals.

13. Interleave this review and retrieval practice by having students work with old material as they are learning new material.

14. Build into your course plenty of assessment opportunities, including low-stakes quizzes, practice tests, in-class exercises, and homework assignments that can tell students how much they are really learning and give them retrieval practice.

15. Start your course with a pretest, which will also serve as (1) a diagnostic test to tell you what your students do and do not know; (2) the first half of a self-regulated learning activity, to be repeated at the end of the term; and (3) the baseline for measuring your students' learning at the end of the term (see chapters 20 and 28).

16. Provide timely, targeted feedback that students can use to improve their performance (see chapter 24).

17. Persuade students that errors are memorable learning opportunities by sometimes giving them the chance to correct their errors (see chapter 20).

18. Integrate *desirable difficulties* into your students' learning. These can help them generate multiple retrieval paths and stretch their abilities (Persellin & Daniels, 2014). Methods include having students recast text material into a graphic format such as a concept map; giving them frequent quizzes; varying the conditions and location of their practice opportunities; having them transfer new knowledge to new situations; assigning especially creative, inventive, and challenging tasks to small groups; and holding your students to high standards (e.g., refusing to accept or grade work that shows little effort). However, be reasonable and don't use yourself as the standard. Very few students will learn your field as quickly as you did or choose the life of the mind as you have.

19. Motivate and reinforce learning with emotions. Make a learning experience dramatic, humorous, surprising, joyous, maddening, exciting, or heart-wrenching. Integrate engaging cases and problems for students to solve and experiential learning opportunities into your courses. Let students reflect, debate, consider multiple viewpoints, record their reactions to the material, and work in groups.

20. Inform your students of the benefits of adequate sleep and exercise, and create a safe, welcoming environment for learning (see chapter 7).

When even an inexperienced instructor implements just some of these research-based principles, students attend classes at a higher rate, are more engaged, and learn twice as much as students in a lecture-based course taught by a seasoned instructor (Deslauriers, Schelew, & Wieman, 2011).

▮ HOW STRUCTURE INCREASES LEARNING

Structure is so key to how people learn and remember material that it deserves an entire section of its own. In addition, structure distinguishes knowledge from mere information.

Students are always talking about "information" when they refer to what they are learning. After all, this is the Information Age, and abundant information is constantly available. It's a snap to find people's phone numbers, the capitals of countries, the years of historical events, directions from one place to another, an area's major industries, and election results, to name just a few common pieces of information. But all of these are only facts: isolated bits of information that do not add up to any generalizations or conclusions about the way the world works.

What isn't so available is *knowledge*, that is, organized bodies of knowledge, which is what we academics have to offer that information-packed websites do not. Knowledge is a structured set of patterns that we have identified through careful observation, followed by reflection and abstraction—a grid that we have carefully superimposed on a messy world so we can make predictions and applications (Kuhn, 1970). Knowledge comprises useful concepts, agreed-on generalizations, well-grounded inferences, strongly backed theories, reasonable hypotheses, and well-tested principles and probabilities. Without knowledge, science and advanced technology wouldn't exist.

Unfortunately our students come to our courses, and usually leave them, viewing our material as a bunch of absolute, disconnected facts and technical terms, meaningful, and memorable as a phone book. They think that these facts and things were out there, and we just discovered them. From this perspective, memorization as a learning strategy makes sense.

Students are not stupid; they are simply novices in our discipline. They lack a solid base of prior knowledge and may harbor misconceptions and faulty models about the subject matter (Hansen, 2011; Svinicki, 2004). Being unable to identify central, core concepts and principles (Kozma, Russell, Jones, Marx, & Davis, 1996), they wander somewhat aimlessly through a body of knowledge, picking up and memorizing what may or may not be important facts and terms and using trial-and-error to solve problems and answer questions (Glaser, 1991). They do not see the big picture of the patterns, generalizations, and abstractions that experts recognize so clearly. As a result, they have trouble figuring out how to classify and approach problems at the conceptual level (Arocha & Patel, 1995; DeJong & Ferguson-Hessler, 1996).

Without that big picture, students face another learning hurdle as well. The mind processes, stores, and retrieves knowledge not as a collection of facts but as a logically organized whole, a coherent conceptual framework with interconnected parts. In fact, it requires a big picture. That framework is what prior knowledge is all about. New material is integrated not into an aggregate of facts and terms but into a preexisting structure of learned knowledge. Without having a structure of the material in their heads, students fail to comprehend and retain new material (Bransford et al., 1999; Hanson, 2006; Svinicki, 2004; Wieman, 2007).

The mind structures knowledge based on patterns and relationships it recognizes across observations. In fact, it is driven to generalize and simplify reality. If it did not, we would experience repetitive events as novel every time they occurred and would learn and remember nothing from them. No doubt, we would find reality too complex to operate within and would perish. Animals too have a need and capacity to recognize patterns. They learn to obtain what they need and survive not just by instinct but by learning—for instance, learning to hide, judge distances, time their strikes, and fool their prey—and they get better with practice. The behaviorists call learning by pattern recognition *operant conditioning,* and they have demonstrated that mammals, birds, reptiles, and fish learn this way.

Human thinking is so wired to seek and build structure that we make up connections to fill in the blanks in our understanding of phenomena if we don't already have a complete explanatory theory handy. Some of these made-up connections stand up to scrutiny and testing and may be elevated to science. Charles Darwin, for example, did not observe mutations happening in nature; rather, he hypothesized their occurrence to fill in the explanatory blanks for species diversity. No one was around to watch the big bang, but the theory fills in quite a few missing links in cosmology. Astronomers have never directly observed dark matter (undetectable matter or particles that are hypothesized to account for unexpected gravitational effects on galaxies and stars), but they believe it makes up 30 percent of the universe. Not all imagined connections, however, stand the test of time or science. Superstitions and prejudice exemplify false patterns. The belief of many people, including many students, that one's intelligence is fixed and immutable also fails under careful study.

The kind of deep, meaningful learning that moves a student from novice toward expert is all about acquiring the discipline's hierarchical organization of patterns, its mental structure of knowledge (Alexander, 1996; Chi, Glaser, & Rees, 1982; Royer, Cisero, & Carlo, 1993). Only then will the student have the structure on which to accumulate additional knowledge. By their very nature, knowledge structures must be hierarchical to distinguish the more general and core concepts and propositions from the conditional, specific, and derivative. Experts move up and down this hierarchy with ease.

What are the odds that a learner will develop such a structure of knowledge on his or her own in a few weeks, months, or even years? How long did it take us? Most, if not all, of our time in graduate school—or longer? People require years of specialized study and apprenticeship to internalize the structure of the discipline and become an expert. Unfortunately, many, if not most, of our students pass through our discipline for only a term or two, not nearly enough time to notice its patterns and hierarchical structure. Yet without having a mental structure for organizing what they learn, they process our course content superficially and quickly forget it. Is it not our responsibility as teaching experts to help our students acquire a structure quickly, so our short time with them is not wasted? Should we not make the organization of our knowledge explicit by providing them an accurate, ready-made structure for making sense of our content and storing it?

Given the central role that structure plays in learning, here are some ideas to foster student learning:

- Very early in the term, give students activities and assignments that make them retrieve, articulate, and organize what they already know (or think they know) about your course material. Then identify any evident misconceptions and address in class how and why they are wrong, and show them that your discipline's mental model is more plausible, useful, and convincing (Baume & Baume, 2008; Taylor & Kowalski, 2014).

- Very early in the term, give students the big picture—the overall organization of your course content. The clearest way to show this is in a graphic syllabus (see chapter 5). Carry through by presenting your content as an integrated whole, that is, as a cohesive system of interpreting phenomena rather than an aggregate of small, discrete facts and terms. Keep referring back to how and where specific topics fit into that big picture.

- Give students the big picture of their learning process for the term—that is, the logical sequencing of your learning outcomes for them. A flowchart of the student learning process for a course is called an *outcomes map* (see chapter 2).

- Help students see the difference between information and knowledge. The previous discussion of the topic, as well as the next section of this chapter, supplies some useful concepts and vocabulary for explaining the difference.

- Teach students the thinking structures that your discipline uses—for example, the scientific method, the diagnostic process, the rules of rhetoric, basic logic (the nature of fact, opinion, interpretation, and theory), and logical fallacies. Where applicable, acquaint them with the competing paradigms (metatheories) in your field, such as the rational versus the symbolic interpretive versus the postmodern perspectives in English literature, pluralism versus elitism in political science, functionalism versus conflict theory in sociology, and positivism (or empiricism) versus phenomenology in social science epistemology.

- Design exercises for your students in pattern recognition and categorical chunking to help them process and manage the landslide of new material. These thinking processes will help them identify conceptual similarities, differences, and interrelationships while reducing the material to fewer, more manageable pieces. The fewer independent pieces of knowledge the mind has to learn, the more knowledge it can process and retain. Cognitively speaking, less is more (Hanson, 2006; Wieman, 2007).

- In addition to showing your students a graphic syllabus and outcome map of your course, furnish them with graphic representations of theories, conceptual interrelationships, and knowledge schemata—concept maps, mind maps, diagrams, flowcharts, comparison-and-contrast matrices, and the like—and then have them develop their own to clarify their understanding of the material. Such visuals are powerful learning aids because they provide a ready-made, easy-to-process structure for knowledge (Hanson, 2006; Wieman, 2007). In addition, the very structures of graphics themselves supply retrieval cues (see chapter 23).

THE COGNITIVE DEVELOPMENT OF UNDERGRADUATES

No matter how bright or mature your students may be, do not expect them to have reached a high level of cognitive maturity in your discipline. Almost all students, especially freshmen and sophomores, begin a course of study with serious misconceptions about knowledge in general and the discipline specifically (Hansen, 2011). Only as these misconceptions are dispelled do students mature intellectually through distinct stages. As an instructor, you have the opportunity—some would say the responsibility—to lead them through these stages to epistemological maturity.

Psychologist William G. Perry (1968, 1985) formulated a theory of the intellectual and ethical development of college students. In its simple four-stage version, students begin college with a dualistic perspective and may, depending on their instruction, advance through the stages of multiplicity, relativism, and commitment (definitions are given in what follows). The research supporting the model accumulated rapidly, making Perry's the leading theory on the cognitive development of undergraduates.

Perry developed his theory using a sample of mostly male students, but some years later, researchers, notably Baxter Magolda (1992), did more study on women students. She identified four levels of knowing—absolute, transitional, independent, and contextual—roughly parallel to Perry's but with most females following a relational pattern and most males the abstract. Table 1.1 displays both models.

While Perry's framework of development applies across disciplines, a student's level of maturity may be advanced in one and not in another. We shouldn't assume, for example, that a sophisticated senior in a laboratory science major has a comparable understanding of the nature of knowledge in the social sciences or the humanities.

The more elaborate version of Perry's theory posits nine positions through which students pass on their way to cognitive maturity. (The stages in Perry's simpler model are italicized in the following paragraphs.) How far and how rapidly students progress through the hierarchy, if they do at all, depend largely on the quality and type of instruction they receive. It is this flexible aspect of Perry's theory that has made it particularly attractive and useful. The schema suggests ways that we can accelerate undergraduates' intellectual growth.

We begin with position 1, the cognitive state in which most first-year students arrive. (Of course, many sophomores, juniors, and seniors are still at

Table 1.1   Stages or Levels of Student Cognitive Development

Perry's Stages of Undergraduate Cognitive Development	Baxter Magolda's Levels of Knowing
1. *Duality*: Black and white thinking; authorities rule	Absolute knowing
⇩	
Uncertainty	
2. *Multiplicity*: poor authorities or temporary state	Transitional knowing
⇩	
Uncertainty as legitimate, inherent	
3. *Relativism*: All opinions equal	Independent knowing
⇩	
Standards of comparison	
4. *Commitment* (tentative) to best theory available	Contextual knowing

this level.) Perry used the term *dualism* to describe students' thinking at this stage because they perceive the world in black-and-white simplicity. They decide what to believe and how to act according to absolute standards of right and wrong, good and bad, truth and falsehood. Authority figures like instructors supposedly know and teach the absolute truths about reality. Furthermore, all knowledge and goodness can be quantified or tallied, like correct answers on a spelling test.

At position 2, students enter the general cognitive stage of *multiplicity*. They come to realize that since experts don't know everything there is to know, a discipline permits multiple opinions to compete for acceptance. But to students, the variety merely reflects that not all authorities are equally legitimate or competent. Some students don't even give these competing opinions much credence, believing them to be just an instructor's exercise designed ultimately to lead them to the one true answer. As they advance to position 3, they accept the notion that genuine uncertainty exists, but only as a temporary state that will resolve itself once an authority finds the answer.

Entering position 4, which marks the broader stage of *relativism*, students make an about-face and abandon their faith in the authority's ability to identify the truth. At this point, they either consider all views equally valid or allow different opinions within the limits delineated by some standard. In brief, they become relativists with no hope of there ever being one true interpretation or answer. Students at position 5 formalize the idea that all knowledge is relativistic and contextual, but with qualifications. They may reserve dualistic ideas of right and wrong as subordinate principles for special cases in specific contexts. Thus, even in a relativistic world, they may permit certain instances where facts are truly facts and only one plausible truth exists.

At some point, however, students can no longer accommodate all the internal inconsistencies and ambiguities inherent in position 5. They may want to make choices but often lack clear standards for doing so. As a result, they begin to feel the need to orient themselves in their relativistic world by making some sort of personal commitment to one stance or another. As this need grows, they pass through position 6 and into the more general cognitive stage of *commitment*. When they actually make an initial, tentative commitment to a particular view in some area, they attain position 7. Next, at position 8, they experience and examine the impacts and implications of their choice of commitment. That is, they learn what commitment means and what trade-offs it carries. Finally, at position 9, students realize that trying on a commitment and either embracing or modifying it in the hindsight of experience is a major part of their personal and intellectual growth. This process is, in fact, a lifelong activity that paves the road toward wisdom and requires an ever open mind.

■ ENCOURAGING COGNITIVE GROWTH

Nelson (2000), a leading authority on developing thinking skills, contends that we can facilitate students' progress through these stages by familiarizing them with the uncertainties and the standards of comparison in our disciplines. He and many others (Allen, 1981, in the sciences, for example) have achieved excellent results by implementing his ideas. (Kloss, 1994, offers a somewhat different approach tailored to literature instructors.)

Exposure to uncertainties in our knowledge bases helps students realize that often there is no one superior truth, nor can there be, given the nature of rational knowledge. This realization helps lead them out of dualistic thinking (position 1) and through multiplistic conceptions of knowledge (positions 2 and 3). Once they can understand uncertainty as legitimate and inherent in the nature of knowledge, they can mature into relativists (positions 4 and 5). Instructive examples of such uncertainties include the following: (1) the range of viable interpretations that can be made of certain works of literature and art, (2) the different conclusions that can be legitimately drawn from the same historical evidence and scientific data, (3) a discipline's history of scientific revolutions and paradigm shifts, (4) unresolved issues on which a discipline is currently conducting research, and (5) historical and scientific unknowns that may or may not ever be resolved.

Our next step is to help students advance beyond relativism through positions 6 and 7, at which point they can make tentative commitments and progress toward cognitive maturity. To do so, students need to understand that among all the possible answers and interpretations, some may be more valid than others. They must also learn why some are better than others—that is, what criteria exist to discriminate among the options, to distinguish the wheat from the chaff. Disciplines vary on their criteria for evaluating validity. Each has its own metacognitive *model*—that is, a set of accepted conventions about what makes a sound argument and what constitutes appropriate evidence. Most students have trouble acquiring these conventions on their own; they tend to assume that the rules are invariable across fields. So Nelson advises us to make our concepts of evidence and our standards for comparison explicit to our students.

By the time students reach position 5, they are uncomfortable with their relativism, and by position 6, they are hungry for criteria on which to rank options and base choices, so they should be highly receptive to a discipline's evaluative framework. To encourage students to reach positions 7 and 8, we can provide writing and discussion opportunities for them to deduce and examine what their initial commitments imply in other contexts. They may apply their currently preferred framework to a new or different ethical case, historical event, social phenomenon, political issue, scientific problem, or piece of literature. They may even apply it to a real situation in their own lives. Through this process, they begin to realize that a commitment focuses options, closing some doors while opening others.

We should remind students that they are always free to reassess their commitments, modify them, and even make new ones, but with an intel-lectual and ethical caveat: they should have sound reason to do so, such as new experience or data or a more logical organization of the evidence, not just personal convenience. With a clear understanding of this final point, students achieve position 9.

Bringing Perry's and Nelson's insights into our courses presents a genuine challenge in that students in any one class may be at different stages, even if they are in the same graduating class. Almost all first-year students fall in the first few positions, but juniors and seniors may be anywhere on the hierarchy. It may be wisest, then, to help students at the lower positions catch up with those at the higher ones by explicitly addressing knowledge uncertainties and disciplinary criteria for selecting among perspectives and creating opportunities for students to make and justify choices in your courses.

Keep your students' cognitive growth in mind as you read this book. If you use the outcomes-centered approach to designing a course (see chapter 2), you may want to select a certain level of cognitive maturity as a learning outcome for your students.

■ TEACHING TODAY'S YOUNG STUDENTS

If you are teaching traditional-age students, you should know some basics about what has come to be called generation Y—aka the net generation, the neXt generation, and, most commonly, the millennial generation. A great deal has been written about it, and this section provides a quick summary of the best-researched generalizations about the bulk of middle- and upper-middle-class students (Arum & Roksa, 2011; Bauerlein, 2009; Babcock & Marks, 2011; Bureau & McRoberts, 2001; Cardon, 2014; Carlson, 2005; Curren & Rosen, 2006; Howe & Strauss, 2000; Levine & Cureton, 1998; Levine & Dean, 2012; Lowery, 2001; Nathan, 2005; Oblinger, 2003; Raines, 2002; Singleton-Jackson, Jackson, & Reinhardt, 2010; Strauss & Howe, 2003; Taylor, 2006; Tucker, 2006; Twenge, 2007).

This generation comprises children born between 1982 (some say 1980) and 1995 (some say 2000) to the late baby boomers. These parents kept their children's lives busily structured with sports, music lessons, club meetings, youth group activities, and part-time jobs. In their spare time, young millennials spent many hours on the computer, often the Internet, interacting with peers, doing school work, playing games, shopping, and otherwise entertaining themselves. Unless they attended private schools or schools in college towns or higher socioeconomic areas, they received a weaker K–12 education than previous generations did. Still, they flooded into colleges and universities starting around 2000. Their combined family and school experience, along with their heavy mass media exposure, made them self-confident, extremely social, technologically sophisticated, action bent, goal oriented, service minded, and accustomed to functioning as part of a team. On the flip side, they are also impatient, demanding, stressed out, sheltered, brand oriented, materialistic, and self-centered. They use, and abuse, alcohol and prescription drugs more than street drugs. Although skeptical about authority, they tend not to be particularly rebellious, violent, or promiscuous. With so much activity in their lives, as well as frequent interaction with friends and family (much of it on computers and cell phones), they have little time or inclination for reflection, self-examination, or free-spirited living.

Another feature of this generation, one that distinguishes it from so many preceding ones, is that millennials do not hunger for independence from their parents. Quite the contrary: they stay close to the parents through college (and often beyond) and turn to their parents for help when organizations don't meet their needs. These parents have earned the descriptor of *helicopter parents* for hovering over their grown children to ensure their well-being and competitive advantage in life.

For college faculty, this generation can be challenging to deal with. Millennials view higher education as an expensive but economically necessary consumer good, not a privilege earned by hard work and outstanding performance. They (or their parents) purchase it for the instrumental purpose of opening well-paying occupational doors on graduation, so they feel entitled to their degree for the cost of the credits. As many of them did little homework for their good grades through high school, they anticipate the same minimal demands in college and often resent the amount of reading, research, problem solving, and writing that we assign them and the standards that we hold for their work. Those whose grades slip in college feel their self-esteem threatened, and they may react with depression, anxiety, defensiveness, and even anger against us. They also have different ideas from ours about what cheating and plagiarism involve. In addition, they hear a lot of bad news from us in their classes: that they didn't learn enough in high school to handle college, that knowledge bases are full of holes and unsolved mysteries, that their beliefs and values are subject to question and debate, and that both college and the real world demand that they work and prove their worth.

Not only are we bearers of bad news, however inadvertently, but we are also very different from them and difficult to fathom and identify with. We prize the life of the mind, we love to read, and we work long hours for relatively little money. We must remember that this generation values money and what it can buy. Aside from the materialism that their parents and the mass media promoted, these young people face the prospect of being the first generation, at least in the United States, that may not afford a standard of living comparable to that of their parents, let alone higher. So while millennials may be hopeful, they also have economic anxieties.

Immigrants, children of immigrants, and students from poverty might be more optimistic about their future prospects of upward mobility. But if they know they will graduate with heavy student-loan debt, they too may carry financial worries.

In any case, our modest material status, coupled with all our education, does not inspire a great deal of their respect. To them, we render customer service, a somewhat menial calling, to a society that doesn't value abstraction, intellectual discourse, or knowledge for knowledge's sake. Therefore, if they are dissatisfied with our services (usually the workload, their grades, or our responsiveness to their desires), they complain to our bosses, often involving their parents to bolster their power. They sense they have the upper hand: that instructors are subject to being disciplined or even fired at administrative will and that institutions want to retain students and keep them happy. In this quasi-corporate model, the customer is always right, whether she is or not. So millennials can be demanding, discourteous, impatient, time-consuming, and energy sapping. For the same reason, college and universities have been upgrading their residence halls, food services, recreational and workout facilities, tutoring programs, computing, and teaching (with an eye toward boosting the student ratings of their instructors).

Despite the difficulties millennials may present, this generation can be easier to reach if we make a few adjustments. After all, they have career goals, positive attitudes, technological savvy, and collaborative inclinations. In addition, they are intelligent enough to have learned a lot, even if it is not the knowledge that we value. Our adjustments need not include lowering our own standards.

Although millennials are understandably cynical about authority (so are we) and don't assume we have their best interests at heart, they value communication, information, and caring, and they respond well when we explain why we use the teaching and assessment methods we do. We can sell them on the wisdom of our reading selections, assignments, in-class activities, and rubrics, reinforcing the fact that we are the experts in our field and in teaching it. As experts, we *should* have solid, research-based reasons for our choices. Why not show our students the respect of sharing these reasons?

Millennials also want to know that we care about them (Granitz, Koernig, & Harich, 2009; Meyers, 2009). Remember that they are still attached to their parents and not far from the nest. They are also accustomed to near-constant interaction, so they do want to relate to us. Showing that we care about their learning and well-being will go far in earning their loyalty and trust (see chapter 7).

Finally, having led a tightly organized childhood and adolescence and not being rebellious, they respond well to structure, discipline, rules, and regulations. If you set up or have them set up a code of classroom conduct (see chapter 9), they will generally honor it. If you promise that you will answer their e-mail at two specific times each day and you follow through, they will not expect you to be available 24/7. Whatever course policies your syllabus states, as long as they are clear and fairly airtight, the students will generally respect them, though a few may try to pressure you to bend your rules. Even their parents will usually withdraw their demands for grade information if you clearly explain any applicable restrictions under the Family Educational Rights and Privacy Act (FERPA). What millennials consider unprofessional is an instructor's (apparent) disorganization, ill preparation, or inability to stick to her own syllabus.

Of course, blanket statements about an entire generation always apply to only a portion of its members. Biggs (2003) has another take in it. He describes an undergraduate profile applicable to both the British Commonwealth nations and the United States, and he puts a face on it—two faces, actually. There is "Susan," the archetypal good student: intelligent, well prepared, goal oriented, and motivated to master the material. Susan came to college with solid thinking, writing, and learning skills. While about three-quarters of today's college students were like her in 1980, only about 42 percent are like her today (Brabrand & Andersen, 2006). The rest (almost 60 percent) are like "Robert," who is much less academically talented, college ready, and motivated to learn (Brabrand & Andersen, 2006). He just wants to get by with the least amount of learning effort so he can parlay his degree into a decent job. He will rely on memorizing the material rather than reflecting on and constructing it. "Good teaching," according to Biggs, is "getting most students to use the higher cognitive level processes that the more academic students use spontaneously" (2003, p. 5), that is, changing Roberts into Susans.

When you divide the student population the way Biggs does, the millennial generation doesn't look so monolithic, and no matter where we teach, we find both types of students in our classes. Many of them are interested in learning and know something about how to do it, even if they are also materialistic, tied to their parents, and frequently texting. While we can generalize about millennials, we must not forget that they are the most diverse generation economically, politically, ethnically, racially, and culturally that North American institutions of higher learning have ever welcomed.

In contrast to the millennials, almost nothing has been written on the next generation, dubbed generation Z, and it should be in college by now or very soon. No clear differences between it and the millennials have yet come to light in the research literature.

■ THE CHALLENGE

With such a heterogeneous student population on so many dimensions, including academic background, we may wonder at what level of student to aim our courses. Some of us find peace aiming at the top 20 percent, where we know our efforts will be intellectually productive. Others aim at the broad middle, hoping to bring as many students along as possible. Of course, where the top 20 percent and broad middle lie varies by type of institution.

In the past, the more selective colleges and universities welcomed only strong academic performers, regardless of cultural and economic background, and students were on their own to survive in college. Now institutions strive to educate as many people as possible in response to the changing demographics of our society. This mission shift in higher education generated teaching and learning centers, higher faculty standards for teaching effectiveness, and an explosion of research on how students learn and respond to different instructor behaviors, teaching methods, and instructional settings. This book draws on and integrates much of this research into a practical reference on the most effective approaches to use for different types of learning outcomes.

CHAPTER 2

Outcomes-Centered Course Design

Teaching has only one purpose, and that is to facilitate learning (Cross, 1988). Learning may occur without teaching, but teaching can, and unfortunately does, occur without learning. In the latter case, the students lose time, money, potential gains in knowledge and cognitive development, and perhaps confidence in themselves or the educational system. But less obviously, instructors lose faith in their students and in themselves. For our own mental health and that of our students, we need to better meld teaching and learning.

The first step toward this goal is to design your courses wisely. Whether you are teaching an established course for the first time, developing a brand-new course, or revising a course you currently teach, first ask yourself what you are trying to accomplish. No doubt, you want your students to learn certain things, to master a body of material. But you can't assess how well you've met this goal unless you have students do something with that material that demonstrates their learning. What they do may involve writing, discussing, acting, creating a graphic or visual work, conducting an experiment or demonstration, making an oral presentation, designing a website, teaching a lesson, or baking a cake. Whatever the display of learning, you have to be able to perceive it though your senses and appraise the quality of the performance. How else can you determine their internal state—what they know, realize, and understand?

WHY OUTCOMES-CENTERED COURSE DESIGN?

This chapter recommends designing your course around what you want your students to be able to do by the end. This approach echoes Wiggins and McTighe's (2005) backward design strategy, which recommends starting the course design process by articulating the learning results you desire. Other approaches exist, such as developing a course around a list of content topics. Before 1990, a course was always described as a range of content, such as "a comprehensive survey of vertebrate animals including their taxonomy, morphology, evolution, and defining facets of their natural history and behavior" or "an introduction to the process of literary criticism." Course catalogues and many syllabi still contain such descriptions. You can also organize a course around your favorite textbook or the one you've been told to use. However, such approaches will not ensure that your course is student active, which we know significantly increases learning.

Outcomes-centered course design also satisfies the accountability requirements of an increasing number of accrediting agencies. These agencies hold an institution or a program accountable for ensuring its students' achievement of certain learning outcomes, as well as for formally assessing its students' progress toward that goal. In other words, they require departments and schools to determine what they want their students to be able to do on graduation and to produce materials that show what the students can do. Some agencies even take it on themselves to specify exactly what abilities and skills that the graduates of a certain area should demonstrate.

This chapter focuses primarily on formulating student learning outcomes because they provide the foundation for proper course development, which include selecting teaching methods and moves (i.e., brief strategies for clarifying content and giving students practice in thinking about and working with it) that will help students achieve those outcomes (see chapter 11) and assessment instruments that will measure students' success in performing those outcomes (see chapters 26 and 27).

■ WRITING OUTCOMES

A learning outcome is a statement of exactly what your students should be able to do after completing your course or at specified points during the course. Some faculty also set outcomes for individual classes and units of the course. Outcomes are written from a student's point of view—for example, "After studying the processes of photosynthesis and respiration, the student should be able to trace the carbon cycle in a given ecosystem."

Of course, outcomes are promises, and you should make it clear that students have to do their part to make these promises come true. So you might state verbally and in your syllabus something like this: "Students may vary in their competency levels on these abilities. You can expect to acquire these abilities only if you honor all course policies, attend classes regularly, complete all assigned work in good faith and on time, and meet all other course expectations of you as a student." (Chapter 5 recommends inserting this kind of disclaimer.)

Before you start composing outcomes, find out from your dean or department chair whether an accrediting agency or the program has already mandated them for your course. For instance, the National Council for the Accreditation of Teacher Education lists the required outcomes for many education courses. The Accreditation Board for Engineering and Technology provides program outcomes, some of which may be useful and even essential for your course. Some departments engage in *curriculum mapping*, which means designating the task of preparing students to meet given program outcomes to specific courses.

If you are free to develop your own outcomes, you might first want to research the history of the course. Why was it proposed and approved in the first place, and by whom? What special purposes does it serve? What other courses should it prepare students to take? Often new courses emerge to meet the needs of a changing labor market, update curriculum content, ensure accreditation, or give an institution a competitive edge. Knowing the underlying influences can help you orient a course to its intended purposes for student learning (Prégent, 1994).

Second, get to know who your students are so you can aim your course to their needs and level. Refer to the first part of chapter 1 for the type of student data you will need—all of which should be available from your institution's admissions office, student affairs office, and career center—to find out the academic background, interests, and course expectations of your likely student population. Ask colleagues who have taught the course before what topics, books, teaching methods, activities, and assignments worked and didn't work well for them. The more relevant you can make the material to the target group, the more effective your course will be.

If you cannot gather much information in advance, keep your initial learning outcomes and course design somewhat flexible. On the first day of class, use index cards and icebreakers to learn more about your students and their expectations (see chapter 7); then adjust and tighten the design accordingly.

Technically an outcome has three parts to it, though usually only the first part appears in the outcomes section of a syllabus. Sooner or later, however, you will have to decide the second and third parts as well:

Part 1. A statement of a measurable performance. Learning outcomes center on action verbs (e.g., *define, classify, construct, compute*; see Table 2.1) rather than nebulous verbs reflecting internal states that cannot be observed (such as *know, learn, understand, realize, appreciate*). For example: "The student will be able to describe the most important differences between sedimentary and metamorphic rocks." "The student will be able to classify rock specimens as igneous or metamorphic." Table 2.2 later in the chapter offers many more examples.

Part 2. A statement of conditions for the performance. These conditions define the circumstances under which the student's performance will be assessed. Will she have to demonstrate that she knows the differences among igneous, metamorphic, and sedimentary rocks in writing, in an oral presentation, or in a visual medium (drawings, photographs)? Will he have to identify the parts of a computer system on a diagram or in an actual computer?

Part 3. Criteria and standards for assessing the performance. By what criteria and standards will you evaluate and ultimately grade a student's performance? What will constitute achieving an outcome at a high level (A work) versus a minimally competent level (C work)? For example: "For an A on essay 3, the student will be able to identify in writing at least three differences between igneous and metamorphic rocks, at least three between igneous and sedimentary rocks, and at least three between metamorphic and sedimentary—for a total of at least nine differences. For a B, the student will be able to identify at least six differences. For a C, the student will be able to identify at least four differences," and so on. Rubrics have such criteria and standards built into them.

TYPES OF OUTCOMES

Virtually every college-level course has *cognitive* outcomes, those pertaining to thinking. But other types may also exist that may be pertinent to your courses. *Psychomotor* skills—the ability to manipulate specific objects correctly and efficiently to accomplish a given purpose—constitute another type that is important in art, architecture, drama, linguistics, some engineering fields, all laboratory sciences, nursing and other health-related fields, and foreign languages. *Affective* outcomes specify emotional abilities you want your students to develop, such as receiving, responding, and valuing (Krathwohl, Bloom, & Masia, 1999). Of course, you cannot perceive your students' inner feelings, but you can observe their *demonstration* of emotions. For example, in nursing, counseling, and the ministry, students must learn to show empathy and open-mindedness toward patients and clients, and performances can be assessed in a role play or a case analysis. Such abilities are also very useful in management, medicine, human resources, marketing, psychology, and architecture. A wide range of disciplines integrate *social* learning outcomes to their courses, since it is now widely accepted that the workplace relies on teamwork and group learning. Many instructors want their students to be able to collaborate effectively in a team, and they consider both the group product and peer evaluations of the group members' social behavior in assessing students' performance. (All too often faculty don't think about *teaching* social skills). In some disciplines, *ethical* outcomes have come to the fore. These outcomes involve taking into account the moral considerations and implications of various options in making professional, scientific, technical, and business decisions. Cases, simulations, role plays, service-learning, fieldwork, and internships provide both learning and assessment contexts for ethical objectives. Exhibit 2.1 gives more specific examples of all five types of outcomes.

Fink (2013) integrates cognitive, affective, and social outcomes in his model of six *categories of learning*, which are cumulative and interactive. The ideally designed course incorporates all six of them as outcomes. In fact, Fink posits that all six categories are essential to create a genuinely significant learning experience. These are his categories of learning:

1. *Foundational knowledge.* Students recall and demonstrate understanding of ideas and information, providing the basis for other kinds of learning.
2. *Application.* Students engage in any combination of critical, practical, and creative thinking; acquire key skills; and learn how to manage complex projects, making other kinds of learning useful.
3. *Integration.* Students perceive connections among ideas, disciplines, people, and realms of their lives.
4. *Human dimension.* Students gain a new understanding of themselves or others, often by seeing the human implications of other kinds of learning.
5. *Caring.* Students acquire new interests, feelings, or values about what they are learning, as well as the motivation to learn more about it.
6. *Learning how to learn.* Students learn about the process of their particular learning and learning in general, enabling them to pursue learning more self-consciously, efficiently, and effectively.

Wiggins and McTighe (2005) propose six *facets of understanding* that also blend cognitive, affective, and social outcomes. While used primarily in elementary and secondary education, their framework transfers smoothly to the college level:

Exhibit 2.1   General Types of Learning Outcomes

Psychomotor—Physical performance; may involve eye-hand coordination. *Examples:* medical/nursing procedures; laboratory techniques; animal handling or grooming; assembling, operating, testing, or repairing machines or vehicles; singing; dancing; playing musical instruments; use of voice, face, and body in public speaking

Affective—Demonstration of appropriate emotions and affect. *Examples:* demonstrating good bedside manner and empathy with patients; showing trustworthiness and concern for clients, customers, subordinates, or students; showing tolerance for differences; showing dynamism, relaxed confidence, conviction, and audience responsiveness in public speaking.

Social—Appropriate, productive interaction and behavior with other people. *Examples:* cooperation and respect within a team; leadership when needed; assertive (not aggressive, passive, or passive-aggressive) behavior in dealing with conflict; negotiation and mediation skills

Ethical—Decision making that takes into account the moral implications and repercussions (effects on other people, animals, environment) of each reasonable option. *Examples:* medical and nursing decisions involving triage, transplants, withholding care, and prolonging life; lawyers' decisions about whether and how to represent a client; managerial decisions involving social, economic, political, or legal trade-offs.

Cognitive—Thinking about facts, terms, concepts, principles, ideas, relationships, patterns, and conclusions. *Examples:* knowledge and remembering, comprehension and translation, application, analysis, synthesis and creating, evaluation.

1. *Explanation.* The ability to connect ideas, events, and actions to concepts, principles, and generalizations; comparable to *integration* in Fink's framework and *comprehension/understanding* in Bloom's and Anderson and Krathwohl's schema described in the next section

2. *Interpretation.* The ability to discern the importance or value of the subject matter; comparable to *caring* in Fink's framework

3. *Application.* The ability to use and adapt knowledge to complex contexts (situations, problems, and the like); contains elements of *application* in Fink's framework and is comparable to *application/applying* in Bloom's and Anderson and Krathwohl's schema

4. *Perspective taking.* The ability and the willingness to shift perspectives and view an issue or experience critically from multiple points of view; contains elements of the *human dimension* in Fink's framework

5. *Empathy.* The ability to find value and meaning in the ideas and behavior of others, no matter how alien or puzzling; contains elements of the *human dimension* in Fink's framework

6. *Self-knowledge.* The ability to self-regulate, practice metacognition, and evaluate one's weaknesses and limitations; similar to *learning how to learn* in Fink's framework

The "Helpful Frameworks for Designing a Course" section later in this chapter examines how an instructor can create learning experiences that interrelate all of these categories synergistically. For the time being, we will focus on writing cognitive outcomes, since they are universal in higher education courses.

■ TYPES OF COGNITIVE OUTCOMES

Bloom (1956) developed a useful taxonomy for constructing cognitive outcomes. His framework posits a hierarchy of six cognitive processes, moving from the most concrete, lowest-level process of recalling stored knowledge through several intermediate cognitive modes to the most abstract, highest level of evaluation.

(Depending on your field, you may prefer to make application the highest level.) Each level is defined:

1. *Knowledge.* The ability to remember and reproduce previously learned material
2. *Comprehension.* The ability to grasp the meaning of material and to restate it in one's own words
3. *Application.* The ability to use learned material in new and concrete situations
4. *Analysis.* The ability to break down material into its component parts so as to understand its organizational structure
5. *Synthesis.* The ability to put pieces of material together to form a new whole
6. *Evaluation.* The ability to judge the value of material for a given purpose

This handy taxonomy is popular to this day, but Anderson and Krathwohl (2000) offer a few friendly amendments to it in their newer model. They use more action-oriented gerunds, update the meaning of *knowledge* and *synthesis*, and rank *creating* above *evaluating*:

Remembering = Knowledge (lowest)
Understanding = Comprehension
Applying = Application
Analyzing = Analysis
Evaluating = Evaluation
Creating = Synthesis (highest)

All of these conceptual terms become more concrete in Table 2.1, which lists common student performance verbs for each of Bloom's and Anderson and Krathwohl's cognitive operations. If this collection fails to meet your needs, Adelman (2015) lists even more verbs classified by purpose, such as certifying information and materials, performing executive functions, communicating in different ways, and rethinking and reconstructing. Once you select the cognitive operations that you'd like to emphasize in a course, you may find it helpful to refer to this listing while writing your outcomes. Another good reference is Table 2.2, which

Table 2.1   Student Performance Verbs by Level of Cognitive Operation in Bloom's Taxonomy and Anderson and Krathwohl's Taxonomy

1. Knowledge/Remembering		2. Comprehension/Understanding	
Arrange	Omit	Arrange	Paraphrase
Choose	Order	Associate	Outline
Define	Recall	Clarify	Recognize
Duplicate	Recite	Describe	Rephrase
Find	Recognize	Explain	Report
Identify	Relate	Express	Restate
Label	Repeat	Grasp	Review
List	Reproduce	Identify	Select
Match	Select	Indicate	Summarize
Memorize	Spell	Interpret	Translate
Name	Tell	Locate	Visualize

3. Application/Applying		4. Analysis/Analyzing	
Apply	Illustrate	Analyze	Distill
Break down	Interpret	Calculate	Distinguish
Calculate	Make use of	Categorize	Divide
Choose	Manipulate	Classify	Examine
Compute	Operate	Compare	Experiment
Demonstrate	Practice	Contrast	Identify assumptions
Determine	Schedule	Criticize	Induce
Dramatize	Sketch	Deduce	Inspect
Employ	Solve	Derive	Investigate
Give examples	Use	Differentiate	Model
	Utilize	Discriminate	Probe
		Discuss	Question
		Dissect	Simplify
			Test

5/6. Synthesis/Creating		6/5. Evaluation/Evaluating	
Adapt	Imagine	Agree	Dispute
Arrange	Infer	Appraise	Evaluate
Assemble	Integrate	Argue	Judge
Build	Invent	Assess	Justify
Change	Make up	Award	Prioritize

5/6. Synthesis/Creating		6/5. Evaluation/Evaluating	
Collect	Manage	Challenge	Persuade
Compose	Modify	Choose	Rank
Conclude	Originate	Conclude	Rate
Construct	Organize	Convince	Recommend
Create	Plan	Criticize	Rule on
Design	Posit	Critique	Score
Develop	Predict	Debate	Select
Discover	Prepare	Decide	Support
Estimate	Produce	Defend	Validate
Extend	Propose	Discount	Value
Formulate	Set up	Discredit	Verify
Forward	Suppose	Disprove	Weight
Generalize	Theorize		

Note: Depending on the use, some verbs may apply to more than one level.

Table 2.2 Examples of Outcomes Based on Bloom's Taxonomy and Anderson and Krathwohl's Taxonomy

Level	The Student Should Be Able to . . .
Knowledge/ Remembering	• Define iambic pentameter. • State Newton's laws of motion. • Identify the major surrealist painters.
Comprehension/ Understanding	• Describe the trends in the graph in one's own words. • Summarize a passage from Socrates' *Apology.* • Properly translate into English passages from Voltaire's *Candide.*
Application/ Applying	• Describe an experiment that would test the influence of light and light quality on the Hill reaction of photosynthesis. • Scan a poem for metric foot and rhyme scheme. • Use the Archimedes principle to determine the volume of an irregularly shaped object.
Analysis/Analyzing	• List arguments for and against human cloning. • Determine the variables to be controlled in an experiment. • Discuss the rationale and efficacy of isolationism in the global economy.
Synthesis/Creating	• Write a short story in Hemingway's style. • Compose a logical argument on assisted suicide in opposition to one's personal opinion. • Construct a helium-neon laser.
Evaluation/ Evaluating	• Assess the validity of certain conclusions based on the data and statistical analysis. • Critically analyze a novel with evidence to support a critique. • Recommend a portfolio of 20 stock investments based on recent performance and projected value.

gives examples of outcomes at each cognitive level in various disciplines.

Bear in mind that the true cognitive level of an outcome depends on the material students are given in a course. If they are handed a formal definition of *iambic pentameter*, then their defining it is a simple recall or comprehension operation. If, however, they are provided only with examples of poems and

Figure 2.1   Rubric for Evaluating and Revising Student Learning Outcomes

Dimension	Excellent	Common Errors	Needs Revision	Missed the Point
Outcomes are observable, assessable, and measurable.	All of the outcomes are assessable and measurable. Instructor can observe (usually see or hear) and evaluate each learner's performance by clear standards, such as how well, how many, or to what degree.	Some outcomes use verbs that refer to a learner's internal state of mind, such as "know," "understand," or "appreciate," which an instructor cannot observe and assess. Or some outcomes are too general to specify standards for evaluation.	Outcomes fail to describe 1) observable performances that are assessable and measurable and/or 2) what the learners will be able to **do**.	Outcomes list the topics the course will cover or what the instructor will do. Or outcomes use verbs that refer a learner's internal state, which an instructor cannot observe and assess.
At least some of the outcomes require high levels of cognition.	Most of the outcomes reflect high levels of cognition—that is, application, analysis, synthesis, or evaluation.	All or almost all the outcomes require low levels of cognition (knowledge and comprehension), such as "recognize," "identify," "define," or "describe."	Not enough outcomes address higher levels of cognition, given the level of the course and the learners.	Outcomes use verbs that describe low-level internal states, such as "know," "understand," or "appreciate."
Outcomes are achievable.	Outcomes are realistic for the course length and credit hours and the level of the learners.	Outcomes are too numerous for the instructor to assess or the learners to achieve.	Outcomes are too advanced for course length/credit hours and/or the learners.	Outcomes don't use action verbs to describe what the learners will be able to **do**.
Outcomes are relevant and meaningful to the learners.	Instructor makes the outcomes relevant and meaningful to the learners and their personal or career goals.	Not all the outcomes and their benefits are relevant and meaningful to the learners and their personal or career goals.	The learners can't make sense out of the outcomes.	Outcomes don't indicate what the learners will be able to **do**.

plays written in it and are asked to abstract a definition from the examples, they are engaging in the much higher-order process of synthesis.

As you check key verbs and draft outcome statements, think about what cognitive operations you are emphasizing. We can foster critical thinking and problem-solving skills only by setting outcomes above the levels of knowledge/remembering and comprehension/understanding. Although these lower levels furnish foundations for learning, they are not the end of education. Even introductory courses can engage students in application, analysis, synthesis, and evaluation. Therefore, whatever your course, it is wise to include some higher-order outcomes to challenge students to higher levels of thinking. Once you draft your outcomes, evaluate them by the rubric shown in Figure 2.1.

To avoid generating too many detailed outcomes, Hansen (2011) recommends deriving them from the big ideas in your discipline and what you hope to be students' *enduring understandings* of your subject matter. Consider how these should shape your students' capabilities and skills. For instance, in chemistry, students should be able to predict and explain the results of two chemicals being combined. In accounting, they should be able to identify and rectify an audit problem in a financial statement. In the arts, they should be able to place an unfamiliar work in its historical context. In education, they should be able to design an effective lesson consistent with cognitive science and educational theory.

◼ SEQUENCING OUTCOMES INTO A LEARNING PROCESS

When you list all your learning outcomes, you will probably notice that some have to precede others. Students have to achieve some of them early in the term to prepare them to achieve more advanced ones later in the course. If they cannot perform the prerequisite outcomes, they won't be able to achieve the latter ones. For instance, if you want your students to be able to develop a research proposal near

the end of the course, they will have to be able to do several other things beforehand:

- Frame a research problem or hypothesis
- Justify its significance
- Conduct and write up an adequate literature review
- Devise an appropriate research design
- Describe the data collection procedures
- Outline the steps of the analysis (which is premised on some methodological expertise)
- Explain the importance of the expected results
- Develop a mock budget

If your course or its prerequisite courses do not include these skills as outcomes, your students will be ill equipped to write a decent research proposal.

From this perspective, a course is a learning process of advancing through a logical succession of outcomes. This sequencing of outcomes serves as scaffolding for an entire course design.

Ultimate Outcomes

The easiest way to develop this logical succession of student learning outcomes is to formulate your end-of-term, or *ultimate*, outcomes first. These are likely to be the most challenging skills and cognitively advanced learning. No doubt they require high levels of thinking (application, analysis, synthesis, or evaluation) and a combination of skills and abilities that students should have acquired earlier in the course. They probably relate to your discipline's big ideas and enduring understandings (Hansen, 2011). They may even constitute the whole goal of the course. Often assessment takes the form of a major capstone assignment or a comprehensive final, or both.

Mediating Outcomes

From here you work backward, determining what your students will have to be able to do before they can achieve your ultimate outcomes. These abilities are your *mediating* outcomes, and you will probably have quite a few of them, each representing a component or lower-level version of one of your ultimate outcomes. You might want to visualize the working-backward process by picturing a branching tree that grows from three or more main trunks (*ultimate* learning outcomes) on the far right and branches back to the left. These branches represent your mediating and foundational (the very first) outcomes, which your students must achieve before attempting the more advanced outcomes to the right.

Your challenge now is to figure out the most logical and efficient order in which students should acquire these mediating abilities. These outcomes may have a logical internal order of their own. The skill-building logic is probably clearest in cumulative subjects such as mathematics, physics, and engineering. However, many courses, especially those within a loosely organized curriculum, allow instructors a lot of discretionary room in sequencing the mediating outcomes. Textbooks may follow a certain order, but the topical sequencing may be largely arbitrary. In introductory survey courses, literature courses, and even certain science and health science courses, the topics students study and the skills they acquire can be logically organized in different ways.

Foundational Outcomes

Once you work your way back to the earliest stages of your course, you will reach your *foundational* learning outcomes: those on which the learning process of the course is predicated. These will involve one or more of the following:

- Your students will master the most basic skills or the first in a sequence of procedures. At the cognitive level, this means being able to recall and paraphrase elemental facts, principles, processes, and definitions of essential terms and concepts.
- They will identify, question, and abandon the misconceptions about the subject matter that they brought into the course.
- They will identify, question, and abandon their dualistic thinking about the subject matter

(a particularly prevalent epistemological misconception) as they come to recognize uncertainties in the field.

These are perhaps the most basic learning objectives we can set for students. After all, they can't apply, analyze, synthesize, or evaluate a discipline's knowledge if they cannot speak or write the discipline's language and summarize or paraphrase its basic ideas. If you organize a course into modules of knowledge that have different sets of basic facts, terms, concepts, or theories, you will probably have foundational outcomes at the start of each module.

Moreover, students cannot accurately map new, valid knowledge onto existing knowledge that is riddled with misconceptions and misinformation. A faulty model will not accommodate the new material you intend for them, so they will not be able to assimilate it, at least not at more than a surface level. To bring about a major shift in your students' worldview, you must create learning situations that reveal the errors in their mental models and the explanatory superiority of your discipline's model.

Let us consider some discipline-specific examples of essential shifts. To master physics on a serious level, students must replace their Aristotelian or Newtonian model of the physical world, both of which are serviceable in everyday life, with Einstein's model. To think like a sociologist, a learner must relinquish an individualistic free-will view to explain people's life courses and replace it with the more deterministic, probabilistic theory that their location in the social structure at birth stacks the deck in favor of or against possible life courses and the acquisition of various rewards. To understand evolutionary biology, students have to stop viewing *Homo sapiens* as the purpose and destination of epochs of evolution and see our species as just another temporarily successful adaptation among millions of others.

In addition, to begin to internalize *any* body of knowledge, students must acquire an understanding of what knowledge actually is and isn't. As explained in chapter 1, knowledge is simply a mental grid that we human beings have created and imposed over a more complex reality to try to understand and manipulate it. This grid encompasses all the major patterns we have identified through our observations, along with our best-supported interpretations of them at this point in time. The fact that that reality is inherently messy and conforms only so far to any grid we can construct is the underlying source of the uncertainty in all disciplines. Because all grids are more or less flawed, disciplines have evolved standards of comparison for distinguishing the better ones. To bring students to these insights, dualism is the first misconception we should discredit before escorting them into our subject matter.

■ HELPFUL FRAMEWORKS FOR DESIGNING A COURSE

Four frameworks—Bloom's (1956) and Anderson and Krathwohl's (2000) taxonomy of cognitive operations, Perry's (1968) and Baxter Magolda's (1992) theory of undergraduate cognitive development, Fink's (2013) categories of learning, and Wiggins and McTighe's (2005) facets of understanding—offer schemata, alone and in combination, for designing courses. You may find one or more of them useful as heuristic devices.

Bloom's and Anderson and Krathwohl's Framework

Both Bloom's (1956) and Anderson and Krathwohl's (2000) taxonomies of cognitive operations are hierarchical, from lower order to higher order. They posit that to be able to perform one level of thinking, learners must be able to perform all the lower-level thinking operations. By extension, a well-designed course should sequence the learning outcomes to lead students up the hierarchy.

It is self-evident that a student has to be able to define certain concepts, state certain principles, and recall certain facts before thinking about them in a more complex way. But beyond that, both Bloom's and Anderson and Krathwohl's hierarchies break down. For instance, the practice of medicine, law, and other professions is all about *applying* knowledge to new, often complicated situations. But before applying knowledge, professionals have to *analyze* the elements of the problematic situation, *evaluate* what knowledge and disciplinary algorithms are most useful and relevant to the situation, and *synthesize* (or *create*) a problem-solving strategy—for example, a legal approach or a medical diagnosis and treatment plan.

Perry's and Baxter Magolda's Framework

The section "The Cognitive Development of Undergraduates" in chapter 1 summarizes both Perry's (1968) and Baxter Magolda's (1992) parallel frameworks. Using one or the other as a course design heuristic, you sequence your learning outcomes to reflect students' progression through the stages or levels, as far as you think you can lead your class. For the primary foundational outcome, which is moving beyond dualism, students would have to explain the multiple competing interpretations or theories for some disciplinary phenomenon or issue, demonstrating that they realize that authorities don't have all the answers or the one right answer on the matter. To achieve a major mediating outcome (moving through multiplicity and relativism), students would have to analyze and critique these interpretations or theories. For the ultimate outcome (tentative commitment), they would have to embrace one of the interpretations or theories and justify their choice, as well as *qualify* it by explicating the limitations of their chosen viewpoint.

While this schema may not apply well to an undergraduate science or engineering course, it can work very effectively in high-uncertainty and interpretive disciplines, such as literature, history, the arts, and philosophy. I used it to design a freshman seminar I taught in the past, Free Will and Determinism. Although it was anchored in philosophy, it featured readings from clinical and behaviorist psychology, sociology, political science, genetics, biochemistry, and sociobiology. These two paragraphs from the syllabus explain the outcomes, starting with the ultimate outcome:

> By the end of this course, you will have developed a well-reasoned, personal position on the role of free will, determinism, compatibilism, fatalism, and spiritual destiny in your own and others' lives. You will be able to express, support, and defend your position orally and in writing while acknowledging its weaknesses and realizing that it can never be validated as "the right answer" and may change over time [Ultimate Outcome: Tentative Commitment]. Hopefully, you will also begin to feel comfortable with the uncertainty and tentativeness of knowledge and with making decisions in spite of it.
>
> To help you attain these major objectives [outcomes], you will also acquire these supporting abilities: to sift out the various positions on free will and determinism (as well as compatibilism, fatalism, and spiritual destiny) in the assigned literature, along with their implicit premises and "givens," and to express them accurately both orally and in writing [Foundational Outcome: Uncertainty]; to draw sound comparisons and contrasts among them; to evaluate their strengths, weaknesses, and limitations [Mediating Outcome #1: Uncertainty as Inherent and Legitimate]; and to distinguish among the stronger and the weaker positions [Mediating Outcome #2: Standards for Comparison].

The final paper closely reflected the ultimate outcome, and the first two papers, the two mediating outcomes.

Fink's Framework

Fink's (2013) categories of learning do not offer a built-in sequencing of outcomes as do the other two frameworks. His approach is not hierarchical but cumulative and interactive. An ideally designed and developed course promotes all six kinds of learning, resulting in a genuinely significant learning experience. The goal is not to order the kinds of learning but to help students interrelate and engage in them synergistically. So a course design based on Fink's framework might start with foundational knowledge and then progressively add outcomes addressing each of the other five kinds of learning one or more times during the course, ensuring that all six kinds are represented by the end.

According to Fink, his framework can accommodate courses of all levels and disciplines, whether face-to-face or online, and he provides a comprehensive, step-by-step procedure for applying it to any course. Here is one generic example. After students acquire some foundational knowledge, have them apply this new knowledge to solve a problem of relevance to them (application) or to resolve a situation where they can see how some phenomenon affects them and others (human dimension). This learning experience should promote their interest in the subject matter (caring). With their interest piqued, they should begin to notice the relationships between the new material and other things they have learned (integration). As they recognize more linkages, they should start drawing additional implications for their own and others' lives (human dimension), as well as other ways to apply the material to improve the quality of life (application). At this point, they should want to learn still more (caring) and realize their need to acquire stronger learning skills (learning how to learn).

This illustration shows that a well-designed course can generate a mutually reinforcing relationship between learning and motivation. Fink also emphasizes course *alignment*—that is, ensuring that the learning activities (teaching methods) and the assessments complement the learning goals (outcomes). (We will revisit his model in chapter 11.)

Wiggin and McTighe's Framework

Because Wiggin and McTighe's six facets of understanding overlap so much with Fink's schema, it should be fairly easy to see how each facet can lead to another.

SHOWING STUDENTS THEIR LEARNING PROCESS

The younger generation of students prefers visuals over text, so it is a wise idea is to illustrate your course design to students so they can see where your course is going in terms of their learning. An *outcomes map* serves this purpose. It is a flowchart of the learning outcomes, starting from your foundational outcomes, progressing through your mediating outcomes, and finally arriving at your ultimate outcomes. Thus, it visually represents the sequence, progression, and accumulation of the skills and abilities that students should be able to demonstrate at various times in the term. It shows how achieving one or more outcomes should enable them to achieve subsequent ones.

Because I have written extensively on charting an outcomes maps elsewhere (Nilson, 2007a),

I will furnish here just a couple of examples that I have developed. Figure 2.2 is an outcomes map for my Free Will and Determinism course. Following Perry's (1968) framework, it contains just a few outcomes that build up to the ultimate commitment outcome. These outcomes parallel those in the two paragraphs from the syllabus in the previous section. Figure 2.3 is the outcomes map for my graduate course, College Teaching. It does not follow any specific course design framework. It has a genuine flowchart look and feel, clearly showing how achieving one outcome equips students to achieve later ones. The students' major assignment is an individual course design and development project, after which they write a statement of teaching philosophy. I make it clear to my students that, of course, I won't be able to assess them on two of the ultimate outcomes—obtaining a teaching position and meeting institutional assessment requirements and

Figure 2.2 Outcomes Map for Freshman Seminar, Free Will and Determinism

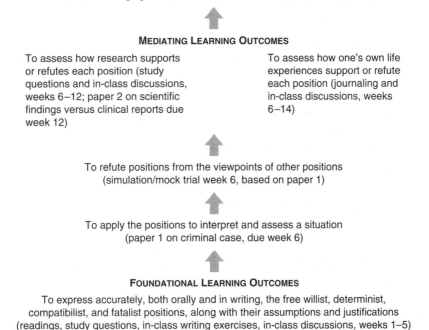

ULTIMATE LEARNING OUTCOME

To develop and explain in writing a well-reasoned personal position on the role of free will, determinism, compatibilism, and fatalism (including spiritual destiny) in your own and others' lives, and to defend it while acknowledging its weaknesses and limitations (capstone paper 3)

MEDIATING LEARNING OUTCOMES

To assess how research supports or refutes each position (study questions and in-class discussions, weeks 6–12; paper 2 on scientific findings versus clinical reports due week 12)

To assess how one's own life experiences support or refute each position (journaling and in-class discussions, weeks 6–14)

To refute positions from the viewpoints of other positions (simulation/mock trial week 6, based on paper 1)

To apply the positions to interpret and assess a situation (paper 1 on criminal case, due week 6)

FOUNDATIONAL LEARNING OUTCOMES

To express accurately, both orally and in writing, the free willist, determinist, compatibilist, and fatalist positions, along with their assumptions and justifications (readings, study questions, in-class writing exercises, in-class discussions, weeks 1–5)

Figure 2.3   Outcomes Map for Graduate Course, College Teaching

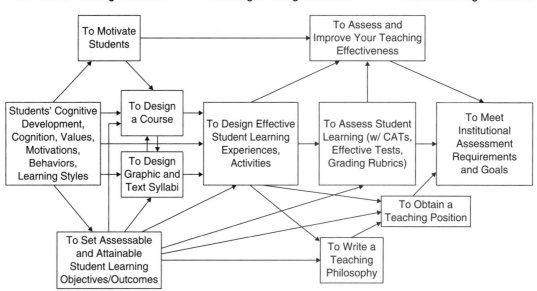

Foundational Learning Outcomes ⟶ *Mediating Learning Outcomes* ⟶ *Ultimate Learning Outcomes*

goals—but they will leave the course knowing how to achieve these in their fast-approaching future.

While these two examples look very different, they cannot possibly illustrate the many ways that outcomes maps can vary: the directions in which they flow; their spatial arrangements; their enclosures and connectors; and their use of type sizes, type styles, shadings, and colors. Outcomes maps may or may not follow one of the four course design frameworks presented earlier. They may or may not supply a time schedule such as the week or class number that you expect students to achieve each outcome. But however they look, they all furnish students with far more information about how their learning will progress through the course than a simple list of outcomes.

If you decide to chart an outcomes map for any of your courses, the process will probably lead you to reexamine your outcomes and their sequencing. You might realize that you've previously missed a step or two in your students' logical learning process or that a different ordering of some of your outcomes would make more sense. So you may find

that you get as much out of your drawing the map as your students do.

■ OUTCOMES-CENTERED COURSE DEVELOPMENT

Your learning outcomes should direct all the other elements of your course, which ensures that your course will be well aligned. Your outcomes map is your course skeleton. With that in place, you start developing your course into a more detailed plan, filling it out by putting muscle and connective tissue on the bone structure.

Course Content

Limit the content to whatever will help your students achieve your outcomes. If you specialize in the content area, narrowing it down will challenge you. Be brutal in eliminating extraneous topics. Instructors, especially new ones, tend to pack too much material into a course. It is better to teach a few topics well than merely to cover the material with a steamroller and wind up teaching very little of anything. You should be able to draw a graphic of the interrelationships among your course topics just as you can draw one of the organization of your student learning outcomes. (We will look at the *graphic syllabus* in chapter 5.)

Students' First Exposure to New Material

If your students' first exposure to new material is assigned readings, then choose books, articles, and websites in line with your learning outcomes and content. You will be fortunate to find a textbook that reflects your disciplinary approach, so you may want to supplement your best available option with additional material. In fact, you don't have to use a textbook at all.

If you flip your classroom, your students' first exposure may take the form of videos or podcasts that you have created of your lectures or found on the web (see chapter 4). Again, they should all serve the purpose of helping your students achieve your outcomes.

It is one thing to assign readings, videos, or podcasts and another thing to get students to read, view, or listen to them attentively and understand them by the time they are due. If you have found students' homework compliance or comprehension to be a problem, you are in excellent company (refer to chapter 21 for solutions).

Teaching Strategies

Think of your teaching strategies as your students' learning activities and experiences, which you create. You have many alternatives to choose from but limited time to manage them and provide feedback. So all of chapter 11 is devoted to helping you make the best decisions—that is, selecting the most effective methods for helping your students achieve your outcomes. The rest of parts 3 and 4 recommend how to implement your best options. You will find the class-by-class bricks and mortar for building a successful

learning experience for your students, ensuring that your teaching translates into their learning.

Indeed, your outcomes can and should guide your choice of activities down to the individual class level. If you want your students to be able to write a certain type of analysis by a certain week of the term, then structure in-class activities and assignments to give them practice in writing that type of analysis. If you want them to be able to solve certain kinds of problems, then design activities and assignments to give them practice in solving such problems. If you want them to research and argue a point of view in class, select activities and assignments to give them practice in research, rhetoric, and oral presentation.

Assessments

Remembering that assessments should mirror outcomes, look to your ultimate outcomes for questions and tasks for your final exam, final paper assignment, or capstone project. After all, these outcomes delineate what you want your students to be able to do by the end of the course. Then move backward through your course and devise assignments and tests that ask students to perform your mediating and foundational outcomes. Once you've written sound outcomes, you've at least outlined your assessments. Chapters 26 and 27 offer good advice about constructing these instruments and assessing student performance on them.

• • •

If you would like to design your course with the guidance of a workbook, I highly recommend Jones, Noyd, and Sagendorf's *Building a Pathway for Student Learning: A How-To Guide to Course Design* (2014), which leads you step by step through the entire process.

■ THE BIG PICTURE

The outcomes map of my Free Will and Determinism course in Figure 2.2 shows not only the sequencing of the learning outcomes but also the activities and assignments for helping students achieve those outcomes and helping me assess their progress. These activities and assignments are listed in parentheses after each outcome, followed by the weeks in the term that they occur. They include readings, in-class and online discussions, journaling, a simulation, study questions, in-class writing exercises, and three papers. Although this flowchart does not provide a class-by-class schedule, it serves well as a general outline for developing the schedule and detailed descriptions of the activities and assignments.

Once you have a sound course design, your syllabus almost writes itself. Chapter 5 presents a concise checklist of all the information that can and usually should be included in this important course document.

The next chapter draws on the course design principles presented in this one to explain how to integrate critical thinking into a course. Research tells us that to foster critical thinking in our students, we have to make it an explicit goal in a discipline-based course and build assessable critical thinking outcomes, learning experiences, and assessments into the course.

CHAPTER 3

Building Critical Thinking into a Course Design

Our courses fail to develop critical thinking in our students unless we explicitly incorporate critical thinking outcomes, learning experiences, and assessments into our course design (Abrami et al., 2008). This finding explains why this topic appears so early in this book. We cannot assume that students acquire critical thinking skills as we move through our content. Conversely, we cannot teach critical thinking in a knowledge vacuum. The skills must be applied to some kind of content or situation. Therefore, students need some knowledge before they can critically examine assumptions, data, arguments, or conclusions (Willingham, 2007).

The literature on critical thinking offers no easy, straightforward prescriptions. It is fragmented into several different perspectives on what critical thinking is and what is required to do it. This may help explain why polls and surveys reveal that few university faculty can define critical thinking or know how to teach it (Paul & Elder, 2013b; Paul, Elder, & Bartell, 2013). Furthermore, the literature includes little empirical testing of teaching techniques that should develop these skills. In one study

on business students, discussions, debates, and guided questioning seemed to work (Braun, 2004). In a study in a research methods course, students learned critical thinking by answering a series of evaluative questions on research-based publications they gathered (Tremblay & Downey, 2004). What the critical thinking literature does provide are questions and tasks that give students practice in critical thinking, and we will look at several sets of these.

THE MANY FACES OF CRITICAL THINKING

Let's take a quick look at the various perspectives so that we can proceed to make some general statements about critical thinking and offer teaching guidelines.

Some scholars avoid the critical thinking literature altogether and endorse existing cognitive models. For instance, Bloom's (1956) higher-order cognitive operations can be cast as critical thinking skills, and the previous chapter supplies lists of verbs that break down these operations into specific skills. Other scholars turn to Perry's (1968) stages of undergraduate cognitive development, which we visited in chapter 1, although these do not easily transfer to everyday life applications. The next five frameworks were developed just for teaching and assessing critical thinking. Let me add the disclaimer that I cannot do justice to any of them in this limited space.

According to Brookfield (2012), critical thinking is all about identifying assumptions, which he broadly defines as any almost kind of statement. He presents four distinct traditions of critical thinking: (1) analytic philosophy, which encompasses logic, logical fallacies, argument analysis, and inductive, deductive, analogical, and inferential reasoning; (2) natural sciences, characterized by the hypothetical-deductive method and principle of falsifiability; (3) pragmatism, which evaluates theories and beliefs according to their practical application; and (4) critical theory, which reveals the hidden dynamics of power and ideological manipulation. As you will see, just about every leading approach to critical thinking embraces analytic philosophy and the natural scientific method, but none takes in pragmatism or critical theory.

Facione and his associates developed the popular California Critical Thinking Skills Test, which assesses thinking skills identified by a large group of philosophers called the Delphi panel (because the group used the Delphi method): overall reflective reasoning, analysis, inference, evaluation, deduction, induction, interpretation, explanation, and numeracy (quantitative reasoning). This perspective falls squarely within the analytic philosophy and natural sciences traditions. The formal definitions of these critical thinking components are at http://www.insightassessment.com/ Products/Products-Summary/Critical-Thinking-Skills-Tests/California-Critical-Thinking-Skills-Test-Numeracy-CCTST-Nl.

Reflecting the same two traditions, Halpern (2003, 2004) proposes a taxonomy of five critical thinking skills: (1) verbal reasoning (identifying weaknesses in persuasive techniques), (2) argument analysis, (3) scientific reasoning (the logic of hypothesis testing), (4) statistical reasoning about likelihood and probability, and (5) decision making and problem solving.

Paul and Elder (2013c), the founding leaders of the Foundation for Critical Thinking, posit eight "universal intellectual standards" by which to evaluate critical thinking around a problem, issue, or situation: clarity, accuracy, precision, relevance, depth, breadth, logic, and fairness (e.g., no conflict of interest). Again, analytic philosophy and scientific reasoning underlie these standards. Paul and Elder's perspective includes a great deal more and will receive more elaboration later. Their website, http://www.criticalthinking .org/, offers a wealth of free resources on the teaching and learning of critical thinking for faculty and students at all educational levels.

Finally, Wolcott (2006) can also boast a comprehensive website on her step-based, developmental framework (http://www.wolcottlynch.com). The instructor's charge is to move students up the "steps for better thinking." Students start at "step 0," where the "performance pattern" is that of the "Confused Fact-Finder." At this stage, comparable to Perry's dualistic stage, students merely repeat whatever information they have read or heard and seek one correct answer to a question or solution to a problem. Once they can move beyond facts and identify a problem or issue, define what information is relevant to it, and accept the uncertainties surrounding it, they arrive at step 1. Although they understand that no one correct answer may exist, they still view their learning task as choosing one answer or solution and gathering evidence to support it. This is why their performance pattern is called the "Biased Jumper." At step 2, students begin to see their own biases and explore other points of view. Fitting the pattern of a "Perpetual Analyzer," they can identify the assumptions and logic of these alternatives, but for them, the goal is to take a detached, noncommittal, relativistic position toward all the options. Students become the "Pragmatic Performer" at step 3. Confronted with a question or problem, they realize that some options are better than others. They evaluate and compare them on relevant criteria in search of the best answer or solution—that is, the one with the strongest evidence and most solid reasoning. No doubt any of us would be happy to guide our students to this lofty performance pattern, but Wolcott's model proposes one more: the "Strategic Re-Visioner." At this final step 4, students view any best answer or solution as provisional and remain open to better ones as they create new knowledge and recast the question or problem. This perspective, which mirrors Albert Einstein's insight, "We can't solve problems by using the same kind of thinking we used when we created them," paves the way for innovative leaps in thinking and problem solving. Only Wolcott's framework ventures beyond analytic philosophy and scientific reasoning to add creativity to critical thinking.

■ COMMON GROUND

What understandings and principles can we take from all these perspectives? Let's start with a definition that we can distill from all of those proposed. Critical thinking entails an interpretation or analysis, then an evaluation or judgment about a claim that may or may not be valid, complete, or the best possible. A *claim* may be a belief, value, assumption, problem definition, interpretation, generalization, analysis, viewpoint, position, hypothesis, prediction, solution, inference, decision, justification, or conclusion. Why question a claim? Perhaps the evidence is uncertain or ambiguous. Or the person or organization making the claim may have an interest in one side or another, or the data or the reasoning from the data are suspect. The issue may engender disagreement, debate, or controversy, and therefore other respectable competing claims. Then again, the problem may be fuzzy and ill defined, or the process for testing the claim unclear or nonstandardized. No doubt logic or scientific reasoning will guide the analytic and evaluative thinking processes.

A point of agreement among all these perspectives is that critical thinking is difficult. Human nature leads us to recognize patterns and generalize from those patterns in an effort to simplify reality. After all, a straightforward, predictable environment quells fear and stress, permits us some measure of control, and facilitates survival. Why question our simplifications unless we have to because they fail us? We feel the same about our beliefs, values, allegiances, and habits of mind—probably more so to the extent that we cherish them and build our identities around them. Challenging them can cause acute discomfort. Therefore, critical thinking takes time to overcome our natural resistance to doing it and change our habits of mind.

As instructors, we can increase our students' willingness to explore different ways of thinking and believing. If we can help them see the costs and fallacies of their current mind-sets—how some kinds of thinking lead to poor decisions and faulty conclusions—we may be able to help them develop a desire to think critically.

This brings us to another common ground among the different perspectives: they all posit that critical thinking extends beyond the cognitive domain and encompasses dispositions, affective attitudes, character traits, and mental health issues. According to Halpern (1998, 1999), a critical thinker must be willing to put effort and persistence into complex tasks; resist impulsiveness and consciously plan and follow through a line of thinking; remain open-minded and flexible; and admit error when necessary and change current thinking strategies for better ones. Paul and Elder (2013d) cite the intellectual traits (or virtues) of intellectual humility, integrity, courage, perseverance, and curiosity; fair-mindedness; and confidence in reason (as opposed to competing sources of knowledge such as revelation, tradition, and authority). Facione and his associates (Facione, Facione, & Giancarlo, 2000) propose a long list of *affective dispositions*, among them broad inquisitiveness, trust in reasoned inquiry, honesty in acknowledging one's own biases, understanding of other people's viewpoints, prudence in suspending and modifying judgments, and diligence in seeking relevant information. My own contribution to the critical thinking literature was pointing out how psychological defense mechanisms (*psychological fallacies*) such as denial, externalization, projection, rationalization, and repression interfere with critical thinking (Nilson, 1997).

Most of the scholars—Halpern (1998, 1999), Facione (2013), and Paul and Elder (2013d)—also contend that critical thinking requires metacognition or self-regulation, which is the habit of monitoring, evaluating, and correcting one's thinking. Only then can students articulate and transfer the thinking skills they are learning to new issues and situations. For instance, students should be able to describe and assess the reasoning process by which they arrived at a certain position or conclusion, including how they gathered and appraised the evidence. They should also be able to explain why they discarded competing positions and conclusions and deemed one to be the best.

With this common ground in mind, let's turn to possible critical thinking learning outcomes for your courses. Then we can examine some the tasks and questions that can give students practice in the type of thinking that will help them achieve those outcomes.

■ CRITICAL THINKING OUTCOMES FOR YOUR STUDENTS

What you want your students to be able to do by the end of your course depends somewhat on your discipline, especially your *type* of discipline. The outcomes listed below do not exhaust all the possibilities, but they cover a lot of learning territory.

Any course in a discipline that takes a scientific approach to its enterprise, such as the natural, social, and applied sciences, should have some critical thinking outcomes related to the scientific method. These skills, some adapted from the ETS Proficiency profile, are good candidates to consider:

- Interpret and display quantitative relationships in graphs, tables, charts, and other graphics.
- Analyze situations or data to identify problems.

- Identify and summarize the problem, question, or position at issue.
- Categorize problems by the appropriate algorithms to solve them.
- Integrate information or data to solve a problem.
- Assess alternative solutions and implement the optimal ones.
- Explain how new information or data can change the definition of a problem or its optimal solution.
- Evaluate hypotheses for consistency with established facts.
- Develop and justify one's own hypotheses, interpretations, or positions.
- Identify the limitations of one's own hypotheses, interpretations, or positions.
- Identify, analyze, and evaluate key assumptions and the influence of context.
- Design and carry out an experiment to test a given hypothesis.
- Evaluate the appropriateness of procedures for investigating a question of causation.
- Evaluate data for consistency with established facts, hypotheses, or methods.
- Separate factual information from inferences.
- Separate relevant from irrelevant information.
- Identify alternative positions or interpretations of the data or observations.
- Evaluate competing causal explanations.
- Explain the limitations of correlational data.
- Evaluate evidence and identify both reasonable and inappropriate conclusions.
- Identify and evaluate implications.
- Identify new information or data that might support or contradict a hypothesis.

Courses in the technical and problem-solving disciplines might be designed around the outcomes above that include the words *problem* or *solution*. However, the criteria for judging the best problem definition or conclusion would include more practical considerations such as cost, time, and client preferences.

In the humanities and some areas of the social sciences, courses focus on arguments anchored in texts, documentary data, logic, and key observations. Their outcomes of choice might include some or all of these:

- Determine the relevance of information for evaluating an argument or conclusion.
- Separate facts from opinions and inferences.
- Locate and use relevant primary and secondary sources to conduct research.
- Analyze explanations for historical and contemporary issues, trends, and problems (Nuhfer, Harrington, Pasztor, & Whorf, 2014).
- Develop explanations for historical and contemporary issues, trends, and problems (Nuhfer et al., 2014).
- Recognize flaws, inconsistencies, and logical fallacies in an argument.
- Evaluate competing interpretations, explanations, evidence, and conclusions.
- Communicate complex ideas effectively.

Finally, courses in the arts have their own distinctive learning outcomes—for example:

- Identify and analyze alternative artistic interpretations of a work.
- Determine how well an artistic interpretation is supported by evidence contained in a work.
- Recognize the salient features or themes in works of art.
- Evaluate works of art according to commonly agreed-on criteria.
- Compare and contrast different works to provide evidence of change or growth through history, across cultures, across locations, or in a particular artist.
- Distinguish between objective and subjective analysis and criticism (Nuhfer et al., 2014).
- Create a respectable piece of art and explain its significance.

Given that metacognition must accompany critical thinking, a course with a critical thinking emphasis should have some self-regulated learning outcomes for students as well. Here are a few suggestions (Nilson, 2013a):

- Identify the main points in readings and lectures.
- Set goals for one's performance on exams and assignments.
- Prepare more effectively for exams.
- Plan how to use feedback to revise an assignment.
- Consciously observe and evaluate one's own thinking and emotional reactions while doing course activities and assignments (reading, listening, organizing, writing, designing, and the like).
- Assess one's improvement in critical thinking skills.
- Explain the usefulness of critical thinking skills beyond the course.
- Describe how one has changed beliefs, values, attitudes, habits of mind, worldviews, and behaviors as a result of the course.

Teaching self-regulated learning generally means (1) explaining to students what it is and how it benefits learners and (2) leading activities and making assignments that engage students self-regulated learning practices. Specifically, students reflect on the meaning of the material and on their strategies for learning, studying for a test, or doing an assignment: How did they define and plan the task? What skills did they use while doing the tasks? What problems did they run into, and how did they solve them? How did they arrive at their response or solution? What learning value did this task have for them? What would they do differently the next time? How did their thinking on the topic change, and why (Nilson, 2013a)? Since chapter 20 contains many self-regulated learning activities and assignments, most of which require little or no grading, we will now move onto another topic.

GIVING STUDENTS PRACTICE IN CRITICAL THINKING

The kinds of tasks you assign and questions you ask your students depend, of course, on your outcomes.

Both in and out of class, give students practice, followed by feedback, in thinking about the content using the skills you have targeted. You should always ask students to explain how they came to the answer, solution, or conclusion that they did. Giving students this kind of practice is your primary strategy for teaching critical thinking.

Halpern's Tasks

Halpern (2003, 2004) suggests teaching students critical thinking skills by assigning tasks like these within a discussion, as a class activity, or as homework:

- Identify and assess assumptions in an argument.
- Identify problems in a situation.
- Explain the connection between new knowledge and prior knowledge.
- Formally plan a strategy to achieve a goal, to include ordering and prioritizing tasks and ranking problems by seriousness and urgency.
- Give and evaluate reasons to support or reject a conclusion.
- Assess degrees of probability and uncertainty.
- Place isolated data into a wider framework or context.
- Recast text-based information into a graphical form.
- Synthesize information from multiple sources.
- Reason through alternatives to select the best option.

Facione's Questions

Facione (1990, 2011) advises that teaching critical thinking starts with what you do in and out of the classroom with your students. You should model the appropriate dispositions, attitudes, character traits, and critical thinking skills in the teaching process. For example, Seesholtz and Polk (2009) modeled critical thinking and civil discourse in their team-taught course by debating issues in front of their students. In addition, you should encourage their curiosity, questions, and skepticism about claims you make. And you should routinely ask them to explain and justify the claims they make.

Facione (2013) lists questions and tasks you can use to teach students the nature of critical thinking and give them practice in doing it. Here is a sample:

- *Interpretation.* What does this mean? How should we understand this? How can we make sense of this? How should we categorize this? Given the context, what was intended by doing this?
- *Analysis.* What do you conclude? Why do you conclude this? Why do you think that? What are your reasons? What are the arguments on both sides? What must we assume to accept that conclusion? Can these two apparently conflicting conclusions be reconciled? If so, how?
- *Inference.* What does this evidence imply? What do these data imply? If we accept/reject this assumption/claim, what are the consequences for us going forward? What unintended consequences may there be? At this point, what conclusions can we draw? What options can we eliminate? What additional information/data do we need? What options have we not yet considered? How do these change our thinking?
- *Evaluation.* How does this claim stack up against the evidence? What reasons might we have to distrust the person making the claim? How sound is the reasoning? Do you see any flaws in the argument? How confident can we be in our conclusion at this point?
- *Explanation.* What exactly did this study/research find? How was the analysis conducted? Why do you favor this answer/solution? How was this decision made?

Facione (2013) also includes a series of self-regulation questions, a topic we have already touched on and will revisit in chapter 20.

Paul and Elder's Model

Paul and Elder (2013a, 2013c) also provide questions to ask students to hold them accountable for meeting the eight standards for critical thinking—questions that we hope students will internalize to ask themselves. Each standard is independent of the others and important in its own right. Paul and Elder call clarity the *gateway standard* because we cannot evaluate a statement until we can understand what it is saying.

1. *Clarity*. Can you elaborate on that point? Can you phrase it in more specific terms and give an example? For example, the question, "How can we solve our energy problem?" fails to define exactly what the problem is. It needs a sharper focus, something that defines an agent and problem parameters, as this question does: "What can power companies do to reduce energy consumption by businesses and households?"
2. *Accuracy*. How can you validate the accuracy of this statement/evidence?
3. *Precision*. Can you be more specific? Can you give more details?
4. *Relevance*. How does that information/variable bear on the issue? For instance, the price of crude oil is not connected to what power companies can do to reduce energy consumption.
5. *Depth*. How does your conclusion address the complexities and most important aspects of the problem? How well does it take feasibility, trade-offs, and options into account? Just telling people to save energy by driving their cars less does not deal with their need for transportation when no other viable alternatives are available.
6. *Breadth*. What is another viewpoint on the problem? How does the other side see the issue?
7. *Logic*. How does this follow from the evidence or previous statements? How can both this and that be true when they lead to such different conclusions?
8. *Fairness*, Do you have a vested interest in one conclusion or another? Do you have any relevant biases? Are you representing the other viewpoints honestly and impartially?

Paul and Elder (2013a) also provide two templates to guide students' analyses of different kinds of texts: one for articles, essays, or chapters and another for textbooks. They also furnish a third template for evaluating an author's reasoning. Each template poses eight questions that ask students to identify the following elements: the main purpose of the text (author); the key question it (the author) addresses; the most important information or evidence it (the author) offers to support the conclusions; the main conclusions or inferences it (the author) draws; the key idea(s) in its (the author's) line of reasoning; the main assumptions (often unstated and taken for granted) behind its (the author's) line of reasoning; the logical implications or consequences, whether stated or not, of its (the author's) line of reasoning; and its (the author's) main point of view.

The third template consists of evaluative questions for each part of the text the students identify. With respect to the author's purpose, is it well stated and justifiable? With respect to the key question, is it clear, unbiased, respectful of the complexities at issue, and relevant to the purpose? Is the most important information accurate, relevant, essential to the issue, and respectful of the complexities at issue? Are the key ideas clear and justifiably used? Are the assumptions questionable, or does the author address any problems inherent in them? Do the conclusions and inferences logically follow from the information given? Does the author consider alternative points of view or lines of reasoning and respond to objections they may raise? Is the author aware of the implications and consequences of her position? These templates show students the process of critical thinking—identifying, analyzing, and evaluating key points—as applied to common academic reading assignments.

Within Paul and Elder's tradition, Nosich (2012) recommends having students go through this four-step procedure, which he calls *SEE-I*, to clarify an issue, claim, or concept:

1. **S**tate briefly and concisely what needs to be clarified.
2. **E**laborate it in your own words with a fuller explanation.
3. **E**xemplify it with a good example.
4. **I**llustrate it visually with a graphic, such as a concept map, diagram, or drawing, or illustrate it verbally with a metaphor, simile, or analogy.

Applying Nosich's (2012) *SEE-I* to the Concept *Bias*

1. Bias is the tendency to make a certain judgment or favor a certain position without good reason.
2. Bias is based on preconceptions or distorted views about some aspect of the world. It can make it impossible for a person to look at evidence dispassionately and come to an impartial conclusion. It can lead to prejudices, favoritism, and injustices.
3. An example of bias is racism.
4. Bias is like wearing blinders. It keeps you from seeing the complete and objective picture of the world.

Wolcott's Task Prompts

Wolcott offers sets of task prompts for giving students step-by-step practice in ascending the ladder of critical thinking. To get them beyond the "Confused Fact-Finder," you must ask them to do more than merely parrot back information; they need practice in identifying problems, finding the information relevant to each problem, and determining the reasons that one approach or solution is neither clear nor certain. The goal is to help students see multiple sides of an issue. This may involve having students collect evidence to make a case for more than one particular approach or solution. Among the questions to pose to them are these:

- Why is there disagreement about this problem or issue?
- What are the different points of view on the problem or issue?
- What is uncertain about this problem or issue or the evidence for one side or another?
- Why does this uncertainty exist?
- Why can't the outcome of an approach or solution be predicted with certainty?
- What are all the possible approaches or solutions?
- What evidence supports each approach or solution?

From here students should progress to the "Biased Jumper" performance pattern. Although they grasp the notion that more than one approach or solution exists, they mistakenly believe that they should simply choose one and amass support for it. Your next task is to help them acknowledge their own biases and entertain other assumptions, interpretations, solutions, or conclusions. Now the questions to present to students are more complex:

- How good is the evidence/data in favor of one position (approach or solution) or another?
- How good is the evidence/data supporting a given approach or solution from other points of view?
- What are the strengths and weaknesses of the various pieces of evidence or data?
- What are the assumptions and interpretations behind each approach or solution?
- How do the different arguments compare and contrast?
- What are your own biases on the issue? How do your own experiences and preferences lead you toward or away from the different approaches or solutions?
- How can you organize the information differently to help you think more thoroughly and complexly about the issue?

Accustoming students to this broader way of thinking should advance them to the pattern of a "Perpetual Analyzer." At this stage, they understand the alternative positions and the reasoning behind them, but their objectivity and relativism paralyze them and they are unable to take a stance. To get them past this on-the-fence attitude, you must ask them questions that help them set priorities, compare their options, and arrive at conclusions:

- What trade-offs does each approach or solution entail? What are your priorities in determining the quality of various approaches or solutions? Which issues or interests are more important and less important in solving the problem, and why?
- How can you select and justify a particular approach or solution?
- How can you defend it against the arguments that support other reasonable approaches or solutions?
- How might changes in priorities lead to other "best" approaches or solutions?
- What does a given audience need to know in order to understand why you selected the approach or solution that you did?
- How should you develop your report/presentation to best communicate your selected approach or solution to your audience?
- Given a different audience or setting, what information and reasoning should you highlight to best communicate your approach or solution?

When students can give intelligent answers to these questions, they mature into the "Pragmatic Performer" pattern. But they may think that their well-reasoned choice settles the matter forever. At this point, you should help them critically examine their approach or solution and acknowledge its flaws and limitations and then encourage them to continue to seek a better option as conditions, information, or their own definition of the problem changes. Posing these questions will help your students emotionally detach from their approach or solution and stay open to revisiting and possibly revising their choice:

- What are the limitations of your chosen approach or solution? What priorities does it fail to serve?
- What are its implications?
- What feasible changes in conditions or new information might motivate you to question your choice?

- Under given conditions ("what if?"), how would you modify your definition of the problem and your chosen approach or solution?
- How can you monitor these conditions and obtain new information relevant to the problem and your approach or solution to it?

Having addressed these issues thoroughly, students attain the highest and most sophisticated performance pattern, the "Strategic Re-Visioner." They can define and justify their priorities; analyze and evaluate alternative approaches and solutions to a problem in view of these priorities; commit themselves, however provisionally, to the best choices; and reexamine these choices over time as conditions change and new information emerges. They can also communicate their thinking processes to others.

Bonwell's Tasks

In case the perspectives summarized thus far in this section fall short of covering all the critical thinking territory, let's look at one more list of tasks for fostering critical thinking, this one offered by Bonwell (2012). Have students practice doing the following:

- Formulate questions for clarification.
- Define the central issue or challenge.
- Classify information by type and level of quality.
- Identify patterns.
- Assess the credibility of a source.
- Distinguish fact from opinion.
- Identify ambiguity.
- Identify the stated and unstated assumptions.
- Identify the stated and unstated reasons for the conclusions.
- Identify errors in reasoning, such as logical fallacies and faulty statistical reasoning.
- Identify omitted evidence and considerations.
- Identify alternative conclusions that fit with the available evidence.
- Analyze compare-and-contrast and cause-and-effect relationships between elements.
- Develop appropriate analogies.

- Predict future trends or outcomes from the available evidence.
- Translate text material into graphic forms (e.g., illustrations, maps, tables, diagrams) and vice versa.

The Best Methods for Practice

A recent meta-analysis to determine the most effective strategies for teaching critical thinking (Abrami et al., 2015) recommends these two methods:

1. Whole-class and group discussions in which the instructor poses questions and presents tasks that require critical thinking. Such discussions may follow readings, videos, simulations, games, role plays, cases, and the like.
2. Opportunities for students to wrestle with and solve authentic or situated problems, such as those related to making life decisions and real-world problems they are likely to face in the future.

Chapter 13 offers proven discussion and questioning techniques and chapters 14 (experiential learning), 17 (the case method), 18 (problem-based learning), and 19 (problem solving in the STEM fields) are all about using authentic and situated problems to foster student learning.

After students complete any critical thinking task or respond to a question, you should ask them to recount how they thought through the task or came up with their answer. How did they arrive at their interpretation, position, solution, conclusion, or evaluation? This is just like asking students to show their work on a math problem, only here the work is their reasoning.

The Socratic Method

Socrates didn't use the term *critical thinking* to describe his questioning method, but his goal was clearly to foster critical thinking among his fellow Athenians at any cost, including his life.

In an instructional context, you open the dialogue on a given topic by posing one planned question that requires a student to take a position or point of view. After she articulates her stance, you construct a question that raises a weakness of or exception to that position, to which she responds with a defense or a qualification of her original position. The student may also assume a new position. In turn, you respond with another question that reveals a possible weakness of or exception to the defense, the qualified position, or the new position, and the student responds as before. And so the dialogue continues. This line of inquiry promotes rational thinking, self-examination, persistence, and pattern recognition, all integral facets of critical thinking.

However, the Socratic method can be a difficult teaching strategy for several reasons.

First, because it relies on a one-on-one interaction, it's difficult to scale in today's classroom. Questioning one student too long can make the rest of the class tune out. Only when you are facing several students who share the same position can you direct the same questions to different students. Because of its scalability problem, the Socratic method in its pure form works best as a tutoring strategy and not a questioning technique in a discussion (see chapter 13). Not that you or, better yet, fellow classmates shouldn't challenge a student's position in a discussion, but the challenges shouldn't evolve into a sustained dialogue with only one student.

Second, the method depends on your ability to craft questions on the spot in response to what a student says. You might not feel comfortable with such a spontaneous, unstructured format. However, with experience, you will be able to anticipate the blind alleys and misdirections students take on specific topics and develop a general discussion plan.

Finally, some students take offense to an instructor hammering them with negative questions, so be very careful to pose your challenges in a lighthearted tone.

■ THE GOAL: CRITICAL THINKING IN EVERYDAY LIFE

We teach critical thinking in the context of academic material, but the real benefits for students of learning and practicing it lie far beyond the classroom. Like writing, speaking, and quantitative reasoning, critical thinking is a life skill that pays off in many everyday settings. It should guide a person's consumer, political, financial, occupational, ethical, medical, and legal decisions (Browne & Keeley, 2010; Facione, 2011, 2013; Nisbett, 1993; Nosich, 2012; Paul & Elder, 2013b). It can even help one make better personal choices, such as who to trust, who to commit to, and how to discipline children. Yes, all life decisions have a strong emotional component, but it helps to be able to distinguish a rational case from an emotional plea for taking action. News commentators, politicians, advertisers, and various authorities throw fallacious arguments at us every day, and most people fall for them. Our students need to know that critical thinking is a real-world skill that is well worth transferring; it is their only protection against being duped and manipulated.

CHAPTER 4

Deciding What Technology to Use

Teaching at its best requires that we consider every educational tool at our disposal to give our students the richest possible educational experience. Educational technology is like any other element of course design. We should choose technologies because they most effectively help our students achieve our learning outcomes, not because students already use them for personal purposes and we want to look cool. In fact, the winners of the teacher-of-the-year awards, sponsored by the Carnegie Foundation for the Advancement of Teaching, use technology modestly at best (Young, 2012). Greatness in teaching is mostly about the relationships between the instructor and the students and among the students.

■ CHOOSING TECHNOLOGIES INTELLIGENTLY

Our fascination with gadgets can make us forget the lower-tech ways of accomplishing the same objective just as well and perhaps better. For example, the board, whether the black or the white variety, holds at least two benefits for our students. First, it slows us down—both our speaking pace and our movement through the material—giving students a few more precious moments to follow, absorb, and take notes on what we are saying and doing. In contrast, when we are using prepared slides or a document projector, we often speed through the material. Second, most of us do a better job of modeling our thought processes while writing on the board. We explain them as they unfold. Slides make more sense for lists and visual materials than for cognitive processes.

In classroom-based courses, even hybrid ones, Costa (2014) recommends viewing educational technology as "a means to an end, not an end in itself" (p. 125). Therefore, our choices should create a richer, more stimulating learning environment than more traditional methods can. Colleges and universities bought $10.4 billion worth of educational technology in 2014 (Derousseau, 2014) despite little or no evidence that it increases student learning (Clark, 2001; Feldon, 2010; Parish, 2013; Toyama, 2015). In fact, Parish (2013), who runs an educational technology company, expresses skepticism about the learning effectiveness of his industry's products:

> College completion is, without a doubt, a serious problem. In fact, for the first time, the current generation of Americans entering the workforce is less educated than the generation that is now retiring. . . . Might technology be the problem rather than the solution?

He also admits that few technologies have been introduced to solve an existing instructional problem.

Still, many high-tech tools offer benefits and conveniences that we can take advantage of as long as we have sound pedagogical reasons, like those listed here (Costa, 2015; Lewis & Wall, 1988; R. Pak, personal communication, May 13, December 12, 2013; Parish, 2013; Sacks, Glazer, & Zhadko, 2014; Tyner, 2010):

- The technology helps facilitate student learning in the best way or the only way possible. For instance, learning objects on the web or a DVD may allow students to experience distant times, places, and events they could not otherwise. A digital simulation may let them perform lab experiments and procedures that would be too dangerous or too expensive to do in reality, such as surgeries, hazardous chemical procedures, and molecular biology experiments.
- The technology provides the best or only available means for you to demonstrate a phenomenon. For example, chemistry and physics instructors can use a digital simulation or animation to show an atomic structure or a chemical or physical force interaction, especially when a phenomenon is too large, too small, or too dynamic to represent in print, static diagrams, or hand gestures.
- The technology increases student engagement, participation, interaction, and activity. VoiceThread, for instance, allows instructors and students to enjoy online audio discussions asynchronously. Participants can append documents, images, videos, and audio files, to which they can add narrations or comments.
- The technology allows students to drill and practice at their own pace. Because we can't regularly give every student individual instruction, computer-based tutorials and interactive online quizzes can function in our place without the time and patience limitations that afflict us mere mortals.
- The technology helps students acquire the technological literacy that their future occupations will require. While they may come to us highly skilled in using certain social media and web search engines, they may have to learn in our courses how to work with career-relevant software that they know little or nothing about: spreadsheets, presentation, database, information management, statistical analysis, geographical information, form development, design, photography, sound, video, publishing, website development, mathematical, drafting, engineering, and the like. While such software advances every few years, it is easier to master a new version after having used the previous one.
- The technology enhances your own and your students' productivity by reducing the time spent on routine record keeping and communication. Grading and attendance records, for example, are most easily managed on a spreadsheet or the learning management system (LMS). Posting announcements, assignments, handouts, and grades on the LMS saves class time. You can also save time word processing your frequently made comments on written assignments and essay exams, since student work often displays similar strengths and weaknesses.
- The technology facilitates collaboration among your students and between you and them, and a great deal of software does this: team and class discussion boards, wikis, blogs, Del.icio.us or Diigo, Google Docs, e-mail, and the Track Changes tool on Microsoft Word. Using one or

more of these, students can exchange files and web resources, provide peer feedback, and edit projects online at any time.

- The technology costs students little or no extra money and time to learn. A steep learning curve drains precious in-class and out-of-class time from the course content. This explains why Second Life lost favor as an instructional tool.

- The technology does not create new problems, such as distractions and temptations that lure students off-task, increase their cognitive load, or interfere with the basic mental processes of their learning. We must consider whether our students have the self-control, focus, motivation to learn, and perseverance to make optimal learning use of the technology.

In this chapter we will not consider how to teach an exclusively online course. This is a complex enough topic to have generated many books, articles, and training programs. Nor can we examine every instructional technology. For instance, we won't look at photo-sharing websites, photo-editing software, virtual reality, Skype or FaceTime, apps, Google tools, e-portfolios, mapping mashups, survey software, or computer-assisted instruction. This last one is generally an institutional, not a faculty, decision made for the purpose of improving student performance in developmental and introductory math courses.

■ HOW FACULTY AND STUDENTS VIEW TECHNOLOGY

Faculty have embraced technology to a good degree. In fact, according to one national survey (*Inside Higher Ed*, 2014), 86 percent report converting a face-to-face course to a hybrid course, most often to increase active learning opportunities, and 94 percent say that they use their institution's LMS at least sometimes, most frequently to distribute the syllabus, record grades, and communicate with their students. However, another national survey (FTI Consulting, 2015) finds that only 20 percent of faculty claim to have adopted hybrid course delivery and only 11 percent have tried it. Similar percentages of faculty have integrated social media or discussion forums into their courses. Only 22 percent report having tried or adopted clickers or other means to obtain real-time student responses. Quite a few more (17 and 29 percent, respectively) say that have tried or adopted the flipped classroom. Why the two surveys' findings differ so much is not clear, but we can guess that the true figures lie somewhere in between.

Yet another national survey found that three-fourths of faculty have tried at least one new technology in the past year. Still, just over a third consider keeping up with technology problematic (Derousseau, 2014). In a smaller survey at three large universities, faculty expressed deep reservations about instructional technologies: that they reap small educational benefits, are adopted to attract student attention or deal with large classes, threaten professional autonomy, and require more work and time than traditional methods (Johnson, 2013).

Students have their own views on the instructional value of various technologies. In a Harvard University (2008) survey, those with experience in using a tool not surprisingly rated its utility higher. Students also said they appreciate the conveniences of online course materials—in particular, syllabi with links to readings and resources—and recorded lectures they can replay at any time. In addition, they like online discussion forums, blogs to connect course material with current events, and YouTube video clips from other countries for learning languages (Harvard University, 2008). In another national survey (Young, 2004), however, students found most online discussions and chats useless, especially when not moderated by the instructor, while course websites and interactive features like preclass online testing on the readings registered high praise. An even larger national survey found that most students prefer a blend of face time with the instructor and moderate use of technology (Kiernan, 2005), as do other studies (Cardon, 2014).

Many don't want a class Facebook page because they prefer to keep their social and classroom identities separate (Cardon, 2014).

LECTURE-RELATED SOFTWARE

Most faculty are very familiar with presentation software, and it can boost the visual quality and impact of lectures and professional presentations. It allows you to create and project text integrated with images, animations, online resources, and video clips, all in full color, as well as sound. You can highlight the text or zoom in on the part of the image you are explaining. If you want to write or draw on your slides, particularly helpful when teaching mathematics, engineering, and the physical sciences, you can project your presentation onto an interactive whiteboard that will save your annotations and digitally distribute the modified slides to your class. (Of course, your classroom students can also make these annotations on their hard copies of your slides.) If your institution has the space and the money, it can redesign a classroom with tables and chairs to sit four to six students with a screen placed on the wall next to each table. The instructor can project her slides onto the student groups' screens and access these screens to project one group's work onto all the screens.

However, instructors commonly overuse slides to display the text they are lecturing about, and this behavior increases student boredom during a lecture (Mann & Robinson, 2009). Here is a list of the most effective uses of slides:

- List of learning outcomes or an outline for the class
- Directions or questions for lecture break activities (see chapter 12 for many options)
- Animations, video clips, and links to instructional websites
- Diagrams, flowcharts, pictures, photos, drawings, and other graphics
- Equations, formulas, and the like that are easily miscopied

- Material that you project onto a Smartboard so you can write or draw on it

Presentation software is merely a complement to lecture and is just as student-passive, so you need to interject student-active breaks by sprinkling reflection and discussion questions, short cases, or problems to give students practice in application. Or you can strategically place concept-oriented multiple-choice questions to assess students' understanding. Fortunately, clickers are designed to interface with PowerPoint (see chapter 12).

Used well, Prezi offers a more organic alternative to standard slides. You can provide a big-picture view of how the parts of the lectures (topics, concepts, principles, examples, and the like) interrelate, the way a graphic syllabus does (see chapter 5), and systematically move from part to part. Unfortunately, the slides that some Prezi users create are not always interrelated.

On text slides, focus on only one concept per slide and use only key words, keeping the information to an absolute minimum. The templates should help you arrange your information in a logical and pleasing way. And never read the slides in class. To students, this is one of the most egregious technological abuses (Young, 2004). In addition, keep the classroom light enough to keep students awake. The best use of this software is to show visually intensive or multimedia material.

One more rule applies: avoid wildly elaborate color combinations, backgrounds, icons, slide transitions and builds, and special effects, and keep the same colors and backgrounds throughout a presentation. In instruction, the fewer the glitzy distractions and the simpler the visuals, the better. Nevertheless, students appreciate your mixing in graphics, animations, and hyperlinks and varying your slide layouts and text colors to enhance design (Clark, 2008). When students create slide presentations, advise them to follow the same design guidelines but still incorporate multimedia vitality and richness. These presentations can be viewed at any time by you or your class and then be revised and preserved in a student's e-portfolio.

■ THE LEARNING MANAGEMENT SYSTEM

An LMS is a package of instructionally useful software for course administration, file exchange, communication, collaboration, tracking, and reporting (e.g., Blackboard, Moodle, and Canvas). Some of the tools are designed to streamline the instructor's duties, such as an online syllabus template, a spell-checker, automatic test grading, and a grade book linked to a spreadsheet program. Other features facilitate and expand opportunities for communication and interaction with and among students, extending the classroom beyond its walls and scheduled meeting times.

Usually an institution decides which LMS all its faculty and students will use, but you can expect yours to have these features (some of which merit elaboration in the subsections that follow): an announcements page; templates for the syllabus, course calendar, pop-up glossary, class roster, student surveys, and student websites; space for posting course materials (text, graphics, multimedia), such as the syllabus, handouts, assigned readings, lecture notes, presentations, and directions for assignments; space for links to library reserve materials; a dropbox for homework assignments and take-home tests; online testing tools (timed, untimed, and multiple-tries option) with automatic grading of closed-ended items; automatic test feedback to students on closed-ended items; an Excel-compatible grade book; e-mail, with a mass mailing option for the instructor; class and team discussion boards, chat rooms, blog space (individual too), and wikis; and online help and search. We could also put blogs and wikis in the "Social Media" section below.

Space to Post Course Material

Students love the one-stop convenience of obtaining all the course materials whenever and wherever they want (Harvard University, 2008; Young, 2004), but consider the impact of posting materials before you do so. If you modify your posted syllabus and assignments, many students may not notice the changes, not even after alerts on the announcements page. So mention such changes in class or on e-mail as well. Posting homework assignments, study questions, review sheets, and the like in advance rarely presents problems, but be careful not to post homework solutions and answers until after you grade and return the students' work. Of course, putting up test questions and answers renders those items unusable in the future.

You can also record your lectures as a video or audio file and let students view or listen to them whenever and however many times they would like. If you post your recorded lectures, complete lecture notes, in-class slide presentations, and class exercises and activities, you won't have students who miss classes coming to you for information and materials. But unless you make every class more valuable than the files you post, your live attendance and even participation are likely to drop (Young, 2004; also see chapter 12).

When we address the flipped classroom below, we will look at the option of making podcasts or videos of your lectures and assigning them as homework. This liberates hours and hours of valuable class time for all the student-active methods described in parts 2, 3, and 4 of this book.

Online Preclass Quizzes

Easily administered from an LMS, regular online quizzes can serve as an incentive for students to keep up with the readings, videos, and podcasts (see chapter 21) or as an inquiry-based diagnostic tool to assess your students' understanding and plan class around clearing up their misconceptions and mistakes (see chapter 16). The latter use is called *just-in-time-teaching* (JiTT). Research attests that this method raises students' level of preparation for class, participation, engagement, and achievement (Bowen, 2012; Marrs & Novak, 2004; Novak, Patterson, Gavrin, & Christian, 1999) as long as the quizzes figure substantially into the final grade (Sullivan, Middendorf, & Camp, 2008). Students seem to know the positive effects of online quizzes on their motivation, engagement, and learning, and they endorse them as a wise use of instructional technology (Young, 2004).

Class E-mail

With this tool, you can send your entire class housekeeping messages, reminders, study questions, assignments, tips on doing the readings, and connections between the course material and current events, all in one mailing (Bowen, 2012). One-to-one e-mail with your students can substitute for live office hours and after-class exchanges but without the restrictions of time and place. Your students can ask you questions confidentially, saving class time that might otherwise go to individual student questions and concerns. Students can also e-mail you their assignments, papers, and presentations as attachments as an alternative to using the drop-box.

A word of warning: some students, especially younger ones, keep very late hours and may not realize that you might not. They may e-mail you with questions, especially right before tests, in the middle of the night, anticipating a prompt reply. Or they may expect you to be online evenings, weekends, and whenever else they are. In your syllabi (see chapter 5) you should set explicit limits with your classes about your online availability.

Discussion Forums and Chat Rooms

While these tools may be essential in online courses, many younger students have lost interest in them as supplements to a classroom or hybrid course. Typically instructors have required students to post a certain number and type of questions and comments, which students have perceived as busywork tasks to check off a list (Wilcox, 2014). Chats have additional problems of requiring synchronized participation, privileging those who think and type fast, inviting netiquette violations, and going off topic. If you are going to grade on the quality of posts, be sure to provide explanations and models of high-quality and low-quality contributions. Consider

having student peers evaluate each other's posts. Be sure to make your presence known by asking for clarification, elaboration, and corrections and synthesizing students' contributions around key points. Of course, team chat rooms can facilitate small-group collaboration, but so can Google Docs, wikis, blogs, and other tools.

Blogs

A blog is a frequently updated personal website similar to a journal or diary where the owner shares opinions, passions, happenings, links, and the like. Posts are easy to make, and only the owner can change them. The blogs built into most LMSs allow students to design the site, invite commentators, and post images, audio files, and videos. Since they are quasi-public (open to the class and specific individuals granted permission), many students do some of their most conscientious writing on them and enjoy adding multimedia to their posts. Individual blogs are particularly well suited to journaling. However, students seem more willing to advocate positions and propose explanations on blogs and to connect course material to their personal experience and intellectual growth in private journals (Foster, 2015). You can also use the class blog as a discussion forum and require that students make a specified number of posts on particular topics. However, blogs do not offer topical threading. If you find your LMS blog wanting, try a commercial host (e.g., Blogger, Livejournal, Squarespace, and WordPress), but be aware that the free sites are stripped down and may display advertising.

If you're going to use blogs, you must integrate them into other aspects of the course and give students an incentive to post regularly, just as with a discussion forum. Although you need to check posts, you need not grade every one. You can, for example, have students write a self-assessment of their posts around midterm, comparing theirs to the best ones they have read in the class. This exercise tends to improve the quality of posts in the second half of the course. Then at the end of the term, you can ask students to select and submit their best three posts for a grade (Lang, 2008).

The blogs of other entities can also be a source of up-to-date reading material. You and your students can sign up to receive updates of the blogs of political and cultural leaders, scientists, corporations, nonprofit organizations, action groups, and social forums. (They usually offer syndication, which means they use an RSS feed to reach subscribers by e-mail.)

Higdon and Topaz (2009) adapted individual blogs to JiTT (see chapter 16). They have their students post their answers to two questions on the readings—the first about the most difficult part of the material and the second about the most interesting part, the material's connection to prior knowledge, or its relevance to their intellectual or career interests. Students submit their responses the night before class and e-mail the link to the blog's RSS feed to the instructor, who (for convenience) aggregates the posts onto a wiki (see the next section). The instructor scans and grades the responses, looking for common difficulties and themes, then adapts the upcoming class to clear the bottlenecks. According to Higdon and Topaz, JiTT blogging enhances students' conceptual understanding, increases their out-of-class time on task, fosters their metacognitive reflection on the material, and improves their ability to transfer knowledge to real-world applications.

Wikis

A wiki is an ever-evolving, collaboratively developed website that allows users to add, remove, edit, revise, update, and make comments to the content. In addition to text, they can accommodate images, video, audio files, and links. Its purpose is to build increasingly higher-quality collective knowledge, so it is ideal for collaborative writing, research, and portfolio assignments, as well as other projects that require sharing, reflection, and evaluation. All the versions of and changes to the document are recorded and attributed, so users (including the instructor) can easily find out who made what change when and, if expected in the comments, why. Thus, wikis build in accountability.

LMSs offer wiki space that is restricted to students and invited guests, but you can find dozens of other hosts at http://c2.com/cgi/wiki?WikiFarms. You can allocate wikis across individual students, teams, and the entire class, along with read-only and edit rights to each one. You may want your students to read but not modify each other's wikis. With edit rights to every class wiki, you can also provide students with formative feedback as their product develops. While wikis are user friendly and intuitive, you may want to orient your students to them with video tutorials at sites such as www.youtube.com/watch?v=-dnL00TdmLY. In fact, you might post wiki instructions on the class wiki and ask students to add tips (Allwardt, 2009).

You can almost guarantee a successful wiki if you (1) have students build a larger body of knowledge than what they could assemble individually and (2) make that knowledge essential to their doing well in the course (Alexander, Lynch, Rabinovish, & Knutel, 2014). University of Michigan business professor Scott Moore (2009) has made extensive course use of class wikis for lecture notes and test questions. For each class, he assigns one student the task of taking notes on the class wiki and encourages other members of the class to make corrections and additions. He also invites students to make up and post objective test items (with answers), which others can then improve or elaborate on. Students can check and study from the items any time they want, and Moore puts about half the items on actual tests. His class wiki is very active.

Not all wikis garner such interest. Some students back away from discussing difficult topics or critiquing the work of their peers, so you may have to require and monitor regular participation, specify appropriate dimensions for critiquing, and promote and reward serious discussion and constructive criticism (Allwardt, 2009). Like every other student discussion tool, you have to be involved with it to make it a success.

■ THE FLIPPED CLASSROOM

In the purest form of the flipped classroom, you record your lectures on video or in podcasts, then post them on the LMS or your course website or send them to your class through an RSS feed, and assign them as homework. In a less pure version, you may also assign online videos or podcasts made by someone else or recordings of campus events, such as speeches, debates, radio shows, interviews, ceremonies, and performances that not all your students can attend live. The recorded materials offer your students the convenience of listening or viewing almost any time and for as many times as they wish. Of course, you may also assign readings. In the loosest use of the term *flipped classroom*, it means ensuring that students get their first exposure to new material outside class (Walvoord & Anderson, 2010).

In every version of the flipped classroom, you have your students do activities in class, perhaps those that were previously homework, such as problem solving, concept mapping, case analyses, simulations, writing, designing, website-building assignments, and the like.

According to Berrett (2012), classrooms that include Mazur's peer instruction (see chapter 12), small group work, discussions, and other activities have been mislabeled *flipped* because they fail to fit the purer definitions. They are more accurately called *student-active*.

If you decide to make videos or podcasts of your lectures, be aware that recording and editing them takes time, and you can't just record and post your classroom-delivered lectures. You have to cut your presentations into short segments of 15, 10, 5, or 2 minutes (depending on whom you ask), each on a single concept. Being concise and logically organized is critical, so you should write a script that includes examples and stories that clarify the concept and eliminate all extraneous verbiage. When using slides, focus on showing visuals and trim the text down to the bare takeaways (Moore, 2013). You should also incorporate transitions between the recorded segments, tying one segment's topic to that of the previous and the next recording. As new knowledge emerges in your field, you may have to re-record the relevant segments the next time you teach the course.

Ask your campus computer specialists about the best locations for recording and the available technology—for example, Audacity or GarageBand for podcasts, and Camtasia, Echo 360, or LectureScribe (available free at http://people.cs.clemson.edu/~bcdean/lscribe/ and ideal for a recording your whiteboard work) for videos. Many instructors make these recordings in their office; others make them in an empty classroom.

If you assign more professionally made online videos and podcasts on certain topics, here are some free sources, the first one for podcasts and the rest for videos, but some of these may be too long for your students in their current form:

- iTunes: https://itunes.apple.com/us/genre/podcasts/id26?mt=2—thousands of podcasts of varying length on hundreds of subjects
- Anneberg Media: www.learner.org—specializing in the arts, literature, language, history, math, social and natural sciences
- Artbabble: www.artbabble.org/partner/national-gallery-art-washington—specializing in art and architecture
- Khan Academy: www.khanacademy.org—over 3,000 lessons, mostly in the STEM fields
- Mindgate Media: http://mindgatemedia.com/ondemand/—films for teaching and learning
- MITOpenCourseware: http://ocw.mit.edu/index.htm—lectures and materials from over 2,200 courses
- OpenYale: http://oyc.yale.edu/—lectures and materials from selected introductory courses
- TED Talks: www.ted.com—hundreds of highly polished lectures of about 20 minutes or less
- TEDEd: http://ed.ted.com—TED talks with short lessons ("flips")
- Videolectures: http://videolectures.net—full-length faculty lectures on many subjects

- YouTube: www.youtube.com; www.youtube.com/edu; and Utubersity: http://utubersidad.com/en/—lessons, lectures, sports, media broadcasts, interviews, and performances (musical, dance, opera, drama, and comedy)

You will find many more websites as well as learning object repositories in the "Web Resources" section below, and all of these represent just a sample.

Your students probably won't know what to watch or listen for in your video and podcast assignments and may not do this homework without a compliance incentive in place. Therefore, treat these assignments as you would any reading assignment and provide students with study questions, a scavenger hunt assignment, or some other homework that ensures and shows evidence of at least basic comprehension. (See chapter 21 for additional compliance and comprehension measures.)

The flipped classroom is a form of blended learning, and we know that the latter, when done well, significantly improves student learning over that in face-to-face or online courses (Glazer, 2011). However, the research on the effectiveness of the flipped classroom has yielded mixed results thus far (Atteberry, 2013; Bowen, 2013; Goodwin & Miller, 2013). Given the newness of the purer versions of the method, we are still learning about its optimal implementation. In addition, some students object to the lack of lecture and the shift to teaching themselves. Talbert (2015) advises addressing these complaints explicitly by explaining not only the benefits of active learning but also the advantages of doing the more difficult work in class and the hard reality that students have to learn how to learn to stay employed in this modern economy.

■ SOCIAL MEDIA

Many documented cases testify that social media has been an effective complement to online courses (Featherly, 2014). However, the results are somewhat mixed in classroom-based courses.

Social Networking Tools: Facebook

A Facebook page allows you to set up your own social network comprising you, the students in one of your courses, and anyone else you allow. For educational purposes, this network can define a learning community. Of course, its value depends on the meaningful participation of all students, which an instructor needs to motivate. While other social networking sites exist, we focus here on Facebook because so many students spend so much time socializing there and they know how to use it. In addition, it allows you to set up collaborative groups, distribute information and media, promote learning resources, and reinforce the sense of community in your course. Students too can post links, images, videos, music, and other media.

Accompanied by Twitter and Skype, Facebook has proven effective in helping entering first-generation students integrate into the college environment according to one study (Hottell, Martinez-Aleman, & Rowan-Kenyon, 2014).

A Facebook course site has two drawbacks. Although it can serve the purpose of an LMS in some capacities, it lacks the templates and most of the features of an LMS. In addition, some students resent using it or Twitter for class purposes because they consider these social media strictly for personal socializing (Cardon, 2014; Marshall, 2015).

Social Bookmarking Tools

These tools help users accumulate and organize websites by topic, so they can facilitate collaborative research that depends on a sizable number of online sources. The simplest alternative is Del.icio.us, which allows users to categorize, annotate, save, manage, and share sites from a centralized collection. It is an add-on you download onto your browser. You can import your favorites into your Del.icio.us collection, and your collection is available from any computer with web access. Go to delicious.com for the software and instructions on how to use it; helpful videos are available on YouTube.

Diigo does what Del.icio.us does and more. Users can highlight material on bookmarked websites, add sticky notes, and create groups to pool resources on specific topics. In addition, they can easily post their findings to their blog (even set up automatic daily posting), send multiple annotated and highlighted pages in one e-mail, and post to social networking sites such as Twitter and Facebook. It also archives web pages. The browser add-ons, including a free version, are available at https://www.diigo.com/sign-up, and video instructions are at http://help.diigo.com/home/get-started. YouTube also offers several video tutorials. Two other social bookmarking options are Slashdot and Netvouz.

Twitter

Twitter is a simple utility for very short messages (up to 140 characters) called *tweets*. Only about one-fourth of students already tweet (Kolowich, 2014), so you may have to have your students set up accounts (they are free) at http://twitter.com/, as well as give some instructions and model substantial tweets. With Twitter, you can quickly send students the tweeting topics to address, brief announcements ("No class today due to snow"), test and due-date reminders, and links to current events or new developments relevant to your course. Students can communicate with you and their peers as well.

A few faculty have experimented with Twitter as a back channel during class, which means students are tweeting class-related questions and comments on the course hashtag site during class. These faculty claim that this back channel engages students and reduces the social distance between them. Students can also privately tweet questions you can answer later. However, students can't pay attention in class while composing tweets, and the exchanges can roam off topic (Young, 2009; Zax, 2009). Some students give into the temptation to go to nonclass sites as well.

Some instructors have used Twitter successfully for homework in a range of disciplines (Lang, 2014). In Koh's (2015) film course, students tweet their interpretations of the films they watch, both in class and out of class, allowing her to gain insight into their reactions and give feedback. Many films have slow moments that permit tweeting without losing information. Ferris (2015) requires his information technology students to regularly post tweets that illustrate the use of statistics as evidence by businesses, survey researchers, and scientists, thereby providing his students many more statistical examples than he or the textbook possibly could. In an experimental study in a first-year seminar for pre–health professional majors (Junco, Heiberger, & Loken, 2010), the students using Twitter for academic and cocurricular discussions showed higher engagement and achievement. However, the treatment group also had additional readings, several reflective writing assignments, and much more extensive faculty support and encouragement, so we can't know how much Twitter was responsible for the favorable results.

■ MOBILE LEARNING IN CLASS

Mobile devices have gained favor in the classroom because almost all students already own them and always have them handy. They cannot accommodate certain software and are not designed for substantial, in-depth writing. Still, Nielsen (2008) enumerates many ways to use cell phones in class, such as having students conduct research, read the news, convert currencies, do language translations, take quizzes, and respond to polls. They are especially popular for polling because clickers cost money and students occasionally forget to bring them to class.

However, if we are to motivate and promote our students' learning, we have a responsibility to direct and focus our students' attention so they can process, encode, and store our material—something we are not doing if we have them using mobile devices in class. A flood of studies, many of them involving very large numbers of students, document that at least 90 percent of students use their cell phone during class for nonclass purposes, such as texting, going to Facebook, tweeting, game playing, web surfing, and shopping, and that their misdirected attempts to multitask reduce their learning, focus, academic engagement, and grades (Clayson & Haley, 2013; Duncan, Hoekstra, & Wilcox, 2012; Foerde, Knowlton, & Poldrack, 2006; Junco, 2012a, 2012b, 2012c, 2015; Junco & Cotton, 2012; Kuznekoff & Titsworth, 2013; Lepp, Barkley, & Karpinski, 2014; McCoy, 2013; Ophir, Nass, & Wagner, 2009; Parry, 2013; Rosen, Carrier, & Cheever, 2013; Tindell & Bohlander, 2012). Seventy percent of these students misuse their cell phone in class for social purposes (to stay connected) (McCoy, 2013). To curtail (though not eliminate) this behavior requires fairly drastic penalties: removal from class or a grade reduction (Berry & Westfall, 2015).

If students do not resist their preferred cell phone use when they are not supposed to be using their device, why would they resist it when the instructor permits these devices in class and they're holding it in their hands? Only about half of the faculty seem to be aware of this problem. Only 53 percent said Facebook has "negative" value for class use and only 46 percent thought the same about Twitter (Moran, Seaman, & Tinti-Kane, 2011).

Why should cell phones disrupt learning? Learning is a highly focused process that multitasking and other distractions undermine every stage of, from attending to new information to rehearsing it for transfer into long-term memory. No matter what students may believe, research documents that multitasking is mostly wishful thinking (Crenshaw, 2008; Loukopoulos, Dismukes, & Barshi, 2009). Mentally working with complex new material demands heavy encoding and all our mental resources: visual, auditory, verbal, and processing. Failures anywhere along the learning process result in information being missed or forgotten, and cell phone activities can cause these failures. Unfortunately, texting, tweeting, reading and posting to Facebook, playing games, web surfing, shopping, and the like make learning impossible. For polling or quizzing students, clickers are the more effective technology because they are not connected to the Internet.

If you still want your students to use their mobile devices in class, they may be able to control themselves better and pay more attention if you follow Cardon's (2014) advice to give them a short break in the middle of the class period to check their devices. In fact, you might want to give your students this kind of break even if you don't use mobile devices in your classes.

Outside class, more frequent visits to Facebook and other distracting Internet sites while doing homework and at other times are also associated with lower GPAs and fewer hours studying per week (Kirschner & Karpinski, 2010; Patterson, 2015). David M. Levy has provided his students with the technology to observe their own computer use while doing homework, and many of them were unpleasantly surprised:

> When students play back the Camtasia recording, they see what was happening on their screens with their own faces displayed in a corner. They watch themselves flit among Words With Friends, e-mail, Words With Friends, Spotify, Words With Friends, and that goofy video of a cat rolling up against a sake bottle. Some are disturbed to observe that they got so distracted they forgot to work on the main task they had set out to accomplish, like reading an article. (Parry, 2013)

Perhaps this pattern of self-inflicted interruptions explains why students have trouble comprehending and remembering the readings and may decide they are not worth doing. But if students barely realize they are task switching so often, they cannot consciously stop it.

■ LAPTOPS IN CLASS

Laptops pose the same distractions and learning pitfalls as cell phones (Bugeja, 2007; Fischman, 2009; Kraushaar & Novak, 2010). In one study, students were on renegade sites about 42 percent of the time in class, and their grades varied inversely with the proportion of time they spent on such sites (Kraushaar & Novak, 2010). Many universities, law schools, and business schools that mandated laptops in class some years ago aborted their initiatives because faculty got fed up with too many students wandering off to non-course-related sites. However, very few of these institutions set up training programs and incentives for faculty to actually teach with laptops and manage student use.

Laptops can in fact be powerful in-class learning tools because they are much more controllable than mobile devices. Size matters; instructors can see students using laptops but not always cell phones so they can enforce course policies that restrict classroom use to certain times. When under faculty control, laptops allow students to engage in many worthwhile in-class activities: running experiments, collecting and graphing field data, analyzing survey data, posting analyses of musical compositions, preparing multimedia educational materials, conducting engineering and computer science labs, and editing papers for publication—all in your presence so you can help and give feedback (Nilson & Weaver, 2005).

In the SCALE-UP type of teaching, students sit in three groups of three at large round tables where they use laptops for activities like labs and problem solving, while faculty circulate to spur their progress with Socratic questions. The research shows that SCALE-UP and similar uses of laptops in class reduce failure rates and improve students' problem-solving skills, conceptual understanding, and attitudes toward the material (Nilson & Weaver, 2005; North Carolina State University Physics Education R&D Group, 2015).

Perhaps the poorest student use of laptops is for taking notes in class; it is much less effective than handwritten note taking (Mueller & Oppenheimer, 2014; Svinicki, 2014), and you should inform your class of this finding. But disabled students or their note takers may have to use laptops.

Here are additional ways to manage students' in-class laptop use (Nilson & Weaver, 2005; North Carolina State University Physics Education R&D Group, 2015):

- Have students work on their laptop assignments in triads, as they do in SCALE-UP classrooms. They are not interested in watching their peers surf, e-mail, play, shop, and the like.
- Set tight time limits for these activities.
- Hold students accountable for accomplishing specific objectives by requiring reporting out or written reports.
- Circulate around the classroom to check students' monitors.
- To test students on their laptops, write exams using secure testing software, such as Respondus Lockdown Browser, and have students download the accompanying software that prevents them from leaving the test site.

■ WEB RESOURCES

The web contains a wealth of free resources that you may want your students to read, view, hear, critique, analyze, play, or respond to as an assignment, in-class activity, or research source. You can easily link to them from your LMS, class Facebook page, or other course websites without violating copyright. Because this electronic space is so vast, your campus library or instructional technology center may offer web search workshops that can save you hours, even days, of roaming around on a browser. Good search engines and your colleagues can also direct you to worthy sites, or you can post your request for recommended sites on one of your discipline's teaching-focused listservs. Also see the discipline-specific sites listed on Clemson University's Office of Teaching Effectiveness and Innovation website at www.clemson.edu/OTEI/resources/instructional.html.

Teaching and Learning Tools

Among the web's resources are an amazing array of free digital teaching and learning resources, many of which fall under the category of learning objects (see the "Learning Objects" section below):

- Realistic demonstrations, animated or on video (e.g., cellular processes at www.cellsalive.com for biology, bioengineering, and the health professions)
- Performances (musical, dramatic, dance, and sport)
- Virtual science laboratories for hazardous or costly procedures and experiments (e.g., the Chemistry Collective at www.chemcollective. org; see chapter 19 for more.)
- Case studies
- Simulations (e.g., in business, management, sociology, urban planning, political science, environmental studies, and biology)
- Drills and exercises for remediation, practice, or review (e.g., mathematics, reading, and foreign languages)
- Teacher resources for K–12 and special education (presentations, exercises, and other activities)
- Tests of greater or lesser validity on temperament and personality, aptitudes, career preferences, political ideology, leadership style, team member type, and other human dimensions, many free
- Multimedia materials useful for research (see below)

Your best source for finding more web resources for teaching and learning is Shank (2014).

Collections for Multimedia Research

Here are some extensive cross-disciplinary collections of well-established, research-worthy multimedia sites that you can safely send your students to:

- Calisphere at www.calisphere.universityofcalifornia.edu/: a huge collection of websites, scholarly materials, images, electronic books, data, and statistics
- Open Learning Initiative at http://oli.cmu.edu/: access to over two dozen online courses and course materials in a wide range of academic fields
- CSERDA Metadata Catalog at www.shodor. org/refdesk/Catalog/: a searchable repository of web-based teaching materials for mathematics, computer science, and the sciences

- Internet Archive (aka the WayBack Machine) at https://archive.org/: a collection of millions of websites, software, and digitized cultural artifacts (images, audio files, animations); also courses, study guides, assignments, books, and recorded lectures under "Education"
- MERLOT (Multimedia Educational Resource for Learning and Online Teaching) at www. merlot.org: tens of thousands of annotated links to free learning materials, most peer reviewed, including entire courses, databases, presentations, and collections
- National Science Foundation Internet Library at https://nsdl.oercommons.org/: rich and technologically sophisticated instructional materials for the sciences, engineering, mathematics, public health, economics, and other fields
- Online Books Page at www.digital.library.upenn. edu/books/: free access to over 2 million books
- New York Public Library Digital Collections at www.nypl.org/collections/: a vast collection of culturally significant images, audio files, videos, print and audio books, articles, maps, DVDs, menus, and research-worthy databases and archives
- Notre Dame's OpenCourseWare at http:// online.nd.edu/ocw/: lecture transcripts, syllabi, and other instructional materials in history and the social sciences
- Smithsonian Institution at www.si.edu: virtual access to the world's largest museum (actually over a dozen museums), nine research centers, and the National Zoo

Learning Objects

These are self-contained, reusable, digital lessons on specific topics, the best of which are animated, interactive, and truly multimedia. Some can provide eye-catching demonstrations to spark up your mini-lectures, while others can make valuable in-class laptop activities as well as out-of-class assignments. Since they provide lessons, students can learn on their own and at their own pace by playing or running them any number of times. Both faculty and students perceive learning objects to be powerful teaching and learning tools (Howard-Rose & Harrigan, 2003; Ip, Morrison, & Currie, 2001; Moore, 2003–2004; Shank, 2014), and one study reports that they most benefit students who need the most help (Biktimirov & Nilson, 2007).

Learning objects are housed in open learning object repositories, many of them searchable by discipline. In some cases, you must join an online community, but this entails no cost. One of the repositories in this list even provides annotated links to additional repositories:

- MERLOT (Multimedia Educational Resource for Learning and Online Teaching) at www.merlot.org: tens of thousands of interactive case studies, simulations, games, and animations for every discipline
- OER (Open Educational Resources) Commons at www.oercommons.org: close to 30,000 materials, many interactive and animated, for college-level and above (much more for K–12) for every discipline
- JORUM at www.jorum.ac.uk: close to 20,000 materials, many interactive and animated, for college-level and continuing education, almost all unique to this site
- Brock University at www.brocku.ca/learning objects/flash_content: 20 high-quality simulations, games, animations, and exercises for English, finance, German, management, mathematics, and psychology
- Wisconsin Online Resource Center at www.wisc-online.com: thousands of animations, games, and interactive exercises for many content areas, as well as for cognitive, communication, and social skills
- Shodor Interactivate at www.shodor.org/interactivate/: dozens of interactive lessons and exercises for the mathematics, statistics, and some sciences
- University of Wisconsin, Milwaukee Center for International Education at http://www4.uwm.

edu/cie/learning_objects.cfm?gid=55: learning objects for global studies and a few more for the social sciences, plus an annotated listing of dozens of learning object repositories across the disciplines

■ MISCELLANEOUS TECHNOLOGIES

This small assortment represents some prominent technologies that fall outside the categories already noted but deserve mention.

E-textbooks and Web-Based Reading Assignments

E-textbooks and web-based readings save students a lot of money, but they have several weaknesses as learning tools. Let's begin by distinguishing e-textbooks, which are used for studying and reference, from e-readers, which are designed for pleasure reading. Memory and retrieval are key in the former and irrelevant in the latter. Unfortunately, people tend to read all material on a screen the same way—quickly and superficially. As a result, students have been found to process and retain less information when they read an e-textbook versus a print textbook (Baron, 2015; Daniel & Willingham, 2012; Daniel & Woody, 2013; Kolowich, 2014; Wästlund, Reinikka, Norlander, & Archer, 2005). Scrolling down web pages similarly reduces comprehension of the text, especially on complex topics and particularly for students with lower working memory capacity (Mangen, Walgermo, & Brønnick, 2012; Sanchez & Wiley, 2009).

Some e-textbooks have another weakness too: they lack at least some of the valuable, effortless retrieval cues that print textbooks offer: page layouts, page location of material, paper texture, colors, and font features. This type of visual and tactile information flows automatically into long-term memory when students are reading a print textbook, and it helps them retrieve the text material. Without it, they have more trouble recalling information (Mangen et al., 2012; R. Pak, personal communication, May 13, December 12, 2013). We can hope that publishers will continue to try to make e-textbooks look more like print textbooks.

Still, students who use e-textbooks report that they are less efficient for studying. Learning takes more time and effort and more frequently detours into digital distractions than for their peers relying on the printed version. No wonder students prefer print to electronic texts, despite the difference in price (Daniel & Willingham, 2012; Daniel & Woody, 2013). These distractions include text-embedded hyperlinks, which are touted as enriching. It turns out that focused reading is a linear mental process (Tanner, 2014; Zhang, Yan, Kendrick, & Li, 2012). Then again, students rarely take advantage of these resources because they prioritize finishing the readings. They are more likely to use an open-access website associated with a printed textbook.

Computer Games

A well-designed educational computer game furnishes players with clear goals, multiple routes to win, and modest costs for making mistakes (Fishman quoted in Fabris, 2015). The developer must also follow the learning principles derived from cognitive research, such as minimizing cognitive load and incorporating practice with feedback (see chapter 1). Under these favorable circumstances, games are as effective (but not more effective) a learning method as other less complicated methods that may have no learning curve (Clark, 2001; Feldon, 2010). In addition, some students are anxious about these games, in particular high achievers (Fabris, 2015) and those who don't play video games for fun. The latter group may find the learning curve a daunting barrier. Chapter 14 has more on games.

Massive Open Online Courses (MOOCs)

MOOCs belong to distance education but deserve mention here because of their potential use in the flipped classroom and hybrid courses. They burst onto the scene around 2011 featuring rock-star professors from renowned universities presenting web-based lectures within a free course. Enthusiasts raved about their potential for educating the world. Indeed, many thousands of people from different countries enrolled in each course, but very few enrollees (often around 3 percent) finished it. It seems that recorded lectures proved even less engaging than the live version, even when the lecturer ranked among the best. In fact, MOOCs tend to appeal to the well-educated person around 30 years old, not a traditional college student (Davidson, 2014).

Soon faculty using a MOOC learned to complement it with relevant graded assignments, collaborative student projects, peer review, and intraclass communication tools, all designed to develop student motivation, engagement, and a sense of community. While these efforts failed to lift the completion rates for all enrollees, between 33 and 63 percent of those who did the first assignment did complete the courses under study (Trumbore, 2014). In a study on a physics course, students in the MOOC learned slightly more than those in traditional live lecture-based courses but dramatically less than those in more student-centered, interactive live courses (Colvin et al., 2014).

Some experts surmise that MOOCs may challenge traditional online education but probably not face-to-face or hybrid courses. In addition, MOOCs rest on a shaky business model: they cost more to produce than they bring in (Burd, Smith, & Reisman, 2015).

■ THE FUTURE OF EDUCATIONAL TECHNOLOGY

It is almost impossible to forecast the future of instructionally relevant technology. Today's high-tech tools and software will be obsolete in a few years, having been superseded by another version, product, or utility that accomplishes the same purposes in some way touted as better. Two safe predictions: in one form or another, the ubiquitous board, as well as electronically delivered and assisted instruction, will stay with us indefinitely.

The younger generation may drive the changes. After all, it didn't take long for texting and tweeting to replace instant messaging on the cutting edge of routine communication. Some younger instructors and early adopters will take to the changes comfortably and quickly, but many older faculty, not being digital natives, will experience future shock.

If you feel pressured to adopt newfangled technologies, review the sound pedagogical reasons given early in this chapter for using technology and keep in mind that as far as we know, *technology rarely enhances learning and can get in the way.* Typically institutions buy these technologies on the word of computer software experts, not the faculty or students, who are the end users. Some of these technologies have a steep and time-consuming learning curve. Be discriminating in selecting them.

CHAPTER 5

The Complete Syllabus

A syllabus is most simply defined as a concise outline of a course of study. But it is also the students' introduction to the course, the subject matter, and *you*. In addition to providing a schedule of class assignments, readings, and activities, it should give students insight into the material and your approach to teaching it. In a sense, then, it is not only the road map for the term's foray into knowledge but also a travelogue to pique students' interest in the expedition and its leader.

■ HOW LONG? HOW EXTENSIVE?

Students usually have many more questions than a brief syllabus of one or two pages can answer. In addition, some courses call for a great deal of first-day information. Most institutions also require a list of learning outcomes, as well as policy statements about academic integrity, disability accommodations, and even the amount of time students should wait in class for an absent instructor. Faculty have come

to the conclusion, many through hard experience, that they often need to include detailed policies on attendance, late work, makeup exams, assessment standards, team freeloaders, civil discourse, sensitive course content, e-mailing the instructor, and classroom conduct. If a policy doesn't exist, students might figure that anything goes; we all have known students who have thought that way. A comprehensive syllabus now easily runs 5, 6, or even 10 pages, and this isn't necessarily too long.

In fact, the syllabus has been evolving over the past two decades into a lengthy, multipurpose document. Grunert's (1997) "learning-centered syllabus" can go on for 20, 30, and even 50 pages or more, becoming in effect a course handbook that includes all the course handouts and the instructions for all assignments—material that instructors typically distribute over the course of the term. It can also include much more: a letter from the instructor; reading, studying, note-taking, writing-style, and exam-taking tips and aids; detailed exam information; a learning-styles inventory and interpretation key;

a learning contract; team-building suggestions; and detailed directions for projects, papers, presentations, and portfolios. This type of syllabus can become so long that it deserves and requires a title page and table of contents. While this über syllabus may provide students up front with all the tools they need to succeed in the course, you must prepare all the elements of your course way ahead of time. Although this frees up time during the term, it also locks you into the assignments and exam formats in the syllabus. In addition, getting students to read such an imposing document, no matter how helpful to them, may present a challenge.

From another view, the syllabus should above all communicate the mutual responsibilities of the students and instructor, including the learning outcomes, the schedule of topics and assignments, mutual expectations, respectful classroom conduct, and the structure of the course (Habanek, 2005). In other words, it should serve as a friendly contract. Slattery and Carlson (2005) agree with this conception and add that a syllabus should also motivate and invite students to become co-learners with the instructor.

Palmer, Bach, and Streifer (2014) go further to recommend that a syllabus begin with learning goals and objectives that encompass all six of Fink's (2013) dimensions of significant learning and go on not only to describe all the major assessment and classroom activities but also to explain their alignment with the goals and objectives. In addition, they advise that the instructor explicitly communicate an encouraging, respectful learning environment in the document by expressing high expectations of students and confidence in their ability to meet them, assuming they are competent and serious learners, explaining the relevance of the course materials to their professional and personal lives, and demonstrating that the planned learning activities are based in research and designed to engage the students socially and individually.

In view of recent efforts to stem sexual assault on campuses, Dawisha and Dawisha (2014) suggest one additional item to include: a statement, such as the one provided here, reminding students that the institution will not tolerate sexual harassment and violence and offers resources to help victims:

> Title IX makes it clear that violence and harassment based on sex and gender is a Civil Rights offense subject to the same kinds of accountability and the same kinds of support applied to offenses against other protected categories such as race, national origin, etc. If you or someone you know has been harassed or assaulted, you can find the appropriate resources here.

In summary, the newest trend in syllabus design includes not only policies and sanctions regarding student behavior but also quasi-philosophical discussions of and justifications for your teaching and assessment strategies, as well as efforts to reach out to your students, validate their abilities, make them full participants in the course, and protect them from harm. Such a document can easily exceed 15 and even 20 pages. You may be concerned that students won't read anything that long, but this chapter contains a section on inducing students to read the syllabus.

■ THE CASE FOR TRIMMING THE SYLLABUS

Not surprisingly, this trend toward long syllabi has generated a backlash to return to the shorter syllabus. In this view, faculty and institutions have overdone the policies and sanctions and have inadvertently created a legalistic, rule-bound document that assumes students must be threatened or bribed to behave courteously in class, submit their work on time, take tests when scheduled, manifest academic integrity, and the like (Schuman, 2014; Singham, 2007). They seem to have reacted fearfully to highly sensitive, grade-anxious students and have adopted the self-protective ethos of the corporatized university (Schuman, 2014). Maybe students would respond better to a less controlling, more learning-focused introduction to the course and even to inviting them to co-create the course and the syllabus with us (Singham, 2007). Perhaps the policies and rules belong in an appendix away from the important information about the course content, schedule, and assignment basics (Schuman, 2014).

This debate on what to put and what not put in the syllabus will no doubt continue to rage. However, we can list some basic information that does belong in the document and allow personal taste, the best interests of our particular students, and common sense to guide us on additional specifics. The next section offers a suggested checklist of the essential information to put in a syllabus, whether printed or online, and you are welcome to add more from the models already presented. The more information you include, the less you have to improvise or decide on the run, and the fewer student questions you will have to answer. You need only remind students that "it's in the syllabus" when necessary. In addition, you can begin to forge a warm, trusting relationship with your class.

◼ ESSENTIAL SYLLABUS ITEMS

Here is an annotated list of all the items that you should probably put in your course syllabi. They represent what your students really want to know: your policies, assignments, and grading methods (Doolittle & Siudzinski, 2010), even if some of these items add a controlling aura to the document.

- *Basic course information:* the course number and title; days, hours, and location of class meetings for classroom-based courses and any synchronous meetings for online courses; credit hours; any required or recommended prerequisites for enrollment, including the instructor's permission; any out-of-class requirements, such as attending a performance; any required laboratories or recitation or discussion sections, with the same information as given for the course; and the titles and location of

any online course materials, exercises, assignments, exams, and supplementary materials that are on the web (give the URL) or in your LMS (specify the folder).

- *Information about yourself:* your full name and title, the way you wish to be addressed, your office hours, office location, office phone number, e-mail address, and home page URL (if you have one). Warmly invite your students to take advantage of your face-to-face office hours. If they aren't geographically close enough to do so, Skype, FaceTime, and similar telecommunication software offer the next best alternative. Advise them that conversation is a much more efficient way to help them understand the material than any kind of text-based electronic exchange. If you decide to give students your home or cell phone number, you may wish to limit calls to certain days and reasonable hours. So that your students do not expect you to be on e-mail 24/7, specify the days and hours that you will be answering their e-mail.

- *The same information about other course personnel,* such as teaching assistants (TAs), technicians, and other assistants, as you gave for yourself. You might encourage section or lab TAs to develop their own syllabi.

- *A briefly annotated list of reading materials,* such as assigned books (including edition), journal articles, class packets, and web materials with full citations, price, location (bookstore, library, reserve status, URL, or LMS folder), identification as required or recommended, and your reasons for selecting them. If you do not plan to give regular assignments from the text, consider making it a recommended supplementary source. If commercially prepared notes are available, say how helpful they might be.

- *Any other materials required for the course,* including cost estimates and where to find them at a good price. (Don't forget eBay and Amazon.com for pricier items.) For example, some science labs require students to have a personal stock of cleaning supplies and safety equipment. Art and photography classes usually expect students to furnish their own equipment, supplies, and expendable materials. If special types of calculators, computers, or software are called for, these too deserve mention. If the materials won't be used immediately, specify when in the term they will be.

- *A course description,* which may be as brief as a few lines describing the content. However, you might want to elaborate on the organization or flow of the course and your rationale for it. You may even want to mention topics the course will *not* cover if past students have held mistaken expectations.

- *Your student learning outcomes for the course.* These should be not just your ultimate outcomes (what students should be able to do or do better at the end of the course) but also your major mediating and foundational outcomes. Chapter 2 gives guidance on developing solid, assessable learning outcomes; designing a course around them; and charting an outcomes map to show students your plan for their learning process. In fact, an outcomes map better orients your students than a list. However, you don't want students to interpret your outcomes as binding promises to them, and you know your students have to apply themselves to achieve these outcomes, so consider adding this caveat or disclaimer: (1) Students may vary in their competency levels on these outcomes, and (2) they can expect to achieve these outcomes *only if* they honor all course policies, attend classes regularly, complete all assigned work in good faith and on time, and meet all other course expectations of them as students.

- *A list of graded course requirements and breakdown of your grading scale,* such as the number and point values of in-class activities, homework assignments, peer-group evaluations, class participation, discussion, electronic communication, tests, papers, and projects, and so on. If you expect students to participate in class discussions, say so. If you want to grade class participation, be sure you have some sort of written record to back up this part of the grade. If you plan to give unannounced, ungraded quizzes to monitor comprehension, let it be known from

the beginning. State if the lowest-scoring work can be thrown out. Finally, explain the grading system you will use (criterion referenced, a curve, or something else; see chapter 27), along with percentage breakdowns (such as 91–100 = A, 81–90 = B, and so on). If you choose, describe the types of in-class activities, homework assignments, and tests and quizzes (how much essay versus objective items; see chapter 26). You might be wise to explain why you are assessing the way you are and how your assessments map onto the learning outcomes.

- *How major assignments (papers, projects, and oral presentations) will be evaluated:* with an atomistic key, a holist rubric, or an analytical rubric (see chapter 27). You might briefly identify the rubric dimensions, but you needn't provide the rubrics. Also explain your policies regarding revisions and extra credit. As with postexam grade protests, the choral call for extra credit can be a nuisance unless you firmly establish your position from the start. One other nuisance you will want to prevent is the frivolous grade protest. You can state in the syllabus that you will deal with a protest by regrading the entire exam, paper, or other product because if you made a mistake in one place, perhaps you made one in another. Or you can require that students submit all grading complaints in writing, tying their justification to specific pages in the readings or dated class periods, within 48 hours.

- *Your policies on attendance and tardiness.* Faculty occasionally debate whether to grade on attendance. As one side argues, how can students learn and contribute to the class without being there? (As Woody Allen once put it, over 90 percent of life is just showing up.) If you take off points for lack of attendance or tardiness, you should state *academic reasons* for your requirements (e.g., you conduct learning activities, you lecture important materials not in the readings, or you give pop quizzes). Taking and grading on attendance does increase class attendance (Friedman, Rodriguez, & McComb, 2001). But others argue that students, being adults, should be free to learn as much or as little as they choose by whatever means they choose. However *you* decide, your syllabus should state your policy.

Including attendance and even tardiness in the final grade (some instructors incorporate it under class participation) is not unusual. Absences are a problem at many institutions, especially in required courses (Friedman et al., 2001). Some colleges and universities require faculty to report students who are excessively absent, so you may have to keep attendance even if you don't intend to grade on it. (Check the academic regulations in your institution's course catalogue.) However, instructors usually excuse absences for documented medical reasons, court obligations, a family death, field trips required for another course, and athletic team commitments.

- *Your policies on missed or late exams and assignments.* Students do occasionally have good reasons for missing a deadline or a test, as they do for some absences, and you may want to ask for documentation for the reason given. State whether students can drop one quiz or grade during the term or schedule a makeup, or if their grade on another exam, like the final, will substitute for the grade on the missed one. If you assess penalties for late work, describe them precisely to prevent any later disputes. Check the academic regulations in your institution's course catalogue so your penalties don't exceed what is allowed.

- *A statement of your and your institution's policies on academic dishonesty, as well as how they apply in your course.* Your institution's policies are boilerplate statements that all but first-semester students have seen and heard before so they might very well belong in an appendix. Yours, however, deserve a more prominent place. Cheating and plagiarism are all too common on today's college campuses, as chapter 10 documents. Unless you make a strong statement about your intolerance of them, your students may assume that you are naive or will look the other way. This statement should include the procedures you will follow in prosecuting violations and the sanctions a student may suffer. (See

your institution's course catalogue, student handbook, or faculty handbook for details.) If your institution has an honor code, state that you will strictly adhere to and enforce it. Another reason to address academic honesty policies is to spell out how you will apply them to group activities and products in your course. If you don't detail your rules, one of two things can happen: your students may inadvertently violate your and your institution's policies, or they may not work as cooperatively as you'd like.

- *A statement of your institution's policies on ADA (Americans with Disabilities Act) accommodations.* Your institution may require you to insert a boilerplate statement somewhere in your syllabus. But you should know some of the accommodations you may have to make. In the traditional classroom, most are quite simple—for instance, giving students extra time or an isolated place to take an exam or welcoming an American Sign Language (ASL) expert in your classroom to sign to a hearing-impaired student what you and your students say. Your institution probably has a disability services office that furnishes quiet exam locations, ASL specialists, and even books on tape for students who need them. In fact, your responsibilities involve little more than cooperating with that office unless you bring online materials into your course.

Your role grows as you move more material online. If you record your lectures, for instance, you should provide a transcript of them. Transcription software like Dragon will create one automatically, but you have to train the software to get used to your voice and way of speaking. If you create a website, you must provide users with navigational help in finding content. All prerecorded audio material, such as podcasts, must be captioned, have a text alternative, or display an ASL-signed version. Prerecorded video and images must have an audio track or description. In other words, all material must be available in *multi*media. Because multimodal teaching is so effective (see chapter 22), many of these accommodations represent teaching at its best for all your students. Other ADA accessibility guidelines lay out technical requirements for audio control, color, contrast, text size control, and text layout. All of the web-content guidelines are at http://www.w3.org/TR/WCAG20/, but you should be able to get help from your campus disability services staff, information technologists, and instructional designers.

• *Policies on classroom decorum and academic discourse.* Such policies may seem controlling, but some students are not familiar with the classroom culture or the effects that their behavior can have on other students as well as on you. For the sake of nondisruptive students, it is your job to create a learning environment that is as free as possible from distractions, annoyances, name-calling, personal attacks, and other demonstrations of disrespect. The policies you may find helpful to set depend on how your students normally behave in class. On some campuses, the main distractions may be mobile devices. On others, it may be interpersonal conflict. Zero in on only the most significant behavioral issues and avoid long lists of don'ts. Phrase conduct codes in positive terms when possible. Explain the benefits of paying attention and engaging in civil discussion along with the consequences for violating the codes (see chapter 9).

• *Proper safety procedures and conduct for laboratories.* While you would hope that students would have the common sense to apply good safety habits to their work, you cannot assume that these habits are intuitive. Specify strict rules for lab dress and procedures. If you threaten to exact penalties for safety violations, stand ready to make good on your word. Remember, it is better to take away a few lab points than to risk the safety of the entire section. These procedures and policies may merit a separate lab syllabus or handbook.

• *Relevant campus support services for students and their locations* for assistance in mastering course software, doing computer assignments, writing papers or lab reports, learning study skills, and solving homework problems. The appendix identifies such resources on the typical campus.

Remember that you don't have to do everything for your students.

• *A week-by-week or class-by-class course schedule* with as much of the following information as possible: topics to be covered; in-class activities and formats (lecture, guest speaker, class discussion, group work, demonstration, case study, field trip, role play, simulation, game, debate, panel discussion, video, computer exercise, review session, and so on); dates of announced quizzes and exams; and due dates of all reading assignments and all other homework. Be sure to accommodate holidays and breaks.

• *A concluding legal caveat or disclaimer.* During the semester, your course schedule may get thrown off for any number of reasons: snowstorms, floods, your own health issues, or your discovering that your students are ill prepared for the material you have planned for them. Usually disruptions slow down the course and force you to diverge from your syllabus. Students may think they are not getting their money's worth if you fail to get through your syllabus by the end of the course. In our litigious society, they may even file a grievance or threaten to sue faculty for failing to follow the syllabus schedule. In fact, the courts have not recognized the syllabus as a legally binding contract on an instructor because the students' registration for the course constitutes voluntary acceptance of the terms of the course and the instructor maintains creative control over the content and methods of instruction (Reed, 2013). Still, you'd be smart to add this caveat/disclaimer regarding changes to the course at the end of the syllabus. This way you make your right to use your own discretion explicit. While this disclaimer mentions policies, it is best to avoid changing those unless they work in the students' favor.

> The above schedule, policies, procedures, and assignments in this course are subject to change in the event of extenuating circumstances, by mutual agreement, and/or to ensure better student learning.

These additional syllabus items are not essential but have merit:

- *Curricular requirements your course satisfies,* such as general education; writing-, speaking-, or ethics-across-the-curriculum; various majors; and any other graduation requirements of your institution or program.
- *Background information about yourself,* such as your degrees, universities you have attended, other institutions where you have taught or conducted research, and your areas of research or special interest. After all, you may be asking your students for some personal and academic information. In addition, most students are keenly interested in you as a professional and a person and appreciate knowing something about you. A little sharing about yourself can also help build their sense of personal loyalty to you.
- *Your teaching philosophy.* So many faculty write such a statement for job applications and reviews that you might want to append yours to your syllabus or include an abbreviated version in the document, preferably within the first page or so. It can express your commitment to education, your hopes and objectives for your students, your knowledge of how people learn, your view of the mutual rights and obligations between instructors and students, the rapport with students you aim to develop, and your preferred teaching and assessment methods (see chapter 28). With it, you can set a fruitful, congenial tone for the term.
- *Other available study or assignment aids.* Students like to know if you plan to distribute study guides, review sheets, practice problems, or practice essay questions.

■ THE GRAPHIC SYLLABUS

A graphic syllabus, like an outcomes map, is a visual tool to communicate your course to your students more effectively. Specifically, it is a flowchart, graphic organizer, or diagram of the sequencing and organization of your course's major topics through the term. It may also notate the calendar schedule of the topics, the major activities and assignments, and the tests. But however much information it contains, it can't include everything that a regular text syllabus should, so it is meant to be a supplement, not a replacement for it. As I have already written extensively about the graphic syllabus (Nilson, 2002, 2007a), the discussion here will be brief.

Perhaps an example is the best way to understand the concept. Figure 5.1 displays the graphic syllabus of an undergraduate Social Stratification course I taught at UCLA some years ago. It is fairly simple and unadorned, but it helped my students see the complex interrelationships among the weekly topics. For instance, it makes clear that the first 3 weeks addressed theory and the rest of the course, empirical research. It illustrates that one of the two major theories has spawned research on two types of inequality (which support *this* theory), while the other major theory has generated research on two other types of inequality (which support *that* theory). During the last few weeks on how social stratification persists, the graphic shows that one explanation derives only from one major theory and its research, while the second one integrates both major theories and their findings, as well as psychology. The flow of course topics takes on a logic and internal cohesion that a list cannot capture.

Aside from clarifying complex relationships among topics, a graphic syllabus offers many other learning benefits. As explained in chapter 1, it gives students an additional level of understanding of the course material by providing the big picture of your course content: the structure of the knowledge as an integrated whole and a cohesive system of interpreting phenomena. With a knowledge structure already in hand, students are better able to process and retain the material. In addition, a graphic syllabus reveals why you organized the course the way you did. No doubt you put substantial time and mental effort into your course design and topical organization, but students, who have no

Figure 5.1   Graphic Syllabus of Social Stratification Course

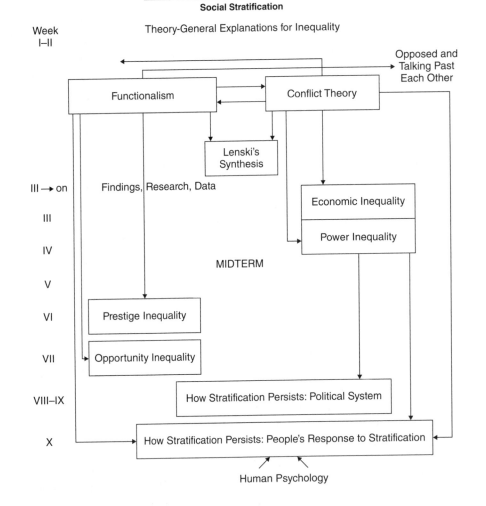

background in the field, can't possibly follow your sophisticated logic. They don't know what many of the words mean or how one concept or topic may relate to another. In a graphic, you can show such relationships using spatial arrangements and arrows.

Additional advantages accrue from a graphic syllabus by virtue of its being a visual representation. Students are more likely to comprehend and remember materials they receive both verbally and visually. In addition, they need not expend as much cognitive energy interpreting a graphic as they do interpreting text because visuals require less working memory and fewer cognitive transformations. They even cue the associated textual information,

which means that simply recalling the shape of the visual can help a student remember the words within it. Moreover, graphics communicate better than text across cultural and language barriers, so they help us meet the learning needs of a diverse student population. Graphics also showcase alternative ways of taking notes, outlining papers, and organizing concepts. Chapter 23 explains and references the evidence for these learning advantages, which apply to visual representations in general.

One final benefit of designing a graphic syllabus is for you. Not only is the activity a creative, right-brain outlet, but it can help you identify any snags in your course organization, such as topics that are chronologically misplaced or missing or that don't fit at all.

Bear in mind that a graphic syllabus shows the structure of your course, not the field, its history, or a theoretical model. These may make fine graphics, but under a different name. In addition, a graphic syllabus should flow in only one direction, as a course does through time. A final warning: don't make it too complex, cluttered, or detailed. Its intent is to *clarify*. And *do* refer to it during the course as you would to a map during a trip.

THE ONLINE "LIVING SYLLABUS"

All online course instructors, as well as many classroom instructors, have an online syllabus. It gives you the opportunity to make it dynamic, growing, and "living" (Wilson, 2008, p. 1). In the first paragraph on Wilson's website for his classroom-based course, History of Life, he informs his students that he will be adding links, images, alternative perspectives on controversial issues, and other information on a weekly basis as the term proceeds, and he requires them to check the site at least once a week.

Those of us who post our course materials on an LMS also add materials ranging from lecture outlines to homework assignments to review questions during the term. But we usually add them to various folders on our course site and rarely link them to the syllabus. If we do link them, however, students wind up reviewing the syllabus again and again. Depending on where we locate the new material in the document, students may need to reread the course requirements, policies, schedule, and previously learned content. Wilson (2008) maximizes the potential value to his students of scrolling through his syllabus by having two content-rich sections of text (350–900 words) for each week's topic—web resources for that week and discipline-related news items—each studded with links to more information on concepts, proper names, and other subjects he mentions.

ENSURING YOUR STUDENTS READ YOUR SYLLABUS

A solid syllabus says good things about you to your class. Among them, it says that you understand students, how they abhor surprises and last-minute assignments, and how they appreciate a tightly organized, explicit course structure around which they can plan the next few months. It says that you respect them, as well as the subject matter of the course.

Even so, you can't expect students to actually study your carefully constructed document. Some instructors field student questions that are answered in the syllabus all term. So unless you maintain an online *living syllabus*, the challenge is getting students to focus on the document. While they may not remember every aspect of the course, they should remember where they can find information. Just reading through the syllabus out loud during your first class meeting isn't enough, and besides, you have other matters to tend to during that class period (see chapter 7). Here are four more effective options.

First, if your syllabus is just a few pages, have your students read it in class; then break into small groups to do one of several possible syllabus activities. For instance, they can simply discuss the document and answer each other's questions about it. Or you can structure their discussion around some question, such as this one: "Compared to the other courses you've taken in college, do you expect this one to be more or less difficult [or require more or less time], and why?" Ballard (2007) has her students make a list of questions that they should never ask her, since the answers are in the syllabus. You can even turn the syllabus into a game by sending the groups on a scavenger hunt for certain critical information. Provide some small prize (candy, for instance) for the quickest and most thorough group.

Another option is to assign the syllabus as homework, answer questions about it the second day of class, and then have each student sign a contract with statements like these: "I have thoroughly read the course syllabus and understand its contents.

I understand the course requirements and the grading and attendance policies stated in the syllabus" (T.D.I. Campbell, personal communication, September 27, 2001). Once students sign the document, they will have no excuse for not knowing about an exam, an assignment deadline, or a policy.

Schuman (2014) takes a third approach: tough love. She assigns the syllabus as the first required reading and warns her students that she will know if they haven't read it. How? At the end of the document, she makes a brief assignment to e-mail her with a question, which she grades pass (for doing it) or fail. She said about half of her students fail an assignment they didn't even know about, but she does accept late submissions.

A fourth alternative, especially for a long syllabus, is to assign it as homework and give a graded test on it the second day of class (Raymark & Connor-Greene, 2002). The test items need not be all factual questions on the number of tests, the point value of assignments, and the like. You can ask interesting and thought-provoking short-answer and short-essay questions, such as: Which of the student learning outcomes for this course are most important to you personally, and why? Of the four papers assigned, which are you least (or most) looking forward to writing, and why? Which of the grading criteria for your oral presentation plays most to your strengths as a learner or a speaker? What are two challenges that you anticipate encountering in this course, and what strategies will you use to overcome them? What campus or course resources can you use to increase your effectiveness in this course, and how and when are you most likely to use them? Answers to these questions will give you insight into your students' aspirations, interests, insecurities, and self-assessments and contribute to their sense of self-efficacy. Such questions will also motivate your students to think about the value of your course to them personally and professionally.

One final option is to distribute your syllabus the first day but wait to review it in class until the third week or so of the term, after enrollment stabilizes and students start to care about the course requirements, assignments, and grading (F. A. McGuire, personal communication, October 12, 2007). This is just-in-time learning at its purest, and you are almost guaranteed an interested audience. Of course, you will still have to refer your class to immediately needed information on the first day, such as the course prerequisites, your office hours and contact information, ADA accommodations, safety procedures (if applicable), classroom conduct policies, and early reading assignments.

▨ ADDING A CREATIVE ELEMENT

Whatever items you incorporate into your syllabus, it need not be a sterile desert of text. Of course, you can design a graphic syllabus to accompany it, but you can also add photos, drawings, clip art, word art, and other graphic features to break up and spark up the text. In addition, you can fashion certain sections of the syllabus, such as the course description and schedule of topics, activities, and assignments, around a metaphor—perhaps an itinerary of a term-long adventure, a program of a concert or conference, or even the menu of a multicourse meal. Students appreciate creative touches like these in an otherwise dry document, and such whimsical enhancements can become your personal trademark.

CHAPTER 6

Copyright Guidelines for Instructors

As you prepare to teach a course—classroom, online, or hybrid—you will likely bump into the issue of copyright. No doubt you will want to assign, play, or show work by people beyond the required books and electronic materials you expect your students to buy.

If so, you have just entered the through-the-looking-glass world of "fair use," "educational purposes," and other such Cheshire cat categories that make most of us instructors think twice before we press the start button on a copying machine, post a document on our course website or LMS, or even consider showing a video in class. This is the unwieldy wonderland in which the only legally correct answer to your simplest query may be "probably," "unlikely," and "it depends on the specific case." For example, Is a classroom a public place? (This issue may affect the legality of showing a video in class.) The answer is that experts disagree and the courts have not yet settled the issue.

In the absence of simple, clear rules of thumb, it is little wonder that we tend to pick up copyright law by word of mouth and wind up swapping myths and misconceptions. The legal ambiguities only feed our fears of what might happen to us if we were actually caught by the copyright enforcers (whoever they may be) violating their rules, even unknowingly.

The laws, guidelines, and enforcement policies are not well publicized in the academic world and may surprise you. Many of them are highly technical, make questionable sense, and are frankly difficult to absorb and remember. Those governing newer technologies also change as lawsuits are resolved and the U.S. Copyright Office issues new regulations and exemptions, some of which have expiration dates.

All of the legal information in this chapter comes ultimately from Title 17 of the United States Code, which includes the Copyright Act of 1976 and its subsequent amendments—literally dozens of them. The Conference on Fair Use (CONFU, 1995–1997), the Digital Millennium Copyright Act of 1998 (DMCA, one of the amendments to the 1976 law), and the Technology Harmonization and Education Act of 2002 (TEACH Act, another such amendment) set the guidelines for multimedia use and online and distance learning, some of which have an ambiguous legal status. This chapter focuses on the fair use exemptions that are granted for educational purposes.

Laws, statutes, and guidelines are written to obfuscate, so credit is due those who have interpreted and translated them into plain English; they have served as invaluable factual sources for this chapter: Davidson (2008), Foster (2008a), Nemire (2007), Orlans (1999), and the University of Minnesota Libraries (2015).

■ WHERE COPYRIGHT DOES AND DOES NOT APPLY

Copyright law does not protect facts, ideas, discoveries, inventions, words, phrases, symbols, designs that identify a source of goods, or some U.S. government publications (you must check on each one). This doesn't mean we don't cite the sources of our facts, other people's ideas, or certain key phrases, for example. We just need not ask permission or purchase a license to use them. Many inventions are protected by patent law, yet another realm of intellectual property.

But copyright law does protect creative works, whether literary (fiction and nonfiction), musical (including lyrics), dramatic (including accompanying music), choreographic, sculptural, pictorial, graphic, architectural, audiovisual (including motion pictures), or sound recorded.

■ COMMON COPYRIGHT MISCONCEPTIONS

Let me dispel some popular misconceptions. First, giving credit to the author of a work is not a way around or substitute for copyright law compliance. All a citation exempts you from is plagiarism. Second, the absence of a copyright notice does not mean the work is not protected. While most works

have a notice, those published on or after March 1, 1989, are protected even without one. Third, changing someone else's copyrighted work here and there will not make it legally yours. In fact, such action may make you doubly liable: for infringement of copyright *and* of the copyright holder's right of modification.

Finally, flattering or showcasing a work is not likely to allay the copyright owner's objections to your free use of the work. This is especially true of multimedia works; their producers view licenses as a new source of income. Freelance writers, music publishers, and musical performers have successfully sued major companies like the *New York Times* for the unauthorized publication or distribution of their work on online computer services.

■ FREE USE: FAIR USE, FACTS, AND PUBLIC DOMAIN

Free use means no license or written permission from the copyright holder is required to copy, distribute, or electronically disseminate the work. However, whether a given case qualifies depends on three rather gray criteria: (1) your use is *fair use*, (2) the material you wish to use is factual or an idea, and (3) the work you wish to use is in the public domain.

In general, fair use means use for noncommercial purposes and specifically for purposes of teaching, scholarship, research, criticism, comment, parody, and news reporting. The courts are most likely to find fair use where the copied work is a factual as opposed to a creative work. However, no legal guidelines are available to distinguish factual material or an idea from something else; determinations are made on a case-by-case basis. Another consideration is whether the new work poses market or readership competition for the copyrighted work.

The amount and the significance of the protected work used also figures into the determination of fair use. Use of a tiny amount of the work should not raise concerns unless it is substantial in terms of importance, such as the heart of the copied work. For instance, a magazine article that used 300 words from a 200,000-word autobiography written by President Gerald Ford was found to infringe the copyright on the autobiography. Even though the copied material was only a small part of the auto-biography, it included some of the most powerful passages in the work.

Public domain is a clearer legal concept but is sometimes redefined. A work that was published in the United States is now in the public domain if (1) it was published on or before 1923, (2) 95 years have elapsed since its publication date if it was published between 1923 and 1977, or (3) 70 years have elapsed since the author's death if it was published after 1977. However, if a work was published between 1923 and 1963 and the copyright owner did not renew the copyright after the 28-year term that once applied, the work has come into public domain. Corporate works published after 1977 enter the public domain 95 years after publication.

The fair use exemption does not permit unlimited copying and distribution. The "privilege" is highly restricted by guidelines with legal force, though they are often ambiguous and arcane, and they do not cover all situations. They were negoti-ated among educators, authors, and publishers. Of course, no copyright exemption excuses you from citing and crediting your sources.

■ PRINTED TEXT

While you may find it restrictive, the realm of print media is the one that most liberally allows fair use. It is, of course, the oldest realm.

Single Copying

As an instructor, you may make single copies, including a transparency or slide, of the following for teaching purposes without obtaining prior per-mission: a chapter of a book; an article from a peri-odical or newspaper; a short story, essay, or poem; and a diagram, graph, chart, drawing, cartoon, or picture from a book, periodical, or newspaper.

Multiple Copying

You may make multiple copies—specifically, one copy per student in a course—without first obtain-ing permission if the work meets the criteria of brevity, spontaneity, and cumulative effect and if each copy contains a copyright notice.

The guidelines define the brevity criterion in this way: (1) an entire poem printed on no more than two pages or an excerpt from a longer poem, not to exceed 250 words copied in either case; (2) an entire article, story, or essay of fewer than 2,500 words or an excerpt of fewer than 1,000 words or less than 10 percent of the work, whichever is less, but in either event, a minimum of 500 words to be copied; and (3) one chart, graph, diagram, draw-ing, cartoon, or picture per book or periodical issue. Multiple copying meets the spontaneity criterion when you do not have a reasonable length of time to request and receive permission to copy. What a "reasonable length of time" may be is not specified.

The cumulative effect is considered acceptably small (permission not required) when your copying is for only one course and you do not make multi-ple copies in more than nine instances per term per course. Furthermore, you may not make multiple copies of more than one short poem, article, story, essay, or two excerpts from the same author or more than three from the same collective work or period-ical volume in one term.

If you want to copy and distribute entire or multiple works in a way that violates the rules above, you must first obtain permission.

Copying Short Works

Short works such as children's books are often fewer than 2,500 words, and you may not copy them as a whole. All you may reproduce without permission is an excerpt of no more than two published pages containing not more than 10 percent of the total words in the text.

Additional "Privileges" and Prohibitions

You are allowed to incorporate text into your multimedia teaching presentations, as can your students into their multimedia projects.

Notwithstanding the previous guidelines, your intentions and the specific work also come into play. You may not make copies under these conditions to create, replace, or substitute for anthologies, compilations, or collective works; to substitute for replacement or purchase of consumable works such as workbooks, exercises, standardized tests, or answer sheets or of the same item term after term; or if you charge students beyond the copying cost or on direction of a higher authority. In addition, you may make copies for your students in only nine instances per term.

▪ IMAGES

The guidelines in this section apply only to photographs and illustrations not in the public domain, which never require permission to use. However, if the one you want to use is part of a copyrighted collection, you should obtain permission for use from the copyright holder.

You may use entire single images but no more than 5 by a single artist or photographer. If you are taking images from a collection, you may use no more than 15 images or 10 percent of those in the collection, whichever is fewer.

If an image is not designated for sale or license, you may digitize and use it if you obtain prior permission and limit access (password-protect) to enrolled students and other instructors of the course. Furthermore, your students may download, print out, and transmit it for personal academic use, including course assignments and portfolios, for up to 2 years. You may also use the image at a professional conference.

An alternative to obtaining permission to show copyrighted visual materials is to take and display photographs of them. This option is legal for fair use as long as the quality of the photographic reproductions is lower than that of commercial reproductions, such as professionally produced slides and prints—in other words, as long as the amateur photographs can't compete in the same market (University of Minnesota Libraries, 2015).

Academic art librarians know where to locate specific pictorial, graphic, artistic, and architectural works and what the restrictions for their use may be. The library may already have permission or a license to display certain works. You can find unrestricted fair use materials (no license or permission required) at the Creative Commons (www.creativecommons.org).

▪ IN-CLASS PERFORMANCES

Assuming your institution is accredited, you and your students can freely show videos, play music, recite poetry, read and perform plays, and project slides in a classroom setting. You can show performances off YouTube and other websites in a live class. None of these actions requires permission. Copying sheet music, however, is restricted to out-of-print music and performances "in an emergency."

You can also play, without prior permission, a DVD or musical CD (or excerpts from it) in class that you have legally bought or rented. But here is the murky part: if a DVD carries the warning "For Home Use Only," the law is unclear on whether you may show it in your classroom. Legal experts reason that you probably can because instructors are clearly permitted to display or perform works in face-to-face teaching situations. Of course, you may show any rented DVD that has been cleared for public presentation as long as it serves a purely instructional objective. Even the hint of entertainment purposes, such as the presence of nonstudents in the classroom, can raise a legal red flag.

Movie studios have built the home DVD industry into a multibillion-dollar business, in part by strictly enforcing the distinction between instruction and entertainment. To illustrate, in 1996 the Motion

Picture Licensing Corporation, a Los Angeles copyright policing agency representing the studios, sent threatening letters to 50,000 day care centers across the nation. The letters demanded up to $325 per year for what they termed "a public-performance video license" for showing children's videos (e.g., *Pooh and Scrooge*) to their "public" of toddlers. Apparently Hollywood does not regard its standard products as educational and therefore exempt from licensing fees under the fair use (Bourland, 1996).

■ RECORDING BROADCAST PROGRAMMING

The rules are ambiguous about whether you can record a television program off-the-air at home and then show it in class. If it is a commercial program, some experts consider this illegal, while others recommend that you demonstrate compliance with the spirit of the law by following the guidelines in this section. These guidelines specify what educational institutions (campus media units) can record off-the-air for educational purposes without obtaining a permission or a license from the copyright holder.

Broadcast Programming (Major National and Local Stations)

These guidelines apply only to off-the-air recording by nonprofit educational institutions, which are responsible for ensuring compliance:

- DVDs may be kept for only 45 calendar days after the recording date. After this time, they must be erased.
- The recording may be shown to students only during the first 10 class days after the recording date and may be repeated only once for reinforcement.
- Off-the-air recordings may be made only at the request of an individual instructor and not in anticipation of an instructor's request. The same instructor can request that the program be recorded only once.

- Duplicate copies may be made if several instructors request the recording of the same program.
- After the first 10 classes allowed for showing, the recording may be used only for evaluation, such as for a test.
- Off-the-air recordings may not be edited or combined with other recordings to create a new work or an anthology.
- All recording, including copies, must contain a copyright notice when broadcast.

Public Television

The Public Broadcasting Service, the Public Television Library, the Great Plains National Instructional Television Library, and the Agency for Instructional Television have somewhat less restrictive rules for off-the-air recording for educational purposes:

- Recordings may be made by instructors or students in accredited, nonprofit educational institutions.
- Recordings may be used only for instruction in a classroom, lab, or auditorium but are not restricted to one classroom or one instructor.
- The use of recordings is restricted to one institution and may not be shared outside it.
- Length of allowed retention varies.

Cable Channel Programs

Cable channels require you to ask permission to show any of its programming, even for fair use purposes, but instructors may be allowed to keep their recordings for much longer. The rules vary by program.

■ ONLINE MATERIALS

Learning management systems and electronic reserves have pretty much replaced course packets and hard copy library reserves, and millions of courses are delivered in part or entirely online. As with print, online content must be accessible only to the students enrolled in the class and only for that term. But because these materials are digitized, the fair use laws governing them are somewhat different, often murky, and more restrictive than those governing course packets.

For starters, the readings on e-reserve should not comprise more than a small amount of all the assigned reading for the course. As specified in the Digital Millennium Copyright Act of 1998, copyright-protected digital materials also include a wide range of content you might not expect: print and electronic books, analog and digital musical recordings, websites, works embedded in websites, print and e-mail messages and attachments, and possibly even databases. In addition, the Technology Harmonization and Education Act of 2002 requires you to add a legal notice in your syllabus that online materials "may" be copyright protected.

Most legal and library authorities argue that you or your institution's library must obtain permission to post any copyrighted digital course content, even when it is available elsewhere on the Internet, is being used in a course for the first time, or is supplemental, unless you get your general counsel's approval to skip obtaining permission. In fact, some university lawyers contend that fair use protection makes permissions unnecessary (Foster, 2008a). Libraries, however, tend to err on the conservative side and routinely obtain permission.

Probably your easiest alternative is providing your class with links to materials that are already available online through your institution's library, which has a license or permission to make the materials available. But what if you want to link to sites not in your library? Here again the law is cloudy. Some say you "may" need the permission of the website owner, and others claim you don't. Another safe bet is to use vendor-provided digital content that is sold along with many textbooks (DVDs and password-protected websites). Because the cost includes the copyright license, no restrictions apply to its educational use.

The legal area surrounding copyright and fair use of electronic materials is the most volatile, as well as the most restrictive. Recall that in traditional face-to-face classrooms, you and your students can listen to music, read poems aloud, perform plays, display slides, view websites, or play excerpts from a DVD, all without prior permission, as long as the purpose is educational. Between 1997 and 2002, you and your students could not do any of these things electronically under fair use protection. The CONFU guidelines required you to obtain a license. Finally, Congress closed this odd legal gap in mid-2002 when it passed the TEACH Act without debate (after the bill languished for an entire year in the House Judiciary Committee). As the rules stand now, you may, without prior permission, download images from the Internet for your teaching, and students may do so for their projects. You may do the same for sound and video files, but subject to severe length limitations: videos to 3 minutes or 10 percent, whichever is shorter, and music to 10 percent of the composition, up to a maximum of 30 seconds. The same length limits apply if you or your students take excerpts from a lawfully purchased or rented DVD or CD. Permission is required only when you or a student wants to exceed these length limits or to post or repost any of the files online.

Don't even think about trying to get permission to put an entire commercially produced motion picture or musical CD on electronic reserve or online. This would require a very costly license.

Electronic copyright law is unsettled, ambiguous, and subject to challenge from both commercial and educational interests. For example, in March 2016, the fair-use status of e-reserves was "mostly" upheld by a U.S. District Court in a lawsuit three academic publishers brought against Georgia State University. I say "mostly" because the decision turned on revenue data, which are not public. So e-reserves remain in foggy territory. Stay tuned to the academic news media to keep abreast of the latest legal developments and clarifications. Another good idea is to make materials available in ways that avoid potential trouble. For example, refer your students to URLs rather than incorporating Internet-based text, images, and performances into your online course materials. Also make the most of any vendor-provided digital content that may accompany your textbooks.

OBTAINING PERMISSION OR A LICENSE

Perhaps you wish to reproduce, display, or play a work or a portion of a work that exceeds the length limits or otherwise violates the guidelines above. Or perhaps your campus library or copy center cannot obtain the necessary permissions or licenses in time for you or your students to use the work. You and your students may follow these procedures to obtain them on your own.

Request in writing (e-mail is okay) the permission of the copyright holder (which is not necessarily the author or creator) to reprint, display, or post online, identifying the exact portion of the work, the number of copies you wish to make and distribute or the planned location on the Internet, the expected readership or viewership, and the purpose or planned use of the work (e.g., instruction in a given course for a specific term at a given institution). A permission granted for classroom use applies only to one course during one term. Or you can contact the Copyright Clearance Center at www.copyright.com. It offers an electronic service that usually obtains your permission within a few days.

You can also request a license of the copyright holder in writing, giving the same precise information as above. Licenses are often required to show a work or portion of a work or to include some nontrivial portion of it in your own scholarship or multimedia production. Licenses always entail fees, but they may be negotiable.

HOW COPYRIGHT VIOLATIONS ARE ACTUALLY HANDLED

What if you forgot to put a long, important journal article on e-reserve, and you decide to make copies of the whole thing and hand them out to your students in class? What penalties might you face? The laws state that you face a judgment of up to $100,000 for each willful infringement, and ignorance of the law won't get you off. What may get you off is a convincing argument that you were acting in good faith, believing on reasonable grounds that your case qualified as fair use. Your institution will probably defend you if you follow its fair use policies.

However, the law doesn't always operate by the law. In the educational arena, institutions, not individuals, are usually sued, and very few of these have been over the past several decades. Obviously colleges, universities, school systems, and private K–12 schools have much deeper pockets than their teaching staff, so copyright enforcers send them threatening letters every once in a while to remind them of the law and potential penalties. Sometimes a threat is based on a tip that violations have occurred. (Some enforcement agencies maintain tip hot lines.) But in any case, the alleged violator, whether an institution or individual, receives not a summons but a cease-and-desist order. Educational institutions have generally induced their violators to cease and desist immediately and have avoided further legal action.

Historically, the most aggressive copyright enforcer has been the Software Publishers Association, which patrols software pirating (installation or reproduction without site licenses). But even it confines its efforts to organizations and stays out of people's home offices.

Corporations, which can rarely claim fair use protection, have never enjoyed such gentle treatment. But then they have the most to gain financially by copyright violations. The copyright cops have ensured that they also have the most to lose. So be aware that publishing houses, which are profit-making corporations no matter how academic they may be, interpret fair use very conservatively.

FOR FURTHER AND FUTURE REFERENCE

These resources provide further detail on copyright protections, restrictions, and exemptions, as well as the latest changes in the laws and guidelines.

Media-Specific Information

- For images: www.vrawebor.ipower.com/organization/pdf/VRA_FairUse_Statement_Pages_Links.pdf
- For online videos: www.cmsimpact.org/sites/default/files/online_best_practices_in_fair_use.pdf
- For documentary films: www.cmsimpact.org/sites/default/files/fair_use_final.pdf
- For poetry: www.cmsimpact.org/sites/default/files/documents/pages/fairusepoetrybooklet_singlepg_3.pdf
- For dance-related material: www.cmsimpact.org/sites/default/files/documents/pages/DHC_fair_use_statement.pdf
- For open courseware: www.cmsimpact.org/sites/default/files/10–305-OCW-Oct29.pdf
- For film or media: http://c.ymcdn.com/sites/www.cmstudies.org/resource/resmgr/files/scms_teaching_statement_-_20.pdf
- For teaching media literacy: http://mediaeducationlab.com/sites/mediaeducationlab.com/files/CodeofBestPracticesinFairUse_0.pdf
- For publishing in media studies: https://c.ymcdn.com/sites/cmstudies.site-ym.com/resource/resmgr/docs/scmsbestpractices4fairuseinp.pdf
- For publishing in communication studies: www.cmsimpact.org/sites/default/files/WEB_ICA_CODE.pdf

General Copyright Information

- American Association of University Professors (AAUP) Copyright, Distance Education, and Intellectual Property: www.aaup.org/issues/copyright-distance-education-intellectual-property

- Copyright Clearance Center Campus Guide to Copyright Compliance for Academic Institutions: www.copyright.com/Services/copyrightoncampus/
- Cornell University Copyright Information Center: www.copyright.cornell.edu/resources/
- Decatur High School Library: http://dhslibrary.csdecatur.net/copyright
- Hall Davidson Copyright Resources: www.hall-davidson.com/downloads.html#anchor923173
- Indiana University Information Policy Office: http://copyright.iu.edu/about/
- Librarian.net 2014 METRO Annual Conference: http://librarian.net/talks/metro/
- Stanford University Libraries Copyright and Fair Use: http://fairuse.stanford.edu/
- U.S. Copyright Office: www.copyright.gov/; 101 Independence Avenue S.E., Washington, DC 20559–6000; (202)707–3000 or 1(877) 476–0778 (toll free); circulars and forms are available free at www.copyright.gov/circs/
- University of Minnesota Libraries Copyright Information and Education: www.lib.umn.edu/copyright/
- University of Texas System Crash Course in Copyright: http://copyright.lib.utexas.edu/

Copyright Tools, Charts, Checklists, and Calculators

- Columbia University Libraries: http://copyright.columbia.edu/copyright/files/2009/10/fairusechecklist.pdf
- Stanford University Libraries: http://fairuse.stanford.edu/charts-and-tools/
- University of Minnesota Libraries: https://www.lib.umn.edu/copyright/fairthoughts

PART 2

HUMAN FACTORS

CHAPTER 7

Creating a Welcoming Classroom Environment for All Your Students

Creating a safe, stimulating, learner-centered classroom environment seems to help students in many ways. They are more likely to achieve the learning outcomes of the course, develop higher-order thinking skills, participate in class activities, behave appropriately in class, be motivated to learn, and be satisfied with the course (Cornelius-White, 2007; Granitz, Koernig, & Harich, 2009). These benefits accrue in online courses too (Lundberg & Sheridan, 2015). Relatedly, having a positive rapport with you enhances students' attitudes toward you and the course, increases their motivation and participation, augments their perceived learning as well as their actual cognitive and affective learning, and raises both their grades and your student ratings (Allen, Witt, & Wheeless, 2006; Frisby & Martin, 2010; Granitz et al., 2009; Meyers, 2009; Wilson & Ryan, 2013).

This primary responsibility for creating this environment lies with you. You have to convey to your students that you designed the course to foster their learning and care very much not only about their learning the material but also about their developing as human beings. Therefore, you will listen to them, honor their voices, seek and respond to their questions and feedback, adapt to their individual and cultural differences, encourage their participation and best thinking, relate to them with honesty and empathy, and convey your enthusiasm about teaching them. Furthermore, you will allow them to speak up, experiment, take risks, and be wrong without evoking a judgmental reaction from you as long as they show respect for you and their fellow classmates (Webb & Barrett, 2014).

Just promising that you will be this way is obviously not enough. You must follow through on those promises and reinforce them throughout the term with a variety of behaviors that this chapter details.

◼ PLANNING A WELCOMING CLASSROOM

The hope is that you will have the chance to write your syllabus days or even weeks in advance.

81

Be careful about the tone, especially in the sections on course policies and assignments. Your goal is to strike a balance between firmly no-nonsense and easy-going softy. For instance, "NO EXCEPTIONS. Don't even ask" sounds inflexible, even threatening. The same substantive method comes through in a positive tenor with, "To be fair, I must hold all of you to the same dates and standards." These words give a good reason for why you will not grant extension requests or otherwise make exceptions. In fact, whenever you describe a disciplinary or regulatory policy or assign a potentially imposing workload or difficult task, justify it in terms of your need to be fair to all students or your high expectations of them. The latter includes your desire to bring out the best in them and motivate them to do their best work.

If you have posted materials on your LMS or course website, check that everything that you want to be there is there. Along with course materials, prepare your agenda for the first class. This chapter contains a range of productive activities to choose from. It may be wise to divide your selections into "essential" and "desirable as time remains." Practice your first-day presentations and your directions for the activities in advance.

A day or two before your first class, tend to some classroom details. First, inspect the room to ensure that all of the technology that you will need is there and in working order and that you know how to access and operate it. Don't forget low-tech needs like chalk, whiteboard markers, and erasers. Check the lights, the clock (if any), and the heating and air-conditioning system as well. If anything is missing or awry, ask your department to correct the problem. Then take a few moments to orient yourself to the setting. Stand at the front of the room and imagine the seats filled with your students. Make eye contact with the sectors of your imaginary class, walk out toward them, move about the room, and practice smiling.

Plan to dress a little more formally for your first day of class than you normally would, at least if you're inclined to more casual attire. A touch of formality conveys professionalism and seriousness. It also gives instructors who are female, young, or physically small an aura of authority and a psychological edge that help separate them from their students (Johnston, 2005; Roach, 1997).

At least a half-hour before the first class, start preparing yourself—specifically, your body and your voice. You want to project a successful instructor persona to your class—one of relaxed confidence, goodwill, and an in-command, no-nonsense presence. This will inspire your students' respect for your authority, their confidence in you, their goodwill in return, and their willingness to honor your rules and policies. You also want to convey enthusiasm, passion, dynamism, and charisma so you can get their attention and keep them engaged for the entire class. If you don't think you're naturally relaxed, confident, in command, and charismatic, take heart in knowing that you can look as if you are by practicing certain behaviors that are listed in chapter 9 under "Preventing Incivility: Your Classroom Persona." You can make these behaviors come more easily and naturally by performing a few vocal and physical exercises shortly before class.

A WELCOMING FIRST DAY OF CLASS

First impressions are lasting ones. Like no other day, the first day of class colors the classroom environment for the entire term. What you do and do not do will affect your students' and even your own expectations and behavior for the rest of the term.

For you, the first day may be cause for anxiety as well as excitement. It may represent innovations and experiments in course content, organization, and design; teaching methods; and assessment methods—not to mention all those new student faces. You may wonder what the day means for your students and what they want you to do: Set up icebreakers, review the syllabus with a friendly tone, explain the how's and why's of the course, or teach content? Certainly, simply reading the syllabus aloud is not among them. Otherwise the research yields conflicting findings on student preferences (Meyers & Smith, 2011). But be reassured that the suggestions here are safe and useful, although social icebreakers may be unruly or impossible to manage in a large class.

Think carefully about the expectations and behaviors you want to establish in your classroom for the next 10 to 15 weeks. Lay out these expectations, and lead the kind of class activities that model the level and type of student engagement you have in mind for the rest of the course. For example, if you hope for considerable discussion, engage your students in discussion, perhaps about their expectations of the course or their current conceptions of the subject matter. If you intend to have a number of in-class writing exercises, start with a short one during that first class. If you plan on group work, prepare a small-group activity for the first day.

Model the behavior you want from your students. Since you expect them to be prompt, set a good example from the start. Arrive in the classroom early, and set a welcoming tone by chatting with students informally as they arrive. Make students feel comfortable with you as a person as well as an instructor, but don't confuse your roles; remember the difference between being friendly and being friends.

No doubt you want to establish a professional classroom atmosphere, and you can communicate this in several ways. First, have a comprehensive, well-structured syllabus posted on your LMS or class website, or hard copies ready to distribute, or both. You may want hard copies if you intend your students to do a scavenger hunt of syllabus information and do not want them to use mobile devices or laptops in class (see chapters 4 and 9). A solid syllabus tells your class that you are careful, well organized, and conscientious about teaching.

Exchanging Information

Information flow should be a two-way street, even (and perhaps especially) on the first day. But you as the instructor initiate the exchange, first by displaying the following information before class convenes: the name and number of your course, the section number (if appropriate), and your name. This information assures students that they are in the right place.

The next several activities need not come in the order presented, but they are strongly recommended for setting an open, safe, and participatory tone for the rest of the term.

Student Information Index Cards

Get to know your students, and let them know that you are interested in them personally, by passing out blank index cards and asking them to write down this information for you: their full name, any preferred nickname, their year in school, their major, and their previous courses in the field of your course. Additional information such as hometown, outside interests, and career aspirations may help you relate class material to your students on a more personal level. Consider also asking them to write out what they expect from this course and why they are taking it (again, aside from requirements), or what topics they would like to see addressed. You may be able to orient the material toward some of their interests and advise those with erroneous expectations to take a more suitable course.

Your Background

Since you're asking students about themselves, it's only fair to tell them something about yourself. (They *are* interested.) You needn't divulge your life history, but giving them a brief summary of your educational and professional background, orally or in your syllabus, helps reinforce your credibility as an instructor and your humanness as a person. A bit of openness also enhances your students' personal loyalty to you. Share some information about your own research and interests, what attracted you to your discipline, why you love teaching it, and the implications and applications of the subject in the world. See this as an opportunity to make the material more relevant to your students.

Course Information

First, say a few words to promote the course and the material. What big questions will your course address? Why is the material so interesting, relevant, useful, and important? How will your students benefit from learning it? Enthusiasm is contagious. Showing some of your own for the subject matter and the opportunity to teach it will motivate your students' interest in learning it and inspire their respect for you as a scholar.

Mark on your copy of the syllabus any points you want to elaborate, clarify, and emphasize. But rather than reading through the whole document, consider choosing one of the options under "Ensuring Your Students Read Your Syllabus" in chapter 5. One option describes several syllabus activities in which student groups discuss the document, raise questions about it, or find information in it. These are ideal for the first day of class. Two other options are to assign the syllabus as homework and follow up with a test or a contract at the next class meeting. Don't otherwise expect students to read the syllabus carefully.

Here are several more do's for the first day:

1. Do mention your office hours and urge students to seek your help outside class. If you are serious about meeting your students individually, face-to-face, tell them that they will not see the results of their first test or assignment unless they come to your office hours.

2. Do explain the teaching and assessment strategies you will rely on the most, along with why you've chosen them. Emphasize the learning benefits they have over other reasonable options, especially if your methods are innovative or collaborative. Your explanation will not only reassure students of your professionalism and commitment to their learning but also reduce their resistance to unusual formats. In addition, they will see your effort as a sign of respect for them.

3. Do state your expectations of students and their responsibilities for preparing for class and participating. For example, if your course calls for considerable discussion, emphasize the importance of their doing the reading, your rules for calling on them, and your criteria for assessing their contributions. You may want to reserve cold-calling as an option, but to keep the classroom atmosphere safe, honor a few rules. Confine cold-calling to material that students should have learned in required readings or another assignment. Explain why you are using it—for example, to help ensure they do the reading. Do it regularly, do it fairly (shuffle cards with students' names on it), address students by name, permit them to pass on responding, and gently correct wrong answers or let their fellow students do so.

4. Do plan to give and enforce rules of classroom decorum. Students expect you to maintain an orderly, civil classroom, with or without their voluntary cooperation. If you don't, your teaching effectiveness and your student ratings will suffer. In fact, many students were never socialized to arrive to class on time, stay seated the whole period, speak only when sanctioned by the instructor, or show respect to both the instructor and their peers. The first or second day of class is the optimal time to set up a code of conduct for the term, and the students who come motivated to learn will love you for it. Chapter 9 offers several effective approaches to getting this somewhat unpleasant job done without alienating your class.

5. Do leave some course policies open for your students to decide. This gives them the opportunity to buy into the policies and take responsibility for the success of the course (Weimer, 2013a). The policies governing classroom conduct and discussions of controversial subjects are ideal candidates. Some instructors have also allowed students to determine the distribution of points across assignments and tests within certain limits, and they claim that the final grade distribution looked much the same as what they developed previously on their own (Dobrow, Smith, & Posner, 2011; Vander Schee, 2009).

6. Do offer your students some advice on how to make the most of class activities by taking notes. Note taking on discussion remains a mystery even to the most verbal students (see chapter 13). If you plan to lecture at all, give students some pointers on your lecture organization and some good note-taking strategies (see chapter 12). Few students took notes in high school.

7. Do share some helpful reading and study skills and problem-solving strategies appropriate to your subject matter. Better yet, integrate some self-regulated learning activities into your classes, assignments, and test debriefings. Chapter 20 provides an array of options, and you'll find a few for the first day later in this chapter in the section "Subject Matter Icebreakers."

You cannot possibly anticipate all the questions that students will have, but here are some likely ones that you should be prepared to field about your testing and grading procedures:

1. What will your tests be like?
2. What types of questions will they have?
3. What kinds of thinking will they require?
4. How should we best prepare for them?
5. Will you give out review sheets?
6. Will you hold review sessions?
7. How will you evaluate papers and other written assignments?
8. How many A's, B's, C's, and so on do you usually give?
9. How possible is it for all students to get a good grade?

Reciprocal Interview

In this two-way interview, which takes about 50 minutes in small classes, you and your students exchange course-related information (Case et al., 2008). You distribute a handout that asks questions like these:

1. What do you hope to gain from this course?
2. How can I help you reach these goals?

3. What concerns do you have about this course?
4. What resources and background in the subject matter do you bring to it?
5. What student conduct rules should we set up to foster the course's success?
6. What aspects of a class or an instructor impede your learning?

Students write their answers to these questions as individuals for the first 5 minutes and discuss them in groups for the next 10 minutes. Then each group spokesperson reports these responses aloud to the class (15 or so minutes, depending on class size). For the second part of the exercise, your handout should also suggest questions to pose to you about your course goals, your expectations of students, and your views on grading. (Students can ask other questions as well.) First as individuals, then back in their groups, students select and develop questions for you, which requires about 10 minutes. Then each group spokesperson reads these questions aloud, which you answer over the next 10 minutes.

According to student feedback (Case et al., 2008), this activity establishes a comfortable class environment, fosters a sense of community, communicates your openness and commitment to student success, and serves as a social icebreaker. Underrepresented students especially appreciate it. If you plan on a lot of group work and class discussion during the term, this exercise will prepare students to participate.

Social Icebreakers: Getting to Know You

If your class size allows it, try to incorporate one or two icebreaker activities on the first day. There are two types: the social or getting-to-know-you variety, which gets students acquainted with each other and begins to build a classroom community, and subject matter icebreakers, which motivate students to start thinking about the material. Feel free to move beyond the examples given here and devise your own.

Let's first consider some social icebreakers. If you plan on discussion or group work, these smooth the way for broad participation and group interaction. First-year students in particular appreciate the opportunity to meet other students, including more senior ones, who can serve as role models.

Simple Self-Introductions

Have students take turns introducing themselves to the class by giving their name, major, their reason for taking the course (once again, aside from fulfilling some requirement), and perhaps something about themselves that they are proud of having done or become. This activity may work best in a smaller class, however, as the prospect of speaking in front of a large group of strangers can mildly terrify some students. If you have your students make speeches or oral presentations in front of the class during the term, this first-day exercise can help them get used to the assignments to come.

Three-Step Interviews

Have students share the same type of self-introductions with a neighbor. Then, without knowing beforehand the second part of the task, each partner can introduce his or her counterpart to another pair of students or to the class as a whole. This exercise also teaches careful listening skills.

Class Survey

Ask students to raise their hands in response to some general questions: How many students are from [various regions of the country]? East/west of the Mississippi? First year, sophomores, juniors, seniors? How many work off campus? How many are married? How many have children? How many like golf? Reading? How many have traveled abroad? To Europe? To Asia? Then you may venture into opinion questions, perhaps some relevant to the course material. Students soon start to form a broad picture of their class and see what they have in common. They will find it far easier to interact with classmates who share their interests and backgrounds.

Scavenger Hunt

For this more structured activity, give students a list of requirements and tell them to move about the classroom seeking fellow students who meet each one. No one may use a given student for more than one requirement. Some possible requirements are "has been to Europe," "prefers cats to dogs," "has a birthday in the same month you do," "can speak two or more languages fluently," and "cries at movies." The "found" students sign their name next to the requirement they meet. You might give prizes to the three fastest students.

Human Bingo

This icebreaker is a variation on scavenger hunt. Instead of a list of requirements, make a page-size four-by-four table with a different requirement in each box, and give one copy of the table to each student. Be sure your class as a whole can meet all the requirements. As in the scavenger hunt, no one may use a given student for more than one requirement. When a student has all the boxes signed by qualified fellow students, she shouts out, "Bingo!" and gets a prize. Bring a few prizes in case of ties.

"The Circles of _____"

Give each student a sheet of paper with a large central circle and six to eight smaller circles radiating from it. Students write their names in the central circle and the names of groups with which they identify most strongly (e.g., gender, age group, year in college, religious, ethnic, racial, social, political, ideological, athletic) in the satellite circles. Then have students move around the room to find the three classmates who are the most or the least similar to themselves.

Like the scavenger hunt and human Bingo, this exercise helps students appreciate the diversity in the class, as well as meet their fellow students. This icebreaker also generates homogeneous or heterogeneous groups of four if you need them for another activity.

Subject Matter Icebreakers

This second type of icebreaker stimulates your students' interest in the subject matter and informs you about what they know, think they know, and know they don't know about it. Some of these can also help you identify or confirm their faulty models and misconceptions about the subject matter.

Diagnostic Activities

Several classroom assessment techniques, developed by Angelo and Cross (1993), activate your students' prior knowledge and help you assess what they know or think they know about your subject matter, such as the Background Knowledge Probe and Focused Listing (see chapter 24). Another option is the knowledge survey, where you assemble an "exam" from your major learning outcomes, assignment tasks, and test questions and problems from previous offerings of the course. But rather than ask students for the answers, you ask them to rate how confident they are that they could answer the question correctly, perform the task competently, or solve the problem (Nuhfer & Knipp, 2003; Wirth & Perkins, 2005, 2008a). While most students, especially the poorest-performing students, tend to overestimate their abilities (Bell & Volckmann, 2011; Ehrlinger, Johnson, Banner, Dunning, & Kruger, 2008; Kruger & Dunning, 1999; Miller & Geraci, 2011), you still get some idea of their background knowledge.

Problem Posting

Ask students to think about and jot down either problems they expect to encounter with the course or issues they think the course should address. Then record their responses on the board or a slide (McKeachie, 2002). Make sure that the whole class has a chance to contribute, even if you have to coax the quiet members. To build trust, avoid appearing judgmental, and check the accuracy of your understanding by restating the students' comments and requesting their confirmation. Finally, identify the problems and issues the course will address, giving students something to look forward to, and identify which ones it will not address and why. You might use problem posting again before you broach a particularly difficult topic.

This exercise accomplishes several purposes. First, it whets students' appetites for the material.

Second, it opens lines of communication between you and your students, as well as among students. Third, it lends validity to their issues and assures them they're not alone. Finally, it reaffirms that you are approachable and interested in listening to their concerns.

Commonsense Inventory

Another way to break students into the subject matter and underline its relevance is to have them judge an inventory of 5 to 15 commonsense statements directly related to the course material as true or false. The trick is to ensure that many of these statements run counter to popular beliefs or prejudices—for example, "Suicide is more likely among women than men." "Over half of all marriages occur between persons who live within 20 blocks of each other." You might break the class into small groups to discuss and debate their answers or to reach a consensus around the statements. Then have a spokesperson from each group explain and defend its position. After these presentations, you can give the correct answers, which may spark more debate, or take the cliff-hanger approach and let the class wait for them to unfold during the term.

Self-Regulated Learning Activities

While this book devotes all of chapter 20 to self-regulated learning, it is worth mentioning here a few activities that can help your students learn how to learn your course content from the first day. The knowledge survey mentioned above as a diagnostic activity serves self-regulating purposes as well because it makes students aware of what they do and do not know. If you repeat the survey at the end of the course and let students compare their pre- and postcourse results, they can also see how much they have learned and how much they overestimated their precourse abilities.

Since most students have mistaken ideas about what learning and thinking really involve, consider assigning a short, corrective reading the first day and leading a discussion on it the second day. If you don't know of a suitable article on the topic, go to chapter 20 for a few recommendations.

One facet of self-regulated learning is goal setting and planning. Help your students set their sights on top-quality performance in your course by having them write this essay, "How I Earned an A in This Course," and date it the day after final exams. The essay can be an in-class or homework assignment and should be followed with a discussion and exchange of strategies, perhaps in small groups. Average students will have to consider what they haven't been doing in their previous courses; the best students, who don't need this assignment, will lead the way for others.

To focus students on the course content, have them reflect on the nature of the subject matter and answer general questions (Kraft, 2008; Suskie, 2009) such as, "Why is the study of [the course content] important?" "What is the nature of science?" "How is science done?" "Why is [the course content] a science?" Or you can ask them more specific questions that reflect the material your course will address—perhaps questions that will reveal their misconceptions and popular myths. Again, if you have them repeat the exercise at the end of the course and compare their reflections with those at the start, they will realize how advanced their thinking has become.

Drawing the First Class to a Close

At the end of this first class and after you answer all of your students' questions, ask students to write down and hand in their responses to general questions like these: What is the most important thing you learned during this first day? How did your expectations of this course change? What questions or concerns do you still have about the course or the subject matter? Such an exercise shows your interest in their learning and their reactions to you and your course (McKeachie, 2002).

Do make productive use of the entire class period. Don't treat it as a throwaway day or dismiss it early. Only if you treat class time like the precious commodity that it is will your students do as well. If you conduct some of the activities in

this chapter, the time will be more than adequately filled and productively spent. Not only will your students enjoy an introduction to the course and its subject matter, but they will also have a chance to get acquainted with you and their classmates, the first step to developing a sense of community in your classroom.

You can find more first-day activities in Weimer (2013b) and on these college and university websites:

http://www.lcc.edu/cte/resources/teachingettes/icebreakers.aspx
http://teachingcommons.depaul.edu/Classroom_Activities/first_class.html
http://www.unm.edu/~tlc/contents/web_resources/first_day_of_class.html

■ LEARNING STUDENTS' NAMES

Most students, especially at smaller and private colleges and universities, expect their instructors to learn and use their name; this conveys that you care about them. Students expect less personal treatment in very large classes (over 100 students), in which case calling them by name will make you a legend. So begin learning and using students' names quickly. If you have trouble remembering names, here are some strategies to help you:

1. Seat students in specific places and make a seating chart. Students may not prefer a seating chart, but they will tolerate it graciously if you say the reason is to learn their names. Seating them in alphabetical order will probably make learning their names easiest for you, and it ensures that proximity-based small groups will be randomly mixed. In addition, it will facilitate your taking attendance (just look for the empty chairs).

2. Alternatively, just let them sit wherever they want, but ask them to stay in those seats for the first three or so weeks. Then make a seating chart. You can capitalize on your strong cognitive

ability as a human to learn and remember spaces. After each of the first few classes, visualize your classroom and populate that space with the images of your students and their names (Foer, 2011).

3. Take notes on the class roster about each student's physical appearance, such as body shape and size, hair color and length, dress style, age, and any distinguishing physical traits. Of course, you should conceal such notes from your students' view.

4. Take roll in every class. While learning names, you can also use the roll to call on students more or less randomly as long as you tell your class what you'll be doing. Or you may use the index cards to call on students. Just shuffle them as you would a deck of cards every so often.

5. Have students wear name tags or badges or display name cards or tents on their desks. To avoid the hassle of making new name tags or cards for every class, print up permanent, convention-style tags or cards, distribute them at the start of each class, and collect them at the end of each session. This is also a subtle way to take attendance.

6. Collect photographs of your students with their names attached, review them, and use them like flash cards to test yourself. (Remember to space your practice sessions, as chapter 1 recommends.) First, check to see whether your institution makes the ID photos of the students enrolled in your classes available to you on your LMS. If not, you can take photographs of individual students or small groups of students; just be sure each person is associated with the right name. Or you can ask your students to give you a picture of themselves with their name on it.

■ THE INCLUSIVE, EQUITABLE CLASSROOM

Today college students vary markedly by gender, race, ethnicity, national origin, sexual orientation, and religion. Time was when only well-to-do white males attended college in the United States. But in 2012 56.5 percent of all undergraduates were female, and only 59.3 percent were white, 15.0 percent African American, 16.0 percent Hispanic, 6.2 percent Asian American, 0.9 percent Native American, 0.3 percent Pacific Islander, and 2.6 percent multiracial, plus 2.6 percent nonresident aliens (U.S. Department of Education, 2013, Table 306.10). In addition, close to 12 percent have a disability ("Profile of Undergraduate Students, 2003–04," 2007.)

While all people learn by the same basic processes described earlier, some of these groups thrive educationally under circumstances that are not always typical in the American classroom. In addition, they often share distinctive values, norms, background experiences, and a sense of community that set them apart and make them feel set apart—and not always in a positive way. Traditionally underrepresented and first-generation groups are more likely to struggle emotionally in college and to leave before attaining a degree.

As an instructor, you are also an ambassador of the academy to these groups, and you are close enough to them to reach out and include them. How you relate to these students has a powerful impact on their performance and retention (Ferguson, 1989; Grant-Thompson & Atkinson, 1997; Guo & Jamal, 2007; Jones, 2004; Kobrak, 1992). You are also a role model to all your students of what equity and inclusion look like in action. Here are some guidelines to help ensure your impact is universally positive:

1. Create a safe climate for the expression of different points of view. With your students' participation, set ground rules for civil discussion in class, and intervene if any students act disrespectfully to others (see chapter 9).

2. Don't let any students get away with insensitive remarks in class. Such incidents open up teachable moments for you to lead an open discussion about cultural differences and stereotyping. Before launching a potentially controversial

discussion, remind students what a civil intellectual discourse comprises.

3. Give attention to all students as equally as possible. After asking a question, lengthen your wait time before calling on anyone by at least 10 to 15 seconds to allow more students to mentally prepare their responses. This will help you broaden participation.

4. Praise students equally for equal-quality responses.

5. Use nonstereotypical examples in presentations. If you use a female in an example, make her a scientist, an accountant, or a surgeon rather than a nurse, a teacher, or an administrative assistant.

6. When possible, integrate course content that includes the scholarly and artistic contributions and perspectives of all genders and all cultural, ethnic, and racial groups that may be represented in your classes.

7. Don't ask diverse students to speak in class as representatives of their group. Whatever the group, it is too internally diverse to be represented by one or a few members.

8. Use gender-neutral language. Try to avoid using the pronouns *he* and *him* exclusively when referring to people in general.

9. Call a group by the name that its members prefer.

10. Develop a personal rapport with your African American, Native American, Hispanic, and female students. Their style of thinking and dealing with the world tends to be relational and interpersonal, which means intuitive, cooperative, holistic, subjective, relationship focused, motivated by personal loyalty, and oriented to socially relevant topics (Anderson & Adams, 1992; Baxter Magolda, 1992). This style contrasts with the analytical, which values analysis, objectivity, logic, reason, structure, sequence, the abstract, debate, challenge, competition, and economic practicality. It is prevalent among European American and Asian American males and in the academy in general (Anderson & Adams, 1992). How closely and easily you relate to your diverse and female students will strongly affect their motivation to learn, their trust in your intentions for them, and their overall satisfaction with college (Allen, Epps, & Haniff, 1991; Gonsalves, 2002; Grant-Thompson & Atkinson, 1997; Kobrak, 1992).

11. Be aware that most international students stand physically closer to others than do Americans, many Asian American women are taught to avoid eye contact, and many Asian Americans and Native Americans have learned to listen quietly rather than jump into discourse.

12. Don't avoid course-appropriate topics related to diverse groups because they are sensitive, controversial, or applicable to only a minority of people. Some students will see your avoidance as prejudicial.

13. Don't avoid giving timely, constructive feedback to diverse students about their work out of fear of injuring their self-esteem or being accused of racism. Indeed, diverse students may interpret your criticisms as racially motivated disrespect, so you should bring up this possibility yourself and explicitly ask them rather than sweeping the issue under the rug. Be very sure that the students really understand your criticisms and recommendations for improvement (Gonsalves, 2002).

14. Don't give inordinate attention to diverse students or make so much of their successes that you imply you didn't expect them to succeed.

15. When possible, allow students to choose the mode in which you will assess their learning (paper, poster, website, video, oral presentation, art form, concept or mind map, and so on).

16. Discretely ask your students with disabilities and non-English-speaking backgrounds whether you can do something in class to make their life easier, such as facing the class when you are talking.

17. Be sensitive to difficulties your students may have in understanding you. International, ESL (English as a Second Language), and hearing-impaired students may have trouble with

idiomatic expressions and accents. Ask such students privately if they do, and urge them to watch your lips and request clarification as needed.

If your class is especially diverse or the subject matter of your course encompasses race, ethnicity, class, gender preference, or gender identity, it's best to bring differences out in the open early if students want to do so. Brookfield and Preskill (2005) describe several classroom activities that acknowledge and honor diversity. In one of them, "Naming Ourselves," students first reflect on the group with which they identify. Then they each introduce themselves as members of their group, stating the label term they prefer for this group and what their identification means to them—for instance, how it has affected their values, beliefs, language, behavior, and so on. In another, "Expressing Anger and Grief," students get into groups and exchange personal experiences of cruelty set off by prejudice or discrimination against the group with which they identify. Then they analyze the stories for common and disparate themes, emotions, and effects.

Equity and inclusion are really about increasing and broadening student participation, not only in discussion but in higher education and beyond.

■ MAINTAINING A WELCOMING ENVIRONMENT

As with any other relationship, you can't just establish a warm, trusting rapport with your students, set it on automatic, and expect it to continue. It will need steady reinforcement and nurturing, but this isn't difficult to do.

First, practice social immediacies, which is a fancy way of saying to be kind, thoughtful, respectful, and amiable. Use your students' names whenever possible. If you pass them on the sidewalk or in the hall, greet them with a cheery hello, as you would a colleague. If you can, arrive 10 minutes before class, set up your technology, and then chat informally

with some of your students as they come in. Be happy to see them. Ask them what they did over the weekend or whether they attended a major campus event. Ask them whether they work and what they do. Ask them about their family. Take an interest in their lives beyond the classroom. Listen to your students; try not to interrupt or rush them. Respond to their e-mail as soon as possible. Meet with them outside class. Encourage them to have high aspirations and to do their best. Tell them you have faith in their abilities. Make eye contact and smile at them in and out of class. Show that you enjoy yourself in their company. Display a sense of humor around them. Tell them that you care about them and their learning. Like everyone else you interact with on a regular basis, they want you to like, respect, and care about them (Meyers, 2009; Webb & Barrett, 2014).

Second, solicit your students' feedback about how the class is going on a fairly regular basis. Your campus teaching and learning or faculty development center probably interviews classes on request, or you can ask students anonymously for their opinion on your own. For specifics, see the "During-the-Term Student Feedback" section in chapter 24.

Third, keep students apprised of their grades on assignments, quizzes, and exams. Your LMS makes this easy for you, but do remind your students that their scores are available and be sure they know how to access them.

Finally, use rubrics to grade all the work that students construct themselves—that is, write, present, draw, design, develop, solve, act out, cook, or compose—and share those rubrics with your students when you make the assignments. Many students regard grading as a mysterious process. After all, they don't have our professional judgment, and if they did, they wouldn't need us! Besides, they have a right to know the criteria on which we will assess them, and we choose these criteria from any number of alternatives.

In the end, establishing and maintaining a welcoming and productive learning environment for all your students simply boils down to following the Golden Rule.

CHAPTER 8

Enhancing Student Motivation

In the context of education, the term *motivating* means stimulating the desire to learn something. In spite of a huge literature about motivation in psychology and educational psychology, we know precious little about the topic. In the educational context, we don't know how to manipulate people's values, attitudes, and belief systems very effectively, at least not as well as politicians and advertisers seem to know. Yet if it is true that when all is said and done, learning is "an inside job," motivating students is our primary task.

▓ INTRINSIC AND EXTRINSIC MOTIVATION

When we in academia use the term *motivation*, we're usually talking about stimulating students' interest in the subject matter—in other words, *intrinsic* motivation. We want to induce in our students a genuine fascination with the subject, a sense of its relevance and practical applicability, a sense of accomplishment

in mastering it, and a sense of calling to it. But this is only one type of motivation.

Extrinsic motivators are unrelated to the subject matter, and we see them operating in our students strongly enough to eclipse their intrinsic motivation. Among the most powerful are the expectations of significant others, such as parents, spouses, employers, and teachers. Many of today's younger students pursue a major because of its earning potential. For them, high achievement in the form of top grades may mean entrance into a professional or business school and ultimately a high-paying occupation. Other students may care about grades only so they can stay in school or have someone else pay for it. A few just want to extend their adolescence and put off adult responsibilities. Returning adult students often have their eye on a promotion or a career change.

While we can't always affect extrinsic forces, we can enhance our subject matter's intrinsic appeal to students, and intrinsic motivators are often more potent than extrinsic one (Hobson, 2002; Levin,

2001; Svinicki, 2004). We know that motivation isn't fixed, but it isn't easily modified in the short term either (Frymier, 1970). How can we develop students' intrinsic motivation? Most of us don't feel very successful at doing it. It seems that students come to us either motivated or not, and they leave the same way. Do we have to reduce their extrinsic drive for good grades first? If we do, how can we? If we don't, why can't we be more effective at getting students engaged in our material?

The vast body of research on the relationships among intrinsic motivation, extrinsic motivation, and student performance comes to no clear conclusions. One stance claims that extrinsic rewards undercut intrinsic motivation (Deci, Koestner, & Ryan, 1999; Kohn, 1993), but some say only under certain circumstances: not if the reward is positive feedback and verbal reinforcement (Deci, 1971) and only if the person was intrinsically motivated to begin with (Svinicki, 2004). These findings have been used to argue against grading, but think about it: Does the fact that you get paid for teaching make it less appealing to you? Another contingent finds almost the opposite: that extrinsic rewards have either no effect or an enhancing one on intrinsic motivation (Cameron & Pierce, 1994; Eisenberger & Cameron, 1996). Still others say the two types of motivators have interactive curvilinear effects on student performance, which is optimized by moderate extrinsic motivation coupled with high intrinsic motivation (Lin, McKeachie, & Kim, 2001). Yet another position is that autonomy of action trumps intrinsic-extrinsic distinctions (Rigby, Deci, Patrick, & Ryan, 1992; Ryan & Deci, 2000). On the extreme end is the argument that intrinsic motivation simply doesn't exist ("Intrinsic Motivation Doesn't Exist, Researcher Says," 2005). A related body of research has addressed the impact of performance goals. Performance-avoidance goals (to avoid looking incompetent) clearly undermine motivation, but the effects of performance-approach goals (to look competent) on both motivation and performance have been positive in some studies and negative in others (Urdan, 2003).

STUDENTS' PERCEPTIONS OF MOTIVATORS IN THEIR COURSES

A couple of studies have solicited college students' opinions of what makes them want to learn, so we have some idea of what students *think* motivates them. Sass (1989) found the critical factors to be the instructor's enthusiasm for the material and teaching it, the relevance of the material, the clear organization of the course, the appropriateness of the difficulty level, active learning strategies, variety in the instructor's teaching methods, the instructor's rapport with the students, and the use of appropriate examples. These are all known to be highly effective in enhancing both student learning and student ratings. More recently, Hobson (2002) identified and ranked the most powerful positive and negative motivators for students. In order of descending importance, the positive motivators are the instructor's positive attitudes and behaviors, a cohesive course structure, a student's prior interest in the material, the relevance of the course content, and the appropriateness of the performance measures. The most potent demotivators are the instructor's negative attitudes and behaviors and a disorganized course structure. Further down on the list are a poor learning environment, boring or irrelevant course content, and a student's prior disinterest in the material.

To the extent students perceive themselves accurately, these findings are good news. Although we cannot control students' attitudes about our material before they come into our courses, we definitely have control over our own attitudes and behavior and the learning environment, and we usually determine the course organization, course content, and assessment measures.

STUDENTS' VALUES ABOUT COLLEGE AND THEIR IMPACT ON MOTIVATION

Motivation at the course level tells us nothing about the more general picture of why students go to college in the first place. Most of them take an instrumental view of college, seeing it as a means to an end. For example, 73.3 percent of the entering college freshmen in 2013 selected "to be able to make more money" as a "very important" reason for attending college; 77.1 percent selected "to get training for a specific career"; and a whopping 86.3 percent chose "to be able to get a better job" (Eagan, Lozano, Hurtado, & Case, 2013, p. 35), and these reasons have gained currency over the past 40 years (Pryor, Hurtado, Saenz, Santos, & Korn, 2007). While students' largely extrinsic reasons for attending college foster their desire for the certificate or diploma, it does not cultivate a thirst for knowledge. Still, these recent freshmen cited intrinsic reasons as "very important" as well: 81.6 percent "to learn about things that interest me," 69.6 percent "to gain a general education and appreciation of ideas" and 45.9 percent "to make me a more cultured person." But extrinsic reasons still predominate.

Unfortunately, the literature fails to clarify the relationships between intrinsic and extrinsic motivation. However, many faculty complain that today's students are not motivated. Given students' intrinsic interest in at least some material, they simply may not be interested in the topics their classes are addressing, or they may not think they will need the material in the future, or they may want to learn the material but *not to work* to learn it. As we saw in chapter 1, millennial students are accustomed to getting good grades without working much, and adult students holding down full-time jobs rarely have time for course work outside class. They may even expect their instructors not to give homework because of this. However, students tend not to know much about what learning for depth and retention requires. Since they are learners, they need to know, and if we don't tell them, who will? (See chapter 20 for what to share with them.) In particular, many of them seem not to understand that learning requires more time, effort, focus, and perseverance than they think it should.

CREDIBLE THEORIES OF MOTIVATION

Before we explore concrete strategies for developing students' motivation, let's consider the major theories that anchor these strategies. In everyday practice, these models work best when two or more are applied together.

Behaviorism

Behaviorism posits two types of reinforcement as powerful shapers of behavior. In the positive variety, students get (are rewarded with) something they want for their behavior, and in the negative type, they avoid something they don't want for the behavior. Either way, the students are the acting agents, and the reinforcement makes them more likely to repeat the behavior. Punishment following a behavior will tend to decrease that behavior's likelihood in the future, but with less effectiveness than reinforcement. Again there are two types. In one type, students get something they don't want for their behavior, and in the other, they are deprived of something they do want for the behavior. The problem is that punishment teaches students what not to do, but it tells them nothing about what they should do.

While behaviorist theory is straightforward and rings true, the key to applying it is determining what students (and people in general) do and do not want. All around the world, the educational system rests on grades as the universal student currency, but even they don't always motivate and they certainly aren't sufficient. But this is not to say that were it not for our institutional obligation to give grades, we should abandon behaviorism in teaching.

In fact, Darby Lewes applies behaviorist principles very effectively in her English literature courses at Lycoming College, a small, private liberal arts institution (Lewes & Stiklus, 2007), and her secret has nothing to do with grades. At the beginning of every course, she confronts her students' natural aversion to the subject matter—one rooted in their fear of failure, a fear they acquired over years of schooling. Until we conquer this aversion, she contends, students will not learn the material at a deep level no matter what we do or don't do. Early in the term, she motivates students to think about a piece of literature and participate in class discussion about it by rewarding each good-faith contribution with a quarter—yes, a 25 cent piece. Money is a more universal currency than grades. A quarter isn't much and it's only a secondary reinforcer (of value only when exchanged), but it motivates her students to partake in literature from the beginning, no mean feat.

Lewes doesn't give out quarters willy-nilly all term. First, she doesn't always give one out for a second contribution during a class, thereby inducing the talkative students to hang back and the quieter ones to speak out. Second, since the effect of pure positive reinforcement weakens over time, she soon replaces regular reinforcement with the selective variety, rewarding only high-quality contributions with a quarter. At this point, the reward provides informational feedback about the relative strength of varying responses, and by this time, she has overcome students' natural aversion to literature. In addition, the delay students encounter in earning the next quarter increases their motivation to work harder and develop their answers more fully. Third, she incorporates regularly scheduled negative reinforcers—in the form of daily quizzes on the readings—to ensure her students are keeping up. Finally, she reserves a jackpot of a $10 bill for extremely special occasions, such as when especially resistant or fearful students volunteer worthy responses. The prospect of earning $10 has made Lewes legendary among students at her college, and anyone who has even observed gambling knows how the possibility of a jackpot positively reinforces behavior. But rather than risking money, these students are learning.

Lewes's approach may be controversial, but her students respond well to it and give her teaching high ratings. They acquire confidence and pride as they learn. Many of them even acquire a taste for literature. It's hard to argue with this kind of success.

Goal Setting

According to goal-setting theory (Locke & Latham, 1990), setting a goal increases students' motivation to attain it. Certainly, mastering some definable body of material and earning a good grade qualify as possible goals for students. This motivation in turn increases the energy, work, persistence, and thought they will give toward achieving it.

For this process to work, a few conditions must hold. First, students must believe that they have freely chosen the goal, and they might not always think they have in what they perceive to be required courses. Second, they have to see the goal as specific and measurable, as an assessment or a grade typically is. Third, they must get feedback about their progress toward the goal, and they almost always do in classes. Finally, students must size up the goal as challenging but achievable. Difficulty does not necessarily discourage; in fact, the higher the difficulty, the more effort a student will put toward the goal.

Goal-setting theory caught on in business and industry, which is why you often hear terms like *sales goals, service goals, training goals, strategic goals*, and the like. It became one of the most widely implemented and tested theories of organization behavior of the past 50 years (Redmond & Perrin, 2014). Does it work with students? Yes, but only to the extent that they regard their goal as freely chosen and not imposed by the program or institution. Some students look at the courses in their major and any general education course, even if they have a choice of 300 of them, as required and therefore not freely chosen. However, you can incorporate choices into your courses, such as different ways to satisfy course requirements and choices among assignments, topics, media used, and the like. Giving students options cultivates that sense of free will.

Goal Orientation

Students who work primarily for good grades have what is called a *performance goal* orientation. They aim to display higher competency than others and to avoid making mistakes and failing in front of others. Given the stakes, they tend to eschew risk taking. For them, learning often exerts stress on their self-esteem and induces insecurity. By contrast, students who work out of a desire to learn have a *learning goal* orientation. Because they don't care about what others may think of their performance, they willingly take risks, make mistakes, and seek feedback so they can improve. As instructors, we want to foster this type of goal orientation because it engenders deeper learning and retention of our material than does the former (Dweck & Leggett, 1988).

Using this model, we can encourage learning over performance goals by doing what we can to create a safe and secure classroom environment (see chapter 7), reduce students' stress over tests and assignments, deemphasize grades and competition, allow alternative ways to satisfy course requirements, reward risk taking and persistence, and role-model a learning goal orientation (Svinicki, 2004). Specific ways to implement these recommendations are in the "Fifty-Five Strategies for Motivating Students" section below.

Relative Value of the Goal

This social cognitive model posits that the more value students give to learning our material, relative to meeting other needs in life, the more motivated they will be to learn (Bandura, 1997). Therefore, we have to create experiences in which their learning serves important needs. In other words, we must add value to their learning.

The purest value we add to our material is to make it more stimulating, interesting, and emotionally engaging—that is, more intrinsically motivating. But we shouldn't stop there. We can also boost its value by giving students some control and choice over the course content, their learning strategies, and their performance options. In addition, we can highlight its practical utility to students, now and in the future. Going deeper into the human psyche, we can position our material to meet some immediate psychological needs, such as those for cognitive

balance, social affiliation and approval, and self-esteem. For instance, we can help students put their learning toward resolving inconsistencies in their beliefs, values, and worldview. We can also make their learning more of a social than an individual enterprise. Finally, we can give students a taste of achievement by encouraging them to tackle some genuine learning challenges and rewarding them accordingly (Svinivki, 2004). More specifics are listed in the section on strategies later in this chapter.

Expectancy of Goal Achievement

Expectancy theory rests on a pragmatic premise: Why aspire to achieve something you know you can't get? Students won't even try to learn something that seems impossibly difficult. To set and pursue a goal, they need to believe they have the agency and the capability. Agency depends on their sense of self-efficacy and their beliefs about the malleability of intelligence and locus of control. Students with low self-confidence, the view that intelligence is fixed by heredity, or the fatalist belief in an external locus of control have a weak sense of agency and a low expectancy of goal achievement. Capability depends on their perception that the goal is reachable and that they have (or soon will have) the skills, prior experience, and support to reach it. Students feel capable when they view the learning task as doable, given their abilities, academic background, and resources: time, encouragement, assistance, and so on (Wigfield & Eccles, 2000).

Although it can be hard to find the right balance, we have to try to make our readings, assignments, and tests just right—neither too long and hard nor too short and easy. Just as important, we must foster our students' beliefs that they have the agency and capabilities to achieve. Too many students sailed through the K–12 system and never had to meet an academic challenge before coming to college (Ripley, 2013). While they may have high self-esteem, they may have a weak sense of self-efficacy at the college level. They may even sabotage their own success by not studying in order to protect their self-esteem since they can blame their lack of studying rather than their lack of ability if they do poorly. It is likely that such students also believe that they can't raise their intelligence.

Other students don't believe they have control over their academic fate. In their experience, studying and working hard seems to make little difference in their grades. They feel they just get lucky when they encounter readings they can understand, test questions they can answer, and assignments they can handle. In their view, most of the control resides in their teachers. Sometimes they get an instructor who likes them and what they turn in, but most instructors don't. With this belief system, students don't perceive themselves earning an A, a C, or an F; rather, they truly think that we give them an A, a C, or an F. While it is true that faculty grading criteria and standards may vary, many of these students lack basic learning skills. They don't know how to focus their mind, read carefully, take decent notes, think critically, study effectively, and write clearly. Without these skills, they may fall short—not on the agency but on the capability to achieve an academic goal. To foster their success, we need to help them learn how to learn (see chapter 20) and to communicate (see the appendix).

Many other specific suggestions for enhancing students' sense of agency and capability, and therefore their expectancy to achieve, are offered among the 55 strategies in the next section.

Self-Determination Theory

This theory posits a set of built-in human needs that can motivate students to action and achievement (Deci & Ryan, 1985, 2002). Like everyone else, students have an innate need to grow, develop, and attain fulfillment as a person. In order to grow and be fulfilled, they must believe they have these three qualities:

1. *Competence*, which requires that they master new knowledge and skills and live through new experiences

2. *Relatedness*, meaning feeling attached to others, valued by them, and integrated into a social group
3. *Autonomy*, that is, the sense that they can freely choose and are in control of their own goals, outcomes, and behavior

Therefore, conditions that help students satisfy these needs should foster motivation. Students develop their competency when they perceive that they are acquiring relevant, interesting skills and knowledge. Faculty need to explain the hidden value of learning tasks that are not obviously interesting, useful, and worth the effort to complete. Students feel more socially connected when someone they respect, such as their instructor, praises their response, piece of work, or contribution. However, they prize their attachments to and approval of their peers just as much, if not more. So we should set up at least a few group activities or assignments (see chapter 15) and cultivate a sense of classroom community (see chapter 7). Finally, students have a stronger sense of volition and control when they can make choices about their assignments, when the instructor pays attention to their feedback, and when they have some input into the course design and topical emphases. You will notice that student choice keeps coming up as a motivating factor.

Social Belonging

Relatedness seems to be such an important factor in student success and retention and has generated enough research to justify its own subsection here. In fact, Chambliss and Takacs (2014) make a strong empirical case that personal relationships play a critical role in determining how academically successful students are or even whether they finish college. Just a small handful of good friends and one or two faculty members who inspire or take an interest in them can make all the difference in their motivation and learning. The effects of social support prove particularly strong among ethnic minorities and first-generation students (Cox, 2011; Dennis, Phinney, & Chuateco, 2005; Jackson, Smith, & Hill, 2003). Moreover, students must be able to perceive this support for the persistence benefits to accrue, so it must be quite explicit (Dennis et al., 2005). Therefore, you should say to a promising but struggling student, "I believe in you. I *know* you can do it."

You may have more importance in your students' lives than you know. Chickering and Gamson (1987) considered frequent in-class and out-of-class contact with faculty the single most powerful motivator of undergraduates' academic commitment. How warm and caring that Native American students thought their professors were predicted their college persistence and retention (Jackson et al., 2003). Umbach and Wawrzynski (2005) studied the effects of faculty behavior on learning and engagement on more than 42,000 students at 137 colleges and universities and reported that instructor interaction, experiential learning, active and collaborative teaching strategies, and a focus on higher-order thinking all led to greater student engagement and learning. Even in large lecture classes, which hinder faculty-student interaction, just talking with students in small groups can help. Student-to-student relationships also increase students' academic motivation as long as the friendships do not foster alcohol use, which depresses motivation (Li, Frieze, Nokes-Malach, & Cheong, 2013).

■ FIFTY-FIVE STRATEGIES FOR MOTIVATING STUDENTS

Fortunately, effective motivational techniques and effective teaching techniques greatly overlap. Of course, by definition, more motivated students want to learn more, so they achieve more. But it is also true that better teaching generates more rewarding learning experiences, which beget more motivation to learn. It is not surprising, then, that you motivate students using the same methods and formats that you do to teach them effectively. To reach as many

students as possible, use as many of the following strategies as you can (Ambrose, Bridges, DiPietro, Lovett, & Norman, 2010; Biggs, 2003; Bjork & Bjork, 2011; Bransford, Brown, & Cocking, 1999; Chambliss & Takacs, 2014; Cox, 2011; Davis, 2009; Dweck, 2007; Gabriel, 2008; Hobson, 2002; Levin, 2001; McGuire, 2015; Paulsen & Feldman, 1999; Persellin & Daniels, 2014; Svinicki, 2004; Theall & Franklin, 1999).

Your Persona

1. *Deliver your presentations with enthusiasm and energy.* Strive for vocal variety and constant eye contact. Vary your speaking pace, and add dramatic pauses after major points. Gesture and move around the class. Be expressive. To your students, your dynamism signifies your passion for the material and for teaching it. As a display of your motivation, it motivates them (see chapters 9 and 12).

2. *Explain your reasons for being so interested in the material,* and make it relevant to your students' concerns. Show how your field fits into the big picture and how it contributes to society. In so doing, you also become a role model for student interest and involvement.

3. *Make the course personal.* Find out your students' birthdays, and when one comes along, put up a slide with "Happy Birthday, ____!" on it. E-mail students with your concern if they haven't been in class for a couple of days. Write students congratulatory letters when they do well on a test.

4. *Get to know your students.* Ask them about their majors, interests, and backgrounds. This information will help you tailor the material to their concerns, and your personal interest in them will inspire their personal loyalty to you. First-generation and nontraditional students may be hesitant to approach you, so make the first move toward them (Cox, 2011).

5. *Let your students get to know you.* Make yourself more human by sharing a little personal information about yourself.

6. *Learn and use your students' names and help them learn one another's names.* You can help by having social icebreakers at the beginning of the term and using their names yourself, especially when you refer to students' previous comments. Name badges and tents serve everyone in the class (see chapter 7).

7. *Foster good lines of communication in both directions.* Convey your expectations and assessments, but also invite your students' feedback in the form of classroom assessment exercises and midterm assessment of your teaching (see chapter 24).

8. *Use humor where appropriate.* A joke or humorous anecdote lightens the mood and has the synapse-building benefits of emotional intensity (see chapter 1). Just be sensitive to context, setting, and audience.

9. *Maintain classroom order and civility* to earn your students' respect as well as create a positive learning environment (see chapter 9).

Your Course and Subject Matter

10. *Design and develop your course with care,* and explain its organization and your rationale for it to your students (see chapter 2).

11. *Allow students some voice* in determining the course content, policies, conduct rules, and assignments. If they have contributed, they will feel more invested and responsible for their learning.

12. *Build in readings and activities that will move students beyond their simplistic dualistic beliefs about your field* (see chapters 1 through 3). The constricted, naive view of learning as memorizing definitions and facts isn't very motivating, even if challenge can seem a bit frightening at first.

13. *Highlight the occupational potential of your subject matter.* Inform students about the jobs and careers that are available in your discipline, what attractions they hold, and how your course prepares students for these opportunities. Whenever possible, link new knowledge to its usefulness in some occupation.

14. For numerous ways to *motivate students to do the readings and other homework on time,* see chapter 21. When students come prepared, you can fill class time with engaging and intrinsically motivating activities.

15. *Create a safe learning environment* in which errors and failure are seen as normal and valuable learning opportunities.

Your Teaching

16. *Explain to your class why you have chosen* the teaching methods, readings, assignments, in-class activities, policies, and assessment strategies that you are using. Students don't assume that everything you do is for their own good.

17. *Help students realize that they can transfer skills* that they have learned in other courses into yours and vice versa.

18. *Explain the value and personal meaning of your material and learning activities.* Connect them to students' futures and the real world to make them meaningful and worthwhile.

19. *Use examples, anecdotes, and realistic case studies freely, and provide students with models of major homework assignments.* Many students learn inductively, experientially, and concretely.

20. *Ensure that students review the material at least two or three times in different modes* (see chapter 22).

21. *Teach by inquiry when possible.* Students find it satisfying and intrinsically motivating to reason through a problem and discover underlying principles on their own (see chapter 16).

22. *Use a variety of student-active teaching formats and methods,* such as discussion, debates, press conferences, symposia, role playing, simulations, academic games, problem-based learning, the case method, problem solving, and others, all covered in later chapters. Schedule short exercises and learning checks every 10 to 20 minutes during your lectures (see chapter 12). These activities directly engage students in the

material and give them opportunities to achieve a level of mastery for achievement's sake.

23. *Share strategies and tips for students to learn your material,* including reading, studying, problem-solving strategies, and metacognitive strategies, and self-regulated learning practices (see chapter 20). Most of your students greatly underestimate the work that learning and thinking involve. It may be best to wait until after the first test or graded homework assignment to bring up learning how to learn because quite a few students will be disappointed by their grade and thus more amenable to changing their learning habits.

24. *Use group learning formats.* They are student active and add the motivational factor of social belonging. Just be sure to set up and manage the groups properly (see chapter 15).

25. *Bring the arts into your teaching to stir student emotions.* This is a standard culture-learning strategy in the foreign languages, but it has far broader application. In mathematics courses, you can show the utility of concepts and equations in visual design and musical composition. In history, anthropology, literature, and comparative politics courses, you can acquaint students with the art of the historical age or the place. If possible, you can have them read native literature and listen to native music. Such experiences give students an intuitive feel for other times and places.

26. *Make the material accessible.* Explain it in common language, avoiding jargon where possible, and make it accessible to students with disabilities.

27. *Hold students to high expectations.* Don't just tell them to do their best. Refuse to accept shoddy work. Give it back to them ungraded, and tell them they have to do the assignment again at a high level of quality to get credit. Be sure to make your expectations clear.

28. *Use Lewes's progressive behaviorist method to overcome your students' aversion* to the material and reinforce their thoughtful contributions to discussion.

Your Assignments and Tests

29. *Reinforce the idea that all students can improve their cognitive and other abilities with practice* and are in control of their academic fates. In other words, build up their sense of self-efficacy, their belief in an internal locus of control, and a growth mind-set. Credit their successes to their effort and focus, not inborn talent or luck (Dweck, 2007).

30. *Give students opportunities for success early in the term.*

31. *Give frequent positive feedback early in the course* to encourage students to believe that they can do well.

32. *Provide many and varied opportunities for graded assessment* so that no single assessment counts too much toward the final grade. Test early and often.

33. *Give students plenty of opportunity to practice performing your learning outcomes before you grade them on the quality of their performance.*

34. *Sequence your learning outcomes and assessments to foster student success.* Learning is a process.

35. *Give students practice tests* with the same types of items that will appear on the actual test.

36. *Provide review sheets that tell students what cognitive operations they will have to perform with key concepts on the tests.* In other words, write out the learning outcomes you will be testing them on.

37. While students must acquire some facts and terminology to master the basics of any discipline, *focus your tests and assignments on their conceptual understanding and ability to apply the material,* and prepare them for the task accordingly. Facts are only tools with which to construct broader concepts and are thus means to a goal, not goals in themselves.

38. *Assign tasks that build in challenge and some desirable difficulty*—not too easy but not overwhelming (see chapter 1).

39. *Set realistic performance goals, and help students achieve them by encouraging them to set their own reasonable goals.* Striving to exceed a personal best is a mighty motivator.

40. *Design assignments that are appropriately challenging* given the experience and aptitude of the class. Those that are either too easy or stressfully difficult are counterproductive.

41. *Assess students on how well they achieve the learning outcomes* you set for them, and remind them that this is what you are doing.

42. *Allow students options for demonstrating their learning,* such as choices in the topics and media of projects and other major assignments.

43. *Design authentic, useful assignments and activities—* those that give students practice in their future occupational and citizenship activities.

44. *Give assignments that have students reflect on their progress.* For example, have students write a learning analysis of their first test in which they appraise how they studied and how they can improve their studying (see chapter 20).

45. *Evaluate student-constructed work by an explicit rubric* (a specific set of criteria with descriptions of performance standards) that students can study and ask questions about before they tackle an assignment (see chapter 27). A well-written rubric makes your expectations clearer.

46. *Be fair.* Make tests consonant with your learning outcomes, topical emphases, and previous quizzes and assignments. Tests should be a means of showing students what they have mastered, not what they haven't.

47. *Give students prompt and constant feedback* on their performance, as well as early feedback on stages and drafts of major assignments.

48. *Accentuate the positive in grading.* Be free with praise and constructive in criticism and suggestions for improvement. Acknowledge improvements made. Confine negative comments to the particular performance, not the performer.

49. *Let students assess themselves.* Of course, you must explicitly teach them how to do this first, and accurate self-assessment is a challenging skill to master.

50. *Inform students about your previous students who have succeeded* in graduate school, professional school, or careers. You needn't name names.

51. *Give students second chances.* Test early and often. Let students drop the lowest quiz or test score. Let them write explanations for their multiple-choice and true/false item answers. Provide chances for them to earn back some of their lost points.

52. *Use criterion-referenced grading* instead of norm-referenced grading (see chapter 27). The former system gives all the students in a class the opportunity to earn high grades.

53. *Use specifications (specs) grading* for some of your assignments or your entire course. Specs grading means assigning grades according to how well students fulfill certain work requirements, as specified in the syllabus or an appendix to it. To get higher grades, students have to successfully complete either more work that shows evidence of more learning or more challenging work that shows evidence of more advanced learning. Under these conditions, students are often more motivated to learn because they have a greater sense of choice of assignments, self-determination, and responsibility for their grade, as well as less fear about creative risk taking and grade anxiety (see chapter 27).

54. *Give extra credit or bonus points only to students who have successfully completed their regular assigned work.* For example, Golding (2008) increased her class attendance and on-time homework turn-ins by giving students bonus problems to work on at the beginning of class in exchange for their assigned homework problems. The same rule can apply to giving students the chance to earn back lost points.

55. *Role-model a learning orientation and encourage it* over a performance orientation. Explain the value of mistakes in learning and retaining the material. Deemphasize grades and competition, and focus on the relevance and utility of the content and skills.

This last recommendation is among the most important, especially for today's generation of students, which needs to learn persistence and experience its payoffs. Persistence works because our brains are so plastic. We can literally "teach ourselves intelligent." Just the idea of this should be motivating, and our students need to own it.

■ NO MAGIC BULLETS

If you implement many of these 55 strategies, you will motivate many of your students. If you implement all of them, you will motivate *almost all* of your students. Just don't expect to motivate every one of your students, no matter what you do. A few will resist your efforts due to their problems with relating to authority, committing themselves to a goal, deferring gratification, and other issues. But don't let those few eclipse your success with many. Celebrate those you inspire.

CHAPTER 9

Preventing and Responding to Classroom Incivility

Student incivility is a national and even international problem in higher education, and yet most institutions have avoided instituting policies against it. Typically, they have left you, the faculty member, on your own to prevent and sanction disciplinary problems and to maintain a controlled, orderly environment that is conducive to learning. Knowing preventive measures and constructive responses to disruption can greatly serve your relationship with your students because even minor incivilities can mar the atmosphere, break your concentration, and get under your skin. And losing your temper is not an option. How effectively you control your classes may even affect your life in general. Boice (2000) found the ability of junior faculty to maintain classroom civility to be the best single predictor of their persistence and success in an academic career.

■ WHAT IS INCIVILITY?

What we call *incivility* encompasses classroom, online, and even out-of-class behaviors that we consider to be inappropriate for any of several reasons. They may distract, disturb, or annoy us and other students, show disrespect or hostility toward us and other students, or waste class time. These are some specific behaviors that qualify as incivil (Ballantine & Risacher, 1993; Boice, 2000; Race & Pickford, 2007; Royce, 2000; Thomason, 2014):

- Talking in class
- Noisily packing up early
- Arriving late to class and leaving early
- Wasting discussion board or class time by being unprepared to contribute, dominating discussion, repeating questions, or asking argumentative or loaded questions
- Speaking or writing to the instructor or another student disrespectfully or discourteously
- Noisily eating or chewing gum in class
- Groaning in a disapproving way
- Making sarcastic remarks or gestures in class
- Taunting or belittling the instructor or another student
- Sleeping in class

- Ignoring a direct question
- Using a computer for nonclass purposes during class
- Using a cell phone for nonclass purposes during class
- Letting a cell phone go off in class
- Coming to class in pajamas or beachwear
- Putting on makeup in class
- Reading a newspaper or magazine or doing any other nonclass activity in class
- Leaving trash in the classroom
- Cheating
- Demand a makeup exam, extension, grade change, or a special favor of the instructor
- Challenging the instructor's knowledge or credibility in class
- Making harassing, hostile, or vulgar comments or physical gestures to the instructor or another student in or out of class or online
- Sending the instructor or another student an inappropriate e-mail
- Threatening the instructor or another student with physical harm

We have all seen, heard, or read at least the milder forms of incivility, and we all hope we never encounter the ultimate incivility that occasionally hits the news: faculty or students being murdered in cold blood.

■ WHY DO STUDENTS BEHAVE THIS WAY?

While no generation of students has behaved like angels in class, senior faculty will tell you that the college students of a few decades ago were quieter in class and much more respectful to both their professor and their peers. Of course, the Internet and online courses did not exist, nor did the accompanying sense of anonymity that leads to "flaming" and other distasteful online behaviors. But we can't blame just the Internet. Both the academy and Western society in general have changed in ways that have exacerbated behavioral and disciplinary problems:

- Increasing diversity has brought in many students who don't share traditional academic values, norms, and communication styles.
- Universities have grown in size, generating an atmosphere of impersonality, distrust, and indifference.
- Relatedly, classes, especially low-level required classes, have grown in size, making students feel anonymous, invisible, and unaccountable for their behavior.
- The K–12 system has done little to enforce discipline, uphold academic rigor, or nurture a love of learning.
- The same could be said of the parents of young college students, some of whom have been indulged and spoiled (Kristensen, 2007).
- College and universities have been working harder than ever before to retain students, so they now sanction only the most serious offensive behaviors.
- Institutions have placed more and more adjuncts in the classroom and online. Because these instructors must get high student ratings to have a chance at keeping their jobs, they cannot afford to enforce much discipline or rigor.
- More young students still live at home and mature more slowly (Kristensen, 2007).
- Much of the mass media portrays uncivil disagreement as normal (Kristensen, 2007).
- Young students and their parents take a consumer attitude toward college, and the students feel entitled to do what they choose in class or online and still get good grades; after all, they think, they bought those grades (Kristensen, 2007; Singleton-Jackson, Jackson, & Reinhardt, 2010).
- Relatedly, many students don't have much respect for faculty. As mentioned in chapter 1, they regard their instructors as well-educated but poorly paid service workers who are supposed to cater to them (Rice, Sorcinelli, & Austin, 2000; Singleton-Jackson et al., 2010).
- Americans have lost trust in and respect for all authority in general. Too many business, religious, and political leaders have proven themselves to

be dishonest, greedy, immoral, and indifferent to the interests of their customers, congregations, and constituencies. Moreover, they have profited from their lack of integrity and corrupt behavior. So while the public has grown cynical of authority, some sectors, including many students, still view these leaders as role models and believe that corruption, dishonesty, and greed help people get ahead. Therefore, this book devotes all of chapter 10 to preserving academic honesty.

• Finally, the culture has become increasingly informal in most forms of self-expression, including dress, language, and behavior. This trend is evident in places of worship, restaurants, stores, offices, airports, and schools, as well as artistic reflections of the culture, such as popular music, television, and movies. No longer do public and private schools at all levels have dress codes for students and faculty, nor do employers insist on business suits, dresses, skirts and blouses, and dress shoes in offices.

In spite of these broad social and cultural changes, most students expect us to establish and maintain an orderly, civil classroom. They too are bothered by their peers' annoying behaviors and expect you to quell such distractions (Young, 2003).

The rest of this chapter provides strategies for minimizing and responding to specific types of incivilities in and out of the classroom and online. Prevention is the preferred outcome, but this is not always in your control, so you'll also find acceptable ways to stop the behaviors. Unfortunately, given the unpredictability of human behavior, none of these strategies is absolutely foolproof. Still, your well-considered efforts at both prevention and response are likely to inspire the respect of the vast majority of your students.

▓ PREVENTING INCIVILITY: YOUR CLASSROOM PERSONA

What kind of personality do you project in the classroom? Is it at all weak, timid, and self-effacing?

Is it innocent and naive about students' instrumentalist attitudes toward education and their efforts to cut corners and do minimal work for their grades? Is it laid back, anything goes, and permissive? Is it one of a protective and overly nurturing pushover who will show endless mercy toward irresponsible student behavior? If so, some students will feel free to take advantage of your apparent vulnerability or tolerance and will walk all over you. Or perhaps you project quite the opposite—that of a cold, distant, condescending professor, possibly with a cynical attitude, a sarcastic sense of humor, an uncaring heart, or a mean, critical streak. (Remember that students are very sensitive and prone to overinterpret small slights.) If so, many students will feel justified in returning your seemingly bad attitude in kind. Either way, you are likely to encounter a disproportionate amount of student incivility.

Part of the performance dimension of teaching involves projecting a persona to your students (Carroll, 2003a, 2003b). So why not consciously fashion one that will command their respect, and perhaps just a touch of fear, and inspire their trust and loyalty? Why not exude relaxed confidence, goodwill, and an in-command, no-nonsense attitude—the elements of a successful faculty image? It is not difficult to do; all it requires is certain concrete behaviors, some verbal and some nonverbal. Whether or not you carry this aura naturally, it is not dishonest to behave in ways that will make you more effective as an instructor. After all, aren't we willing to do almost anything to help our students learn?

Commanding Class Attention

Sometimes students become restless, apathetic, and potentially disruptive because their attention is wandering or they're bored. Your practicing good platform (public speaking) skills both projects a strong persona—one who is relaxed, confident, in command, and no-nonsense—and enables you to attract and hold student attention and engagement for longer periods of time. These skills come up briefly again in chapter 12 because they strongly influence the motivational and teaching effectiveness of a lecture. They also affect how easily you can keep students awake, quiet, orderly, and on task for all or part of a class period.

These skills encompass many different behaviors, most of them small, but they add up to a tremendous difference in the way students will regard and receive you. If you observe a charismatic speaker closely, you will see that charisma can be broken down into a number of small but powerful behaviors carefully orchestrated in combination. Following is a simple listing of powerful behaviors (adapted from Toastmasters International speech manuals and related materials):

1. *Effective use of voice.* Volume adjusted to be audible for the room and audience; words enunciated clearly; rich, resonant voice quality, projected from the chest and diaphragm; vocal variety (changes in intonation to complement the content and for emphasis); volume variety (either extreme for emphasis); varied and appropriate speaking pace (never hurried and dramatically slower for more important content); pregnant pauses for emphasis before and after major points; imagery plays on words (e.g., drawing out *slow* and *long*, saying *icy* in an icy tone, saying *soft* softly, saying *strong* with especially deep resonance).

2. *Effective use of body.* Solid, natural stance (unless moving, legs comfortably apart, knees slightly bent, arms hanging at sides, shoulders relaxed, and back straight); natural movement around the lectern or stage and out toward the audience (for emphasis and to complement the content); abundant gestures to complement the content (especially broad ones before large audiences); word dramatization (e.g., momentarily acting out *timid, angry, anxious, huge*); varied facial expressions (more dramatic in a large room), including smiles where appropriate; only occasional glances, if any, at notes; steady eye contact with the audience (at least 3 seconds per audience sector or quadrant are recommended).

3. *Effective use of visual aids and props.* Smooth transitions to and handling of visual aids; uses of visual aids or props that clarify or dramatize a point.

4. *Emotions to project.* Relaxed confidence and conviction; enthusiasm, excitement, passion, a sense of drama, curiosity; sincerity, concern, honesty, openness, warmth, goodwill, caring, a sense of humor.

5. *Minimization or elimination of distracting behaviors.* Um, uh, you know, like, sort of, kind of, and-and, that-that; mispronunciations; false sentence starts; midsentence switches to the start of a new sentence; volume fade-outs at end of sentences; pacing, swaying, or other repetitive movements; leaning on the lectern, against the wall, against the chalkboard; lengthy checks of notes; ritual apologies to audience (e.g., "I hoped to have prepared this lecture more carefully").

6. *Not speaking for too long.* As you will read in chapter 12, students have a rather short attention span for lecture. Unless you already project a charismatic persona, you're inviting disruptions if you lecture beyond 10 to 20 minutes at a time. Whenever you spot a bored expression or glazed eyes while you are lecturing, pause and change the pace. Pose a question, open the floor for questions, or use any of the student-active breaks suggested in chapter 12. If you don't shift your students' attention to a learning activity, they will shift their attention to a nonlearning activity.

Assembled together, these skills seem impossibly numerous and precise to master. But you probably have inadvertently learned most of them already and may need to polish only a few. For now, the most important skill you should check is your eye contact with your students, a powerful form of crowd control. In large classes, it is easy to forget the far half of the class, and that is exactly the half you usually need to control the most. Eye contact also personalizes your comments, encourages students to return your attentiveness to them in kind, and enables you to read their faces to gauge their interest and understanding.

Another key skill to monitor is your voice. Its tonal variety and pace reflect your level of engagement in the material and your enjoyment of teaching. A voice can sound monotone to an audience because the person speaks at the same pitch or at the same pace for long periods of time. If you find yourself droning this way through a dry section of your lecture, try consciously to modulate your voice and vary your speaking pace to keep student interest.

Singers and actors do warm-up exercises for their voices and bodies before they perform, and as performers in our own right, we might consider doing the same to get ready for class. For example, to enhance your vocal variety, resonance, and projection, you can sing scales, alternate high and low pitches, or read children's books aloud with exaggerated changes in pitch and pace. To loosen up, relax, and eliminate tension from your body, take three or four slow, deep breaths from your diaphragm and push out all the old air before inhaling again. This breathing is also good for your vocal resonance and projection, as well as your brain, since oxygen increases cognitive functioning. Another excellent exercise is standing with your legs about a foot apart and stretching every part of your body in every direction you can. It's best to stretch slowly, stop when you feel any strain, and hold the position for a few moments. Finally, extend your arms out in front of you and send energy along them and out your fingertips. This mental practice develops your ability to send energy out to your audience.

Taken together, these physical exercises will help you fill up your life space in front of your class. Your relaxed state, coupled with your improved blood flow, will make an open body posture feel natural and will add energy, spring, and flow to your movements. You will seem larger, more animated, and more dynamic. Add greater vocal variety and richer voice quality, and your persona will begin to take on charisma.

Balancing Authority and Approachability

Most students accept the authority of a mature tenure-track faculty member without question. But some students are reluctant to accord the same respect to an adjunct, a graduate student, a TA, or an instructor who violates the traditional professorial stereotype of the older, white male with an imposing stance and a low, deep voice. Clearly if you look young, have a relatively high voice, or are nonwhite, physically small, or female, you may encounter some student resistance. If you project weakness, nervousness, softness, or too easy-going an attitude, you may find some students pushing the envelope with you, behaving discourteously, and expecting special favors of you. A few of these simple strategies will add the air of authority to your persona and help you take stronger control of your classes:

- Stand up rather than sit in front of your class, move around the room, and use broad gestures. The dramatic effect is designed to make you appear larger than life. Increasing one's apparent size is a common aggressive and defensive posture throughout the animal kingdom.
- Try to deepen your voice slightly and project it further by speaking from your diaphragm. Also avoid ending a declarative sentence with a questioning rise in pitch.
- Favor more formal dress to convey that you are serious and business minded, especially if you are a woman (Johnston, 2005).
- Add an air of formality and dignity to your classroom. For instance, address students by their last names, and ask that they address you by your title (Dr. or Professor) and last name.
- Refer in class to your own scholarship where appropriate. This establishes you as an authority on the subject and elevates you in your students' eyes.

In particular, some female instructors should take measures to reinforce their legitimacy and authority. Students tend to underestimate the educational attainment of female instructors, even controlling for many other instructor characteristics (Miller & Chamberlin, 2000). Students are also more likely to challenge female and minority instructors about their legitimacy, expertise, opinions, and teaching methods (Moore et al., 1996; Turner & Myers, 2000). In addition, some students expect women to display an empathetic softness that they think they can take advantage of.

Other instructors face the opposite problem of intimidating students. They can do so by too perfectly matching the somewhat chilly professorial stereotype or by coming off as domineering. From your students' viewpoint, you may fall in this category if you are male and are some combination of very tall, physically large, deep-voiced, rugged looking, serious and reserved, or have an aggressive or curt social style. The following behaviors can warm up your persona, making you seem more approachable and likable:

- Assume a relaxed posture in the classroom. Sit down or perch casually on the corner of a desk.
- Speak more softly (but audibly) in class.
- Interact with the class on a regular basis, perhaps by tossing out questions to answer or problems to solve.
- Dress down slightly; for example, wear a loosened tie and a sports jacket, a two-piece suit rather than a three-piece suit, or no jacket or suit coat at all.
- Chat casually with students before and after class so they can see you as friendly, warm, and personable. Address students by their first names. (If you are a TA, consider asking them to call you by your first name.) Consciously practice social immediacies (see the next section).
- Smile whenever appropriate.
- If you are a TA or a faculty member still taking courses, mention that you too are a student, so you can identify with the academic demands they are facing.

Showing That You Care

Wherever your persona falls on the authority-approachability continuum, you can help prevent class incivility and conflict by practicing social immediacies—that is, conveying both verbally and nonverbally that you care about your students as learners and as people. Like everyone else in the world, students want to be loved on some level. You can verbally express, for example, concern for their learning and future success, high expectations for them, interest in their activities outside class, empathy with their learning challenges and stress, and your availability to help them outside class. You can also learn and use their names. Nonverbally, you can communicate your respect for and interest in them by making regular eye contact, speaking with energy and enthusiasm, listening to them intently without interrupting, standing with an open body posture, and smiling frequently. When students raise a problem in the course, you can clarify your course objectives and schedule and enlist students to help resolve the issue.

All of these instructor behaviors, along with teaching interactively, are associated with more civil student conduct and greater student attentiveness in class (Meyers, 2003; Meyers, Bender, Hill, & Thomas, 2006; Wilson & Taylor, 2001). They may even override any negative effects of being female, adjunct, less experienced, or a member of a minority group (Meyers et al., 2006).

Setting Ground Rules

All the literature on classroom management considers setting ground rules, and most students respond very well to them; they want to know what is expected of them. In addition, ground rules convey that you are in command and no-nonsense. Therefore, announce on the first day, especially in a large class, exactly what disruptive behaviors you will not tolerate in your course, and why. Your most convincing reason, and one that is research based, is that such behaviors annoy the other students in the class. This conveys your goodwill. You might reiterate this reason when handling a noisy disruption.

Some conduct rules also belong in your syllabus. Focus on the most common incivilities you encounter, such as side conversations, unauthorized cell phone use, and displays of disrespect for fellow students. Just don't make the list too long. You may prefer to emphasize appropriate behaviors rather than disruptive ones. If so, express your rules in a positive way—for example, "Students are expected to hand in assignments on time," rather than, "Students will be penalized for late assignments." Either way, you must specify and enforce the consequences for violating the rules. The same applies to online incivilities, such as flaming and attacking fellow students for their opinions. You can find college-level netiquette guidelines at these sites:

http://edtech2.boisestate.edu/frankm/573/netiquette .html
http://learning.colostate.edu/guides/guide.cfm? guideid=4
http://www.studygs.net/netiquette.htm

Some classroom instructors have reduced incivilities by having their students collectively draw up a classroom-conduct contract, or set of rules for behavior to which they will agree. Here's the procedure, and it can be adopted to the online classroom. On the first day of class, lead a discussion on the student behaviors that genuinely bother the members of the class. As a member, you can add one or two behaviors to the list. Then from the notes you take, type up a contract for all students to sign at the next class meeting in which they promise not to engage in the disruptive behaviors listed. If someone refuses to sign it, let the other students decide what to do; after all, it's their contract. Instructors who use contracts claim that for the rest of the semester, students pretty much police themselves, keeping even minor violations to a minimum (Baldwin, 1997–1998; Ballantine & Risacher, 1993). A few institutions publish a student code of conduct, but students often don't buy into what they don't feel they own.

A variation on a class contract starts out as a student bill of rights and leads to a larger life lesson (Nilson & Jackson, 2004). Students should have no problem coming up with rights for themselves, and you should ensure these are written down. A few will quickly realize, however, that all rights come with responsibilities. For instance, the right to be evaluated fairly obligates students to hand in work that accurately reflects their best abilities. The related right to receive timely and consistent feedback from the instructor requires that they hand in work on time and use that feedback in improving their work. The right to be safe to express their opinions in turn commits them to respect the opinions of other students and the instructor. And the right to a well-organized course with well-prepared classes obligates students to come to class prepared to make the most of the course. Because students generate these rights and responsibilities themselves, they are likely to police themselves, as in the case of a contract. When they don't, all you have to do to enforce the rules is to smile at the offenders and gently remind them by saying *contract* or *bill of rights*.

Rewarding Civil Behavior

As we saw in the case of motivating students (chapter 8), applying behaviorism wisely can change student behavior for the better. Of course, setting ground rules and course policies and ensuring that violators face unpleasant consequences, whether social pressure or lost points, represent the negative reinforcement and punishment side of the equation. But what about using positive reinforcement, which is more powerful than negative reinforcement and punishment, to discourage such violations?

In addition to noticing and sanctioning misbehavior, you can notice and reward good behavior. You can compliment a class when everyone arrives on time or when attendance is especially high. (This shows that you do notice these things.) When a student is often late, you should not only correct the behavior by speaking to her in private about it but also thank her when she does arrive on time. When a noisy class quiets down, express your appreciation. Research shows that these little positive reinforcers are effective at the workplace as well as in the classroom. They also help create a pleasant and fruitful learning atmosphere (Daniels, 2000; Daniels & Daniels, 2004; Wiesman, 2006, 2007).

Modeling Correct Behavior

Sometimes classroom incivility starts with the instructor's behavior toward the students, such as being rude, sarcastic, condescending, indifferent, insensitive, or inflexible. Your efforts to model good manners do not guarantee that students will always imitate you. But students will consider your standards and requirements fairer if your behavior reflects them, and no doubt more students will honor them. For instance, if you don't want students to interrupt one another during discussions, judiciously try not to interrupt students yourself. If you value punctuality, come to class ahead of the bell and complete your board work before class begins. If you want assignments turned in on time, return papers promptly. If you expect students to come to your office hours, keep to your schedule faithfully. These constitute instructor rights and matching responsibilities.

Nevertheless, students may have somewhat different conceptions of unacceptable faculty behavior than we do. The TA program at Michigan State University conducted a small ($N = 50$) but revealing survey of undergraduate perceptions of irritating instructor behaviors. More than 20 percent of the students mentioned these six:

1. Showing up late for class
2. Not showing up for office hours
3. Making students feel stupid (put down, inferior, dumb) or showing disrespect
4. Not getting to know students
5. Writing on the board while blocking the information or talking to the board
6. Not following the syllabus

Less frequently mentioned were not preparing for class, being disorganized, giving inadequate explanations of difficult material, not controlling the class, assigning busywork, lecturing too quickly, speaking too softly or in a monotone, reading lecture notes, starting class early and ending it late, not grading assigned work, and assigning too much homework (Teaching Assistant Program, Michigan State University, n.d.). We may not think of talking to the board, straying from the syllabus, or talking fast as offensive, but it is to students. In fact, after a first-day-of-class discussion of what *they* shouldn't do, we should ask them in turn what they don't want *us* to do.

From their point of view, defining and modeling correct behavior means meeting their learning needs and showing them respect by living up to their professional expectations of us. We can start by reversing all the don'ts above into do's. For instance, we should display a brief agenda, outline, or list of student outcomes at the beginning of every class. Not only will we appear well prepared and organized; we will also communicate nonverbally that we are in command of the classroom.

We show students respect when we explain why we have chosen the readings, teaching methods, class activities, and assignments that we have without their having to ask. They don't assume that we do what we do for their own good or because of our knowledge of how people learn, so we need to convince them. We can tell them how many other inferior textbooks we reviewed, how much research stands behind the effectiveness of our methods, and how well our assignments will prepare them for their future careers. We might even summarize our teaching philosophy (see chapter 28 on writing one).

Yet another way to show respect for students is to hold them to high expectations. Communicating this point may initially require some tough love, such as refusing to accept shoddy work (in this case, you quickly return it to the student and require him to revise it up to standard before you will grade it). The work may be docked for being late, but at least it will merit some points. Taking this strong action early in the term will motivate students to stretch their abilities, and you'll probably not have to take it again.

◼ RESPONDING WISELY TO INCIVILITY

If you encounter a discipline problem in your classroom, stay calm and in control. Count to 10, breathe deeply, visualize a peaceful scene—or anything else to keep you from losing your temper. No matter how much an offensive student tries to bait you, you lose credibility if you lower yourself to his level. If you keep your composure, you win the sympathy and support of the other students. Viewing an incivility as a teaching moment may help you stay cool. Consider how your class as a whole might learn something from this. Even if the comment or behavior appears to be directed at you, try to make the exchange not about you but about the students and their learning. If you handle the situation well, they may even start using social pressure to discipline the offenders themselves.

For instance, whenever you sanction a student for mild, garden-variety uncivil behavior, smile through your firmness. A smile conveys not only warmth and approachability but also unflappable cool and relaxed confidence. It says you don't take the misconduct personally, that you are just doing your job to maintain a productive learning environment, and that student misbehavior doesn't get under your skin. With this kind of cool, students sense they can't bait you, so they won't.

Keeping your composure, however, does not mean accepting and tolerating the abuse. It is critical that you do not ignore or otherwise tolerate the behavior. You must respond immediately. The worst thing you can do is ignore the behavior (Meyers et al., 2006). The longer you let the incivility continue, the higher the level of response you will have to take later. Here are some specific, appropriate measures you can take in response to disruptive behaviors (Ballantine & Risacher, 1993; Boice, 2000; Feldmann, 2001; Gonzalez & Lopez, 2001; Meyers et al., 2006; Race & Pickford, 2007; Thomason, 2014). Always be especially strict in enforcing the rules early in the term.

Talking in Class

Occasional comments or questions from one student to another are to be expected. However, chronic talkers bother other students and interfere with your train of thought. To stop them, you have several options. The simplest is to pause, allowing their voices to fill the silence. You may also want to accompany your pause with a long stare at the offenders. Staring at them with a smile suggests you're nonplussed by the violation. Another option is to walk over to the offenders while you continue to teach. Still another, and an especially classy alternative, is to handle it with a little humor, such as an invitation to share the conversation with the class. If appropriate, refer to the classroom conduct contract or bill of rights and responsibilities that the class authored and signed. If you don't have a contract, pleasantly say something like, "I really think you should pay attention to this; it might be on the test" or "You are disturbing your classmates." If the problem persists, get stern with the offenders outside class. Public embarrassment is a last resort that should be avoided, since it can turn some students against you.

Packing Up Early

Routinely reserve some important points or classroom activities—a quiz, clarification of the upcoming readings, study guide distribution, or a review activity—until the end of class. Or have students turn in assignments at the end of class. Paper rustling and other disruptive noise during class can be stopped the same way as talking in class.

Arriving Late or Leaving Early

State your policies clearly on these offenses in your syllabus and on the first day of class, and never reteach material for the tardy. You can insist that students inform you in advance of any special circumstances that will require them to be late to class. You can even subtract course points for coming late and leaving early as long as you set this policy at the start. You might draw attention to offenders by pausing as they walk in and out. Alternatively, you can set aside an area near the door for latecomers and early leavers. Finally, as you can do to discourage packing up early, you can routinely schedule important class activities at the beginning as well as the end of class.

Chronic offenders of these policies deserve their day in court—that is, talk to them or e-mail them privately about the problem. They may be late because the previous hour's class tends to run late or is a long walk away. Or they may have to leave your class a little early to get to their job on time.

Cheating

Academic dishonesty is such a serious and widespread problem in higher education today that the entire next chapter is devoted to preventing and responding to it.

Coming to Class Unprepared

This problem too is so widespread that all of chapter 21 addresses getting students to do the readings and related homework assignments on time.

Dominating Discussion

If certain students habitually try to monopolize class time, tell them to speak with you after class to clarify their questions and discuss more of the issues. You can also broaden the discussion and call attention away from the disruptive student by extending your wait time after your questions or asking the rest of the class for the answers. If a student is rambling around or off the subject, take control by seizing the chance to interrupt her and paraphrase whatever meaning you can salvage. Then supply an answer and move along. Alternatively, you can defer answering it for the sake of saving class time and advise her to raise it outside class.

Asking Questions You've Already Answered

A student asks you about the procedure for doing an assignment that you've already explained. Rather than putting down the student ("Where were you when I gave the assignment?"), just answer the question civilly and quickly, or say that you already answered the question and will repeat the answer

only outside class. Another option is to refer that student to the written instructions you've provided and ask exactly which part needs clarification. Still another is to get students in the habit of referring their questions to "three [peers or other sources] before me" in class or on a discussion board (Millis & Cottell, 1998).

Asking Wheedling Questions

Occasionally students try to wheedle answers out of you to avoid having to work out the answer for themselves. In class, you can invite other students to suggest leads and possibly get a discussion going. But one-on-one, the best way to avoid giving in is to answer each of the student's questions with another question that should help him think through the answer. A student who is asking questions solely to pry answers out of you will soon tire of your questions and go away.

Asking Argumentative Questions

A student who tries to entrap you in an argument for the sake of arguing either wants attention or has an authority problem. Just acknowledge his input and quickly move on. To lower yourself to the bait jeopardizes your credibility with the class. If another incident occurs, tell the student you will discuss the issue outside class. After class, inform him in private that you do not appreciate and will not tolerate such uncalled-for hostile behavior in your classroom. Also mention that it disturbs other students and wastes their class time. Another strategy is to handle questions through a different medium. You can collect written questions in a box and briefly address some of them at the next class meeting. You can also encourage students to e-mail their questions to you or put them on the course website. While less personal, these options offer a less confrontational format.

Asking Loaded Questions

The rare nefarious student may design a question solely to embarrass you and put you on the defensive. Like the argumentative student, this type is also probably seeking attention and respect from his peers and deserves the same response. You may also be able to turn the loaded question back on the student asking it:

STUDENT: You're not really saying . . . ?
INSTRUCTOR: What I'm saying is . . . Now, what is your perspective on this topic?

Demanding a Grade Change

To discourage nuisance grade complaints, set a policy in your syllabus that if a student wants to protest a grade, either you will regrade the entire test or assignment or, better yet, will not accept a grade protest unless the student submits a formal written justification for the change, citing exact book pages and class period dates, within forty-eight hours.

If a student still comes to you demanding a grade change, try to neutralize her emotion and delay dealing with the issue until she calms down. Schedule an appointment with her in your office at least a day or two later. Then open with a positive, empathetic statement: "I understand your frustration. Let's take a look at your paper [or test] and talk about the grading." Have the student read her answer aloud to help her hear her errors. Maintain eye contact and try to agree with her whenever possible. If necessary, explicitly disassociate the grade from her worth as a person. Even if you can't turn the student's opinion around, you can reduce both your own and her anxiety levels by showing yourself to be an ally (at least partially). Finally, try to give her a graceful way to retreat from the situation. Just don't be intimidated into changing the grade.

It is very rare that an instructor feels physically threatened by a hostile student, and it invariably happens when others are not around. While verbal hostility usually calls for a private approach, the physical version requires quite the opposite: try to move yourself and the student into as public a place as possible, even if just the hallway. A colleague or student may call campus security on your behalf.

Using a Computer or Cell Phone in Class for Nonclass Purposes

Some students claim they are facile at multitasking, so they can read and respond to their e-mail, text a friend, type a tweet, make a purchase, surf the web, *and* pay attention in class at the same time. But if this were true, people could simultaneously talk on their cell phones and drive safely (a low-concentration cognitive task), and we know that no one can do this. Furthermore, we know that so-called multitasking is simply rotating from task to task, an inefficient and error-ridden practice (Crenshaw, 2008).

If your students are using a computer in class, you can't monitor their screens unless you teach from the back of the room, and you may or may not be able to roam around to see what they are doing. But you can take the measures recommended in chapter 4 to focus students on an in-class computer task. Keep them extra busy by giving them minimal time to complete it. Also have them work in small groups, each group at one laptop or terminal. Chances are that three or four students won't be able to agree on a renegade site. Finally, hold them accountable for completing the task by requiring report-outs or written reports. Between in-class assignments, have them turn off their computers or close their laptops.

Monitoring and controlling students' cell phone use poses tougher challenges because the devices are much smaller and easier to hide. Between 90 and 92 percent of college students admit to using their cell phones in class for nonclass purposes, such as texting, checking Facebook, tweeting, playing games, web surfing, and the like (McCoy, 2013; Tindell & Bohlander, 2012). This behavior borders on addiction. Predictably, it is most common in large classes and long classes and during lectures versus group activities (Berry & Westfall, 2015).

You may ban the use of laptops and cell phones in class, but you have to keep a sharp eye out for offenders and enforce your ban. Your syllabus should warn students that their engaging in renegade computer or cell phone activities will bring serious consequences, such as removal from class or a grade reduction (e.g., being marked absent or losing points). According to students, only fairly drastic measures like these work; public or private reprimands do not (Berry & Westfall, 2015).

If you prefer a more flexible policy, you might give students a short break in the middle of the class period to check their devices (Cardon, 2014), as suggested in chapter 4. This may help them to control themselves better and pay more attention during class. For laptops in particular, you may allow individual students to use them to take notes in class if they request it, but you should seat these students in the front of the room, where their peers can monitor them, or in the back, where they can't distract others. You should also tell them that note taking on a laptop is less effective than doing it longhand (Mueller & Oppenheimer, 2014). In fact, you can use these findings to say no to their request. Of course, students with certain disabilities or their note takers may have to take notes on a laptop.

Cutting Classes

These are the top three reasons students give for cutting class: (1) attendance is not taken or does not affect the grade, (2) the instructor does not see or care if a student is missing, or (3) the class content is available elsewhere. Attendance also drops off in required, large, and lecture-oriented classes (Friedman, Rodriguez, & McComb, 2001).

From these findings, the best ways to increase attendance, especially when used in combination, suggest themselves: basing part of the course grade on attendance; taking attendance regularly (even if you don't calculate it in the grade); basing part of the course grade on participation in discussion (see chapter 13); making the class more interactive and participatory; giving frequent graded quizzes; regularly taking up homework to be graded; covering in class a great deal of material that isn't in the reading; not allowing commercial production of your lecture notes; not putting your lecture notes online (skeletal outlines are okay); requiring students to catch up with any classes they have missed on their own;

having group activities in class and grading students in part on peer performance evaluations (see chapter 15); and conducting other frequent, graded in-class activities.

Asking for Extensions and Missing Assignment Deadlines

In your syllabus, specify penalties for late work (e.g., docking a portion of the grade), with or without an approved extension. Some instructors feel comfortable strictly enforcing this policy, while others prefer to be flexible. Students occasionally have good reasons for not meeting deadlines, but they also occasionally lie. You must assess each extension request and excuse on a case-by-case, student-by-student basis, perhaps allowing a single, documented incident but drawing the line at the second.

A student with a habitual problem deserves a private talk and the full penalties. You might ask other instructors in your department for the names of any chronic cases that they have encountered.

Showing Disrespect in General

If your prevention measures fail, talk to offenders privately and explain that their behavior is affecting their fellow students' ability to learn. Avoid showing or inciting anger by keeping your voice low. Be aware that sometimes students show disrespect to get the attention they believe they can't get through any other means. They want to vent their anger toward authority or express some other deep-seated emotional problem. Leave such cases to the professionals, and refer these students to your institution's psychological or counseling center.

If your warnings fail or you face grievous and repeated displays of disrespect and abuse in class, don't hesitate to order the offenders out of the classroom, at least for that day. Should they refuse to leave, call campus security. After the incident, review it with the students in class so they can serve as witnesses, tell your department chair, and make a written record of the verbal exchange. While calling security is a last-resort response, it's a good idea to memorize the number or store it in your phone. Taking this tack should end your incivility problems in the class for the rest of the term (Carroll, 2003a).

If the disrespect takes the form of an abusive online post to a discussion board, first delete the post. Then e-mail or phone the perpetrator to point out the inappropriateness of the post and the consequences of doing this again. A reasonable penalty is blocking his or her posts for the rest of the term, an action that should hurt the offender's grade.

■ SEEKING ASSISTANCE

You are not alone in having to deal with student incivilities. Ask respected colleagues how they handle them. Requesting their advice will not lead them to believe you are an ineffective teacher. Another source of strategies is the student affairs staff. These officers usually understand students and their worlds and how to communicate with them better than many faculty, and the dean of student affairs should know about even mildly threatening incivilities. In addition, refer students with ego, authority, or anger management problems to your institution's psychological or counseling center. Finally, speak outside class with your best-behaved students, enlisting them to help you keep an orderly learning environment. You might ask them to subtly communicate their disapproval of the misconduct during class or talk to the offending students outside class.

CHAPTER 10

Preserving Academic Integrity

Student cheating mirrors the ethics and behavior of the broader society. An overall decline of public morality started in the self-centered 1970s and 1980s and has since gotten worse. Media depictions of the good life motivate students to quest after a lifestyle that they are not sure they will be able to afford. Moreover, the scandalous antics of leaders in business, politics, sports, and even education make unethical behavior seem normal, and the often small price these leaders pay makes it look profitable. These impressions have recently been reinforced by several large-scale cheating scandals at well-known universities, some with honor codes. No wonder those who cheat in college intend to violate norms and rules in the future to get ahead (Lovett-Hooper, Komarraju, Weston, & Dollinger, 2007).

The term *cheating* refers to a wide variety of behaviors generally considered unethical, at least by faculty. In its basic form, it is misrepresenting one's knowledge and effort. Plagiarism, a type of cheating, is claiming the ideas or words of others to be one's own, if just passively by not referencing their true source—in short, theft of intellectual property. A student who plagiarizes a report, fails to cite sources, copies an answer on a test, or pays someone to write a paper has dishonestly obtained information and has lied in passing off the product as her own original work.

■ HOW PREVALENT IS CHEATING?

The most recent figures of self-reported cheating in college at least once vary from 65 percent (McCabe, Butterfield, & Treviño, 2012) to 82 percent, the latter figure coming from an alumni survey (Yardley, Rodríguez, Bates, & Nelson, 2009). Predictably, other studies (Rettinger & Kramer, 2009) give figures in between (73.4 percent). The most common forms of cheating are getting information about an exam from a peer who has already taken it and collaborate with others on an individual assignment (McCabe, 2005). Furthermore, 90 percent of college students admit to using the Internet to cheat (Berry, Thorton, & Baker, 2006).

Plagiarism is also quite common in that 36 to 38 percent say that they have copied or copied and pasted "a few sentences" without crediting them to their source, but only 6 percent claim that they have plagiarized from public material on a paper (McCabe, 2005; McCabe et al., 2012). However, the fact that these two figures were much higher in past surveys (1962–1963 and 1993–1994) (McCabe et al., 2012) suggests that plagiarism-detection software may serve as a real deterrent. This does not necessarily imply that student values have radically changed. Not even 30 percent of those who cheat regret doing it, and getting caught deters only 7 percent of them from doing it again, according to a survey conducted by CollegeHumor (cited by Poythress, 2007).

Cheating in high school bears a strong relationship to cheating in college (Harding, Mayhew, Finelli, & Carpenter, 2007). In a 2012 national survey of high school students, 51 percent admitted to cheating on at least one test, 32 percent to plagiarizing at least one assignment from the Internet, and 55 percent to lying to a teacher about a significant matter—all within the previous year. Like the figures for college students above, the percentages of self-reported cheating behavior have dropped, however modestly, over the past several years. Still 45 percent of the boys and 28 percent of the girls agree that "a person has to lie and cheat at least occasionally in order to success." Yet 93 percent claim to be "satisfied with my own ethics and character," and 81 percent say that they are more ethical than most other people (Josephson Institute, 2012).

■ WHO CHEATS AND WHY?

Some college student demographics and activities are related to the prevalence of cheating. Cheating is more common among student who are younger (traditional age), are international (Grasgreen, 2012), earn lower grades (Hutton, 2006; McCabe et al., 2012), have joined a fraternity or sorority, are very involved in extracurricular activities, or engage in heavy drinking and partying behavior (Grasgreen, 2012; Hutton, 2006; McCabe et al., 2012).

When asked why they cheat, here are some top-ranking reasons:

1. Laziness (Center for Academic Integrity survey cited in Hutton, 2006)
2. Need for better grades (Center for Academic Integrity survey cited in Hutton, 2006); grades too low to get into desired program or obtain desired honors, or scholarship at risk (Grasgreen, 2012; Lang, 2013; Yardley at al., 2009)
3. Pressure to succeed (Center for Academic Integrity survey cited in Hutton, 2006); competitive pressures (Josephson Institute, 2012)
4. Time pressures (Grasgreen, 2012; Yardley et al., 2009)
5. Difficulty of the course (Yardley et al., 2009)
6. Difficulty of the test or assignment (Yardley et al., 2009)
7. Inadequate preparation for the test or assignment (Yardley et al., 2009)
8. To help a friend (Yardley et al., 2009)
9. Disinterest in the material (Kleiner & Lord, 1999; Lang, 2013)
10. Instructor not focused on academic integrity (Grasgreen, 2012)
11. Faculty not enforcing academic integrity, not reporting cheaters, which half the faculty admit to (McCabe, 2005; McCabe et al., 2012; Nadelson, 2007; Young, 2010)
12. Uncertainty about what constitutes cheating or plagiarism (Burt, 2010)
13. Pervasiveness of cheating that students see; acceptability of cheating in the student culture (Anderman, Freeman, & Mueller, 2007; Hutton, 2006; McCabe et al., 2012; Rettinger & Kramer, 2009)
14. Perceived opportunity to cheat due to the low chances of getting caught or the low sanctions for getting caught, associated with large class size, reliance on multiple-choice tests, or faculty indifference (Kerkvliet & Sigmund, 1999; McCabe, 2005; Nadelson, 2007)

15. Adjunct or graduate student instructor (Kerkvliet & Sigmund, 1999), a situation that frequently occurs in larger, research-oriented public universities

16. Instructor "not worthy of honesty" due to unfairness, arbitrary assignments, irrelevant material, focus on grades, or lack of concern about student learning (Anderman et al., 2007; Hutton, 2006; Kerkvliet & Sigmund, 1999; Yardley et al., 2009)

17. Institutional indifference to academic integrity (Bok, 2006; Haney & Clarke, 2007)

■ DETECTING CHEATING

Catching incidences of cheating is not rocket science. During tests, an observant eye can often see wandering glances and students passing notes, cheat sheets, and even blue books to one another. Sometimes you can spot a ringer by an unfamiliar face. Other tip-offs are a heavily erased exam, suspicious behavior (e.g., leaving the room during the exam, rustling through one's things, hiding a cell phone in one's lap, repeatedly looking at one's hands and arms), and, of course, a considerable number of identical answers, even incorrect ones, across exams. Be concerned, too, if a student improves his exam performance meteorically without having seen you or your TA for extra help.

Plagiarism is possible when a student hands in a paper (1) without quotations or references; (2) with references that don't fit the text; (3) with odd, esoteric, or inaccessible references; (4) on a topic other than the one assigned; (5) with a format different from your requirements; (6) with a cover page typeface different from the text's; (7) late; (8) on a recently changed topic; (9) with a shifting writing style; (10) with familiar-sounding sections; (11) heavy on facts not tied together; (12) very similar to another student's paper; (13) that is photocopied; or (14) that is just too perfect and mature for the student in question (Suarez & Martin, 2001). Also be suspicious if a student electronically sends you a corrupted file of a paper, as students have done this just to get an extension (Tallahassee Community College Library, 2013).

Many first-year and international students do not know what plagiarism is. High schools didn't teach it, and most international students follow a different set of values and norms, particularly those from what are called *high-power-distance* cultures, which include all of Asia, most of the Middle East, much of Europe and Latin America, and some of Africa. This kind of culture exalts those in authority and requires deference to them (Dimitrov, 2009). Copying their published work pays tribute to their expertise and acknowledges that the student cannot phrase the message as well (Fox, 1994). This attitude hardly reflects theft.

You can teach students about plagiarism or assign one of several websites that explain what it is, how to avoid it, and how it differs from paraphrasing (e.g., www.virtualsalt.com/antiplag.htm, and www.brocku.ca/learningobjects/flash_content/LO/PProject-Paraphrase.html). In an experiment involving 500 students, Dee and Jacob (2012) found that having students take an interactive online tutorial on plagiarism before they turned in a paper reduced their incidence of plagiarism by two-thirds. Also instructive is to have your students put their paper drafts through some plagiarism-detection software.

Realize that you may not be able to trace all purchased papers to their source, and there are dozens of paper mills on the web. However, you can uncover most cases of plagiarism by using plagiarism-detection software or by typing, in quotation marks, a distinctive suspect phrase or sentence into one or more web search engines.

■ FORTY-TWO WAYS TO PREVENT CHEATING

Research suggests that about 20 percent of students never cheat, and another 20 percent will cheat no matter what precautions you take or how motivating you are (Teddi Fishman, director of the International Center for Academic Integrity, quoted in Supiano, 2014). The web has plenty of sites, including videos of "creative" ways to cheat on tests. But you can at least reduce academic dishonesty in your classes with proven prevention measures. Most of these either make cheating more difficult or heighten students' perceived chances of getting caught and facing dire consequences, and the rest reduce students' motivation to cheat (Brauchle, 2000; Braumoeller & Gaines, 2001; Grasgreen, 2012; Hutton, 2006; Johnson & Ury, 1998, 1999; Kerkvliet & Sigmund, 1999; Kleiner & Lord, 1999; McCabe et al., 2012; McCabe & Treviño, 1996, 1997; Supiano, 2014; Tallahassee Community College Library, 2013):

1. Motivate your students' interest in your subject, and help them understand its relevance to their careers and the broader world so they will want to learn it (see chapter 8). Deemphasize grades.

2. Define cheating and plagiarism to your students, and give examples and hypothetical cases. Your students may not understand these terms. Also teach them how to cite sources correctly.

3. State verbally and in writing your own and your institution's policies on academic dishonesty and their applications to each assignment and test you give. State that you strictly enforce these policies and what penalties violators are risking. Include these statements in your syllabus (see chapter 5).

4. If you're a graduate student or adjunct instructor, be especially assertive. Students may think they can get away with more in your class since you're supposedly less savvy and more sympathetic to students than regular faculty are.

5. Make your exams as original as possible to reduce student reliance on old tests for study. Solicit potential new test questions from TAs and students.

6. Ensure equal access to study aids by placing a file of old tests and assignments on your course LMS or website for all students to use.

Fraternities and sororities often keep test files for their members.

7. Ban the use of cell phones, tablets, laptops, and other electronic devices during tests. Students can use them to store information, photograph the exam for friends, text friends for answers, and search the Internet.

8. If students must use laptops for the test, download the instructor version and have students download their version of Lockdown Browser or similar software that prevents them from leaving the test site. Generally institutions have to buy a license for this kind of software.

9. Ban water bottles, food, hats, and extra writing devices. Students have used all of them to write crib notes. They also use their body parts, such as their skin beneath a hole in their jeans. Only your diligent vigilance can discourage this behavior.

10. Make up different forms of tests, especially multiple-choice tests, by varying the order of the questions. The test tools in LMSs usually can do this for you.

11. If your class is so large that you can't recognize all your students, check student IDs or driver's licenses against your enrollment roster before distributing tests.

12. Firmly remind your class before each test that academic integrity is important to you, your institution, and the larger society, and that you will enforce it using all the institutional means you have available.

13. Although even good students don't want to squeal, appeal to their social ethics and their desire to protect their own intellectual property to report cheating.

14. During tests, if the room permits, seat students with space between them and place their personal belongings, especially cell phones, far away from them (e.g., at the front of the room).

15. In large lecture halls, have assigned test seats, and keep a chart of students' names.

16. Supply scratch paper if needed.

17. Have students clear all calculators before passing out a test, or ban calculators altogether.

18. If you have students bring their own blue books, have them turn theirs in just before the test; then redistribute them randomly.

19. Proctor tests judiciously, enlisting the aid of your TAs and colleagues. Don't allow yourself or your assistants to work on any other project while proctoring. Charge only one proctor (perhaps yourself) with answering any questions during the test.

20. Monitor students sitting at the back of the room during the test.

21. Check for cheat notes in nearby restrooms.

22. Collect tests from students individually to avoid a chaotic rush at the end of class.

23. When grading tests manually, clearly mark incorrect answers with an X or a slash in ink. To make any later additions or changes more obvious, draw a line down the answer sheet through the answers and place a mark at the end of each short answer or essay in colored ink.

24. Return exams, papers, and assignments to students in person or electronically.

25. Collect your test questions after you review the tests. If the test question forms are separate from the answer sheets, have students put their names on the forms to ensure you can account for all of them.

26. Assign paper topics that are unique and specific and require original critical thinking or critical self-examination.

27. Give explicit collaboration rules for all out-of-class assignments.

28. Change your writing assignments as often as possible to discourage paper recycling.

29. Explain the relevance and purpose of all assignments and in-class activities.

30. Take class time to discuss difficulties in the assignments and how to overcome them.

31. Make specific format requirements, and grade in part on adherence to them.

32. Require a certain combination of sources in an assignment: so many from the web, so many from print material in the campus library, so many from videos in the campus collection, and so on.

33. Teach students how and when to cite sources.

34. Warn students in advance that you always check the originality of their papers with plagiarism-detection software.

35. Require a personal interview as a source, preferably taped or conducted over e-mail, with the documentation to be turned in.

36. Meet with students early and often to monitor their progress on a major assignment and to gauge the development of their ideas.

37. Guide and monitor students through the process of researching and writing. Have them complete assignments in stages and turn in progress reports.

38. Require students to submit first drafts. This ensures you see a work in progress and allows you to provide early feedback.

39. Require students to turn in photocopies of at least the first page of the print and Internet material they use.

40. Require students to turn in the original of their paper and a copy for your files. You can refer to the file copy if you suspect piracy later.

41. Strive to be fair, clear, and authentic in all the ways you assess. Explain to students your rationales behind your assessment instruments and grading standards.

42. Clearly and repeatedly communicate to your students how much you care about them and their success in your course and their lives beyond. In addition to telling them explicitly, tell them implicitly by showing them respect, kindness, and understanding.

If you suspect any form of academic dishonesty, take swift, decisive action. Know your institution's policies and the person to whom to report the violation. (Ask your dean or chair, or refer to your institution's faculty handbook, student handbook, or course catalogue.) Our hope is that the judicial process won't be discouragingly time-consuming, laborious, and biased in the student's favor. Some instructors don't take the official route and instead handle cases quietly on their own—for example, giving an F to papers and tests where plagiarism or cheating is evident (Schneider, 1999). Ask senior colleagues how much de facto discretion you have and should take. Usually an instructor's ad hoc penalties are more lenient than institutional ones and don't go on a student's record.

If your institution's official process of reporting and providing evidence for cheating cases is laborious and discouraging for faculty, the best thing you can do is work to change it (Grasgreen, 2012; McCabe et al., 2012).

We don't know very much about the incidence of cheating in online classes, but what we do know is discouraging. Milliron and Sandoe (2008) uncovered evidence of cheating on low-stakes online quizzes involving 20 percent of the 300 students in their hybrid introductory information systems course. Most frequently, students were taking the quizzes in groups or giving one another answers. After their hybrid course ended, Haney and Clarke (2007) surveyed their students about their quiz-taking practices: 54 percent admitted to exchanging answers, and 79 percent were aware of online cheating. Perhaps the intimacy of small, online courses counteracts the anonymity, and older students who don't know each other outside the course are probably less likely to cheat. But it's almost impossible to know who is taking an online exam unless the students have webcams on their computers or a remote proctor is available (Carnevale, 1999).

■ HONOR CODES

Campuses with a well-established and well-enforced honor code have historically had a somewhat lower incidence of cheating, by as much as 25 percent, than those that do not (McCabe & Treviño, 1996; McCabe, Treviño, & Butterfield, 2001). Students are responsible for policing one another. In fact, they run the honor system themselves either completely (as at Washington and Lee and the University of Virginia) or largely (Rettinger & Searcy, 2012). Cheating violations usually carry a heavy penalty, such as expulsion. Typically students pledge their adherence to the honor code in writing on every graded test and assignment, which serves to remind them of the code and reinforce their commitment to it. However, the real reason for the difference in cheating rates lies in campus culture's regard for academic integrity and honor (McCabe & Pavela, 2005; McCabe & Treviño, 1996; McCabe et al., 1999). In most cases, valuing honesty is part of a tradition that dates back more than 100 years. Such campuses are predominantly private and modest in size (the University of Virginia excepted) and tend to nurture bonds of trust and caring between students and faculty (Hutton, 2006). But the success of honor codes does indicate that the student culture has an impact independent of the larger societal culture.

In the hopes of changing the culture, several large, public institutions have tested the efficacy of modified honor codes. While instructors still proctor tests and check for plagiarism, students take an honor pledge, sign a document renewing it on all assignments and tests, and to an extent police themselves (Wasley, 2008). For instance, a student-dominated judicial board is often established to try alleged violators and decide their fate. At least initially, cheating has dropped to rates about midway between those of honor-code campuses and those of no-code campuses on the campuses that have adopted modified codes (McCabe & Pavela, 2000). In addition, students have reported many more cheating cases than they once did (McCabe & Pavela, 2005). But the research on these experiments has not continued.

A more recent study (Shu, Gino, & Bazerman, 2011) has confirmed the importance of signing an honor-code statement. While just reading an honor code before a test reduced cheating somewhat, signing the code eliminated it completely. However, this research was conducted in a laboratory, not a real-life setting.

CHANGING STUDENT VALUES

What about the future of this larger culture? As studies cited early in this chapter found, younger students feel little remorse about cheating, and they consider themselves ethical in spite of it. We are facing the prospect that this generation's culture of cheating will carry over into the broader society and economy (Lovett-Hooper, Komarraju, Weston, & Dollinger, 2007). It seems that many, if not most, students don't perceive cheating as wrong. Can we possibly convince them that it is?

No doubt, we can convince some. According to a survey by Staats, Hupp, Wallace, and Gresley (2009), only 24 percent of the students definitely planned to cheat in the future, and almost 30 percent were uncertain. Perhaps this undecided group can be swayed. Wueste (2008) is even more optimistic. He believes that we can persuade as many as 60 percent of our students by pointing out the damaging consequences, the injustice, and the character implications of cheating. He offers these seven specific arguments to share with students:

1. Cheating misleads employers into thinking you have mastered knowledge and skills that you haven't. What harm will you do to the world because you lack that knowledge and those skills?

2. Relatedly, cheating cheapens your degree. If you graduate poorly prepared, you will lower your institution's regard among employers and your fellow citizens.

3. Cheating undermines the faculty's ability to give you honest feedback and evaluation of your work.

4. Cheating gives you an unfair advantage over your fellow students who do not cheat.

5. Cheating violates the social contract that you voluntarily entered into with your institution when you arrived here.

6. Cheating damages your character. If you cheat now in college, you will cheat later in other contexts—in the workplace, on your taxes, in marriage, and so on.

7. Cheating obstructs any hope of your achieving excellence in whatever matters to you. You will never accomplish what you are capable of; you won't even know what you're capable of.

We can add to Wueste's list Staats et al.'s hopeful findings (2009): compared to cheaters, academically honest students hold a higher opinion of others and score higher on measures of courage, empathy, and honesty in general.

Will reasoning this way with students change their values? If we have taught long enough, we know firsthand that we indeed have the power to create learning experiences that induce students to change their values. We also know that our prevention and policing efforts haven't solved the cheating problem. Maybe it's time to try Wueste's and Staats et al.'s approach.

PART 3

TRIED-AND-TRUE TEACHING METHODS

CHAPTER 11

Matching Teaching Methods with Learning Outcomes

Your selection of teaching methods is critical to your students' learning. Derek Bok (2006) argues that it is even more important than the content you select, and he bemoans that faculty discussions neglect the topic of pedagogy. He points out the discouraging research finding that the average student cannot remember most of the factual content of a lecture within 15 minutes after it ends, but lessons learned through more active learning methods can leave students changed forever. In Bok's (2006) own words:

> In contrast, interests, values, and cognitive skills are all likely to last longer, as are concepts and knowledge that students have acquired not by passively reading or listening to lectures but through their own mental effort. . . . The residue of knowledge and the habits of mind students take away from college are likely to be determined less by *which* courses they take than by *how* they are taught and *how well* they are taught. (pp. 48–49)

Let's turn to the critical issue of how you will teach your courses. This chapter extends the course design process in chapter 2 into course development: selecting the best teaching methods for enabling students to achieve your learning outcomes. If your outcomes map is your skeleton, your methods are the muscles on the bones. Fortunately, some of your fellow faculty have devised and conducted research on numerous teaching innovations over the past few decades, so you have plenty of worthy options to choose from. Both part 3 of this book, which opens with this chapter, and part 4 focus on a wide range of well-researched methods that we know can generate powerful learning experiences, assuming they are implemented properly and for appropriate purposes. Chapters 12 through 19 lay out ground rules for setting up and managing them correctly, and this chapter gives an overview of which methods to use when, with the *when* depending on your learning outcomes.

As Figure 11.1 shows, your student learning outcomes provide the foundation for every aspect of your course, and you should align all the other components with them. As the ends of your instruction, your outcomes inform your choice of

Figure 11.1   The Logic of Aligned Course and Curriculum Design

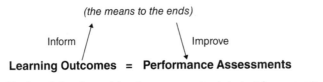

Teaching Methods/Learning Experiences to Help Students Achieve Outcomes

(the means to the ends)

Inform   Improve

Learning Outcomes   =   Performance Assessments

(the foundation, the ends)   *(measurements of students' progress to the ends)*

teaching methods (the means of your instruction), which encompass all the learning experiences you give your students in the form of assignments and activities (active listening is an activity), whether as homework or in class. The most appropriate means of instruction will afford your students practice, plus feedback, in the performances specified in your learning outcomes. This practice should imitate the way you plan to assess student performances for a grade: by multiple-choice items, a case analysis, a literary analysis, a creative multimedia project, a concept map, a diagram, a design, a solution to a real-world problem, solutions to mathematical word problems, and so on. If it does, it should improve your students' performance on your assessment instruments. These instruments—quizzes, test questions, assignments, and other course components on which you see student results—should mirror your outcomes very closely. Note the equals sign in Figure 11.1 between outcomes and assessment. If you want your students to be able to do X, Y, and Z, assess their progress by having them do X, Y, and Z.

If your outcomes go beyond students' recognizing and regurgitating correct facts, terms, equations, and algorithms—and they should go beyond these knowledge-level cognitive operations—you should be familiar with multiple means to help your students achieve your ends. As eminent psychologist Abraham Maslow once said (1966, p. 15), "... it is tempting, if the only tool you have is a hammer, to treat everything as if it were a nail." In the not-so-distant past, faculty knew and used the lecture almost exclusively, and there was precious little research to suggest that other methods were more effective for most purposes. We have since learned

that you can't craft effective learning experiences just by hammering lectures into students' heads. The material doesn't stick well. But now we have a toolbox full of options. As an instructor, one of your most critical tasks is to choose the best tool for the job—or, more accurately, choose among the best tools for the job, as you can usually identify several means to reach your ends.

■ TYPES OF TOOLS

A complete teaching toolbox contains three types of tools to select from: course formats, major teaching methods, and teaching moves. *Teaching moves* refers to the ways you explain and elaborate on material, the learning-to-learn strategies you share with your class, the short in-class activities and exercises you have students do (during interactive lecture breaks, for example), and the questions you ask them to contemplate.

Course Formats

A course format defines the course meetings—specifically, the setting and expected activities for the class period. It may be lecture meetings only, lecture meetings with discussion sections, lecture meetings with laboratories, lecture meetings with skill activity sessions, discussion meetings with some lecture, discussion meetings with skill activity sessions, skill activity sessions alone, or a seminar. In a seminar, as opposed to a discussion section, students prepare their contributions in advance, whether research presentations, arguments, points of view, or interpretations.

In a skill activity section, students have the chance to practice something, so it may be scheduled in a room other than a regular classroom, such as a computer lab, a language lab, a studio, a stage, a music room, or a clinic with medical equipment or a simulated human body. It may take place outside or off-campus, perhaps in a botanical garden, a forest, a clinic, or a hospital.

We don't know the relative learning impact of different formats, but we do know quite a bit about the effects of closely related variables: the degree of in-class student activity (or lack thereof; see chapter 1) and class size. Hoyt and Perera (2000) identified not the actual impact of formats but the success that faculty perceive formats having for certain learning objectives. These objectives were somewhat different from the outcomes presented in chapter 2 for course design. In Hoyt and Perera's study, they ranged from "substantive knowledge" (of facts, principles and theories, and applications) to much higher-order abilities such as general cognitive and academic skills (communication and critical thinking), life-long learning skills (research and interest), personal development (broad liberal knowledge and values development), and other skills and competencies (team skills and creativity). Hoyt and Perera found that faculty consider lecture/discussion, lecture/lab, and lecture/skill activity pretty ineffective—"average" at best—in equipping students to meet these objectives. (Lecture/lab achieved a high average on factual knowledge, as did lecture/discussion on values development.) Discussion/lecture did better on general cognitive and academic skills and personal development (liberal knowledge). Skill activity alone earned high ratings on developing students' communication skills, creative capacities, and liberal knowledge but average on the other objectives. The only formats that faculty saw as highly effective on almost all of the objectives were discussion/skill activity and seminar. Not surprisingly, both have a great deal of student activity and small-size classes.

You may not think you have control over your formats, but you may be able to negotiate a change. Introductory courses are typically lecture based, perhaps with discussion, lab, or skill activity sections, while freshman seminars are set up as seminars or discussion sessions. Courses in the major may be anchored in the lecture, discussion, skill activity, or seminar format. If you believe that a different format from the one currently attached to your course would strengthen student learning, make a case to your department chair. Point out that you have learning outcomes that your students are unlikely to achieve because, for all practical purposes, the current format prohibits implementing the effective teaching methods and moves. You have nothing to lose by asking, and you and your students have a great deal to gain.

The next two sections address which teaching methods and moves are most effective for various learning outcomes.

Major Teaching Methods

The tools in this category comprise major methods—that is, multiweek assignments or in-class activities that require considerable time. We may schedule one on a regular or semiregular basis during a course or devote one or more class periods to it. For instance, we rarely have just one discussion or one small-group activity during a term-long course. If we do plan just one, it probably won't work very well because it will violate students' expectations. If we choose to give interactive lectures, we probably give many of them. If we use the case method to teach, we probably assign and debrief at least several cases during the term. We may have just one simulation, one substantial problem-based learning assignment, or one service-learning project, but each of these is likely to require students to put in hours of class time or homework.

Before turning to the outcomes each method serves well, let us review the basic definitions of these methods. Most of them merit their own chapter or a section of a chapter in parts 3, 4, or 5 of this book.

- *Lecture:* Instructor presenting material and answering student questions that arise (chapter 12)

- *Interactive lecture:* Lecture with 2- to 15-minute breaks for student activities (such as answering a multiple-choice objective item, solving a problem, comparing and filling in lecture notes, debriefing a minicase, doing a think-pair-share exercise, or a small-group discussion) every 12 to 20 minutes (chapter 12)
- *Recitation:* Students answering knowledge and comprehension questions (chapter 13)
- *Directed discussion:* Class discussion that follows a more or less orderly set of questions that the instructor has crafted to lead students to certain realizations or conclusions or to help them meet a specific learning outcome (chapters 13)
- *Writing and speaking exercises:* Any of many informal assignments and activities, usually in-class and ungraded, to help students learn material, clarify their thinking, or make progress on a formal assignment (chapter 22)
- *Classroom assessment techniques:* Informal assignments and activities, usually in-class and ungraded, to inform the instructor how well students are mastering new material just presented or read; often overlap with writing and speaking exercises (chapter 24)
- *Group work/learning:* Students doing a learning activity or creating a product in small groups of two to six in or out of class; must be carefully managed by the instructor (chapter 15)
- *Student-peer feedback:* Students giving one another feedback on a written or an orally presented product, usually a written draft or practice speech (chapter 24)
- *Cookbook science labs:* Pairs or triads of students conducting a traditional, often predictable experiment following prescribed, cookbook-like procedures (chapter 19 recommends and illustrates more effective inquiry-based labs)
- *Just-in-time-teaching:* Instructor adjusts class activities and lectures to respond to the misconceptions revealed by students' electronic responses to conceptual questions; an extension of electronic daily quizzes to motivate students to do the readings (chapters 16 and 21)

- *Case method:* Students applying course knowledge to devise one or more solutions or resolutions to problems or dilemmas presented in a realistic story or situation; an individual, small-group, or whole-class activity (chapter 17)
- *Inquiry-based or inquiry-guided learning:* Students learning or applying material in order to meet a challenge, such as to answer a question, conduct an experiment, or interpret data (chapter 16)
- *Problem-based learning:* Student groups conducting outside research on student-identified learning issues (unknowns) to devise one or more solutions or resolutions to fuzzy problems or dilemmas presented in a realistic story or situation (chapter 18)
- *Project-based learning:* Students (as individuals or in groups) applying course knowledge to produce something, such as a report (written or oral), process or product design, research or program proposal, or computer code; often paired with group work
- *Role plays:* Students acting out instructor-assigned roles, improvising the script, in a realistic and problematic social or interpersonal situation (chapter 14)
- *Simulations:* Students playing out, face-to-face or on computer, a hypothetical social situation that abstracts key elements from reality (chapter 14)
- *Service-learning with reflection:* Students learning from the experience of performing community service and systematically reflecting on it (chapter 14)
- *Fieldwork and clinicals:* Students learning how to conduct research and make sound professional judgments in real-world situations

The outcomes we will consider should sound familiar. As you will recall from chapters 1 and 2, the first six on this list come from Bloom (1956) and Anderson and Krathwohl (2000), the seventh from Perry (1968), and the last from Nelson (2000):

- *Knowledge/remembering:* To memorize or recognize facts, terms, principles, or algorithms

- *Comprehension/understanding:* To translate, restate in one's own words
- *Application/applying:* To use, apply, make useful
- *Analysis/analyzing:* To identify and examine components, compare and contrast, identify assumptions, deduce implications
- *Synthesis/creating:* To make connections, identify new relationships, design something new (new to students)
- *Evaluation/evaluating:* To make a judgment, assess validity, select and defend
- *Cognitive development:* To progress from dualism to multiplicity to relativism to a tentative commitment to the most worthy perspective available; to come to understand the nature of knowledge as inherently uncertain but subject to definite standards of comparison
- *Shift in mental models:* to replace a faulty understanding of a phenomenon with the discipline's more valid mental model

Table 11.1 brings these outcomes and the major methods together in answering the question, "Which methods for which outcomes?" Two caveats are in order. First, this table represents the general findings of a large body of literature on the methods listed. The references are embedded in the chapters and chapter sections on each method. Second, the efficacy of the interactive lecture, directed discussion, and group work depends entirely on the tasks you have students do or the questions you have them discuss. For identifying productive tasks and questions for your outcomes, see chapters 12 and 13 as well as Exhibit 11.1 in the next section, which lists short in-class assignments and activities that help students master each of Bloom's cognitive operations.

Davis and Arend (2013) propose another model, shown in Table 11.2, relating methods to outcomes, but with different categories of outcomes. They also identify the origins and theories behind the appropriate methods.

The overlap between the models in Tables 11.1 and 11.2 is considerable. For instance, Davis and Arend identify "presentations" and "explanations" as appropriate methods for acquiring knowledge, which roughly equate to lectures, interactive lectures, and recitation in Table 11.1. Their "decision making" and "practicing professional judgment" rely mostly on analysis and evaluation. However, Table 11.1 encompasses only cognitive outcomes, while Davis and Arend give some attention to psychomotor ("building skills") and affective ("exploring attitudes, feelings, and perspectives") outcomes as well. In fact, the only disagreement between the two models pertains to how many methods experiential learning encompasses. In this book, *experiential* includes what they categorize as "virtual realities" (see chapter 14).

Teaching Moves

Teaching moves are strategies for clarifying content and giving students practice in thinking about and working with it, as reflected in your learning outcomes. The practice you give them should at least resemble the ways you plan to assess their learning.

Compared to major methods, these minimethods entail much less time and commitment. You may use a dozen or more of them in a given class period—one to help students recall the readings, the next to clarify a knotty point, another to explain new material, yet another for a lecture break in which students apply the material, and so on. If one doesn't seem to work well, you can immediately try another. When a teaching move involves the students in an activity, not only do they get practice, but you obtain immediate feedback on their misconceptions, misunderstandings, and mastery. In turn, you can give them or they can give each other immediate feedback. Thus, many of these moves serve to assess as well as teach.

Exhibit 11.1 lists effective teaching moves by the learning outcome they serve. Some of them specify what you can do or say in class to familiarize your students with different ways of thinking

Table 11.1   Teaching Methods Found to Be Effective for Helping Students Achieve Different Learning Outcomes

	Knowledge	Comprehension	Application	Analysis	Synthesis	Evaluation	Cognitive Development	Shift in Models
Lecture	X							
Interactive lecture	X	X	[a]	[a]	[a]	[a]	[a]	
Recitation	X	X						
Directed discussion		X	[a]	[a]	[a]	[a]	[a]	[a]
Writing/ speaking exercises		X	X	X	X	X		
Classroom assessment techniques		X	X	X		X		
Group work or learning		X	[a]	[a]	[a]	[a]	[a]	
Student-peer feedback		X		X		X		
Cookbook science labs		X	X					
Just-in-time-teaching	X	X						X
Case method			X	X	X	X	X	
Inquiry based or inquiry guided	X[b]	X	X	X	X	X	X	X
Problem-based learning	X[b]		X	X	X	X	X	
Project-based learning	X[b]	X	X	X	X	X		
Role plays and simulations		X	X	X		X		X
Service-learning with reflection			X	X	X	X		X
Fieldwork/ clinicals	X		X	X	X	X	X	X

Note: An X indicates this method can help students achieve this learning outcome if the method is properly implemented to serve this outcome. Poor implementation or implementation for other ends may mitigate against students' achieving the outcome.

[a]Depends on the lecture-break tasks, the discussion questions, or the group tasks assigned.

[b]The knowledge acquired may be narrowly focused on the problem or project.

Table 11.2 Davis and Arend's (2013) Model of Learning Outcomes, Ways of Learning, and Teaching Methods

Intended Learning Outcomes: What Students Learn	Ways of Learning: Origins and Theory	Common Methods: What the Teacher Provides
Building skills Physical and procedural skills where accuracy, precision, and efficiency are important	*Behavioral learning* Behavioral psychology, operant conditioning	Tasks and procedures Practice exercises
Acquiring knowledge Basic information, concepts, and terminology in a discipline or field of study	*Cognitive learning* Cognitive psychology, attention, information processing, memory	Presentations Explanations
Developing critical, creative, and dialogical thinking Improved thinking and reasoning processes	*Learning through inquiry* Logic, critical, and creative thinking theory, classical philosophy	Question-driven inquiries Discussions
Cultivating problem-solving and decision-making abilities Mental strategies for finding solutions and making choices	*Learning with mental models* Gestalt psychology, problem solving, and decision theory	Problems Case studies Labs Projects
Exploring attitudes, feelings, and perspectives Awareness of attitudes, biases, and other perspectives; ability to collaborate	*Learning through groups and teams* Human communication theory; group counseling theory	Group activities Team projects
Practicing professional judgment Sound judgment and appropriate professional action in complex, context-dependent situations	*Learning through virtual realities* Psychodrama, sociodrama, gaming theory	Role playing Simulations Dramatic scenarios Games
Reflecting on experience Self-discovery and personal growth from real-world experience	*Experiential learning* Experiential learning, cognitive neuroscience, constructivism	Internships Service-learning Study abroad

Source: From Davis, J. R., & Arend, B. D. (2013). *Facilitating seven ways of learning: A resource for more purposeful, effective, and enjoyable college teaching.* Sterling, VA: Stylus, p. 38. Reprinted with permission from the publisher.

Exhibit 11.1   Effective Teaching Moves for Six Learning Outcomes (Bloom's Cognitive Operations)

KNOWLEDGE

For You to Do

- Suggest prior knowledge to which students can link new and future information and knowledge.
- Chunk knowledge into coherent groups, categories, or themes.

- Share devices to improve memory such as mnemonic patterns, maps, charts, comparisons, groupings, highlighting of key words or first letters, visual images, and rhymes.
- Point out parts, main ideas, patterns, and relationships within sets of facts or information.

For Students to Do

- Practice recalling and restating information.
- Practice recognizing or identifying information.
- Practice recalling and reproducing information.
- Practice restating concept definitions and principles.

COMPREHENSION

For You to Do

- Outline new or upcoming material in simple form.
- Concept-map or mind-map new or upcoming material.
- Explain with concrete examples, metaphors, questions, or visual representations.

For Students to Do

- Restate or paraphrase and summarize information or knowledge.
- Describe or explain phenomena or concepts using words different from those used in the initial teaching.
- Identify the correct meaning of concepts or terms.
- Add details or explanations to basic content.
- Relate new to previously learned content.
- Construct visual representations of main ideas (mind or concept maps, tables, flowcharts, graphs, diagrams, or pictures).

APPLICATION

For You to Do

- Give multiple examples of a phenomenon that are meaningful to students.
- Define the procedures for use, including the rules, principles, and steps.
- Provide the vocabulary and concepts related to procedures.
- Explain steps as they are applied.
- Define the contexts, problems, situations, or goals for which given procedures are appropriate.
- Explain the reasons that procedures work for different types of situations or goals.
- Ensure students' readiness by diagnosing and strengthening their command of related concepts, rules, and decision-making skills.
- Provide broad problem-solving methods and models.
- Begin with simple, highly structured problems and gradually move to more complex, less structured ones.
- Use questions to guide student thinking about problem components, goals, and issues.

- Give students guidance in observing and gathering information, asking appropriate questions, and generating solutions.

For Students to Do

- Generate new examples and nonexamples.
- Paraphrase the procedures, principles, rules, and steps for using or applying the material.
- Practice applying the material to problems or situations to gain speed, consistency, and ease in following the problem-solving steps.
- Practice choosing the types of problem-solving strategies for different situations.
- Solve simple, structured problems and then complex, unstructured ones.
- Practice recognizing the correct use of procedures, principles, rules, and steps with routine problems, then complex ones.
- Demonstrate the correct use of procedures, principles, rules, and steps with routine problems, then complex ones.

ANALYSIS

For You to Do

- Point out the important and the unimportant features or ideas.
- Point out examples and nonexamples of a concept, highlighting similarities and differences.
- Give a wide range of examples, increasing their complexity over time.
- Emphasize the relationships among concepts.
- Explain different types of thinking strategies, including how to think open-mindedly, responsibly, and accurately.
- Emphasize persistence when answers are not apparent.
- Ask students questions that require their persistence in discovering and analyzing data or information.
- Encourage students to self-evaluate and reflect on their learning.
- Ask questions that make students explain why they are doing what they are doing.
- Explain and model how to conduct systematic inquiry, detect flaws and fallacies in thinking, and adjust patterns of thinking.

For Students to Do

- Classify concepts, examples, or phenomena into correct categories.
- Summarize different types of thinking strategies.
- Use types of thinking strategies to analyze and evaluate their own thinking.
- Practice choosing the best type of thinking strategy to use in different real-world situations and explaining why their choice is superior.
- Detect and identify flaws and fallacies in thinking.
- Identify and explain instances of open- and closed-mindedness.
- Identify and explain instances of responsible versus irresponsible and accurate versus inaccurate applications of thinking strategies.
- Answer questions that require persistence in discovering and analyzing data or information.

SYNTHESIS

For You to Do

- Promote careful observation, analysis, description, and definition.
- Explain the process and methods of scientific inquiry.
- Explain and provide examples of how to identify a research problem, speculate about causes, formulate testable hypotheses, and identify and interpret results and consequences.
- Model inquiry and discovery processes.
- Encourage independent thinking, and avoid dead ends and simplistic answers.
- Show students examples of creativity to solve problems.
- Encourage students to take novel approaches to situations and problems.
- Explain phenomena using metaphors and analogies.
- Give students examples of reframing a problem—turning it upside down or inside out or changing perceptions about it.
- Explain and encourage brainstorming.
- Pose questions and problems with multiple good answers or solutions.
- Give students opportunities for ungraded creative performance and behavior.

For Students to Do

- Explain their experiences with inquiry activities and the results.
- Resolve a situation or solve a problem that requires speculation, inquiry, and hypothesis formation.
- Resolve a situation or solve a problem requiring a novel approach.
- Design a research study to resolve conflicting findings.
- Write the limitations section of a research study.
- Write the conclusions section of a research study.
- Develop products or solutions to fit within particular functions and resources.
- Manipulate concrete data to solve challenging thinking situations.
- Practice reframing a problem—turning it upside down or inside out, or changing perceptions about it.
- Explain phenomena using metaphors and analogies.

EVALUATION

For You to Do

- Create conflict or perplexity by posing paradoxes, dilemmas, or other situations to challenge students' concepts, beliefs, ideas, and attitudes.
- Explain how to recognize and generate proof, logic, argument, and criteria for judgments.
- Explain the consequences of choices, actions, or behaviors.
- Provide relevant human or social models that portray the desired choices, actions, or behaviors.
- Explain with examples how factors such as culture, experience, desires, interests, and passions, as well as systematic thinking, influence choice and interpretations.

For Students to Do

- Evaluate the validity of given information, results, or conclusions.
- Draw inferences from observations, and make predictions from limited information.

- Explain how they form new judgments and how and why their current judgments differ from their previous ones.
- Identify factors that influence choice and interpretations, such as culture, experience, desires, interests, and passions, as well as systematic thinking.
- Detect mistakes, false analogies, relevant versus irrelevant issues, contradictions, and faulty predictions.
- Critique a research study.
- Use research and analysis to devise the best available solutions to problems, and explain why they are the best.
- Choose among possible behaviors, perspectives, or approaches, and provide justifications for these choices.

Note: Partially adapted from Goodson (2005) with permission.

about and working with the material. The rest are activities and exercises for your students to give them practice and you feedback on their learning. The existing literature addresses these mini-methods only in terms of their relationship to Bloom's cognitive operations (Goodson, 2005). But these operations do represent key learning outcomes and easily map onto Anderson and Krathwohl's (2000). This list is not exhaustive, but it is a rich heuristic device that may inspire you to devise additional teaching moves to serve your purposes.

A TOOL FOR ORGANIZING YOUR COURSE

Fink and Fink (2009) provide a useful tool for putting all the elements of your course together and ensuring they are well aligned. It is a simple three-column table, shown in Table 11.3. The "learning goals" are equivalent to learning outcomes and the "learning activities" to teaching methods and moves. The examples given represent material from an anthropology

Table 11.3 Fink and Fink's Three-Column Tool for Developing a Well-Aligned Course

Learning Goals	Assessment Activities	Learning Activities
1. Describe the differences in social stratification systems among bands, tribes, chiefdoms, and states.	Daily quizzes Multiple-choice and multiple true/false questions on tests	Readings Interactive lectures
2. Apply knowledge of social stratification systems to predict what the system looks like in given societies.	Written homework assignments around case studies of societies Stimulus-based multiple-choice questions on tests	Break activities during interactive lectures Discussions around cases studies
3. Evaluate the effects of a person's status in a social stratification system on his or her self-esteem, mental and physical health, and material aspirations.	Reflective written homework assignments Essay questions on tests	Readings Break activities during interactive lectures Discussions Reflective writing

or sociology course. Fink and Fink (2009) offer additional examples from a variety of courses.

Once you have formulated your learning outcomes, you can refer to Tables 11.1 and 11.2 as well as Exhibit 11.1 to decide on and design your most effective learning activities. We will get to assessment in part 6, and chapters 26 and 27 will help you choose and implement the most appropriate activities for your outcomes.

■ HAS OUR KNOWLEDGE CHANGED OUR TEACHING?

As we accumulate knowledge on the effectiveness of different teaching formats, methods, and moves for various learning outcomes, we run out of excuses for relying on traditional lecture. In 2006, Bok didn't mince words accusing the faculty of avoiding pedagogical debates for their own self-protection from change:

> It is relatively easy to move courses around by changing curricular requirements. It is quite another matter to decide what methods of pedagogy should be altered. Reforms of the latter kind require much more effort. . . . To avoid such difficulties, faculty have taken the principle of academic freedom and stretched it well beyond its original meaning to gain immunity from interference with how their courses should be taught. . . . Teaching methods have become the personal prerogative of the instructor rather than a subject appropriate for collective deliberation. The result is to shield from faculty review one of the most important ingredients in undergraduate education. (p. 49)

He implies that if faculty continue to dodge the evidence in favor of student-centered methods, they shouldn't be completely free to choose their pedagogy. Maybe they should only be allowed to choose from a limited range of methods and moves known to be effective.

This idea isn't absurd. Departments, institutions, and regional and professional accreditation agencies already mandate learning outcomes, so why shouldn't they or some other unit mandate methods?

Fortunately, the faculties are heading off the threat of external regulation by beginning to choose better teaching strategies on their own. In a 2013–2014 survey, almost 83 percent of faculty said they use discussion in all or most of their undergraduate courses, up from about 70 percent in 1989–1990. In this same time period, fewer faculty reported using lecture in all or most of their courses: just under 51 percent versus about 56 percent. In addition, more faculty stated that they used cooperative learning, group projects, and peer feedback on students' work in 2013–2014 than they did in 1989–1990 (Eagan et al., 2014).

Call this modest progress, but it is change, and it has taken place against some student resistance. While most students enjoy active learning strategies, some do not (Amador, Miles, & Peters, 2006; Qualters, 2001; Thorn, 2003). In fact, a few of the best teaching methods for helping students acquire high-level thinking skills (e.g., problem-based learning) can lower an instructor's student ratings. Some students protest that these methods require too much work, lack sufficient structure, demand more independence than they can or want to manage, or cause undue grade anxiety because they are being asked to do things they've never done before. Some complain that they have to teach themselves too much and that their instructor isn't doing her job. At the same time, colleges and universities are striving to serve and retain students. In this crunch, which should take higher priority: student satisfaction or student learning? This is a values matter that only institutions can resolve for themselves. But we can help ourselves tremendously by explaining to our students why we choose certain teaching methods and moves over others. When we refer to the research standing behind our selections, we reaffirm to our students our commitment to do our best by them.

CHAPTER 12

Lecturing for Student Learning

In the late 1980s, new teaching methods began to emerge that researchers found far superior to the lecture, particularly in promoting deeper-level student learning and development. In fact, student-active methods like discussion, experiential methods, inquiry-based learning, group work, and writing-to-learn exercises did a better job of helping students think conceptually, examine and possibly change attitudes and values, develop critical thinking and problem-solving skills, transfer knowledge to new situations, retain knowledge, explore controversial or ambiguous material, master a performance technique or technical procedure, improve communication skills, and cultivate a lasting interest in the material (Bligh, 2000; Bonwell & Eison, 1991; Canfield, 2002; Hake, 1998; Jones-Wilson, 2005; McKeachie, Pintrich, Lin, Smith, & Sharma, 1990). More recently, critics of the lecture have disparaged it as a "teacher-centered" versus a "student-centered" method.

In addition, research dating back to the 1920s documents that most lecture material fades from students' memory rather quickly. The much-replicated *forgetting curve* for the average student is 62 percent recall of the material just presented, 45 percent recall 3 to 4 days later, and only 24 percent recall 8 weeks later (Menges, 1988).

After so many studies documenting the lecture's weaknesses, people don't conduct research on it anymore. Yet lecture is still the single most used technique by faculty (Smith & Valentine, 2012), so it is well worth exploring how to use it wisely. In fact, it serves certain purposes very well if it is carefully prepared, eloquently delivered, interspersed with thought-provoking student activities, and processed effectively by students.

■ WHEN AND HOW MUCH TO LECTURE

As chapter 11 advises, student learning outcomes should guide your choice of methods. Already listed above are outcomes that lecture doesn't serve well. According to Table 11.1, straight lecture has proven effective only in helping students acquire knowledge, and given its forgetting curve, it hasn't done a great job of that.

When Lecture Works Well

Knowledge is at the heart of our enterprise. Therefore, for at least segments of a class period, the lecture may be essential. The following short list sets out occasions when it is probably the most effective and efficient option (Bligh, 2000; McKeachie, 2002):

- You want to model a problem-solving approach or a kind of higher-order thinking before asking your students to try it themselves.
- You want to give your students material not available in print or video, such as a brief summary of background knowledge, the very latest findings, your own related research, or other material too advanced for students to understand on their own.
- You want to present a particular organization of the material that clarifies the structure of the reading, the course, or the field.
- You want to add your personal viewpoint on the subject matter.
- You want to pique your students' curiosity and motivation to learn if your style is very expressive.

Do *not* lecture material that simply duplicates the assigned readings or other course materials. Repetition and redundancy have their place, but student-active exercises requiring application, analysis, synthesis, and evaluation can replicate the material at a higher cognitive level. Deleting a redundant lecture frees plenty of class time for student activities. Besides, if a lecture primarily repeats the readings, any rational student will decide either to do the readings or to attend lecture (see chapter 21)—no doubt not what you intend.

Attention Span Limits

One literature review raises methodological questions about the research on students' attention span and claims we know little that is reliable about the topic (Wilson & Korn, 2007). Still, we have all noticed the pattern identified by the studies cited in Bligh (2000), Bonwell and Eison (1991), and Middendorf and Kalish (1996): a lecture begins with a 5-minute settling-in period during which students are fairly attentive. This attentiveness extends another 5 to 10 minutes, and then students become progressively bored, restless, and confused. Focus and note taking increasingly drop until the last several minutes of the period, when they revive in anticipation of the end of class. Bligh (2000) reconfirmed this pattern using students' heart rates as a measure of arousal. Even medical students, who tend to be highly motivated and self-disciplined, display similar patterns of concentration levels: an increase over about 15 minutes, followed by a sharp decrease. So what can we expect of our undergraduates? No doubt enthusiastic, engaging lecturers can extend that time horizon. But aside from improving our platform skills and teaching students how to take notes, what else can we do when we must lecture?

In a word, pause. One study supports the practice of pausing at least three times during each lecture to allow pairs or small groups of students to discuss and clarify the material (Rowe, 1980). Another recommends pausing for 2 minutes every 15 to 18 minutes to permit student pairs to compare and rework their notes (Ruhl, Hughes, & Schloss, 1987). This latter study was designed experimentally with a control group receiving a series of traditional nonstop lectures and a treatment group hearing the same lectures with periodic pauses. Both groups took free-recall quizzes during the last 3 minutes of each lecture (i.e., students individually wrote down everything they could remember from the lecture) and the same 65-item multiple-choice test 12 days after the last lecture. In two different courses repeated over two semesters, the treatment group performed much better than the control group on both the quizzes and the test—better enough to make a mean difference of up to two letter grades (17 percentage points), depending on the cutoff points. Translated into learning terms, sacrificing the least important 12 percent of your lecture content for periodic 2-minute pauses can increase the learning of your current C students to that of your current B students and even A students. In other words, a little less can be a lot more.

Inserting short break activities during the lecture transforms the lecture into a series of minilectures. Later in this chapter, you will find many other options for such activities.

Using and Posting Presentation Slides

Recent research (Mann & Robinson, 2009) reports that 30 percent of college students consider most or all of the lectures they attend boring, and 59 percent find half of the lectures boring, leading students to skip classes. The personality trait of Boredom Proneness best explains why students experience boredom, and this trait plus low class attendance go far in accounting for the inverse relationship between boredom and grade point average (Mann & Robinson, 2009). But among the other factors, faculty overuse of presentation slides, especially for text, ranks at the top (Mann & Robinson, 2009). So look at chapter 4's "Lecture-Related Software" section to find out how best to design and use slides.

Now let's turn to posting these slides on the LMS before or after a live lecture. Many faculty do this because their students ask them to. If you are using slides in the most effective ways as listed in chapter 4, then by all means post them, at least after class. But to the extent that your slides are primarily text based, be wary. Many students claim that they benefit from downloading the lecture slides before class so they can listen more intently and write fewer of their own notes. Some contend that reading the notes and slides reinforces hearing them (Clark, 2008).

But these arguments have a few holes. How deeply are students processing a lecture when they are just following along with prepackaged material? If they are not taking notes, they are not judging what is more or less important, translating the material into their own words, or distilling it down to an abbreviated version (see the "Inducing and Teaching Students

to Take Good Notes" section later in this chapter). In addition, both reading and hearing words involve receiving material verbally, so this simultaneous redundancy does little to contribute to learning (Kress, Jewitt, Ogborn, & Charalampos, 2006; Tulving, 1985; Vekiri, 2002). Not surprisingly, then, slides and handouts that duplicate the lecture presentation seem not to increase student learning or improve exam performance (Kinchin, 2006; Noppe, Achterberg, Duquaine, Huebbe, & Williams, 2007). Of course, posting these will save you some time because fewer students who miss class will come to you for information and materials. But unless you make every class more valuable than the documents you post, your live attendance and even participation are likely to drop (Young, 2004).

Therefore, post selectively. The best document to post in advance is a *skeletal outline* of your lecture. While you can create it in a presentation program, using a word-processed document is even better. Allow plenty of white space between major topics, and advise your students to print out the document and bring it to class for note taking or use it while listening to your recorded lecture. It will enable them to follow your organization. In fact, skeletal notes are the most effective learning aid you can furnish to your students for lectures. Because these notes improve note taking, students perform better on tests, suggesting they learn more (Cornelius & Owen-DeSchryver, 2008; Hartley & Davies, 1986; Potts, 1993).

▇ MAKING THE LECTURE HOMEWORK

In the flipped classroom option described in chapter 4, faculty record their lectures and assign watching or listening to them as homework. In hybrid and traditional courses, face-to-face class time is then reserved primarily for student activities. While students can view or listen to the lectures many times, remember that their short attention spans limit you to recordings of 5 to 20 minutes, and you can't ensure that students will do any activities you assign unless you require them to hand in evidence of their having done the activities.

■ PREPARING AN EFFECTIVE LECTURE

Bligh (2000) lays out several organizational models for lectures, but they share the common ground summarized here.

Class Outcomes

First, determine your student learning outcomes for the class period or recording. What precisely do you want your students to learn to do? How will you express your outcomes to the class? If a lecture serves only one or two of the multiple objectives you have for the class, then it should fill only part of the period.

Overview

Whenever possible, limit a lecture or recording to one major topic. Some students find it difficult to pick up a lecture from one period to the next, and some need to see the big picture before any of the details and examples will make sense to them. Also lay out a time-content schedule, bearing in mind the two most common lecturing errors: trying to include too much material and delivering the material too fast. While you're lecturing, you will have to proceed slowly enough, including pausing after major points, for students to take notes. So if anything, underbudget content.

To start planning your lecture, subdivide the major topic into 15- to 20-minute chunks. If you will lecture live, plan student-active breaks of 2 to 15 minutes between these chunks. Don't let class size deter you. Most of the break activities in this chapter can be—and have been—conducted in large lectures of hundreds of students as well as smaller classes. Finally, allow 2 to 5 minutes for a recap activity at the end.

Let us turn to the internal organization of your lecture. The skeleton for any lecture is the introduction, the body, and the conclusion (McKeachie, 2002).

Introduction

For a class-long lecture, the ideal introduction has three parts, the order of which is really an aesthetic decision: (1) a statement that frames the lecture in the context of the course outcomes, (2) a statement reviewing and transitioning from the material covered in the previous class period, and (3) an attention grabber for the new material. Effective attention grabbers include an intriguing question the lecture will answer, a story or parable that illustrates the new subject matter of the day, a demonstration of a nonobvious phenomenon, a reference to a current event or movie, a case or a problem that requires the lecture's information to solve, or a strong generalization that contradicts common thought. The idea is to draw in the class with surprise, familiarity, curiosity, or suspense.

Body

The body is your presentation and explication of new material. It is within this section that you subdivide the major topic into minilectures, each of which should revolve around only one major point. There is no best logic to follow in organizing a minilecture except to keep it simple. You can choose from an array of options: deduction (theory to phenomena/examples); induction (phenomena/examples to theory); hypothesis testing (theory and literature to hypothesis to evidence); problem to solution; cause to effect; concept to application; familiar to unfamiliar; debate to resolution; a chronology of events (a story or process)—to name just some common possibilities.

Organizational Outline

Make whatever organization you select explicit to students. For instance, tell the class, "I am going to describe some common manifestations of dysfunctional family behavior and then give you a definition and general principles that apply to the phenomenon." In addition, furnish students with a skeletal outline of each lecture that they can print out and use to take notes. At the very least, provide a general outline of the main points of your lecture on the board or a slide to help students follow your logical flow.

Finally, try to integrate as many of these learning aids as you can:

- *Visuals*. As you plan the material, think about how you can convey or repackage it visually—in pictures, photographs, slides, graphic metaphors, diagrams, graphs, or concept or mind maps (spatial arrangements of concepts or stages linked by lines or arrows). Prepare these graphics for presentation to the class. Such visual aids facilitate almost everyone's learning (see chapter 23).
- *Examples*. Think about illustrating abstract concepts and relationships with examples. Ideally these examples should be striking, vivid, current, common in everyday life, and related to students' experiences (past, present, or future). Making them humorous also helps students remember them.
- *Restatements*. Consider how you can restate each important point in two or three different ways—in scholarly terms, lay formal language, and informal language. Restatements not only demystify the material, making it more comprehensible, but they also build students' vocabulary and encourage their own paraphrasing of the material.

Conclusion

For learning purposes, the conclusion should be a 2- to 3-minute recap of the most important points in your lecture. It is too important to be rushed after the bell. You should plan and direct the recap activity, but the students should do it. The prospect of having to retrieve the material helps keep all students on their toes. The recap activity may take the form of an oral summary presented by one

or more students, a free-recall writing exercise (see chapter 20), or a quiz.

Whether graded or ungraded, a quiz at the end of the class period is a particularly effective means to ensure students retain more lecture content. Recall lecture's infamous forgetting curve: 38 percent of the material gone within minutes, 55 percent in 3 to 4 days, and 76 percent in 8 weeks. Now recall from chapter 1 that people learn less by reviewing material and more from being tested or testing themselves on it, because the latter activities involve greater cognitive processing and practice retrieving (Brown, Roediger, & McDaniel, 2014; Dempster, 1996, 1997; Dunlosky, Rawson, Marsh, Nathan, & Willingham, 2013; Karpicke & Blunt, 2011; Roediger & Karpicke, 2006; Rohrer & Pashler, 2010; Winne & Nesbit, 2010). This is why giving some kind of test right after a lecture doubles both factual and conceptual recall after 8 weeks (Menges, 1988).

Your Lecture Notes

Your lecture notes should be easy to read at a glance and as sketchy as you can handle. After all, you know the material, so all you need is a map showing your next conceptual destination. Therefore, consider laying out the lecture graphically in flowcharts, concept maps, tree diagrams, Venn diagrams, or network models, including any visual aids you plan to put on the board. Some instructors like to color-code their notes for quick visual reference. If a graphic organization does not appeal to you, make a sketchy outline of your lecture. But be sure it's very sketchy. In any case, write big and leave a lot of white space. Confine the words in your notes to key concepts and phrases, transitions to make explicit to the class, and directions to yourself (e.g., *board, pause, slide, survey class, ask class question, break activity #2—voltage problem*). The habit to avoid is writing out sentences (except direct quotes). That may tempt you to read them in class, in which case you will lose spontaneity, expressiveness, flexibility, eye contact, and, most important, psychological contact with your class.

■ DELIVERING AN EFFECTIVE LECTURE

A lecture can be highly motivational, but its success depends on the lecturer. An expressive, enthusiastic instructor can ignite students' interest in the material, and a reserved, boring one can douse it. The platform skills that convey energy, dynamism, and charisma can be isolated (they are listed in chapter 9) and learned. Public speaking courses and clubs help people develop and practice eye contact, effective verbal pacing and pausing, vocal quality and variety, facial expressions, gestures and movements, lectern and microphone use, visual aid display, and so on. Those who start out weak in these skills but work on them diligently can achieve impressive results within a year. Others seem to have a knack for them.

Don't dismiss such presentation techniques as mere acting. They have a powerful impact on students' motivation and learning, as well as on their student ratings (see chapter 28). But this is true only to the extent that an instructor relies on the lecture format. With the variety of teaching methods available, no instructor need rely on it much at all.

Therefore, instructors have a choice. Those who have an expressive, dynamic public personality or are willing to acquire the trappings of one can afford to use the lecture more in their teaching. (For the sake of student learning, however, even the most charismatic instructor should not depend on it exclusively.) Those who do not project such a persona can avoid lecturing whenever possible and employ more student-active methods. In brief, you should play to your natural and acquired strengths. The wide array of effective teaching methods should put to rest the notion that good teachers are born and not made.

■ INCORPORATING STUDENT-ACTIVE BREAKS: THE INTERACTIVE LECTURE

During these breaks, students should be in some way interacting with the material (and often one another) for brief, controlled periods of time. With the appropriate activities, you can help your students achieve the highest-level cognitive outcomes. Ideally the breaks should give them the opportunity to practice performing your learning outcomes or working with the lecture content you just gave. How well they complete the break task should furnish you with a diagnosis of their understanding. After all, you shouldn't move onto the next chunk of material unless almost all your students comprehend this one.

To keep the breaks brief and controlled, carefully time-control them. Inform your students that they will have exactly X number of minutes (or seconds) to complete the activity you assign them. Strictly enforced, those limits keep students focused on the task. When in doubt, allocate a little less time than you think some of them will need, but feel free to extend the limit a bit if they are working diligently. To make managing easier, bring a timer or stopwatch to class. Also circulate around the classroom to let students know you are listening to them and are willing to answer any procedural questions.

These breaks work well in any size class. In larger classes, however, having students work with their neighbors (in ad hoc pairs or triads) is quicker and easier than having them get into preorganized small groups unless you arrange for group members to sit together during every class.

Ask students to work and talk as quietly as they can, but expect the classroom to get noisy anyway. After their activity time is up, you can bring even the largest class to silence within seconds by taking this tip from cooperative learning researchers. Set the rule that you will raise your hand when the time is up. Tell your students that as soon as they see your hand up, they should immediately stop talking and raise their hands. The rest of the class will quickly follow suit.

Ideas for Student-Active Breaks

Below are some commonly used break activities, along with the number of minutes each typically takes. (They come mainly from Bligh, 2000;

Bonwell & Eison, 1991; Angelo & Cross, 1993; Cuseo, 2002; Mazur, 1997; McKeachie, 2002; and informal collegial exchanges.) Some of them recommend randomly calling on individual students or groups to hold them accountable for participating in the activity. Let these examples serve as your inspiration to conceive and experiment with your own innovations:

Pair and Compare

Students pair off with their neighbor and compare lecture notes, filling in what they may have missed. This activity makes students review and mentally process your minilecture content. Time: 2 minutes.

Pair, Compare, and Ask

This is the same as pair and compare but with the addition that students jot down questions on your minilecture content. Students answer one another's questions; you then field the remaining ones. Time: 3 minutes, plus 1 to 2 minutes to answer questions.

Periodic Free-Recall, with Pair-and-Compare Option

Students put away their lecture notes and write down the most important one, two, or three points of your minilecture, as well as any questions they have. The first two times you do this, use a slide, overhead, or the board to give instructions. After that, just telling them will do. Again, this activity makes students review and mentally process your minilecture content. Students may work individually, but if they work in pairs or triads, they can answer some of each other's questions. Time: 3 minutes, plus 1 to 2 minutes to answer students' questions.

Active Listening Checks

This is the same as the previous activity, except that you have your students hand in their three most important points, and then you reveal what you intended as most important. Lovett (2008), the researcher who devised this activity, uses it to improve her students' listening and note-taking skills. From the first time she did this in class to the third time, the percentage of students who correctly identified her three most important points rose from 45 to 75 percent. Time: 2 to 3 minutes.

Reflection/Reaction Paragraph

Students individually write out their affective reaction to the minilecture content (or video or demonstration). Ask a few volunteers to share. Time: 3 to 4 minutes.

Solve a Problem

Students solve an equational or word problem based on your minilecture. They can work individually or, better yet, in pairs or triads. Randomly call on a few individuals or groups to sample their answers. Time: 1 to 3 minutes for problem solving, depending on the problem's complexity, plus 1 to 2 minutes for surveying responses.

Multiple-Choice Item

Put a multiple-choice item, preferably a conceptual or application type, related to your minilecture on the board or a slide, and give four response options. Survey your students' responses (the next section, "Surveying Student Responses," explains various ways to do this). You can also ask students to rate their confidence level in their answer. Then give them a minute to convince their neighbor of their answer, and resurvey their responses. This activity makes students apply and discuss your minilecture content while it's fresh in their minds, and it immediately informs you how well they have understood the material. You can then clarify misconceptions before proceeding to new material. Time: 3 minutes, plus one 1 to 3 minutes to debrief and answer questions.

Multiple-Choice Test Item

In contrast to the previous multiple-choice item task, this one puts students in pairs or small groups to compose multiple-choice items on your minilecture for a test you will give in the future. As we know, this is no easy task, so provide your students with some training in good test-item writing. Teach them Bloom's taxonomy. Tell them the characteristics of plausible distractors (see chapter 26). Show them examples of well-constructed and poorly constructed items, then lower-order recall and higher-order thinking items. Students will be motivated to write test items you will want to use because they will know the answers to the ones they submitted. And you will never have to write multiple-choice items again. Nor will students ever again blame you for items they find tricky, ambiguous, or too hard. Of course, you should reserve the right to tweak their submissions. Time: 1 to 3 minutes for each item they write.

Listen, Recall, and Ask; Then Pair, Compare, and Answer

Students only listen to your minilecture, no note taking allowed. Then they open their notebooks and write down all the major points they can recall, as well as any questions they have. Instruct students to leave generous space between the major points they write down. Finally, they pair off with their neighbor and compare lecture notes, filling in what they may have missed and answering one another's questions. Again, this activity makes students test themselves, and practice retrieval of your lecture content. Time: 3 to 4 minutes for individual note writing plus 2 to 4 minutes for pair fill-ins and question answering.

Pair/Group Graphic

Students develop a concept map, mind map, thinking map, graphic organizer, picture, diagram, flowchart, or matrix of your minilecture content in pairs or small groups. What they are actually doing is integrating and reassembling their understanding of the content into a big-picture graphic. It is one of purest constructivist activities you can have them do, and it yields powerful learning benefits (they are detailed in chapter 23). Because these graphics provide you with deep insight into your students' interpretation of the material, you may want to collect and peruse them. You may also want to return them with some feedback—at the very least, pointing out any misconceptions and oversimplifications they reveal. Time: 3 to 10 minutes in class.

Quick Case Study

Students debrief a short case study (one to four paragraphs) that requires them to apply your minilecture content to a realistic, problematic situation. (Chapter 17 addresses the case method, including tips on developing your own cases.) Display a very brief case on a slide; put longer ones in a handout. You may add specific questions for students to answer or teach your class the standard debriefing formula: What is the problem? What is the remedy? What is the prevention? Instruct students to jot down their answers. Students can work individually or, better yet, in pairs or small groups. Time: 3 to 5 minutes, depending on the case length and complexity, plus 5 to 10 minutes for class exchange and discussion.

Pair/Group and Discuss

Students pair off with their neighbor or get into small groups to discuss an open-ended question that asks them to apply, analyze, or evaluate your minilecture content or to synthesize it with other course material. This question should have multiple possible correct answers. (Refer to chapter 13 for helpful questioning schemata and question framing techniques.) Have students outline their answers in writing. This activity makes students examine and extend, as well as process, your minilecture content and serves as an effective prelude to a general class discussion. Time: 3 to 10 minutes, depending on the question's complexity, plus 5 to 10 minutes for class exchange and discussion.

Pair/Group and Review

This is the same as the previous activity but with an essay question designed for preexam review. Randomly select student pairs or groups to present their answers to the class. Then mock-grade them based on your assessment criteria (explain these before the exercise). You can also have the rest of the class mock-grade these answers to help students learn how to assess their work. Time: 3 to 10 minutes, depending on the question's complexity, plus 5 to 15 minutes for pair/group presentations.

• • •

Here are several other break activities that apply to a wide range of content areas. Johnston and Cooper (1997) developed them under the apt name "quick-thinks." Each takes 1 or 2 minutes, plus 1 to 3 minutes to survey responses.

Correct the Error

Using immediate minilecture content, students correct an error that you have intentionally made in a statement, equation, or visual. The error may be an illogical or inaccurate statement, premise, inference, prediction, or implication.

Complete a Sentence Starter

Students accurately complete a sentence stem related to your minilecture content. The completed statement may be a definition, a category, a cause-and-effect relationship, an implication, a rationale, or a controversy. Present students with a sentence starter that requires reflection and higher-order thinking, not just rote knowledge, to complete.

Compare and Contrast

Students identify similarities or differences between parallel elements in your minilecture, such as theories, methods, models, events, problems, solutions, or artistic or literary works. To comprise a true analysis task, students must work on elements that have not been compared and contrasted in your minilectures or the readings.

Support a Statement

Students garner support for a statement you present: a conclusion, inference, theory, opinion, or description. Sources of support may be your minilecture, the readings, or evidence they generate on their own.

Reorder the Steps

Students correctly sequence items that you present to them in mixed order. These items may be elements of a procedure, process, cycle, method, plan, strategy, or technique.

Reach a Conclusion

Students logically infer the implications of facts, concepts, or principles drawing from data, opinions, events, or solutions. The inferred conclusions can be probable results, probable causes, or outcomes.

Paraphrase the Idea

Students put an idea—a definition, theory, statement, procedure, or description—into their own words. This task can be just a check on their comprehension or a little more when you add the twist of targeting the paraphrase to a specific audience.

Seventh-Inning Stretch

This least cognitively active break is what Kodani and Wood (2007) coin the *seventh-inning stretch*. For a few minutes, they play some music and have their students get out of their seats and stretch. Afterward their classes seem more alert. When Kodani and Wood surveyed their classes, their students overwhelmingly appreciated this break and believed it enhanced their learning. But a few would have preferred it to be content focused.

• • •

You will find still more options for lecture breaks in chapter 15 (on group learning), chapter 20 (on teaching students how to learn), and chapter 24 (on feedback).

Surveying Student Responses

When you develop a lecture break around a multiple-choice item—or, for that matter, a true-false item—follow up by surveying your students' responses before and after they discuss their answers with their neighbors. The fact that students commit to an answer makes them more interested in finding out what the correct response is, and the results furnish you with valuable feedback on their understanding.

You can collect those responses in several ways. First, you can ask for a show of hands for each response. While this option is very simple, it has its weaknesses. In a large class, you can't know for sure whether everyone is participating, and since you don't have time to count all the hands, you may get only a vague measure of the distribution of responses. You have no record of these responses either. One additional problem is that responses are not anonymous, so students may mindlessly change their answers just to follow the crowd.

Second, you can distribute four or five cards as small as 5-by-8 inches (you can use heavy cover stock) of different colors to each student, where each color signifies an answer—for example, red for a, blue for b, yellow for c, and green for d. Then have students put up the color of card that signifies their response choice. With this alternative, you can get a somewhat better idea of your participation rate and response distribution, especially if you have students put the stock directly in front of their faces. If you see a face, you can coax the student to make a choice. With students' faces covered by their choices, the answers become more anonymous as well. The only problem is that you have no record of the responses.

Third, you can use clickers, more formally known as personal or classroom response systems, or their online equivalent, such as Poll Everywhere or Socrative with students' mobile devices. These technologies also allow free response polls, which resemble fill-in-the-blank and very short answer items. With clickers, students simply push a button indicating their response or type in their answer, and a receiver connected to your computer picks up the signals and immediately tallies all the answers, displaying them in a histogram or word cloud on your monitor. You then have the option of revealing these results to the class.

Of course, this electronic alternative involves more advanced technology, which means that your institution, your students, or both have to pay for the clickers and your receiver. In addition, you have to learn the technology. However, you can tell exactly who isn't participating (and coax them to respond) and exactly how the responses distribute, and you can archive the survey results. The process is completely

anonymous to the class, so only you know how each student is responding. This also means you can take a confidential survey on sensitive attitudinal or behavioral topics. If you think students may be concerned about your knowing their individual responses, you can turn off your receiver's identification function and tell them that you have done so.

With the polling software, students similarly click on or type in their answers, and you get an appropriate distribution graphic on the web or on a presentation slide. You can take anonymous or respondent-identified polls and also archive the results. Bear in mind, however, the warning in chapter 4 about letting students use their mobile phones in class. They might click in their answer and immediately switch to a renegade activity.

Almost all of the research on the impact of this lecture break technique—posing a multiple-choice question and surveying student responses before and after a short pair discussion—has been conducted on clickers. Compared to a traditional lecture, incorporating clicker breaks enhances student learning substantially, often by an entire letter grade on tests (Bruff, 2009; Crouch & Mazur, 2001; Deal, 2007; Fagen, Crouch, & Mazur, 2001; Gauci, Dantas, Williams, & Kenn, 2009; Kaleta & Joosten, 2007; Mazur Group, 2008; Reay, Li, & Bao, 2008; more references at Bruff, 2016). The good news is that lower-tech survey methods, at least colored cards, produce learning gains just as impressive as clickers (Lasry, 2008). The payoff comes from the lecture break activity itself, not the technology. Therefore, the vast majority of the learning-relevant research involving clickers applies to hand raising and colored cards as well.

The student learning benefits of this lecture break technique over traditional lecture derive from its very specific effects. The literature reports that this technique increases class attendance, broadens class participation to literally the entire class, multiplies the chances for both student-to-student and student-to-faculty interaction, affords students regular practice in higher-order thinking, teaches them to critically examine and defend their thinking, provides formative assessment of learning, provides instant feedback to students and the instructor on their understanding and short-term retention, heightens students' attention and alertness in class (even early and late in the day), enhances their engagement in the material, and develops their metacognition, allowing for mindful and self-regulated learning (Bergtrom, 2006; Bruff, 2009; Crouch & Mazur, 2001; Deal, 2007; Fagen et al., 2002; Kaleta & Joosten, 2007; Mazur Group, 2008; Radosevich, Salomon, Radosevich, & Kahn, 2008; more references at Bruff, 2016). You can also use this technique to assess students' prior knowledge and launch discussion.

Clickers offer additional opportunities to do the following: take attendance instantly, with or without posing a question; grade participation, even in a large class, based on the number of correct responses to questions; play academic games, such as Millionaire; and give objective-item quizzes, as long as considerable cheating isn't likely. While some faculty use clickers for quizzes, this is not the purpose they were meant to serve. They are best used for learning and formative feedback.

Of course, these benefits depend on the questions; they must require higher-order thinking and problem-solving skills. For example, they may ask students to choose an example of a principle or to choose a principle to explain an example. They may survey an opinion, pose an ethical dilemma, have students classify a concept, or challenge them to make a prediction. If clickers collect the responses anonymously, the questions can address controversial or personal matters, such as students' opinions on hot-button issues or private experiences that illustrate a theory, principle, or finding (Bruff, 2007, 2009).

Since this lecture break technique started in large science classes, the STEM fields (science, technology, engineering, and mathematics) already have large online collections of well-tested questions and other resources for using clickers (e.g., www.cwsei.ubc.ca/resources/clickers.htm#questions). Other resources for a wider array of disciplines are available at Bruff (2016) and http://cft.vanderbilt.edu/docs/classroom-response-system-clickers-bibliography/.

INDUCING AND TEACHING STUDENTS TO TAKE GOOD NOTES

Many students come to college—and often leave it—with poor note-taking skills. The average student's notes include only 10 percent of the lecture (Johnstone & Su, 1994) and 40 percent of its critical ideas (for first-year students, just 11 percent) (Kiewra, 1985, 2005), and only about a third of students take decent notes (Johnstone & Su, 1994). One reliable way to get your material into those notes is to write it on the board. But students also make errors in copying, particularly diagrams, equations, numbers, and the contents of slides and transparencies, through which we often move too quickly. They also tend to leave out the instructor's corrections, descriptions of demonstrations, examples of applications, the structure of arguments, and technical definitions (Johnstone & Su, 1994).

Some students don't take notes at all, especially when they have a hard copy of the lecture's presentation slides. But having these slides often gives them a false sense of security that all the material they need to know for the test lies in front of them, and they may think they will remember what they have heard and read at the same time. We must realize that most young students did not take notes in high school, and for good reason: teachers often provided handouts with all their notes and gave easy tests. If students succeeded academically without taking notes before, they may question why they should now. So they don't even know that they should take notes, let alone how to take good ones.

Selling Students on Note Taking

Before teaching your students how to take good lecture notes, you have to motivate them to take them by selling them on the benefits. Fortunately, you can make your case from plenty of research

(Carrier, 1983; Johnstone & Su, 1994; Kiewra, 1985, 2005; McKeachie, 1994; Potts, 1993; numerous studies cited in Bligh, 2000). Although these studies may seem dated, the human mind has not changed since they were written. Students who take their own notes and review them later reap numerous cognitive payoffs over those who just listen. The practice fosters attention to and concentration on the lecture, accurate judgments about the relative importance of content (from nonverbal cues), understanding of the development and structure of the knowledge, far-transfer application of the material, and deep cognitive processing. In deep processing, learners engage in more thoughtful and active listening. They paraphrase, interpret, and question while integrating the new material into their organized bank of prior knowledge. Perhaps most compelling to students, taking notes cements the knowledge in their memories, especially if they review their notes later. This means note takers perform better on all types of tests than non–note takers. Of course, it is just as important that students review their notes, but you can incorporate lecture breaks and end-of-class activities to ensure they review them at least once (see the "Ideas for Student-Active Breaks" section above).

Kiewra (1985) conducted some intriguing research on the relative value of students studying from their own lecture notes versus the instructor's lecture notes. On factual tests, students who studied only the instructor's notes performed better than those who studied only their own notes. In fact, this former group did better even if they did not attend lectures! However, the highest factual test scorers were those who studied both the instructor's notes and their own notes. When students took tests requiring higher-order thinking, the instructor's lecture notes were of no help to them. It seems, then, that for higher-order cognitive outcomes, the greater focus and deeper thought processes that note taking engages really pays off.

Teaching Note Taking

After selling students on note taking, acquaint them with some note-taking systems (Bligh, 2000; Ellis, 2006; Kiewra, 2005). Show them how to make a formal outline with first-level headings, second-level headings, and so on. (Points of equal importance or generality should start at the same distance from the left margin.) Tell them about the Cornell system: drawing a line down each page one-third in from the left, taking lecture notes on the right two-thirds of the page, and reserving the left one-third for reviewing activities, such as condensing the notes and rewriting the most critical content. Display or hand out your own lecture notes just once or twice early in the term to provide students a model of how they should be taking notes. You might also teach your students how to reorganize their notes into concept maps, mind maps, graphic organizers, matrices, and diagrams so they can take advantage of the learning and memory benefits of visual representation (see chapter 23). No one strategy is equally effective for everyone, so advise students to try out at least a couple.

In addition, explain to your students that the real art of taking notes is putting the most knowledge into the fewest possible words—preferably their own words. It is not mindless transcription, which is what students tend to do when taking notes on their laptop. Students should avoid writing complete sentences unless the specific wording is crucial. So advise them to take notes sparingly in longhand, dropping all unnecessary words and recording only the words and symbols needed to recall the idea they signify later. To convince them, share the research results that students who take notes in longhand, versus on laptops, take fewer notes, use more of their own words, and wind up performing better on tests of both factual and higher-order conceptual learning (Holstead, 2015; Mueller & Oppenheimer, 2014; Svinicki, 2014).

Finally, share with your class some proven note-taking pointers, such as those listed in Exhibit 12.1 (Bligh, 2000; Ellis, 2006; Kiewra, 2005; Mueller & Oppenheimer, 2014; Svinicki, 2014).

Making Note Taking Easier for Students

You can do a lot to help students take good lecture notes; these strategies have already been detailed in

Exhibit 12.1   Sixteen Tips for Taking Good Class Notes*

1. Arrive early to class to warm up your mind. Review your notes from the previous class and the assigned readings. Ask your instructor to clarify what doesn't make sense.

2. Avoid taking notes on your laptop, and write your notes in longhand instead. Laptops tempt you to transcribe the lecture mindlessly, while writing forces you to reflect on the material and take notes sparingly in your own words. The best note takers compress the most knowledge into the fewest possible words and symbols. Besides, your laptop invites too many distractions.

3. Avoid cramming your notes or writing too small. Strive for easy readability. Leave a generous left margin for rewriting important words and abbreviated key content later.

4. Occasionally glance back over the last few lines of notes you have taken, and clarify any illegible letters, words, or symbols.

5. Make key words, important relationships, and conclusions stand out. Underline, highlight, box, or circle them, or rewrite them in the left margin.

6. Organize your notes according to your instructor's introductory, transitional, and concluding words and phrases, such as "the following three factors," "the most important consideration," "in addition to," "however," "on the other hand," "nevertheless," "by contrast," and "in conclusion." These phrases signal the structure of the lecture: cause and effect, relationships, comparisons and contrasts, exceptions, examples, shifts in topics, debates and controversies, and general conclusions.

7. Identify the most important points by watching for certain instructor cues: deliberate repetition, pauses, a slower speaking pace, a drop in pitch, a rise in interest or intensity, movement toward the class, showing a slide, and writing on the board.

8. Pay close attention to your instructor's body language, gestures, and facial expressions as well as vocal changes and movements around the room. Your instructor's subtlest actions punctuate and add meaning to the substance of the lecture.

9. Whenever possible, draw a picture, concept map, or diagram to organize and abbreviate the relationships in the lecture material. You may want to do this after a lecture. Almost everyone can recall a visual more easily than a written description.

10. Develop and use your own shorthand, such as abbreviations and symbols for common or key words—for instance, *btw* for "between," + for "and," *b/c* for "because," *rel* for "relationship," *df* or = for "definition," *cnd* for "condition," *nec* for "necessary" or "necessitates," *hyp* for "hypothesis," Δ for "change," *T4* for "therefore," + for "more," − for "less," ↑ for "increasing," ↓ for "decreasing," → for "causes," ← for "is caused by," and two opposing arrows for "conflicts with."

11. Take notes quickly and at opportune times. Use your instructor's pauses, extended examples, repetitions, and lighter moments to record notes. You can't afford to be writing one thing when you need to be listening closely to another.

12. To help speed your note taking, try different pens until you find an instrument that glides smoothly and rapidly for you.

13. If your instructor tends to speak or to move from point to point too quickly, politely ask him or her to slow down. You are probably the most courageous student of many others who cannot keep up either.

14. If you lose focus and miss part of a lecture, leave a space and ask a classmate, a TA, or your instructor to help you fill in the blank.

15. Separate your own comments and reactions from your lecture notes.

16. Review, edit, clarify, and elaborate your notes within 24 hours of the lecture, again a week later, and again a month later, even if for just a few minutes. While reviewing, recite, extract, and rewrite the key concepts and relationships. The knowledge will become yours forever.

*Most of these tips also apply to taking notes on readings, videos, and podcasts.

this chapter. Still, they are worth highlighting here. For starters, we can organize our lectures clearly and simply, giving each an introduction, a body, and a conclusion and making the organization explicit in class. You can deliver your content using nonverbal cues (vocal variety, gestures, movement) to signal the most important points. You can chunk the content into minilectures, each making one major point, with student-active breaks between them. You can also schedule lecture breaks and end-of-class review activities that allow students to review, fill in, and revise their notes, individually or in pairs (Bligh, 2000; Kelly & O'Donnell, 1994; McKeachie, 2002; O'Donnell & Dansereau, 1993). Finally, you can display or hand out your own lecture notes once or twice early in the term to provide students with a model of how they should be taking notes.

The most effective learning aid you can furnish is a skeletal outline of your lecture that provides just the main headings and subheadings of your lectures and appropriately sized blocks of white space below them. Word-process the outline to prevent students from getting that false sense of security that printouts of presentation slides give them, and post them well in advance of the class so that students can download them. With an even sketchy lecture outline in front of them, students tend not to get lost, and they quickly figure out from the amount of white space how much note taking to do on their own. As a result, they not only take better notes

on skeletal outlines but also perform better on tests (Cornelius & Owen-DeSchryver, 2008; Hartley & Davies, 1986; Potts, 1993).

To make the most of skeletal notes, include the type of material that students often miscopy (equations, formulas, and like) and insert a heading and white space for them to record what they frequently leave out: discussions, demonstrations, examples of applications, the structure of arguments, and technical definitions (Johnstone & Su, 1994). Also include some of the material appropriate for presentation slides, such as the learning outcomes for the class, directions or questions for lecture-break activities, and graphics.

■ MAKING THE LECTURE EFFECTIVE

A well-crafted lecture can be a student-centered and student-active learning experience. You can enliven it with stimulating lecture-break activities, graphics, video clips, demonstrations, animations, and the like. Furthermore, you can facilitate it with a skeletal outline and enrich it with learning skills, such as note taking and activities that give students practice in active listening, conceptual thinking, problem solving, knowledge application, reflection, and retrieval of material—skills that encourage and enable academic success and lifelong learning.

CHAPTER 13

Leading Effective Discussions

Discussion is a productive exchange of viewpoints, a collective exploration of issues involving higher-order thinking. To bear fruit and not degenerate into a free-association, free-for-all bull session, you as the instructor must chart its course and content, steer it in the right direction, and keep hot air from blowing it off course. But to keep it flexible and fluid, you might go with the breezes occasionally. Your challenge is to strike that delicate balance between structure and flow. Finding that balance helps you broaden participation and keep all hands on deck.

Contrast with *recitation,* which is asking students to reproduce, either verbatim or in their own words, material that they are supposed to have already learned from assigned readings, videos, podcasts, or live lectures—that is, performing knowledge/remembering and comprehension/understanding cognitive operations.

■ WHEN TO CHOOSE DISCUSSION

Well planned and well managed, discussion can help your students achieve every type of learning outcome with the possible exception of knowledge/remembering, and it isn't bad at that either. In fact, discussion shines in developing many of the skills and attitudes on which lecture is weak (Bligh, 2000; Bonwell & Eison, 1991; Brookfield & Preskill, 2005; Dallimore, Hertenstein, & Platt, 2008; Delaney, 1991; Ewens, 2000; Forster, Hounsell, & Thompson, 1995; Gilmore & Schall, 1996; Howard, 2015; Kustra & Potter, 2008; McKeachie, 2002; Robinson & Schaible, 1993; Springer, Stanne, & Donovan, 1999):

- Examining and possibly changing attitudes, beliefs, values, and behaviors
- Exploring unfamiliar ideas open-mindedly
- Deep, conceptual learning

- Active listening
- Critical thinking
- Problem solving
- Communicating orally
- Synthesizing and integrating ideas
- Transferring knowledge to new situations
- Retaining the material
- Wanting to learn more about the subject matter

The problem-solving skills that discussion fosters apply not only to math problems but to all other kinds of solution-oriented tasks, whether they call for one correct answer, one best answer, or many possible correct answers. Such tasks include resolving ethical dilemmas; designing a research project; explaining deviations from expected results; writing a computer program; solving a case study; evaluating various positions on an issue; analyzing a piece of literature; and developing approaches to tackling real-world social, political, economic, technological, and environmental problems. Because discussion models democracy, it may even promote civic engagement and good citizenship (Brookfield & Preskill, 2005; Lempert, Xavier, & DeSouza, 1995).

Contrast with *recitation,* which serves other respectable outcomes:

- Recalling and restating knowledge, terms, and facts
- Speaking the language of the discipline (Leamnson, 1999)
- Expressing important material in one's own words, thereby demonstrating understanding
- Practicing what requires drill and repetition to learn
- Retaining and retrieving the basic knowledge students need for discussion and other higher-order thinking activities

■ SETTING THE STAGE FOR DISCUSSION AT THE START OF YOUR COURSE

Students need to be primed for discussion, especially since they spend so much of their classroom time passively listening to an instructor. They have learned to expect that they need only *look* attentive in class while relying on their talkative peers to assume responsibility for participating (Howard, 2015). Therefore, if you plan to make discussion an integral class activity, even if not a primary one, inform and prepare your students on the first day of class. Let them know the primary ground rule: everyone's participation is expected and no backbenchers will be allowed. Announcing the key role that discussion will play in your course will encourage students to take the activity seriously. So will telling them your reasons for using discussion—for instance, how the research supports its effectiveness in helping them achieve your learning outcomes. Follow up by explaining how class discussions will relate to other parts of the course, such as readings, written assignments, and tests. When you can, build homework, quizzes, and tests around both the readings and the discussions about them.

Explain the true nature of discussion as the expression of different, legitimate points of view. Disagreement enriches the learning experience. In fact, college is all about hearing, trying on, and appraising different perspectives. Students should listen actively and respectfully to every opinion put on the table, evaluate the evidence for and against that claim, and be prepared with evidence to defend their own positions. Their contributions are truly valuable.

Then lead your class in a discussion—if not about the syllabus (see chapter 5), then about their prior knowledge of, experience with, and interest in the course material. Try to get every student to say something that day. You might draw out students by directing questions to them individually, such as, "Janet, what interested you in this course?" or, "Matt, what topics would you like to see addressed in this course?"

"Education is the ability to listen to almost anything without losing your temper or your self-confidence."
—Robert Frost

◼ POLICIES TO ENCOURAGE PARTICIPATION

The biggest challenge facing you is eliciting broad and active participation. If you can do that, most of the other problems that go wrong in a discussion—domination by one or two students, topical tangents, silent sectors of the room—simply disappear. Just about all the recommendations in this chapter help ensure that all of your students will come to a discussion prepared, comfortable, and willing to contribute.

Grading on Participation

You may or may not wish to include the quality and quantity of class participation in your final grading scheme. But doing so will increase the likelihood of your students coming to class prepared and participating (Dallimore, Hertenstein, & Platt, 2006). If you do, you should make this very clear in your syllabus and your first-day presentation. Also explain your conception of adequate quality and quantity. To help articulate your standards, put the phrase "class participation grading rubric" in a search engine and peruse the examples your colleagues use.

To head off uneven participation, especially the problem of a couple of dominant students, you can limit the number of contributions each student can make each class before everyone has spoken. To keep track, have students display a colorful sticky note on the front of their desk for each of their contributions. You can combine this system with grading by giving students a participation point for their first two or three comments but no more points for any subsequent ones (Lang, 2008).

Consider the class level and size in deciding the weight to give participation in the final grade. First-year students may feel comfortable with 20 percent in a class of 20 to 25 students but may find it unreasonably stressful in one of 45 to 50. More advanced students should be able to handle a higher percentage weight even in a large class. You might have students vote on the percentage (give them options) and follow the majority rule.

Setting Ground Rules for Participation

How do you foresee conducting class discussions? Students want to know how you will call on them. The two most common options are calling on raised hands or cold-calling students by random selection, such as shuffling and drawing index cards with their names or choosing students who haven't spoken recently.

The first method keeps the class relaxed but does little to motivate preparation. Most important, participation is bound to be uneven, with a few verbal individuals monopolizing the floor and most students playing passive wallflowers. You may even wind up inadvertently reinforcing social inequities unless you make special efforts to draw out and validate your minority students. The second method, cold-calling by random selection, obviously ensures broad participation and motivates preparation, but some instructors resist it for fear it will cause students undue discomfort. Actually there is no evidence to support this concern, at least not for advanced students. In addition, cold-calling combined with graded participation is effective in increasing both the frequency of student contributions and preparation for discussion (Dallimore et al., 2006).

You may want to vary your methods for calling on students. For example, when the raised-hands method fails to generate broad enough participation, you might shift to cold-calling, perhaps targeting students who have been silent for a while.

If you cold-call, a good ground rule to set is the escape hatch, permitting students to pass on answering a question. It is demoralizing to the class and counterproductive to the discussion to badger, belittle, or otherwise put a person on the spot for not having a comment when you demand it. A student with nothing to say may simply have nothing new to contribute. While it's possible he isn't prepared, he may simply agree with other recent remarks, or may have no questions at the time, or may be having a bad day and not feel like talking. To cover these possibilities, inform your class that you will occasionally accept responses such as, "I don't want to talk right now" or "Will you please call on me later?"

You should make it clear, however, that you will not tolerate certain negative behaviors: purposefully steering the discussion off-track; trying to degenerate it into a comedy act; instigating an inappropriate debate; personally attacking a fellow student; displaying one's temper; asking wheedling, argumentative, or loaded questions; or engaging in more general uncivil classroom behaviors (see chapter 9).

Alternatively, you can lead a class discussion on what the rules of civility should be (Kustra & Potter, 2008). Ask the students to recount the qualities of the best discussions they have participated in. How did their classmates behave? How did they show mutual respect? Then ask them about the worst discussions in their educational experience. How did people treat each other? What behaviors induced the silence, anger, or fear of others? From this point, the class can generate their own ground rules, and you can supplement them as necessary.

Setting ground rules is particularly important in a diverse classroom, which can introduce controversy and discourse that students may not know how to handle. If the topic may provoke racist or discriminatory remarks, stand poised to intervene and return to the discussion on the subject at hand. Regardless of how you feel about the various positions raised, do not project those emotions onto the students who express them. Protect both the attacked and the attacker. Then have the students calm down, step back, and think about what has just happened. You may go from here to turn the situation into a teachable moment. Have students write a reflection paper on the incident expressing not only their feelings but what they learned. Or ask those involved in the incident to restate and explain their views calmly. Or defer discussing the issue until later, and do bring it up later, after you have a strategy for handling the conflict (Derek Bok Center for Teaching and Learning, 2006). For more ideas on ensuring equity in your classroom, see chapter 7.

One final rule to set yourself is a reassurance: "The only stupid question is the one you don't ask." Students are downright terrified by the prospect of looking stupid or foolish to you or their peers. They appreciate being told that you will welcome all questions and ensure that they are answered. A similar but modified rule should apply to all answers as well: you will welcome all contributions given with good intentions. But this doesn't mean that you won't correct faulty answers or allow other students to correct them.

■ SKILLFUL DISCUSSION MANAGEMENT

First and foremost, you are the discussion *facilitator*, which means to make it easy for students to participate. The process can begin before class. By arriving a little early and casually chatting with students as they arrive, you can loosen them up for dialogue. Facilitating also entails starting off the discussion and adding to it when necessary. But once the discussion takes off, your role largely involves directing traffic. Still, at all times, you serve as manager-on-call to control the focus, structure, and tone of the exchange.

Depending on the circumstances, you may briefly assume a wide variety of roles: coach, moderator, host, listener, observer, information provider, presenter, counselor, recorder, monitor, instigator, navigator, translator, peacemaker, and summarizer. During contentious exchanges, you may even find yourself playing referee. Congratulate yourself when students start speaking to each other directly rather than through you. Your goal is to make yourself superfluous.

The next several sections list ways to achieve some of the goals you need to meet to ensure a productive discussion with the broadest possible participation. You needn't follow all the recommendations below, and some may not work in your class, but implementing a few will increase your success.

Ready the Class and Ignite the Exchange

Students come to class with all manner of things on their mind, and the subject matter of your course may not rank among them. So before launching into a discussion, warm up the class to the topic of the day (Brookfield & Preskill, 2005; Jones, 2008; McKeachie, 2002).

- Put up a written outline/road map for the discussion/class period.
- Start out by asking students to summarize the previous class.
- Start out with a few recall questions on the readings.
- Start out by asking for students' emotional reactions to the readings.
- Start out with a reference to a well-known current event or an experience from your previous class, such as a video, demonstration, or role play.
- Start out with a highly controversial question.
- Start out by having students read aloud important text passages (rather than you doing it).
- Start out with a writing prompt—that is, a reading-relevant question or provocative statement that students can reflect on and write about for a few minutes.

- Start out by having students brainstorm what they already know about a topic or what outcomes they anticipate of a situation or an experiment.
- Start out by taking the role of devil's advocate and arguing in favor of a position that you know that some students will argue against. As a few students may interpret your representing "the devil" as manipulative, untrustworthy, and confusing, explain what you're doing beforehand. While you're assuming the role, you might even wear a hat or a sign with "Devil's Advocate" written prominently on it.

Lower Social Barriers and Reduce Shyness

We may find it easy to speak in front of a class, but remember that few of your students do. Here are some ways to make speaking out in class less stressful for them:

- Arrange seats in a circle.
- Have icebreakers the first day of class.
- Have students fill out index cards the first day, letting them share any information they'd like about their student and personal lives.
- Call students by name.
- Help students learn their classmates' names; use name tags or tents.
- Casually chat with students before and after class.
- Get to know students through office hour appointments. (Frequently pass around a sign-up sheet.)
- Make eye contact with all students.
- Establish physical proximity with all students by sitting in different places and moving around the room.
- Have students read aloud important text passages (instead of your doing it).
- Refer back to the previous contributions of students (by name) during discussions.
- Frequently break your class into small groups to solve problems and answer complex questions.

- Extend students' participation by having them post to a class blog, wiki, discussion board, or chat.
- Have students jot down answers to complex questions before calling on anyone.
- Direct some questions to quieter sectors of the room and to quieter individuals.
- See quiet students in your office hours and ask them why they haven't participated; they may be dealing with a major emotional problem. Still, encourage them to become involved. You might give them one or more discussion questions in advance of the next class and let them rehearse their answers with you.

Motivate Students to Prepare

You have to take some measures to ensure that students have something to contribute:

- Include participation in the course grade (10 to 30 percent or as bonus points).
- Distribute study guide questions on the readings.
- Have a random-selection "calling-on" policy. This technique works especially well when you provide study questions on the readings in advance.
- Use some of the many reading compliance strategies in chapter 21, such as requiring students to take reading notes, write answers to study guide questions, or submit written questions on readings; or giving daily quizzes on the readings; or setting up in-class games or simulations that require doing the readings to do well.
- Allow students to use their reading notes, answers to study questions, and the like to answer the discussion questions.
- Have students mark passages in the readings that are puzzling to them, especially important, or related to other readings or discussion themes, and then read them aloud in class and explain why they selected them. After all the students have shared their passages, each in turn responds to classmates' choices and insights, recounting what they have found most meaningful, interesting, or novel (SCCtv, Boyer, & Harnish, 2007).

Motivate Students to Pay Attention

Too many students tune out of discussions because they fail to see the value of their peers' thoughts. Here are some ways to keep their attention on task:

- Advise students on how to takes notes on discussion.
- Advise them specifically *when* to take notes.
- Refer frequently to your discussion outline/road map.
- Write the major points made on the board.
- Include the content of discussions in assignments and exams (and say you will do this).
- Ask students to comment on and react to one another's contributions.
- In small-group discussions, randomly select a few groups to summarize their progress, answers, conclusions, and so on, and within each group randomly select the spokesperson.
- Regularly select a student to summarize the discussion at the end of class; then invite other students to add major points.
- End class with a *one-minute paper* (but budget 2 to 3 minutes)—that is, ask students to write down anonymously (1) the most important things they learned during the class and (2) any questions or points they found the most confusing. Do collect these to ensure students do them, and sample a few to see how students experienced the class.

Moderate to Maintain Momentum

As some of the response options suggest, you often best facilitate by doing and saying very little, acting only as the resource of last resort. Your goal is to shift the spotlight from you to your students every chance you get. Regard your task as directing traffic:

- Before commenting on an answer yourself, ask other students to react to their peers' contributions.
- Ask students to address comments directly to one another.
- Ask students to help you clarify points.

- If the class is splitting into camps on an issue, set up a spontaneous debate, allowing students to change their mind as it progresses. For a twist, have each side argue in favor of the opposition.
- Step in, preferably with a thoughtful follow-up question, only if no student supplies the needed clarification, correction, or knowledge or if the discussion strays off track.
- Be sure a topic is settled before moving on. Ask if anyone has something to add or qualify.
- Ask a student to summarize the main points made during the discussion of the topic. Then move on, making a logical transition to the next topic.

What if traffic comes to a screeching halt and no one says a word after a generous wait time? Break the silence and tension with a touch of humor: "Helloooooo, is anybody out there?" But you should definitely ask students why they are silent. Perhaps your question was ambiguous or too complex or used words your students didn't understand, or they misunderstood your meaning.

Respond Honestly to Student Responses

Give approval, verbal or nonverbal, to all student contributions by nodding, looking interested or accepting, or recording the response on the board. But provide verbal feedback suitable to the response. Students want to know how correct and complete their own and their classmates' answers are, but they want you to deliver your judgment in a diplomatic, encouraging way. Here are some verbal response options you may wish to use:

- *When the answer is correct,* praise according to what it deserves.
- *When the answer is correct but is only one of several correct possibilities,* ask another student to extend or add to it. Or frame a question that is an extension of the answer. Avoid premature closure.
- *When the answer is incomplete,* follow up with a question that directs the student to include

more—for example, "How might you modify your answer if you took into account the _____ aspect?"
- *When the answer is unclear,* try to rephrase it, and ask the student if this is what she means.
- *When the answer is seemingly wrong,* follow up with one or more gently delivered Socratic questions designed to lead the student to discover his error—for example, "Yes, but if you come to that conclusion, don't you also have to assume ____?" (See the box on the Socratic method near the end of chapter 3.)
- Vary your response to faulty answers so students simply don't translate a stock phrase as, "You're wrong."
- Avoid identifying and correcting errors yourself for as long as possible.

Pause and Wait for Responses

To eliminate needless delays in students' responding, ask only one question at a time. Resist the temptation to pose another related question if you don't get an instant response to the first. Putting multiple questions on the table confuses students.

Once you pose a well-crafted question, allow sufficient time for students to respond—5 to 15 seconds, depending on the difficulty of the challenge. This rule applies no matter what method you use to call on students. While a few students may jump at the chance to say anything, even if it is incorrect, most need time—more time than we might expect—to think through and phrase a response they are willing to share publicly. After all, they are struggling with new knowledge and thinking in what is a foreign language to them—the language of the discipline. They need time to retrieve and sort through the knowledge for an intelligent response and then figure out how to express it. Extending your wait time can dramatically increase the number of students with a response.

If the question is particularly difficult, lengthy, or complex, advise students to outline their answer in writing first. This step will boost their confidence and yield higher-quality answers. This way, too, you can feel free to call on anyone—in particular, the quieter students.

Watch for nonverbal cues of students' readiness to respond, especially changes in facial expression. Still, refrain from calling on anyone until you see several raised hands or eager faces. When you have many possible students from whom to select, you can spread the attention and participation opportunities across students who haven't spoken recently.

■ QUESTIONING TECHNIQUES

Questions are the heart of a discussion, and framing thoughtful ones is a key teaching skill and has been for millennia. Socrates honed it to such a fine art that an entire method of questioning is attributed to him. Not just any type of question can launch and carry a discussion, however. Questions that demand only recall and rephrasing serve recitation well but not discussion. Many a delightful review session conducted as *Jeopardy* or *Millionaire* games has relied on such questions with very short answers (Kaupins, 2005), but they haven't started a discussion. Other types of questions serve no purpose whatsoever—in particular, a string of questions an instructor may nervously fire off to fill an awkward silence and vague questions that may sound open but are actually too confusing or unfocused for anyone to know how to answer. For example, this one calls for logical acrobatics: "Who else knows what else doesn't fall into this category?" This one is too global: "What about the breakdown of the family?" Students resist taking the risk required to attack such questions. Two common questions that represent well-meaning attempts to help rarely get an honest answer: "Does everyone understand this?" and, "Any questions?"

Crafting Good Discussion Questions

Constructing questions that ignite and sustain discussion involves much more than turning around a couple of words in a sentence and adding a question mark. Well-crafted ones take thought and creativity in order to evoke the same from students. They all have one feature in common: multiple respectable answers. Therefore, they encourage broad participation and in-depth treatment. (Of course, they have multiple faulty answers as well.)

Perhaps the most open invitation to students to contribute is to ask them to brainstorm ideas, topics, interpretations, examples, similarities, differences, problems, solutions, and like. Here are a few examples: "What issues does Hamlet question in the play?" "What social trends in the past couple of decades have increased classroom incivility at the college level?" "How might the public be convinced to care about ecological imbalances?" At the start of a brainstorming session, the instructor tells the class to withhold judgment and criticism for the time being and records all the responses on the board, a slide, or a flip chart. Only after all brains stop storming do the students begin editing, refining, combining, eliminating, grouping, and prioritizing, using criteria they generate themselves.

Another strategy is to have students choose a viewpoint or position from several alternatives and back up their choice with reasoning and evidence. Students may develop and defend their own opinions, adopt those of a particular author, or assume a devil's advocate stance—for example: "Do you think that Marx's theory of capitalism is still relevant in today's postindustrial societies? Why or why not?" "To what extent is Ivan Illich a victim of his own decisions or of society?" "Is the society in *Brave New World* a utopia, a nightmare of moral degeneration, something between the two?" You might play devil's advocate on an issue or make a contentious, controversial statement and invite your students to react against it. Such questions may spark a healthy debate. Before letting the issue rest, ask for possible resolutions or analyses of the conflict if they don't evolve on their own.

You might even pose questions that, as of yet, have no clear correct answer, such as contradictory findings that haven't been reconciled, the meaning or sources of anomalies, questions challenging the discipline, best next steps in a line of research, and other unresolved scholarly issues. Do tell your students that these questions represent genuine unknowns in your field. Not only will they feel freer to speculate in responding, but they will also begin to grasp the fact that your discipline faces uncertainties and its knowledge base is not a frozen collection of terms, principles, and procedures. With this understanding, your students can begin to ascend Perry's stages of cognitive development (see chapter 1).

Let's look at a couple of question typologies that offer additional ideas for developing multiple, varying points of view on an issue. Note that all of these question types require higher-order thinking.

McKeachie's Discussion Questions

McKeachie (2002) suggests four types of fruitful, challenging questions, which vaguely overlap with Bloom's cognitive operations of analysis, synthesis, and evaluations:

1. *Comparative questions* These ask students to compare and contrast different theories, research studies, literary works, and so on. Indirectly, they help students identify the important dimensions for comparison.

2. *Evaluative questions* This type extends comparisons to judgments of the relative validity, effectiveness, or strength of what is being compared.

3. *Connective and causal effect questions* These challenge students to link facts, concepts, relationships, authors, theories, and the like that are not explicitly integrated in assigned materials and might not appear to be related. These questions are particularly useful in cross-disciplinary courses. They can also ask students to draw and reflect on their personal experiences, connecting these to theories and research findings. When students realize these links, the material becomes more meaningful to them.

4. *Critical questions* This type invites students to examine the validity of a particular argument, research claim, or interpretation. Such questions foster careful, active reading. If the class has trouble getting started, you can initiate the discussion by presenting an equally plausible alternative argument. Asking for comments on what a student has just said is also a critical question. Used in this content, it fosters good listening skills.

Brookfield and Preskill's "Momentum" Questions

Brookfield and Preskill (2005) propose seven types of questions that serve the express purpose of sustaining the momentum of a discussion. These questions are designed to make students probe into issues more deeply, reconsider positions in novel and more critical ways, and stay intellectually stimulated:

1. *Questions requesting more evidence* As the name states, such a question asks a student to defend his position, especially when the evidence for the position is questionable or another student challenges it as unsupported. You should pose the question in a matter-of-fact way as a simple request for more information—data, facts, passages from the text—so as not to alienate the student.

2. *Clarification questions* This type invites the student to rephrase or elaborate on her ideas to make them more understandable to the rest of the class. You can request an example, an application, or a fuller explanation.

3. *Cause-and-effect questions* These questions coax students to consider the possible causal relationship between variables or events and, in effect, formulate hypotheses. You can use them to challenge a conventional wisdom or introduce the scientific method.

4. *Hypothetical questions* These are "what-if" inquiries that require students to think creatively to make up plausible scenarios to explore how changing the circumstances or parameters of a situation

might alter the results. They can induce imaginative thinking and even send a discussion off on fanciful tangents, but students still have to use their prior knowledge and experience to come up with supportable extrapolations. Hypothetical questions can extend cause-and-effect questions. If, for example, the class established the impact of education on income, you could pose this hypothetical scenario to help students define the limits of the relationship: "What if everyone in the society got a bachelor's degree? Does that mean that everyone would make a similarly high income?"

5. *Open questions* These questions invite risk taking and creativity in problem solving and have the greatest potential for expanding students' intellectual and affective horizons. No matter how they are phrased, they are truly open only if you welcome all well-meaning responses and aren't fishing for a preferred answer. You can accept the weaker contributions as opportunities for the students to build and expand on them and follow up with clarification questions, requests for more evidence, cause-and-effect questions, and hypothetical questions.

6. *Linking or extension questions* A high-quality discussion depends on students' actively listening to each other's contributions. Linking or extension questions encourage this by asking students to think about the relationships between their responses and those of their classmates.

7. *Summary and synthesis questions* To enhance the learning value of discussion, you should close with a few wrap-up questions that ask students to summarize or synthesize the important ideas shared during the exchange. Students have to review and reflect on the discussion, identifying and articulating the intellectual highlights. These questions can take a variety of forms. They can ask outright for the one or two most important ideas that emerged or for some key concept that best encapsulates the exchange. Or they can ask what points the discussion clarified, what issues remain unresolved, or what topics should be addressed next time to advance the group's understanding.

ORGANIZING DISCUSSION QUESTIONS

The most engaging discussions are not just a list of loosely connected questions. Rather, they have a direction and a destination. They comprise a purposeful sequence of questions that guides students through a more or less orderly process of thinking about a topic more deeply.

Working Backward from End-of-Class Outcomes

Backward design can be applied to designing a discussion session as well as an entire course. First, jot down your ultimate outcomes for the class period: the one, two, or three things you want your students to be able to do (classify, explain, analyze, assess, and so on) by the end of class. For each performance, create one or two key questions that will assess the students' facility. Then for each key question, develop another two or three questions that logically proceed and will prepare the students to answer the key questions intelligently. In other words, work backward from the key questions you want your students to answer well at the end through the questions that will lead them to that facility.

When class begins, launch the discussion with one of the last questions you framed. You can lend structure to the discussion by displaying all of your questions (key assessment ones last) on the board or a slide or in a handout with note-taking space below each question. Still, unless you have framed too many questions, you can afford to be flexible. You can allow the discussion to wander a bit, then easily redirect it back to your list of questions.

The next section on Bloom's hierarchy of questions suggests a logical sequencing scheme for the working-backward strategy.

Guiding Students Up Bloom's Hierarchy of Questions

You can view Bloom's (1956) taxonomy of questions as a hierarchical ladder of cognitive levels for leading your students from knowledge, the lowest thinking level, to evaluation, the highest. This schema was set out in chapter 2, where we applied it to developing learning outcomes. The lists of verbs associated with each cognitive operation are just as useful here for framing questions, so refer back to Table 2.1.

To structure a discussion as a process of inquiry, you might start off with knowledge (recitation) questions on the highlights of the previous class or the reading assignment. A factual recall exercise serves as a mental warm-up for the students and gives those who come in unprepared the chance to pick up a few major points and follow along, if not participate later. As you can see in Table 13.1, knowledge questions often ask *who*, *what*, *where*, and *when*, as well as *how* and *why*, when

Table 13.1　Examples of Questions at Each Cognitive Level of Bloom's Taxonomy/Hierarchy

Cognitive Level	Questions
Knowledge	• Who did _____ to _____? • What did you notice about _____? • What do you recall about _____? • What does the term _____ mean? • When did _____ take place? Where did it take place? • How does the process work? (Describe it.)
Comprehension	• In your own words, what does the term _____ mean? • How would you explain _____ in nontechnical terms? • Can you show us what you mean? • What do think the author/researcher is saying?
Application	• What would be an example of _____? • How would you solve this problem? • What approach would you use? • How would you apply _____ in this situation?
Analysis	• How are _____ and _____ alike? How are they different? • How is _____ related to _____? • What are the different parts of _____? • What type of _____ is this? How would you classify it? • What evidence does the author/researcher offer? • How does the author/researcher structure the argument? • What assumptions are behind the argument? • What inferences can you draw about _____?
Synthesis	• What conclusions can you come to about _____? • What generalizations can you make about _____? • How would you design (structure, organize) a _____? • How would you adapt (change) the design (plan) for _____? • How can you resolve the differences (paradox, apparent conflict)? • What new model could accommodate these disparate findings?
Evaluation	• What would you choose, and why? • What are the relevant data, and why? • Why do you approve or disapprove? • Why do you think the conclusions are valid or invalid? • What is your position (opinion), and how can you justify it? • How would you rank (rate, prioritize) the _____? • How would you judge (evaluate) _____?

students have already read or been told the correct answer. Avoid questions that call for one- or two-word answers; aim for multisentence responses. But do not spend more than several minutes on this level, especially if you depend on raised hands to call on students. The boredom potential aside, students will not answer many recitation questions because they may fear their classmates seeing them as apple polishers—bailing you out, so to speak. Besides, we have more important thinking skills to develop in our students.

Rapidly move the discussion up the hierarchy through comprehension so you can find out whether your students correctly understand the material and can put it in their own words. Draw on the questions in Table 13.1. At this juncture, you can identify and correct any misconceptions they have about the subject matter that might get in the way of their deeper learning. If they do comprehend the material, they should be able to answer application questions and think of appropriate examples and use the material to solve problems. If they can do this, they should be ready to progress to analysis of the material: distilling its elements; drawing comparisons and contrasts; identifying assumptions, evidence, causes, effects, and implications; and reasoning through explanations and arguments.

Once students have explored the material, they are prepared to step outside its confines and attempt synthesis. As illustrated in Table 13.1, this type of question calls for integrating elements of the material in new and creative ways: drawing new conclusions and generalizations; composing or designing a new model, theory, or approach; or combining elements from different sources. When students can synthesize material, they have mastered it well enough to address evaluation questions. They now can make informed judgments about its strengths and shortcomings; its costs and benefits; and its ethical, aesthetic, or practical merit.

Structured as a hierarchy, Bloom's taxonomy helps rein in students from leaping into issues they aren't yet prepared to tackle. Often they are all too eager to jump to judging content without thoroughly understanding and examining it first. In addition, if you teach the taxonomy to your students, they acquire a whole new metacognitive perspective on thinking processes and levels. If you label the level of your questions, you maximize your chances of obtaining the level of answers you are seeking. Students also quickly learn to classify and better frame their own questions.

The taxonomy should be used flexibly, however. Some discussion tasks, such as debriefing a case (see chapter 17), may call for an inextricable combination of application, analysis, synthesis, and evaluation. Moreover, a comprehension question in one course may be an analysis task in another. How any question is classified depends on what the students have previously received as "knowledge" from you and the readings you assign.

■ TURNING THE TABLES

You need not always be the person leading the discussion and posing the questions. If you model and teach good discussion facilitation and questioning techniques, you can have your students lead discussions and develop and organize the questions. The quality of these questions tells you how diligently your students are doing and reflecting on their readings (see chapter 21).

The next chapter offers other teaching formats that put the spotlight and the responsibility for learning squarely on students.

CHAPTER 14

Coordinating Experiential Learning

This chapter covers a potpourri of teaching methods that allow students to discover and construct knowledge by direct experience, either simulated or real. These activities rank even higher than discussion on a continuum of student engagement, ranging from moderately engaging to extremely so, and the intense emotions they often evoke cement the experiences into students' memories. Research documents that experiential learning methods, such as simulations, games, and role playing, ensure higher student motivation, more learning at higher cognitive levels, greater appreciation of the subject matter and its utility, and longer retention of the material than does the traditional lecture (Berry, 2008; Bonwell & Eison, 1991; Bowen, 2012; Carnes, 2014; Hertel & Millis, 2002; Howard, Collins, & DiCarlo, 2002; Specht & Sandlin, 1991). These methods also meet a wider range of instructional goals than do less active ones (see chapters 1, 2, and especially 11). We start here with the moderately engaging and move to the more powerful, which generally require more setup and direction on your part.

■ STUDENT PRESENTATION FORMATS

Employers place a high premium on communication skills, and many complain that new college-graduate employees are weak in these skills. To address this problem, faculty have integrated student presentations into many of their courses. Formal presentations are not in themselves experiential, except to the extent that students learn all the preparation, platform skills, and rehearsal that go into a good presentation. However, oral communication takes many forms, and the activities described in this section give students public speaking opportunities within experiential learning contexts. As such, they add reality and pizzazz to student presentations. In addition, most of them give students experience in conducting research on a topic, controversy, position, person, role, or school of thought.

Variations on Debate

Every field has topics amenable to a two-sided (at least) fact-based argument. A debate format can be as simple as statements of the affirmative and the negative, plus rebuttals, each with a strict time limit. But the variations below foster deeper student learning and critical thinking. To obtain the best results, you may have to teach your students rhetorical structure, the basic rules of evidence, and common logical fallacies before having them debate.

In a *change-your-mind debate*, you designate different sides of the classroom as "for the affirmative" or "for the negative," with the middle as "uncertain/undecided/neutral." Before the debate, students sit in the area representing their current position and can change their seating location during the debate as their opinions sway. After the debate, lead a debriefing discussion focusing on the opinion changers ("What changed your mind?") and the undecided students, who are likely to provide the most objective analysis of both the debate and the issue at hand.

In *point-counterpoint* (Silberman, 1994), you divide your class into groups—as many groups as there are positions on an issue—and tell each group to come up with arguments in favor of its assigned position. Select one student to launch the debate by presenting one argument for his group's stance; then call on each group in turn to give a different argument or counterargument. Conclude with a class discussion comparing the various positions.

Yet another variant is *structured controversy* or *academic controversy*, in which two pairs in a group of four students formally debate each other on an issue, then switch sides, and finally synthesize a joint position (Johnson, Johnson, & Smith, 1991). Done properly, this activity requires that students conduct considerable outside research and write a final report.

One final version is to randomly assign students to one position on a controversial issue, which will compel some of them to argue against their own.

Along with the debate, each student writes a reflection paper on the strengths and weaknesses of both positions and, after the debate, another paper evaluating how well her group and the opposing group applied the course material and additional literature in arguing their position. Students can clearly see and assess both sides (Chrisler, 2013).

When students have to research and debate a position counter to their own, their minds open to both their own biases and the other side of the issue; sometimes they even change to that of other side. In addition, they realize the key role of understanding in civil discourse (Budesheim & Lundquist, 2000; Chrisler, 2013; Trujillo-Jenks & Rosen, 2015).

Panel Discussion, Symposium, and Town Meeting

In a *panel discussion*, four or five students briefly present different points of view on a topic, usually representing authorities or historical figures—for example, Freud, Jung, Adler, Skinner, and Rogers in a psychology course; Franklin, Jefferson, Burr, Madison, and Washington in an early American history course; or Swift, Wordsworth, Coleridge, Burns, and Fielding in an 18th-century English literature course. Then the class addresses thoughtful questions and challenges, preferably prepared in advance, to the various panel members.

The *symposium* is a similar format, often used in advanced seminars, where individual students or teams present their independently conducted research papers that express their own ideas. The rest of the class asks probing questions and offers constructive criticism, which is especially useful if students revise their work. In addition, you may assign one or two discussants to interrelate and critique the papers for each class period. Discussants should have at least a couple of days to review the symposium products in advance.

You can also make the entire class into a panel by calling a *town meeting* on a multisided issue or complex case (Silberman, 1994). After doing some outside research on the issue or situation, students prepare to voice their views within a time limit you set, following the format that each speaker calls on the next speaker.

Press Conference

You or a student assumes the focal role, posing as a noted scholar, a leader in some realm, or a representative of a particular position or school of thought, while the rest of the class plays investigative reporters, each student or small group with an assigned audience or readership, such as local residents, residents of another area or country, a special interest group, a specific company, or some public agency. These reporter students ask probing, challenging questions of the focal person.

Two planning caveats are in order. First, the focal role should represent a broad-ranging, controversial decision or stance. Defining such a role is easy in political science, history, or philosophy, but in other fields, it requires more creative thought. In psychology or sociology, for example, the focal role may be a criminologist or criminal psychologist whose testimony leads to the probation of a violent convict. In economics, the focal role may advocate an uncertain or risky intervention strategy. In the sciences and medical fields, it may stand for a controversial environmental or public health position—perhaps on global warming, endangered species preservation, genetically engineered cattle, prescription drug restrictions, human cloning, or the like. Second, in addition to assigning audiences or readerships to the students playing reporters, you can require them to research and write out their questions and challenges in advance. Having them then write a mock article incorporating the press conference is an excellent optional follow-up assignment.

You need not confine the activity to one focal person. You can have a succession of them with different viewpoints and perspectives.

■ ROLE PLAYING

You assign students roles in a true-to-life, problematic social or interpersonal situation that they act out, improvising the script. The situation must incorporate potential conflict between the roles and some need

for the players to reach a resolution (Halpern & Associates, 1994). When one player is not supposed to know the full story about another player's intentions, problem, or goals, you should provide written descriptions for each role for the players to review in private. You also must decide what information to give to the rest of the class. Following the enactment, you lead a debriefing discussion. You should ask the players how they felt in their role at crucial junctures and what intentions and interests motivated their actions and ask the rest of the students what behavioral patterns they observed and how these behaviors reflected concepts and principles addressed in the course.

While role playing relies on make-believe, however realistic, scenarios in the classroom, students learn experientially by identifying with the roles they play and observe. This technique is used successfully in both therapy and instruction, especially in the humanities, social sciences, counseling, clinical psychology, and nursing. In political science or history, students can take the identity of key leaders or decision makers with conflicting goals or the role of collective constituencies that face an important task. You may also play a role, especially when you want to model certain behaviors, such as how to conduct a family therapy session, negotiate a contract, mediate conflict, or open a formal meeting.

Here are some examples of role plays to inspire your own ideas:

- A professional (doctor, lawyer, or clergy, for example) and client disagree over an approach to the client's problem.
- An executive promises a financially pinched union negotiator (or up-start worker) a major promotion and salary increase for keeping quiet about an impending plant closing, a behind-the-scenes corporate takeover, future layoffs, or planned benefit cuts.
- Worker representatives try to convince executives not to close an unprofitable plant.
- A human resource executive must make a tough hiring decision among various male, female, minority, and nonminority candidates with different job qualifications and personalities.

- An instructor has to decide what to do in response to one or more students complaining about a grade, a course policy, an assignment, or their team's dysfunctional dynamics.
- A politician experiences role and ethical conflict between partisan and administrative roles or between ideological stance and the need for campaign funds.
- A couple or family argues over money, (un)employment, discipline of the children, authority, autonomy, communication, moving, in-laws, domestic violence, or alcohol or drug use. This scenario may spotlight the roles of social worker, physician, clergy, law enforcer, lawyer, or therapist.

If you teach a foreign language, feel free to make a role play of any situation your students might encounter while traveling, and it need not be contentious. While students may not learn much through empathy, they will get useful conversational practice in the target language. If you teach literature, consider casting students in the roles of the characters and letting them play out a hypothetical scene that extends the piece of literature. In other fields, search out case studies that you can adapt to role playing.

The higher percentage of the class involved in a role play, the more the activity takes on the characteristics of a simulation.

■ SIMULATIONS AND GAMES

Simulations and games share the prospect of winning something desirable: money, power, territory, profits, being correct, doing the job well, getting one's way, or simply a sense of satisfaction. But the biggest win is in learning. Simulations and games can bring the course material to life and emotionally engage an entire class as few other methods can.

Games

Many academic games are modeled on traditional games, such as Bingo and Go Fish, and classic television game shows, such as *Jeopardy, Family Feud, Wheel of Fortune, Password,* and *Who Wants to Be a Millionaire?* Recently some faculty have adapted *Survivor* to subjects as disparate as physiology (Howard et al., 2002) and music theory (Berry, 2008). The questions and answers come from the course material and can easily capture knowledge, comprehension, and application levels of thinking, if not higher. Games provide an effective and painless, even fun, review format (Kaupins, 2005; Moy, Rodenbaugh, Collins, & DiCarlo, 2000), and in this context, students can sometimes submit the questions and even run the game.

Games can also supply a format for almost every class period. After opening her music theory classes with a minilecture, Berry (2008) assigns "tribes" of students their "challenge" for that day, such as a timed workbook exercise on the minilecture topic. The tribe members correct their work and tally their individual and tribal scores with the goal to get the highest possible. Personal pride and peer pressure motivate individual achievement, even though the tribes don't vote off the lowest-scoring member.

A new category of games, called *serious* or *educational*, is gaining in popularity. You can find an assortment at http://edugamesresearch.com/ and http://teachingnaked.com/games/; some are free. Free history games are available at http://playinghistory.org/ for many educational levels, including college. If you teach biology, medicine, or nursing, you can find free serious games at http://www.nobelprize.org/educational/. Your best source of information on educational games, particularly those available online, is Bowen (2012). Serious games enthusiasts even have their own annual award competitions, the Games for Change Festival and the Serious Games Showcase and Challenge. In 2014, the latter honored National Geographic's game, The Underground Railroad: Journey to Freedom, and the University of Washington's Nanocrafter. However, these games are pitched more to middle and high school students than to postsecondary. Thus far, few college-level computer-based games have been produced, and none has become a phenomenon, with the possible exception of Reacting to the Past, which is not exactly a game.

Reacting to the Past

In the mid-1990s, Barnard College history professor Mark C. Carnes started conducting his classes around a game he called Reacting to the Past, but it has the realism of a simulation. Students assume the identity of historical figures and write papers and make oral presentations that reflect their figure's beliefs, values, and ideas. In addition, they strategize ways to win the game. Winning entails persuading uncommitted parties to one's side while operating within the given historical and social context. Therefore, Socrates may be acquitted, and Louis XVI may retain power after the French Revolution. A student game book supplies all the essential historical background and rules information, as well as primary source readings. Students learn history because the game accurately incorporates the cultural, sociological, economic, political, and technological contexts of the period and place under study. However, even though they learn the actual history, they can play history differently than the actual figures did and generate different historical outcomes.

As the instructor, you have your own manual and role as gamemaster. You have to dedicate a sufficient number of class periods, most commonly from 8 to 12, for the game and set it up. But then students pretty much run the game on their own. In fact, Reacting is famous for motivating tremendous engagement, effort, and research on their part.

Reacting has spawned a cottage industry of conferences and workshops (see http://reacting. barnard.edu/conferences-events), publications (listed at http://reacting.barnard.edu/node/3034), social media sites (access at http://reacting.barnard.edu/ instructors), and Reacting games. Ten games have been published by W. W. Norton & Company (listed at http://reacting.barnard.edu/curriculum/ published-games), about as many are under review (listed at http://reacting.barnard.edu/curriculum/ games-in-development), and dozens more have

been developed and used by faculty at over 300 North American institutions (listed at https:// docs.google.com/spreadsheet/pub?key=0AslH quj5C_74dHZoX3MycjBzbzdtam80WWxJS 0JMYUE&output=html). Carnes (2014) draws on these resources as he outlines the history of Reacting and amasses evidence of its teaching effectiveness. If you want to incorporate the game into your own history, political science, political sociology, or area courses, do read his book first.

Simulations

By abstracting key elements from reality, simulations allow students to live out the hypotheses and implications of theories, giving them intense emotional, cognitive, and behavioral experiences that they will otherwise never have. This method developed a strong faculty and student following during the 1970s and the early 1980s around a growing market of simulations of societies, formal organizations, corporations, markets, urban areas, cultures, world politics, and other complex macrosocial realms. These were strictly face-to-face enactments of hypothetical social situations, unmediated by computers, some requiring many hours and an array of supporting materials. Some of the early simulations that have endured are Barnga and Bafa' Bafa, both of which sensitize students to cultural differences and clashes.

Among these early simulations was a variant called a *frame simulation*. It offers instructors different scenarios or settings to choose from or to develop on their own. Some are now on interactive computer sites and still serve an important instructional purpose. For example, students can play the Prisoner's Dilemma under various conditions and payoff rules that illustrate different psychological and sociological principles (http://serendip.bryn mawr.edu/playground/pd.html). Another frame simulation, structured like a mock trial, comes with a free suite of actual cases relevant to several disciplines (http://www.streetlaw.org/en/Page/63/ Civil_mock_trials). In fact, frame simulations can revolve around any decision-making body: a court, a board of directors, a review board, a legislature, or an administrative agency (Hertel & Millis, 2002). In large classes, some may work best as role plays.

Computers ushered in an expanded selection of products available on the web or in software packages. They range from individual tutorial programs (computer-assisted instruction) to full-blown multimedia simulations. Among the latter are history and political science simulations on the Civil War and World War I at http://www.historysimulation.com and highlights of American history through the Vietnam War at http://caho-test.cc.columbia.edu/main/sim/index.html. Many more options in the social sciences are available at http://teachinghistory.org/teaching-materials/ask-a-master-teacher/23691 and http://fod.msu.edu/oir/simulations-and-serious-gaming-resources-design-and-use-higher-education-classroom.

The field of business may have the most simulations, and they tend to be marketed under straightforward titles such as Airline, Corporation, Supply Chain, Manager, Marketer, Human Resource Management, Collective Bargaining Simulated, and Entrepreneur. Several companies produce and sell computerized business simulations (e.g., http://goventureceo.com/, http://www.bsg-online.com/, http://www.capsim.com/), as does Harvard Business School Publishing (http://hbsp.harvard.edu/list/simulations/). For the economy-minded, BusSim offers free web-based simulations for introductory courses in business, marketing, operations, finance, human resources, and enterprise (http://bussim.org/).

The sciences and engineering also have simulations, enhanced by animation and interactivity. Among these are hundreds of virtual laboratories allowing students to conduct experiments and manipulate parameters in ways that would be too dangerous or too costly in real life. In hydraulics, for instance, students can solve complex canalization problems by varying the delivery, inflow, outflow, and power of various pumps. In electrical engineering, they can manipulate the performance of an electrical network and study overloading, breaks, and the like. You will find the URLs for free simulations listed in chapter 19. In the health sciences, faculty can program SimMan and other medical software to simulate specific diagnostic situations. To obtain data for diagnosing the symptoms, students can even ask questions of the hypothetical patient and get answers, as well as run hypothetical tests.

Simulations are not just for young students. They are mainstays of adult education and job training. The military runs battle simulations, hospitals and emergency response agencies hold disaster preparedness simulations, and companies use them to teach their employees new skills.

Running Games and Simulations

A game or simulation and its debriefing take a good deal of class time—at least an hour for the very simplest. In addition, to grab your students' full attention, you should assess them on the quality of their strategy. Here is the conventional wisdom for running simulations. First and foremost, be prepared. Read the instructor's manual or directions at least twice at a leisurely pace well in advance. Mark the directions you will give students at each stage of the game or simulation. In general, it's best not to give all the instructions at the beginning because too much information will confuse students. Rather, parcel them out. List your preclass setup tasks. Know the sequence of events and the schedule of distributing artifacts and materials, but don't hesitate to refer to the manual. Finally, to grab your students' full attention, you should inform them that you will assess them on the quality of their strategy.

Most facilitators run games and simulations at too slow a pace. The challenge is to keep the experience moving, even if the tempo puts pressure on the students. They need a long enough time to realize the constraints, costs, and benefits of their decision-making options, but not necessarily long enough to answer every question that arises, come to a full consensus, or feel completely comfortable with their decisions. After all, a game, and especially a simulation, must imitate life as much as possible. (For more detailed advice, see Hertel & Millis, 2002.)

Debriefing Simulations and Substantive Games

The debriefing process is an essential component of a simulation or a substantive game. It disengages students from the emotional aspects of the experience and settles them back into the classroom reality, allowing them to transform what they experienced into meaningful learning. They should be able to identify the disciplinary concepts and principles illustrated in the simulation and game and assess their own decision-making abilities. In addition, a debriefing brings out the disparate perceptions, feelings, and experiences each player had (Hertel & Millis, 2002).

So important is the debriefing that you should prepare the questions in advance. They should progress through three phases (Hertel & Millis, 2002). First, ask students to recount their experience and their feelings about it. A successful simulation or game may evoke some pretty strong emotions, both negative and positive. Second, have them explain their actions within the context of their roles, specifically their intentions and motivations behind their decisions. If different roles had different information, students can reveal what they knew and didn't know, what their goals were, and what strategy they had for attaining them. Finally, return students to their true role as learners with questions about the connection between their simulated experiences and the concepts, principles, theories, and hypotheses they have studied in your course. Help them translate the concrete into the abstract and derive generalizations related to the subject matter.

Resources for Simulations and Games

You can find games and simulations as well as ways to maximize their instructional value in these journals and books:

- *Decision Sciences: Journal of Innovative Education* published by the Decision Sciences Institute (economics and business disciplines). Available free online at www3.interscience.wiley.com/journal/118499600/home

- *The International Simulation and Gaming Research Yearbook* published by the Society for Academic Gaming and Simulation in Education and Training as the proceedings of the society's annual conference. See http://gamesbs.com/229594–11846801–0749433973-The_International_Simulation_Gaming_Research_Yearbook_International_Simulation_and_Gaming_Research_Yearbook.html

- *Simulation & Gaming: An Interdisciplinary Journal of Theory, Practice and Research,* published bimonthly by an international consortium of professional associations, including the Association for Business Simulation and Experiential Learning. See http://sag.sagepub.com/

- Squire, K. (2011). *Video games and learning: Teaching and participatory culture in the digital age.* New York, NY: Teachers College Press. Providing an easy-to-read introduction to educational games, Squire recounts how he uses the complex game Civilization to induce many layers of learning in his students.

- Steinkuehler, C. Squire, K., & Barab, S. (Eds.). (2012). *Games, learning, and society: Learning and meaning in the digital age.* Cambridge, UK: Cambridge University Press. Leading game designers and scholars review the research on learning through games.

- Whitton, N. (2014). *Digital games and learning: Research and theory.* London, UK: Routledge. Whitton links game design to learning research and analyzes the range of genres and forms that games take: explorable worlds, motivations tools, experimental spaces, and learning technologies.

If you choose to design your own simulation or substantive game, follow Hertel and Millis's (2002) advice to keep in mind your learning outcomes, the number of hours you have available, and the number of students you want to involve. First, look for the real-life or realistic scenarios to structure your simulation or game around. Good sources are case studies, textbooks, journals, magazines, newspapers, and your personal experience. Next, develop your characters and the interests they will pursue, ensuring conflict or competition among your primary roles. Then fill out the situation with secondary and supporting roles, which the primary characters may use to further their interests. Be sure that none of the acting roles know too much. They have to be challenged and allowed to make bad decisions, even to fail. Finally, select the geographical setting, write the necessary documents, and develop the instructions, action constraints, and procedural rules (Hertel & Millis, 2002). Further help is available at http://fod.msu.edu/oir/simulations-and-serious-gaming-resources-design-and-use-higher-education-classroom.

■ SERVICE-LEARNING AND CIVIC ENGAGEMENT: THE REAL THING

Service-learning, sometimes called *community engagement*, is a method by which students acquire various skills and knowledge while working in community service. The more recently coined term, *civic engagement*, applies when students render service to governmental or civic institutions (e.g., registering people to vote and improving public buildings). Primary and secondary schools gave many of our younger students experience in both forms of service.

Service-learning and civic engagement represent classic learning by doing, and nothing teaches experientially like direct experience. If you want students to understand the characters in a piece of modern literature, let them interview the human counterparts. If you want them to comprehend the dynamics of poverty, let them work with the poor and the homeless. If you want them to appreciate the problems and crises of other countries, let them help émigrés and refugees. If you want them to understand prisoners, children, or any other group, let them spend productive time with some of these people.

According to instructors and "graduates," service-learning is almost uniformly a positive, life-changing experience for students—the kind they never forget. It teaches not just in the abstract

but in a concrete, real-world context. Most faculty also find it effective in meeting certain course objectives. Because the experience often stimulates emotions, it helps students progress toward achieving certain affective, social, and ethical learning outcomes, as well as higher-order cognitive outcomes. In addition, the emotions themselves strongly enhance learning and memory (see chapter 1).

Campus Compact, an organization that promotes and provides information on service-learning and civic engagement, reports that its membership numbers more than 1,100 postsecondary institution of all types, representing over a quarter of all colleges and universities, and has been growing by an average of 70 campuses per year over the past 5 years (Campus Compact, 2014). Almost all (96 percent) of these institutions have set up at least one office devoted to community and civic engagement, and more than 60 percent have two or three such offices (Campus Compact, 2012). These units furnish interested faculty with information and funding and coordinate the services to balance them across clients (outside organizations and agencies receiving services). However, only a sliver of the faculty, about 7 percent, teach service-learning courses (Campus Compact, 2012), probably because community or civic engagement takes a great deal of time to implement (see the next section) and bears little relationship to the content of most courses.

Being the older and more general method, service-learning has been studied extensively for its effects on students. Research conducted some years ago found that it enhances the following (Astin, Vogelgesang, Ikeda, & Yee, 2000; Eyler, Giles, & Gray, 1999):

- Students' personal development (sense of identity and efficacy, spiritual and moral growth)
- Students' social and interpersonal development (leadership, communication, ability to work with others)
- Students' cultural and racial understanding
- Students' sense of civic responsibility, citizenship skills, and societal effectiveness

- Students' commitment to service in their career choice and future voluntary activities
- Students' relationships with faculty
- Students' satisfaction with college and likelihood of graduation
- Relations between the institution and the community
- In many studies, students' academic learning and abilities on some dimensions: writing skills, the ability to apply knowledge to the real world, complexity of understanding, problem analysis, critical thinking, and cognitive development (but no clear effect on grades, grade point average, or later standardized test scores)

Another national study (Gray, Ondaatje, Fricker, & Geschwind, 2000; Gray, Ondaatje, & Zakaras, 1999) found more mixed effects. On the positive side, students in service-learning courses were indeed more satisfied with their courses than were students in non-service-learning courses. In the same comparison, students perceived that their service-learning experience slightly enhanced their civic engagement, their interpersonal skills, and their understanding of people of different backgrounds from their own. However, they reported no effect on their academic skills (writing, analytical, quantitative, or knowledge) or their professional skills (confidence in their choice of major and career, expectation of graduation, or career preparation). In fact, students who opted out of service-learning felt that they *did* advance their academic and professional skills.

In a more recent, small-scale study, students who opted for a service-learning experience in a rehabilitation services course scored no higher on the objective tests of medical facts and procedures but did perform better on the cases studies requiring an assessment of the services being given than the students who didn't (Mpofu, 2007).

According to a meta-analysis of the best-designed studies, service-learning has a moderate, statistically significant impact on students' understanding of the course material, their ability to

transfer course content and skills to different settings, and their capacity to reframe complex social issues, which requires critical thinking (Novak, Markey, & Allen, 2007). In summary, then, service-learning provides some modest academic benefits, as well as some social and affective ones.

How positive the service-learning experience is depends on several factors. The single most powerful determinant is a student's degree of interest in the subject matter before the experience. Therefore, service-learning is best reserved for upper-level courses in a major (Astin et al., 2000). Other known influences are under the instructor's control: how much students can share and discuss their experiences in class; how much training they have for the experience; how many hours per week they perform service; how well tied the experience is to the course content; and how much written and oral reflection students are asked to do, especially in tying the experience back to the course content (Astin et al., 2000; Gray et al., 1999, 2000; Zlotkowski, 1998). Fewer than 20 hours of service dulls its impact (Gray et al., 2000).

Implementing Service-Learning or Civic Engagement

Is service-learning or civic engagement right for your courses? First, examine your learning outcomes. These methods merit consideration if you have outcomes that are affective, ethical, or social beyond working effectively in a group, or if your cognitive outcomes are served by students' practicing on an outside clientele. If either of these is true, try to identify community needs that truly complement your subject matter. For example, if you teach children's literature and want your students to be able to critique works from a child's point of view, then their reading books to children makes sense. If you teach public relations, having your students conduct a PR campaign for a local nonprofit organization clearly benefits their learning. If you teach public health or community nursing, your students can better master the subject matter if they plan and implement a community health or health education effort. If you teach political science, consider a civic engagement project where your students learn how to navigate the politics at the various levels of government by conducting partnership projects in your course (Redlawsk, Rice, & Associates, 2009).

Second, be aware of the ethical questions that some engagement experiences raise, even though requiring them is legal. If the experience involves working for social change, is it appropriate to require students to do this, no matter how they feel about the changes aimed for? Should they have to give service even if their current politics and ethics don't warrant it? Will they be placed in physical danger?

Third, consider your time constraints and commitment. Service-learning and civic engagement require more planning and coordination than most other methods, especially your first foray into this area, and you should start laying the groundwork at least a few months in advance. Before you contact any agency, consult with the community and civic engagement office. It already has ties with local organizations and can recommend appropriate clients that need and want students' help. This unit may also save you time by contacting potential clients. If your campus doesn't have an engagement or volunteer office, start contacting local agencies, such as schools, medical and mental health facilities, social service agencies, and the local United Way. Then schedule a face-to-face meeting with the key contact person to find out about the organization's needs and expectations and to explain your own ideas for your course. Ensure that the agency will orient and supervise your students. Alternatively, have students find their own agency and work out the project details.

Then start making course design decisions. Will the service-learning or civic engagement be required, optional, or extra credit? Will you offer an alternative assignment? How many hours will be required? How much will it count toward students' final grade? What will be the requirements of the service-learning experience? How will you assess and grade it? How will you link the service

to the course content? When will you have students discuss their experiences? What writing tasks will you assign for reflection? (It is best to have multiple reflection assignments.) How will you grade these reflection assignments? This information will be needed for your syllabus. What previous course components will be eliminated to make time for engagement activities?

Finally, make the necessary logistical arrangements: getting help with liability issues from your institution's risk management office (such as release forms); creating student teams if appropriate (highly advisable to mitigate any physical danger); helping students and the agency coordinate schedules; ensuring students are oriented and supervised at the agency; arranging for student transportation, even if just car pools; and devising a system to monitor students' hours of service.

Two journals and several books offer additional guidance for instructors and a wealth of ideas for solid engagement projects, including exemplars:

- *Journal of Higher Education Outreach and Engagement,* an open access journal available at http://openjournals.libs.uga.edu/index.php/jheoe/
- *Michigan Journal of Community Service-Learning,* issues available for purchase at http://ginsberg.umich.edu/mjcsl/
- Campus Compact. (2003). *Introduction to service-learning toolkit: Readings and resources for faculty* (2nd ed.). Boston, MA: Author. Strong on learning theory, teaching strategies, and practical advice in implementing the method.
- Clayton, P. H., Bringle, R. G., & Hatcher, J. A. (Eds.). (2013). *Research on service-learning: Conceptual frameworks and assessment, Vol. 2A: Students and faculty.* Sterling, VA: Stylus. Rich on the research on both students and faculty.
- Howard, K. (2013–2014). *Community-based learning at Centre College: Faculty handbook.* Centre College Center for Teaching and Learning. Available at http://ctl.centre.edu/assests/cblhand

book.pdf. Essential (and free) for an instructor incorporating service-learning for the first time. Has links to syllabi of service-learning courses in many disciplines and practical how-to tips.

- Zlotkowski, E. (Ed.). (1998). *Successful service-learning programs: New models of excellence in higher education.* San Francisco, CA: Jossey-Bass. Detailed descriptions of strong service-learning courses.

In addition, you can go to www.youtube.com, put "community-based learning" into the search box, and watch dozens of examples of the method in action.

■ MAXIMIZING THE VALUE OF EXPERIENTIAL LEARNING

While student presentation formats don't call for debriefing and reflection, the more engrossing and impactful forms of experiential learning definitely do. This chapter already recommended debriefing discussions after role plays, simulations, and community and civic engagement experiences. But discussions alone may not ensure students get maximum mileage out of the experience. Substantial role plays, games, simulations, and engagement activities deserve some kind of written reflection to give students the time and emotional distance they need to glean additional insights. In fact, service-learning without reflection is merely service.

Do supply students with direction to ensure their thinking doesn't dissolve into a stream of consciousness. Guide students toward developing their metacognitive and meta-emotional awareness and control—that is, their self-regulated learning skills (Nilson, 2013a). So what questions might you ask them to answer? After a role play, game, or simulation, any of these probes may be appropriate:

- What were your goals, and how did they change during the experience?

- How did you change your strategies during the experience? How did you use feedback from the simulation or game and other players?
- How did your emotions change during the experience? How did you overcome discouragement, fatigue, and any other emotional barrier?
- If students solved a problem: How did you arrive at your best solution? What was your reasoning in defining the problem, deciding what principles and concepts to apply to it, developing alternative solutions, assessing their relative worth, and determining the best one?
- Evaluate your goal achievement, strategies, problem-solving decisions, and overall performance.
- Why was this experience valuable? What did it teach you? What skills did it develop? How did it help you progress toward achieving any of the course learning outcomes?

After a service-learning or civic engagement experience, pose questions like these:

- What are the links between your experience and the outcomes and content of the course?
- What feedback did you receive from the people and the agency you served, and how did you use it?
- What academic and personal value did the experience have for you? What did you learn from it? What intellectual and personal strengths and weaknesses did it reveal in you?
- What skills did you gain or improve? When do you think these skills will prove useful in the future?
- How would you assess the value of your contribution?
- What would you do differently if you could?

Chapter 20 explores self-regulated learning in detail, but it merits mention here because it truly transforms engaging experiential learning activities from just experience into learning.

CHAPTER 15

Managing Productive Groups

In learning as in business, two heads are better than one, three heads are better than two, and for some tasks, four, five, or even more heads are best. When we put students in pairs or small groups to hash out an issue or solve a problem, we are conveying the underlying message that people working together with a cooperative ethos can accomplish much more than they can as individuals working apart. We are also implying that students are responsible for their own learning and socially constructing their knowledge. Learning is not listening to some expert's words. Our role transforms from an all-knowing authority figure to facilitator, coach, and consultant who unobtrusively circulates, observes, monitors, and answers questions (Millis, 1990). Group work also says a lot about a seismic shift in higher education's mission. No longer is it focused on sorting, classifying, and screening out students. Its primary goal now is to educate them—all of them.

A GROUP BY ANY OTHER NAME ...

This teaching method has become popular enough to take on multiple labels. These days, the most commonly used terms are simply *group work* and *group learning*. Most of the research conducted on it in the 1980s and 1990s relied on the term *cooperative learning* (Millis & Cottell, 1998), defined as a structured teaching method where small student groups work together on a common task. The name *collaborative learning* emerged in the 1990s as the one favored in the sciences and engineering. Following Mazur's (1997) lead, these disciplines have also used the terms *peer instruction* and *peer tutoring* when referring to student pairs or small groups in class explaining their answers to multiple-choice items to one another. Now the label *collaborative* has largely replaced *cooperative* across the disciplines. However, not everyone sees these terms as referring to the same thing. Some (e.g., Davidson & Major, 2014) view *cooperative* learning groups as more structured than *collaborative* ones.

However, there is a much more structured version of group work known as *team-based learning.* It builds in mutual, positive interdependence and individual accountability more than any other version. To ensure preparation for class, students take team as well as individual tests, and both may count equally toward their grade (Michaelsen, 1997–1998; Michaelsen, Knight, & Fink, 2004; Sibley & Ostafichuk, 2014; Sweet & Michaelsen, 2012). Team-based learning is so distinctive that it merits its own section in this chapter.

Because the terms *group work* and *group learning* are so commonly used, they are the choices here. The terms *group* and *team* will be used interchangeably except when describing *team-based learning.*

■ THE CASE FOR GROUP LEARNING

The evidence supporting the effectiveness of group over individual learning is so overwhelming that I can cite several meta-analyses. Among the earliest was Johnson, Johnson, and Smith's literature review (1991), which reported that most of the hundreds of studies published to that point found that cooperative learning was superior to competitive and individual approaches to teaching, and the other studies found no detrimental effects to using groups.

However, group learning had a slow start in higher education. Faculty hadn't learned that way, and, because they had no trouble learning individually, it was hard for them to understand why their students would. Faculty also had to relinquish the control and the center stage of the classroom, not a satisfying prospect for comfortable, committed lecturers. Besides, the method hailed from the distant K–12 world.

The research on the effects of group learning has focused on several variables—achievement/productivity (learning), positive attitudes and ethics, the quality of interpersonal relationships, and psychological health—and group work enhances all of them

for students at all educational levels and of all backgrounds (Johnson & Johnson, 1989, 1994; Johnson, Johnson, & Smith, 1991, 2014; Pascarella & Terenzini, 2005; Romero, 2009; Springer, Stanne, & Donovan, 1999). Light (1990, 1992) reported similar results for out-of-class study groups in the Harvard Assessment Seminars. According to Hattie's (2009) mega-meta-analysis of over 800 meta-analyses on the effects of various teaching and learning strategies on student achievement, group work has an effect size of .59—that is, a one standard deviation increase in group learning experiences leads to just under three-fifths of a standard deviation increase in learning.

Not that groups should supplant whole-class discussion, experiential learning, and every other method. Rather, group work is a supplementary technique suitable for various classroom activities (Millis, 1990), from interactive lecture breaks (see chapter 12) to problem-based learning (see chapter 18) to inquiry-guided STEM activities (see chapter 19). And it needn't be used all the time to boost student achievement. Nor should it. Students have to acquire and practice some skills on their own as individuals. Reading, writing, and speaking, for instance, are individual skills and responsibilities. However, peer feedback, especially on written work, can be very valuable (see chapter 24).

■ CAUTIONS ABOUT GROUP LEARNING

A few caveats are in order. Study groups may not always enhance learning. Arum and Roksa (2011) found that these groups didn't unless they were organized and monitored by a campus learning-assistance unit. In addition, group learning relies on the brighter students to teach the slower ones. While a person usually learns a subject most thoroughly by teaching it, many talented students learn very effectively on their own and benefit little from the reinforcement of teaching it. Furthermore, the time that the brighter students spend tutoring their classmates is time that they are not getting additional challenges and acquiring more advanced knowledge and skills. In addition, the weaker students in a group may freeload off the stronger ones. Moreover, the latter students so desperately want to get an A in the course that they often take over and do all the work. No wonder gifted students often resist group learning. It clearly benefits average students, but at some cost to the talented ones.

Another concern is students' lack of maturity and understanding of group member responsibilities. Although most younger students have been learning in groups all through school, we should not expect them to monitor and sanction each other for poor team behavior. In fact, some faculty perceive that students have become so close over their school years that they hesitate to evaluate each other's group contributions and performance honestly. Frequently they cover up for social loafers and refuse to sanction them, showing more loyalty to their peers than to learning. Students didn't always do this; early studies found that group members punished their dysfunctional peers (Ferris & Hess, 1984; Jalajas & Sutton, 1984; Murrell, 1984). But now students expect *you* as the instructor to know about the freeloaders and administer justice by giving different individual grades on the group product, even if you have explained that their grades will depend solely on quality of the group product (Jassawalla, Malshe, & Sashittal, 2008). Their expectations no doubt reflect their many years in K–12 group work, where teachers handed down the rules of engagement and intervened when violations occurred, so they come to college ill prepared and ill trained for adult-level team dynamics. We have to dispel them of their immature view of group work and teach them to bear collective responsibilities (Jassawalla et al., 2008).

In addition, your students may know very little about group dynamics, including the typical stages of team development—forming, storming, norming, and performing (Tuckman, 1965). If you are putting students in long-term, stable groups, they need to know these stages, especially the fact that storming is normal and not symptomatic of team breakdown. Teach them some basic principles of group dynamics,

like communication patterns. Draw a few simple graphics on the board with circles standing for individuals and arrows designating the direction of communication. Show your students one-way and two-way (double-arrow) communication between two individuals, then a group with leader-directed communication (all one-way), and a group with balanced communication (arrows connecting multiple individuals). Finally, have your students sketch the patterns of some of the group communication patterns they have experienced and consider how these patterns affected their participation. Ask them to share their drawings and participation experiences with the class or in their groups. This exercise should sensitize them to the benefits of balanced communication (Kustra & Potter, 2008).

To give your students a crash course in group dynamics as well as the wisdom and the tools to collaborate successfully, refer them to Kennedy and Nilson's (2008) free online book, *Successful Strategies for Team* (http://www.clemson.edu/OTEI/documents/teamwork-handbook.pdf). It is written simply and is colorfully illustrated for undergraduates.

Setting up and managing group learning may be the most challenging method you ever use, so start small. Begin with in-class ad hoc groups (also called informal groups; see the next section) doing a small-scale, pretested technique, like those in the "Tried-and-True In-Class Group Activities" section below, perhaps in an optional help or review session. It may not work perfectly (any strategy can fall short the first time tried) and your time estimate may be off one way or another (Johnson et al., 1991; Millis, 1990). In addition, sell group work to your class by explaining that decades of research document its superior effectiveness.

■ MANAGING AND TROUBLESHOOTING IN-CLASS AD HOC GROUPS

These groups present fewer management challenges than formal, long-term, project-based groups and entail virtually no setup because students work with one to three peers sitting close to them in the classroom. Many lecture break activities rely on them unless you have formal, long-term groups sit together in class. Still, the success of these groups depends on your following these guidelines:

1. *Give groups a specific, structured task with an end product* (problem solution, a list of ideas, or a group test answer sheet) to prevent any confusion. It may be a written product as informal as handwritten notes, in which case you randomly cold-call on groups to report out. Or it may be a group-signed and -submitted document, which you can use to take attendance or to give group members a point.

2. *Make the task more challenging than what you would give an individual student.* It should go beyond what students have learned and require group synergy to complete.

3. *Give the task a tight time limit to keep groups focused*—just enough time for an on-task group to finish. Bring a timer or stopwatch with you to class.

4. *Cold-call on individual group members randomly to report out, or have groups assign a recorder or a spokesperson.* The first time you do the latter, tell students to point to one fellow member on the count of three. Then assign the student receiving the most points the task of appointing the recorder/spokesperson. The element of surprise adds humor to the moment.

5. *Change the composition of the groups two or more times during the term* so diligent students aren't stuck with slackers the whole term. You might have a seating chart, which you can use for taking attendance and learning names, and rearranging seating.

6. *Set the rule of "three before me"*—that is, insist that students ask at least three other students their questions before they ask you; accept only group questions.

7. *Control noise levels by setting rules* such as "no unnecessary talking" and "only one group member talking at one time." Another helpful hint

(mentioned in chapter 12) is to bring the class to silence by informing students that you will signal when time is up by raising your hand. They should then stop talking and raise their hands as soon as they see yours up. This technique enables you to silence a large lecture hall in seconds.

Tried-and-True In-Class Group Activities

This sampler of proven, safe group activities comes from Barkley et al. (2014), Johnson et al. (1991), Michaelsen (1997–1998), Millis (1990), and Millis and Cottell (1998), and these sources offer still more options. Many of these activities work well as student-active lecture breaks (see chapter 12), and some double as classroom assessment techniques (see chapter 24). Although a few may sound adolescent, all have been used effectively at the postsecondary level.

Think–Pair–Share

Give students a question or problem, and ask them to think quietly of an answer or solution. Have them discuss their responses with their neighbor and then share them with the class. You can also set the requirement that they come to a consensus or submit one piece of written work as a pair. Set a time limit of 1 or 2 minutes for the pair exchange. You can extend this format by having each pair in agreement join another pair in agreement to come to a consensus together.

Pairs Check

Partners coach each other on worksheet problems or check their class or reading notes for completeness and accuracy. This 2-minute activity is similar to the lecture break "pair and compare" in chapter 12.

TAPPS (Talking Aloud Paired Problem Solving)

Pairs of students solve a problem or resolve a case by taking turns playing different roles—one that talks through the process of reaching a solution, while the other listens, asks questions, and provides feedback.

STAD (Student Teams Achievement Divisions)

After a lecture, video, or demonstration, teams of three or four receive a worksheet to discuss and complete. When members feel that they have reached acceptable solutions, you give a brief oral or written quiz to the group, a representative, or each individual member to assess their mastery of the material. In her music theory class, Berry (2008) integrates STAD within the academic game Survivor (see chapter 14). For the daily challenges, she distributes workbook exercises for the "tribes" to complete, then administers individual quizzes. These quiz scores are totaled for a tribal score. Although tribes don't vote off weak members, students perform diligently due to peer pressure, their personal pride, and their sense of responsibility to their tribe.

Jigsaw

Each member of a *base group* is assigned a minitopic to research. Students then meet in *expert groups* with others assigned the same minitopic to discuss and refine their understanding. The base groups re-form, and members teach their mini topics to their teammates.

Structured/Academic Controversy

Pairs within a group of four are assigned opposing sides of an issue. Each pair researches its assigned position, and the group discusses the issue with the goal of exposing as much information as possible about the subject. Pairs can then switch sides and continue the discussion (see chapter 14).

Group Investigation

Assign each group, or let each group choose, a different topic within a given subject area. Groups are free to organize their work and research methods and even to determine the form of the final product, such as a video, play, slide show, website, demonstration, presentation, or paper.

Numbered Heads Together

Assign a number to each member of a team of four. Pose a thought question or problem, and allow a few minutes for discussion. Call out a number, designating only students with that number to act as the group spokesperson. This exercise promotes individual accountability.

Talking Chips

This method guarantees equal participation in discussion groups. Each group member receives the same number of poker chips (or any other markers, such as index cards, pencils, or pens). Each time a member wishes to speak, he tosses a chip into the center of the table. Once individuals have used up their chips, they can no longer speak. The discussion proceeds until all members have exhausted their chips. Then they reclaim their chips and begin another round.

Send a Problem

Each group member writes a question or problem on a card. The group reaches consensus on the correct answer or solution and writes it on the back. Each group then passes its cards to another group, which formulates its own answers or solutions and checks them against those written on the back by the sending group. If groups disagree, the receiving group writes its answer as an alternative. Stacks of cards continue to rotate from group to group until they are returned to the original senders, who then examine and discuss any alternative answers or solutions given by other groups.

■ SETTING UP, MANAGING, AND TROUBLESHOOTING FORMAL, PROJECT-BASED GROUPS

For this type of group to be successful, your task is more challenging. You must build certain features into the structure of the groups by the way you assemble them, design tasks, manage activities, and determine grades. The cooperative learning scholars have best explained these essential features (Felder & Brent, 2001; Johnson et al., 1991; Johnson & Johnson, 1994; Millis, 1990; Millis & Cottell, 1998).

Positive Interdependence

For a long-term, project-based group to function effectively, each member must feel a sense of personal responsibility for the success of her teammates. In addition, her success must depend at least in part on the group's. In brief, members must feel they need one another to complete the task at the desired level of quality. To ensure this element, you can do one or more of the following:

- Assign a group product on which all members sign off and are given a group grade. You can also separately grade individual contributions if you choose.
- Give group as well as individual quizzes and tests that count toward each member's individual grade.
- On individual tests, give group members bonus points if they all score above a given level.
- Allocate essential resources or pieces of information across group members, requiring them to share (materials interdependence).
- Assign each member a different part of the total task (task interdependence).
- Randomly select students to speak for their group in class.
- Require that all members edit one another's work using Word's Track Changes tool, a wiki, or Google Docs.
- Assign group members different roles. Common roles are recorder, spokesperson, researcher, summarizer, checker/corrector, skeptic, organizer/manager, spy (on the progress of other groups), observer, writer, timekeeper, conflict resolver, and runner/liaison to other groups or the instructor. Less-known ones are coordinator, driver (of the group's operating style), finisher (lends a sense of urgency to the task), implementer (of group decisions), supporter (harmonizer), monitor-evaluator, originator (of ideas), and resource investigator (Belbin, 2004). For online groups, roles such as data gatherer, data manager, and multimedia specialist may be more appropriate (Barkley, Major, & Cross, 2014).

Individual Accountability

All members must be held responsible for their own learning as well as for the learning of other group members. At the same time, no member should feel that he or she is giving more (or less) than an equal share of effort to the group task. In other words, no freeloaders, social loafers, or hitchhikers are allowed. You can build in this element in several ways, some of which overlap with those above:

- Base final grades predominantly on individual quizzes, tests, papers, and other assignments.
- Count the team grades only for students who are passing the individual quizzes, tests, and written assignments.
- Assign group members different roles (see the previous subsection for possible roles).
- Assign group members primary responsibility for different parts of the team project and grade them on their part (e.g., one member develops the bibliography, another conducts the research, and another does the write-up).
- Add an individual assignment in which students reflect on the process of completing their designated portion of the group work (Huang, 2014).
- Give groups time as soon as you form them for members to discuss, develop, and agree on a contract detailing their policies and expectations, including when and where they will hold out-of-class meetings, how they will divide the labor and responsibilities, how they will evaluate each other, when the sections of the project will be due (unless you set these dates), and how they will sanction members for skipping meetings, not preparing for them, not contributing, not sharing resources, and not completing assignments on time. These documents reduce group problems and keep students more honest and responsible (Barkley et al., 2014; Oakley, Brent, Felder, & Elhajj, 2004). You may want to review them before students sign them.
- Allow teams to fire a noncontributing member (after a verbal and a written warning) and have them put this in the contract.

- Allow an overburdened member to resign from a group of freeloaders and seek membership on another team.
- Base a significant portion of the project grade on peer performance evaluations, and break the project into stages to help ensure that students write honest evaluations after each stage.

This last strategy deserves elaboration. At the end of the term or the group work unit, have members assign each of their teammates a letter grade for their group contributions, or estimate the percentage of the work they contributed, or allocate a limited number of points across their teammates. If you use percentages or points, you may want to forbid students from giving equal percentages or points across their teammates.

Of course, students must have criteria on which to grade their peers on being a good team member, such as attendance, preparation, promptness, leadership, quality of contributions, quantity of contributions, and social skills. You can have students brainstorm criteria in a whole-class discussion or have the groups develop their own to incorporate into their group contract, or you can provide them. If you choose the last option, you should include these five criteria—contributing to the team's work, communicating effectively, striving for a high-quality product, doing one's share of the work, and making every effort to solve team problems and resolve conflicts—because students value these behaviors the most in their teammates (Crutchfield & Klamon, 2014). In any case, the peer portion of the final grade should reflect the amount and importance of group work in the course—at least 5 to 20 percent but no more than 30 percent.

How valid and accurate are peer performance evaluations? If your students are merciless in penalizing freeloaders, social loafers, slackers, couch potatoes, sandbaggers, control freaks, ego trippers, bullies, whiners, martyrs, and saboteurs, chances are that the evaluations are valid and accurate. But, as mentioned before, students more often give all their teammates high evaluations, sometimes to protect the poor contributors. To help counter this

tendency, have students write peer performance evaluations two, three, or four times during the term and schedule them right after major project sections are due. This way any anger or frustration toward errant group members will come out in the heat of the moment. Another way to counter cover-ups is to say you will toss out any peer performance evaluations that give As to all teams members.

Appropriate Group Composition, Size, and Duration

According to the research, groups that are heterogeneous in terms of ability, race, gender, and other characteristics help students develop social skills, understand and get along with those of differing social backgrounds, and learn the material better (Heller & Hollabaugh, 1992; Heller, Keith, & Anderson, 1992; Johnson et al., 1991; Johnson & Johnson, 1994; Millis, 1990; Millis & Cottell, 1998). When group composition is diverse in ability or content background specifically, the slower students learn from the brighter ones often better than they do from us because students seem to speak one another's language. The brighter ones can benefit by teaching the material, at least if they didn't learn it thoroughly on their own.

Depending on your course, it may be more important that you maximize heterogeneity on a variable other than ability or content background. For example, if you want your groups to debate ideas and critically examine their own, you might want to find out students' views the first week of class (have them do a free-write, for instance) and assign teams based on varying opinions and value systems. Expediency may also have to take priority. If you want teams to meet face-to-face outside of class, you may have to consider students' schedules in assigning groups. The research also indicates that students should not form their own long-term groups. Such a composition reinforces existing cliques and homogeneity, encourages discussion of extracurricular topics, and can favorably bias the members' peer performance evaluations. However, it does reduce intragroup conflict.

Optimal group size varies with the open-endedness of the task. Several group activities described earlier in this chapter and in chapter 12 rely on pairs. But most other activities require groups of three to five to ensure lively, broad participation and prevent freeloading. A threesome seems to be optimal for mathematical and scientific problem-solving tasks that allow alternative means to one correct answer (Heller & Hollabaugh, 1992). Four or five is best for tasks with several possible good answers or solutions. Still, teams of up to seven members can function effectively and offer the added benefit of greater diversity (Michaelsen, 1997–1998; Sibley & Ostafichuk, 2014).

Ideal group duration also depends on the task. Long-term group assignments facilitate major projects and ongoing tasks, since duration fosters group loyalty and refines members' collaborative skills. But students can get acquainted with more classmates if groups change with each short-term project or every several weeks. What often happens, however, is that students develop team loyalties quickly and plead to keep the same groups throughout the term.

Face-to-Face or Sufficient Virtual Interaction

If at all possible, allocate some class time to team meetings because often students can't meet face-to-face outside class. Virtual interaction may be the easiest, if not the only, way that students can collaborate. Make students aware of virtual group communication channels such as text, audio, and video chat, chat rooms, discussion boards, wikis, Word's Track Changes tool, and Google Docs. The latter three work well for sharing and editing. If group members communicate on your LMS, you can keep track of their collaboration.

Genuine Challenge

A group task must make students *learn* something, not just *do* something. It should go beyond the course material, be a harder task than you'd assign to students working alone, and demand group synergy and higher-order thinking processes (application, analysis, synthesis, evaluation). In addition, it should be complex enough to have multiple respectable answers or multiple means to the best answer.

This setup rule for group work is too often forgotten. Students find doing a routine activity in a group boring busywork. Such a task also undercuts much of the learning payoff of group work. Students learn more in groups not only because they discuss the material and teach each other but also because they should be tackling a more challenging task than they otherwise would. Anything less especially sours the brighter students against working in groups.

Explicit Attention to Collaborative Social Skills

Working together effectively in long-term, stable groups require good team-member behaviors—not only those that students think to put in their contract but also listening actively, taking turns in talking, not interrupting, encouraging others, cooperating, being open-minded, giving constructive feedback, tactfully defending one's views, compromising, and showing respect for others. Young students in particular need occasions for reflection and feedback on their social and communication skills. They have to acquire the courage to express criticism constructively to their peers. Unfortunately, some instructors shy away from overseeing group processing sessions largely because they don't know how to run one. But it's really quite easy.

Processing best begins with students' assessing themselves as teammates, referring to the contract and answering questions such as these (Kustra & Potter, 2008):

- How many of my group's meetings did I attend?
- How well prepared was I for each meeting?
- How consistently did I complete whatever task I was assigned to do?
- How well did I listen to others in my group? How open was I to their ideas?

- Did I ever interrupt them or get angry with them?
- When I disagreed with one or more teammates, was I tactful and sensitive to their reactions? Did I try to find common ground or otherwise resolve the conflict? Did I propose or agree to a compromise?
- How much did I comment productively on my teammates' ideas, including giving them praise and encouragement?
- How well did I play my assigned roles?
- How consistently did I share my knowledge and resources with my group?

Students should present their self-assessments orally or in writing within their groups. (You can make these self-assessments an out-of-class writing assignment.) Then their teammates should provide feedback, couching it in the same terms as a response to the self-assessment. Counsel students to make their feedback helpful, not hurtful, to their teammates; this is not the time to unload. In addition, they should supply positive as well as negative evaluations. Furthermore, they should describe specific behaviors, not judge the person, and ask whether he understands the feedback, recalls the behaviors mentioned, or has questions. Following this procedure, students are more likely to take the feedback seriously and accept it (Kustra & Potter, 2008).

After the individual self-assessments and feedback, the students should address some questions within their groups while a recorder takes notes:

- How well have we included and encouraged all our members in our discussions?
- How evenly have we shared the work?
- How well have we handled conflict?
- How could we accomplish our tasks more effectively and enhance their quality?
- How could we function as a group more smoothly?

The recorder should save these notes and read them aloud at the next group processing session.

Then the group members can assess how much they have improved (Kustra & Potter, 2008).

Criterion-Referenced Grading

Chapter 27 examines different grading systems, but in group learning, all students and all groups must be able to earn an A. An absolute grading scale like criterion-referenced grading gives all students an equal chance to achieve. Grading on a curve (i.e., norm-referenced grading) undercuts the spirit of cooperation and the prospect of group success on which group learning relies.

■ TEAM-BASED LEARNING

Unlike an occasional in-class activity or a strategy for organizing students on a major project, team-based learning is a way of designing and running a course that relies on in-class group learning almost exclusively. It requires you to structure, or restructure, a course in a very specific way. It works well for any academic discipline or subject matter as long as you incorporate the following four essential elements, all of which team-based learning enthusiasts have tested for their effectiveness (Michaelsen, 1997-1998; Michaelsen et al., 2004; Sibley & Ostafichuk, 2014; Sweet & Michaelsen, 2012):

1. *Heterogeneous, term-long teams of five to seven members.* As the instructor, you should create them yourself; never let students form their own.
2. *The Readiness Assurance Process (RAP) at the beginning of each topical module (1 to 1½ hours).* Designed to ensure that students prepare for class, this process begins with assigning readings, video, or podcasts that students will need to complete to do the in-class problem-solving and application activities. The next two stages, which open the class that starts the module, are an individual multiple-choice test on the assigned material, followed by the same test taken by the teams. Both tests must be graded immediately, which is why

team-based learning faculty usually use IF-AT (Immediate Feedback Assessment Technique) cards and match the correct answer (A, B, C, D, or E) to the letter designated as correct on each item on the cards. (You can purchase these cards from Epstein Educational Enterprises.) Teams invariably score higher than its members do in the individual tests. Teams that disagree with an answer can go through the Appeal Process, which requires them to write a formal justification for their opinion. In the last stage, you judge the validity of any appeals and clarify any points of confusion. This double-testing procedure greatly improves students' retention of the content over individual tests (Cortright, Collins, Rodenbaugh, & DiCarlo, 2003).

3. *Challenging, structured problem-solving and application activities* (2 to 5 hours). To develop these activities, follow the 4 S framework:

   a. Make the problems *significant*, complex, and open to different perspectives. They may have more than one correct answer.

   b. Give all teams the *same* problems to work on at the same times. While they are working, you move from team to team to track student progress and clear up any confusion, but allow students to struggle with the problem on their own.

   c. Require each team to come to consensus on a *single, specific* choice among the possible answers or on a very short answer, such as one or two words, a number, or a location on a graphic. Teams have to prepare to defend their choice.

   d. Have all teams reveal their answer *simultaneously* using "voting cards" (with A, B, C, D, and E on them), sticky notes, pushpins, or a small whiteboard. Then cold-call on specific students to justify their team's answer, rotating the task around the team so that over time all members have the experience of being spokesperson. Differences of opinion are bound to launch a lively discussion. As you can see, team-based learning inherently runs like a flipped classroom.

4. *Individual accountability for class preparation, including to teammates.* Students are loathe to let down their teammates during the RAP and in-class activities, and they are later evaluated by their peers for part of their grade. Thus, freeloaders are much rarer than in other forms of project-based group work.

Course grading strategies vary, and some instructors don't calculate the in-class problem-solving and application activities into the final grade at all. Here is one model:

Individual readiness assurance tests	10 percent
Team readiness assurance tests	10 percent
Peer performance evaluations	5 percent
Individual homework assignments	20 percent
Midterm (individual)	20 percent
Final (individual)	35 percent

Team-based learning does not devote time to a discussion of good team-member behavior or group processing. Such behavior is considered intuitive, and teams must resolve any internal conflicts and inequities on their own without instructor intervention (which may include firing the offending member). After all, the work world is not interested in a team's interactional problems and preferences.

When designing a team-based learning course, you still start with your student learning outcomes and design RAP tests, problem-solving and application activities, and other homework assignments and tests to support and assess student performance on these outcomes. But you may also want to incorporate social outcomes and even aim to shift students' mental models of people, learning, responsibility, and collaboration. This happens with team-based learning as with no other group structure. Planning such a course requires a new gestalt on what a course looks like, as well as considerable work on your part, especially developing the RAP tests and other in-class activities. But you'll never have to prepare and deliver a lecture again. Besides, research documents that students learn as much or more in a team-based learning course than they do in courses using other instructional methods (Kubitz, 2014).

The most comprehensive online resource on implementing team-based learning is www.team basedlearning.org. Aside from plenty of how-to advice, you'll find numerous recorded interviews of faculty who have used the method and students who have learned through it.

■ PREPARING STUDENTS FOR LIFE

Younger college students are intent on learning what they will need to succeed in the real world they are about to enter, while older ones want to know how they can function more effectively in it at a higher level. Group work—team-based learning, in particular—helps them meet their goals. Course-related groups imitate those in the workplace just so far, however, because the latter generally have managers who monitor how well the members meet their responsibilities; freeloading and other team misbehavior can have profound career consequences. Still, collaboration is the way the world works because well-functioning teams generate more innovative and creative ideas and devise better solutions to problems than do individuals with a competitive ethos. We must prepare students to become high-functioning team members as both leaders and followers. This means we must implement group learning with care, teaching students to assume collective responsibility and share a collaborative ethos.

PART 4

INQUIRY-BASED METHODS FOR SOLVING REAL-WORLD PROBLEMS

CHAPTER 16

Inquiry-Guided Learning

Inquiry-guided learning also goes by the names *inquiry-based learning, inquiry learning, guided inquiry,* and *guided discovery.* In addition, it has several definitions in the literature that are not entirely consistent with each other. In chapter 11, it was defined very generally as "students learning or applying material in order to meet a challenge, such as to answer a question, conduct an experiment, or interpret data" so as to accommodate the range of more specific definitions.

▇ DEFINITIONS OF INQUIRY-GUIDED LEARNING

As with critical thinking, inquiry-guided learning has spawned different schools of thought with different definitions of the concept. According to Hudspith and Jenkins (2001), it is "a *self-directed, question-driven search for understanding*" (p. 9, italics in original)—more specifically, a process that begins with students exploring a subject for research, then identifying a central research question, developing a research strategy guided by anticipated results, and finally answering the central question with the results. Guiding students through this entire process might take two terms, Hudspith and Jenkins openly admit. After all, it will take many weeks for students to explore a subject thoroughly enough to come up with decent research questions and narrow their inquiry to one central question. In addition, the instructor must develop and facilitate many training sessions on a list of essential topics and skills: understanding the inquiry process itself, developing researchable questions, anticipating answers, conducting types of research (library, Internet, survey, interviews, focus groups), assessing evidence, and writing up or presenting the results.

The definition forwarded by Lee, Green, Odom, Schechter, and Slatta (2004) describes a similar process that starts with students formulating good questions and following the scientific method to answer them. They add that the good questions are likely to have multiple respectable answers. But the authors also have a very open view of inquiry-guided learning, as they see it happening within the interactive lecture, discussion, group work, and every other student-active teaching method listed in Table 11.1. In at least some of these situations, however, students are likely to be furnished with the questions.

Prince and Felder (2007) do not see students developing questions as a necessary part of the process. Quite the contrary, to them inquiry-guided learning involves giving students a challenge, such as a question, a hypothesis, or simply data to interpret, and they learn whatever they must to meet that challenge, which may or may not go beyond the course material. The inquiry may have a very narrow scope—for instance, one question that a segment of the lecture raises—or a very broad one entailing a major term project based on outside research. Prince and Felder also consider inquiry-guided learning an umbrella for several major methods—the case method, problem-based learning, discovery learning, project-based learning, and just-in-time-teaching (JiTT)—all of which they call *inductive teaching*. These methods all launch the learning process with a realistic, problematic situation and require that students research and assemble facts, data, and concepts to resolve it. Giving students challenging problems in the STEM disciplines also qualifies as inductive teaching.

For purposes here, we will use Prince and Felder's definition of *inquiry-guided learning* and view the methods they list as close variations of it. The first two, the case method and problem-based learning, as well as solving challenging STEM problems, merit their own chapters in this book (17 and 18), as they are complex, well researched, and widely used across the disciplines. The remaining three—discovery learning, project-based learning, and JiTT—require less explanation and are treated within this chapter.

■ THE EFFECTIVENESS OF INQUIRY-GUIDED LEARNING

However you define inquiry-guided learning, its inductive nature makes it a powerful learning method

(Bransford, Brown, & Cocking, 1999). It typically involves acquisition and comprehension of knowledge, analysis of data, evaluation of evidence, application of findings to a situation or problem, and synthesis of one or more resolutions. In short, it requires that students engage in multiple modes of higher-order thinking. Some forms of it may even spur cognitive development by introducing students to multiple perspectives on a problem and the uncertainty that arises in choosing among solutions. In addition, it introduces *desirable difficulties* into the learning process, which, as we noted in chapter 1, promote deep learning and long-term retention of the material (Bjork, 1994, 2013; Bjork & Bjork, 2011).

Compared to lecture-based instruction, inquiry-guided learning does a much better job of fostering students' academic achievement and improving their critical thinking, problem-solving, and laboratory skills (McCreary, Golde, & Koeske, 2006; Oliver-Hoyo & Allen, 2005; Oliver-Hoyo, Allen, & Anderson, 2004). In addition, engagement in inquiry-guided activities is related to a student's perceived gains in science and technology understanding, intellectual development, and vocational preparation (Hu, Kuh, & Li, 2008; Justice et al., 2007; Pascarella & Terenzini, 2005). To be fair, however, it does have a negative effect on perceived gains in general education and personal development, and its positive impacts fade as we move from high-performance to low-performance students (Hu et al., 2008).

■ THE NEED FOR STUDENT GUIDANCE

Like every other teaching method, the benefits of inquiry-guided learning depend on its implementation. To be effective, students must have sufficient guidance and scaffolding through the inquiry process—that is, explicit directions about what to do and how to do it, assuming they are dealing with new material. In fact, an overwhelming amount of research documents this need, as well as the failure of minimally guided, problem-centered instruction, commonly called *discovery learning* or *open discovery* (Aulls, 2002; Kirschner, Sweller, & Clark, 2006; Klahr & Nigam, 2004; Mayer, 2004; Moreno, 2004; National Survey of Student Engagement, 2007). In other words, constructivism has its limits. Students are unlikely to discover the basic principles of science by following the investigative techniques of professional researchers. However, the stronger the students' background knowledge in the subject matter, the less guidance they need (Kirschner et al., 2006), so an instructor can withdraw scaffolding as they acquire more knowledge (Hmelo-Silver, Duncan, & Chin, 2007). As students begin thinking more like experts, they are better able to identify key characteristics of a problem as well as the procedures and algorithms to solve it, thereby drawing on "internal guidance" (Kirschner et al., 2006). Acquiring this knowledge base may require somewhat more conventional learning strategies.

The literature endorses two forms of guidance, or scaffolding, both of which make up for a weak or incomplete command of basic knowledge. The first form is *worked examples*, which serve as models of problem-solving schemata for students. They illustrate the procedures and logic for approaching and working through problems (Chi, Glaser, & Rees, 1982). When students can follow a model, they have enough working memory available for processing these procedures and the reasoning behind them. Without worked examples, they have to divert much of their working memory to searching their long-term memory for possible strategies (Kirschner et al., 2006). Numerous studies from the 1980s and 1990s show that students learn more when they can study worked examples before tackling comparable problems on their own (Kirschner et al., 2006).

The second form of guidance is *process worksheets*. These lay out a proven sequence of problem-solving steps for students to follow, sometimes with hints and rules of thumbs. With this structure, students don't rush headlong into problems without first identifying the useful information they do and don't have, classifying the problem, visualizing it (in mathematics, the physical sciences, and engineering),

and performing whatever other steps are prescribed for reasoning through the type of problem. As a result, students display improved task performance (Nadolski, Kirschner, & van Merriënboer, 2005). Chapter 19 recommends using both forms of guidance to teach problem solving in STEM fields.

You can easily vary the amount of guidance and challenge (Lee, 2011). To increase guidance, you can do more modeling, use journal articles as models, add guiding questions, share heuristics, provide assessment rubrics, assign readings, or minilecture on background knowledge or relevant inquiry skills, such as hypothesis development or data analysis. To augment challenge, you can introduce irrelevant information, expand the scope of the inquiry, withhold helpful information, and suggest multiple perspectives. Experience will teach you where the optimal balance lies (Lee, 2011).

■ OBJECTS OF INQUIRY

What might students inquire about? Unless you have the course time to let them explore a new subject and frame research questions, you will have to supply the object of their inquiry. The following are categories of objects that apply to many disciplines, as well as possible questions to pursue (Hudspith & Jenkins, 2001):

- *A phenomenon:* Does it exist? If so, to what magnitude? What are its causes? What are its effects? Examples: black holes, bone cancer, dual coding, election fraud, plate tectonics, near-death experiences, a change in the violent crime rate.
- *The absence of an expected phenomenon:* What prevents (prevented) it from happening? Examples: acceptance of evolutionary theory in the curricula of many K–12 school systems, the Malthusian "population bomb" forecast in the 1960s, a certain nation's economic collapse.
- *A perceived relationship:* Does it exist? To what extent? To what extent is it causal or spurious? Examples: the links between education and

income, religiosity and political affiliation, global warming and human activity, diet and cancer, capital punishment and violent crime rates.

- *A controversy:* What underlies it? Examples: Why do scientists disagree about the cause of the Great Extinction? Why do physicians disagree about the role the mind plays in healing? Why do some people believe that tax cuts on dividends and interest stimulate the economy and others do not?

- *A theory:* How well grounded is it in fact or observation? How well does it explain and predict a phenomenon? How is it related to one or more other theories? Examples: evolutionary biology, the "great man" theory of history, the big bang theory, functionalism/pluralism versus conflict theory/elitism.

- *A complex concept:* What is its meaning? How well grounded is it in fact or observation? Examples: addiction, dark matter, genetic marker, constructivism, cultural drift.

- *A process:* How does it work? Examples: How does lupus undermine the immune system? How does economic development lower birthrates? How does the U.S. Census Bureau determine what to ask and how to ask it on the census questionnaire? How do people make decisions about purchasing a house?

- *A solution to a problem:* How can a given problem be solved? Examples: How can we reduce the incidence of AIDS on the African continent? How can we determine the reasons behind the demise of the Neanderthals? How can we respond effectively to another Ebola epidemic? How can we stem the trend of increasing economic inequality?

- *A course of action:* How sound or desirable is it? Examples: producing genetically engineered foods, setting the legal drinking age at 21, allowing electronic machine voting without a paper trail, instituting charter schools to spur improvement in the public school system, allowing private corporations to oversee health care, charging young illegal immigrants in-state college tuition.

MODES OF INQUIRY

Another way of getting your mind around inquiry-guided activities, especially if you teach in the sciences, engineering, or technical fields, is to consider various modes of inquiry (Arons, 1993). Students can tackle tasks such as these:

- Observe phenomena qualitatively and interpret what they perceive, trying to identify patterns.
- Formulate concepts out of their observations.
- Develop and test models that reflect their observations and concepts.
- Examine a new piece of equipment, and figure out how it works and how it can be used.
- Use a new piece of equipment to make measurements, analyze the data, and present the results.
- Distinguish explicitly between what they have observed and what they are inferring in interpreting the results of observations and experiments.
- Answer probing questions about a given research study, such as, "How do we know . . . ?" "Why do we think . . . ?" and "How strong is the evidence for . . . ?"
- Ask and answer "What will happen if . . . ?" questions (called *hypothetical-deductive reasoning*) about an experiment or other type of research study. If possible, students can follow up by proposing hypotheses and testing them in an experiment that they themselves design.

All of these modes are as useful for the social sciences as they are for the physical and biological sciences. Even those involving physical equipment may apply to psychology, and data-analytical software may be considered a type of equipment.

In fact, inquiry-guided learning works very well in the arts and humanities. Perhaps the most varied examples of this method's implementation appear in Lee's edited volume (2004), which showcases the teaching scholarship of North Carolina State University faculty. In addition to inquiry-based courses in food science, microbiology, physics, paper science and engineering, forestry, and psychology, you can read about such courses in history, design, music appreciation, French culture and civilization, and Spanish language. In history, for example, students do what historians do: find, evaluate, and analyze primary sources and then develop logical arguments supporting particular historical interpretations with evidence from their research (Slatta, 2004). In Spanish for Engineers, students research how the Spanish culture, in history and today, influences and informs technology (Kennedy & Navey-Davis, 2004). In music appreciation, they investigate the scientific aspects of music (sound, acoustics, hearing, and recording technology), as well as the artistic (musical expression, interpretation, meaning, and value). While the former aspects allow experimentation and testing, the latter, lacking universally agreed-on standards, permit students to develop and defend their own reasoned judgments (Kramer & Arnold, 2004). Across the disciplines, students have the opportunity to learn inductively and critically think their way to their own conclusions.

◾ VARIATIONS OF INQUIRY-BASED LEARNING

We already examined discovery learning and concluded from the research that this minimally guided, highly constructivist version of inquiry works most effectively for students who already have solid background knowledge and are prepared to practice quasi-professional research methods. So let's turn to JiTT and project-based learning.

JiTT

As a complement to their reading assignments, students receive conceptual questions on these readings, usually multiple choice, shortly before each class through the LMS. (Because this material has not yet been discussed in class, JiTT is considered inductive.) The instructor then designs or adjusts his plan for the upcoming class based on students' answers. The goal is to address and challenge students' misconceptions on the subject matter before they become further ingrained and inhibit learning of new material.

The research on this method attests to its learning effectiveness. Novak, Patterson, Gavrin, and Christian (1999) credited it with reducing attrition by 40 percent and raising students' normalized gains on the Force Concept Inventory by 35 to 40 percent in physics courses that were previously lecture based. A study on a large introductory biology course found comparable and additional benefits to JiTT: higher normalized pretest-posttest gains and lower attrition, plus improved student preparation, study habits, and class participation (Marrs & Novak, 2004). Research in general chemistry and organic chemistry courses also documented higher student achievement and engagement due to JiTT (Slunt & Giancarlo, 2004).

Some instructors are discouraged from trying JiTT because they have to prepare conceptual questions on all the readings. However, these items are the same type as those used in the interactive lecture, and some disciplines, especially the sciences, already have dedicated websites with many conceptual multiple choice questions for collegial use (see chapter 12).

Project-Based Learning

This method comprises a major assignment in which students, often in teams, design or create something, such as a piece of equipment, a product or architectural design, a computer code, a multimedia presentation, an artistic or literary work, a website, a scientific poster, or a research paper involving the collection, analysis, and presentation of real data. Service-learning and civic engagement projects generally fall within this category as well. To complete their project, students may draw solely on course material or supplement it with outside research.

Duda (2014) has transformed his lecture-based quantum mechanics course for physics majors into what he called "project-based" by centering classes and homework around four open-ended, ill-defined, real-world problems that he elaborates in stages. Each problem has a different project deliverable—a new-findings research manuscript, a review article manuscript, a paper for presentation, or a poster—and considerable class time goes to helping students overcome difficulties. Interestingly, the weaker students benefit most from Duda's new approach. While he considers his method project based, it also qualifies as problem-based learning (see chapter 18). Alternatively, Wurdinger and Qureshi (2015) ask their education graduate students to propose their own projects.

Compared to more conventional methods, project-based learning contributes to students' conceptual understanding, problem-solving skills, and attitudes about learning, and their performance on content-focused tests is the same or better (Mills & Treagust, 2003; Thomas, 2000). Wurdinger and Qureshi's students have reported significant improvements in their communication, creativity, problem solving, self-direction, and sense of responsibility. However, a major project shifts students' out-of-class time away from the standard course content to specialized subject matter, so their mastery of the fundamentals often suffers (Mills &

Treagust, 2003). Because Duda provides the necessary background material in readings, homework problems, and minilectures, his students score just as well on standardized quantum mechanics exams as have those in traditional offerings of the course.

UPCOMING INQUIRY-GUIDED METHODS

The next three chapters go into much further detail on three more complex and more commonly used inquiry-guided techniques: the case method, problem-based learning, and problem solving in the STEM disciplines. In fact, the case method dates back to the late 1800s, problem-based learning is at least several decades old, and problem solving in the STEM fields goes back from 5,000 years (mathematics) to just a few decades (engineering and technical fields). All of these methods predate the coining of the terms *inquiry-based learning, inquiry learning, guided inquiry,* and *guided discovery* and have a great deal of research documenting their strengths and challenges.

CHAPTER 17

The Case Method

In this complex world full of daunting challenges, students must learn how to solve problems. Different disciplines focus on different types of problems, and different types of problems call for different teaching methods. Both the case method and problem-based learning (chapter 18) help students learn how to solve open-ended, high-uncertainty problems that have multiple respectable solutions—some better than others, to be sure. These two methods are variants of inquiry-guided learning and appropriate to any discipline with real-world application. Chapter 19 suggests ways to construct tutorials and laboratories to teach students the process of scientific problem solving.

The case method exposes students to problematic, real-world situations and challenges them to apply course knowledge to analyze the issues and formulate workable solutions. It is based on real or realistic stories that present problems or dilemmas that are quite well structured but lack an obvious or clear resolution. Cases are usually text-based, but some are available dramatized on video. Those in web-based learning objects may add the dramatic realism of interactivity. If canned cases do not suit your instructional purposes, you can write your own at no cost but your time. Anyone with a bit of storytelling flair should find case writing an entertaining activity. To guide you in writing or selecting cases, this chapter identifies the qualities of a good case and describes the many types of cases.

THE EFFECTIVENESS OF THE CASE METHOD

Aside from the fact that students enjoy the case method, good cases are rich educational tools for a host of reasons:

- They require students' active engagement in and use of the material (Sharkey, Overmann, & Flash, 2007).
- They help make up for students' lack of real-world experience.
- They accustom students to solving problems within uncertain, risk-laden environments, thus

promoting cognitive development from the dualistic mode of thinking to informed judgments about the best approaches and solutions to difficult problems (Fasko, 2003; Levin, 1997; Lundeberg, Levin, & Harrington, 1999).

- They foster higher-level critical thinking and cognitive skills such as application, analysis, synthesis, and evaluation, all of which come into play in the process of thinking through and developing solutions to a case (Dinan, 2002; Gabel, 1999; Habron & Dann, 2002; Yadav, Shaver, Meckl, & Firebaugh, 2014).

- They raise awareness of the ethical side of decisions (Lundeberg et al., 2002).

- They demand both inductive and deductive thinking, compensating for higher education's usual focus on the latter.

- They serve as excellent writing assignments, paper topics, and essay questions, as well as springboards for discussion, review, and team activities.

- They increase class attendance (Lundeberg & Yadav, 2006a, 2006b).

- They improve the students' perceptions of and confidence in their learning, as well as faculty attitudes about teaching (Lundeberg & Yadav, 2006a, 2006b; Sharkey et al., 2007).

- They enhance students' achievement of their learning outcomes in their instructors' eyes (Lundeberg & Yadav, 2006a, 2006b; Rybarczyk, Green, Odom, Schechter, & Slatta, 2007).

On the student-involvement continuum from didactic methods (lecture) on the low end to experiential methods (such as role plays, simulations, and service-learning, as addressed in chapter 14) on the high end, the case method falls somewhere in the middle, depending on the case. The more it resembles a simulation, the more experiential the learning is. A case more closely approximates a simulation when it is written in the second person (placing the student in the story's key role), the present tense (happening now), and extended stages (see later in this chapter). But the second person and the present tense don't belong in a case taken from reality. No matter how they are written, cases only approach the experiential because students don't act them out. However, the last type described in this chapter, sequential-interactive, blurs the distinction.

■ THE SUBJECT MATTER AND WEBSITES FOR CASES

The case method accommodates any discipline or subfield that has a context for application or use. This is why professional schools have adopted it as a central instructional method. Business and law did so decades ago; in fact, Harvard Business School built a whole curriculum and publishing company around it. Medicine, nursing, clinical psychology, educational administration, and pastoral studies followed. So have many engineering and science fields, as well as music history (Chiaramonte, 1994), philosophy (ethics), economics (macro, legal aspects), political science (policy analysis, public administration, constitutional law), sociology (social problems, criminology, organizations), experimental and organizational psychology, biology (resource management, ecology, paleontology), mathematics, and research methods (study design and implementation to test a given hypothesis).

You can find well-tested cases in the sciences, engineering, or mathematics at any of these websites:

- For all sciences (over 500 cases, all peer reviewed): http://sciencecases.lib.buffalo.edu/cs/
- For all sciences (over 350 cases): http://www.cse.emory.edu/cases/index.cfm
- For biology, chemistry, physics, and earth sciences (over 70 cases for college level): http://www1.umn.edu/ships/modules/index.htm
- For biology, especially molecular (almost 40 cases): http://www.caseitproject.org/

- For engineering (over 250 cases): http://www. civeng.carleton.ca/ECL/5index.html
- For ethics in engineering (over 40 cases): http://www.depts.ttu.edu/murdoughcenter/products/cases.php
- For ethics in engineering (over 100 cases): http://ethics.tamu.edu/NSFReport.aspx
- For statistics (26 cases): http://www.stat.ucla.edu/cases/

A Chemistry, Geology, or Environmental Engineering Case

As an environmental chemist with the Environmental Protection Agency, you are charged with directing the remediation of a residential area with lead levels in the soil of 700–900 ppm. Your funding for this project is limited. Your advisory team is bitterly divided between two strategies: physical removal of the lead-contaminated soil and phytoremediation.

If you teach physics or mathematics, you can find many dozens of *context-rich problems*, which are essentially minicases, at http://groups.physics.umn.edu/physed/Research/CRP/on-lineArchive/ola.html and learn to write your own at http://groups.physics.umn.edu/physed/Research/CRP/crcreate.html.

Two excellent sources of advice and strategies for teaching science with cases are Using Case Studies to Teach Science at http://actionbioscience.org/education/herreid.html#primer and Teaching with the Case Method at http://serc.carleton.edu/sp/library/cases/index.html. The University of Buffalo website, http://sciencecases.lib.buffalo.edu/cs/, also features two training videos: one on leading a case-based debriefing discussion and the other on using cases with team-based learning (see chapter 15).

These sources offer relevant cases in medicine, nursing, the allied health fields, and public health:

- For environmental medicine (4 cases): http://library.med.utah.edu/envirodx/index.html
- For epidemiology and public health (8 cases for purchase): http://www.cdc.gov/epicasestudies/
- For pathology (over 850 cases): http://path.upmc.edu/cases.html
- For the health fields on allergies (18 cases): http://www.allergyadvisor.com/Educational/index.html

Even faculty and TA development has embraced the method. It uses cases portraying problems that instructors may encounter with classes and individual students—for example, challenges to authority, hostile reactions to sensitive material, accusations of discrimination, grading and academic honesty disputes, and difficulties implementing new teaching and assessment techniques.

A Faculty Development Case

A couple of weeks after the final exam, a student with a poor grade in your course approaches you saying that her performance will seriously worsen her father's heart condition. In the middle of the meeting, she breaks into tears.

WHAT MAKES A GOOD CASE, AND HOW TO WRITE YOUR OWN

A good case may be written in the second or third person and in the present or past tense, and it may be almost any length. What is important is that it have the following four qualities.

1. *Realism.* Real or hypothetical, a case should depict a currently relevant situation with which students can empathize or identify. Realism is further enhanced by technical detail, character development, historical context, the inclusion of irrelevant as well as relevant information, and extension over time or a decision-making process (see the next section).
2. *Opportunities for synthesis.* Cases should require students to draw on accumulated knowledge of the subject matter to analyze the problems and formulate solutions. Without some review built into the situations, students may forget to apply the basics in real decision-making situations in their careers.
3. *Uncertainty.* Although some solutions will be better than others, a case should offer room for multiple solutions and valid debate. Several solutions may be viable, but you may have students select just one course of action or rank-order their options and justify their decisions. The uncertainty surrounding the solutions may be due to uncertainty in the knowledge base (a trait of all bodies of knowledge), information missing in the case (as is often true in reality), or the genuine validity of different approaches to the problem.
4. *Risk.* The decisions students make must have some importance, even if it is only hypothetical—for example, a character's employment, health, or life;

an organization's survival or success; a country's welfare; the outcome of a legal case; social justice; or public security. Something valuable must be at stake.

Be sure to incorporate the following qualities in any case that you author, and make sure your case complements your course material and learning outcomes. You can get good ideas for your cases from other cases and from sources like these:

- News, journal, or magazine articles
- Product descriptions or advertisements
- Provocative statements by experts or leaders
- Testimonials and complaints by patients or users
- Excerpts from memos, letters, primary sources, ethnographies, laws, or public policies
- Data sources, such as spreadsheets, graphs, charts, clinicals, and public records
- Your own professional or personal experience

TYPES OF CASES

A good case may range from brief to very long. *Bullet cases* make one teaching point in just two or three sentences. They serve as good small-group discussion topics and short essay questions. *Minicases* are a tightly focused paragraph or two; if dramatized in a minute or two, they are called *vignettes.* They generate more discussion and analysis than do bullet cases. You can easily modify either type by confining the possible solutions to four or five reasonable options, much like a multiple-choice question. Then students must identify and justify their selection of the best solution (Waterman & Stanley, 2005). At the other extreme are cases like those that Harvard Business School publishes, which range from a couple of pages to over 40.

A Minicase for Physics or Mathematics

You are a consultant for a semiprofessional baseball team attending an important play-off game. During this windless evening, a hit baseball that could have been a home run bounces off the top of a light pole in left field. The team's front office asks you to calculate how far the ball would have traveled if the pole hadn't been in the way. You find out that the pole is 97' tall and 370' from home plate. You must estimate anything else you need to know.

Most cases, and virtually all bullet cases and minicases, represent a one-time snapshot of a situation. Depending on their length, they can occupy students for 15 to 20 minutes, a class period or two, or a single homework assignment. Longer cases can either elaborate the specifics in a snapshot or tell an unfolding story in segments over real or condensed time, in which case they are *continuous cases.* As real-life situations usually evolve over time, this structure adds realism. For instance, some faculty development cases describe an instructor's shifting relationship with a class over a term, with each minichapter presenting different issues to consider. Some medical and nursing cases follow the progression of a disease or a pregnancy in a hypothetical patient.

A final type, the *sequential-interactive case,* tells a continuing story that shifts directions according to student decisions. It leads students through a process of narrowing down their solutions or decisions by providing additional information *as the students request it.* Approaching the experiential realism of a simulation, this type of case casts students in the key decision-making role throughout, requiring that at least their minds act it out. Here is a step-by-step outline of how you can structure such a case across subject matter, with the medical or clinical variant in parentheses:

1. Students study a case giving limited information on the nature or root cause of a problem. First, they brainstorm all interpretations or causes (diagnoses) and their solutions (treatment plans). Then they rank-order the interpretations or causes (diagnoses) according to the ease and feasibility for verifying or eliminating them (ease and safety of testing).

2. Students request specific additional information, beginning with what they have ranked as the easiest and most feasible to obtain (easiest and safest to test) to help them narrow down the possible interpretations or causes (diagnoses).

3. You provide the information as they request it. (You should have additional information in hand for any likely request.)

4. Students again rank-order the possible interpretations or causes (diagnoses) in light of the new information and repeat step 2.

5. You repeat step 3.

6. Students select the most likely one or two interpretations or causes (diagnoses) and their solutions (treatment plans).

Depending on the subject matter and the problem, you may also want to include the ease and feasibility of implementing a solution (treatment plan) as a rank-ordering criterion. After all, if students identify widespread poverty as the root cause of a problem, they may not be able to develop a workable, action-oriented solution. Alternatively, you may wish to focus attention on the relative importance or likelihood of a cause. The case method is extremely flexible.

▪ DEBRIEFING CASES

For cases to function well as homework assignments, paper topics, essay exam questions, or discussion springboards, you must guide students through a productive debriefing. That is, you have to challenge them with good questions about the case—questions that engage them in application, analysis, and synthesis of the material, plus critical evaluation of their proposed interpretations and solutions (see chapter 13).

The simplest formula for debriefing a case is problems-remedies-prevention, that is: "What are the problems?" "What are the solutions?" and, if applicable, "How could these problems have been prevented?" The structure for sequential-interactive cases often follows this basic formula.

While the problems and solutions are the essential issues, you might ask other questions to direct students back to the course material to find answers. Cases that you debrief following a list of questions are called *directed* (Waterman & Stanley, 2005). Good cases often contain other matters and important details well worth students' consideration—for example, possible reasons behind a character's action or inaction; reasons that such action or inaction fails to solve or even worsens a problem; the impact of the historical context, the organizational culture, or financial constraints; or how the situation might play out if one ingredient were different. Providing your questions in writing will keep the debriefing focused on the key points.

You can launch a case discussion with the entire class (see chapters 13) or have students discuss a case in groups (see chapter 15). Using groups offers still more options:

- All groups can work on the same case with the proviso that each group reach a consensus on its answers (otherwise majority rules). This format works well only with cases that can generate widely different interpretations.
- All groups can work on the same case, but with each group addressing different questions.

- After a general class discussion identifying the problems in the case, half the groups address solutions and the other half preventions.
- Each group works on a different case and presents a descriptive summary and debriefing to the rest of the class.

A POSTSCRIPT FOR PIONEERS

If the case method is rarely, if ever, used in your field but you can see a place for it in your course, trying it poses very little risk. It is a tried-and-true method in many fields, and course evaluations show that students find it both highly instructive and enjoyable. The key is in the quality of the case. You might show drafts of your own creations to colleagues before using them in class. Remember too that you will undoubtedly continue to improve your cases over time.

CHAPTER 18

Problem-Based Learning

Both the case method and problem-based learning (PBL) present students with real-world, human-situational, open-ended, high-uncertainty, and risky challenges with multiple respectable solutions, some better than others. However, PBL problems tend to be messier and fuzzier, and the course material alone cannot provide viable solutions. Students must do outside research, which usually makes the problem-solving process a sizable project best conducted by teams of at least four (Duch, Groh, & Allen, 2001).

The McMaster University Medical School in Ontario, Canada, introduced PBL in the late 1960s to move medical education away from straight lecture and memorization tests and toward actual practice. Medical students worked in groups with a precept to discuss, research, and diagnose hypothetical medical cases. From the 1970s on, PBL spread to several dozen North American medical schools (Jonas, Etzel, & Barzansky, 1989; Kaufman, 1985; Kaufman et al., 1989; Kirschner, Sweller, & Clark, 2006). It is applicable in all the same subject areas that the case method is: the social sciences, psychology, history, philosophy, business, law, educational administration, medicine, nursing, clinical fields, the biological and physical sciences, engineering—any discipline or profession that presents unclear and uncertain challenges in an applied context.

HOW PBL WORKS

PBL tends to leave students more or less on their own to research their problem and devise solutions to it. But they should follow this series of steps (Amador, Miles, & Peters, 2006; Bridges, 1992; Duch, Allen, & White, 1997–1998; Edens, 2000):

1. Team members review the problem, which is typically ill structured, and clarify the meaning of terms they do not understand.
2. They analyze and define the problem. (You may provide guidance.)
3. They identify and organize the knowledge they already have to solve the problem. This may

also mean identifying and ignoring extraneous information given in the problem.

4. They identify the new knowledge they need to acquire to solve the problem—the *learning issues.*

5. They organize and rank-order the learning issues and set objectives for outside research. (You may or may not provide references.)

6. They divide the work among themselves.

7. They conduct the assigned research individually by agreed-on deadlines.

8. They continue to meet to share research findings and conduct additional research as needed.

9. They merge their newly acquired and previous knowledge into what they consider to be the best possible solution. (This step qualifies PBL as a constructivist method.)

10. They write up or orally present their solution.

Once the instructor guides students through the basic procedures, the teams should work as independently as possible. Each devises its own internal organization and decision-making rules for evaluating alternative formulations of and solutions to the problem. Members integrate course materials with outside library, Internet, interview, survey, documentary, or field research. Depending on the problem, the assessable product may take any of several possible forms: a lengthy memo, a report, a scholarly manuscript, a budget, a plan of action, or an oral presentation to the class or a hypothetical decision-making body.

PBL's Experiential Potential

While PBL usually doesn't require students to play roles, that's not to say that it can't. Some elaborate PBL problems allow an optional experiential dimension, which adds an early step: the team members decide on the roles they will play in a kind of open-ended simulation. Students might assume professional roles, such as members of a council with varying political interests to be taken into account. In the lengthy educational administration problem that Bridges (1992) developed, students take the role of personnel selection committee members, with one acting as project leader, another as facilitator, another as recorder, and the rest as members. He also incorporates specific role plays and minisimulations, such as conferences, interviews, field observations, in-basket exercises, and progress presentations.

PBL's experiential realism is grounded not only in the problems, activities, and (sometimes) roles, but also in time factors. A project may be designed to proceed in real time. In a multistage rollout problem, the challenge may unfold over time as you supply students with pieces of additional information (Duch et al., 2001). Solving one problem can entail weeks of research and group meetings in and out of class. In fact, a substantial problem can absorb most of a term. But you can find or design problems that take only a week or two to solve.

Assessing PBL Projects

Beyond balancing group and individual grading (see chapter 15), you must decide in advance the specific criteria on which you will grade the product and set bottom-line standards for various grades or point ranges. Then you must develop a rubric describing the product for each level of quality on each criterion (see chapter 27). You must also convey those criteria and levels to your students before they begin the project so they will have some structure within which to direct their efforts. Appropriate dimensions may include the clarity of the problem definition, the breadth of outside sources used, the feasibility of the solution, the cost-effectiveness of the solution, the extent to which the solution resolves all aspects of the problem, and the rationales for the solution selected.

Because the PBL literature offers little assessment guidance, grading these projects can present challenges. It can be difficult to take points off because the teams are supposed to work independently, so you don't monitor your students as carefully as you might with other teaching methods. Another potential complication stems from the high degree of student engagement. Grading down a project can touch emotional nerves unless you can clearly justify your assessments.

GOOD PBL PROBLEMS AND WHERE TO FIND THEM

Good PBL problems and good cases have the same key characteristics: realism, opportunities for students to synthesize material, uncertainty, and risk—and all the better if they resemble problems that students will experience in their careers (Duch et al., 2001). Some generic workplace problems include managerial miscommunications, low organizational morale, difficult policy implementation, negative public relations, and ethical dilemmas. In addition, a good PBL problem for your course is one that gives students practice in the abilities that you target in your learning outcomes and directs students to the knowledge you want them to acquire beyond the course material.

You can also judge the quality of problems using Bloom's (1956) taxonomy of cognitive operations (see chapter 2). A poor problem requires only knowledge or comprehension, as do typical end-of-textbook-chapter problems. A fair problem adds a story element but entails no more than application. A good problem demands analysis, synthesis, and evaluation to solve. It is highly realistic, full of researchable unknowns, and open to more than one solution (Duch & Allen, 1996). Its description is usually much longer as well.

Here's a simple example. Let's say that the readings, lectures, and class activities in a biology course have familiarized students with the structure and function of DNA, the function of various enzymes involved in DNA synthesis and replication, and radio-labeling techniques. The instructor then gives teams this PBL problem: "A rare blood disorder has been identified in a particular family in Europe. [The problem describes the symptoms.] Devise the least expensive method to determine the disorder's cause and to locate the defective gene, and suggest diagnostic tests for identifying potential victims." Solving this problem presumably requires the students to conduct outside research on topics like blood DNA, DNA research methods, and genetic testing. Once the teams complete their task, they explain their solutions to the class, which then engages in discussion to evaluate the various methods suggested.

Because the case method is more popular and most cases are less complex, well-tested PBL problems are not as plentiful as cases. However, quite a few are available in the sciences and business, and several in the social sciences and medicine. The best source across the disciplines is http://www.udel.edu/pbl. This site also has some articles on teaching with PBL. The literature offers a few additional problems in biology (Allen & Duch, 1998; Duch & Allen, 1996; Mierson, 1998) and physics (Duch & Allen, 1996). Edens (2000) gives brief summaries of 10 problems in biology, physics, chemistry, business, art history, educational leadership, medicine, and criminal justice, along with their sources. Depending on what knowledge is and isn't included in your course materials, you may also be able to use some of the cases at the University of Buffalo site: http://ublib.buffalo.edu/libraries/projects/cases/case.html.

A Short Medical PBL Problem

Your group is an infectious disease team at a university hospital in Nashville, Tennessee. A female patient in her late 30s comes into the office presenting a red rash on her legs, thighs, and forearms; muscle and joint aches in the same areas; and fatigue. Your team concurs the cause could be (1) a fungal infection prevalent along the Texas Gulf Coast, (2) Rocky Mountain spotted fever (from a southeastern U.S. tick bite), or (3) a not-yet-identified food allergy. What is the wisest sequence of actions for your team to take to diagnose and treat the disease? Justify each decision you decide to take.

• • •

Note: Timing is critical to solving this problem. The students' research should inform them that the results of the tests for conditions 1 and 2 will take at least 1 week and food allergy testing at least 2 weeks. Before a diagnosis can be determined, the team should treat the patient for Rocky Mountain spotted fever because it can cause debilitation and death within a few days of the described symptoms appearing.

▨ PBL'S EFFECTIVENESS

Theoretically PBL has strong credentials. It is based on the well-tested principle of students learning by actively doing (see chapter 1), and they typically get to practice a variety of higher-order and social skills: recording, scheduling, conducting meetings, discussing, prioritizing, organizing, planning, researching, applying, analyzing, integrating, evaluating, making decisions, compromising, cooperating, persuading, negotiating, and resolving conflict. Beyond these basics, you decide and determine what your students will learn to do and what additional knowledge they will acquire by their research in your choice or design of a problem.

According to the research, PBL is especially effective in developing the following abilities in students (Albanese & Dast, 2014; Albanese & Mitchell, 1993; Banta, Black, & Kline, 2000; Bridges, 1992; Dochy, Segers, Van den Bossche, & Gijbels, 2003; Edens, 2000; Hintz, 2005; Hung, Bailey, & Johassen, 2003; Lieux, 1996; Major & Palmer, 2001; Mierson & Parikh, 2000; Prince, 2004; Prince & Felder, 2006; Strobel & van Barneveld, 2009):

- Teamwork
- Project management and leadership
- Oral and often written communication
- Emotional intelligence
- Tolerance for uncertainty
- Critical thinking and analysis
- Conceptual understanding and deep learning
- High-level strategies for understanding and self-directed study
- Application (transfer) of content knowledge
- Clinical performance (health fields)
- Application of metacognitive strategies
- Research and information-seeking skills
- Retention of knowledge
- Decision making
- Problem solving (of course), including knowledge transfer, often across disciplines

In addition, PBL activates prior knowledge and imparts new knowledge in the context in which it will later be used. In this way, it builds in enough redundancy to ensure the knowledge is well understood and retained. If the problem mirrors situations that students will encounter in their future occupations, PBL develops career realism as well as skills.

A Short Geoscience PBL Problem

Having earned your Ph.D. in geoscience and attained a head research position at a respectable university, you and your team are contracted by the U.S. Department of the Interior (DOI) to assess a claim forwarded by a group of your colleagues: that the mega-magna chamber below Yellowstone National Park is leaking increasing amounts of sulfur dioxide into the atmosphere and will cause a catastrophic mass extinction within 70,000 years. They rest their claim on the mass extinction that wiped out over

90 percent of all life 250 million years ago. Your task is to evaluate this claim, including its premises and reasoning, and to decide whether the DOI should accept it. [*Optional hint:* Among conducting other investigations, you and your team will want to research and compare the projected hydrospheric, atmospheric, and biospheric conditions of the Earth to those of 250 million years ago.]

PBL has its weaknesses and its critics. In the most methodologically rigorous studies, few of PBL's positive effects are strong (Albanese & Dast, 2014). At the same time, implementing PBL is difficult and time-consuming, starting with finding the right problems to fit your course or writing your own (guidelines given at the end of the chapter). Given such challenges, fully committed and well-prepared instructors are essential to PBL's success, and their shortage may explain the mixed impact of the method on medical education (Glew, 2003; Kirschner et al., 2006). In addition, when instructors don't provide enough structure and scaffolding, PBL stumbles into the same pitfalls as discovery learning. Students with weaker knowledge backgrounds may require more just-in-time instruction to help them over problem-solving hurdles (Hmelo-Silver, 2004; Kirschner et al., 2006; see chapter 16).

Another unsettled question is whether PBL courses cover less content. If students are drilling deeply into a specialized problem, they are not learning the subject matter more broadly. But research on undergraduate PBL courses finds no such content or test performance loss (Banta et al., 2000; Duda, 2014; Edens, 2000; Hung et al., 2003), so it is apparent that instructors can structure a PBL course to encompass a wide range of topics. Even if such a loss does occur, many PBL enthusiasts may not care because they value application and research skills over content mastery (Biggs, 2003).

WHAT STUDENTS THINK

Many younger undergraduates feel uncomfortable with PBL, which might be considered another weakness of the method. While they report developing skills such as problem solving, critical thinking, communication, and taking responsibility, they tend to perceive they are working harder but learning less, even though test results don't confirm this (Banta et al., 2000; Edens, 2000; Lieux, 1996; Woods, 2001). Many students, especially the highest achievers and those in their first year, express frustration with the open-endedness, complexity, and ambiguity of the problems; the lack of task structure and guidance; and the murky standards for performance (Edens, 2000; Lieux, 1996). Such stressful conditions can breed intragroup conflicts and problems.

This does not mean that PBL courses necessarily get low student ratings and critical comments (Mierson, 1998). But instructors new to PBL may not know how to improvise through unexpected schedule changes or how to handle the student protests and sticky situations that can arise. Such novices may indeed suffer a temporary drop in their ratings (Lieux, 1996). So before you embark on PBL, evaluate how much risk you can afford to take.

CREATING YOUR OWN PBL PROBLEMS

When you are looking for PBL problems, start by reviewing those already published. Finding one to fit your course can be difficult, however. A PBL problem in a colleague's course may not be a case in yours because your course materials and activities already address the solutions. Feel free to modify published problems to your purposes, but don't feel constrained to use them at all. Two of the best things about college-level teaching are the creativity and autonomy it allows. Just as you can write your own cases tailored to your course and student needs, you can compose your own PBL problems. This may be your best alternative, if not your only one, because you maintain full control over your students' learning issues. These learning issues are what distinguish a PBL problem from a case and what push students to practice the highest levels of thinking.

If you want to compose your own PBL problem, follow these steps (adapted from D. Johnston in Biggs, 2003, and Mastascusa, Snyder, & Hoyt, 2011):

1. Identify the concepts, knowledge, and skills required to propose a good solution.
2. Write out your student learning outcomes for the PBL project.
3. Find a real problem that fits your learning outcomes and that your students may encounter in their careers or civic lives.
4. Write your problem as you would a case: in the present tense, with specific data and a practitioner role or multiple roles that students can assume. Embellish the problem with unnecessary information, dramatic detail, character development, and the like.
5. Consider omitting some information that you know students can either estimate or find out in the course of their research.
6. Consider structuring your problem as an extended rollout type, letting realism be your guide.
7. Define the deliverable—for example, a decision, a lengthy memo, a manuscript, a report, a budget, a plan of action, or a persuasive presentation—and develop a rubric for assessing student products (see chapter 27). Be sure the deliverable integrates decisions that students have to make.

After testing and refining your problem in your course, you can even publish it if you also write a facilitator's guide. Include in the guide the information in the steps above, and add content background for facilitators and suggested resources for students.

CHAPTER 19

Problem Solving in the STEM Fields

One of the most difficult tasks instructors face is teaching students to be good problem solvers in mathematics and in the math-reliant scientific, technical, and engineering fields. Students must learn how to identify different types of problems so they can choose the appropriate algorithms for calculating the solutions. Unfortunately, novice problem solvers often misidentify a problem because they fail to understand it in terms of concepts and principles. Instead, they try to find a similar problem that either they or their instructor has solved in the past and too often choose a template problem based on a superficial resemblance to the new problem (e.g., both involve falling objects). Then, in their impatience to find a numerical solution, they dive into algebraic manipulations. They neither qualitatively analyze the problem nor systematically reason through a strategy for solving it. When they arrive at any solution, they are satisfied and don't take the time to check it (Heller, Keith, & Anderson, 1992; Kalman, 2007).

To the extent your students can get the right answers by whatever means, you might not even notice the shallowness of their understanding. Unless the problems you assign elucidate the underlying disciplinary principles and the quantitative reasoning process, your students may merely be going through the motions, repeating the problem-solving pattern you showed them, and using the *plug-and-chug* approach. In addition, they expect there to be only one way to arrive at a solution, even though there may be several viable alternatives. They also come to expect problems to be easy; after all, the instructor breezes through them and the book examples seem straightforward. Unprepared for hurdles, they become discouraged by difficult problems and stop trying. Then they may mistakenly conclude that only a special few people are meant for the discipline. Fortunately, the research suggests strategies to help students acquire conceptual understanding and overcome their faulty problem-solving approaches.

WHERE STEM EDUCATION FALLS SHORT

Thanks to two classic works, Tobias (1990) and Seymour and Hewitt (1997), we know quite a bit about why so many students come to dislike, lose interest in, and switch out of STEM majors. At the top of the list is poor teaching, manifested as faculty with a weed-out mentality about their courses, poor communication and public speaking skills, attitudes of indifference or even condescension toward students, little understanding of how students learn, and lessons that lack application and illustration—all exacerbated by too much material being crammed into too little time (Seymour & Hewitt, 1997). Other influential turn-offs are the heavy reliance on lecture, the emphasis on factual memorization in both teaching and assessment, the predominance of mechanical *how* over more meaningful *why* explanations, the need for quantitative operations, and the focus on technique—all at the expense of theory, creativity, interconnected concepts, and discussion (Tobias, 1990).

Although the STEM fields engage in the discovery and identification of facts, they are not just mountains of factoids. Yet undergraduate science education often gives that impression. One reason lies with the overreliance on lecture, often the instructor's technique of choice because it maximizes the amount of factual information that can be conveyed. It also feels comfortable and easy to manage, especially with large classes, because the instructor exercises total control. The lecture has its appropriate uses, but it is not digestible as a steady diet. In physics courses that serve it exclusively, students take away no more than 30 percent on average of the key concepts that they didn't already know at the beginning of the course (Hake, 1998). As chapter 12 explains, lecturing much beyond 15 minutes or so pushes students' ability to process and retain the material and becomes counterproductive. A series of in-class experiments has revealed that only 10 percent of students can recall a non-obvious fact and illustration of it just 15 minutes

after the professor says them (Wieman, 2007). In addition, the lecture does a relatively poor job of teaching students how to do something, such as reason, think critically, formulate a hypothesis, solve a problem, design and conduct an experiment, and use lab equipment safely.

The laboratory that typically accompanies large science and engineering lectures also fails to capture the excitement of getting results from an experiment or making a breakthrough on a problem. All too often, labs are treated like second-class, tacked-on learning experiences at best—poorly coordinated with the readings and lectures, hampered by a shortage of functioning equipment, shunted off on poorly paid graduate students, and dulled by cookbook procedures leading to predictable answers that haven't been of scientific interest for decades. Students rightfully come to regard such labs as tedious, irrelevant tasks to hurry through, get done, and forget.

Finally, STEM education has a problem with problems. Those in most textbooks (Stephan, Bowman, Park, Sill, & Ohland, 2014 excepted) present unrealistically shallow and formulaic situations that presume one method of reaching a single solution. Denying students the desirable difficulty that benefits their learning, they provide all the information needed and not a datum more. Students don't have to use their prior knowledge to determine the type of problem they face, select the most efficient method or algorithm, sift through extraneous information, or estimate unknowns. They will never face such simplistic problems in the workplace or their lives.

IMPROVING STUDENT LEARNING IN STEM COURSES: GENERAL ADVICE

Before we examine the revolutionary developments in STEM lectures and labs, let's introduce some general principles that should guide STEM education.

First and foremost, instructors have to anticipate and address any misconceptions about the subject matter that students bring into the classroom (see chapter 1). If you don't already know your students' faulty mental models, you can discover them by giving a diagnostic exam the first week, asking students to explain a certain phenomenon, having them apply concepts to a realistic problem, or having them draw a concept map or flowchart of some basic material or process (Mastascusa, Snyder, & Hoyt, 2011). Expect misconceptions especially in the sciences because the layperson's intuitive understandings of natural phenomena are so often wrong. You have to discredit these mistaken models while making the scientific explanations more plausible and persuasive and equally clear and comprehensible. Only after students adopt the expert's paradigm can they learn the discipline at a deep, meaningful level.

Second, students need help filling in the paradigm—that is, acquiring the discipline's hierarchical mental structure of knowledge (Hanson, 2006; Wieman, 2007). They are not likely to see this hierarchical organization unless we tell them about it explicitly, and a concept map can help (see chapter 23). After all, it took us years to develop it in our own minds because, most likely, no one told us about it when we were in school. Why not alleviate our students' struggle and quicken their learning by showing them how experts structure their vast knowledge? By distinguishing the more general and core concepts and propositions from the condition-specific and derivative ones, a hierarchy reduces the need to memorize while making long-term storage, retrieval, and appropriate application of knowledge much easier (Hanson, 2006; Wieman, 2007; also see chapter 1).

Third, we need to do whatever we can to reduce the heavy cognitive load that learning science imposes on students (Mastascusa et al., 2011). Teaching them the hierarchical structure of the discipline's knowledge helps accomplish this purpose, but we can also show them how to recognize patterns across concepts, principles, and problems and how to chunk knowledge into categories based on such patterns (Hanson, 2006; Wieman, 2007). After

showing them, we should give them practice in these mental operations, preferably in small groups to start. Another way of reducing cognitive load is to supplement the verbal delivery of knowledge with visuals—diagrams, figures, flowcharts, concept maps, and the like—and to have students draw their own whenever possible (Hanson, 2006; Wieman, 2007). Not only do graphics package information more efficiently and succinctly than do words, but by their very nature, they also display an organization of knowledge. In fact, visuals facilitate learning in such powerful ways that they merit an entire chapter (23), so we will leave detailed explanations for later.

Fourth, we must help students learn to transfer their knowledge to new situations, and it may not happen unless we have a strategy to teach them. The case method is useful here. First, we lead students through two or three contrasting cases that are structured around the same underlying concepts and principles—for example, flow rate and pressure interdependence, or rain forests as illustrated in temperate and tropical climates. Then we present a problem or question that coaxes students to identify the commonalities across the cases and construct a general abstract model based on the commonalities (Mastascusa et al., 2011).

One final principle to facilitate science education—in fact, learning in any discipline—is to encourage metacognition. That is, students need to acquire the expert's habit of monitoring their own thinking, of honestly assessing how deeply they understand the material (Hanson, 2006; Mastascusa et al., 2011; Wieman, 2007). Some teaching techniques build in the process of self-monitoring—for example, group problem solving of context-rich problems, collaborative inquiry–guided learning, and stepwise problem-solving procedures that require students to represent the problem visually and check the answer for plausibility. This chapter deals with these techniques in a later section. The next chapter revisits metacognition as a dimension of self-regulated learning and offers a number of ways to foster it in our students.

■ IMPROVING STUDENT LEARNING IN STEM COURSES: SPECIFIC STRATEGIES

An enormous amount of research on STEM education all leads to the same conclusion: inquiry-guided, problem-focused, and collaborative, alternative teaching strategies are more effective than traditional lecture. Students who learn by these newer approaches leave their STEM courses with better skills in higher-order thinking, problem solving, and experimental design (Beichner et al., 2007; Burrowes, 2003; Cortright, Collins, & DiCarlo, 2005; Duda, 2014; Freeman et al., 2014; Freeman et al., 2007; Giuliodori, Lujan, & DiCarlo, 2006; Haak, HilleRisLambers, Pitre, & Freeman, 2011; Hake, 1998; Hanson, 2006; Hanson & Wolfskill, 2000; Hodges, 2015; Jones-Wilson, 2005; Knight & Wood, 2005; Lewis & Lewis, 2005; Lord, 1997; McCreary, Golde, & Koeske, 2006; Oliver-Hoyo & Allen, 2005; Oliver-Hoyo, Allen, & Anderson, 2004; Oliver-Hoyo & Beichner, 2004; Reddish, 2003; Reddish, Saul, & Steinberg, 1997; Prince & Felder, 2007; Schroeder, Scott, Tolson, Huang, & Lee, 2007; Wieman, 2007, 2014; Wilke, 2003; Wilke & Straits, 2001; Wood & Gentile, 2003; Yadav, Shaver, Meckl, & Firebaugh, 2014) and stronger conceptual understanding of the content (Crouch & Mazur, 2001; Hanson, 2006; Hodges, 2015; Jones-Wilson, 2005; Oliver-Hoyo & Beichner, 2004; Wieman, 2007, 2014; Yadav et al., 2014). Furthermore, these gains come with no loss in content coverage (Duda, 2014; Jones-Wilson, 2005) or students' content mastery, whether the class is small or large (Cortright et al., 2005; Lord, 1997, 1999; Wilke & Straits, 2001).

These alternative strategies vary from relatively small, inexpensive changes, such as interspersing conceptual multiple-choice questions throughout the lecture and having individual students and then groups choose the right answer (Crouch & Mazur, 2001; Eddy & Hogan, 2014; Freeman et al., 2014; Haak, HilleRisLambers, Pitre, & Freeman, 2011; Hodges, 2015; Wieman, 2007; see chapter 12), to complete course redesigns, such as combining lecture, recitation, and laboratory into a tutorial or workshop format (Beichner et al., 2007; Breslow, 2010; Deslauriers, Schelew, & Wieman, 2011; Duda, 2014; Hodges, 2015; Laws, 1991; Oliver-Hoyo & Allen, 2005; Oliver-Hoyo, Allen, & Anderson, 2004; Oliver-Hoyo & Beichner, 2004; Reddish, 2003; Reddish et al., 1997).

Making Modest Changes to the Lecture

Let's start with the modest changes you can make in your STEM courses within a lecture format:

- *Interspersing conceptual multiple-choice questions* and having individual students and then groups choose the right answer (see chapters 4 and 12).
- *Integrating case studies and problem-based learning scenarios,* which abound in the sciences, as in-class activities or homework (Yadav et al., 2014; see chapters 17 and 18 and the "Online Resources in STEM Education" section later in in this chapter).
- *Incorporating just-in-time-teaching.* Research finds that this reduces attrition, raises standardized test scores, and improves student preparation (Marrs & Novak, 2004; Novak, Patterson, Gavrin, & Christian, 1999; see chapter 16).
- *Doing experimental demonstrations* during lecture, whether live (not requiring data collection) or online interactive simulations that double as virtual labs (Wieman, 2007; see the URLs below for sources). Students become involved when they not only watch but also discuss what they have observed and interpret the results. In the course of the discussion, you explain the concepts and principles illustrated and the real-life applications. With the students having time to discuss the experiment, this teaching method is called an interactive lecture demonstration (Sokoloff & Thornton, 1997, 2001).
- *Modeling expert reasoning*—in particular, problem-solving strategies—but perhaps more self-consciously and explicitly than you have before. Recall from chapter 16 that novice learners grappling with new material need guidance and

scaffolding through the inquiry process—that is, explicit directions about what to do and how to do it. The research recommends two forms of guidance. One form, *worked examples,* provides students with a problem-solving model (Chi, Glaser, & Rees, 1982). Following a logical set of procedures frees up enough of the learners' working memory to let them process the reasoning behind the procedures. We know from numerous studies that students learn more when they can study worked examples before trying to solve comparable problems on their own (Kirschner, Sweller, & Clark, 2006). However, the way instructors typically demonstrate problem-solving fails to capture the real process. They show students what experts do when they run through an exercise, not how to attack a real problem, which involves quantitative reasoning. To accomplish this goal, you must model the cognitive processes involved in genuine problem solving and explicitly describe the steps and flow of your thinking. Only then can students grasp the techniques for solving problems and appreciate what these techniques can do for them.

- *Teaching the steps of problem solving.* The second form of inquiry guidance that benefits novice learners is *process worksheets*—that is, an optimal sequence of problem-solving steps for students to follow, supplemented by hints and rules of thumbs when available. This reasoning structure improves students' problem-solving performance by making them carefully examine and recast problems in conceptual terms, thus preventing them from rushing headlong into misdirected calculations (Nadolski, Kirschner, & van Merriënboer, 2005). The literature endorses teaching students a tried-and-true stepwise method for tackling and solving problems that is adaptable to any quantitatively based discipline (Heller et al., 1992; Kalman, 2007). During your interactive lecture (see chapter 12), you can build in problem-solving opportunities and insist students follow and display this method in this exercise and again in their homework. This

five-step procedure requires students to translate the problem into different representations, each more abstract and more mathematically detailed than the last:

Step 1: Visualize the problem. Sketch or diagram the main parts of the problem. Identify the known and unknown quantities and other constraints. Restate the question in different terms to make it more understandable.

Step 2: Describe in writing the principles and concepts at work in the problem. Then translate the diagram into symbolic terms, and symbolically represent the target variable.

Step 3: Plan a solution. Identify the equations necessary to solve the problem, and work backward from the target variable to see if enough information is available to arrive at a solution.

Step 4: Execute the plan. Plug in the appropriate numerical values for the variables, and compute a solution.

Step 5: Check and evaluate your solution. Is the solution complete? Are the proper units used? Is the sign correct? Is the magnitude of the answer reasonable?

Some students may profit from incorporating a few more steps: reading the problem at least twice, preferably aloud, before trying to restate it (step 1); thinking about the relationships among the different pieces of information given before describing the relevant principles and concepts (step 2); if the complexity of the numbers in the problem is getting in the way, substituting simpler numbers before planning the solution (step 3); and pausing while computing (step 4) to review their intuitive understanding of each concept (Pauk, 2001).

Supplementing or Replacing the Lecture

Experience has taught us that making major substantial course modifications, such as turning classes into a studio or workshop experience where carefully assembled student groups solve complex, realistic problems, probably requires departmental action (Breslow, 2010; Wieman, Perkins, & Gilbert, 2010). But if you are teaching a lecture course with recitation sessions, you may be able to make those sessions inquiry guided, problem focused, interactive, and collaborative by modeling them on McDermott and Shaffer's (2002, 2011–2012) physics tutorials or Laws's (1991) workshop physics. In this format, student groups answer conceptual questions on a worksheet while the instructor and TAs rotate around the groups asking them Socratic questions. On occasion, students work with a few simple laboratory items, but the activity is usually paper and pencil (or on a laptop). Compared to traditional recitation sessions, the tutorials/workshops (or *suites*) increase students' learning gains by over 50 percent (Reddish et al., 1997) and raise course completion rates (Preszler, 2009). These improvements in learning, performance, and retention extend across all types of students but are greater for females and, with respect to grades, underrepresented minority students (Preszler, 2009). In lieu of worksheets, you can bring cases and context-rich problems (see below and chapter 17) into these sessions.

Physics tutorials and workshop physics were designed not just for recitation sections but as replacements for lecture as well. When they constitute *the* method for teaching physics, students score significantly greater gains on the Force Concept Inventory and the Force Motion Conceptual Evaluation than those in lecture-based physics classes and measurably greater than those in lecture-based classes supplemented by student-active tutorials (Reddish, 2003; Reddish & Steinberg, 1999; Wittmann, 2001). However, the students' perceptions of the curriculum's effectiveness depend heavily on how well their teams function (Reddish & Steinberg, 1999).

Two more encompassing transformations in science and engineering education go under the acronyms of POGIL (process-oriented guided inquiry learning) and SCALE-UP (student-centered active learning environment for undergraduate programs). While the instructor may lecture during some class meetings or give minilectures at the beginning of most class meetings, both innovations replace a great deal of lecture with hands-on, small-group activities, such as answering critical thinking questions, developing concepts, or inquiry-guided problem solving. Since SCALE-UP places three students around one laptop, these triads may also engage in computer-based simulations or hypothesis-testing labs. These activities are known as *tangibles* and *ponderables* (Beichner et al., 2007). While the students are working, the instructor and TAs circulate around the class posing Socratic questions. Near the end of the class, at least some of the groups make oral reports, and all turn in written ones or completed worksheets (Beichner et al., 2007; Hanson, 2006). In other words, students spend much of the lecture period engaged in the activities they might do during a recitation section.

Both POGIL, which started in chemistry courses, and SCALE-UP, which was introduced in physics, have proved highly successful in promoting student learning. Compared to traditional lecturing and, in one case, interactive lecturing, POGIL has been found to increase student interest in the subject matter, raise student ratings of the instructor and the course, improve learning skills and test performance, and reduce the D-F-W (D grade-fail-withdraw) rate to statistically significant degrees. In addition, students prefer POGIL to traditional lecturing and deem the activities challenging and valuable for their learning (Hanson & Wolfskill, 2000; Lewis & Lewis, 2005).

SCALE-UP has achieved similar significant results. Students display deeper conceptual understanding, better problem-solving skills, higher test scores, and more favorable attitudes toward the discipline (Beichner et al., 2007; Oliver-Hoya & Beichner, 2004). (However, according to Breslow, 2010, the SCALE-UP-based TEAL Initiative at MIT initially encountered strong student pushback and even some from faculty.)

Not surprisingly, POGIL and SCALE-UP have spread to other disciplines. For the sciences, engineering, and mathematics, you can find plenty of online inquiry-guided activities. Start with the websites listed in the "Online Resources in STEM Education" section later in this chapter.

SCALE-UP requires some serious investments in new facilities. Short of constructing new buildings, institutions must tear out some of their lecture halls and replace them with large, one-level, computer-smart classrooms and large round tables, each with nine movable chairs and electrical outlets. In addition, either the students or the institution have to purchase laptops—one for each student triad (Beichner et al., 2007). Class sizes must decrease because a lecture hall that once held over 200 students may accommodate only 90 in the SCALE-UP format.

Making Problems More Real and Challenging

Unlike typical textbook problems, real-world ones furnish more interesting, meaningful, and challenging contexts for students to apply and hone their skills. Heller and Hollabaugh (1992) devised the idea of *context-rich problems* in physics as part of their approach to promote good problem-solving skills. As mentioned in chapter 17, these problems are short cases about real objects and realistic events, more like those that students encounter in the real world and actually care about. They thus incorporate the motivation to understand the problem, perform the calculations, and find a solution. (One such problem involves planning a skateboard stunt, another deciding whether to fight a traffic ticket.) These problems also have these additional characteristics:

- They may not refer specifically to the unknown variable.
- They may include irrelevant information not needed to solve the problem.
- They may require students to supply missing information from common knowledge or educated guessing.
- They do not specifically mention the reasonable assumptions that may be necessary to reach a workable solution.

If you teach physics, you can find a collection of context-rich problems at http://groups.physics. umn.edu/physed/Research/CRP/on-lineArchive/ ola.html. If your courses include introductory engineering, you can draw on the problems in Stephan et al.'s textbook (2014). Otherwise, you can learn to write your own such problems at http:// groups.physics.umn.edu/physed/Research/CRP/ crcreate.html.

Context-rich problems are designed to be difficult—too difficult for most students to generate satisfactory answers working on their own. Therefore, they are perfect for group work. Group learning spreads the thinking and reasoning load over several students and gets them discussing the concepts and principles behind a problem and the possible strategies for solving it. Ultimately students must choose the type of problem and approach to reaching a solution from among the alternatives suggested, which weans them away from the mechanical application of algorithms and builds their individual problem-solving skills.

To identify the most successful group arrangement and structure, Heller and her associates experimented with different group compositions, including random, homogeneous, and heterogeneous on various variables. Initially they assembled the groups randomly. After the first exam, they reconstituted the groups based on abilities, teaming together students of high, medium, and low abilities, as the cooperative learning literature advises (see chapter 15). Generally students in these heterogeneous ability groups developed their problem-solving skills as fully as did the homogeneous high-ability groups in previous experiments. The optimal group size proved to be three, with members rotating among the roles of manager, skeptic, and checker/recorder. Pairs lacked the critical mass to arrive at more than one or two strategies and were more easily sidetracked onto a fruitless path. And groups of four or more gave some members the opportunity to freeload on other members' reasoning (Heller & Hollabaugh, 1992).

Heller et al. (1992) also found that the students in their experimental program developed higher problem-solving expertise than those taught in the regular lecture and discussion section format with assignments of standard physics problems. They concluded that problem-solving groups working on context-rich problems offer a preferable alternative to the traditional approach (confirming Treisman, 1986). With students relying on each other to resolve their concerns and questions immediately as they arise, groups also free you to circulate and help the students in genuine need.

■ GETTING REAL IN THE LAB

Real, everyday science often involves solving problems in a laboratory, even if the data are collected and partially analyzed in the field. If lab work is so central to science, it should also be in science education. It should imitate the reality of scientific methodology in the lab—that is, devising hypothesis-testing strategies and procedures using reasoning and trial-and-error to meet the experimental objectives with valid and reliable findings. All the evidence indicates that traditional lab designs and manuals are outmoded, ineffective, and ripe for replacement with inquiry-guided labs.

Starting the Lab

Recall that science defectors cite a lack of theory and conceptual links as reasons for leaving. When the lab is disembodied from concepts, it lacks meaning and relevance, so it is critical to place it in the bigger scientific picture before proceeding into the actual activities. Given the time constraints of many lab activities, you may be tempted to forgo explaining the objectives to be achieved or the principles to be illustrated and simply launch into the day's work with a brief synopsis of the procedures. While this shortcutting gets students out of the lab more quickly (which they usually appreciate, especially in traditional labs), it robs the lab of its educational value.

Begin a lab by asking students to review the previous week's material. You might have them do a 2-minute free-write to activate their memory (see chapter 22). After you ask a couple of students to read their responses aloud, tie this particular lab to the course's progression of topics and labs, sketching as cohesive a big picture as possible. Then introduce the day's objectives or principles and ask the students to explain the hypotheses to be tested or questions to be answered.

Designing the Lab

In many science and engineering courses across the continent, laboratories have been completely revamped to incorporate these characteristics (Felder & Brent, 2001; Hodges, 2015; Howard & Miskowski, 2005; Kimmel, 2002; Laws, 1991; Odom, 2002; Reddish, 2003; Reddish & Steinberg, 1999; Sokoloff & Thornton, 1997):

- They reflect the *inquiry-guided learning* model—that is, they have students learn or apply material to meet some kind of a challenge, such as to answer questions, solve problems, conduct an experiment, or interpret data. In one way or another, students conduct real scientific investigations, identifying and solving problems the way scientists actually do, only with the instructor's guidance. They must develop their own strategy to test a hypothesis or find answers, along with the procedures to carry it out. The lab manual provides neither, and the lab results are not predictable.
- They focus on developing students' *critical thinking, decision making, and complex reasoning skills,* including inductive thinking, by giving students opportunities to practice them. In addition to developing an experimental strategy and procedures, they must devise one or more explanations for unexpected results and include them in their lab reports.

- They foster genuine *teamwork and collaboration.* Since the labs are novel and challenging, students mutually need each other, as they would in a professional setting. In many cases, each lab group turns in one report and shares a group grade. (In Kimmel's labs, students also keep their own individual lab notebook, which is graded.) In addition to sharing their discoveries, results, and conclusions, students may even exchange their lab reports for peer review (Odom, 2002).
- They feature *modern technology,* such as industry equipment in current use and updated software (e.g., spreadsheet, database, statistical, and mathematical) for analyzing the data and displaying the results.

For clarification, here is an example of an actual inquiry-based lab: a pendulum lab in a sophomore-level calculus-based physics course (Odom, 2002). First, students use their laptops to access the online lab manual. The manual gives a background lesson on the basic mechanics of a pendulum, including the equation to describe its period and the simplified version for small angle approximations (first-order expression). Students then receive the two lab objectives or outcomes:

1. Determine the maximum angle for which the period of a simple pendulum is valid. In other words, determine the cutoff angle for when the small angle approximation fails.
2. Use a simple pendulum to determine the value of g, the acceleration due to the earth's gravity.

Each lab group is supplied with equipment: a pendulum stand, clamp, string, and bob (an aluminum rod with its center of gravity marked); a protractor; a computer timing device (on the lab website); and meter sticks (located around the classroom). In addition, groups receive 10 "nudge" questions to answer and a lab report template (on the lab website) with five problems to solve, all of which lead the students through the process of meeting the lab objectives. They receive no other directions. This lab requires about 6 hours over 2 weeks. Odom (2002) also got rid of the 3-hour-a-week-lab restriction that constrains most science curricula.

Innovations such as Odom's are not isolated. Developed by Sokoloff and Thornton (1997), real-time physics labs begin with phenomena and lead students to derive the principles inductively. The labs rely on the power of small groups answering challenging questions and performing nonroutine tasks with the assistance of a floating instructor or teaching assistant. Typically students receive most or all of the data they need electronically, along with analysis tools, so they focus less on collecting data and more on interpreting them.

The results of these experimental programs have been so positive that the hosting institutions have adopted them into their regular curriculum. Students actually discuss and even argue about the best plan of attack, and they divide the labor on their own. Compared to students in courses with traditional cookbook labs, they hand in higher-quality lab reports, do significantly better on tests, have higher final grades, give the course higher evaluations, and enjoy the labs more (Felder & Brent, 2001; Hodges, 2015; Howard & Miskowski, 2005; Hufford, 1991; Kimmel, 2002; Luckie, Maleszewski, Loznak, & Krha, 2004; Odom, 2002). In addition, they make greater improvements in scientific reasoning (Benford & Lawson, 2001), as well as other higher-order thinking skills, such as data analysis and interpretation (Howard & Miskowski, 2005). They retain the lab material longer as well (Lord & Orkwiszewski, 2006; Luckie et al., 2004). In Kimmel's labs, the C students show the greatest gains in achievement. In addition, students' attitudes in his new labs are better than those in the old. Specifically, students are more motivated and more engaged, they perceive they are learning more in the course and the labs, and they assess their team functioning more favorably (Kimmel, 2002).

ONLINE RESOURCES FOR STEM EDUCATION

A rich variety of POGIL, SCALE-UP, tutorial/ workshop activities, and inquiry-guided labs is available online as virtual labs, field trips, problem scenarios, and simulations for all the STEM fields:

Physics

http://phet.colorado.edu; http://apphysicsb.homestead.com/vls.html (links to many virtual labs); http://web.mit.edu/8.02t/www/802TEAL3D/ Workshop physics: http://physics.dickinson .edu/~wp_web/WP_homepage.html Physics tutorials in print only in McDermott, Shaffer, & Physics Education Group (2012)

Chemistry

http://www.chemcollective.org/find.php; http://onlinelabs.in/chemistry; http://www.chem.uci.edu/undergrad/applets POGIL textbooks http://www.pogil.org/ resources/curriculum-materials/textbooks (chemistry and biochemistry)

Biology

http://www.hhmi.org/biointeractive/vlabs/; http://onlinelabs.in/biology; http://highered.mcgraw-hill.com/ sites/0072437316/student_view0/online_labs.html; http://www.biologylabsonline.com/; http://bio.rutgers.edu/; http://www.phschool.com/science/biology_ place/labbench/

Zoology

http://www.abdn.ac.uk/~clt011/zoology/ virtuallaboratory/

Human Anatomy

http://onlinelabs.in/anatomy

Geography

http://homepages.abdn.ac.uk/p.marston/pages/ geography/virtualfieldtrip/

Geology

http://onlinelabs.in/geology

Engineering

http://www.jhu.edu/~virtlab/virtlab.html; http://virlab.virginia.edu/VL/contents.htm

Statistics

http://www.math.uah.edu/stat/; http://onlinestatbook.com/rvls.html

Multidisciplinary sites

http://www.planetseed.com/science/lab-activities; http://matdl.org/virtuallabs/index.php/ Main_Page; http://www.merlot.org/; http://virtuallaboratory.colorado.edu; http://jersey.uoregon.edu/; http://www.shodor.org/interactivate/ POGIL problems http://serc.carletonvdu/sp/ library/pogil/examples.html (81 in all sciences) POGIL instructor's guide http://www.pogil.org/ resources/implementation/instructors-guide

WHY STEM EDUCATION IS SO IMPORTANT

We are forever hearing that our nation is falling behind other countries in scientific literacy and quantitative reasoning at all grade levels and that we are facing a shortage of STEM professionals. At least so far, internationals have been filling in the openings in the United States, but for how long?

If these reasons to improve STEM education aren't pressing enough, then consider the broader place of these disciplines, especially the sciences, in our country. In a truly enlightened, democratic society, people must be scientifically and quantitatively literate—not only conversant in but also comfortable with these fields. Everyone who teaches in these disciplines plays a crucial role in fostering a society that is well informed enough to govern itself intelligently. Self-government requires not only a well-informed populace but also one that can solve its own problems. Problem solving of every type—open-ended and closed-ended, qualitative and quantitative, high-uncertainty and formulaic—is STEM's stock-in-trade. This fact alone makes it an essential component of higher education. But we have to ensure that students learn how problem solving and knowledge building really proceed—not like a well-ordered textbook but in a zigzag, trial-and-error, collaborative manner that demands complex reasoning, strategic thinking, and inventiveness.

PART 5

TOOLS AND TECHNIQUES TO FACILITATE LEARNING

CHAPTER 20

Helping Students Learn How They Learn

People may be born to learn, but they are not born knowing the best strategies to learn all the declarative, procedural, and conditional knowledge that they encounter in life. It's not that everyone learns differently, though on some level that may be true. Rather, some principles of learning apply across everyone, but schools don't teach them. K–12 teachers may expose students to some mnemonic devices, such as the acronym HOMES for the names of the Great Lakes, and a few study and test-taking tips that students may or may not apply on their own. But they don't explain how the mind processes new information, how to facilitate and deepen that processing, and what interferes with it. If our students don't learn how to learn from *us*, where will they learn it?

■ LEARNING AS AN "INSIDE JOB"

Learning is something that one does to oneself. Admittedly, this is a controversial position because it seems to eliminate teaching from the learning process. It really doesn't, but let's explore the claim further.

Figure 20.1 shows the major mental processes involved in learning and memory. Note that while a person may not be in total control of the surrounding sensory information, all the processes that move sensory stimuli from the environment into long-term memory and make it retrievable are completely under her control. The learner decides where to direct her attention and how long to focus it there. She decides whether to subject the information to elaborative rehearsal and eventual encoding by thinking about it—thinking specifically about what it means and how it fits into what she already knows about the topic. If it doesn't seem to fit, she may decide to reject and forget it, or she may decide to reconsider the validity and organization of her prior knowledge—that is, her mental model. If she wants to remember this new information well enough to recall it on demand, she will practice retrieving it every so often. Learning, then, rests solely with the learner.

Figure 20.1   Model of Learning and Memory Processes

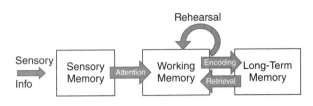

Or does it? If you don't know how learning works, then you don't know how to control the process well enough to make it happen. This is definitely where teaching comes in—specifically, teaching students how they, and people in general, learn. Certainly most students know little or nothing about learning otherwise. Undergraduates are known to blame their poor performance on their instructors' "ineffective" teaching and the irrelevance or advanced level of course material and, as a result, they don't feel responsible for their own learning (Curren & Rosen, 2006; Singleton-Jackson, Jackson, & Reinhardt, 2010; Twenge, 2007). Even many graduate and professional students see themselves as somewhat passive recipients of knowledge and skills. In one study, veterinary students most commonly identified the quality of their faculty's teaching, including the workload and curriculum, as having the biggest impact on their learning and rarely cited their own effort or learning strategies (Ruohoniemi & Lindblom-Ylanne, 2009). With these beliefs about learning, these students may never become independent, self-directed learners.

We can certainly make it easier for students to lead themselves through the learning process. First, we can inspire their interest in the material by displaying our passion for it and explaining its relevance to the world and their own lives. We can catch their attention with intriguing class openers, humor, eye contact, vocal variety, physical movement, expressiveness, our reasons for our choice of teaching methods and assignments, and interesting activities for them to do in class. We can minimize distractions by discouraging unsanctioned uses of technology and other disruptive classroom behaviors (see chapters 4 and 9). We can jump-start

students' elaborative rehearsal and encoding of new material by pausing frequently for them to reflect on it, discuss it, write about it, or apply it to a problem. And we can give them retrieval practice by quizzing them, leading recitations, having them do a free-recall exercise, or having them graphically represent it. But ultimately students have to choose to maintain their attention, continue the rehearsing and encoding, and practice retrieving on their own to recall the material during the next test, for the final exam, and beyond. Participation in class-time activities alone cannot complete the learning process.

Deep, long-lasting learning is self-aware, which is an internal state of mind. In other words, a learner is aware of his learning. First, he thinks about his learning goals. If he is reading a book chapter, does he want to be able to recognize, reproduce, apply, or critique the important information? Then he chooses a strategy for accomplishing this goal—perhaps note taking, jotting down answers to study questions, writing marginalia, visually representing the material, occasionally self-quizzing, reviewing, or writing a summary. While he's following his plan, he checks his learning every so often to assess how well it's going. What can he recall? How is the information organized? What are the main points or themes? If his strategy doesn't seem to be working well, he replaces it with a more promising one. Finally, he checks his learning at the end. How well did he meet his goals? What did he learn about his learning?

This process, called *self-regulated learning*, is the conscious planning, monitoring, and evaluation of one's learning with the intention of maximizing it. Most students do not practice it. If they did, more of them would answer your invitation, "Does anyone have any questions on the readings [or lecture]?" with questions. Their silence belies the fact that they haven't seriously asked themselves, let alone assessed, what they have and haven't understood. The material made sense when they read it or heard it, so they optimistically assume they *have* understood it and will therefore remember it.

Self-regulated learning proceeds through three stages:

1. Planning a strategy before the learning or performance task, which includes conducting a task analysis
2. Monitoring one's learning during the task
3. Evaluating one's learning after the task

In addition, the process takes place in three dimensions:

1. The *metacognitive*, which constitutes metacognition, often defined as "thinking about one's thinking"
2. The *meta-emotional*, which involves monitoring and directing one's emotions to ensure sufficient motivation, justified confidence, open-mindedness to challenging ideas, and perseverance
3. The *environmental*, which entails finding and setting up the best physical conditions for one's learning

At this juncture, we can distinguish between self-regulated learning and metacognition. The latter is mainly cognitive (Flavell, 1976; McGuire, 2015), although some scholars (e.g., Hostetter & Savion, 2013) include a few emotional and environmental elements (motivation, study context) in their definition of the former. Self-regulated learning encompasses metacognition and more.

■ THE LEARNER'S QUESTIONS

If we cross the three process of self-regulated learning by its three dimensions, we get Table 20.1 with nine cells of questions that the savvy learner will ask herself in the process of learning something.

The learner might not ask herself all the questions every time she starts a task because she may already know the answers. For example, she may know what kind of task it is because she's done it successfully hundreds of times before, which means she probably knows the best strategy to use. Presumably she heard about various approaches over the years, experimented with them, and identified the ones that work most effectively for her.

Table 20.1   Questions That Self-Regulated Learners Ask Themselves

	Metacognitive	Meta-emotional	Environmental
Planning before a learning or performance task (task analysis)	• What kind of a task is this? • What is my goal? How will I know I have reached it? • What do I already know about the topic? • What additional information, if any, will I need? • What strategies should I use: actively listening, taking notes, outlining, visually representing the material, occasionally self-quizzing, reviewing, or writing a summary? • What strengths can I bring to the task? • What are my weaknesses, and how can I make up for them?	• How interested and motivated am I to do the task, and how can I increase my interest and motivation if they are low? • What's the value or relevance of what I'll be learning? • How confident am I in my ability to learn this material? If not very, how can I increase my belief in my ability to learn it without becoming overconfident? What similar tasks can I recall doing well in the past?	• What is the best environment for the task that I can create? • Am I in a good physical place and position to do this task? • Is the temperature right for me? How about the background sounds? • Have I had enough sleep? • Have I had the right amount of coffee today? • Have I put potential distractions far away? • How much time and what resources will I need? Are these resources handy?

(continued)

Table 20.1 (*Continued*)

	Metacognitive	Meta-emotional	Environmental
Monitoring during a learning or performance task	• Am I sure I know what I am doing? • Does my approach to the task make sense? • Am I making good progress toward my goal? • How well are my strategies working? • What changes in approach or strategies should I make, if any? • How focused am I? Am I getting tired? If so, how can I keep myself focused and alert? • What material is the most important? • What material am I having trouble understanding? • How does what I am learning relate to what I already know? • How is my thinking on the topic changing?	• If my interest and motivation are sagging, how is what I'm learning relevant to my experience or my future? • What material is challenging what I've thought about the subject? Am I resisting it? • Am I starting to get discouraged or give up? Am I thinking I'm just no good at this subject? How can I change this negative thinking? What similar tasks can I recall doing well in the past?	• Should I try another environment to see if it works better? • How about another physical position? • How are the temperature and background sounds working out? • Am I staying away from distractions? If not, I have to get farther away from them. • Do I need a short break to refresh my mind and body?
Evaluating after a learning or performance task	• How well did I achieve my goal or master what I set out to learn? • What can I recall, and what do I need to review? • What were the most important points I learned? • Can I see and organize the interrelationships among them? • What am I still having trouble understanding? • What questions do I have to ask my instructor? • How does what I learned relate to other things I've been learning or have experienced? • How has my thinking on the topic changed? • Which approaches and strategies worked well? • Which didn't? • What do I need to do differently next time I take on a similar task?	• How am I reacting emotionally to my evaluation of my learning? Being pleased reinforces a learner's motivation and other positive emotions she generated about the material and her ability to learn it. Being disappointed may lead either to improving her learning strategies or her defensively withdrawing her energy from task. This last reaction in turn undermines the positive emotions needed to begin the next learning or performance task.	• How well did I avoid distractions and stay on task? • If not that well, how can I avoid distractions more effectively in the future? • Do I need to experiment more with different physical factors to find the best working environment and break schedule for myself?

Source: Some questions are adapted from Schraw (1998) and Tanner (2012).

But she will still have to monitor her progress, understanding, focus, reactions, and mental connections and evaluate her learning at the end. Emotionally, she may never have to question her confidence in her ability to do the task well, but she still has to examine and monitor her motivation and interest in the material, buoy them up if they sag, check for affective resistance to the content, and assess her emotional response to her metacognitive evaluation of her learning. Similarly, she may be quite familiar with her optimal learning environment, but she still needs to monitor herself for mental fatigue, time her breaks, and resist distractions.

■ THE EVIDENCE FOR SELF-REGULATED LEARNING

Perhaps the strongest evidence that self-regulated learning enhances student achievement and performance comes from Hattie's (2009) mega-meta-analysis of more than 800 meta-analyses on the effects of different teaching and learning methods and teacher competencies on student learning and achievement at all educational levels. While he found that all the causal factors have some positive impact, some have a much more powerful one than others.

Hattie looked specifically at the effect size of the various methods and teacher skills. Among the strongest factors was the teacher's clarity in communicating, with an effect size of .75. This number means that when clarity increases by 1 standard deviation, student learning/achievement increases by three-fourths of a standard deviation. Getting feedback had a slightly weaker effect size of .73; spaced (as opposed to mass) practice .71; and metacognitive strategies, which are only the cognitive aspect of self-regulated learning, .69. This last effect size was measurably larger than those of mastery learning, group work, computer-assisted instruction, time on task, and test-taking strategies. McGuire (2015) recounts many cases of struggling students who became A students just by using the metacognitive strategies she taught them.

We find more evidence in a series of research studies conducted in developmental courses at the New York City College of Technology, also known as City Tech (Zimmerman, Moylan, Hudesman, White, & Flugman, 2011). The first study measured the effects of self-regulated learning activities and assignments in a semester-long developmental mathematics course enrolling 140 students in six sections. In the randomized experimental design, three of the sections received traditional instruction and served as the control group, and the other three incorporated self-regulated learning activities and served as the treatment group. In all the sections, faculty administered the same 15- to 20-minute quizzes with four or five problems every two or three class periods, as well as the same major exams and final exam.

However, at the beginning of the course, the instructors of the self-regulated learning (SRL) sections explained to their classes how errors offer learning opportunities, and they modeled and provided practice in error detection and strategy adaptation. In addition, they asked students not only to show all their work in their problem solutions but also to rate their confidence in their ability to solve each problem, first before they tried to solve it and again after solving it, so overconfident students learned to correct their inflated self-assessments. On the quizzes, students also had the chance to earn back lost points by completing a self-reflection form for each missed or incomplete problem where they wrote an analysis of their error and re-solved a similar problem.

The results, shown in Figure 20.2, were statistically significant and unequivocal. Sixty-eight percent of the students in the SRL treatment-group sections passed the course, versus 49 percent of those in the control-group sections. In addition, 64 percent of the former students passed the gateway test in math required for admission into credit-bearing courses, versus only 39 percent of the latter students.

Following the same randomized experimental design and treatment structure, the study was replicated on students enrolled in sections of

Figure 20.2   Percentages of City Tech Students Passing the Course and Gateway Exam in Traditional versus SRL Sections of Developmental Math

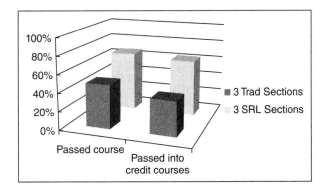

served as the control group, but they otherwise had the same lessons, quizzes, and exams. The quizzes and exams asked students to do writing tasks such as paraphrasing or summarizing a passage of text. But in the SRL sections, students received revision sheets after their quizzes were returned where they could redo any writing task that they didn't do correctly. They also answered questions on where they erred in the quiz, how they prepared for it, and how they would prepare better next time.

The strategy of having students identify and correct their errors worked just as effectively in writing as in math. Seventy-two percent of the treatment-group students passed the gateway exam in writing, while only 52 percent of the control-group students did. The following fall semester, 65 percent of the former students successfully completed a credit-bearing writing course, compared to only 32 percent of the latter students.

an intensive 5-week developmental math course offered in the summer. As Figure 20.3 shows, 84 percent of the students in the self-regulated learning sections passed the course versus 63 percent of the control-group students. The following fall semester, 60 percent of the former students successfully completed a credit-bearing math course versus only 34 percent of the latter.

The City Tech developmental writing faculty decided to follow Zimmerman et al.'s lead and conducted a similar study on the students taking a five-week intensive writing course offered in the summer (http://www.selfregulatedlearning.blogspot.com/). Again, some sections were infused with self-regulated learning activities and assignments and the others

You can find the results of more experimental studies on the effects of self-regulated learning at the Self-Regulated Learning Program website (http://www.selfregulatedlearning.blogspot.com/). This additional research includes students enrolled in a variety of courses at a number of 2-year, 4-year, and secondary institutions. Every study reports that students performed much better in classes and following classes that incorporated self-regulated learning activities and assignments.

Figure 20.3   Percentages of City Tech Students Passing the Summer Course and a For-Credit Fall-Semester Math Course in the Traditional versus SRL Sections of Developmental Math

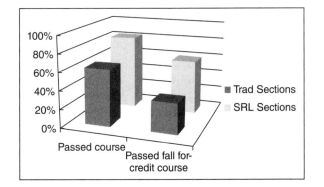

Figure 20.4   Percentages of City Tech Students Passing the Gateway Exam and a For-Credit Fall-Semester Writing Course in the Traditional versus SRL Sections of Developmental Writing

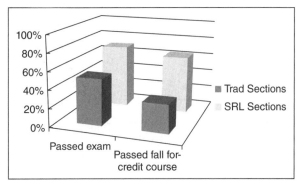

ACTIVITIES AND ASSIGNMENTS FOR EVERY OCCASION

At this point, you may be asking how you can enhance your courses with self-regulated learning components. This section will acquaint you with a sample of self-regulated learning activities and assignments. You'll find dozens more in Nilson (2013a). Some of these focus on planning (e.g., goal setting), others on monitoring, and still others on evaluation. Several are intended for the beginning and the end of a course. Those that take place during a lecture are sometimes called *lecture wrappers*; those designed to accompany readings, *reading wrappers*; those piggybacked on assignments, *assignment wrappers* or *meta-assignments*; and those associated with quizzes or exams, *exam wrappers*. If they generate homework to hand in, the reading wrappers also serve to enhance reading compliance and comprehension (see chapter 21).

Students don't mind these additional tasks because they are short, low stress, low stakes, and useful for learning about themselves and improving their grades. You don't mind them either because you don't have to grade the in-class activities and you can grade most of the assignments pass/fail, credit/no credit at a glance. If the assignment is worth 5 points, students will earn all 5 points if their work meets all the specifications that you set for the assignment—for example, all the questions are answered, the problem is attempted in good faith, the short essay addresses the topic and is at least 150 words long—or no points at all if it doesn't. This standard motivates students to read the directions and take the assignment seriously. Only lengthy reflections and self-evaluations may require actual grading using a rubric, such as those that accompany substantial experiential learning activities like fieldwork, service-learning, a lengthy simulation, or a complex role play. And even these can be graded pass/fail (see the "Specifications Grading" section in chapter 27).

Following are self-regulated learning activities or assignments and the course components they are designed for. The first, however, presents four paired activities or assignments to book-end a course.

Course Bookends: Paired Activities for the Beginning and End of a Course

Beginning of the Course	End of the Course
Informal essay: How I Earned an A in This Course (Zander & Zander, 2000)	Informal essay: How I Earned an A in This Course—or Not
Reflections on the nature of the course material (Kraft, 2008; Suskie, 2009)	Repeat reflections and compare.
Take-a-stance-and-justify essays on course material	Correct first essays and rewrite them using course content; usable as the final exam (J. M. Coggeshall, personal correspondence, 2010–2011).
Knowledge survey (student confidence survey) on course learning outcomes and related knowledge and skills (Nuhfer & Knipp, 2003; Wirth & Perkins, 2005, 2008a)	Repeat knowledge survey and compare.

For Live Lectures: Periodic Free-Recall

1. Students listen to a 10- to 20-minute minilecture, then close their notebook when the instructor pauses.
2. They write down all the important points they can recall and any questions they have, leaving space between the points.
3. They pair up to compare, fill in, and fine-tune their free-recall notes, as well as answer each other's questions.

(Bonwell & Eison, 1991)

For Live Lectures: Active Listening Checks

1. Students listen to a 10- to 20-minute minilecture, paying special attention for the three most important points (they may take notes).
2. The instructor pauses, and they write down the three most important points and turn these in.
3. The instructor reveals the three most important points.
4. Students assess their listening skills.

(Lovett, 2008)

For Reading, Videos, or Podcasts: Minute Papers

- What is the most useful or valuable thing you learned?
- What is the most important point or central concept?
- What idea or fact surprised you?
- What stands out in your mind?
- What helped or hindered your understanding?
- How does the content connect or conflict with your prior knowledge, beliefs, or values?

(Chew, quoted in Lang, 2012; Wirth, n.d.)

For Live Lectures, Readings, Videos, or Podcasts: Reflective Writing

- What are the most important concepts or principles you just heard/read, and what you don't understand clearly?
- What comparisons and connections can you make between what you just heard/read and your prior learning, preconceptions, existing framework of knowledge, or other courses?
- How did you react emotionally to what you just heard/read? Explain how the material reinforced, challenged, or modified your attitudes, values, or beliefs.

(Araujo, quoted in Schell, 2012; Kalman, 2007; Mezeske, 2009; Wirth, n.d.)

For Readings, Videos, or Podcasts: Read, Recall, Review

1. Read (or watch or listen). Then put away the book and any notes.
2. Recall all you can, and write it down (to turn in for homework).
3. Review the reading for what you misunderstood or forgot, and write down these points (also to turn in for homework).

(McDaniel, Howard, & Einstein, 2009; Roediger & Butler, 2010; Roediger & Karpicke, 2006)

For Live Lectures, Readings, Videos, or Podcasts: Visual Representations of the Content

See chapter 23, the section "Types of Visuals for Learning."

For Math-Based Homework Problems

- "Think aloud": Student pairs talk through solving a few homework problems in class and guide each other through the process (Whimbey & Lochhead, 1999).
- For each problem solved incorrectly or not at all, students write an error analysis or a description of the correct strategy and solve the same or a similar problem (Zimmerman, Moylan, Hudesman, White, & Flugman, 2011).

For Papers, Projects, and Portfolios: Reflective Writing

- Describe the research (or writing) process you went through while completing this assignment, including what steps you took, what strategies you followed, what problems you encountered, and how you overcame them.
- Describe your reasoning to define the problem, decide what principles and concepts to apply, develop alternative solutions, and determine one solution as the best possible.
- For a portfolio: Evaluate all of the samples of your work and explain the progress they show you made over the term. Evaluate your strengths, weaknesses, and achievements as a writer.
- Write a paraphrase of my feedback.
- Identify your goals and strategies for your revision.
- Explain the value of this assignment to you. What knowledge did you gain? What skills did you gain or improve? When do you think this knowledge or these skills will be useful in future?
- How will you do a better job on a similar assignment next time?
- What advice on this assignment do you have for the students who will take this course the next time it is given? How should they best prepare? What strategies do you recommend? What problems and pitfalls can you warn them about? What are they likely to gain from doing the assignment?

(Jensen, 2011; MacDonald, 2013; Mezeske, 2009; Rhode Island Diploma System, 2005; Suskie, 2009; Zubizaretta, 2004, 2009)

For Experiential Learning (Service-Learning/Community Engagement, Fieldwork, Simulation, Game, or Role Play): Reflective Writing

- Connect specific aspects of your experience to the learning outcomes, key concepts, key principles, and other content of the course.
- Explain and evaluate your goals, strategies, decisions, and responses to other players. How and why did these change during the experience?
- Evaluate how well you achieved your goals, how effective your strategies were, and how well you performed overall.

(Brown & Rose, 2008; Nilson, 2013a; Suskie, 2009; Tai-Seale, 2001)

For Graded Exams: Reflective Questions

1. Compare your expected and actual performance.
2. How do you feel about your grade?
3. How many hours did you study, and was this enough time?
4. How did you study? What exactly did you do to prepare for this exam?
5. Where and why did you lose points? Do you see any patterns?
6. Set your performance goal for the next exam and design a study game plan. What will you do differently?

(Barkley, 2009)

For Graded Exams: Test Autopsy

Error analysis form; reflective questions may be added

Question Profile			Reason Answer Was Incorrect			
Question Missed	Points Lost	Type of Question	Carelessness	Unfamiliar Material	Misinterpreted Question	Did Not Finish

(Academic Success Center, Iowa State University, 2011; Achacoso, 2004)

Self-Correcting Exams

Students take a multiple-choice exam in class, submit their answers on a form, and have until the next class meeting to use all their course resources to correct any wrong answers. They receive 2 points for each correct answer on the original test and 1 point for every wrong answer they correct (Gruhn & Cheng, 2014).

■ SELF-REGULATED AND SELF-DIRECTED LEARNING

Self-directed learning has a range of definitions. Knowles's (1975) is so inclusive as to overlap with self-regulated learning:

> In its broadest meaning, "self-directed learning" describes a process by which individuals take the initiative, with or without the assistance of others, in diagnosing their learning needs, formulating learning goals, identifying human and material resources for learning, choosing and implementing appropriate learning strategies, and evaluating learning outcomes. (p. 18)

Representing the more limited and more popular definitions is Gibbons's (2002): "any increase in knowledge, skill, accomplishment, or personal development that an individual selects and brings about by his or her own efforts using any method in any circumstances at any time" (p. 2). What these two conceptions share in common is this: a self-directed learner is self-motivated to take on a learning task and successfully complete it while relying on his own efforts and learning strategies. One could argue that only a self-regulated learner can be self-directed, but not the other way around. Self-directed learning uniquely emphasizes having a choice in what to learn, which adults out of school typically have. Self-regulated learning does not presume such autonomy and is better suited to the formal educational context.

■ SOURCES FOR TEACHING YOUR STUDENTS HOW TO LEARN

You can teach your students how to learn by sharing the information on learning in this book, especially chapters 1, 4, 22, and this one. Or if you don't have the time or feel comfortable doing that, you can assign any of several readily available readings about learning, all written for students:

- "Learning (Your First Job)," by Robert Leamnson (2002) at http://www.udel.edu/CIS/106/iaydin/07F/misc/firstJob.pdf (12 pages of wise advice on the effort that studying and learning involve)
- "Learning to Learn," by Karl R. Wirth and Dexter Perkins (2008b) at http://www.macalester.edu/academics/geology/wirth/learning.pdf (29 pages of more advanced, detailed, and technical material than Leamnson's article)
- *The New Science of Learning: How to Learn in Harmony with Your Brain*, by Terry Doyle and Todd Zakrajsek (2013). Sterling, VA: Stylus. (126 pages; an easy-to-read learner's manual for the mind)

The messages in these readings will probably come as sobering news to your students and should easily spark discussion, so leave some class time for it.

CHAPTER 21

Ensuring Students Prepare for Class

Some faculty say that they don't have the luxury of leading engaging activities in class because so many of their students don't do the assigned homework, whether this means reading print or online material, watching videos, or listening to podcasts. Or if they do their homework, they do it too superficially. Indeed your students have to prepare for class if you intend to run an active classroom. Their first exposure to the material should be on their own outside class so that they can work with it in class (Walvoord & Anderson, 2010). In fact, many students wait until the next exam to do any homework, by which time too many classes have been dulled by too many lectures and too little student participation. In addition, students do not learn the material as deeply from listening to lectures without doing the readings in advance (Fernald, 2004).

The research on how to induce students to prepare for class is confined to readings, but we can safely assume that without an incentive, many students will skip assigned videos and podcasts too.

And just the fact that you assign homework isn't incentive enough. Estimated from their performance on pop quizzes, about 80 percent of the students normally did the readings in 1981, but only 20 percent of them did in 1997 (Burchfield & Sappington, 2000). More recently, the percentage may have risen—in Hoeft's (2012) study, to 46 percent—perhaps because some faculty have instituted reading compliance measures. But only 21 percent of these students read the material more than once, and only 45 percent demonstrated basic comprehension of it. Did some of the students lie about their compliance, or did they not know how to process it?

In this chapter, we dispassionately examine why students come to class unprepared. They have their reasons, right or wrong, and we often make it easy for them. But we can take measures that will motivate the vast majority of students to do the readings, view the videos, or listen to the podcasts—and help them to get value from them—while making it costly for them to ignore the homework.

WHY STUDENTS DON'T PREPARE

Let's examine all the reasons that some students habitually do not do the homework, at least not when it's due. Don't worry about the student who occasionally doesn't do the readings because of some short-term life interference, and eliminate those who overburden themselves by trying to combine a full course load with more than half-time employment.

Poor Reading Abilities, Habits, and Persistence

Despite the trend toward assigning videos and podcasts, readings provide the mainstay of higher education. Yet roughly half of the high school graduates in the United States do not have the reading skills that college-level work requires (Kuh, Kinzie, Schuh, Whitt, & Associates, 2005). According to the 2003 National Assessment of Adult Literacy, the latest such survey available, relatively few students achieve reading proficiency by the end of their higher education; in prose literacy, only 19 percent of those with a 2-year degree and 31 percent of those with a 4-year degree, and in document literacy, only 16 percent and 25 percent, respectively (Kutner et al., 2007). One problem that gets in the way of students' reading comprehension and speed is their inability to focus for more than a few minutes (Blue, 2003). They may not realize that reading is a mind activity, not an eye activity, and a very engrossing one that demands concentrated, sustained attention. With limited reading experience, they lack a sophisticated vocabulary, which slows their reading speed, impedes their comprehension, and discourages them from further reading.

Whether as a cause or a result, many students don't seem to enjoy reading, at least not for learning purposes, and do very little of it—much less than earlier students used to. Americans ages 15 to 34 spend on average about 1 hour per week reading, and the percentage of adults ages 18 to 24 who read literature dropped by 17 percent over the two preceding decades. However, a more recent study (Huang, Blacklock, & Capps, 2013) reports that college students read quite a bit—almost 21 hours a week—just not for their courses. On a weekly basis, they dedicate almost 9 hours to reading on the Internet, chiefly social media such as Facebook, Instagram, and Twitter, and a little over 4 hours to extracurricular reading, such as the news, graphic novels, and nonacademic books. But they give only 7.7 hours to academic reading. They complain that reading textbooks is tedious and time-consuming, and some admit they do it only if they have to for an exam.

Higher-Priority Activities

Students also have more compelling or more attractive options for their nonclass time. We can easily understand their obligations to their jobs, their family, other more important courses, and community service arrangements. However, we have to accept the fact they may prioritize socializing (virtual, phone, or face-to-face), fraternity and sorority activities, playing sports and games, watching television, listening to music, web surfing, shopping, drinking, sleeping, working out, reading a novel or magazine, doing more interesting course work, or engaging in extracurricular activities such as clubs and hobbies. Some of these activities mix well—for example, socializing and drinking—making the combination all the more appealing. Our courses have stiff competition for students' time.

No Perceived Need

Many college students never or rarely did the readings in middle and high school and did very well, thank you. In fact, two-thirds of the entering first-year students in fall 2003 claimed to have spent less than 6 hours a week doing homework in their senior year in high school, and almost half of these students graduated from high school with an A average (Higher Education Research Institute, 2004). Furthermore, 70 percent of all students entering college in 2003 rated their academic ability above average or within the top 10 percent of their age group (Higher Education Research Institute, 2004). Basing their expectations of the present on the past, many students believe that they shouldn't have to work any harder in college than they did in high school, and they see themselves as intelligent enough to slide thorough their college courses. Clearly they consider reading tangential to their learning (Bradley, 2007).

Furthermore, students assess their short-term need to do the readings on time. If they don't have to hand in any homework on the readings, won't be quizzed on the material in class, and won't have to publicly discuss the material, most of them will skip the readings (Hoeft, 2012; Nathan, 2005). They figure they will pick up the gist of them during the next class, especially if you normally lecture. Or their friends will tell them about the class. Or they will go to you to get lecture notes. Or they can read your notes on the LMS. Of course, the wisdom of these strategies depends mostly on you.

No Perceived Payoff

Today students are practical instrumentalists. They view college as a means to an end—the end being a high-paying job that can support their consumer habits. This is particularly true of millennials (see chapter 1), but the somewhat older generation Xers share with them the demand for course material of immediate relevance and utility. Neither generation received the quality K–12 education that taught them to appreciate learning for its own sake, apply themselves to academic pursuits, or defer their gratification for a longer-term purpose. Therefore, they tend to view assignments, readings, and tests as barriers on their path to a degree and college in general as a game about grades. In their minds, the readings, recorded lectures, and the like have nothing to do with their aspirations in life or their definition of success, so they are not worth the time and effort.

These young people misperceive the real world, as reading ability correlates strongly with income. In 2003, only 13 percent of the below-basic readers earned $850 a week or more, while almost 60 percent of the proficient readers did (National Endowment for the Arts, 2007). In other words, poor readers become poor students who become poorly paid workers, and good readers become good students who become better-paid workers.

When you examine all the possible reasons that students habitually don't prepare for class, they boil down to three: (1) they don't want to (due to poor reading skills or compared to other activities), (2) they don't think they have to, and (3) they really don't have to—that is, they face no dire consequences if they don't.

■ HOW WE CAN EQUIP AND INDUCE STUDENTS TO COME PREPARED

Let's accept that fact that most students approach the assigned readings, videos, and podcasts with a somewhat cavalier and pragmatic attitude, combined with varying degrees of anxiety and dread. To address this negative posture, we have to see the issue from their point of view given their life circumstances to avoid projecting our identities and values onto them. When we were in college, most of us ranked among the best students, or we wouldn't have made it through graduate school and into the academy. We exceeded the average in our reading abilities and persistence, our enjoyment of the activity, the importance we attached to it, the learning benefits we derived from it, our interest in at least some subjects, and our raw intelligence. At the same time, we probably weren't perfect students ourselves. No doubt we cut some corners, skipped some readings, spent some nights cramming, and prioritized certain extracurricular activities over some of our courses. And we were gifted enough to get away with it.

Here we are years later, happily wedded to our fields and expert readers in them, selecting the readings that we value for our novice students. We may not have noticed that we have internalized a large disciplinary vocabulary that is a foreign language to them. We have also learned a variety of cognitive shortcuts that make our reading easy. For us, a single term may recall an entire mental structure of concepts, principles, assumptions, and implications that enriches our understanding of the sentence and foreshadows the next sentence. The unending flow of meaning allows us to move through the text quickly with unwavering focus. Even our brightest students stumble over technical vocabulary and bring shallow, if any, associations to their academic readings. And they can't possibly appreciate their value or our reasons for selecting them.

Moreover, from our students' standpoint, some of us don't seem very serious about the readings. We assign them but make little or no effort to sell the students on them. This might not be so odd if everyone else weren't trying to sell them something. Many of us lecture the readings in class, as if we don't expect our students to do them either. In addition, few of us have introduced incentive or sanction mechanisms to hold our students accountable for doing the readings, viewing the videos, or listening to the podcasts when they are due. A big test is too distant a concern. So why should they do the homework?

Stop Lecturing the Readings and Never Lecture the Videos or Podcasts

None of the strategies in this chapter for increasing reading and other homework compliance will work very well if we lecture the same material in class. Certainly we should use class time to extend and update the content and clarify what we know from experience confuses students. But otherwise we should be leading activities on the material, specifically making students practice it, apply it, examine it, and work with it. These activities ensure better learning and retention of the readings while holding students accountable for doing them. (See the "Holding Students Accountable for the Readings" section below.) Just imagine what you and your students could do in class if most of them came prepared!

• • •

The next several sections address ways you can teach your students how to read academic material and, for that matter, view academic videos and listen to academic podcasts. In view of our students' reading skills, habits, and persistence, we must not assume that they know how to read and study a textbook, a research article, an essay, or a piece of literature. Nor should we assume that they know how to gain academic value from videos, which they might view like a television show, and podcasts, which they might listen to like music. They probably do not know what they should be looking or listening for, how to take notes, and what they should retain for class. We may not be interested in teaching these skills, but if we don't help our students acquire them, they will leave our classes having learned very little, not least of which is how to learn.

Give Students the Grand Tour of a Book

Chances are that your students don't know how each genre of assigned reading is organized, so spend a little time leading students through an exploration of a textbook's or nonfiction book's structure and purpose. Insist that they bring their books to class for this, which means you must also insist that they buy the required books, which you have a right to do. Have them read the title and the Preface or Foreword and discuss what they think the book is about. Then tell them to examine the Table of Contents, and ask them how the book is organized, what its major sections and subsections are, and how they can identify them. If the work is a point-of-view nonfiction book, have students look for the author's thesis, issue, or position and how the book develops it. Not only will this exercise ensure they have the required book, but it will also get them over the hump of opening it and acquaint them enough with it to get more out of reading it.

Teach Students Proven Reading Methods

The simplest proven reading method, at least for factual and problem-solving material, is what is sometimes called active recall or the 3R (read-recite-review) strategy (McDaniel, Howard, & Einstein, 2009; Roediger & Karpicke, 2006). Students read a section of text, then close the book and recite aloud or write down as much as they can remember, and finally reread the section looking for what they missed or misunderstood. In other words, they reinforce their reading by reproducing the material and practicing retrieval with self-testing. In terms of student performance on multiple-choice and problem-solving tests, this technique works as effectively as note taking in less time and better than rereading the text multiple times (McDaniel et al., 2009; Roediger & Karpicke, 2006).

While this technique has been studied on reading, the general learning principle is the *testing effect*, which states that being tested or self-testing provides retrieval practice, which facilitates remembering the material later (Roediger, & Butler, 2010; Roediger, & Karpicke, 2006; Rohrer, Taylor, & Sholar, 2010; see chapter 1). It should apply to viewing and listening to media as much as it does to reading.

Similar multiple-step reading strategies date back many decades (e.g., Adler, 1940) and now proliferate on study-skills sites all over the web. One or more of the steps make excellent writing assignments that students can hand in as proof of their having done the homework. You can select the strategies and tips you find the most effective for your course (some sites recommend different reading techniques for different subjects) and refer your students to them. There are several major sites:

- http://www.collegeatlas.org/college-study-guides.html
- http://www.how-to-study.com/pqr.htm
- http://www.mindtools.com/rdstratg.html
- http://www.ucc.vt.edu/academic_support_students/study_skills_information/
- http://studygs.net/

The strategies tend to overlap. For example, SQ3R stands for survey-question-read-recall-review, and PQR3 is short for preview-question-read-recite-review. Just about all of them advise students to do the following:

1. Scan the reading to get a sense of what it's about, how it's organized, and where it's going, noting the titles, subtitles, graphics, bold and italicized words, conclusion, and summaries.
2. Review the purpose for reading. Since few students approach their reading with a purpose, we have to give them one or teach them how to devise their own purpose (see the next section).
3. Read with purpose to find what you are looking for, while thinking about what you are reading and paraphrasing what you are finding (most effectively in written notes).
4. Review the main points of the reading. We may have to induce students to complete this step by giving them a structured review assignment (see the "Require Students to Review" section later).

If you think about these steps, you may realize that you've been following them for years. For example, when you pick up a research article, you don't usually read it straight through from the first word to the last. Rather, you read the abstract, thumb through the pages to glance at the tables and figures, then scan the conclusion, and perhaps work your way back to the results or methods. The last thing you may read is the literature review, which normally comes right after the abstract. This is the way an expert approaches a piece of academic reading, which is quite different from the way one reads a magazine article or a novel. Our students have not yet learned to make the distinctions.

Unfortunately, not all of these reading techniques easily export to videos and podcasts. You can't scan or thumb through these media, although you can view or listen to them once through to get the gist, then go back for more details and then the main points a second and third time through.

Give Students a Purpose for Their Reading, Viewing, and Listening

Having a purpose for reading is the hallmark of the expert reader. When you pick up a scholarly article or book, you're usually looking for something relevant to your research, a course you teach, or a long-term interest. One of the reasons that you scan it first is to see if you have a purpose for reading it. If you find you do, your scan informs you where to focus. By contrast, students approach their readings with little or no purpose except to get it over with. They may not have a preexisting interest in the material, and they probably don't know what they are supposed to look for, which is why they complain that they can't tell what is and isn't important. We don't help them any by telling them that all the material is important.

We must give our students a purpose—that is, things to look for or a strategy for devising their own purpose—for the readings, videos, and podcasts we assign. Possible purposes include seeking answers to questions, and the best questions are our own study questions—what Maurer and Longfield (2013) call "reading guides." Developing our own questions allows us to direct our students' attention to what we deem important and worth gaining in the assignments. In addition, we can ask students to apply, analyze, synthesize, and evaluate the material, getting them to deep-process it and think both practically and critically about it. For a point-of-view nonfiction piece of work, we can provide students with several generic thinking questions that ensure solid comprehension and analysis:

- What is the author's position or claim?
- What are the main arguments given in support of this position or claim?
- What evidence or data does the author furnish to support his or her position or claim?
- Evaluate the author's case, identifying any questionable evidence or data, missing information, or flaws in logical or analysis.

In problem-solving disciplines such as mathematics, physics, and engineering, the purpose may be solving the assigned problems. Advise students to review the questions or problems before they read, watch, or listen so they will be primed to be on the lookout for the answers or the solution strategies.

Alternatively, we can show students how to create their own purpose at least for readings, especially a textbook, by turning the chapter headings and subheadings into questions for them to answer (Doyle, 2008). For example, if the heading reads "The Causes of Type 2 Diabetes," the question for students to ask themselves and answer is, "What are the causes of type 2 diabetes?" When students initially scan the reading, they can get a sense of the questions they will be addressing.

To guarantee that students process the content with the purpose we have in mind, we have to make them write out their answers or solutions and turn them in as daily graded homework or in a journal we collect and grade occasionally. While some students may not enjoy the process, you can sell them on it by telling them that they will never have to read the text, watch the video, or listen to the podcast again. Don't let the word *grade* scare you. In the "Hold Students Accountable for the Readings, Videos, and Podcasts" section later, you will see what the term means for you in practice.

Teach Students to Watch for Transitions and Verbal Signals

Some words serve as verbal signposts that make logical connections between ideas. These connections provide the key to comprehension, as they build the structure of the knowledge being explained or the arguments being presented. It is critical that we teach our students to watch and listen for them and ensure they know what the terms mean. Transitions or signal words or phrases fall into several categories (Langan, 2007):

1. *Addition* words signal that the author is making multiple points of the same kind. Examples: *also,*

in addition, another, next, first, second, third, finally, likewise, similarly, moreover, and *furthermore.*

2. *Cause-and-effect* words indicate that the author is about to address the results or effects. Examples: *because, since, consequently, therefore, thus, as a result, so that,* and *if-then.*

3. *Comparison* words point out a likeness between two ideas. Examples: *like, likewise, similarly, equally, alike, just as,* and *in the same way.*

4. *Contrast* words highlight a change in direction or a difference between two ideas. Examples: *but, yet, still, however, nevertheless, in contrast, on the contrary, on the other hand, otherwise, conversely, although,* and *even though.*

5. *Emphasis* words tell the reader to pay close attention to a particular idea. Examples: *most of all, above all, a primary concern, a significant factor, a major event, a principal item, a key feature, a distinctive quality, a central issue, in particular,* and *especially.*

6. *Illustration* words signal that the author is giving one or more examples to clarify a general point. Examples: *for example, for instance, to illustrate, specifically, like,* and *such as.*

Teach Students to Write Marginalia and to Highlight or Underline Wisely

These two techniques apply only to reading and are useful only to students with solid academic reading skills. These are advanced techniques because they presume the reader can sort out and distill the important points independently, as we do when we're studying new material. If your students seem prepared to make such judgments on their own, a few in-class practice sessions may ensure their readiness. These techniques also require students to buy the assigned books and mark them up, reducing what little resale value they have. Still, as expert readers, we know that the only way to study a book in depth is to mark it up; it's part of the learning and learning-how-to-learn process. We have the right to require this commitment of our students. If they choose not to make it, they have the option to drop your course.

Marginalia are notations we write in the margins to summarize the gist of the content or our reactions to a passage of text. Often, reviewing our reactions later makes us recall the substance of the text. We can task our students with writing summaries, their reactions, or both as homework and can check their compliance by asking them to read their marginalia in class and giving feedback as needed. To teach them to write useful marginalia, we can impose some rules on what they can write—perhaps three to five words per paragraph. The best readers enrich their marginalia by underlining key words, phrases, and sentences as well.

Underlining or highlighting is an advanced method, but too many poor readers rely on it. They typically highlight or underline too much text, which does little to improve their recall of the selected material and actually dulls their recall of unselected material (Kiewra, 2005). To sharpen our students' judgment in sifting out the important material, we can lead them through scavenger-hunt exercises to find the main idea in paragraphs. Along the way, we can tell them how textbooks are typically written: the topic sentence is usually the first sentence of a paragraph; if not there, it's probably the last sentence (Doyle, 2008). Weimer (2013a) has taught her students intelligent highlighting or underlining in three class periods. She has them mark their readings as homework and then has a discussion about what she selected as important, what they selected, and why. She asks them to explain her decisions as well as to justify their own. Over time, they approach a consensus.

Require Students to Review

Although all the study-skills and reading-skills books and websites recommend taking this final step, students usually don't do it. We may have to push them to do what is best for them by assigning a written homework exercise that makes them consolidate and integrate the new knowledge they have gained in the readings, videos, and podcasts. The simplest review assignment for students is to write out the main points and put them together into a one- or two-sentence summary. Another review strategy, one that requires less writing but more thinking, is to have students draw a graphic of the material, such as a concept map, mind map, concept circle diagram, flowchart, or whatever else is appropriate. In a graphic, students must construct their understanding of the organization of the concepts and principles. If their understanding is valid, the product gives them a mental structure with which to retain and elaborate on the knowledge. If your students haven't done this in other classes, teach them how by modeling the method in class; then having them work in small groups to map, diagram, or chart some material a few times; and finally assigning the task as individual homework. Chapter 23 explains a variety of graphic aids to learning and ways to teach them to students.

A third type of assignment, *reflective writing*, relies on freewriting about the readings, in response to open-ended thinking questions (Wirth, n.d.) or section by section (Kalman, 2007). In the latter, students read a section or two of the assigned chapter while highlighting, jotting down marginalia, or doing whatever else helps their comprehension. Then for roughly two-thirds of a page, they free-write about the section—not summarizing it but writing about what it means and then about what they don't understand. By this process, they generate questions to ask in class. In reflective writing, students are reviewing not just the material but also their understanding of it, and this should work equally well with videos and podcasts.

Assign Realistic Workloads

Chapter 4 gives sobering advice about how short your assigned videos and podcasts have to be. True, we can assign several of them at a time, but we have to be careful. With reading assignments, we have to be even more careful not to overload, given our students' reading challenges. Less can be more because students are more likely to complete shorter ones that longer ones (Hobson, 2004). In one study, when the instructor assigned six different readings, the vast majority of students in the class barely glanced at three of them. They were much more likely to do the readings when only two articles were assigned. Even so, students rarely completed all the readings (Bradley, 2007). Still, the evidence suggests that we should require only the most essential readings, those most crucial to our learning outcomes.

We also should take measures to ensure our readings are aimed at students' level—that is, at marginally skilled readers (Hobson, 2004). Even if we teach them how to read the material, they will need practice before they become fluent at it. A few readability indexes are available on the web at http://www.editcentral.com/gwt1/EditCentral.html. Just copy and paste some text into the calculator, and you obtain both a grade-level and a reading ease score.

Sell the Readings, Videos, and Podcasts

To an extent, we can motivate some students to do the assignments by promoting them. We can explain their purpose, relevance, and our reasons for choosing them over other options. In the syllabus, we can emphasize how central they are to the course and learning outcomes. Each day or week, we can preview and promote the next assignment, noting what questions it will answer and what value it will hold for their immediate learning and later lives and careers. We can also place it in the context of the next class, later assignments, upcoming in-class activities, and the larger course and curriculum (Hobson, 2004).

Let's not underestimate the potential impact of such efforts. Students cite their personal desire to learn as their single strongest motivator for doing the readings, far above wanting to participate in discussion or feeling obligated (Bradley, 2007). Chances are we can influence their desire with a short, persuasive pitch.

Hold Students Accountable for the Readings, Videos, and Podcasts

Making the assignments more accessible, doable, and valuable to students may go far. Once students start doing them, they may enjoy the learning and sense of achievement enough to continue. But these helpful strategies may not go far enough. You may also have to induce students to prepare for class for extrinsic reasons—that is, to set up incentives and sanctions related to their own self-interest.

We know that most students are motivated by grades, just as people in general are motivated by material and monetary rewards. We also know that people are motivated by pride. They don't want to look bad in front of others, especially superiors and peers. These two cost-benefit values suggest ways to make students accountable for doing the homework. So whether they want to do it or not, most students will decide that they have to do it to attain their goals and avoid unpleasant consequences.

Here we review four categories of tools that hold students accountable:

1. *Written homework* on the readings, videos, or podcasts to hand in
2. *Quizzes* on them
3. *In-class activities* (problem-solving or written exercises) on them
4. *Cold-call recitation* on them

Abundant research documents that these methods work for at least readings (Barrineau, 2001; Carney, Fry, Gabriele, & Ballard, 2008; Connor-Greene, 2000; Eddy & Hogan, 2014; Fernald, 2004; Hoeft, 2012; Leeming, 2002; Lin, 2014; Maurer & Longfield, 2013; Mazur, 1997; Nathan, 2005; Nilson, 2007b; Ruscio, 2001; Thompson, 2002; Thorne, 2000). In fact, Nathan (2005) claims that students decide if they will do the readings for a given day based on whether they have homework on the readings to hand in, will be tested on the material, or will have to speak publicly on the material in class. If none of these conditions applies, Nathan explains, chances are good that most students will skip the readings.

To make any of these tools work effectively as accountability mechanisms, follow these guidelines:

- Use these tools or some combination of them on a regular or near-regular basis on the class days that assignments are due. Your students should expect to be held accountable for *every* assignment. Randomly administered (chance) quizzes also raise reading compliance (Fernald, 2004;

Lin, 2014; Ruscio, 2001), but not as much as regularly occurring ones (Carney et al., 2008; Lin, 2014). Generally the more frequent the quizzing, the stronger the inducement to prepare and the higher the student learning and achievement (Carney et al., 2008; Leeming, 2002).
- Grade the products in some way, even if on an informal scale, such as 1 to 4 points, 0 or 1 point, √+/√/√-, √/0, or P/F. You don't have to grade on quality or provide feedback as you would with a formal assignment. Since you're looking only for evidence of students' having done the assignment, you can give full credit to a complete product or a good-faith effort—that is, one that addresses the assigned content and meets your length or elaboration requirements. You can assess on these criteria at a glance. You may get equally good results with grading only some of written homework some of the time as you would with grading all of it all of the time (Carney et al., 2008). The grades on the products in total must count significantly toward the final grade. We know that 5 percent is too little (Sullivan, Middendorf, & Camp, 2008) and that 20 percent is an effective incentive (Kalman, 2007).
- Make the readings, videos, and podcasts the only available source of their content—that is, don't lecture them in class or post outlines or summaries of them.

Pride becomes a powerful secondary motivator when the accountability tool is cold-call recitation or an in-class group activity for a group grade. In the latter situation, most students feel a sense of responsibility to their teammates (see chapter 15).

■ SPECIFIC TOOLS FOR HOLDING STUDENTS ACCOUNTABLE

The tools described here—some obvious, others not—come from a variety of sources, and certain forms of homework also teach students how to read and comprehend the material (see above).

Homework

Some research finds that required written homework for submission motivates students to prepare for class more regularly and carefully than does any schedule of quizzes, even if it is not always graded (Carney et al., 2008). In fact, Hoeft (2012) found that her daily, graded journal assignments on the readings more than doubled the percentage of reading-compliant students (from 46 to 95 percent), and Eddy and Hogan (2014) reported similar results. With some forms of homework, you may want your students to submit two copies: one for them to refer to and take notes on in class and another to submit (probably electronically) for grading before class. You may even make the written product a requirement for entering class. The options for homework on the readings, videos, or podcasts are almost limitless:

- Notes on or an abstract or summary (Barrineau, 2001; Kalman, 2007; Kalman & Kalman, 1996; McKinney, 2001; Peirce, 2006)
- An outline or graphic (Peirce, 2006)
- One or more questions on the content written on cards or posted electronically (Martin, 2000; McKinney, 2001; Millis & Cottell, 1998). You may even ask for specific types of questions (multiple choice, true-false, essay, and so on) for possible use in future tests.
- Answers to study, reading-response, journaling, or end-of-chapter questions (Carney et al., 2008; Eddy & Hogan, 2014; Hoeft, 2012; McKinney, 2001; Peirce, 2006). Questions that make students reflect on the personal relevance of the material also enhance their perceptions of their ability to participate productively in class discussions (Carney et al., 2008; Wirth, n.d.).
- Solutions to problems
- Any type of outside material that illustrates an important point in the readings or an application of them—for example, a magazine or news article, a printed advertisement, a photograph, a website, or an object

For comprehension, however, quizzes may surpass homework. Because Hoeft's (2012) students merely skimmed the readings for answers to her journal questions, only 42 percent of them demonstrated basic comprehension.

Quizzes

Frequent, regular quizzes are proven accountability tools (Barrineau, 2001; Carney et al., 2008; Connor-Greene, 2000; Hoeft, 2012; Lin, 2014; Mazur, 1997; Nathan, 2005; Nilson, 2007b; Ruscio, 2001; Thompson, 2002; Thorne, 2000), and they induce homework compliance more effectively than randomly administered (chance or pop) quizzes (Carney et al., 2008). They also enhance student performance on major exams and increase class attendance (Lin, 2014; Mazur, 1997). With daily quizzes, Hoeft (2012) reported a 74 percent reading compliance rate, which is low compared to other studies, and a 53 percent basic comprehension rate among the compliant, which surpassed answering journal questions.

You can administer accountability quizzes in class or online shortly before class. Either way, they should focus on the major points and concepts, not details, and the items should be easy for you to grade quickly—either multiple choice or short essay. One study found short essay questions more effective than multiple-choice items in helping students gauge their own learning (Sullivan et al., 2008). Remember that you can grade the answers as simply as acceptable/not acceptable (credit/no credit) based on whether they address the question and meet the required length.

Just-in-time-teaching, an inquiry-based method described in chapter 16, is a type of daily quiz on the readings or other assignment. Students submit their answers online to conceptual multiple-choice items 30 to 60 minutes before each class, giving you just enough time to adjust your lesson plan to clarify any comprehension problems they had. We know this method raises students' level of preparation for class, participation in class, engagement, and achievement (Marrs & Novak, 2004; Novak, Patterson, Gavrin, &

Christian, 1999) as long as it appreciably figures into the final grade (Sullivan et al., 2008).

With in-class quizzes, you can dictate the questions or display them on a slide. You can also have students make up the questions as homework submitted earlier. Finally, you can follow the individual quiz with a group quiz where students have the chance to discuss the material (see the "Team-Based Learning" section in chapter 15).

In-Class Activities

Such activities include problem solving and written exercises. With problems, students can solve them or design new ones for future tests. Written exercises encompass a one-minute paper, a reading response mini-essay, a summary, or any of a wide assortment of short writing assignments described in chapters 20 and 22 and classroom assessment activities suggested in chapter 24. They can even be graphics, such as a map, diagram, or flowchart of the material (see chapter 23).

To encourage high-quality work, you might allow students to use their in-class products during future tests. One summary exercise that is particularly effective at motivating students to seriously study the readings, videos, or podcasts is a *mind dump*. You allow students 5 or 10 minutes to write down everything they can remember from their studying. Then you collect these recollections and return them to their authors at the beginning of tests. While students may have little time to hunt through them during tests, they will feel less anxious and no doubt will have better mastery of the material just for having written about it.

While individual accountability is critical for reading compliance, some of these exercises are adaptable to groups. In fact, the more challenging ones, such as writing higher-order multiple-choice items for future tests, may benefit from the synergy of multiple minds. You can find many more structured group activities in chapter 15.

You will need to keep individual students and groups on task and accountable. You can have them sign and hand in their exercises or problem

solutions. If valid answers emerged during class, you don't have to correct or write feedback on them. Just check off that they completed the task. Or randomly call on several students or groups to read their answer, explain their solution, or display their graphic. If the exercise or problem has one right answer and not everyone comes up with it, don't correct those with wrong answers. Let students with different results debate them.

Recitation

As explained in chapter 12, recitation is students' recalling and reproducing, either verbatim or in their own words, material they are supposed to have already learned from assigned readings, videos, podcasts, or live lectures—that is, performing knowledge/remembering and comprehension/understanding cognitive operations. It's then easy to move into higher-order discussion questions. In classic recitation, you pose recall questions and cold-call on students in a way that looks or actually is random. Shaffer (n.d.), for instance, asks his students to print their names on 3-by-5-inch cards, which he collects and uses during the semester to pick students to answer questions. At times he shuffles the deck. At other times, he stacks the deck before class. He then grades students' answers on the fly, marking a plus or minus on their card (or 0 versus 1 point). These oral performances count 15 percent of the course grade and open most class periods. Since he calls on 30 to 60 students in a typical class, they get plenty of participation opportunities.

These variations on recitation also allow you to grade students on the fly:

- Randomly call on students to present their written homework on the readings, videos, or podcasts (questions, answers to questions, problem solutions, summaries, reading responses, outside material, and so on), either in addition to or instead of handing it in to you. Over the term, you can no doubt call on all your students at least once and possibly many times.

- After an in-class exercise or problem-solving session, ask some students or groups to explain their answers or solutions to the class.
- Have students bring in questions on the material (for future tests, discussion, or clarification) and ask them to call on other students to answer them.

◼ MANAGING YOUR WORKLOAD

Before you conclude that accountability tools would generate too heavy a workload for you, consider how much time the tools actually demand and what other tasks they can eliminate. Yes, you will have to find or create short homework assignments, quiz items, recitation questions, or in-class exercises and activities, and you will have to grade them in some fashion. However:

- You can have your students make up questions and problems for you, whether for quizzes, tests, in-class activities, or recitation.

- You can make the grading quick and effortless (Connor-Greene, 2000; Kalman, 2007; Thompson, 2002). With written homework, short essay quizzes, and submitted in-class activities, you need only check the work for completeness or a good-faith effort, and you can grade recitation on the fly in class.
- You can give fewer major tests and assignments, saving yourself considerable preparation and grading time.
- You can require and collect all written homework, but you only have to grade some of it some of the time (Carney et al., 2008).
- You need not prepare lectures.

Finally, consider how much more your students will learn and how deeply you can take them into the material if they prepare for class. Imagine the discussions and other activities you could lead! In fact, most accountability tools serve multiple purposes and can provide a springboard or an entire framework for an engaging class period. Perhaps these tools can *save* you time.

CHAPTER 22

Teaching in Multiple Modes

This chapter replaces the one on learning styles that appeared in previous editions of this book. Too much respectable research has accumulated debunking the existence of learning styles and types of intelligences, despite the fact that dozens of models have vied for attention. While students may voice learning preferences—that is, their liking for one teaching method over another—studies have found no evidence that teaching to a person's style enhances her learning (Coffield, Moseley, Hall, & Ecclestone, 2004; Glenn, 2009; Kirschner, Sweller, & Clark, 2006; Kratzig & Arbuthnott, 2006; La Lopa, 2013; Pashler, McDaniel, Rohrer, & Bjork, 2009; Riener & Willingham, 2010; Stahl, 1999; Willingham, 2004, 2005a, 2005b; Winne & Nesbit, 2010). However, before abandoning learning styles and moving on to multimodal learning, we will examine the still-valid aspects of two models.

■ KOLB'S LEARNING CYCLE

Kolb's (1984) model of learning styles has weak predictive validity—too weak even to support its business training applications—and low test-retest reliability (research summaries in Felder & Brent, 2005 and Kirschner et al., 2006). And since he developed it as a business tool, the learning styles classification instrument is available only for purchase at http://www.haygroup.com/leadershipandtalentondemand.

However, the learning *cycle* Kolb describes maps well onto the structure of the brain (Zull, 2002). The cycle moves the learner through feeling, perceiving, thinking, and acting in four phases: concrete experience (CE), reflective observation (RO), abstract conceptualization (AC), and active experimentation (AE). He may enter the cycle at any point. For instance, those who begin learning something through concrete experience (CE) proceed to the reflective observation (RO) phase as they observe others and reflect on their own and others' experiences. Next, they try to assimilate their observations and perceptions into logical theories, thus moving into the third phase of abstract conceptualization (AC). When they later use concepts to make decisions and solve problems, they enter the fourth and final stage of active experimentation (AE).

To elaborate on the phases, the *concrete experience* stage relies more on feeling than on thinking to solve problems. People interpret human situations in a very personal way and focus on the tangible here and now. The *reflective observation* phase emphasizes intuitive thinking to observe and understand situations, permitting a learner to grasp the meanings and implications of ideas and situations quickly and examine situations and phenomena empathetically from different points of view. It fosters patience, objectivity, and good judgment. The use of logical thinking and conceptual reasoning characterizes the *abstract conceptualization* stage. It focuses on theory building, systematic planning, manipulation of abstract symbols, and quantitative analysis and can generate personality traits such as precision, discipline, rigor, and an appreciation for elegant, parsimonious models. Finally, the *active experimentation* mode is directed toward the practical and concrete (like the CE) and rational thinking (like the AC). But its objective is purely pragmatic results: influencing people's opinions, changing situations, and getting things accomplished.

Now visualize a graph with two axes: the *x*-axis from active (on left) to reflective (on right), and the *y*-axis from abstract (at bottom) to concrete (at top). This arrangement places the concrete experience at 12 o'clock, reflective observation at 3 o'clock, abstract conceptualization at 6 o'clock, and active experimentation at 9 o'clock. Connecting the phases by arrows going clockwise, you can see Kolb's proposed learning cycle.

■ FELDER AND SILVERMAN'S LEARNING STYLES MODEL

While first developed for engineering students, Felder and Silverman's (1988) model of learning styles applies to learners across the disciplines. Furthermore, it is the most scientifically grounded framework of all the major models. The 44-item Index of Learning Styles questionnaire (Felder & Soloman, n.d.a) has high to moderate construct validity, internal consistency reliability, test-retest reliability, total item correlation, and interscale correlation (Felder & Spurlin, 2005; Litzinger, Lee, Wise, & Felder, 2007; Zywno, 2003). You can also take it free at http://www.engr.ncsu.edu/learning styles/ilsweb.html.

Felder and Silverman don't posit learning styles per se. Rather, they propose four independent, cognitive dimensions, each anchored by pure types. One dimension identifies how a student prefers to process information and knowledge: *actively* through physical activity or discussion or *reflectively* through introspection. Another pertains to the sensory mode in which a student prefers to receive information and knowledge: *verbally* in written or spoken words or mathematical equations or *visually* in pictures, graphics, videos, and demonstrations. A third continuum considers the type of information that a student most readily perceives: internally based *intuitive* experiences (hunches, insights, possibilities) or externally based *sensory* experiences. The final dimension focuses on how a student acquires understanding: *sequentially* in incremental steps or *globally* in holistic leaps.

A student may have a strong, moderate, or weak leaning toward one end of a continuum or the other. Furthermore, she may lean in one direction for some tasks and in the other direction for other tasks. The most effective learners and problem solvers tend to cluster around the middle, functioning well in both polar modes. Those who strongly prefer one style or another may miss important aspects of learning, such as crucial details, the big picture, alternative approaches, cognitive shortcuts, or possible applications. But the model recommends ways to teach to both poles on all four dimensions (Felder, 1993; Felder & Silverman, 1988; Felder & Soloman, n.d.b).

Active versus Reflective

Active learners gain the most out of doing something with the material: discussing it, explaining it to others, applying it, trying things out, experimenting with how things work, or bouncing off ideas. They like to solve problems, evaluate ideas, and design and conduct experiments. They learn best from group work, discussion, problem solving, and experiential and inquiry-guided activities. To study most productively, they should follow up their reading with study-group members who take turns explaining different parts of the material to each other. To retain material, they should associate it with ways it can be applied. To prepare for tests, they should work in a group organized around guessing the questions and answering them.

By contrast, reflective learners need some quiet time to process the material internally. Then they can generate good ideas and theories, define problems effectively, and propose possible solutions. As instructors, we need only build in brief pauses in the middle of lectures or after classroom activities to allow them a few moments to think. We might also pose reflection questions such as, "What does this all mean?" or, "What do you think was the point of this activity?" During recitation and discussion, we should wait at least several seconds before calling on anyone. Reflective learners should study alone and practice summarizing the material or making up and answering questions about it.

Verbal versus Visual

All people learn better when they receive information and knowledge in both the verbal and the visual modes, and the most facile learners can accommodate input in either mode. But some learners process and remember material better if it is presented in one mode or the other. Strongly visual learners get the most out of flowcharts, diagrams, mind and concept maps, pictures, diagrams, graphs, time lines, matrices, videos, animations, and demonstrations (see chapter 23). By contrast, those leaning toward the verbal pole find it easier to process symbols such as words, whether spoken or written, and equations. They benefit most from reading, listening to lectures and podcasts, taking notes, and doing written exercises and assignments. To prepare for tests, they

should write summaries or outlines in their own words or join study groups where they can listen to others explain the material and explain it out loud themselves.

Intuitive versus Sensing

Since higher education tends to emphasize concepts and principles, intuitive learners have an edge because they grasp and remember abstractions, relationships, generalizations, and mathematical formulas quite easily. They tend to work quickly and efficiently and conceptualize problems and interpret material in imaginative ways. However, they dislike repetition, standard procedures, detail work, plug-and-chug courses, and the memorization of facts.

Sensing learners work best with whatever information they receive through their senses from the outside world. They are comfortable memorizing facts, patiently observing phenomena, carefully tending to details, doing routine assignments, and solving problems by well-established methods. Like active learners, they are practical minded and can remember material better when they can see its connections to the real world in examples or applications. In addition, they need a lot of practice performing higher-order cognitive operations. As instructors, we need to furnish that practice and pepper our lessons with plenty of examples and real-world applications of concepts and principles. We can also advise them to study by translating the abstract and general into the concrete and specific, both alone and in study groups.

Sequential versus Global

Representing the majority of students, sequential learners absorb new material in linear steps, each logically following the one before. They solve problems the same way, following a logical series of steps. While most of us organize our courses sequentially, these learners can get lost if we (or the textbook) skip steps or change topics without making explicit transitions. They study best when they outline the lecture and the readings using their own organizational scheme.

Because they can miss seeing connections among topics or between new and previously learned knowledge, their learning can be pretty shallow, so we should pose explicit questions about these relationships and help students make these links on their own.

While we are struggling to fully grasp new material, we all experience sudden insights and gestalts that make the pieces fall into place. However, before the flash, sequential learners are usually able to work with the material at some level, enough to do the homework and pass the tests. What marks global learners is their inability to do much of anything with the material until they have made the grand leap to complete understanding. In the meantime, they simply absorb new material as unrelated pieces. Once they grasp the big picture, they may still have trouble with the details, but they may be able to solve complex problems quickly or synthesize ideas in novel and creative ways, even if they can't explain how they have done it. Interestingly, we can help global learners the same way we can help their sequential counterparts: by encouraging them to see the relationships between new material and what they already know. We can also advise them to skim through a reading assignment before actually reading it to get a content overview. While neither Felder nor his coauthors mention it, global learners may also profit from seeing or creating graphics that capture the big picture (see chapter 23).

The Teaching Challenge

Wherever your students may lie on whatever continuum, Felder (1996) recommends using multiple teaching strategies to reach them all. Accompany abstract, theoretical, and conceptual content with concrete examples, applications, demonstrations, experimental results, and problem-solving tools. You might even furnish students with data, examples, or observations and invite them to infer the general principle. Illustrate the magnitudes of calculated quantities using demonstrations and physical analogies. Keep your classes student-active with group work, discussion, problem solving, and the like, but build in some quiet time for students to reflect on and write about the material. Balance lectures, podcasts, and readings with graphics such as pictures, matrices, graphs, diagrams, flowcharts, and big-picture concept and mind maps, as well as demonstrations. Display and explain the logical flow of your students' learning outcomes with an outcomes map and your course topics with a graphic syllabus while highlighting the big picture that these graphics show (see chapters 2 and 5) and pointing out links between your course material and other courses, other disciplines, and everyday life.

◼ MULTIMODAL LEARNING

According to both previous models, we should give students multiple opportunities to learn the same material in different ways. In fact, all learning style models recommend this strategy if we teach many students in the same class, and, of course, we always do. (These models run aground when they advise teaching *individuals* according to their learning style.) Interestingly enough, cognitive psychological research comes to the same conclusion, but from a very different angle. It has found that people learn new material best when they receive it multiple times through multiple senses and in multiple modes (or modalities), which are learning channels in different parts of their brain (Feldon, 2010; Kress, Jewitt, Ogborn, & Charalampos, 2006; Mayer, 2005, 2009; Metiri Group, 2008; Tulving, 1985; Vekiri, 2002). Scholars dispute the number and types of modes, but all agree that the more modes learners activate, the more learning that occurs. As Feldon (2010, p. 19) explains it, each modality has "limited bandwidth," so it is best to distribute new information across several modes. Therefore, all students should read, listen, talk, write, see, draw, act/experience, and ultimately think new material into their system. They should go through new material in at least two or three different modes, and it's our job to arrange the learning experiences to ensure they do so.

Of course, we should teach using most appropriate modes for the content (Willingham, 2005a)—for example, visuals for inherently visual material (art and art history, cartography, geology, biology, physics); reading and listening for poetry and literature; listening, seeing, and acting (experience) for drama; and seeing and experiencing for physical procedures. Learning relatively recent history can draw on almost every mode. In fact, just about every kind of knowledge can and should be conveyed in more than one mode.

The Reading Mode

Typically reading is students' first exposure to new material, but as we saw in chapter 21, most of today's students lack good reading comprehension skills. Chapters 20 and 21 and "The Writing Mode" section below offer a number of ways to improve those skills and make the most of the reading mode, including pairing or following reading with an activity in the writing, speaking, or visual mode (see below). Prepared visuals complement readings especially well for comprehension purposes as long as both are in close proximity to each other (Mayer, 2005, 2009; Metiri Group, 2008).

The Listening Mode

The expression "in one ear and out the other" overstates the weaknesses of listening. The problem occurs when students confuse listening with hearing or being within earshot, just as they may confuse reading with running their eyes over a page. Both listening and reading presume focusing *attention* on the words—specifically, interpreting their meaning, making decisions about the importance of the message, translating the message into written shorthand symbols, relating it to what one already knows, and perhaps dialoguing with or questioning it. This deep processing constitutes elaborative rehearsal and eventual encoding of the message into long-term memory.

Few students know how to listen actively like this, but we can teach them. Refer back to the self-regulated learning activities in chapter 20 that are designed for live lectures, podcasts, and videos: periodic free recall (Bonwell & Eison, 1991); active listening checks (Lovett, 2008); minute papers (Chew, quoted in Lang, 2012; Wirth, n.d.); reflective writing (Araujo, quoted in Schell, 2012; Kalman 2007; Mezeske, 2009; Wirth, n.d.); and Read (or listen), Recall, Review (McDaniel, Howard, & Einstein, 2009; Roediger, & Butler, 2010; Roediger & Karpicke, 2006). These exercises, especially periodic free-recall and active listening checks, give students the chance to test the effectiveness of their listening and, if necessary, practice listening more intently. With podcasts and videos, they can review by replaying the recording to find out what they may have missed.

Listening also has a benefit over reading: it is at least sometimes easier for the brain to process material delivered orally than in written form. For instance, listening to a narrative that accompanies visual material (a graph, video, or animation) carries a lower cognitive load than does reading about the visual material (Mayer, 2005, 2009; Metiri Group, 2008).

The Speaking Mode

Speaking is inherently more active than listening in that a person must think through what he wants to say and how to put it into words. Even the *chance* to speak in response to someone else's words typically makes one's listening more active. This is why students learn so effectively from discussion. They learn even more when the exchange takes place in a small group where they can enjoy plenty of opportunities to speak and respond to others.

Chapter 20 presents two self-regulated learning activities that rely on pairs using the speaking mode: periodic free recall, in which students help each other reconstruct a lecture (Bonwell & Eison, 1991), and think-aloud, where they help each other talk through solutions to math-based problems (Whimbey & Lochhead, 1999). Speaking makes sharp and explicit ideas and strategies that would otherwise lie fuzzy and unformed and would probably be forgotten.

The Experiential Mode

Of course, real experience can be a powerful way to learn, but so can acting out a role in a realistic situation, as acting affords a vicarious, empathy-based experience. Either way, experience still requires focused and systematic reflection, preferably using the modes of discussion and writing, to generate actual learning. Chapter 14 details experiential learning and accompanying reflection questions (also see chapter 20).

The Writing Mode

No other chapter in this book explores writing as a learning medium, so the topic will receive closer attention here than the other modes. Specifically, we'll explore *writing-to-learn* exercises, which may be checked in but not graded.

Writing is not just a medium of communication but a powerful method for thinking and learning in several ways (Bean, 2011; Walvoord, 2014; Young, 2006). First, writing about content helps students learn it better and retain it longer—whatever the subject and whether the exercise involves note taking, outlining, summarizing, recording focused thought, composing short answers, or writing full-fledged essays. Second, writing makes students think actively about the material, and, depending on your prompt, you can make your students think at higher-order cognitive levels, as well as affectively and ethically. Third, writing exercises can define audiences other than the instructor and therefore develop students' sensitivity to the interests, backgrounds, and vocabularies of different readers. A fourth benefit of writing is for classroom assessment (see chapter 24), that is, to find out quickly, while you're still focusing on a particular topic, exactly what your class is and isn't learning. This way you can diagnose and clarify points of confusion before you give the next exam and move on to other topics (Angelo & Cross, 1993). Reading such short, infor-

mal writing assignments takes no more time than any other type of class preparation. Finally, many writing exercises give students the chance to learn about themselves—their feelings, values, cognitive processes, and learning strengths and weaknesses. This is why so many of the self-regulated learning activities and assignments (described in chapter 20) involve writing.

Elaborated by Bean (2011), Smit (2010), Wright, Herteis, and Abernehy (2001), and Young (2006), here is a small sample of writing-to-learn exercises, some of which can double as self-regulated learning exercises.

Free-writing

Students write about a predetermined topic for a brief, specified number of minutes (1 to 3) as fast as they can think and put words on paper. The objective is to activate prior knowledge or generate ideas by free association, disregarding grammar, spelling, punctuation, and the like. Free-writing serves as effective in-class warm-up exercises. It can help students recall the previous class meeting and assigned reading. Frequent free-writing on the readings also puts students on notice that they had better keep up with the course. Here are some possible free-writing topics:

- Have students write down all the important points they can remember from the previous discussion.
- Have them summarize the most important points from the assigned readings (or from the day's lecture or class activities).
- Write three key words on the board from the previous class (or assigned reading) and ask students to explain their importance.
- Have students define a concept in their own words, explain the parts of a complex concept, give real-life examples of a concept, or compare concepts from the today's class with those from the previous class.
- Write a seed sentence on the board—that is, a major hypothesis, conclusion, or provocative

statement related to class or readings—and have them write their reactions.

- Have them apply a principle to their own experience.
- Have them free-write answers to test review questions to prepare for a tightly timed essay test.

Of course, free-writing needn't be private. Students can share them with one another, in which case the activity is called *inkshedding* (Hunt, 2004). They can trade and comment on one another's freewriting. Their purpose is not to evaluate the other's writing but to understand it. After such an exercise, the class is ready for discussion.

Free-writing can also be assigned as homework, as Kalman (2007) does to ensure his students prepare for class and process the readings (see chapter 21). After students read a section or two of a chapter, they begin free-writing about what they just read and what they don't understand. Then they go on to the next section and free-write again. At the end of the assigned chapter or unit, they write three sentences, one on each of three key concepts they have identified in the readings. Students usually write three or more pages of notes and reflection.

The one-minute paper, discussed in chapters 13 and 24, is a type of free-writing designed to close a learning experience, such as a minilecture, in-class activity, or reading. It helps students absorb, digest, elaborate, and internalize new material, moving it into long-term memory. It also makes them think about the material, especially what they didn't understand, which is precisely what you need to know before wrapping up a topic.

Journals

Students summarize what they are learning or how they are reacting, cognitively and emotionally, to the lectures, discussions, readings, laboratories, homework problems, or other written assignments. They do this regularly at the end of each lecture, discussion, or lab or as a meta-assignment (see chapter 20). Journals help them keep up with the course, as well as read and listen actively. They also induce students to think about the material and what they are learning. Some instructors require just one weekly journal-writing session, either in class or as homework, on any or all aspects of a course. Students should have a special notebook, blog, wiki, or word-processing file solely for their journal.

Students need your guidance on the topics their journals should address. Here are some possible probes:

- What is new to you about this material, and what did you already know?
- Does any point contradict what you already knew or believed?
- What patterns of reasoning (or data) does the speaker/author offer as evidence?
- How convincing do you find the speaker's/author's reasoning or data?
- Is there any line of reasoning that you do not follow?
- Is this reasoning familiar to you from other courses?
- What don't you understand?
- What questions remain in your mind?

You should collect and check off journals regularly or intermittently, but you need not grade them. If you do, don't weigh them very much toward the final grade. But do write comments in them to develop a personal dialogue with each student. If you want to try journaling, consult Stevens and Cooper (2009) for more ideas and guidelines.

Dialectical Notes

Students read and take notes on a relatively short, important, self-contained passage that you select from course readings. On the left side of their note paper, they write their reactions to the text as they read it: where they agree, where they disagree, where they are unsure, where they are confused, where they have questions, and so on. At some later time, they review the passage and their left-side notes and write their reactions to these notes on the right side of the note paper.

Dialectical notes encourage students to read a text carefully, interact with it, analyze it critically, and reevaluate their initial reactions to it. They have special value in disciplines that require close readings of difficult texts, such as literature, philosophy, history, political science, religious studies, law, and social theory. However, they easily adapt to problem solving in mathematics, economics, engineering, and physics as well. Students work the problem in mathematical symbols on the left side of the paper and explain in words what operations they are performing, and why, on the right side. Later, in small groups, students can read and discuss each other's approaches and solutions.

These notes demonstrate the nature and value of scholarly dialogue and debate, and they make superb springboards for discussion. After students get used to the exercise, you might consider collecting and grading their notes.

One-Sentence Summaries

As an in-class activity or a short homework assignment, students answer these questions on a specific topic in one (long) grammatical sentence: Who Did What to Whom, How, When, Where, and Why (WDWWHWWW)? The topic may be a historical event, the plot of a story or novel, or, by substituting another What for Who/Whom, a chemical reaction, mechanical process, or biological phenomenon. This technique makes students distill, simplify, reorganize, synthesize, and chunk complex material into smaller, essential units that are easier to manipulate and remember. You should do the exercise first and allow students twice as much time as it takes you. You can collect and comment on the summaries yourself or let your students exchange them and write comments on each other's.

The Visual Mode

One other finding from cognitive psychology should guide our teaching: we should introduce the visual mode whenever possible because it so effectively facilitates learning, memory, and retrieval. In fact, for people in general, it is the most powerful mode. Therefore, it deserves its own chapter, which is the next chapter.

■ COMBINING MODES

Students should receive new material multiple times but not repeating the same learning activities. Just rereading a text again and again, for example, is an inefficient use of time (McDaniel, Howard, & Einstein, 2009; Roediger & Butler, 2010; Roediger & Karpicke, 2006) and, sadly, our students' default strategy. Rather, students need to process the same material through different parts of their brain. It's pretty easy to provide these opportunities, and you may already be doing it. Let's say you assign a reading and give a short essay quiz the day it's due. Then you have students get into groups and discuss what they wrote. You have already led them through the material in three different modes. Or maybe you assign a podcast of your lecture and give students study questions on it to answer in writing as homework. Then in class you ask some recitation and discussion questions, or break students into groups to draw a concept map of the video, or have them do a role play or short simulation based on the video. Again, you have furnished a solid set of multimodal learning experiences.

Not just any combination of modes works effectively. For instance, students are bored and frustrated when they are assigned a reading, then the instructor lectures the reading, and the presentation slides outline the reading and the lecture (Cardon, 2014). All three renditions are verbal, and two involve reading, so students will rationally chose their favorite (or least taxing) medium to get the material. They correctly anticipate that going through the same material several times in one mode or two very similar modes will do them little good, and they aren't likely to process the material deeply or retain it. In other words, to keep our students' interest and facilitate their learning, we must avoid redundancy in the repetition we provide.

CHAPTER 23

Making the Most of the Visual Mode

We humans have relied on our sight for survival more than any other sense. Through most of the ages, we were dependent on it for hunting, fishing, gathering, making fire and tools, determining the edible versus the poisonous, identifying and avoiding predators, planting and harvesting, and reading the sky for the time of day and time of year. At some point, we used our sight to fashion shelters, clothing, and personal decorations and to paint animals on the walls of our caves. Even if our eyes could never compete with the eagle's, we were able to distinguish colors, shapes, and distances rather well for a mammal. Besides, we didn't enjoy the olfactory or auditory sentience of so many of our four-legged neighbors. In time, after we refined spoken language and invented the story, we added a strong oral component to our culture. But once we devised writing and later printing, we relied more on sight for communication.

Still, reading and writing aren't quite as effortless as spotting a lion. The brain processes visual information up to 60,000 times faster, as instantaneous as one-tenth of a second, than it decodes text (Semetko & Scammell, 2012). The left side of our cerebrum needs time to interpret the textual symbols our eyes are seeing and translate our thoughts into visual symbols. Pure visual images, unfettered by text, convey information more directly, efficiently, and quickly. Marketing professionals understand and take advantage of these findings (Kusinitz, 2014).

Visuals, then, can serve our instructional purposes very effectively. They come in many forms—flowcharts, diagrams, graphs, tables, matrices, pictures, drawings, figures, even animations—offering countless options for depicting course material. They can be created and displayed on a computer, but they can be just as powerful when hand-drawn. We can provide them to help students learn and to become accustomed to using visuals, so they can go on to develop graphic representations of their own understanding of the subject matter.

Chapters 2 and 5 introduced two visual teaching tools: the outcomes map for showing your students' progression through learning outcomes in your course and the graphic syllabus for displaying the topical organization of your course (Nilson,

2007a). Both commonly take the form of a flow-chart or diagram to illustrate the sequencing of outcomes or topics over time. Like the most powerful visuals we will examine in this chapter, they provide students with the big picture of your course and the internal structure of its major components, either outcomes or topics. As the next section details, these visual schemas can give students the scaffolding they need to better understand and remember the learning process you have planned for them and your course content.

HOW VISUALS ENHANCE LEARNING

The evidence that graphics of all kinds facilitate comprehension, transfer, and retention of course material has generated a large body of research and several sizable literature reviews (e.g., Vekiri, 2002; Winn, 1991). Many of the studies center around specific visual tools, such as concept maps and mind maps, and these are summarized in the next section on the leading types of graphics. Whatever the type, visuals cue the text, helping students remember the indicated relationships and the contents inside the boxes, circles, or cells. You may even remember recalling material during a test by picturing the page of the textbook where the material was located and reading it in your mind's eye.

Other research focuses on multimedia learning. For instance, adding a visual to either text or auditory material enhances retention and facilitates later retrieval (Fadel, 2008; Mayer, 2005; Medina, 2008). In fact, according to Ginns's (2005) meta-analysis, pairing graphics with spoken text enhances student learning significantly more than combining graphics with printed text. However, auditory information alone has little staying power. People can retrieve only 10 percent of auditory input after 3 days, but if that material is complemented with a visual, the retrieval rate soars to 65 percent (Kalyuga, 2000; Mayer & Gallini, 1990). This strong effect reflects the fact that our brains process visual, text, and auditory

material through independent channels, which means that each medium reinforces the learning of the other (Fadel, 2008). Visuals foster deeper learning because they show the relationships among concepts (Medina, 2008; Vekiri, 2002)

More generally, Marzano (2003) documents that "nonlinguistic representations" of material, which include graphics, images, metaphors, and art forms, have an effect size on learning of .75, meaning that students exposed to them score .75 standard deviation higher on tests than students not so exposed. This effect size is comparable to that of collaborative learning and reinforcement and feedback. Hattie's (2009) meta-analysis of meta-analyses obtains a lower effect size of .57, but it is only for concept maps. This figure, too, approximates that for cooperative learning.

Cognitive psychology explains how visuals work—specifically, dual-coding theory, the visual argument theory, and cognitive theory.

Dual-Coding Theory: Redundancy and Reinforcement

Dual-coding theory addresses how visuals work in conjunction with text, which is typically a mode in which students receive material. It posits that the human mind has two memories, the semantic and the episodic, corresponding to the verbal and visual-spatial systems, respectively (Paivio, 1971). Neurological findings that the brain processes and stores verbal and visual-spatial information in separate cognitive systems have lent physiological evidence to this theory (Vekiri, 2002). So when presented with complementary text or audio and visuals, learners process it twice, through both systems, without overloading their working memory (Moreno & Mayer, 1999). As a result, they retain the material better and longer and can access and retrieve more easily than they can when they learn it in just one mode using just one system (Clark & Paivio, 1991; Kosslyn, 1994; Mayer & Gallini, 1990; Mayer & Sims, 1994; Paivio, 1971, 1990; Paivio & Csapo, 1973; Paivio, Walsh, & Bons, 1994; Svinicki, 2004; Tigner, 1999; Vekiri, 2002).

Another way of interpreting dual-coding theory is with reference to brain hemispheres. As the left side of the brain processes verbal symbols and the right side visuals, material presented in both modes activates both sides of the brain, roughly doubling the number of neurons firing and synapses forming.

Of course, the learning and comprehension benefits accrue only if the student receives the verbal and visual versions together and is able to integrate them cognitively (Mayer, 2005; Metiri Group, 2008). In addition, the visual must clearly and accurately depict the verbal.

The Visual Argument Theory: Greater Efficiency

According to this theory, visuals work so effectively because, compared to text, they convey information more efficiently—that is, visual information requires less working memory and fewer cognitive transformations to process and draw inferences from (Larkin & Simon, 1987; Robinson, Katayama, DuBois, & Devaney, 1998; Robinson & Kiewra, 1995; Robinson & Molina, 2002; Robinson & Schraw, 1994; Robinson & Skinner, 1996; Waller, 1981; Winn, 1987). In other words, it is less taxing on the mind to derive meaning from graphics than from words. In addition, a good graphic does a much better job than text of (1) inducing learners to attend to the conceptual relationships rather than just memorize terms; (2) enabling them to recognize patterns among concepts; (3) helping them elaborate their cognitive schemata by inferring new, complex relationships; and (4) helping them integrate new knowledge into their existing cognitive structures (Hyerle, 1996; Robinson & Kiewra, 1995; Robinson & Schraw, 1994; Robinson & Skinner, 1996; Robinson et al., 1998; Winn, 1991).

According to Larkin and Simon (1987), visuals offer "perceptual enhancement" by communicating information through both their individual components and the spatial organization of those components. As a result, they allow learners to process all the relevant concepts and the relationships among

them simultaneously as a whole. This ability facilitates understanding because bodies of knowledge are typically structured as a hierarchy of concepts with relationships among them. So just showing learners a picture of this organization teaches them a great deal about the nature of knowledge—for one, that it is not a list of loosely linked ideas but a tightly structured web of interrelated categories and principles. In addition, the mind need not interpret or infer the conceptual interrelationships because they are transparently displayed in the spatial arrangements, the shapes of the enclosures, the types of lines, the directions of the arrows, the colors, and any other graphic features the designer may use to distinguish causal links and direction, strength of relationship, level of generality, and the like.

Contrast the relatively effortless, holistic learning that visuals allow with the slower and more complicated process of extracting information from printed material. Text unfolds components and interrelationships among them linearly, sequentially, one piece at a time, as though they comprise a list. The mind must then interpret the pieces and connections and, to integrate and retain the knowledge, reconstruct the hierarchical organization, hopefully discerning the superordinate from the subordinate concepts, the more general and abstract from the more specific and concrete, exactly the way the text intended. The task demands a great deal of working memory and several cognitive transformations, allowing plenty of room for misunderstandings, shifts in meaning, and just plain error. In the meantime, the mind is too occupied to think very much about the material it is translating, such as to link it to prior knowledge, question it, draw inferences from it, trace its implications, or apply it toward solving a problem. Going back over the text to find specific information also takes more time and cognitive energy than does locating it on a graphic. The reader has to search through paragraphs, if not pages, or refer to the Contents page or the index (Larkin & Simon, 1987; Vekiri, 2002).

McMaster University professor Dale Roy (cited in Gedalof, 1998) demonstrated the superior efficacy of graphics on a faculty audience, a group highly skilled in processing text. He asked participants to prepare a brief oral presentation, which included developing one text-based and one visual transparency. After the participants delivered their minilesson, he had the rest of the audience reconstruct it. Consistently the faculty were able to reproduce almost all of the visual material but no more than half of the text-based presentation.

Cognitive Theory: The Big Picture

Chapter 1 has already addressed the critical importance of learners' seeing the organized big picture of knowledge, which includes recognizing patterns in how the world works. It is having this big picture of our field that makes us experts. In our mind's eye, this structure resembles a complex web of patterns that our contemporary and ancestral colleagues have identified and verbalized. It equips us with an intricate filing system that enables us to easily assimilate new information and store and retrieve from a vast collection of concepts, facts, data, and principles (Alexander, 1996; Chi, Glaser, & Rees, 1982; Novak, 1977; Reif & Heller, 1982; Royer, Cisero, & Carlo, 1993). We developed this schema over many years of intensive study—probably the hard way without the help of conceptual maps.

Without such a valid and robust mental structure, our students are disciplinary novices. They bring to our courses little background knowledge, no filing system for new knowledge, and often faulty models and misconceptions about the subject matter (Svinicki, 2004). After all, the mind is so wired to seek patterns that it can make mistakes in its quest. Students are unfamiliar with the hierarchy of concepts and principles, cannot discern patterns and generalizations, and lack the algorithms that facilitate applying knowledge to solving conceptual problems (DeJong & Ferguson-Hessler, 1996; Kozma, Russell, Jones, Marx, & Davis, 1996). As a result, they wander through a knowledge base picking up pieces of it on a superficial level, memorizing isolated facts and terms, and using trial-and-error to

solve problems and answer questions (Glaser, 1991). What they need to advance beyond novice is an empirically grounded big picture of the hierarchical structure of the body of knowledge—one convincing enough to override their misconceptions, as well as accurate and comprehensive enough to accommodate new knowledge and multiple conceptual networks (Baume & Baume, 2008; Posner, Strike, Hewson, & Gertzog, 1982). This is their entrée into expert thinking and a framework for deep, meaningful learning. In fact, students can't really learn and get beyond memorizing without it. The mind depends on organization; it acquires and stores new knowledge only if it perceives its organization and its logical place within the mental structure of prior knowledge (Baume & Baume, 2008; Bransford, Brown, & Cocking, 1999; Hanson, 2006; Reif & Heller, 1982; Royer et al., 1993; Svinicki, 2004; Wieman, 2007; Zull, 2002, 2011).

Since the chances are very slim that students will independently build such cognitive schemata in a semester or two of casual study, we would be wise to furnish them with relevant structures of our discipline, with valid, ready-made frameworks for filing this content (Kozma et al., 1996). They need to internalize this scaffolding, especially at the introductory level, where they have little prior knowledge of the subject matter on which to map new knowledge, before we elaborate it with details, conditions, and qualifications (Ausubel, 1968; Carlile & Jordan, 2005; Zull, 2002, 2011). In addition, we should help students become aware of any faulty mental models they may harbor and guide them in reconciling these with more accurate cognitive structures. Specifically, we can give them practice in reinterpreting their prior observations and experiences. Otherwise, if all we impart are masses of content, they will graduate mentally unchanged and uneducated, with only memory traces of their college years.

Because mental structures of knowledge are so crucial to students' learning, we need to convey them in the most transparent and efficient way possible. We know that the cognitive models of experts like ourselves look like hierarchical networks of complexly interrelated concepts and principles (Hanson 2006; Wieman, 2007). Many types of visuals are similarly structured to display component parts in hierarchical or web-like arrangements. Therefore, well-crafted graphics should do an excellent job of depicting disciplinary schemata. The next section examines four types that are suitable to the task.

■ TYPES OF VISUALS FOR LEARNING

Ausubel (1968) coined the term *advance organizer* decades ago to apply to any graphic that offered an opening overview of a lesson, whether a flowchart, diagram, chart, table, matrix, web, map, figure, or something else. In this section we focus on the major types of graphics that spatially display the relationships among ideas and concepts. Such visuals can serve as an advance organizer; a constructivist assignment for student groups or individuals; or a planning and memory aid for managing projects, solving problems, running meetings, organizing papers and presentations, integrating and summarizing material, and even writing creative works (Buzan, 1974; Svinicki, 2004; Wycoff, 1991). In other words, we can use graphics not only to help students acquire and retain knowledge but also to teach them tools that will facilitate their work in college and beyond and engage the creativity of the visual-holistic side of the brain. In addition, having students draw their own graphics can make excellent homework assignments—for example, summarizing their understanding of the readings or reviewing for tests—as well as challenging group activities during class and even test questions. The products can help you diagnose students' misconceptions and assess their conceptual, analytical, and synthesis skills without your having to read essays.

Concept Maps

A concept is human-defined pattern or common ground across a category of objects, events, or properties. For instance, concepts that represent objects include *force, light, food, population, weather, pressure,* and *energy.* Examples of those describing events are *rain, photosynthesis, osmosis, conversion, fission,* and *marriage.* Among those designating properties are *taste, density, life-giving, volume,* and *texture.* A concept map graphically displays the hierarchical organization of several (up to 20 or so) concepts and often examples of them, from the most inclusive/general/broad/abstract concept at the top to the most exclusive/specific/narrow/concrete concepts at the bottom. Therefore, it frequently looks like a network or spider web, typically pyramidal in overall shape, in which the lines link concepts or ideas to one another.

When Angelo and Cross (1993) suggested using such maps as a classroom assessment technique (see chapter 24), they described them as "drawings or diagrams showing mental connections that students make between a major concept . . . and other concepts they have learned" (p. 197). These connections may be categorical, causal, or logical relationships or even comparisons and contrasts. They may also designate a process or sequence of events, in which case they may resemble a chain or flowchart. Because of the many possible links, the lines between concepts should usually be labeled to specify the relationship.

You can teach your students how to draw a concept map by having them follow these steps (Wandersee, 2002b):

1. Identify key concepts, perhaps 12 to 20, from the readings, your last lecture, or another source.
2. Write each concept on a small index card or sticky note.
3. Identify the main topic or concept, and place it at top center. This is called the *superordinate* concept. It is either the most inclusive, general, broad, or abstract or the first stage in a process or sequence.
4. Rank-order or cluster all the remaining ideas, called *subordinate* concepts, from the most inclusive, general, broad, or abstract, placing these higher up and closer to the main concept, to

the most exclusive, specific, narrow, or concrete, placing these lower down. In the case of a process or sequence, order the concepts chronologically. The object is to structure the concepts and their interrelations correctly.

5. Arrange the concepts in a linkable hierarchy.

6. Draw the entire hierarchy on a piece of paper with enclosures around the concepts and linking lines that are labeled to specify the relationship. The linked concepts together with the labeled link are called a *proposition*. Because the map's presumed direction is downward, arrows are not necessary.

7. Check for cross-links (connections going across the branches); draw these links as dotted lines, and label them.

In addition, several universities have created and posted training videos on YouTube (recommended in Persellin & Daniels, 2014):

https://www.youtube.com/watch?v=eYtoZRmWLBc

http://www.youtube.com/watch?v=Gm1owf0uGFM

http://www.youtube.com/watch?v=P0DBS-YbRc0&list=TLacCperJK3vA

http://www.youtube.com/watch?v=vuBLI6ijHHg

Figure 23.1 shows several examples of very simple concept maps with just two or three concepts and one or two links. In a class, these maps would be only part of a larger map. Figure 23.2 elaborates the very simple map in which "population" is the superordinate concept, extending it by seven additional concepts arranged on three levels. Where a concept falls in the hierarchy depends on the lesson. In one map, a concept may be superordinate and in another subordinate. As Figure 23.3 illustrates, "photosynthesis" may be on the lowest (fourth) level in a concept map that starts with "energy," ranking below "light" and "life-giving," but "photosynthesis" can also be a superordinate concept, in which case "light" may be subordinate.

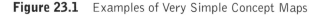

Figure 23.1 Examples of Very Simple Concept Maps

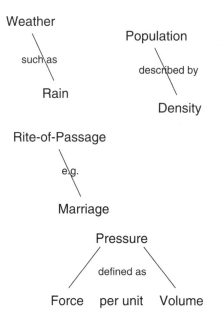

Concept maps are quite easy to write instructions for and to assess, which is why they make good gradable assignments and tests. The key evaluative dimensions are:

- The number of concepts included, unless you provide them
- The number of valid propositions (links between concepts)
- The number of valid levels in the hierarchy
- The number of valid cross-links
- The number of valid examples

Therefore, you can instruct students to draw a map with a given number of concepts interrelated with a given number of links, spanning a given number of hierarchical levels, with a given number of cross-links and examples. Novak and Gowin (1984), who devised the leading scoring model for concept maps, recommends giving 1 point for each valid link, 5 points for each valid level, 10 points for each valid cross-link, and 1 point for each valid example. Quicker still is a computer-based technique that scores maps by the number of links

Figure 23.2   Concept Map of "Population" with a Total of Nine Concepts

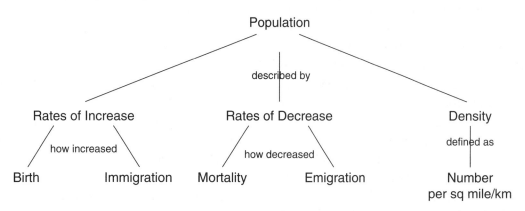

Figure 23.3   Two Simple Concept Maps Illustrating How Concepts in One Map Can Change Levels in Another Map

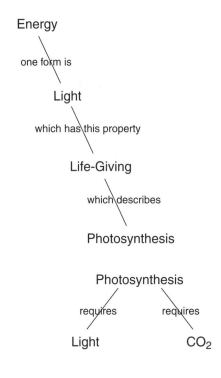

and the geometrical distances between concepts (Taricani & Clariana, 2006).

Many researchers have found that concept maps facilitate students' mastery of content and development of cognitive skills. In fact, concept maps have proven their value in some of the most challenging subjects, such as accounting (Leauby & Brazina, 1998), applied statistics (Schau & Mattern, 1997), biology (Briscoe & LaMaster, 1991; Cliburn, 1990; Kinchin, 2000, 2001; Wallace & Mintzes, 1990), chemistry (Regis & Albertazzi, 1996), conceptual astronomy (Zeilik et al., 1997), geoscience (Rebich & Gauthier, 2005), marine ecology (Beaudry & Wilson, 2010), mathematics (Brinkmann, 2003), medicine (Hoffman, Trott, & Neely, 2002; McGaghie, McCrimmon, Mitchell, Thompson, & Ravitch, 2000; West, Pomeroy, & Park, 2000), and nursing (Baugh & Mellott, 1998; King & Shell, 2002; Schuster, 2000; Wilkes, Cooper, Lewin, & Batts, 1999), among others. In Zeilik et al.'s (1997) experimental study, the astronomy students who developed concept maps scored higher than the control group on three kinds of conceptual examinations: one measuring the ability to relate concepts, another of multiple-choice items designed to identify faulty models, and a third fill-in-the-blank concept map. Among the skills that concept maps are known to enhance are postsecondary reading comprehension (Katayama, 1997; Mealy & Nist, 1989; Robinson & Kiewra, 1995; Robinson & Schraw, 1994), writing (Beaudry & Wilson, 2010), critical thinking (King & Shell, 2002; Nixon-Cobb, 2005; Schuster, 2000; West et al., 2000; Wilkes et al., 1999), and problem solving (Baugh & Mellot, 1998; Beissner, 1992; Kalman, 2007; Okebukola, 1992).

Of course, the effectiveness of concept maps, like every other teaching tool, depends on how it is used, and instructors have often maximized their interactive, constructivist potential by having students develop them along with the instructor or in peer groups, as well as alone. When students draw the maps, they are actively constructing their own knowledge (Kinchin, 2000, 2001), clarifying and organizing it (Hoffman et al., 2002; McGaghie et al., 2000), reinforcing their understanding of the material, and integrating it with prior knowledge (Plotnick, 2001). In addition, they are making explicit to both the instructor and themselves any misconceptions they may have and the progress they are making in correctly and complexly structuring the subject material (Romance & Vitale, 1999; Vojtek & Vojtek, 2000).

Concept maps work well for most knowledge construction tasks because all but the process variety presume an overall hierarchical structure of carefully integrated elements (Leichhardt, 1989; Plotnick, 1996; Romance & Vitale, 1999). As we will see, mind maps presume the same but have a different look and layout.

Mind Maps

Mind maps are the more colorful and whimsical cousin of concept maps. The mind-mapping method was developed by Buzan (1974) for note taking. Over the years, Ellis (2006) and authors of other books on college success popularized it as a technique for organizing course material for study, review, and paper writing. It follows steps similar to concept mapping:

1. Write the central concept, topic, or idea in the center of a large piece of paper, the board, or a landscape-set screen. This is the *primary* idea.
2. Identify up to six or seven closely related concepts, topics, or ideas (e.g., subordinate concepts, subtopics, properties, descriptors), and write each of them on the end of a thick line (with arrows) radiating from the center. Use key words only (the briefest and sharpest expression of the idea). These are the *secondary* ideas.
3. For each secondary concept, topic, or idea, identify up to six or seven closely related subordinate

concepts, subtopics, or ideas (properties, descriptors, examples, or the like), and write each of them on the end of a thinner line (arrows are optional) radiating from the secondary idea. Again, use key words. These are the *tertiary* ideas.
4. Look for cross-relationships, and draw thin lines between related ideas.
5. Add color, suggestive icons, and appropriate symbols. Color-code the lines and key words by secondary-idea branch.

In addition, Persellin and Daniels (2014) recommend the training video at http://www.youtube .com/watch?v=MlabrWv25qQ.

A couple of examples will bring the power of mind maps to light. Figure 23.4 is a graphic syllabus of the advanced corporate finance course designed and taught by Ernest N. Biktimirov, a finance professor at Brock University in St. Catharines, Ontario, Canada. He uses mind maps and other visual tools extensively in his teaching. His course, the primary idea, is graphically conveyed with a drawing of a bank check. It has three major segments (the secondary ideas): an overview of financial markets and instruments, symbolized by the struggle between the bear and the bull; portfolio theory, represented by a briefcase full of money; and financial instruments, illustrated by an investment certificate. These visual representations capture the major topics in an eye-catching way. The chapters addressing these topics are the tertiary ideas.

Figure 23.5 shows a more elaborate, icon-rich mind map that Biktimirov created to summarize course material on futures contracts and make it memorable for his students. In the center he represents the primary idea, types of futures contracts, by a flying saucer and a crystal ball to communicate two ideas: in a futures contract, a buyer and a seller agree on a price today for a future transaction; and the prices of futures contracts on different underlying assets help investors forecast the futures prices of these assets (E. N. Biktimirov, personal communication, April 13, 2009). Radiating from the center are three lines, one for each type of

Figure 23.4   Mind-Mapped Graphic Syllabus of Advanced Corporate Finance Course

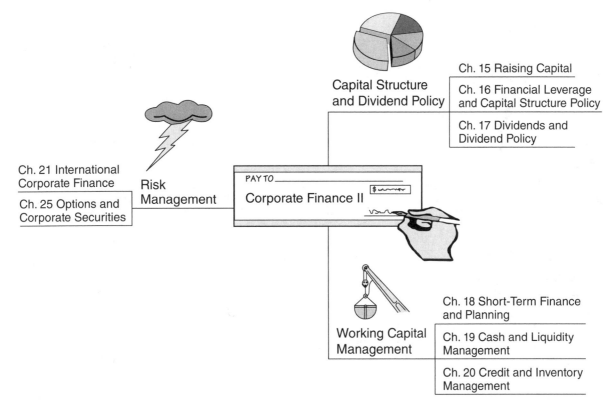

Source: Created by Ernest N. Biktimirov. Reprinted with his permission.

contract (secondary ideas): commodities, of which there are five types (tertiary ideas); weather, which affects cooling to heating needs all over the world (tertiary ideas); and financial, of which there are four types (tertiary ideas). The connection between each idea and its visual representation is transparent and sometimes amusing—for example, a piggy bank symbolizing financial types of futures contracts. This mind map extends out to quaternary ideas on the commodities branch and quinary ideas on the financial branch. It would be easy to recast this graphic as a concept map, but the end product wouldn't be nearly as visually evocative without the icons.

While not as well researched as concept maps, mind maps have proven to be effective learning tools in business (Driver, 2001), business statistics (Sirias, 2002), economics (Nettleship, 1992), executive education (Mento, Martinelli, & Jones, 1999), finance

(Biktimirov & Nilson, 2006), marketing (Eriksson & Hauer, 2004), and optometry (McClain, 1987). In another study, 50 second- and third-year medical students who used mind mapping as a study aid improved their factual recall of their readings 1 week later (Farrand, Hussain, & Hennessy, 2002). Mind maps can be graded the same way as concept maps.

Although the secondary and tertiary ideas radiate out from the center of a mind map, this graphic reflects a hierarchy of ideas. But unlike a concept map, it uses icons, symbols, color, and line thickness to communicate meaning and does not normally label the lines. Of course, you and your students can mix and match features of concept and mind maps to serve your learning purposes. Similarly, graphic syllabi and outcomes maps may also incorporate the visual cues of mind maps. Such colorful and whimsical touches not only add fun to instructional materials but also

Figure 23.5   Mind Map of Types of Futures Contracts

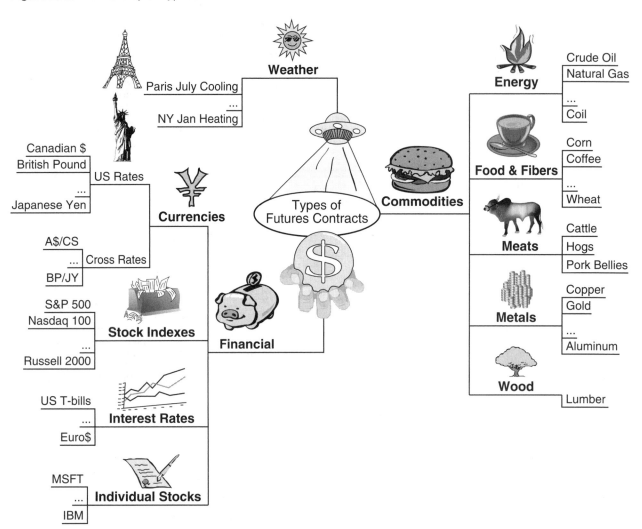

Source: Created by Ernest N. Biktimirov. Reprinted with his permission.

contribute to learning and retention. Specifically, unexpected novelty and humor attract attention and arouse emotions, releasing neurotransmitters from the limbic system that reinforce associated synaptic connections (Leamnson, 2000; Mangurian, 2005; see chapter 1). Besides, such personal extras testify to your sense of humor, creativity, openness to new ideas, and comfort with students and yourself.

Concept Circle Diagrams

The least well known of the graphics we will look at here, concept circle diagrams illustrate the relationships among concepts in terms of the distances and the overlaps among circles and the relative sizes of the circles. When drawn by the instructor, they can disentangle complex conceptual interrelationships for the students and serve as a memorable image. Of course, students can create their own to clarify their understanding of conceptual interconnections, in which case they should also draw their diagram and write an accompanying sentence or two to explain its meaning (Wandersee, 2002a).

Here are some basic guidelines for creating these diagrams (Wandersee, 2002a):

- The relative sizes of the circles reflect the relative importance, quantities, variable values, or level of generality of the concepts.
- A smaller circle drawn within a larger one indicates that the latter concept encompasses the former.
- Partially overlapping circles mean that one concept includes some instances of the other concept.
- Superimposed circles show that the concepts are equivalent and share all the same instances.
- Completely separate circles denote unrelated or independent concepts.
- Broken circles convey that the conceptual boundaries are not well understood.
- Adding color enhances the diagram, especially when the colors of overlapping areas accurately reflect the combination of the circle colors.
- Detail in a diagram can be shown by projecting out a new diagram of an enlarged section of the original diagram (called *telescoping*).

Unfortunately, YouTube does not offer videos on drawing concept circle diagrams, except for one type, Venn diagrams, and only in the context of philosophy and set theory.

Venn diagrams, which illustrate overlapping concepts and categories by overlapping circles, are the most widely used kind of concept circle diagrams. The simplest example is two partially overlapping circles. How much they overlap depends on the content. If you wish to show the relationship between deviant behavior and illegal behavior, you might overlap the circles about a quarter of the way because some deviant behavior is not illegal (e.g., cross-dressing) and some illegal behavior is not deviant (e.g., exceeding the speed limit by 5 or 10 miles per hour). The video at https://www.youtube.com/watch?v=YAjxRUGS0Gc gives a good tutorial

The more complex Venn diagram showcased in Figure 23.6 demonstrates the full potential of this type of graphic. It illustrates the complicated relationships among different classifications of explicit, first-order, ordinary differential equations (ODEs).

Its creator, Daniel D. Warner, professor of mathematical sciences at Clemson University, designed it for his sophomore course for engineering and science majors on differential equations and his calculus course for life science majors. He gives it to his students along with the assignment of constructing an example of an ODE that is exclusive to each portion of the diagram. (Possible correct answers are in brackets, where a, b, r, N, and Ta are constants.) As the diagram has eight portions, the solution involves eight different ODEs (D. D. Warner, personal communication, April 8, 16, 2009).

1. General and neither separable nor linear [$dy/dt =$ a + b cos(t) exp(y)]
2. Separable and neither autonomous nor linear [$dy/dt =$ a cos(t) sin(y)]
3. Linear and not separable [$dy/dt =$ a − y/(b − t), a mixing model, or $dy/dt =$ -m g t − b y, like an object falling with air resistance]
4. Autonomous and not linear [$dy/dt =$ r(1 − y/N) y, logistic growth]
5. Autonomous and linear but not quadrature [$dy/dt =$ r y, Malthusian growth, or $dy/dt =$ r (Ta − y), Newton's law of cooling]
6. Quadrature and not autonomous [$dy/dt =$ r t + a, variable velocity, constant acceleration]
7. Linear and separable but neither autonomous nor a quadrature [$dy/dt =$ (t + a) (y − b)]
8. Autonomous and quadrature (a very small set, but not empty) [$dy/dt =$ r, constant velocity].

Another type of concept circle diagram is the context map (Hyerle, 1996), which is composed of two or more concentric circles. The outer circles represent the contexts, settings, environments, or frames of reference of the inner circles or the external influences on the inner circles. For instance, sociologists sometimes use a context map to show the different levels of socialization that affect the individual. If you place individuals in the innermost circle, their primary groups—immediate and near-immediate family, close friends and neighbors, and one's minister—occupy the closest concentric

Figure 23.6   Concept Circle Diagram (Venn Diagram) for the Classification of Explicit, First-Order, Ordinary Differential Equations

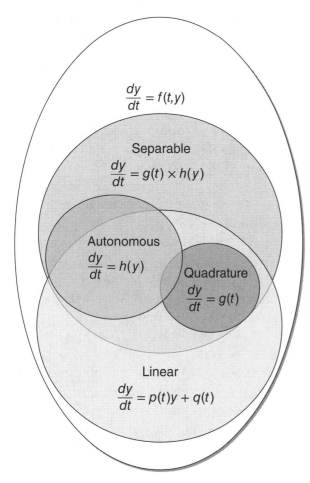

Source: Created by Daniel D. Warner. Reprinted with his permission.

circle because these groups have the most direct impact on the focal person. In the next concentric circle are secondary groups, with which an individual may occasionally have direct contact of a more formal type. These include most relatives, school and work associates, colleagues, fellow church members, distant friends, acquaintances, most neighbors, and people with whom one does business. While their influence on the individual is weaker, they often have indirect effects through members of the primary group. The outermost concentric circle represents the broader society, which socializes the individual both directly—through the mass media, political institutions, law enforcement, and economic markets, for instance—and indirectly through its impact on the secondary and primary groups.

Since concept circle diagrams can take on several shapes and forms, no scoring formula is available. However, Wandersee (2002a) suggests several evaluative dimensions to consider when assessing a student product: (1) its legibility, clarity, and interpretability; (2) the relevance of the concepts selected to the assignment; (3) the validity of the relationships shown among concepts; (4) the relevance of the title to the diagram; (5) the accuracy and fit of the written explanation; and (6) the appropriate use of graphic options, such as color and telescoping.

Matrices

Matrices may be the least constructivist visual of those considered here, as they are constrained by a table-like format. Yet they can transform linear text and notes into much more useful two-dimensional schemata that invite comparing and contrasting objects, concepts, or categories by any number of properties. As text or notes alone are not set up to engage higher-order thinking, students usually wind up just memorizing them. Matrices also enhance storage and retrieval (Atkinson et al., 1999; Derry, 1984). Kiewra (2005) strongly recommends matrices as learning devices for organizing, analyzing, reviewing, and remembering material, and he furnishes examples that display categories of literature, different schedules of psychological reinforcement, properties of various biological species, and types of atomic particles. If used for assessment purposes, matrices are easy to score on a cell-by-cell basis.

Table 23.1 shows a data retrieval matrix comparing and contrasting aspects of the seven major wars in which the United States has fought during the 20th and 21st centuries. The matrix asks students to identify the length of each war, the causes, the precipitating incidents, and the positive and negative impacts on the country. The level of thinking required to complete it depends partially on what the students can and cannot gather directly

Table 23.1 Matrix Comparing and Contrasting Aspects of the Major Wars of the United States in the 20th and 21st Centuries

	Duration in Years, Months	Causes	How Started	Positive Effects for United States	Negative Effects for United States
World War I					
World War II					
Korean War					
Vietnam War					
Desert Storm					
Iraq War					
Afghanistan War					

from course materials. For instance, if the materials have provided the effects of these wars but have not distinguished the favorable from the unfavorable effects, students must evaluate the broader, longer-term ramifications of each war on the country.

■ THE FUTURE OF VISUALS IN LEARNING

Due to the dominance of television, movies, video games, and the Internet, our culture has been deemphasizing text to communicate information in favor of graphics for decades (Fischman, 2001; Hartman, 2006). The millennial generation has grown up with the full dose of these visual media, and as far as we can tell, subsequent generations will too. This "visual explosion," as Felten (2008, p. 60) terms it, has spread from the popular culture into the scholarly arena. We can now use high-quality digital libraries and galleries—historical, scientific, and artistic—and educational resources, such as those archived on these websites:

http://www.merlot.org/

http://www.brocku.ca/learningobjects/flash_content

http://www.wisc-online.com/

http://www.shodor.org/interactivate/

http://www4.uwm.edu/cie/learning_objects.cfm?gid=55

Many of these resources showcase the power of adding interactivity and animation to graphics, generating many of today's cutting-edge teaching tools in online education and computer-assisted instruction: learning objects, virtual and augmented realities, and simulations. These may come to dominate the educational media, elevating visual literacy to an essential skill for understanding and interpreting complex sets of information. Such innovations represent just a few of the new high-tech instructional tools (see chapter 4).

One more benefit of graphics—this one particularly important in the global village we now inhabit—is that they communicate across cultures. Many of the conventions used in visuals, such as spatial proximity among closely related elements and the use of arrows to indicate direction or movement, seem to be universal, anchored in the basic human processes of visual perception (Tversky, 1995, 2001).

CHAPTER 24

Improving Student Performance with Feedback

The purpose of feedback is to help the recipient perform some skill better, and it usually does. After all, practice doesn't make perfect if, as is typical, you start out doing something imperfectly and never get feedback on how to do it better. In his meta-analysis of 800 meta-analyses, Hattie (2009) found that feedback has an impressive average effect size of .73 on student achievement, placing it among the most powerful teaching and learning methods available. In a smaller meta-analysis, he and Timperley (2007) reported an even larger average effect size of .79. Feedback to students can come from any number of sources: the instructor, of course, but also peers and oneself. But it's a two-way street. To improve student achievement, we need feedback from students to assess their progress and suggest how we might enhance their learning. The chapter addresses all these facets of feedback. Yet, however helpful it can be, feedback does not always succeed with students, and we'll first examine why this happens.

◼ WHY FEEDBACK FAILS

Feedback can fail for so many reasons that we should appreciate the times it succeeds. Feedback failure has received too little attention in the literature, so we must rely on one essay (Falkenberg, 1996), which offers four possible explanations for it.

First, for whatever reason, a student may just not be capable of meeting the higher standards the feedback given sets as a goal, at least not within the time limit allowed. People have different abilities, and some require far longer than a week or even a semester to bring certain skills up to par.

A second possibility is that a student may not agree with our performance standards, in which case it falls on us to change her mind. But can we? For instance, faculty and students have quite different definitions of cheating and plagiarism in terms of what is and isn't ethical (see chapter 10). Thus far, we have not found successful ways to convince students to adopt our values. Many students also believe that we should grade them not just on performance but also on effort, and some maintain they are entitled to an A just for showing up in class or paying tuition (Singleton-Jackson, Jackson, & Reinhardt, 2010). In this case, we can enforce our grading criteria, but have we gained converts? Another area of disagreement is writing standards. Students who in our view write poorly may argue that they have always written this way and have gotten good grades and been understood by their friends. We can tell them that the workplace will expect a writing style closer to our criteria, but will they believe us? They may also oppose our scientific perspectives on religious grounds, pitting our material against their years of socialization. Perhaps the best we can do is to persuade them to accept and compartmentalize science as a separate worldview.

A third reason feedback may fail is that a student may not correctly perceive our performance standards. For example, we may counsel him that he frequently writes sentence fragments, but if he continues to write them, it may be that he doesn't understand what a sentence fragment is. We may be able to overcome this barrier by clarifying our standards in different words, providing more models, or tutoring the student individually.

Finally, a student may not correctly evaluate her performance against our standards for any of several reasons. If it is because of simple error, all we need to do is supply additional feedback that gives new information or an alternative interpretation. But the block may represent ingrained error—that is, she has been performing the skill wrong for so long that it feels right to her. Even so, we can possibly reach her by furnishing more models and tutoring. However, if the student is too immature to accept criticism or is out of touch with reality, we really can't do anything to get through. This may explain the students we have known who have cut classes, turned in failing work, and refused our help.

While Falkenberg's insights shed light on our apparent failures, they don't diagnose the reasons a given student fails, so we must probe further and try to provide more clarification, feedback, and models

before we give up. When we can intervene, we should enlist other students to help us. Often they can furnish the additional clarification, information, interpretation, models, and even tutoring, especially when they work in small groups to provide peer feedback on their drafts of assignments (see the next section). We should also refer students to campus resources such as the writing or academic assistance center (see the appendix).

■ STUDENT PEER FEEDBACK

Drafts of written work—essays, lab reports, proposals, papers, and the like—that will be turned in later for formal grading fall into a gray category that we might call "writing-to-learn-to-write-better" assignments. Just like professionals, students improve their writing in response to well-informed feedback on drafts. As the instructor, you may provide the best-informed critique, but students can benefit from peer feedback as well, from both getting it and giving it. Peer feedback not only provides students with more varied, immediate, and frequent feedback than any one instructor can give, but it also helps them develop communication, critical thinking, collaboration, and lifelong learning skills (Dochy, Segers, Van den Bossche, & Gijbels, 2003; Topping, 1998).

However, the validity, reliability, and accuracy of peer feedback are uneven, some tainted by personal relationships and traits (such as race) and typically too lenient, superficial, and unfocused (Mowl & Pain, 1995; Orsmond, Merry, & Reiling, 1996). This should not be surprising, as students have loyalties to one another and concerns about criticizing a peer's work. In addition, they lack the disciplinary background to know and apply professional standards, at least in lower-level courses, and they give only as much feedback as the questions provided absolutely demand. So in answer to the question, "Is the central idea clear throughout the paper?" most students will say only yes or no and will not reference specific passages unless told to do so.

Instructors can obtain much more valid, neutral, useful, and detailed student peer feedback by putting a different kind of item on the feedback forms. Rather than requiring an evaluation about the adequacy, effectiveness, clarity, or logic of some aspect of the work, you can ask students to identify features or parts of the work, as each student sees them, or give their personal reactions to the work (Nilson, 2002–2003, 2003). For example, instead of forcing a judgment with, "Does the opening paragraph lay out a clear thesis statement for the rest of the paper?" rephrase the question as one requiring simple identification: "What do you think is the thesis of the paper? Paraphrase it below." Rather than asking, "Is the title of the paper interesting, appropriate, and sufficiently focused?" solicit instead students' personal reaction: "What three adjectives would you use to describe the title of the paper?" Rather than requesting an evaluation such as, "How well written is the paper?" give students this innocuous task: "Highlight any passages you had to read more than once to understand what the writer was saying."

The revised questions are emotionally neutral and require only basic rhetorical knowledge to answer, yet they demand close attention to the work and often references to its particulars. They do not allow students to give biased, uninformed, or superficial feedback. Rather, the responses they solicit tell the writer how readers have understood and reacted to the paper and what they got out of it. If most of the readers do not identify the intended thesis, the writer knows she must strengthen and clarify the thesis statement. If she doesn't like the way her readers described her title, she knows she should change it. If they highlight several passages as hard to read, she knows she needs to work on rewriting those sections. With peer feedback, students find a genuine audience—a role that instructors cannot play—and they can come to care about how and what they communicate (Nilson, 2002–2003, 2003).

If you are teaching an advanced course, your students may be cognitively and emotionally mature enough to actually appraise each other's work. In this case, teach them to do so by modeling and explaining your assessment process. Provide your own detailed comments on the first draft of the first product, review your feedback methods with your class, and then comment on your students' comments on the next piece of work. After feedback from you on their feedback, they should be able to provide useful evaluations on their own.

SELF-ASSESSMENT

Students' ability to assess their work does not develop just by their getting our assessments. We have to set self-assessment as a learning outcome and incorporate activities that will teach them and give them practice in how to do it. In addition, we must lay out very clear quality standards for a given assignment (Boud, Lawson, & Thompson, 2013).

Students report that they start out quite insecure about their own judgment, but their anxiety subsides with experience. They also say that self-assessment benefits them in many ways: raising their grades, increasing their motivation, lowering their stress, sharpening their focus on an assignment's key elements, and helping them pinpoint the strengths and weaknesses in their work (Andrade & Du, 2007). Even so, they do not develop their own judgment so much as they come to better understand what their instructor wants. In addition, only a few transfer their self-assessment skills to their other classes (Andrade & Du, 2007).

If students receive both practice and instructor feedback on their self-assessments, most learn how to self-assess quite well—that is, their judgments converge more and more with their instructors'. As a result, these students improve their performance in the course. However, this is true only of the midrange achievers, who tend to assess their performance quite accurately, and the high achievers, who tend to underestimate their performance. Low achievers start out and unfortunately end up overestimating their performance to about the same degree and are therefore unable to improve (Boud et al., 2013; Falchikov &

Boud, 1989; Kruger & Dunning, 1999). The main reason is that they simply cannot perceive their errors and shortcomings, even beyond the classroom and when given incentives to be accurate (Ehrlinger, Johnson, Banner, Dunning, & Kruger, 2008). This is a perfect example of how feedback can fail. No doubt some students cannot understand the quality standards they are supposed to apply in self-assessing, and others may even disagree with those standards.

Leading students through the evaluation stage of self-regulated learning is more straightforward in that we can pose questions that require them to gather accurate data about their learning. Among the "Learner's Questions" in chapter 20 are self-testing queries such as, "What can I recall . . . ?" "What were the most important points I learned?" and "Can I see and organize the interrelationships among them?" If students have little or nothing to say in response, they know they haven't learned the material as well as they should.

In addition to the clarity of your assessment criteria, the effectiveness of your training in applying them, and the quality of your students, two other factors affect how well your students will learn how to self-assess: the level of your course and your discipline. More advanced students and those in the scientific and mathematical courses learn to self-assess more accurately than the less advanced and those in other kinds of courses, such as those in the humanities (Edwards, 2007; Falchikov & Boud, 1989). More advanced students are presumably more motivated and more familiar with the standards of the discipline. In addition, scientific and mathematical courses focus on solving problems with one correct answer and therefore offer clearer quality criteria. So be discriminating in choosing the courses to incorporate self-assessment.

■ STUDENT PORTFOLIOS

A portfolio is a collection of samples of a student's work during the term, one that you and he may assemble together, along with his written reflections on the products or his own intellectual progress through writing them. It may take the form of a notebook/folder or a website; if the latter, it is called an electronic portfolio or e-portfolio. The samples may be the student's best work, the widest variety of his good work, or the history of one or more major pieces of work, such as notes, outlines, peer and instructor reviews, and multiple revisions in response to those reviews (Bernhardt, 1992; Zubizarreta, 2009). You can assess and document your students' progress across written or otherwise created products without attaching grades. You grade only the total portfolio and the student's reflections, typically at the end of the course. To the extent that you want these reflections to incorporate self-assessment, you must teach students how to assess their work against specific criteria.

Beginning in the 1980s, student portfolios started to acquire a strong following among English instructors from primary through postsecondary levels. Those who use them testify that portfolios encourage constructive dialogue between students and the instructor and motivate students to attempt more varied and adventuresome writing, take instructor and peer feedback seriously, and revise their work, often several times. Instructors in many disciplines, even mathematics and business, have developed their own versions of the portfolio, most of which encourage more creative demonstrations of learning than do traditional assignments and tests (Belanoff & Dickson, 1991; Crowley, 1993; Zubizarreta, 2009).

Consider, for example, the imaginative range of assessment artifacts that a mathematics portfolio can contain: samples of journal entries; written explanations for each mathematical step of a complex problem solution; a mathematics autobiography focusing on changing attitudes and new insights; multiple solutions to a challenging problem, each reflecting a different approach; an elegant proof, either intuitive or formal depending on the student's abilities; student-developed lesson plans for teaching a particular mathematical concept; student-developed word problems; student-drawn visual representations of problems; student-made concrete representations; and reviews of mathematical books and journal articles—all in addition to examples of traditional student output, such as tests, quizzes, and homework (Crowley, 1993; Stenmark, 1989, 1991).

Portfolios are not without their problems. For example, postponing grading until the end of the course will not necessarily save you grading time. Quite the contrary. While you may not have to affix letters or points to a student's work until the end, you will probably assign more and more varied writing projects and put more time and effort during the term into giving formative feedback and holding student conferences. Without this detailed, personalized feedback, few of the potential benefits of portfolios will accrue. In addition, you will otherwise suffocate at the end of the course under an avalanche of paper or websites filled with only vaguely familiar writing samples (Bernhardt, 1992; Zubizarreta, 2009).

For many students, the lack of grading during the term presents serious problems. They may be anxious not knowing where they stand and how they are doing, and some need to know early in the term to decide whether to stay in the course. Academic regulations may not even allow such postponement of grades. At some institutions, faculty are required to disclose midterm grades or to submit deficiency reports on students earning a C- or lower, and curriculum committees will not approve new courses unless a substantial part of the final grade is determined by the middle of the term.

A final challenge with using portfolios pertains to grading standards. If a portfolio contains only students' best work, how can anyone in the class not receive a good grade? But the converse problem also arises: some instructors resist assigning deservedly low grades to students who have worked hard during the term. Even with herculean effort, some students barely pass a course, and it can be very difficult for an instructor to break the bad news to them after all the time spent counseling and conferencing with them.

Therefore, before adopting student portfolios, consider the following issues about delayed grading: how your students might respond to it, whether your institution's academic regulations accommodate it, and whether you can uphold your quality standards in spite of it. Then ask yourself if you can make the time to give your students' work the detailed, ongoing feedback that is required.

▨ INSTRUCTOR FEEDBACK: HELPING STUDENTS IMPROVE WITH IT

Summative feedback is what we write or say to students to help them improve their work on a subsequent assignment, and it usually accompanies some kind of grade. Students may view it more as our justification for the grade we give. By contrast, *formative feedback* comprises all the recommendations we or their peers give them for improving their work at an early stage, before it receives a grade, with the expectation that they will revise it accordingly. If you attach a grade to such drafts, it should be mainly to motivate student effort during the work's development and should count only for a portion of the work's final grade.

This type of feedback benefits both you and your students in several ways. For you, it yields better student products, practically eliminates plagiarism, and changes your role from judge to facilitator or coach. For them, it encourages steady writing and work habits, gives them criteria on which to improve their work and their communication skills, and teaches them the professional creation process, which always involves extensive revision.

These suggestions will make formative assessments of papers and projects more productive:

• *Set and enforce deadlines for students to complete a major work in stages* to find topics, gather resources, develop an outline, and submit a first draft. Each stage provides an occasion for feedback.

• *Set clear criteria for what a draft must accomplish, what elements it must contain, and what questions it must answer. Then grade the drafts pass/fail.* Students receive all of the points if they meet all the criteria and no points if they miss any. This will ensure that students attend to your requirements and submit high-quality drafts, which they otherwise may not do (Nilson, 2015). Chapter 27 more fully explains this type of grading, called *specifications* (or *specs*) grading because you grade work pass/fail based on whether it meets the necessary specifications.

- *Ensure students understand that formative feedback focuses on major problems in their work* and that making the suggested changes does not guarantee them an A.

- *Comment more on major writing issues,* such as content, reasoning, and organization, and less on style and grammar.

- *Make your comments constructive, improvement directed, and process centered.* Suggest how to correct and improve the work in relation to your predefined criteria. Give praise where deserved because students often do not know what they are doing right. But focus on praising the effort and the process students went through to produce the work, not on their intelligence or the product itself, to help ensure they keep putting forth the necessary effort (Coffield, 2014; Dweck, 2007; Halvorson, 2014). No one excels by sitting on their laurels.

- Whether you are giving students formative or summative feedback, *make a follow-up assignment in which they must paraphrase or summarize your feedback back to you.* If you are using a rubric, they should include your standards as feedback as well (Doyle, 2008). This way, they have to read all of your feedback carefully and make sense of it. Without having to do so, they often ignore or don't try very hard to understand our comments and corrections (Duncan, 2007; Hattie & Timperley, 2007) and rarely ask us to clarify what they don't comprehend. We in turn will find out how our students interpret our comments and corrections and can clarify what they misunderstand. Perhaps the words, abbreviations, and symbols we use are alien or ambiguous to them. Only when students attend to and accurately understand our feedback can we expect them to improve their work in their revisions or later assignments.

- *When students will be revising a piece of work, have them also write out their goals and plans for revision.* They should explain the changes they make in the work in response to the feedback they've received.

- Whether feedback is formative or summative, *we should provide it as promptly as we can;* we know this. But *how* we provide it—that is, our feedback medium—also matters to students. In a recent survey, over three-quarters of students said that they find face-to-face feedback "very" or "extremely effective," no doubt because we can best convey our meaning using our whole person and students can ask for clarification on the spot. Almost the same proportion, close to 70 percent, viewed written or typed comments just as favorably. But only around a third of students found video- or audio-recorded comments "very" or "extremely effective" (Turnitin, 2014).

CLASSROOM ASSESSMENT TECHNIQUES

No doubt you can recall classes when you would have liked to have known what your students were learning from your lesson and whether you should proceed with the next one. Perhaps you found out what they missed from a test you gave three weeks later. Obviously it is much more effective to assess your students' learning while in progress, before their shortfalls in understanding adversely affect their grades and motivation. Such information can also help you assess, and ultimately enhance, your teaching effectiveness because it helps you shape and focus your subsequent teaching. It can do the same for your students' subsequent learning by directing their attention to the areas they need to study more. In fact, in Hattie's (2009) meta-meta-analysis, furnishing "formative evaluation" to instructors has a remarkable effect size of .90 on student achievement, even larger than the feedback we give to students.

Classroom assessment techniques (CATs) were developed precisely to serve these purposes (Angelo, 1991a). You can use them regularly or intermittently without violating the structure and content of your course and quickly identify trouble spots your class is encountering. Knowing what your students did not process the first time through the material, you can turn around a potentially disappointing situation. Perhaps classroom assessment is not all that much different from the informal, sometimes unconscious gauges you already use, such as reading your students' expressions and body language and asking and answering questions. But these are unreliable and rarely encompass the whole class. CATs formalize and systematize the process, ensuring that you assess your whole class. Given their purpose, they are especially appropriate for student-active lecture breaks, but they make stimulating warm-up activities at the beginning of class and good wrap-up exercises at the end of class.

Selecting Appropriate CATs

Different CATs are designed to measure students' progress in different types of learning. So before selecting a CAT, consider which type you wish to assess (Angelo, 1991b). *Declarative learning* is learning *what*—that is, learning the facts and principles of a given field. In terms of Bloom's (1956) taxonomy of cognitive operations (see chapter 2), declarative learning focuses on knowledge and comprehension at the lower-level end of the scale. *Procedural learning* is learning how to do something, from the specific tasks of a given discipline to universal skills such as writing, critical thinking, and reasoning. Its emphasis is application. The third type, *conditional learning*, is learning when and where to apply the acquired declarative knowledge and procedural skills. Too often taught only implicitly through example and modeling, it can be better taught explicitly using the case method, problem-based learning, role playing, simulations, and service-learning (see chapters 14, 17, and 18). While conditional learning clearly entails application, it also involves analysis and synthesis. Finally, *reflective learning* is learning why, which engages students in analysis, synthesis, and evaluation. It directs their attention to their beliefs,

values, and motives for learning about a particular topic. Without this reflection, higher education is little more than job training.

Some Proven CATs

Chapters 20 and 22 introduced several popular CATs that also serve as self-regulated learning and writing-to-learn exercises, such as the one-minute paper and the one-sentence summary. Angelo and Cross (1993) describe dozens of other techniques, among which are these:

Background Knowledge Probe

This is essentially a diagnostic pretest to administer on the first day of class or when you begin a new unit of instruction. It can consist of 2 or 3 short-answer or essay questions or 15 to 20 multiple-choice items about students' attitudes and understanding. This CAT can provide information not only on your students' prior knowledge but also on their motivation, beliefs, values, and misconceptions about the subject matter and, if you use open-ended questions, their writing skills. The results also tell you what material to cover and what existing knowledge you can use to map on new knowledge. Finally, probes activate students' prior knowledge, readying them for additional learning.

Focused Listing

You can use this technique to activate students' prior knowledge before you teach a topic and to help them review afterward. Direct students' attention to a single important name, concept, or relationship and ask them to list as many related concepts and ideas as they can. You might limit the exercise to 2 to 3 minutes or 5 to 10 items. With these constraints, the results give you a pretty accurate picture of the features students identify and recall as salient and not just those they think you want to hear.

Muddiest Point

Ask your students to write down what they perceived as the muddiest point in a lecture, a reading, a video, or a demonstration. Reserve some time at the end of class to ask and answer questions; then collect the students' responses. You can clarify the muddy points during the next class. Struggling students who are not comfortable asking questions publicly find it to be a lifeline. In addition, it enables you to see the material through your students' eyes, reminding you of the many different ways they process information. Finally, knowing that they will have to identify a muddy point induces students to pay closer attention in class. And when the time comes for the CAT, they have to review whatever learning experience they are reflecting on.

Paper or Project Prospectus

A prospectus is a detailed plan for a project or paper—perhaps even a first draft that focuses students on the topic, the purpose, the issues to address, the audience, the organization, and the time, skills, and other resources needed—in fact, whatever guidelines you provide for the final product. First, students need to understand these guidelines—that is, the important facets and likely pitfalls of the assignment. For the prospectus itself, you might compose a list of three to seven questions that students must answer. Advise students not to begin substantive work on their actual assignment until they receive feedback on their prospectus from you and possibly other students. This CAT is a major assignment in itself, so you may want to make it required and grade it, but without counting it heavily toward the final grade. The prospectus accommodates many different types of assignments and teaches crucial, transferable planning and organizational skills. In addition, it gives students early enough feedback to help them produce a better product.

Everyday Ethical Dilemmas

For this CAT, you first locate or create a brief case study that poses an ethical problem related to the material (see chapter 17). Then write two or three questions that make students take and defend a position. This activity encourages students to try on different values and beliefs, thus helping them develop moral reasoning skills. It also affords you probing, personal glimpses into their ethical and cognitive maturity. With these insights, you can foster their continuing growth by introducing values and opinions that they have not yet considered. Let your students turn in their written responses anonymously, thus giving you an honest overview of the prevailing class opinions and values. Students will need some time to reflect and develop their arguments, so you might assign this CAT as homework.

Application Cards

After a lecture segment, demonstration, or video on procedure, principle, or theory, have students write down on a card or piece of paper one or more real-world applications of the material. As you read through them, select the best ones to read to the class at the next meeting. This CAT gives students practice in transferring knowledge to useful applications.

• • •

The "Surveying Student Response" section of chapter 12 describes a lecture break activity that quickly gives you feedback on your students' understanding while enhancing their learning: you display a multiple-choice or true/false item on the topic you were just talking about and, using clickers, online polling, or colored cards, survey your students' responses before and after they discuss their answers with their neighbors. Crouch and Mazur (2001) devised and tested this technique under the name of "peer instruction."

■ DURING-THE-TERM STUDENT FEEDBACK

Recall Hattie's (2009) finding that furnishing "formative evaluation" to instructors has a whopping effect size of .90 on student achievement. That formative feedback entails not only classroom assessment but also midterm feedback solicited directly from your students. Most students take the opportunity to give their instructors in-progress feedback more seriously than they do end-of-term evaluations. When the course is over, why should they make thoughtful judgments and remarks when it won't do them any good? The best time to gather student feedback is early enough in the term for their input to make a difference.

You have the option to gather and analyze your own midterm student feedback. You can collect it anonymously online using the polling tool in your LMS or a polling or survey website; Survey Monkey (www.surveymonkey.com) has course evaluation templates. Or you can have students fill out a paper form or index card in class. You can use items similar to those on your institution's or department's official ratings form or tailor items to your needs. For instance, you can set up a 1-to-5 agree-disagree scale for statements like these: "This class stimulates my interest in the subject matter." "I learn a great deal from answering clicker questions in class." "The daily quizzes help me keep up with the readings."

You can also ask students a set of open-ended questions, such as, "What things are helping you learn in this class? What would help you learn more? What things are getting in the way of your learning?" These are also popular open-ended probes: "To help my learning: Keep doing _____. Stop doing _____. Start doing _____." If you try a new teaching technique, ask the students anonymously how it helped or didn't help their learning. Or you can ask about the effectiveness of specific teaching methods, activities, assignments, or readings. Just be sure to focus your students' attention on their learning. Students don't always know when they are and aren't learning, but they will appreciate your interest in their reactions.

Alternatively, ask your institution's teaching and learning center (see the appendix) to collect and analyze student feedback. The typical procedure, often called a *small group instructional diagnosis* (SGID), a *small group analysis* (SGA), or a *class interview*, relies on focus-group methodology. You leave your classroom, and a center staff member explains the procedure to your students, breaks them into groups of three to six, and gives each group one form to complete. The form asks open-ended questions like those above or similar ones, such as, "What are your instructor's primary teaching strengths?" and, "What are your instructor's primary teaching weaknesses?" Your students discuss their answers and generally concur on what they write on the form. The staff member then has the groups share their responses and may even survey student agreement with these responses. A day or so later, she prepares a write-up and meets with you to review the results. Research shows that soliciting early student feedback and having an interpretive consultation with a specialist result in significantly higher student ratings at the end of the term (Finelli et al., 2008), as well as course improvements (Millis, 2004). Typically, any effort you make to gather midterm student feedback lifts your ratings at least modestly.

You should discuss the results with your class as soon as possible (Davis, 2009). Start out by thanking your students for their honest and thoughtful suggestions. You can pick and choose among the changes your students may request, explaining to them why you are making some of the changes they recommend and not others. In fact, you can address many of their concerns just by providing your reasons for the teaching and assessment decisions you have made. (They may have forgotten the reasons you already gave.) Again, this book supplies plenty of research-based rationales for effective choices.

■ THE POWER OF FEEDBACK

The combination of providing quality feedback to your students and, in turn, soliciting and using it from them can have a greater positive impact on student achievement than just about anything else you can do. True, not all your students will understand and use your feedback or that of their peers all the time, but those who do will benefit immensely. Just build in an assignment to ensure they read and process the feedback they receive.

PART 6

ASSESSMENT AND GRADING

CHAPTER 25

Preparing Students for Exams

R ecall your undergraduate days. Did you ever experience the feeling of dread or anxiety when your professors announced an exam? Did you ever walk into a test feeling pretty well prepared, only to freeze when you saw the first question? Did you ever leave an exam thinking that you aced it, only to be sorely disappointed in your grade? If any of these situations rings true, you can probably empathize with some of the emotions your students experience before an exam.

The first question students usually ask is, "What will be on the test?" While this is not a valid question, another common query is, "What will the test format be?" So is, "What will I have to be able to do in order to do well on the exam?" In fact, honest answers to those questions pretty much tell students what will be on the test.

We'd like to believe that students will perform well on any type of exam with adequate study. But different types of exams call for different types of study strategies, and most students learn based on how they are tested (Wergin, 1988). Factual memorization for a recall-oriented objective test requires a different kind of study effort from that for analyses of problems or situations. It is that latter type of studying that helps students develop critical thinking skills, and they need experience in the higher-level cognitive processes of analysis, synthesis, and evaluation. In fact, students perform better on the multiple-choice portion of a test if they know there will be an essay question on it (Drake, 2009). In other words, studying to use higher-order thinking on a test better prepares a learner to perform whatever level of cognitive operation is required. Of course, multiple-choice items can call for much more thought than just recall and comprehension (see chapter 26).

TEST PREPARATION MEASURES

If we accept that tests can be instruments of learning as well as evaluation, then preparing students to perform well on them is also an excellent teaching strategy. Here are some easily implemented ways to help students get ready for tests.

Reading and Review Strategies

You begin preparing your students from the very first day by teaching them proven techniques for taking notes on your lectures and class activities, provided in chapter 12, and for reading academic material effectively, given in chapter 21. Of course, students should review the relevant readings and their notes before a test. More than 80 percent of the studies conducted on reviewing lecture notes find that the activity leads to better test performance (Bligh, 2000). But just reading notes over, even multiple times, will not help much for the test. As research cited in chapter 20 indicates, the quickest, most efficient, and most effective way to study written material, at least for factual and problem-solving tests, is *active recall* or the *read-recall-review* strategy (McDaniel, Howard, & Einstein, 2009; Roediger & Karpicke, 2006). Following this method, students read a section of their text or notes, then put the material away, recite aloud or jot down as much as they can remember, and finally review the section to find what they missed or misunderstood. In addition to reinforcing their reading by restating and hearing the material, students practice retrieval, which is exactly the skill they will need during the test.

Other exam preparation techniques worth sharing include drawing visual representations of the material in which students organize and integrate the concepts, principles, processes, and similarities and differences among phenomena that your course has recently introduced. Depending on the content, the most suitable representations may be concept maps, mind maps, concept circle diagrams, flowcharts, cycles, or compare-and-contrast matrices (see chapter 23). Students who learn inductively from examples may also benefit from reviewing particularly fitting examples of concepts and processes, explaining why they are such fitting examples, and formulating different ones on their own.

Alternatively or in addition, you can have successful students from recent offerings of your courses recommend study techniques to your current classes. At the end of a course, have your students write a letter to future students of the course on how they can do well in the exams and assignments, as well as what they can look forward to learning (MacDonald, 2013; Weimer, 2013a). To save yourself time in a large class, you may prefer to solicit letters from only the A students (G. R. Davis, 2015). Before passing on these documents, obtain your students' permission to do so. For these students, the letter writing serves as a self-regulated learning exercise during which they review the course material, assess what they have learned, and accept responsibility for their performance (see chapter 20). Later cohorts benefit by getting solid advice that they will take to heart probably more than anything we can tell them.

Study Groups

Several of the chapters in this book point out how groups facilitate learning. Study groups that meet regularly outside class can also enhance student performance (Treisman, 1986). Since member commitment can make or break them, consider formalizing them by having students sign up for such groups early in the term. Then distribute a list of all the groups with their members' names and contact information. The more tightly organized the groups are, the more positive their effects will be. Casual study groups may even undermine learning (Arum & Roksa, 2011).

Review Guides

This study aid helps many students prepare for a test, especially first-year and second-year students who do not yet know what college-level assessment involves. You can make a review guide as simple as a list or outline of important topics that you have emphasized, but this alone will not tell students how to study this content.

Students gain much more from a sample test or a list of review questions that mirror your student learning outcomes and represent the variety of item formats that will appear on the test.

If you plan to use some factual and terminological multiple-choice questions on the test, then put some examples of those items on the review sheet. If you intend to test analysis and synthesis, develop some questions that require those same cognitive operations. This method demands much more of your time and effort because you do not want to duplicate the sample items on the real test. But it is highly effective, and you can draw appropriate items from previous tests.

Perhaps the best option for students is what is called a *test blueprint* (Suskie, 2009). It can also help you design a test that assesses your students' achievement of your outcomes, so have your syllabus and outcomes map (see chapters 2 and 5) handy. To make a test blueprint, begin by listing all the major content areas that your test will address; then designate their relative importance by the percentage of the test (or number of points) to be devoted to each area. Within each content area, write down what you want students to be able to do or demonstrate, using action verbs and avoiding internal-states verbs such as *know, understand, realize,* and *appreciate* (see chapter 2). These statements should reflect your learning outcomes, though probably on a more microlevel than in your syllabus or outcomes map. Finally, allocate points or items across these outcome statements according to how central they are in this part of the course. In other words, instead of just listing concepts for students to "know," tell them more specifically that, for instance, they should be able to *recognize* the definitions, purposes, and examples of a list of concepts and be able to *reproduce* a given list of principles. Then let these statements serve as the blueprint for your test questions.

With podcasts becoming more common, you may want to audio-record and post your review questions online. Advise your students to pause the file after each question to practice retrieval of the content and verbalize an answer (Guertin, 2011).

Unless you scrupulously collect or otherwise guard your exams from previous offerings of your course, you should make your earlier versions available to all your current students. This helps to even the playing field for those who don't have access to your previous tests through membership in fraternities, sororities, and other organized campus groups. To students, these earlier exams make excellent review sheets.

Review Sessions

About three-quarters of the students say that they want a pretest review session (Mealy & Host, 1993), so you may want to schedule one during a class or outside class, as do many instructors. But it is likely to work well only if students have already made significant progress in their independent or small-group studying. Therefore, you should make it clear that you will not be summarizing the past few weeks of lectures and readings or dispensing the answers to the review questions.

The most productive way to conduct a review session is to insist that students come prepared to ask specific questions on the material and answer any review questions on their own. With respect to their questions, always ask the class for answers before saying anything yourself. With respect to the review questions, have the entire class participate in brainstorming and refining the answers. For example, you can assign different questions to small groups and have them develop and orally present their answers. Invite other students to evaluate the group's answers and then offer your own assessment.

Chapter 12 describes a variation on this format, *pair/group and review*, in which student pairs or small groups develop answers to review questions, after which you randomly select a few of them to present their answers to the class. You then mock-grade the answers and explain your assessment criteria or, better yet, have the rest of the class mock-grade them to help students learn how to assess their own work.

Similarly, about a week before the exam, you can assign students the task of reviewing the material and bringing in short-answer and essay questions, passages for identification, or whatever types of item you intend to use on the test. (Tell them you won't accept test bank questions.) To the extent that they submit good questions, you can put the items in a review guide and on the test itself (J. B. Jones, 2010).

One more variation, this one tailored to an essay exam, is the *question shuffle* (Millis, 2005). Students attending the review session must bring in two essay questions, each on an index card, that they think would be appropriate for the test. The students pair off, review their four questions, and select the best two. Then all the pairs circulate for a few moments, shuffling their two cards among other pairs. From the two questions they wind up with, the pairs select one to answer, and each student writes out an answer within a time period that replicates what the exam will allow for such a question. This activity furnishes a test-taking rehearsal, which generally reduces anxiety and enhances performance. The students in each pair compare and evaluate their different approaches to the question, giving them practice in critical thinking. As time permits, you can repeat the shuffle. You can then collect the questions (and responses) and use the best ones on the test. Not only does this review exercise supply you with an already-vetted test (or discussion) question bank, but it also serves as a classroom assessment technique (see chapter 24), informing you about your students' understanding of the material and possibly giving you the chance before the test to clear up their misconceptions and help them improve their essay writing (Millis, 2005).

Help Sessions or Course Clinics

This measure takes the review session one step further by establishing weekly meetings of an hour or longer during which you or your TA answers questions. A regularly scheduled meeting motivates students to keep up with the course and not wait until the last minute to cram for a test. It also reduces stress by encouraging them to study without the impending threat of an exam.

Lessons from Previous Exams

The best preparation for any given exam may be analyzing where one went wrong in similar previous exams, and we should never miss an opportunity to help students learn by their mistakes or realize their control over their academic performance. As described in chapter 20, Barkley (2009) recommends giving students a list of reflection questions to answer in class or as homework when returning their graded exams. The test autopsy, also introduced in chapter 20, turns students' attention to the errors they made during previous exams to help them identify their faulty strategies, such as misreading questions and failing to budget their time (Academic Success Center, Iowa State University, 2011; Achacoso, 2004).

In his version of the activity, Felder (1999) writes a memo to students who are disappointed with their test grade, no matter how high their grade was, followed by a list of probes about how they've been doing their homework and how they prepared for the exam. The probes lay out best practices for learning. He then recommends that any students who admitted that they didn't typically follow at least two of these practices change their ways.

Finally, you can capitalize on students' mistakes by having them redo tasks that they did not complete or do properly on the exams. If they failed to solve a problem correctly, they can get back some of the points they lost by explaining why they didn't or laying out the correct strategy, and then re-solving the same or a similar problem (Zimmerman, Moylan, Hudesman, White, & Flugman, 2011). If their written product missed the mark, they can redeem some points by explaining where they went wrong on the exam and rewriting their response (http://selfregulatedlearning.blogspot.com/). Like the other procedures in this section, these build students' self-regulated learning skills (see chapter 20) while improving their performance on the next exam.

■ MEASURES TO ENSURE STUDENTS UNDERSTAND OUR LANGUAGE

Students, especially in their first year, often do poorly on exams because they are not exactly sure what a question, especially an essay question, is asking them to do. They do not know what the verb designating the task means, at least not the way we use the verb. This sometimes explains why some students fail to follow directions. So it may be safest to provide them with written definitions of common exam verbs, along with review questions or sessions that give them practice in the cognitive operations (Anderson & Krathwohl, 2000; Ellis, 2006; Reiner, Bothell, Sudweeks, & Wood, 2004):

- *Analyze:* Break something down into parts, such as a theory into its components, a process into its stages, or an event into its causes. Analysis involves characterizing the whole, identifying its parts, and showing how the parts interrelate.
- *Assess/criticize/critique/evaluate:* Determine or judge the degree to which something meets or fails to meet certain criteria. If the criteria are not provided in the question, develop them for making judgments.
- *Categorize/classify:* Sort into major, general groups or types that you name or identify.
- *Compare/contrast:* Identify the important similarities and differences between two or more elements in order to reveal something significant about them. Identify similarities if the command is to compare and differences if it is to contrast.
- *Create/devise:* Put together, organize, or reorganize elements to make a new approach, product, process, or solution.
- *Defend/justify:* Give good reasons to support a position, and explain how or why something happened.
- *Define/identify:* Give the key characteristics by which a concept, thing, or event can be understood. Place it in a general class; then distinguish it from other members of that class.
- *Describe:* Give the characteristics by which an object, action, process, person, or concept can be recognized or visualized.
- *Develop:* Create, elaborate on, or make more effective, detailed, or usable.
- *Discuss/examine:* Debate, argue, and evaluate the various sides of an issue.

- *Explain/justify:* Give the basic principles of or reasons for something; make it intelligible. Explanation may involve relating the unfamiliar to the more familiar.
- *Generate:* Think up, devise, or brainstorm good ideas or alternatives.
- *Infer:* Logically conclude on the basis of what is known.
- *Interpret/explain:* State what you think the author or speaker of a quotation or statement means, and why.
- *Illustrate:* Use a concrete example to explain or clarify the essential attributes of a problem or concept, or clarify a point using a diagram, chart, table, or other graphic.
- *List/enumerate:* Give the essential points one by one, in a logical order if applicable. It may be helpful to number the points.
- *Outline/review/state:* Organize a description under main points and subordinate points, omitting minor details and classifying the elements or main points.
- *Predict:* Infer from facts, trends, or principles what will happen in the future.
- *Propose:* Suggest or present for consideration.
- *Prove/validate:* Establish that something is true by citing factual evidence or giving clear, logical reasons.
- *Summarize:* Briefly restate the main points.
- *Synthesize:* Put together elements in a new way so as to make a novel theory, approach, product, process, or solution.
- *Trace:* Describe the course or progress of a phenomenon, trend, or development.

ANXIETY-REDUCTION MEASURES

Moderate anxiety is normal before an exam and can motivate and energize students. From their review of the test anxiety literature, Mealy and Host (1993) identified three types of anxious students. Those of the first type lack adequate study skills and are aware of the problem; they are not well prepared for exams and worry about performing poorly. The second group comprises students who have adequate study strategies but become severely distracted during a test. Those of the final type mistakenly believe that they have adequate study skills but do poorly on exams, then wonder what the problem could be. They may blame instructors and "unfair exams" for their falling short of their high expectations.

Mealy and Host (1993) also asked students how an instructor can affect their anxiety before, during, and after a test. They received four kinds of responses:

1. The vast majority of students want some kind of review before the test and are less anxious after attending one. They feel more confident if they are sure they have correct information in their notes.
2. Students become stressed when their instructor tells them that the test will be hard. Many do not mind a challenging exam, but they want to hear how they should study, followed by some words of reassurance.
3. Most students get nervous when their instructor walks around the room during a test and looks over their shoulders. While this may help keep cheating in check, it also raises the anxiety of stress-sensitive students.
4. Many students resent interruptions during a test. Even if you break in to correct or clarify an exam item, it throws off their train of thought.

In summary, taking measures to prepare your students for tests, such as providing quality review sheets and review sessions, along with building their self-confidence and minimizing test interruptions, will help allay their test anxiety. So will these actions:

1. Have your test schedule written in your syllabus, and stick to it as closely as possible.
2. Have in your syllabus a clear grading system and your policies on missed quizzes and tests.

3. Consider dropping your students' lowest test or quiz score from your final grade calculations; anyone can have a bad day or a legitimate reason for missing a class.
4. Test frequently, reducing the relative weight of each test so that one poor performance will not cost students dearly.
5. Tailor your tests to the time allotted. If it takes you so many minutes to complete one of your tests, figure that it will take your students three times as long. Not being able to finish a test discourages students, even if you tell them they are not expected to finish it.
6. Teach students relaxation techniques, such as deep breathing, counting to 10, and visualizing a successful test session (Ellis, 2006).

Occasionally you may have a student for whom test anxiety is a debilitating problem. Refer this individual to your institution's counseling center, as you should for other emotional and psychological problems, or its academic assistance center, or both (see the appendix).

■ WHAT THE EFFORT IS WORTH

Taking measures to prepare your students for a test is one way to ensure that they review, synthesize, and retain the material. Some of these measures can also help you better plan and organize a test so that it assesses exactly what you want to assess. Whatever else you can do to reduce your students' test anxiety allows them to better demonstrate their actual learning and gives you a more valid assessment of their understanding and skills. It is only by seeing their honest achievement that you can appraise how successful your teaching has been. In your performance review, you may also want to use some of your students' tests to document your teaching effectiveness, a topic addressed in chapter 28.

CHAPTER 26

Constructing Student Assessments for Grading

When you assess student performance for a grade, score, or rating, you are conducting a *summative assessment*. Typically, tests or exams, quizzes, assignments, projects, and some in-class activities fall under this category. This chapter presents the advantages and disadvantages of various types of assessments. It also summarizes best practices for designing meaningful test items and assignments: first, objective test items, and then test items and assignments that require students to construct a response. The time and effort invested in writing a good test or assignment are not without reward. It is heartening to see your students perform well on a challenging task or for you to receive a compliment on the task from a student. Both indicate that your test or assignment was a worthwhile learning experience as well as a fair evaluation.

■ GENERAL TESTING GUIDELINES

Summative assessment is serious business to your institution and especially to your students. If they are consistently performing poorly on your tests, you might find the reasons in this section.

It's All About Outcomes

As chapter 2 explains, teaching at its best begins with developing and sequencing assessable student learning outcomes and then selecting the teaching formats, methods, and moves that are most effective for helping students achieve those outcomes. Excellent teaching also entails appropriate assessment—specifically, constructing instruments that measure, as directly as possible, students' success in achieving those outcomes. In the end, all three phases of instruction—outcomes setting, teaching, and assessing—should be woven into a multifaceted arrangement of interdependent parts, each reflecting and reinforcing the others.

Therefore, before you begin writing a quiz or an exam, think seriously about what you are trying to accomplish with it. A test can assess just short-term memory skills or the abilities to comprehend, apply, analyze, synthesize, and evaluate the material as well (see chapter 2). Review your learning outcomes, and identify the cognitive level of each one. If they focus primarily on knowledge, comprehension, and application, then so should your test questions. Unless you have taught your students and given them practice in thinking at higher levels, questions pitched at lower levels will not measure their attainment of your outcomes. In other words, your tests will not be valid (Suskie, 2009; Walvoord & Anderson, 2010). In addition, your students will be doomed to perform poorly.

Lessons Learned by Experience and Research

The following recommendations represent much of the conventional wisdom on test construction (Jacobs & Chase, 1992; Ory & Ryan, 1993; Suskie, 2009; Walvoord & Anderson, 2010).

- *Test early and often.* Frequent testing and quizzing yield benefits for you and your students. Early testing furnishes students with feedback they can use to optimize their course performance. Frequent testing gives them more opportunities for success, reducing the penalties for any single poor performance. It also enhances the reliability of your overall assessment—that is, its stability, repeatability, and internal consistency. Over more test items and occasions, the effects of random errors, such as students' misinterpretations and distractions, tend to weaken. Students get better grades, are less likely to withdraw from the course, and are more satisfied with the course and instructor (Myers & Myers, 2007).

- *Compose test questions immediately after you cover the material in the class.* The material and the cognitive levels at which you taught it are fresh in your mind. Practiced regularly, this strategy ensures you a stock of questions to use when quiz and exam times arrive. Alternatively, you can have your students develop these questions at the end of class or as homework. They will want to compose clean, challenging ones to increase

the odds that theirs will appear on a future test. After all, they know the answers to the ones they made up.

- *Give detailed, written instructions for all tests.* Remind students about your and your institution's policies on academic dishonesty (see chapter 10). Also specify how much time the test is allotted; how many questions of each type; how many points each item is worth; where to record answers; whether to show work; and whether books, notes, or calculators may be used. Do not assume that your students committed all this information to memory just because you said it in class, in a handout, or somewhere on the LMS.

- *Start the test with some warm-up questions.* Asking a few easy questions at the beginning gives students some low-stress practice in retrieving the material and builds their confidence.

- *Have a colleague review the test for clarity and content.* This is a particularly good idea if you are somewhat inexperienced at teaching or writing test items. You may have written a quiz or exam that seems crystal clear to you, only to find out later that certain items were double-barreled, ambiguously phrased, or awkwardly constructed. Writing good test items is a hard-to-learn craft, and you need not learn it all by bad experience.

- *Proofread the test form for errors.* Check for spelling and grammar mistakes, split items (those that begin on one page and continue on the next), inconsistencies and errors in format, missing or ambiguous instructions, and inadequate space for constructed responses. It is best to have another set of eyes proofread the test form too.

- *After the test, conduct an item analysis of your new objective items.* If your completion, true/false, matching, multiple-choice, and multiple true/false items are machine or computer graded, check whether the overwhelming majority of your students missed certain questions. If so, these items are suspect, so you should examine them carefully for unclear or ambiguous wording. Check also for any items that all or almost all the students answered correctly. These items are also suspect; they probably were too obvious or easy to guess right due to unintentional cuing in the wording. This type of item analysis is the basic one. To refine your analysis, identify the best 10 to 15 percent of your students in the class, in which case you must have either tested the class previously or accessed all your students' academic records. Either way, your best students' item responses become your point of comparison. If all or almost all missed an item, it is probably faulty. If they answered an item correctly and only a few in the rest of the class did, it is highly discriminating.

■ OBJECTIVE TEST ITEMS

Objective items include completion (fill-in-the-blank), true/false, matching, multiple choice, and multiple true/false, the least known and used on this list. Famous for measuring knowledge and comprehension, the last three types can also assess most kinds of higher-order thinking very efficiently. When they do, they are called "performance tasks," and we too often gloss over assessing such thinking skills (Chun, 2010). Since most objective items can be graded by computer, they make regular assessment in large classes possible. However, none can measure students' abilities to create, organize, communicate, define problems, or conduct research.

Good objective questions, the unambiguous and discriminating ones, take time and thought to write. Professional test writers may produce only 8 or 10 usable questions a day. However, be wary of test bank items that come with your textbook. They are rarely, if ever, composed by professionals, and they tend to tap only factual knowledge, sometimes of the trivial variety.

The rest of this section lays out the advantages and disadvantages of each type of objective item and furnishes guidelines for constructing them (Brookhart, 1999; Jacobs & Chase, 1992; Jacobsen, n.d; Ory & Ryan, 1993; Sibley, 2014; Suskie, 2009; Waugh & Gronlund, 2012). Each type has its place,

and using a variety of questions helps students feel more secure with the exam format. Remember that you can also teach your students to write good questions before the test.

Completion (Fill-in-the-Blank)

These items measure only how well students have memorized facts, terms, and symbols, but some material is so basic that students have to be able to reproduce it. This type of item is well suited to the foreign languages, since they require precise representations of words. They are also a good fit for mathematical problems, assuming you don't insist on students showing their work, because they have only one exact right answer, and students can't work backward from given options as they can from multiple-choice items. However, in other fields, the one right answer may have several acceptable versions. If the correct answer is John Fitzgerald Kennedy, you might consider John F. Kennedy, John Kennedy, Jack Kennedy, J. F. Kennedy, Kennedy, J. F. K., and some of the possible misspellings of *Kennedy* acceptable. In such cases, you cannot computer-score completion items unless you can anticipate and specify every possible variation of the correct answer that you will accept as right. Your alternative is to restrict all fill-ins to one word and insist on the correct spelling.

Advantages

- Easy to prepare and grade
- Can assess knowledge, recall, spelling, and vocabulary well
- Eliminates guessing
- Can test a lot of material in a short time

Disadvantages

- Cannot assess higher levels of cognition
- Highly structured and inflexible; may require an all-or-nothing response
- Not useful as a diagnostic tool
- Vulnerable to grammatical clues

- Difficult to construct so that the desired response is unambiguous
- Difficult to computer-grade if more than one version of the right answer may be correct

Construction

- Estimate 30 seconds to 1 minute for students to answer each item.
- Use clear wording to elicit a unique response.
- Avoid grammatical cues; use *a/an* and *is/are,* for instance, to reduce cluing.
- Omit only significant words from the statement.
- Omit words from the middle or end of a statement, not the beginning.
- Make all fill-in lines the same length.
- Place the response lines in a column to the left or right to facilitate grading by hand.
- Use familiar language that is similar to what you and the readings have used to explain the material.

True/False

This type of item encourages guessing because students have a 50-50 chance of getting an item right. It also tends to focus on recall of terms and facts, sometimes trivial ones. You can avoid both limitations by having students correct false statements. But then you cannot use a computer to grade these items; the job will fall to you.

Advantages

- Usually easy to prepare and grade
- Can test a lot of material in a short time
- Useful as a diagnostic tool if students correct the false statements
- Can tap higher levels of cognition by having students correct the false statements

Disadvantages

- High guessing factor for simple true/false questions
- May be difficult to think of unequivocally true or false statements

- Encourages testing of trivial factual knowledge
- Often fails to discriminate the more from the less knowledgeable students because the best students may see too many nuances, read in multiple meanings, or conceive of exceptions
- Can be ambiguous
- May include verbal clues (e.g., questions with *usually, seldom,* and *often* are frequently true, while those with *never, always,* and *every* are commonly false)

Construction

- Estimate 30 seconds to 1 minute for students to answer each item.
- Use statements that are only entirely true or entirely false.
- Focus each statement on a single idea or problem.
- Write positive statements; negative and double-negative statements are confusing.
- Avoid verbal cues to the correct answers (e.g., *usually, seldom, often, never, always,* and *every*).
- Use familiar language that is similar to what you and the readings have used to explain the material.
- Roughly (but not exactly) balance the number of true and false answers.
- Avoid always making true statements long and false statements short, or vice versa. Students quickly pick up on these patterns.
- Avoid direct quotes from lectures or readings requiring only rote memorization.
- Add higher-level cognitive challenge and assessment validity by having students rewrite false statements to make them true.
- Allow students to write a rebuttal to your marking their answer wrong for a small percentage of the items.

Matching

One way of looking at matching items is as a set of multiple-choice items that share the same set of response options (Suskie, 2009). The key to composing them is to assemble homogeneous items in the stimulus or question column with homogeneous items in the response or option column, such that every response is plausible for every stimulus. Common matches include theories with their originator; people with their major achievement or work; causes with their effect; terms with their definitions; foreign words with their translation; and pieces of equipment, tools, lab apparatus, or organs with their use or function. If you wish, you can list stimuli with multiple correct responses; just inform students that some items may have more than one answer or specify the number for each stimulus. Check to see whether the testing tool in your LMS can grade multiple-answer matching items.

Matches can also involve visuals, such as concepts or chemicals with their symbol, pictures of objects with their name, or labeled parts in a picture with their function. In fact, if your matching responses are embedded in one large graphic, such as a representation of a cell, a part of human anatomy, an electrical system, or a machine, you can have students describe a process by specifying a sequence of responses (Laird, 2004).

The examples thus far assess only lower-level thinking, but you can test higher-order cognitive skills by having students match causes with *likely* effects; concepts with *new* examples of them; and *new* hypothetical problems with concepts, tools, or approaches needed to solve them (Suskie, 2009). Of course, new examples or problems need just be new to your students.

Advantages

- Easy to grade
- Can assess knowledge and recall as well as higher levels of cognition
- Relatively unambiguous
- Can test a lot of material in a short time

Disadvantages

- Difficult to construct a common set of stimuli and responses
- High guessing factor
- Not useful as a diagnostic tool

Construction

- Estimate 30 seconds to 1 minute for students to answer each item.
- Keep stimuli and responses short and simple.
- List the possible responses in some logical order—alphabetical, numerical, or chronological—to reduce student search time.
- Add challenge and reduce process-of-elimination thinking by inserting one or more unmatchable responses or one or more responses that match more than one stimulus. Just be sure to add this statement to the directions: "Some responses may be used more than once and others not at all."
- To add even more challenge, include a few stimuli that require multiple responses or a sequence of responses. Inform your students by adding this or a similar statement to the directions: "Some items require multiple responses or a sequence of responses describing a process."
- Limit the list of stimuli and responses to 15 or fewer.
- Keep all stimuli and responses on one page.
- If students write down their response choice, have them use capital letters to avoid ambiguity.

Multiple Choice

No doubt multiple-choice items are the most popular type of objective test item in North America. Educational Testing Services and publishers' test banks rely on them heavily. You would think good ones would be easy to write, but they aren't. A solid, clean multiple-choice question avoids two tricky pitfalls: diverting a knowledgeable student away from the correct response and cluing a poorly prepared student toward the correct response (Suskie, 2009). Faulty phraseology and construction can do either. Test bank items that accompany textbooks usually avoid these flaws, but they do so at the cost of challenging students and assessing their higher-order thinking. To meet these higher standards, you have to search out proven, concept-oriented multiple-choice items or compose your own. If your area is the sciences or mathematics, you should be able to find some high-quality items in the clicker question databases you can access at http://www.cwsei.ubc.ca/resources/clickers.htm#questions. For STEM and other disciplines, check out http://cft.vanderbilt.edu/docs/classroom-response-system-clickers-bibliography/ and Bruff (2016). You might also search the web using "'clicker questions' + teaching" and look for your discipline. But don't be discouraged from writing your own and teaching your students how to write good ones.

One way to guarantee that your multiple-choice questions will assess higher-order thinking is to compose what are called *interpretive exercises* (Suskie, 2009) or stimulus-based items. These are a series of multiple-choice items based on a new (to the students), realistic stimulus—a table, graph, diagram, flowchart, drawing, photo, map, schematic, equation, data set, description of an experiment, report, statement, quotation, passage, poem, situation, or short case—that students must interpret intelligently to answer the items correctly. The process of interpreting and reasoning from the stimulus normally requires, in addition to knowledge, also comprehension, application, analysis, synthesis, or evaluation. If you prefer, you can look at the types of thinking involved as interpretation, inference, problem solving, generalization, and conclusion drawing.

This type of multiple-choice question frequently appears in professionally written standardized tests, such as the Scholastic Assessment Test, the Graduate Record Examination, and the California Critical Thinking Skills Test (CCTST), as well as licensing exams, such as the National Council of Licensure Examinations for registered nurses and practical nurses. Here are two college-level examples (reprinted with permission from the Learning Sciences, University of Texas at Austin, 2015), the first of which focuses on an experiment and the second, on a situation or minicase. Correct answers are marked with an asterisk.

Scenario 1: Statistics

Two researchers were studying the relationship between amount of sleep each night and calories burned on an exercise bike for 42 men and women. They were interested if people who slept more had more energy to use during their exercise session. They obtained a correlation of .28, with a two-tailed probability of .08, and the alpha was .10.

1. Which is an example of a properly written research question?
   a. Is there a relationship between amount of sleep and energy expended?*
   b. Does amount of sleep correlate with energy used?
   c. What is the cause of energy expended?
   d. What is the value of rho?
2. What is the correct term for the variable amount of sleep?
   a. Dependent
   b. Independent*
   c. Predictor
   d. *y*
3. What is the correct statistical null hypothesis?
   a. There is no correlation between sleep and energy expended.
   b. rho equals zero.*
   c. *R* equals zero.
   d. rho equals *r*.

4. What conclusions should you draw regarding the null hypothesis?
   a. Reject*
   b. Accept
   c. Cannot determine without more information
5. What conclusions should you draw regarding this study?
   a. The correlation was significant
   b. The correlation was not significant.
   c. A small relationship exists.*
   d. No relationship exists.

Scenario 2: Biology

One day you meet a student watching a wasp drag a paralyzed grasshopper down a small hole in the ground. When asked what he is doing, he replies, "I'm watching that wasp store paralyzed grasshoppers in her nest to feed her offspring."

1. Which of the following is the best description of his reply?
   a. He is not a careful observer.
   b. He is stating a conclusion only partly derived from his observation.*
   c. He is stating a conclusion entirely drawn from his observation.
   d. He is making no assumptions even though he should.
2. Which of the following additional observations would add the most strength to the student's reply in question 1?
   a. Observing the wasp digging a similar hole
   b. Observing the wasp dragging more grasshoppers into the hole
   c. Digging into the hole and observing wasp eggs on the paralyzed grasshopper*
   d. Observing adult wasps emerging from the hole a month later
3. Both of you wait until the wasp leaves the area; then you dig into the hole and observe three paralyzed grasshoppers, each with a white egg on its side. The student states that this evidence supports his reply in question 1. Which of the following assumptions is he making?
   a. The eggs are grasshopper eggs.
   b. The wasp laid the eggs.*
   c. The wasp dug the hole.
   d. The wasp will return with more grasshoppers.
4. You take the white eggs to the biology laboratory. Ten days later, immature wasps hatched from the eggs. The student states that this evidence supports his reply in question 1. Which of the following assumptions was he making?
   a. The wasp dug the hole.
   b. The wasp stung the grasshoppers.
   c. The grasshoppers were dead.
   d. Paralyzed grasshoppers cannot lay eggs.*

Whether you use this type or the standard kind of multiple-choice item, these are the plusses and minuses and, if you or your students write them, the best practices in constructing them:

Advantages

- Easy and quick to grade
- Reduces some of the burden of teaching and assessing in large classes
- Can assess knowledge, comprehension, application, analysis, synthesis, and evaluation and do so more efficiently than can constructed response questions
- Useful as a diagnostic tool since students' wrong choices can indicate weaknesses and misconceptions
- Familiar to students

Disadvantages

- Difficult and time-consuming to construct
- Can be ambiguous to students
- Encourages students to find the correct answer by process of elimination

Construction

- Estimate 1 to 2 minutes for students to answer each question.
- Address one problem or concept per question.
- Strive for clarity and conciseness; avoid wordiness.
- Include in the stem any words that may repeat in the response alternatives.
- Avoid lifting phrases directly from your lecture or the readings and thereby requiring only simple recall.
- Still, use familiar language that is similar to what you and the readings have used to explain the material.
- Use the words *no, not, never, none,* and *except* sparingly, and make them stand out by italicizing, bolding, or underlining them.
- Write the correct response first, then the distractors.

- Develop the distractors by juggling the elements of (or the variables in) the correct response. For example, if you have students interpret a table from which they should conclude that more industrialized nations have lower birthrates and infant mortality rates than less industrialized nations, the elements (or variables) are a nation's degree of industrialization, birthrate, and infant mortality rate. You can mix these variables together in an assortment of ways. You might also use other variables that students often confuse with the elements—for instance, population density and population growth, which some students mistakenly equate with birthrate.
- Make all responses equally plausible and attractive. Absurd options only make guessing easier.
- Make all responses grammatically parallel and about the same length.
- Present the options in some logical order—alphabetical, numerical, or chronological—to reduce the possibility of cluing students or falling into a pattern.
- Avoid grammatical cues to correct answers. These can be subtle, but test-wise students look for them. For example, the correct answer usually includes the elements that most commonly appear in the distractors. In other words, a term that appears in most of the options will probably appear in the correct one. Conversely, a term that appears in just one option cues the student that the option is incorrect (Sibley, 2014).
- Use three to five responses per item six at the outside.
- Make sure each item has only one correct or clearly best response. Questions with multiple correct answers confuse students (but see the "Multiple True/False" section next).
- Incorporate graphics where appropriate.
- If you want to use *none of the above* or *all of the above*, use it liberally, not just when that answer is correct. These options discriminate the more from the less knowledgeable students; even the "all of the above" option makes an item more challenging to students (Huang, Trevisan, & Storfer, 2007).

Stimulus-based multiple-choice items (or interpretive exercises) have a few additional construction guidelines:

- Give students prior practice in interpreting the types of stimuli you put on the test and in performing the cognitive operations each item requires.
- Minimize interlocking items—that is, items that responding to correctly requires having responded correctly to previous items in the series.
- Longer and more complex stimuli should yield a longer series of multiple-choice questions.
- Start looking for good stimuli, and you will find them; they are all around you.

- Be creative with the stimuli and use different kinds.

Multiple True/False

Perhaps the least used, least known, and yet statistically strongest objective test question is the multiple true/false item. Like a multiple-choice item, it has a stem and a list of responses, and it may (or may not) involve interpreting a stimulus. But students do not select one right response; they decide whether each option is true or false in relation to the stem. Therefore, a multiple true/false item is flexible enough to accommodate multiple correct answers. Here is an example with the true and false responses marked:

When constructing a completion (fill-in-the-blank) test item, it is recommended that you:

T 1. Estimate 30 seconds to 1 minute for students to answer each item.

F 2. Locate the word(s) to fill in at the beginning of the sentence, not in the middle or at the end of it.

F 3. Vary the length of the fill-in lines according to the length of the correct answer.

T 4. Omit only significant words from the sentence to complete.

Note that this single stem, one multiple true/false item, presented four decision points: two distractors and two correct responses. In essence, it created four separate objective items, and it did so efficiently using no more words than for one item. With 10 stems, then, you can easily generate 40 to 50 items, and a test with 50 items is much more reliable than one with only 10. In summary, multiple true/false items are more flexible, efficient, and reliable than multiple-choice and most other objective test items (Ebel, 1978; Frisby & Sweeney, 1982.)

Multiple true/false items share a great deal with true/false and multiple-choice questions in terms of their advantages, disadvantages, and construction guidelines. However, they have a few of their own:

Advantages

- Superior flexibility, efficiency, and reliability

- Easier and quicker to develop than multiple-choice items
- Adds challenge and eliminates process-of-elimination thinking

Disadvantage

- One faulty stem undercuts the value of multiple items.

Construction

- Take extra care to write clear, concise, unambiguous stems.
- Be sure the distractors are clearly true or false in relation to the stem.
- Consider allowing students to write a rebuttal to their wrong answer for a small percentage of the items.

Short Answer

Instructors typically use a short-answer question to test recall, comprehension, or application. Given its length limitation, it does not allow students to construct or justify a deeply considered response.

Advantages

- Easy to construct
- Can assess recall, comprehension, and application
- Requires a command of vocabulary or problem-solving skills
- Very useful as a diagnostic tool
- Encourages instructors to give students individual feedback

Disadvantages

- Time-consuming to grade given the amount of knowledge tested
- Difficult to standardize grading due to variability across answers

Construction

- Estimate 2 to 5 minutes per item.
- Be very specific and concise in identifying the task that students are to perform. See the advice below for constructing essay questions and writing assignments.
- Use familiar language that is similar to what you and the readings have used to explain the material.
- Indicate whether diagrams or illustrations are required or are acceptable in place of a written answer.
- Require students to show their work for full credit on problems.
- Leave an appropriate amount of space for the answers. Too much space invites students to write too much.

■ CONSTRUCTED-RESPONSE TEST ITEMS AND ASSIGNMENTS

A constructed-response instrument is an interrogatory statement (a question) or an imperative statement (a task description) that an instructor composes to assess student achievement of one or more learning outcomes (Ory & Ryan, 1993). It is usually an essay item on a test or an assignment. Typically students write their answers, but complex graphics, such as concept maps, mind maps, matrices, and concept circle diagrams (see chapter 23), may do the job just as well. For an assignment, so may more creative media like video productions, musical compositions, artistic performances, visually rich websites, oral presentations, poster presentations, and the like.

Constructed-response instruments can have just one correct answer with limited leeway for phraseology, such as science lab reports and mathematically based problem solutions; Suskie (2009) calls these *restricted response* instruments. Here is an example from a finance exam: "What are the six major capital budgeting techniques? Define them (you need not give their formula). Under what two categories are they normally grouped? Categorize all six techniques." Every introductory finance textbook supplies the answers to these questions. This next set is less clear: "What is the difference between experimental research and survey research? What do they have in common?" If the course addresses experimental research and survey research independently and never draws comparisons or contrasts between the two methods, then these questions demand higher-order thinking. Similarly, an application question or task must use problems, cases, diagrams, graphs, data sets, and the like that students have not seen before to assess higher-order thinking skills.

Unless you are testing students on material they have to memorize, it is more efficient to use objective items to assess their recall, recognition, and comprehension. Constructed responses are best reserved for *extended response* (Suskie, 2009) questions and tasks that have multiple respectable answers and require professional judgment to assess. This is because they take more time and effort to grade than do objective items, even with the time-saving grading methods that chapter 27 recommends. If students write the product, as they usually do, you must interpret their sometimes rambling thoughts, distracting grammar and spelling, and confusing punctuation, and then evaluate variable content. Therefore use constructed-response instruments with discretion, such as when the learning outcome you are assessing requires students to generate, as opposed to select, an answer. If your outcome calls only for selection, then you might as well use objective items (Reiner, Bothell, Sudweeks, & Wood, 2004).

Constructed-response instruments, especially essay tests, have been misnamed *subjective* (as opposed to *objective*). This poorly chosen descriptor makes a mockery of professional judgment and gives students the mistaken impression that faculty have no clear standards for evaluating their work. We do have standards, of course, but they often do not boil down to a dualist right or wrong answer. Moreover, each of us may prioritize different criteria on given essay questions and assignments. This is why we should explain our grading criteria and standards to students at the same time we talk about the test or the assignment (see chapter 27).

Below are the advantages, disadvantages, and construction guidelines for constructed response instruments. Those that apply only to essay test items are marked with a †.

Advantages

- Quick and relatively easy to construct (but specify exactly what you want students to do, following the guidelines in the next section)
- Encourages students to study in a deeper, more integrated manner†
- Discourages last-minute cramming†
- Can assess all types of higher-order thinking

- Can assess students' abilities to logically compose and present an argument
- Can assess their reasoning skills (you get inside their heads)
- Can assess them authentically, that is, on tasks that they are likely to do in real-world work
- Can encourage creativity and originality
- Requires students to have a solid command of the material
- Gives practice in writing
- Makes cheating more difficult and reduces its incidence†
- Encourages instructors to give students individual feedback
- Varies the type of assessment from objective tests (yet yields the same student rankings as do multiple-choice tests, according to Jacobs & Chase, 1992)†

Disadvantages

- More time-consuming to grade than objective items (but see chapter 27 for ways to trim that time)
- Difficult to standardize grading because of variability across answers as well as length of answers (but see chapter 27 for ways to handle the variability)
- Cannot test broad content with any one question†
- Penalizes students who read or work slowly, have poor writing skills, or are nonnative English speakers
- Can mislead students if they do not understand the verbs used in the questions or don't read the entire question carefully
- Encourages grading protests if the scoring seems subjective, inconsistent, or unjustified (but see chapter 27 for ways to nearly eliminate protests)
- Easy to make a question or task too broad for students to zero in on the answer
- Allows students to pick up credit for bluffing and padding

- Produces poor, hasty writing, and students do not learn to improve it†

Construction

- Specify exactly what you want the students to do, following the guidelines in the next section.
- Estimate 15 minutes to 1 hour per essay question.†
- Put on the test your estimate of how much time an answer should require to help students budget their time wisely.†
- Give the point value for each essay.†
- Give several shorter essay questions rather than one or two long ones. This strategy covers more material and spreads the risk.
- Consider giving students a choice among several essay questions. Having options lowers their anxiety and lets them show you the best of what they have learned.
- If you let students choose among several questions, limit their choices—for example, to 5 out of 7 options rather than 5 out of 10.

Making Constructed-Response Instruments Specific Enough

Be specific and concise in describing the task you want students to perform or the answer you expect to the questions you ask. Identify the key points that students should address. You might even specify the cognitive operations and the general content that students should use in their responses. Rather than beginning a question with an interrogative pronoun such as *why, how,* or *what,* start with a descriptive verb (see chapter 25 for a list of common test and assignment verbs and their definitions) and state exactly how elaborate the answer should be and, to an extent, how it should be organized (Reiner et al., 2004)—for instance: "*Describe three ways* that social integration could break down in the modern world, according to Durkheim. Then *assess* how closely *each one* applies to the United States today."

All you have to do is to decide exactly how you would like an excellent answer to read. Then you can transform a vague question like, "What were the causes of the collapse of the Ming dynasty?" into a well-defined, multistage task:

> Select *three key* causes of the collapse of the Ming dynasty, and decide which was *most* important, which was *second* in importance, and which was *last* in importance. Write a paragraph on each cause, not only describing its impact on the Ming dynasty, but also arguing why you rank-order it as you do. Explain any interrelationships that exist among the causes.

By incorporating the proper procedure to follow, the instructions reinforce students' understanding of historical interpretation and analysis while assessing their ability to do it. Similarly, the rudderless task, "Explain Shakespeare's view of women as reflected in his plays," can be elaborated into a review of basic literary analysis:

> Pick *three* of Shakespeare's plays that feature a woman in a major role, and analyze these characters to identify *four* patterns in his views of women. Consider not only what these female characters do and say but also what other characters do and say to them.

If the content lends itself, it is also an excellent strategy to situate an essay question or writing assignment in a novel (but not foreign) problem (Reiner et al., 2004). Problem-focused assessment gives students practice in real-world application, and for this reason is authentic. You can take a theoretical task such as, "Explain how a nurse should handle a person who threatens suicide," and place it in a realistic situation:

> In the emergency department, a patient tells the nurse that he plans to commit suicide and agrees to a voluntary admission to the psychiatric unit. What specific issues should the nurse discuss with the patient when he asks, "How long do I have to stay there?" (Adapted from http://findarticles.com/p/articles/mi_qa3689/is_200408/ai_n9444981.)

The last example of an essay question or writing assignment that needs and gets a makeover asks students to perform a low-level and vaguely stated task: "Summarize the most important trends in social inequality that we have seen in the United States since the 1960s." The revision assumes that students can perform this low-level task and requires that they analyze and synthesize that knowledge in a new way to address a contemporary real-world paradox:

> Recall the trends in social inequality that we have seen in the United States since the 1960s. Also recall that during this time, (1) the relationship between educational and income attainment has been consistently positive and (2) educational attainment has increased. How then is it possible that the distributions of income and wealth have become more polarized over this time period? Resolve this apparent contradiction, taking into account other major determinants of income, the role of the occupational structure, and the type of economy in the United States.

With direction, organization, and hints in the instructions, you can prepare your class to perform truly high-order cognitive operations. But do remember that you have to give your students prior practice in the types of thinking you ask them to do in graded assessments. If you identify these types of thinking from the start in your learning outcomes, you will be able to select and implement the teaching formats, methods, and moves that will create the learning experiences to give your students the practice they need.

If you want to use an essay question or give a writing assignment that students may view as controversial or value-based, do assure them in advance that you will assess their work strictly on the validity of their arguments, the strength of their evidence, or the quality of their presentation, not the opinion or viewpoint they express. Be sure to incorporate whatever grading dimensions you define in your grading rubric (see chapter 27).

Ideas for Good Test Essays and Writing Assignments

For a little inspiration, consider how you might adapt these general ideas for engaging test essays and writing assignments to your course material:

- Discuss the relevance of course material to a life decision.

- Argue against a position you believe in.
- Set the conditions under which a relationship or concept does and does not apply.
- What if _____ [a specific change occurs, time or place shifts, or an assumption is violated]? Would a relationship still hold? How would it be changed?
- Push an idea to its limits, to the point of absurdity.
- Determine whether a problem can or cannot be solved given available information.
- Separate relevant from irrelevant information to solve a problem.
- Break a problem into subproblems.
- Explain a specific complex phenomenon to a 12-year-old.
- Design a study to test a relationship.
- Consider why a relationship may be causal or spurious.
- Suggest reasons that different research studies may obtain different results.
- Design a study to reconcile different results across several studies.
- Imagine you are a _____ with the following problem to solve: _____. Draw on course material to structure an approach to the problem or to propose a solution.
- Design a society, government, private or public organization, or funding agency to accomplish a certain purpose.

■ STUDENT ASSESSMENTS AS TEACHING ASSESSMENTS

How your students perform on your summative assessments provides the best data you can use for your personal self-assessment of your teaching. So pay close attention to the subject areas where your students underperformed and try to figure out why.

- Did you assign the relevant readings without a compliance incentive or a comprehension exercise?
- Did you use teaching methods or moves that weren't among the most effective for the material?
- Did you limit your students' learning experiences to one modality?
- Did you give your students too little practice in the required cognitive operations?
- Did you fail to emphasize the content in class or in your review guide or session?
- Did the content challenge misconceptions, beliefs, or values that your students hold dear?

These are just a few of the reasons that your students may have faltered. You can even ask them directly why their performance fell short of what you expected, and their answers may prove helpful. Diagnosing the difficulty now means that you will reduce or eliminate your disappointment next time and become a better instructor.

CHAPTER 27

Grading Student Assessments

G rading is a task that most of us view with dread and disdain, but our institutions absolutely require it and it furnishes essential feedback to your students on their performance and to you on your teaching effectiveness. Of course, grades cannot provide the whole picture on your teaching because assessment standards vary radically across the academy and some students are unable or unwilling to learn, no matter what you do. In fact, the way we now grade seems not to motivate students; rather, it just focuses their attention on grades (Schinske & Tanner, 2014).

■ GRADING SYSTEMS

Summative assessment occurs at the end of a learning process, which may be after a section of a course or at the end of the course. It typically follows one of two basic grading standard systems, norm referenced or criterion referenced.

Norm-Referenced Grading

Commonly called *grading on a curve,* this type of grading standard system assesses each student's performance relative to all other students' performances. Its relative nature gives it some serious flaws. First, it places students in competition with each other for class ranking so you cannot expect them to work cooperatively together in graded group work. Second, it statistically assumes a bell-shaped (*normal*) distribution of student scores, a phenomenon that doesn't always occur. Third, the grades the system yields are unrelated to any absolute performance standard. So if all students in a class perform poorly, some inadequate performances will receive an A anyway. Conversely, in a high-achieving class, some good performances will unjustly get a C, D, or F.

Nevertheless, this system also has strengths. The best and worst performances set the parameters within which other performances are judged, so an instructor can give a highly challenging test without unduly lowering his students' grades or an easy one while still differentiating the quality of student performance. It also ensures any class grade point average an instructor considers reasonable, so it can combat grade inflation.

In the past couple of decades, norm-referenced grading has fallen into disfavor for at least a couple of reasons. For one, higher education has widely embraced group work, and for another, it no longer aims to screen out the low achievers. The retention rate has replaced the attrition rate as an institution's badge of honor.

Criterion-Referenced Grading

This type of grading standard system requires instructors to set absolute standards of performance (grading criteria) in advance, giving all students sole responsibility for their own grades. Compared to norm-referenced, criterion-referenced grading better serves the purpose of assessing how well students achieve given learning outcomes. It allows the possibility that all students will attain A's or, conversely, that all students will fail. In addition, it does not discourage cooperation and collaboration among students.

To be sure, criterion-referenced grading has drawbacks. In particular, it is difficult to develop meaningful, valid standards for assigning grades based on absolute knowledge acquisition (Ory & Ryan, 1993). Instructors who are unfamiliar with their student population may have no idea how scores will distribute on any given test or assignment. (As the nightmare goes, all the scores cluster around 95 percent or all lag below 70.) But with more experience, instructors learn how to design and grade tests and assignments to differentiate performances.

▆ GRADING CONSTRUCTED RESPONSES

Grading answers to constructed-response questions requires considerable thought and strategies to ensure accuracy, consistency, and fairness within reasonable time frames (Jacobs & Chase, 1992; Ory

& Ryan, 1993; Suskie, 2009; Walvoord & Anderson, 2010). Certain practices help ensure those qualities (also see chapter 24):

1. Removing students' names from their work to avoid grading biases
2. Providing a grading rubric (defined later in the chapter) along with the directions for an assignment or before an essay test, or distributing a detailed grading key when returning student work
3. Supplying samples of exemplary work and helping students understand what makes them excellent, along with the directions for an assignment or before an essay test
4. Allowing students to make revisions after providing formative assessments on first drafts
5. Commenting as generously as your time allows, including on what the student did right
6. Making specific comments, not a cryptic "What?" or "?"
7. Identifying a few key areas for improvement, especially those emphasized in your grading rubric, and specific remediation methods
8. Directing comments to the performance, not the student
9. Reviewing exams when you return them so that students understand what you wanted and how they can improve their performance, with a focus on frequently made errors
10. Referring some students to your institution's academic assistance center for special help (see the appendix)

Because grading constructive responses takes so much time, here is another good practice that will save you time and focus your students on your most important expectations. (They will almost always meet them.) Set *gateway criteria*, requirements that students must meet before you grade their product (Walvoord & Anderson, 2010). These criteria may center around proper grammar and punctuation, organization, labeling of graphs and tables, types or number of references, reference style, or any other features that you consider bottom-line signs of a good-faith effort. (You may want to adjust your language-related criteria for nonnative English speakers.) Rejecting a piece of work presents a timely opportunity to refer a student to the campus writing center (see the appendix). At your discretion, you can accept a revision of the work but dock the grade as a late submission.

Beyond having gateway criteria, you can choose from three commonly used grading methods (Ory & Ryan, 1993; Rodgers, 1995; Stevens & Levi, 2012; Suskie, 2009; Walvoord & Anderson, 2010): atomistic, holistic, and analytical grading.

Atomistic Grading

This grading technique follows a key. To develop one, you first list the components of an ideal response on paper and then allocate point values among the components. As you read a student's work, you mentally check off the components on your list or write the number of points earned next to the component on the student's work. You typically give partial credit to an incomplete or partially correct answer. Then you total the point values for the grade. This approach helps inexperienced instructors become accustomed to the quality range of student work and the grading process.

This method is content focused and serves well for grading test items and assignments that require only knowledge or comprehension and have one correct response. It can also be used with criteria that have fairly clear standards of right and wrong: conformity to specified format, organization, quality of data or evidence, logic of reasoning, style (sentence structure, word choice, and tone), and mechanics (grammar, punctuation, and spelling). You can easily keep track of four or five dimensions and, if you wish, give each a different point value or weight—for example, 20 points for content, 15 for organization, 10 for style, and 5 for mechanics, for a total of 50 points. In terms of allocating points on such criteria, this method resembles analytical grading, addressed later in the chapter. If you have general assessment dimensions like these, do explain them and their point values to your class in advance,

perhaps when you give the assignment or conduct a review for the test. Your students need to understand the criteria on which you will evaluate their work.

Atomistic grading takes a great deal of time because it requires attention to minute detail and because most instructors feel obligated to explain what is wrong or missing on each student's work. It may be more efficient to show students a copy of the key when returning the test or paper. While atomistic grading seems highly objective, it still invites grading protests and point mongering, especially for partial credit. It often involves hair-splitting the total point value for a question into fractions for flawed answers. If an instructor could be totally consistent in hair-splitting points, students might not try to argue for a point or two more. But student answers are unique, and no key can cover every possible imperfection. In addition, it is difficult to remember precisely how one graded a similarly but not identically flawed response 20 or 30 papers ago. Consistency across multiple graders can also be difficult to maintain. Perhaps a more serious weakness in atomistic grading is its rigidity when applied to essays and assignments that require higher-level thinking and have multiple respectable answers. The key can quickly become unruly if you try to lay out standards for grading every possible acceptable response, and it may not include all such responses.

Holistic Grading

Over the years, this method has been called *global grading* and *single impression scoring*. As the name implies, an instructor grades a student-constructed response on her overall evaluation of its quality. The technique is relatively quick, efficient, reliable, and fair when backed by instructor experience, practice, and familiarity with the student performance range at the institution. In addition, it easily accommodates essays and assignments that demand higher-order thinking and have multiple respectable responses.

With inductive holistic grading, which is suitable for small classes, you read quickly through all the responses or papers, rank each above or below the ones you have already read, from best to worst, and then group them for assigning grades. Finally, you write up descriptions of the quality of each group and give them to students when you return their work. To personalize the feedback, you can add comments to each student's sheet or highlight the most applicable parts of the appropriate description. While the descriptions are customized to the student products, this schema presents a couple of problems. Because it relies on your comparative evaluations of students' responses and papers, it contains an element of norm-referenced grading (curving). Moreover, students cannot know in advance the dimensions on which you will assess their work.

With deductive holistic grading, which is suitable for any size class, students do know in advance and in some detail how their work will be evaluated. At the same time you compose the writing assignment or essay question, you decide the four or five dimensions on which you will assess the student product. Four or five criteria are a reasonable number to explain to your students and to remember while you are grading. Furthermore, your students cannot do their best on more than a handful of dimensions at one time. We carry around in our heads 20 or more criteria on which we judge scholarly work, all of which come out when we read a journal article or book in our discipline. But students cannot work on so many in one assignment or essay; they don't even know what all these criteria are. Besides, it is unfair to them to critique their novice efforts on the full array of professional dimensions, even if we don't expect high performance. So select just a few as the most important skills for students to demonstrate in any given piece of work, and forget the rest. You can focus on other dimensions in other assignments and essays.

Your relevant assessment criteria will vary according to your discipline, the course level, the nature of your material, and the task you are assigning. Here are just 14 of the possible options:

1. Satisfying the assignment, following directions (particularly salient for first-year students)

2. Accurate statement of facts, figures, definitions, equations, or text material

3. Proper use of technical terminology

4. Demonstration of accurate understanding of the materials and texts

5. Proper references to texts and other sources

6. Organization, conformity to the required organizing framework of format

7. Precision of measurement, quality of data

8. Specification of limits, qualifications to results, and conclusions

9. Clarity of expression or explanations

10. Conciseness, parsimony

11. Strength or tightness of arguments (internal consistency, evidence, and logic)

12. Mechanics (spelling, grammar, and punctuation)

13. Writing style, as suitable to the discipline and assignment

14. Creativity of thought, design, or solution

After choosing the criteria of interest, you then write out descriptions of what the student product will look like at the different levels of quality. If you are assigning letter grades, you will describe the qualities of A, B, C, D, and F work on the dimensions you selected for the assignment or essay. If you are allocating points, you will describe the work for each point or range of points. You might link words to the grades or point ranges, such as *exemplary, competent, developing,* and *unacceptable.* The document you generate is called a *rubric,* defined as an assessment and grading tool that lays out specific expectations for an essay or assignment (writing, speaking, multimedia, and so on) and describes each level of performance quality on selected criteria. In holistic grading, these descriptions take the form of paragraphs in which each sentence typically addresses a different dimension in the rubric.

An example should clarify. Let's say our assignment is to write a classic five-paragraph essay arguing in favor of norm-referenced grading or criterion-referenced grading, drawing on several readings on the topic. Let's assume our rubric focuses on satisfying the assignment (with an emphasis on following the classic five-paragraph essay format), demonstrating an accurate understanding of the readings, backing one's argument with evidence from the readings, and mechanics. The holistic rubric can look like this:

- An *A essay* strictly follows the classic five-paragraph essay format, stating the thesis (position) in the first paragraph, providing evidence in each of the next three paragraphs, and concluding with a summary or synthesis. It consistently makes appropriate and accurate references to the readings. It also provides all the evidence available in the readings to support its argument. Finally, it contains no more than two spelling, punctuation, or grammatical errors.

- A *B essay* follows the classic five-paragraph essay format with no more than one minor deviation. While generally accurate in referring to readings, it shows a thin, incomplete, or shaky understanding of some readings in a couple of places. It also misses some parts of the readings that would lend more evidence to the argument. It contains more than two but fewer than eight spelling, punctuation, or grammatical errors.

- A *C essay* breaks significantly from the classic five-paragraph essay format—perhaps failing to state a clear position in the first paragraph, mixing arguments across paragraphs, or closing with a new argument or information. While it refers to the readings, it demonstrates a spotty or superficial understanding of them. It also misses opportunities to use them for evidence. It contains quite a few (eight or more) spelling, punctuation, or grammatical errors, though not enough to make parts of it incomprehensible.

- A *D essay* does not follow the classic five-paragraph essay format, failing either to state a clear position or to use the rest of the essay to bring evidence from the readings to support it. It demonstrates little understanding or knowledge of the readings.

In addition, it draws little relevant evidence from them. The frequent and serious errors in spelling, punctuation, and grammar are distracting or render the essay incomprehensible in places.

- An *F essay* fails to address the assignment in topic or format, or the frequent and serious errors in spelling, punctuation, and grammar render the essay incomprehensible, or it is not turned in.

Alternatively, you can increase your flexibility by associating a grade or number of points with "all or almost all" or "most or many" of several characteristics. This arrangement also breaks out your assessment criteria more clearly:

- An *A essay* contains *all or almost all* of the following characteristics:
  - Classic five-paragraph essay format
  - Thesis (position) stated in the first paragraph
  - Evidence provided in each of the next three paragraphs
  - Conclusion with a summary or synthesis
  - Appropriate and accurate references to the readings
  - All evidence to support its argument drawn from the readings
  - No more than two spelling, punctuation, or grammatical errors

- A *B essay* contains *most or many* of the following characteristics:
  - Classic five-paragraph essay format previously described with no more than one minor deviation
  - Generally accurate and appropriate references to the readings
  - A thin, incomplete, or shaky understanding of the readings in a couple of places
  - All evidence to support its argument drawn from the readings
  - Missing some parts of the readings that would lend more evidence to the argument
  - More than two but fewer than eight spelling, punctuation, or grammatical errors

- A *C essay* contains *most or many* of the following characteristics:
  - Significant deviations from the classic five-paragraph essay format described earlier—for example, failing to state a clear position in the first paragraph, mixing arguments across paragraphs, or closing with a new argument or information
  - A spotty or superficial understanding of the readings referred to
  - Missing some parts of the readings that would lend more evidence to the argument
  - Quite a few (eight or more) spelling, punctuation, or grammatical errors, though not enough to make parts of it incomprehensible.
- A *D essay* contains *most or many* of the following characteristics:
  - Failure to follow the classic five-paragraph essay format—for example, failing to state a clear position or use the rest of the essay to bring evidence from the readings to support it, or both
  - Little understanding or knowledge of the readings
  - Little or no relevant evidence drawn from the readings
  - Frequent and serious enough errors in spelling, punctuation, and grammar to be distracting or to render the essay incomprehensible in places
- An *F essay* contains *either* of the following characteristics, or it is not turned in:
  - Failure to address the assignment in topic or format
  - Frequent and serious enough errors in spelling, punctuation, and grammar to render the essay incomprehensible overall

Distribute copies of these performance descriptions to your students along with the assignment directions or review sheet (preferably a test blueprint, as described in chapter 25), and explain them with examples. This way students will know to concentrate on the dimensions that are most important to you, and they will understand the quality of work you expect. To save paper and increase the odds that they will study your rubric again, you might ask them to attach the document to the product they hand in. (Of course, this does not apply to electronic turn-ins.) Then you need not hand back another copy with their work.

When you grade the essays or papers, you decide which performance description best fits the work and write that grade on the paper or essay. That is really all you have to do, and this can reduce your grading time to a fraction of what atomistic grading requires. The rubric explains the reasons for the grade, although you should write personal comments as time permits.

The literature offers examples of holistic rubrics written in paragraphs for many types of assignments: letters (Montgomery, 2002); portfolios (Stevens & Levi, 2012); integrative essays (Benander cited in Walvoord & Anderson, 2010); oral presentations, class participation, and journals (Baughin, Brod, & Page, 2002); essay tests and website designs (Brookhart, 1999); and mathematical problem solving (Baughin et al., 2002; Benander, Denton, Page, & Skinner, 2000; Montgomery, 2002). As these models demonstrate, it is best not to abbreviate the descriptions of the B, C, and D products because students are likely to focus only on the description of their own grade. However, the description of F work may be briefer because such serious shortcomings often transcend the rubric.

This holistic approach can shortchange students if the rubric provides an overall rationale for each grade without making the grading criteria clear and obvious enough to furnish meaningful feedback. After all, it is quite possible that a student's work contains elements of two, three, or even more performance levels. For example, the work may follow the organizational format perfectly but demonstrate a poor understanding of the readings and contain a moderate number of mechanical errors. In this case, you need a rubric that allows you to mark or highlight the salient descriptors on different performance levels. Between the two models above, you would probably find it easier to do this using the second model, where the criteria are broken out. Of course, you can always write personalized comments on each student's work, but this sacrifices the efficiency and time-saving advantages of holistic grading.

As a result, many instructors favor a synthetic rubric that combines some of the specificity of atomistic grading with the efficiency and professional judgment involved in the deductive holistic method. In fact, the second holistic model above approaches this kind of rubric.

Analytical Grading: The Effective Synthesis of Atomistic and Holistic

This grading technique follows the procedures of deductive holistic grading—focusing on four to six assessment criteria, writing descriptions for each performance level, and providing students with the rubric in advance—and shares the advantage of speed and efficiency. But rather than writing an overall description of the student product for each performance level, you write a brief description for each performance level on each criterion and assess the product not overall but independently on each criterion. Then you total or average the points gained across all the criteria to derive an overall point total grade.

This grading method certainly requires you to write more descriptions than does the holistic method—as many as the number of performance levels times the number of criteria—and you may find yourself writing more extensive or specific descriptions. However, these furnish your students with more detailed instructions, expectations, and feedback as well as clearer justification for your assessment. In addition, you can give different weights to your criteria reflecting their relative importance in the piece of work. Just don't make your system too difficult for your students to follow.

While you can write the descriptions in full sentences and even paragraphs, you can also use more succinct phrases. In addition, you can display the rubric in an easy-to-read matrix or table for clarity, listing the assessment dimensions down the left side of the page to define rows and the levels of performance (usually the possible numbers of points) across the top to create columns. The cells contain your descriptions of the performance quality on each dimension.

For purposes of illustration, let's return to that essay assignment arguing in favor of norm-referenced or criterion-referenced grading and transform the holistic rubric shown above into an analytical one (Table 27.1). (Only holistic rubrics with well-defined, consistent dimensions easily convert into an analytical version.)

Table 27.1 Analytical Grading Rubric for a Hypothetical Essay Assignment

Grade Criteria	A/19–20	B/16–18	C/13–15	D/10–12	F/Below 10
Format	Follows the classic five-paragraph essay format strictly, stating the thesis (position) in the first paragraph, providing evidence in each of the next three paragraphs, and concluding with a summary or synthesis	Follows the classic five-paragraph essay format with no more than one minor deviation	Breaks significantly from the classic five-paragraph essay format— failing to state a clear position in the first paragraph, mixing arguments across paragraphs, or closing with a new argument or information	Does not follow the classic five-paragraph essay format—failing to state a clear position or use the rest of essay to bring evidence from the readings to support it	Fails to address the assignment in topic or format, or frequent errors in spelling, punctuation, and grammar render the essay incomprehensible, or not turned in

(continued)

Table 27.1   (*Continued*)

Grade Criteria	A/19–20	B/16–18	C/13–15	D/10–12	F/Below 10
Command of readings	Consistently makes appropriate and accurate references to the readings	Generally accurate in referring to readings, but shows a thin, incomplete, or shaky understanding of some readings in a couple of places	Refers to the readings but demonstrates a spotty or superficial understanding of them	Demonstrates little understanding or knowledge of the readings	
Evidence from readings	Provides all the evidence available in the readings to support its argument	Provides evidence available in the readings, but misses some parts that would lend evidence to the argument	Misses opportunities to use the readings for evidence	Draws little relevant evidence from the readings	
Mechanics	No more than two spelling, punctuation, or grammatical errors	No more than several spelling, punctuation, or grammatical errors	Quite a few spelling, punctuation, or grammatical errors, though not enough to make parts of the essay incomprehensible	Frequent errors in spelling, punctuation, and grammar that are distracting or render the essay incomprehensible in places	

When you use your rubric to grade, first test it out on three or four pieces of student work. While you are ethically bound not to make substantive changes, you may tweak it if needed. As you read a student product, mark (underline, highlight, check, star, or circle) the applicable phrases in the descriptions on the student's copy of the rubric. This grading method accommodates wide differences in a student's performance across criteria. Then calculate the point total or letter grade from the distribution of your markings, and write that in a discrete place on the student's work. Add your personalized comments on the work or the rubric only as your time permits. If you have composed a good rubric, you shouldn't have much more to say. Finally, return the work with the student's copy of the rubric.

With a little experience, you will be able to develop rubrics quickly and at the same time that you design an assignment or write an essay test question. For the latter use, you can prepare a generic rubric that doesn't give away the question. When students can work on an assignment or study for a test with the rubric in front of them, they are less likely to explain away a poor performance with, "I didn't know what he wanted."

You will find more examples of analytical rubrics in matrix/table form than any other kind, and models are available for every grading purpose. Look in the assessment literature (Baughin et al., 2002; Brookhart, 1999; Leahy, 2002; Montgomery, 2002; Rodgers, 1995; Stevens & Levi, 2012; Suskie, 2009; Walvoord & Anderson, 2010) and on dedicated websites, such as RubiStar (http://rubistar.4 teachers.org/), Teachnology (http://www.teachnology.com/web_tools/rubrics/), iRubric (http://www.rcampus.com/rubricshellc.cfm?mode=gallery&sms=home&srcgoogle&gclid=CNSCsu 3PmZMCFQv_sgodPBO_xA), and Tech4Learning (http://myt4l.com/index.php?v=pl&page_ac=view&type=tools&tool=rubricmaker). All of these sites feature not just models but also rubric generators, allowing you to create your own for specific assignments.

For many types of assignments, RubiStar, for instance, offers a drop-down menu of appropriate criteria to choose from. When you select a dimension, it displays descriptions of four quality levels, which you can then edit to your needs. While designed primarily for and by K–12 teachers, many of the models and generated rubrics easily adapt to college-level work.

The next chapter contains another example of an analytical rubric, and this is one you can use as you write a statement of your teaching philosophy.

■ GRADING LAB REPORTS

While this is a specialized kind of grading for a specialized kind of writing, the guidelines for grading constructed responses still apply. No doubt, you'll be examining these features: the student's presentation of the problem, the hypothesis, and the results; her analysis of the results; and her ability to follow the scientific method. In lower-level science courses, you can familiarize your students with the proper format and content by providing them with models, perhaps from other courses. You can also have them organize their reports with an outline or flowchart and practice-write the various sections.

Another excellent way to help your students produce good reports is to give them the grading rubric in advance. Rodgers (1995) developed a detailed analytical rubric, presented in an easy-to-read matrix, to grade his students' chemistry lab reports. His rubric has a daunting 21 assessment dimensions, but they fall within four more general criteria—focus, appearance, content, and structure—and have only three levels of point allocations: 2, 4, and 6. For example, under "focus," Rodgers has nine dimensions (1995, p. 21)

1. Shows understanding of the experimental objectives

2. Abstract describes what was done and what the major results were
3. Concise, no unnecessary statements or observations
4. Introduction shows depth.
5. Written with an objective, scientific tone
6. Give suggestions for improvement and further study in conclusions
7. Relates the experiment to other known chemical principles
8. Shows detailed understanding of the scientific method
9. Distinguishes between a theory and a proof

While nine dimensions seem imposing, many of the cells have only one- or two-word descriptors, such as "very clear," "demonstrated," or "unsophisticated." Even when the descriptor is considerably longer, it is very easy to simply check, circle, or highlight the most appropriate option. At the end, you total the points accumulated across all 21 dimensions by calculating or eyeballing.

Rodgers (1995) recorded how long it took to grade a lab report using his old atomistic method versus his new method. He timed both himself and his trained TAs. The results were quite startling. His previous grading technique required 15 to 20 minutes per report, while the new one took only 3 1/2 minutes (for him) to 4 minutes (for his TAs) per report. In other words, atomistic grading took four to five times longer than analytical. Rodgers was also pleased with the reliability and overall grading results.

■ HOW TO GRADE AND TEACH MECHANICS AT THE SAME TIME

Many instructors decide to avoid grading mechanics, even though they bemoan their students' writing—or perhaps because they do. They may say that they have tried to improve their students' writing—they have spent laborious hours copyediting it—but their students neither looked carefully at the corrections nor improved their writing. Once you return an essay test or written assignment with a grade on it, most students will read the rubric description associated with their grade and maybe your written comments but give scant attention to your copyediting, even if their faulty mechanics cost them points. Many of our corrections make little sense to them. Besides, the work already has a grade, so what's the point?

First, let's define the meaning of *mechanics* here as spelling, grammar, punctuation, and sentence structure. Bean (2011) explains the conflict some instructors may have about grading students on the basis of their conforming to the rules. On the one hand, enforcing edited standard written English (ESWE) is imposing formal white, well-educated, middle- and upper-class language conventions on others who happen to be in this country. On the other hand, not writing ESWE and not speaking standard English will likely prevent students from obtaining the kinds of jobs they want. Departures from the standard that are associated with low educational and socioeconomic status (e.g., no subject-verb agreement and double negatives) irritate business managers and leaders the most. Students need to know how their future employers and business associates judge different versions of the English language.

With any grading method involving multiple criteria, it can be difficult to distinguish among evaluative dimensions. We should try not to let a poor grammatical construction devalue a good idea, but if we can't easily decipher the idea, the writing issue must be serious. Indeed, some departures from ESWE are more serious than others, and we should concentrate on helping students understand the nature of the more serious ones, such as sentence fragments, run-on sentences, lack of parallelism, and erratic capitalization. Other apparent errors may be so trivial as to reflect just taste and preference (e.g., the Oxford comma before the *and* in a series).

Various factors increase or decrease the frequency of mechanical errors. Not surprisingly, both the cognitive challenge of the assignment and careless editing and proofreading increase errors, while writing multiple revisions of a work and reading a draft out loud decrease them (Bean, 2011). You might consider, then, building revisions into more difficult assignments and having students get into groups in class to read their work to each other before submitting it. Errors also drop when students write for a public audience, whether that "public" is the online world or just the rest of the class (Bean, 2011).

Before grading mechanics, you should take at least a couple of the steps noted above to minimize avoidable student errors. Then you can fairly use the efficient way described below to grade mechanics and do it in a fraction of the time it takes to copyedit writing. Furthermore, you will ensure that your students learn some grammar, spelling, punctuation, and sentence structure rules along the way and use what they learn in their subsequent writing.

When you make an assignment, tell students that you will be grading their mechanics by choosing one page from their work—but don't tell them which page in advance—to note their mechanical errors. You determine how many errors on the page will affect the grade in what ways and state that in your rubric—for example, up to 5 errors merit 20 points (total possible) for mechanics, 5 to 10 errors merit 15 points, 10 to 15 errors merit 10 points, 15 to 20 errors merit 5 points, and more than 20 errors merit no points. On that page, you will be placing a check mark at the end of a line for every serious grammar, spelling, punctuation, and sentence structure error in that line without identifying what the error is or correcting it.

After returning the graded work to your students, make the required follow-up assignment of identifying and correcting the mechanical errors they made on that page (or as many as they can) to gain back a portion of the points they lost. They will get credit only for accurate corrections. Do refer them to one or more English language or writing handbooks. (The web has a variety of free ones, including *The Grammerly Handbook* at http://www.grammarly.com/handbook/, World-English at http://www.world-english.org/writing.htm, and the University of Wisconsin-Madison Writing Center's Writer's Handbook at http://writing.wisc.edu/Handbook/.) But it's no matter to you whether they use a handbook, go to the writing center, or ask a family member for help. They will learn how their writing departed from ESWE and how to correct it through the process of discovery.

To motivate students to get the mechanics right the first time, give them only partial credit for each correction, certainly no more than half the value of the points they lost. Instruct them to make their corrections on the actual page of the paper in a different color ink (or pencil) from black and the color you used for grading. Give them 3 to 4 days to complete this follow-up assignment. When you collect these corrected pages, you need only look at the number of check marks you made in the margin and the corrections made. Moreover, students will remember the errors they identified, researched, and corrected and will not want to repeat the same ones again. If, on average, they learn just a half-dozen new spelling, punctuation, grammar, and sentence structure rules of ESWE, these are a half-dozen rules they otherwise might not learn at all.

In the next writing assignment, grade on mechanics the same way, selecting another page for noting mechanical errors. Chances are that you will see fewer departures from ESWE than before and, for each student, different ones from those you marked before. This time students will learn a few more rules. With just several writing assignments and a modest amount of your time, your students will radically improve their writing.

The writing of students who are not native English speakers may reflect the cultural conventions of their heritage. We need to make them aware that American English is particularly direct and concise compared to other languages, but this should constitute more of a learning than an evaluative experience for them. In grading their writing, we should be more lenient and note only the errors that interfere with the reader's ability to understand the message. There's no point in overwhelming these students. Usually their errors tell you a lot about their native language—for example, the way and extent to which it uses articles before nouns. If advisable, refer them for personalized help to your institution's ESOL (English for Speakers of Other Languages) center, its writing center, or its academic assistance center (see the appendix).

■ SPECIFICATIONS (SPECS) GRADING

This section briefly summarizes a new way of grading that I proposed elsewhere, specifications (specs) grading (Nilson, 2015). It rests on the premise that students can achieve more than what we have demanded of them. Research shows that specs grading promotes high standards, motivates students to do higher-quality work, and saves you time grading. In addition, most students prefer it to traditional methods. Although you can adopt just pieces of this new system and combine it with features of traditional grading, the greatest benefits derive from its pure version, which I describe here in three parts.

First, you grade all assignments and tests satisfactory/unsatisfactory, pass/fail, or full credit/no credit, depending on whether the student work meets the specifications, or specs, that you laid out for it. You can think of the specs as a one-level rubric. However, you set the passing bar at B work or even higher. The specs may be as simple as "completeness"—for instance, all the questions are answered, or all the problems are attempted in good faith, or the work follows the directions and meets a required minimum length. Or the specs may be more complex—for example, a description of a good literature review or the required contents (questions that must be answered) and length of each section of a proposal, a report, or a reflection. You might also recommend how many hours students should put into a given assignment. In any case, you must write the specs very carefully to describe exactly what features in the work you are going to look for. In fact, most of our assignments follow a formula. The specs should simply lay out that formula. At your discretion, they can also include on-time submission.

From the students' point of view, they must read and follow the specs because there is too much at stake not to. They can't slide by and depend on partial credit for a slipshod, 11th-hour product. We are not asking too much of our students simply to follow directions and put some effort into their work. Other academics (cited in Nilson, 2015) have implemented pass/fail grading of assignments and tests and have reported gratifying results.

Second, you add flexibility and second chances for your students with a virtual token system. Students start the semester with, say, three tokens that they can exchange for a 24-hour extension on an assignment or the chance to revise an unsatisfactory assignment, take a makeup exam, or have an absence or late arrival to class not count against them. You have to keep track of students' tokens as you would points, but you don't have to listen to excuses and requests for special treatment. If you choose, students can also earn tokens by submitting satisfactory work early, doing an additional assignment, or having perfect attendance all term. Of course, students who do what they are supposed to do (submit satisfactory work the first time and on time, attend class, and take their exams when scheduled) will not lose any tokens. Perhaps because of the gamelike quality of a system, students prize their tokens and try not to use them, especially if, at the end of the course, you reward the students with the most tokens with the option to skip the final exam or a gift certificate for a pizza. The token system meshes with any type of grading.

How do you wind up with letter grades at the end of course? If you want to maintain the point system, then you make each passed test or assignment worth so many points (all or nothing), total the points, and convert them to percentages. However, you don't have to use points anymore or ever haggle

with students about points again. Rather—and this is the third aspect of specs grading—you base a student's course grade on the *bundle* of assignments and tests he completes at a satisfactory level. The bundles for higher grades require some combination of more work (more learning) and more challenging work (more advanced learning)—that is, students have to jump more hurdles or higher hurdles for higher grades—or both. More advanced, challenging work may require higher-order cognitive skills in Bloom's (1956) hierarchy, higher-stage thinking in Perry's (1968) schema of undergraduate development, or higher-step skills in Wolcott's (2006) framework of critical thinking. Or it may involve solving more complex problems.

Ultimately, students have the freedom to choose the grade they want on the basis of their motivation, time available, needs, and commitment. If a student chooses a C because that's all she needs in your course, you can respect that. You may be able to schedule the deadlines for the C and D bundles before the end of the term, send those students aiming for a C or D on their way, and then direct your attention to the more motivated students. However, we should encourage all our students, especially the underprepared and first-generation ones, to vie for the higher grades.

Bundles allow you to associate each grade with the learning outcomes that are achieved by successfully completing a bundle. In our current grading system, a course grade provides no clue as to the outcomes a student has achieved, except an A if it is rigorously awarded. If our grades did reflect the outcomes achieved, programs wouldn't have to assess students' competencies for accreditation. A simple four-bundle example will clarify:

- For a D, students must successfully complete/ pass all the exams and assignments in the easiest and most basic bundle. Doing so requires only knowledge and comprehension (or perhaps the knowledge and skills required by the accrediting agency).

- For a C, students must successfully complete/ pass all the work in that basic bundle and a second bundle, somewhat more challenging, that requires application.
- For a B, students must successfully complete/ pass all the work in the first and second bundles, plus a third bundle, still more challenging, that requires analysis.
- For an A, students must successfully complete/ pass all the work in the first, second, and third bundles, plus a fourth bundle, even more challenging, that requires synthesis (creativity) and evaluation.

Unless all your students aspire to an A, you have less work to grade, especially the kind that consumes your time: the lower-quality attempts at cognitively complex assignments. Because your students chose their final grade, they are more likely to see it as their own responsibility. They should also be motivated to work harder not only because more is at stake but also because they clearly control their own outcome, at least if the specs are clear. This should reduce their grade anxiety and shift their orientation more toward learning than performance (Bandura, 1997; Deci & Ryan, 1985; Dweck & Leggett, 1988; Locke & Lantham, 1990; Wigfield & Eccles, 2000).

This very brief introduction to specs grading has probably left you with more questions than answers, and understandably so, because specs grading demands a whole new gestalt on something we've done one way for so long that we can't imagine another way. The answers to your questions and many more details and examples are in Nilson (2015).

▪ RETURNING STUDENTS' WORK

Under the provisions of the Buckley Amendment (the Family Educational Rights and Privacy Act), it is illegal to publicly display scores or grades with any identifying information, including entire or partial social security numbers. Therefore, to protect students' privacy, return their work in any order except grading rank and record points or grades inside the test or paper, never where they can be seen.

Grade and return tests and assignments as promptly as you can; students cannot learn from your feedback on a piece of work they have long forgotten. Allow class time for review, questions, problem re-solving exercises, and self-regulated learning exercises (see chapter 20) so students can learn what they did not the first time. It is best not to proceed to new material until students assure you that they understand what they did wrong. Some instructors give a statistical grading summary showing the distribution of points, the class mean and median, the standard deviation, and the cutoff lines for grades (already built into the criterion-referenced system). No doubt these data increase students' interest in elementary statistics; they also encourage point mongering.

If students submit their tests and assignments online, you can return them online, along with a statistical summary and your key or rubric, if you choose.

Returning graded work in class can take precious time but need not. You can assign each of your students a number and place their graded work into correspondingly numbered slots in an accordion file (McIntosh, 2010). You can let them pick up their work before or after class or during a break. For a large class, use multiple accordion files. Just let students know that they must go only into their own slot. You can also take attendance with this method; any slot with paper left in it tells you the student was absent.

Students have trouble seeing their mistakes on their graded work as learning opportunities. They see only the points they missed. But if you give them any kind of credit for it, most will eagerly diagnose and correct their errors. Chapter 20 suggests several in-class or homework activities for helping students learn by their mistakes or poor study strategies. The reflective questions and the test autopsy also help students take responsibility for their test performance.

Returning student work brings us to the unpleasant topic of grade disputes. No matter how carefully you grade, a few students will be dissatisfied with their scores. The holistic and analytical grading methods discourage (but do not prevent) such challenges because, unlike atomistic grading, they rely heavily on professional judgment, which is too sophisticated for most students to debate. Rule number one is never to discuss a grade with an emotional student. Rather, require him to cool off and submit his case for a grade change formally in writing (not in a text or e-mail) with justifications citing specific material in the readings or your lectures, within a time limit of 48 to 72 hours. Students who cannot make a case in 2 or 3 days probably do not have one. Alternatively, agree to regrade the entire test or paper, which means you may find a grading error that does not work in the student's favor. Or agree to regrade the item in question, but should you find no cause for a point change, you will subtract the number of points disputed. However you decide to respond to grade challenges, clearly state your policy in your syllabus and stick to it.

THE REAL PURPOSE OF GRADES

In the best of all possible worlds, we would not give grades at all. Rather, we would furnish our students with individual feedback on how to improve their work. So we should keep grades in perspective and see them for what they are: an institutionally mandated shorthand used to screen, sort, sanction, motivate, and reward—with mixed results. What grades cannot do is inspire students to want to learn. That admirable task is ours, and our success depends on our teaching methods, motivational strategies, enthusiasm, rapport with students, and other qualities and behaviors that we examine in the next and final chapter.

CHAPTER 28

Defining and Documenting Teaching Effectiveness

Over the past few decades, teaching has taken on greater weight in the faculty review process, including tenure and promotion decisions. With this trend has come an increasing focus on how to document teaching success. This chapter starts out by defining teaching effectiveness and examining the ways that institutions try to measure it. It summarizes the major research findings on the one tool almost all institutions use, *student evaluations of teaching*, or the more appropriate term, *student ratings*, including how these ratings relate to student learning, what they actually measure, and how you can improve yours. We move on to explain and evaluate other approaches to measuring teaching effectiveness: peer evaluation, the teaching philosophy, the teaching portfolio, measures of learning in a course, and the Teaching Practices Inventory. For each approach except the first, you will find guidelines for implementing it if you choose to or are asked to do so. Finally, this chapter lays out a comprehensive faculty evaluation system that assesses every aspect of the faculty's role. Evaluating teaching effectiveness turns out to be more complex than judging the merits of a colleague's research or service.

WHAT IS TEACHING EFFECTIVENESS?

Virtually every institution of higher learning assesses faculty on *teaching effectiveness*, but the criterion eludes a clear definition because we measure it so indirectly. At the very least, it is an instructor's degree of success in facilitating student learning. To break this down, the more knowledge and skills students learn, the more advanced the cognitive level (and affective, ethical, social, and psychomotor levels, if applicable) at which they learn it, and the better they can communicate what they have learned, the more effective an instructor's teaching. From another view, the higher the level at which students achieve an instructor's learning outcomes and the more students who do so, the more effective the teaching has been.

Therefore, why shouldn't faculty be assessed on their students' learning? After all, colleges and universities measure learning to evaluate and accredit programs, departments, colleges, and entire institutions. They use student portfolios, student interviews, standardized test results, and whatever evidence they can glean from courses.

Of course, student learning is not completely under faculty control. Students may or may not be willing and able to learn the material in a given course, despite the instructor's best efforts. But programs and institutions encounter the same issues. And student ratings are not completely under faculty control either, as the next section documents.

Ideally, we would assess learning using independently developed standardized tests that were tailored to each course and administered at the beginning and end of a course. But such tests exist for very few introductory courses (e.g., physics and chemistry), and they capture only the cognitive learning. As a result, institutions have been using substitutes for learning—in particular, student ratings. We will first examine the validity of this substitute measure and proceed to consider several better alternatives.

■ WHAT STUDENT RATINGS DO AND DO NOT MEASURE

Student ratings directly tap students' perceptions of and affective reactions to an instructor and a course, specifically student satisfaction with them. The forms that institutions use to collect these data often have flawed, homespun items with questionable validity and reliability (Arreola, 2007; Nuhfer, 2010). But more obviously, satisfaction is not the same as learning, and the two variables aren't even related.

How did student ratings come to be used to measure teaching effectiveness? In the 1970s and early 1980s, student ratings (the global items) had a moderately strong positive correlation with student learning, as measured by an external exam—

between .44 and .47, according to Cohen's (1981) meta-analysis. Two more meta-analyses (Feldman, 1989; Marsh, 1984) reported slightly higher correlations between a few criterion-specific items and learning. These three meta-analyses supplied the reason to use student ratings to substitute for student learning in faculty reviews. In other words, these studies provided the basis for the *validity* of student ratings. The stronger the relationship between student ratings and learning and the fewer and weaker the biases in ratings, the more valid ratings are and the better they serve as proxies for direct measures of learning. As Cohen (1981) put it:

> It [teaching effectiveness] can be further operationalized as the amount students learn in a particular course. . . . If student ratings are to have any utility in evaluating teaching, they must show at least a moderately strong relationship to this index. (p. 281)

Since that time, the college student population has changed markedly in demographics, values, attitudes, motivations, aspirations, percentage employed, academic preparation, and reasons for attending college. We could expect such profound shifts to have an impact on student ratings, and they have. Today, some students—and it does not take many to affect ratings—object to active learning strategies, student-centered courses, and an emphasis on critical thinking, and they accordingly penalize instructors on their rating forms (Edens, 2000; Lieux, 1996; Rhem, 2006; Thorn, 2003; Weimer, 2013a). More generally, recent research finds little or no relationship between ratings and learning, as measured by student performance on a final exam or in follow-up courses, and in some studies the correlation is negative (Braga, Paccagnella, & Pellizzari, 2014; Carrell & West, 2010; Deslauriers, Schelew, & Wieman, 2011; Johnson, 2003; Marks, Fairris, & Beleche, 2010; Weinberg, Hashimoto, & Fleisher, 2009). In fact, not one study first published after 1990 reports a positive relationship between ratings and learning (Clayson, 2009), with the exception of Marks et al.'s (2010) study, and the relationship they document is weak. Findings on the link between ratings and students' *perceived* learning are mixed, and perceived and actual learning are unrelated (Bowman, 2011; Johnson, 2003; Weinberg et al., 2009; Williams & Ceci, 1997).

The data regarding biases have changed as well. In earlier days, students brought only a few biases into a course (e.g., their prior interest in the subject matter, their expected grade, the level of course, the discipline, and the perceived purpose of the ratings), and all but prior interest had relatively weak effects (Cashin, 1995). Studies involving today's students document additional, stronger, and, one might say, uglier biases (see Nilson, 2012, for the citations and references). Many of these biases revolve around perceived instructor characteristics: charisma, physical attractiveness, personality (congeniality, confidence, optimism, and enthusiasm), age, rank, gender in the sciences and engineering, gender in general (MacNell, Driscoll, & Hunt, 2014), membership in a disadvantaged racial group, and Asian accent. Clayson (2011) estimates that instructor personality alone explains 50 to 75 percent of the variance in student ratings. Course and class features factor in too: the length of the class meeting, in that longer meetings lower ratings; the timing of the ratings, in that collecting the data shortly before tests and due dates of major assignments and after returning graded work depresses ratings; class size; the number of rows in the classroom; the quality of the curriculum; and the functionality of the classroom's technology.

One final bias deserves special attention: students' anticipated grade in the course. The evidence for this bias is strong and getting stronger (see Nilson, 2012); the correlation used to be .10 to .30 but is now .45 to .50 (Clayson, 2011). And this relationship does *not* reflect the effects of better teaching and more learning on student ratings. Rather, Clayson, Frost, and Sheffet (2006) find the clearest evidence for the *reciprocity* hypothesis, which states that student ratings mirror what students perceive to be the instructor's evaluation of them.

As far as course rigor, challenge, and required student effort are concerned, the results are mixed.

Some studies find that students' scores on the relevant items vary negatively with instructor ratings (Centra, 1993; Steiner, Holley, Gerdes, & Campbell, 2006; Weinberg, Fleisher, & Hashimoto, 2007; others cited in Clayson, 2009). However, others document a positive relationship (Beyers, 2008; Dee, 2007; Martin, Hands, Lancaster, Trytten, & Murphy, 2008). It may depend on the institution.

Unfortunately, few studies have examined the honesty or factual accuracy of student ratings, but those that have (Clayson & Haley, 2011; Sproule, 2002; Stanfel, 1995) show that student responses on the forms often misrepresent reality, even on the most fact-based issues—for instance, how quickly graded work was returned. In Clayson and Haley's (2011) survey, about a third of the students confessed to stretching the truth on their rating forms, 56 percent said they knew peers who had, and 20 percent admitted to lying in their comments.

In summary, student ratings no longer serve as valid proxies for student learning, and their factual accuracy is questionable, so they should not be used to measure teaching effectiveness. If they lack validity, their reliability is a moot point. However, they do seem to measure student satisfaction with an instructor and a course. The fact that administrators still rely on student ratings in making personnel decisions suggests that they value student satisfaction over student learning.

■ HOW TO IMPROVE YOUR STUDENT RATINGS

As long as institutions use student ratings to evaluate faculty, you should know how to raise yours if you have to. For each class, carefully analyze your statistical summary and student comments, looking for areas of repeated criticism (ignore isolated complaints) and try to identify patterns and trends. Mentally correct for the negative biases associated with large classes, introductory courses, required courses (required in students' minds), and the like.

Remember that these forms collect students' perceptions and affective reactions, not objective reality. You may not think you behaved a certain way that alienated your students (e.g., condescending, impatient, disorganized), but you apparently did or said something that gave some of them that impression or that angered them. What could that be?

Then consider the factors related to ratings that you can and cannot control. For instance, you cannot change your race, accent, gender, age, rank, discipline, the curriculum, the specific subjects you teach, the required or elective nature of your courses, the condition of your classroom, or the size of your classes. You probably cannot do a great deal to improve your physical appearance either. Nor can you affect your students' prior interest in the subject matter, their academic commitment, or their motivation to take your course. But here's what you can change, along with the chapters in this book that can help you:

Changes You Can Make	Relevant Chapters in This Book
1. Improve your use of class time, your preparation (real and apparent), the organization of your course (even if it is just making that organization more apparent to students with a graphic syllabus and an outcomes maps), and your public speaking skills.	2, 5, and 12
2. Add warmth, empathy, and caring to your instructor persona by learning students' names, encouraging their success, smiling, and exhibiting a few other simple immediacy behaviors.	7 and 8
3. Cultivate a sense of community, safety, and comfort in your class.	7, 8, 13, and 15
4. Enhance your instructor persona by projecting more enthusiasm, energy, relaxed self-confidence, authority, and in-command leadership—qualities that will stimulate students' interest in the material and maintain their respectful attention; balance authority and approachability.	8, 9, 12, 13, and 21
5. Give students choices and control when possible.	8
6. Explain why you teach and assess the way you do, emphasizing the evidence-based learning benefits to students; also explain why you focus on the content that you do, emphasizing its relevance for work and life in general.	8
7. Vary your teaching and assessment activities and assignments, and avoid doing any one thing for too long.	8, 22, and 23
8. Help students see how much they are learning by providing plenty of feedback and having them reflect and write about their newly acquired or improved skills.	20 and 24
9. Solicit feedback (at least some of it anonymous) from students on how well they think they are learning in the class and what can be improved; thank them and fine-tune your course accordingly, or explain why you will not make a requested change.	8, 20, and 24
10. Explain how important student ratings and comments are to your institution and to you personally.	

While some of these behaviors have little to do with student learning, at least none of them undermines learning and a few of them actually enhance it—notably, improving your use of class time, being better prepared, organizing your course more transparently, attracting and maintain student attention, increasing student choice and control, having students work in groups, giving them quality feedback, and getting feedback from them. However, some of these do require either your time outside class or actual class time, which leaves less time for the content. I could counsel you to grade more leniently, but in good conscience, I can only advise you to grade no more stringently than your colleagues. Since the findings are mixed on how course rigor, challenge, and required effort affect ratings, I cannot give definitive advice. But again, avoid roaming too far from your department's norms. In addition, promote rigor and challenge by explaining the rewards they will bring: what they will enable your students to do and how they will help them grow (Geddes, 2014).

■ DOCUMENTING YOUR EFFECTIVENESS

Without exception, all scholars interested in student ratings, regardless of what they think about these ratings, recommend that you include other teaching-related data in your reviews as well (Arreola, 2007; Berk, 2005; Nuhfer, 2010; Seldin, Miller, & Seldin, 2010). Therefore, while your institution probably requires you to submit your student ratings, you should always provide additional evidence; the reviewers will usually look at whatever you supply. Aside from the fact that these ratings measure anything but learning, current students are in no position to judge your course content, every facet of your instructional design and delivery, or the longer-term impact of your teaching. Although submitting the materials described in this section cannot guarantee you a favorable review, they may make the academic reward system more responsive to your teaching achievements (Seldin et al., 2010).

Peer Evaluations of Teaching

Peers have the expertise to advise on and judge your course content, book selections, online resources, class activities, demonstrations, and the technical aspects of instructional design, such as the syllabus and assignments. In fact, a committee of your colleagues should evaluate your course documents as part of every major review. When used for formative purposes, peer observations may provide feedback that can help you improve your teaching, especially your presentation skills. However, your peers cannot adopt the perspective of a novice (Ambrose, Bridges, DiPietro, Lovett, & Norman, 2010) and judge, as a student would, the clarity of your course organization and explanations, the challenge of your tests

and assignments, or the degree of motivation and interest you inspire. Therefore, like student ratings, they should not be weighted heavily in a review.

In fact, it is questionable whether peer observations should be included in a review at all. In some departments, politics can trump professional judgment. And in almost every department, the observers have no training in conducting an observation, nor are they instructional experts familiar with the wide range of best teaching practices. Some of them may not understand the more innovative methods and activities you are using in your classroom. So peer (and administrative) observations do not belong in promotion and tenure reviews, unless (Millis, 1992):

- The observers are formally trained in classroom observation and the use of a good evaluation form.
- They meet with the instructor beforehand to discuss her teaching philosophy, preferred methods, characteristics of the course and students, and learning outcomes for the course and the specific class.
- They observe the instructor's class at least seven or eight times during the term.
- They schedule the classroom visits with the instructor in advance.

Some of these conditions are difficult to impossible for busy faculty, department chairs, and deans to meet, but such a professional observation program has been developed and tested (Millis, 1992).

The Teaching Philosophy

This one- to two-page single-spaced statement is often a required part of an academic job application and faculty review materials, including a teaching portfolio. It does not document your teaching effectiveness as much as it shows you have reflected on your teaching and use presumably effective strategies. Following an essay format with an introduction and conclusion, it is a personal statement written in the first person and incorporating both cognitive and affective elements. It should explain your theory of how learning occurs and how teaching can foster it; the values, goals, or ideals that motivate you to teach; and the specific teaching methods you use, linking them to your learning theory or your motivating values, goals, or ideals, or both (Berke & Kastberg, 1998; Chism, 1997–1998; Johnston, 2003; Schönwetter, Sokal, Friesen, & Taylor, 2002).

If you can identify a key belief that is central to how you teach, you can generate a statement of your teaching philosophy just by answering these questions: What assumptions about teaching, learning, students, education, and the like underlie your key belief? What values, principles, goals, or ideals does it reflect or spring from? What teaching strategies logically flow from it? Your key belief should align with your assumptions, values and goals, and methods.

If you have trouble articulating key beliefs, a theory of teaching and learning, or your motivations for teaching, complete one or both of these free online teaching inventories: the Teaching Goals Inventory at http://fm.iowa.uiowa.edu/fmi/xsl/tgi/data_entry.xsl?-db=tgi_data&-lay=Layout01&-view and the Teaching Perspectives Inventory (TPI) at http://www.teachingperspectives.com/tpi/. In addition to finding out more about your own teaching identity, you will learn richly descriptive terms for various teaching aims and approaches that you can use in your statement.

If appropriate, two other topics belong in a teaching philosophy. First, you should at least mention any research on teaching you have done, even if you have not published it. If you have published it, refer your reader to the section of your curriculum vitae where you list it. Second, you should explain, if possible, any problematic student evaluations you have received in recent years. As mentioned earlier in this chapter, some students have been known to penalize instructors who stretch students' abilities, emphasize critical thinking, or use student-centered practices. If your evaluations have suffered for any of these reasons and you have continued to teach the way you do because you know it increases student learning, then state this in your philosophy as an illustration of your strong educational principles.

Make your statement inviting. Do not try to cram in more text by covering all the available white space. Leave margins of at least 1 inch all around and use 11- or 12-point type. Write clearly, simply, and with conviction, and use transitions generously to shepherd your readers through the document. Once you have a good draft of your statement, appraise it against the teaching philosophy rubric in Table 28.1, and revise it to meet the specifications and qualities under "Excellent."

Table 28.1   Rubric for Assessing and Revising a Statement of Teaching Philosophy

	Excellent	Needs Some Revision	Needs Considerable Revision	Needs a Complete Rewrite
Content; coverage of essential topics	Thoroughly and thoughtfully presents a theory of teaching and learning; teaching values, goals, and ideals; and compatible teaching methods.	Addresses the three essential topics but does so too briefly or superficially.	Fails to address one of the three essential topics.	Fails to address two of the three essential topics.
Balance of personal and professional	Well balanced; formal in tone but maintains the sense of "I."	Occasionally too informal or too impersonal.	Often lapses into an inappropriate informality or loses the sense of "I."	A personal stream of consciousness or a totally impersonal essay with no sense of "I."

(continued)

Table 28.1 (*Continued*)

	Excellent	Needs Some Revision	Needs Considerable Revision	Needs a Complete Rewrite
Structure and organization	Essay is coherent with a clear introduction, a strong conclusion, and logical transitions between paragraphs and sentences.	Essay is generally coherent but lacks either a clear introduction or a strong conclusion. Has some logical transitions between paragraphs and sentences.	Essay lacks a coherent structure and organization. Some paragraphs seem out of place, unconnected to the surrounding text. Lacks either a strong introduction or a clear, strong conclusion. Has few logical transitions between paragraphs and sentences.	Essay is incoherent and unstructured. Lacks a clear introduction, a clear conclusion, and logical transitions between paragraphs and sentences.
Writing style and mechanics (grammar, punctuation, spelling, and sentence structure)	Writing is clear, concise, and smooth. It follows the rules of standard written English. Each sentence is connected to the ones before and after. Structure of sentences varies. Very few, if any, mechanical errors.	Writing follows rules of standard written English with few errors in sentence structure and syntax. Sentences are usually connected. Some minor mechanical errors.	Writing violates some rules of standard written English and is sometimes awkward and difficult to understand. Some sentences seem unconnected and out of place. Frequent mechanical errors.	Writing often violates rules of standard written English and is generally awkward and difficult to understand. Sentences are unconnected, monotonously structured, and full of mechanical errors.
Presentation and length	Neatly typed, single-spaced, 11- or 12-point type. Optimal length: one to one and a half pages, possibly two pages if very experienced.	A bit too long or too short.	Somewhat too long or too short.	Sloppy, double-spaced, type too small, cramped, or much too long or too short.

The Teaching Portfolio

This is a collection of materials that you assemble to highlight your major teaching strengths and achievements, comparable to your publications, grants, and scholarly honors in your research record (Seldin et al., 2010). It opens with a 5- to 10-page statement where you furnish basic information about your teaching responsibilities: the courses you teach, your student learning outcomes, your approach to course design, your expectations for student progress, and your assessment strategies. The statement should also annotate and evaluate the content you selected for your portfolio, specifically explaining and justifying your criteria for assessing your teaching effectiveness.

Institutions that use teaching portfolios require different components and organization, so check first with your chair. For example, your institution may want you to integrate your teaching philosophy, 5-year teaching goals, self-evaluation, course updates and improvements, and teaching-related professional activities into your teaching statement.

Or it may recommend you write your annotations a certain way. To ensure objectivity and cogency in selecting materials, prepare your portfolio in consultation with a trusted colleague, your department chair, or a teaching and learning center consultant.

If the following items are not incorporated into your teaching statement, they probably belong in your portfolio (Seldin et al., 2010):

- Your teaching philosophy
- Your teaching goals for the next 5 years
- A brief self-evaluation with your teaching improvement strategies and efforts, including the teaching and learning center services, workshops, and programs you have taken advantage of
- Descriptions of improvements and updates in your course assignments, materials, and activities
- A list of your teaching-related professional activities, such as instructional research (the scholarship of teaching and learning), publications, journal editing and reviewing, conference presentations, and invited teaching workshops. Include abstracts or reprints of your published research and summaries of your unpublished research in the appendix.
- Syllabi and other important course materials
- A list of students you have advised or supervised in research projects
- Teaching awards, honors, and other types of recognition, such as teaching committee appointments
- A recording of one of your class periods
- Student ratings and comments from all your courses

Ask whether your department or institution would like any of these testimonial-type materials:

- Statements from peers or administrators who have observed your teaching
- Statements from peers who have reviewed your course materials
- Statements from peers on how well you have prepared your students for more advanced courses

- A statement from your chair or supervisor about your past and projected departmental contributions
- Statements from employers about graduates who studied a great deal with you
- Statements from service-learning clients on the impact of your students' projects
- Statements from your advisees and research mentees about how you have influenced them
- Statements and letters, solicited and unsolicited, from former students about your longer-term teaching impact

Finally, your reviewers may be interested in more data from and about your students:

- Student feedback that reflects improvement, perceived learning, or satisfaction—aside from student ratings and comments
- Samples of student work on graded assignments. Do include samples of varying quality with your feedback and your reasons for the grades you assigned.
- Surveys of student knowledge at the beginning and the end of a course
- Improvements in students' attitudes about the subject matter, as documented by final reflection or personal-growth essays or by attitudinal surveys you administer at the beginning and the end of the course
- Students' opinions of their success in achieving your learning outcomes (an extra student ratings form item if you can add one)
- A list of your successful mentees in the discipline
- Information on how you have influenced students' postgraduate and career choices
- Students' scores on standardized tests, especially the sections of national and licensing exams that reflect your courses

You can see examples of high-quality teaching portfolios in Seldin et al. (2010) or at http://cft.vanderbilt.edu/guides-sub-pages/teaching-portfolios/, http://www.mcgill.ca/edu-e3ftoption/portfolios, and http://cetalweb.utep.edu/sun/cetal/resources/portfolios/samples.htm.

Teaching portfolios are tenuous reflections of student learning. Their contents vary, and no doubt faculty put in whatever makes them look best. In addition, no clear guidelines exist for evaluating them, and they require a great deal of time from both the reviewee and the reviewers.

An alternative to the teaching portfolio is the course portfolio, a collection of materials summarizing how you planned, taught, managed, and now evaluate a particular course. You would assemble one on every course you regularly teach (Cerbin, 1994; Hutchings, 1998). It ultimately serves the same purpose—and has the same problems—as the teaching portfolio, but in contrast, the course portfolio never took off.

Measures of Student Learning in a Course

Standardized tests and student portfolios are used to measure student learning on the institutional, school, and program levels, but they do not transfer well to the course level. As mentioned earlier, course-specific standardized tests are very rarely available, and student portfolios are too cumbersome and time-consuming for colleagues and administrators to evaluate. A measure of learning in a course must be easy to determine and reduce to a single number; otherwise administrators will not use them in faculty reviews. If possible, an instrument should also do double-duty as a learning enhancement or major assessment that the instructor would normally give. (A longer version of this section appears in Nilson, 2013b).

The instruments presented in Table 28.2 can meet these conditions and have all been used to measure learning for one purpose or another. They are classified by when the instructor collects the data—only at the end of the course or at the beginning and the end (pre- and posttest)—and whether the data tap learning directly or indirectly, where *indirectly* means as perceived by students. Recall from the section on student ratings that few students correctly perceive

Table 28.2 Course-Level Measures of Student Learning Classified as End-of-Course-Only or Pre- and Posttest and Direct or Indirect Measures

Type	Indirect Measure	Direct Measure
End-of-course only	Perceived student learning gains (SALG)	Capstone paper, journal entry, or essay final exam (integrative or targeted)
Pre- and posttest	Knowledge surveys (student self-confidence)	First-week writing (ungraded) and correction exercise as final exam
		First-week essays (ungraded) and value-added essay final exam
		First-week final exam (ungraded) and final exam

Source: Table adapted from Nilson, L. B. (2013). Measuring student learning to document faculty teaching effectiveness. In J. E. Groccia & L. Cruz (Eds.), *To improve the academy: Vol. 32. Resources for faculty, instructional, and organizational development* (pp. 287–300). San Francisco, CA: Jossey-Bass.

their own learning (Bowman, 2011; Johnson, 2003; Weinberg et al., 2009; Williams & Ceci, 1997). In addition, Falchikov and Boud's (1989) meta-analysis of the student self-assessment literature tells us that students tend to rate their abilities more favorably than faculty do, especially in non-STEM and introductory courses. Therefore, indirect measures of learning are flawed. However, so are direct methods because the instruments (our exams and assignments) are not validated (Wieman, 2015).

Indirect, End-of-Course-Only Measures

Here you ask students about their *perceived* learning gains. The best-known and most widely used instrument of this kind is the Student Assessment of Learning Gains (SALG) survey at http://www.salgsite.org. Students assess not only their learning gains—general, conceptual, skill, attitudinal, and integrative—but also how much the main course components—class activities, assessments, specific learning methods, laboratories, and resources provided—helped them achieve those gains. Response options vary from "no gains" to "great gains" or from "no help" to "great help" on a 5-point scale. In validity tests of the current instrument, the student scores overall correlated moderately but significantly ($r = .41$) with student scores on the final exam. For unexplained reasons, the comparable correlations in specific topical areas ranged between .49 and 0.

You can easily adapt the questions to any course in any discipline, and SALG results have been submitted as evidence of student learning in faculty reviews. To obtain a single number, just average the scores on the relevant learning-gains items. The instrument also gives students a chance to reflect on what they have learned, which has value as a self-regulated learning activity.

Indirect, Pre- and Posttest Measures

We encountered knowledge surveys in chapter 7 as first-day diagnostic activities and chapter 20 as self-regulated learning exercises. They have also been used to measure student learning (Nuhfer & Kripp, 2003; Wirth & Perkins, 2005, 2008) and can claim scientific legitimacy as pretest and posttest instruments. However, they can underestimate student learning because students coming into a course often overestimate what they know (Boud et al., 2013; Falchikov & Boud, 1989; Kruger & Dunning, 1999). If you are teaching a somewhat advanced STEM course, you are on safer ground. You can reduce your measure of student learning to a single number by using one of the calculation methods in the section below on direct, pre- and posttest measures.

Direct, End-of-Course-Only Measures

This type of measure easily doubles as a final exam or capstone assignment. Of course, it should reflect at least your ultimate (end-of-course) student learning outcomes and perhaps some mediating outcomes as well. Here are two examples of this type of measure

in the literature. You can have students review and summarize the most important and valuable course material they learned in an integrative essay or journal entry (Atlas, 2007). Or you can ask them to imagine themselves in a real-world situation and explain how they would use the course material to solve the problem presented or perform the task at hand. For example, Weimer (2007) places her students in a job interview where they are asked to recount the most important things they learned in the course and demonstrate their skills in applying these things. You can report your students' learning as the average percentage score on the final exam or capstone assignment.

In terms of weaknesses, end-of-course-only measures cannot identify and remove the skills and knowledge that students brought into the course. It is also easy to inflate students' performance by grading more leniently, so peer reviewers should examine the questions students answered, the grading rubric, and some samples of student work.

Direct, Pre- and Posttest Measures

This is the most scientifically legitimate type of measure because it removes students' precourse skills and knowledge from the end-of-course assessment. You must assess your students' course-related knowledge and skills at the beginning of the course and again at the end using the same or very similar assessment. For example, Griffith (2010) gives her students an ungraded, in-class writing assignment the first week in her Miscarriage of Justice course. It emphasizes facts, terms, and processes they know little or nothing about. For the final, she places her students in the role of professor to critique and grade their first-week assignments. They correct their earlier errors, poor reasoning, and misconceptions and then answer the same questions again drawing on the course material. For another example, anthropology professor John ("Mike") Coggeshall (personal communication, 2010–2011) also gives his students an ungraded, in-class writing assignment the first week of class. He presents seven claims—some true but most commonly believed myths (e.g., that the arrival of the Europeans was responsible for Native Americans developing complex societies)—and asks students to agree or disagree and explain why. For the final exam, he has them critique and rewrite four of their original answers, drawing their evidence from the course and explaining how and why their thinking has changed, if it has. He grades these *value-added* essays on the quality of the evidence students use to justify their end-of-course position, which reflects his central ultimate learning outcome. For his faculty reviews, he reports the percentage of students who supported their positions with anthropological evidence, and all of his reviewers accept this figure as evidence of student learning.

A final option, one that works well for objective tests, is to give the final exam twice—first as an ungraded diagnostic test at the beginning of the course and later as the final. Give the diagnostic test in class—students will need little time to complete it (and tell them not to guess)—to prevent them from copying it, and don't let them photograph it. If you tell them later that they already took the final exam, they will try to remember all they can and watch for relevant material during the course. If you feel uncomfortable with this arrangement, use a previous final exam as the pretest if you have one that reflects the current content of your course. Also use a previous final exam if you teach online, as you do not want students downloading the current final.

Even though you do not grade the pretest, you do score it so you can calculate your students' learning gains during your course. Two methods are available, and these work for pre- and posttest knowledge surveys as well. The first method gives the percentage by which students increased their knowledge of the course subject matter during the course.

$$\frac{(\text{Average posttest\%} - \text{Average pretest\%}) \times 100}{\text{Average pretest\%}}$$

Therefore, if the students' average score was 20 percent on the pretest and 75 percent on the final, they increased their knowledge and skills in the subject matter by 275 percent during the course:

$$\frac{75 - 20}{20} = \frac{55}{20} = 2.75 \times 100 = 275$$

However, you obtain a more meaningful measure of student learning by calculating the *average normalized gain*, which is ratio of the *actual* average learning gain (posttest minus pretest) to the *possible* learning gain in the course (100 in the posttest minus the pretest) (Hake, 1998). This tells how much the students learned of all that they *could* have learned in the course:

$$\frac{(\text{Average posttest\%} - \text{Average pretest\%}) \times 100}{(100\% - \text{Average pretest\%})}$$

Given the same average percentage scores as in the example above, the students learned 68.75 percent of the knowledge and skills that they *could* have learned in the course:

$$\frac{(75 - 20)}{(100 - 20)} = \frac{55}{80} = .6875 \times 100 = 68.75$$

Tell your reviewers which equation you use and interpret the results correctly for them.

The Teaching Practices Inventory (TPI)

The newest measure of teaching effectiveness is an inventory of teaching practices that research documents as highly effective in promoting student learning. Developed by Wieman and Gilbert (2014) for use in science and mathematics courses, it accommodates most face-to-face classes (not seminars, instructional labs, or project-based class) in most disciplines (perhaps not the humanities) (Wieman, 2015). It was extensively tested on instructors and reviewed by many faculty and experts. For the most part, the TPI asks an instructor to check a box if he uses a certain practice in his course (form in Wieman & Gilbert, 2014). These practices fall into eight categories:

1. Course information provided to students
2. Supporting materials provided

3. In-class activities (whole class and small group), demonstrations, simulations, and videos
4. Homework assignments
5. Feedback, testing, and grading policies
6. Other (e.g., diagnostics, new methods, assessments, and student reflections and choice)
7. Training and supervision of TAs
8. Collaboration/sharing with other faculty and use of teaching and learning literature

While the form takes just 10 minutes to complete, a colleague should review the course documents and observe one or (preferably) more classes without prior notice to corroborate the instructor's responses. This colleague should receive training in the classroom observation protocol (Smith, Jones, Gilbert, & Wieman, 2013).

The TPI measures the means or methods of good teaching in an attempt to measure the ends of good teaching, which is student learning. So it is an indirect measure of learning. As such, it is possible that an instructor who uses good teaching methods either implements them poorly—for instance, poses low-level clicker questions or gives cryptic feedback on exams—or fails to relate well to students. The TPI does not pick up such flaws, and they can undermine learning.

Choosing among Alternatives

Every method we use to document teaching effectiveness has weaknesses as well as strengths. Keeping this in mind, departments and institutions would be wise to triangulate and use more than one method to base their promotion, tenure, and reappointment decisions.

■ A COMPREHENSIVE FACULTY EVALUATION SYSTEM

The key, and the challenge, to instituting any comprehensive faculty evaluation system is forging a departmental (or college) consensus on appropriate faculty activities, their relative value, the relative value of their components, and the relative value of their information sources. The decision-making process is all about publicly articulating values. Arreola's (2007) system, now used in whole or in part at hundreds of North American institutions, includes detailed, step-by-step guidelines for implementing faculty evaluation on a comprehensive scale, starting with these departmental decisions:

Step 1. Determine and list all the faculty activities worth evaluating at your institution: research, teaching, advising, community service, professional service, university service, and so on.

Step 2. Weight the importance of each activity in percentages that add up to 100 percent.

Step 3. Define each activity as a list of components—that is, observable or documentable products, performances, and achievements. For example, a department may agree to define teaching in terms of content expertise, instructional design skills, instructional delivery skills, impact on student learning, and course management.

Step 4. Operationalize each component—that is, break it down into measurable chunks. For example, faculty may break down content expertise into content currency, importance, and balance (more examples below).

Step 5. Weight the components of each role, again in percentages.

Step 6. Determine the best sources of evaluation information—for example, students, department peers, outside peers in specialized areas, the department chair, or someone else.

Step 7. Weight each information source by its appropriate worth. (A spreadsheet can do all the arithmetic required in steps 2, 4, and 6.)

Step 8. Determine how to gather the information from each source, such as by using forms or questionnaires.

Step 9. Select or design the appropriate policies, procedures, protocols, and forms for your system. Model forms are available in Chism (2007) and Arreola (2007).

Once the department sets the parameters and implements the system, each faculty member under review ends up with a composite rating, usually between 1.0 and 4.0 or between 1.0 and 5.0, that represents the collective judgment of that individual's performance in each faculty role (one for research, one for teaching, and so on). These numbers are weighted (as in step 2) and added to create an overall composite rating, which is then compared against the evaluative standards set by the top-level administration. Therefore, faculty are not compared against each other but against an absolute standard. In a 1.0-to-4.0 system where 1.0 denotes "unsatisfactory" and 4.0 means "exemplary" or "exceptional," 3.0 may designate the "acceptable" level. This system easily adapts to any review: reappointment, tenure, promotions, raises, and posttenure.

Steps 4 through 8 deserve clarification with an extended example. In step 4, content expertise was operationalized as currency, importance, and balance. Let's look at how the other components of teaching effectiveness suggested in step 3 might be operationalized.

Instructional Design Skills

Comprehensive syllabus
Well-organized course
Attainable, assessable student learning outcomes
Activities and assignments that help students achieve outcomes
Assessment instruments that measure students' achievement of outcomes

Instructional Delivery Skills

Well-organized classes (activities, demonstrations, presentations)
Sufficient student activity/engagement
Enthusiasm, creation of student interest
Clear communication (explanations)
Good public speaking skills

Impact on Student Learning

Tests and assignments challenging? (student perceptions)

Learning outcomes met? (student perceptions)
Want to learn more about the subject? (student perceptions)
Perceived learning gains (student perceptions)
Preparation for later courses
Pre- to postcourse learning gains

Course Management

Course paperwork processed on time
Books and other course materials available on time
Field trips well planned
Grades submitted on time
Other policies and procedures followed

To continue with this example, these components might be weighted by percentages and the best assessors of the operationalized components determined, as shown here:

Content expertise	15%	Department peers
Instructional design	30%	Students and department peers
Instructional delivery	20%	Students and department peers
Learning impact	30%	Students for "perceived"; department peers and faculty reviewee for "actual"
Course management	5% 100%	Department chair

Then the judgments of the assessors would be weighted proportionally and the assessment data specified, as this example shows:

Content expertise	15%	Department peers	1.00	Syllabi reviewed, peer observations
Instructional design	30%	Students	.50	Student ratings on design items
		Department peers	.50	Syllabi, activities and assignments, and graded work and tests reviewed

Instructional delivery	20%	Students	.75	Student ratings on delivery items
		Department peers	.25	Peer observations
Learning impact	30%	Students	.25	Perceived learning gains items
		Department peers	.50	Graded work and tests reviewed; peers' experience with students
		Reviewee	.25	Pre- to post-course learning gains
Course management	5%	Department chair	1.00	Chair's records

The final worksheet for evaluating a faculty member's teaching effectiveness might look something like this:

Content expertise	15%	Peers	1.00	$4 \times .15 \times 1 = .60$
Instructional design	30%	Students	.50	$3 \times .3 \times .50 = .45$
		Peers	.50	$3 \times .3 \times .50 = .45$
Instructional delivery	20%	Students	.75	$3 \times .2 \times .75 = .45$
		Peers	.25	$2 \times .2 \times .25 = .10$
Learning impact	30%	Students	.25	$3 \times .3 \times .25 = .23$
		Peers	.50	$4 \times .3 \times .50 = .60$
		Reviewee	.25	$4 \times .3 \times .25 = .30$
Course management	5%	Chair	1.00	$2 \times .05 \times 1 = .10$
Composite rating for teaching				*3.28*

To review, the first column on the far left is the component of the teaching role; the next columns, the percentage weight of that component, then the best assessing parties, and then the proportional weight of the judgment of each assessing party. The next column, which shows numbers from 2 to 4 in bold, designates the rating the faculty member received from each assessing party on the 1.0-to-4.0 scale, where 1.0 denotes "unsatisfactory" and 4.0, "exemplary" or "exceptional." The number is multiplied by the weight of the component, then by the weight of the assessing party. Finally, the numbers in the far right column are summed to obtain the overall composite rating. In this example, the faculty member under review achieves a 3.28, which exceeds the acceptable level of 3.0.

Some academics have complained that such a step-by-step system undermines professional and administrative judgment, but all it really does is eliminate a review party's discretion to say one thing and do another—for example, to claim to value teaching and service but to decide the fate of faculty careers solely on the research record. By demanding integrity and making the review process transparent, such a system can only benefit those who value, practice, and document teaching at its best.

■ COMPLEX BEYOND MEASURE

Documenting and evaluating teaching effectiveness is genuinely challenging. Just showing that you *try* to excel in your teaching requires considerable documentation. In addition, learning involves an array of outcomes—cognitive, affective, social, ethical, and psychomotor—and standardized tests cannot possibly tap them all. We have to rely on soft evidence like a teaching philosophy or teaching portfolio, flawed evidence such as measures of learning in a course or the Teaching Practices Inventory, or poor evidence like student ratings.

At its core, teaching is all about relationships between the instructor and every student in every one of her classes over many terms. Superimposed on these many relationships are those among all the students who ever interacted in a class. What instrument, what assembly of data could possibly capture this elusive, multilayered, multifaceted transaction in which one individual tries to induce other individuals to process new knowledge, acquire new skills, and change their thinking? In addition, the "other individuals," the students, bring their own unique backgrounds, abilities, aptitudes, attitudes, interests, and aspirations to the table, and the "one individual," which is you, can motivate, persuade, explain, inspire, and nurture learning only as far as each student will allow. You cannot bring everyone with you, but if you strive for teaching excellence, you can bring most students with you—enough to give your professional life magnificent meaning.

Instructional Support and Resources at Your Institution

Teaching well at the college level starts with becoming familiar with your institutional environment. Instructors, especially new ones, need to realize that they cannot and *should* not try to handle all the many challenges of their jobs single-handedly. Every college and university is a large, multilayered organization—a few rivaling small cities in size and complexity—each with its own unique subculture, norms and values, official power structure, informal power networks, and infrastructure of services and support units. Even seasoned faculty in a new institution feel unsettled as they anticipate unfamiliar policies, forms, procedures, expectations, and types of students.

Most colleges and universities offer a wealth of instructional support services and resources—the library and computer services being among the most obvious. But the instructional help available from some individuals and units may not be obvious from their titles or names alone. The people and campus offices described below are well worth your getting to know. The referral services they provide can save you countless hours, and the information they furnish can prevent costly, however innocent, mistakes.

FOR FACULTY, STAFF, AND STUDENTS

Colleagues, especially senior ones, are perhaps the most conveniently located and sometimes the most knowledgeable sources of information on discipline-specific issues, including how best to teach certain material, what to expect of students in specific courses, how to motivate students in a given subject, how to locate appropriate guest speakers, how to prepare for tenure and other faculty reviews, how to obtain special services or funding, and what assistance to request from department support staff. Colleagues are also excellent sources of informal feedback on teaching; most will be happy to serve as a classroom observer or reviewer of a recorded class. (Also see the "teaching and learning center" later).

Department chairs can offer broader, departmental perspectives on discipline-specific issues.

They are especially well informed on departmental curriculum matters and can advise you on proposals to develop new courses and revise established ones. They may also provide the best counsel on standards and procedures for promotion and tenure. Finally, since they have the opportunity to study the student evaluations of all the courses and sections in the department, they can help interpret your student ratings and written comments as well as suggest ways to improve them.

The *dean's office* of your college, school, or division can advise you about promotion and tenure matters, student characteristics, curriculum issues, and course design and development from a still broader perspective. Demographic and academic data about the student body will prove particularly valuable in helping you decide on the objectives, outcomes, design, and content for each of your courses. You will also need information about curriculum policies and procedures: What general education or breadth requirements do your courses satisfy? What percentage of students will enroll in a particular course because they are required to take it? How do you propose and get approval for a new course? What components and assignments must a course have to qualify for *honors, writing,* or any other special designation? Finally, the dean's office may be the place to turn for help with classroom matters—for example, if the classroom you are assigned doesn't meet your class size, ventilation, or technological needs, or if you need a room reserved for special class activities and sessions. In large universities, departments may control a set of classrooms and handle such matters.

The *library* is no longer just a place to find books. Having adapted to the technological age in record time, libraries have expanded into one-stop shops for electronic information as well as print resources, and librarians have evolved into the sentinels of information literacy.

You don't have to *go* to the library for many of these resources. Just visiting its website will give you easy access to an impressive range of academic search engines, indexes, and databases, such as Academic OneFile, LexisNexis, InfoTrac, OneSearch, Ingenta, Web of Science, and EBSCO Host, which allow you to find scholarly publications by subject, author, publication type, and other criteria. These resources can also help your students broaden their research horizons beyond Google, and librarians will teach your class how to use them for the assignments you have in mind.

While libraries still provide most traditional services, the card catalogue, library requests, and interlibrary loan are usually online. Beyond print and electronic resources, libraries also maintain a collection of instructionally useful videos, CDs, and DVDs.

A *teaching and learning, faculty development,* or *instructional development center* has become an increasingly common resource on research as well as teaching-oriented campuses. It usually provides instructional consultation and training services to faculty and TAs, such as class recordings, classroom observations, class interviews, midterm student feedback, advisory consultations, orientations for new instructors, teaching workshops, teaching webinars, teaching certificate programs, preparation for faculty reviews, and assistance in classroom research. Often these centers also maintain a library, run lecture series, publish a newsletter and teaching handbook, organize writing groups, consult to departments and colleges on curricula and assessment, consult on the teaching aspects of grants, award mini-grants for teaching innovations and travel to teaching conferences and workshops, and maintain a website with links to online teaching resources. Some house language testing and training programs for international TAs.

On a number of campuses, these centers also offer consultations and training in instructional technology and online teaching, such as the most effective pedagogical applications and the how-to's of available software (see chapter 4). Certainly those with "instructional development" or "technology" in the title do, and these may be housed within larger technology units. But most campuses have specialized, stand-alone teaching and learning centers.

A *center for academic computing, information technology,* or *instructional technology* is the most likely unit to handle the faculty's, as well as students' and staff's, computing needs, from setting up e-mail accounts to replacing old terminals. Its major functions are client support in both hardware and software and training workshops in commonly used office, technical, and instructional software. This support usually includes buying the software and licenses and installing the software on request. Almost all campuses have some brand of learning management systems, such as Blackboard and Canvas. These centers also transformed most traditional classrooms into smart classrooms equipped with software-rich computer terminals or laptop stations, LCD projectors, and DVD players. Scheduling, maintaining, and updating these classrooms are a full-time job.

Centers vary in how much instructional design they do for faculty who are teaching wholly or partly online. On one extreme, some universities expect instructors to learn the necessary software for website design, animation, photo and video digitizing and editing, and so forth in specialized workshops and on their own. On the other extreme are the institutions that employ instructional designers and technologists to do much of the materials development and all the technical work for the faculty.

A women's center often provides a wider variety of services than the lecture series, library, and support groups that you would expect. It is well worth asking if the one on your campus also sponsors self-development and health workshops, career planning forums, and book and study groups. No doubt it offers legal and policy information about sexual harassment as well as emotional support for those who may have a complaint. However, complaints are probably processed by the "equal opportunity" unit described below.

Multicultural and *racial/ethnic cultural centers* similarly may be a richer instructional resource than one might expect—and an essential one on today's highly diverse campuses. They usually offer symposia and lectures on cultural topics and coordinate multicultural celebrations and commemorations. Many of them maintain libraries of print materials and videos—most valuable if you are teaching multicultural subjects—and a few sponsor art exhibits and musical performances. They may also provide support services for students of colors.

Of particular value to faculty and staff are their cultural awareness programs, including diversity training workshops. These centers can also answer your private questions about the minority student population on your campus and cultural differences among various groups. They will help you resolve any concerns about relating to students of color in the classroom.

An *international center* typically administers study-abroad and international internship programs and sets up new ones to meet the demands of a rapidly changing world economy. For example, many universities have recently added programs in China, Southeast Asia, the Middle East, and India. Often in conjunction with an area studies center, this kind of unit may also equip students and faculty traveling abroad with some basic global competencies, such as information on the social and cultural differences between Americans and natives of the host country. In addition, the center provides acculturation counseling and support for international students and their families, as well as legal advice on visas, work permits, taxes, and so on. On some campuses, the international center is also responsible for ESL (English as a Second Language) or ESOL (English for Speakers of Other Languages) testing and courses.

An *equal opportunity center* may go by any number of titles, but you should look for key words such as *opportunity development, affirmative action, access, equality, equity,* or *civil rights.* Its purpose is to coordinate state and federally mandated programs designed to ensure equal opportunities for minorities, women, individuals with disabilities, and other disadvantaged groups. It also serves as a source of information for students, faculty, and staff members who may have questions or complaints related to equal opportunity in education, employment, and campus programs and activities. If a complaint is judged valid, it will also advise on grievance procedures.

Sexual harassment falls under the equal opportunity umbrella. Often in collaboration with a women's center (see above), an equal opportunity office disseminates information on the legal definition of sexual harassment, the institution's policy regarding it, specific types of harassment behavior, its prevalence, its prevention, procedures for filing a complaint or a grievance, and confidential support and counseling services.

A *disabilities services center* issues written certifications of students' learning and physical disabilities for instructors, although they probably do not conduct tests for these disabilities. As required by the Americans with Disabilities Act (ADA) of 1990, this type of center ensures that people with disabilities have equal access to public programs and services. Therefore, it also recommends the special accommodations, if any, that instructors should make for identified students in their teaching and testing.

Most accommodations are minor (e.g., an isolated test environment, a longer test period), and the center may provide special facilities for them (such as a proctored testing rooms). In any case, it will advise you about exactly what accommodations are needed. For the hearing-impaired classroom student, you may have to stand or sit where the student can lip-read. For a visually impaired classroom student, you may have to vocalize or verbally describe any visual materials you present or distribute to the class. Appropriate testing may require you to make a large-print copy of the exam or allow the students use of a reader, scribe, or computer during the test.

Online learning demands more extensive adaptations, although sometimes the student's own specialized computer hardware and software will take care of access. Still, instructors must be mindful to keep websites uncluttered and to provide captions or transcripts for audio materials and text alternatives for visual materials. Instructional designers can best advise on online course accessibility issues.

■ JUST FOR STUDENTS

The centers previously described may serve your own or your students' needs. Let's consider now the units and individuals who specialize in serving students.

Students seeking general academic counsel should be referred to their academic advisers; those requesting information or assistance with respect to a specific course should be sent to the instructor or the department. At times, however, students need help with other problems, some that most instructors are ill equipped to address. These include learning disabilities, math or test anxiety, severe writing problems, poor study and test-taking skills, weak academic backgrounds, emotional difficulties, and career planning questions. These cases call for a referral to a unit in the next group.

Almost all campuses have a facility designed to help students improve their academic skills. It is often called a *learning, learning skills, learning resources, academic assistance, academic support,* or *academic success center,* and its services typically include individual counseling in academic skills, individual and small group tutoring, and workshops in learning strategies, such as reading skills, study skills, note taking, test preparation, and test taking. Some tutoring may be geared to specific courses or subject matter that are known to give students trouble, such as calculus, chemistry, physics, biology, economics, and foreign languages. This type of center may also offer ESL testing and courses.

A *writing* or *communication program* may be housed in a learning center or comprise its own stand-alone unit. It is likely to provide individual and small-group tutoring in the mechanics of grammar and punctuation as well as the structure of exam essays, short papers, critical papers, and research papers. It may even schedule formal writing workshops. Staff members are trained not to outline or edit student work, but rather to show students how to master the stages of the writing process on their own. If "communication" is in the title, the unit may also help students improve their public speaking and presentation skills.

A *psychological* or *counseling center* is the place to refer students who manifest any type of psychological or emotional disorder. It gives free individual counseling for psychological, emotional, and sometimes academic problems, and it may coordinate group programs for personal growth, self-improvement, and self-awareness. If it is associated with a medical facility or it has a physician on staff, it may also prescribe drugs and administer shots.

A *career center* helps students identify and achieve their occupational goals. It typically provides assessment tests in skills and interests and resources for career exploration as well as information on internship opportunities and summer jobs. Workshops on job search strategies, résumé preparation, communication and decision-making skills, and job interview techniques may also be available.

Some centers hold campus job fairs and help graduates obtain jobs.

• • •

All of these campus units will welcome your requests for further information and will point you to their website or send you their brochures, newsletters, and any other materials they furnish for students. As service centers with a service orientation, they are well worth learning about. They exist to meet your and/or your students' needs—instructional, learning, professional, or personal. Unless their resources are already stretched beyond capacity, they actively pursue and benefit from increasing use. So if they can make your life as an instructor easier or more fulfilling, if they can save you class and office hour time, if they can handle any of the many student requests and problems that pass through your office door, by all means take advantage of their expert services.

Abrami, P. C., Bernard, R. M., Borokhovski, E., Wade, A., Surkes, M. A., Tamim, R., & Zhang, D. (2008). Instructional interventions affecting critical thinking skills and dispositions: A stage 1 meta-analysis. *Review of Educational Research, 78*(4), 1102–1134. doi: 10.3102/0034654308326084

Abrami, P. C., Bernard, R. M., Borokhovski, E., Waddington, D. I., Wade, C. A., & Persson, T. (2015). Strategies for teaching students to think critically: A meta-analysis. *Review of Educational Research, 85*(2), 275–314. doi: 10.3102/0034654314551063

Academic Success Center, Iowa State University, Ames, IA (2011). Exam prep: Test autopsy. Retrieved from http://www.asc.dso.iastate.edu/sites/default/files/resources/handouts/test/Exam%20Prep--Test%20Autopsy.pdf

Academic Success Center, Purdue University, West Lafayette, IN. (n.d.). Post exam reflection. https://www.purdue.edu/studentsuccess/academic/asc/documents/ASC_Handouts_PostExamSurvey.pdf

Achacoso, M. V. (2004). Post-test analysis: A tool for developing students' metacognitive awareness and self-regulation. In M. V. Achacoso & M. D. Svinicki (Eds.), *New directions for teaching and learning, No. 100: Alternative strategies for evaluating student learning* (pp. 115–119). San Francisco, CA: Jossey-Bass.

Adelman, C. (2015). To imagine a verb: The language and syntax of learning outcomes statements. National Institute for Learning Outcomes Assessment, Occasional Paper 24. Retrieved from http://learningoutcomesassessment.org/documents/Occasional_Paper_24.pdf

Adler, M. J. (1940). *How to read a book: The art of getting a liberal education.* New York, NY: Simon & Schuster.

Albanese, M. A., & Mitchell, S. (1993). Problem-based learning: A review of the literature on its outcomes and implementation issues. *Academic Medicine, 68*(1), 52–81.

Albanese, M. A., & Dast, L. (2014). Problem-based learning: Outcomes evidence from the health professions. *Journal of Excellence in College Teaching, 25*(3&4), 239–252.

Alexander, M. M., Lynch, J. E., Rabinovich, T., & Knutel, P. G. (2014). Snapshot of a hybrid learning environment. *Quarterly Review of Distance Education, 15*(1), 9–21.

Alexander, P. (1996). The past, the present, and the future of knowledge research: A reexamination of the role of knowledge in learning and instruction. *Educational Psychologist, 31*(2), 89–92.

Allen, D. E., & Duch, B. J. (1998). *Thinking toward solutions: Problem-based learning activities for general biology.* New York, NY: Saunders.

Allen, M., Witt, P. L., & Wheeless, L. R. (2006). The role of teacher immediacy as a motivational factor in student learning: Using a meta-analysis to test a causal model. *Communication Education, 55*(1), 21–31.

Allen, R. D. (1981). Intellectual development and the understanding of science: Applications of William Perry's theory to science teaching. *Journal of College Science Teaching, 10,* 94–97.

Allen, W., Epps, E., & Haniff, N. (1991). *College in black and white: African American students in predominantly white and historically black public universities.* Albany, NY: SUNY Press.

Allwardt, D. (2009, April). *Using wikis for collaborative writing assignments: Best practices and fair warnings.* Poster session presented at the Third Annual Innovations in Teaching Forum, Western Illinois University, Macomb.

Amador, J. A., Miles, L., & Peters, C. B. (2006). *The practice of problem-based learning: A guide to implementing PBL in the college classroom.* San Francisco, CA: Jossey-Bass/Anker.

Ambrose, S. A., Bridges, M. W., DiPietro, M., Lovett, M. C., & Norman, M. K. (2010). *How learning works: Seven research-based principles for smart teaching.* San Francisco, CA: Jossey-Bass.

Anderman, L., Freeman, T., & Mueller, C. (2007). The "social" side of social context: Interpersonal and affiliative dimensions of students' experiences and academic dishonesty. In E. Anderman & T. Murdock (Eds.), *Psychology of academic cheating* (pp. 203–228). Burlington, MA: Elsevier.

Anderson, J. A., & Adams, M. (1992). Acknowledging the learning styles of diverse populations: Implications for instructional design. In L. Border & N. V. N. Chism (Eds.), *New directions for teaching and learning: No. 49. Teaching for diversity* (pp. 19–33). San Francisco: Jossey-Bass.

Anderson, L. W., & Krathwohl, D. R. (2000). *A taxonomy for learning, teaching, and assessment: A revision of Bloom's taxonomy of educational objectives.* White Plains, NY: Longman.

Andrade, H., & Du, Y. (2007). Student responses to criteria-referenced self-assessment. *Assessment and Evaluation in Higher Education, 32*(2), 159–181.

Angelo, T. A. (1991a). Introduction and overview: From classroom assessment to classroom research. In T. A. Angelo (Ed.), *New directions for teaching and learning: No. 46. Classroom research: Early lessons from success* (pp. 7–15). San Francisco, CA: Jossey-Bass.

Angelo, T. A. (1991b). Ten easy pieces: Assessing higher learning in four dimensions. In T. A. Angelo (Ed.), *New directions for teaching and learning: No. 46. Classroom research: Early lessons from success* (pp. 17–31). San Francisco, CA: Jossey-Bass.

Angelo, T. A., & Cross, K. P. (1993). *Classroom assessment techniques: A handbook for college teachers* (2nd ed.). San Francisco, CA: Jossey-Bass.

Arocha, J. F., & Patel, V. L. (1995). Novice diagnostic reasoning in medicine: Accounting of clinical evidence. *Journal of the Learning Sciences, 4,* 355–384.

Arons, A. B. (1993). Guiding insight and inquiry in the introductory physics lab. *Physics Teacher, 31*(5), 278–282.

Arreola, R. A. (2007). *Developing a comprehensive faculty evaluation system: A guide to designing, building, and operating large-scale faculty evaluations systems* (3rd ed.). San Francisco, CA: Jossey-Bass/Anker.

Arum, R., & Roksa, J. (2011). *Academically adrift: Limited learning on college campuses.* Chicago, IL: University of Chicago Press.

Aslanian, C. B. (2001). *Adult students today.* New York, NY: College Board.

Astin, A. W., Vogelgesang, L. J., Ikeda, E. K., & Yee, J. A. (2000). *How service learning affects students.* Los Angeles, CA: Higher Education Research Institute.

Atkinson, R. K., Levin, J. R., Kiewra, K. A., Meyers, T., Kim, S., Atkinson, L., Renandya, W. A., & Hwang, Y. (1999). Matrix and mnemonic text-processing adjuncts: Comparing and combining their components. *Journal of Educational Psychology, 91,* 342–357.

Atlas, J. L. (2007). The end of the course: Another perspective. *Teaching Professor, 21*(6), 3.

Atteberry, E. (2013, December 5). "Flipped classrooms" may or may not have any impact on learning. *USAToday.* Retrieved from http://www.usatoday.com/story/news/nation/2013/10/22/flipped-classrooms-effectiveness/3148447/

Aulls, M. W. (2002). The contributions of co-occurring forms of classroom discourse and academic activities to curriculum events and instruction. *Journal of Educational Psychology, 94,* 520–538.

Ausubel, D. (1968). *Educational psychology: A cognitive view.* New York, NY: Holt.

Babcock, P., & Marks, M. (2011). The falling time cost of college: Evidence from half a century of time use data. *Review of Economics and Statistics, 93*(2), 468–478. doi: 10.1162/REST_a_00093

Baldwin, R. G. (1997–1998). Academic civility begins in the classroom. *Essays on Teaching Excellence, 9*(8), 1–2.

Ballantine, J., & Risacher, J. (1993, November). *Coping with annoying classroom behaviors.* Paper presented at the 13th annual Lilly Conference on College Teaching, Oxford, OH.

Ballard, M. (2007). Drawing and questioning the syllabus. *National Teaching and Learning Forum, 16*(5), 5–6.

Bandura, A. (1977). Self-efficacy: Toward a unifying theory of behavioral change. *Psychological Review, 84*(2), 191–215.

Bandura, A. (1997). *Self-efficacy: The exercise of control.* New York, NY: Freeman.

Banta, T. W., Black, K. E., & Kline, K. A. (2000). PBL 2000 plenary address offers evidence for and against problem-based learning. *PBL Insight, 3*(3). Retrieved from http://www.samford.edu/pbl

Barkley, E. F. (2009). *Student engagement techniques: A handbook for college faculty.* San Francisco, CA: Jossey-Bass.

Barkley, E. F., Major, C. H., & Cross, K. P. (2014). *Collaborate learning techniques: A handbook for faculty.* San Francisco, CA: Jossey-Bass.

Baron, N. (2015, February 13). The plague of tl;dr. *Chronicle of Higher Education Review.* Retrieved from http://chronicle.com/article/The-Plague-of-tl-dr/151635/

Barrineau, N. W. (2001). Class preparation and summary note cards. *National Teaching and Learning Forum, 10*(4), 5–6.

Bauerlein, M. (2009). *The dumbest generation: How the digital age stupefies young Americans and jeopardizes our future (or Don't trust anyone under 30).* New York, NY: Tarcher.

Baugh, N. G., & Mellott, K. G. (1998). Clinical concept mapping as preparation for student nurses' clinical experiences. *Journal of Nursing Education, 37*(6), 253–256.

Baughin, J., Brod, E. F., & Page, D. L. (2002). Primary trait analysis: A tool for classroom-based assessment. *College Teaching, 50*(2), 75–80.

Baume, D., & Baume, C. (2008). *Powerful ideas in teaching and learning.* Wheatley, UK: Oxford Brookes University.

Baxter Magolda, M. B. (1992). *Knowing and reasoning in college: Gender-related patterns in students' intellectual development.* San Francisco, CA: Jossey-Bass.

Bean, J. C. (2011). *Engaging ideas: A professor's guide to integrating writing, critical thinking, and active learning in the classroom* (2nd ed.). San Francisco, CA: Jossey-Bass.

Beaudry, J., & Wilson, P. (2010). Concept mapping and formative assessment: Elements supporting literacy and learning. In P. L. Torres & C. V. Marriott (Eds.), *Handbook of research on collaborative learning using concept mapping* (pp. 449–473). Hershey, PA: Information Science Reference.

Beichner, R. J., Saul, J. M., Abbott, D. S., Morse, J. J., Deardorff, D. L., Allain, R. J., Bonham, S. W., Dancy, M. H., & Risley, J. S. (2007). *The student-centered activities for large enrollment undergraduate programs (SCALE-UP) project.* Retrieved from http://www.per-central.org/document/ServeFile.cfm?ID=4517&DocID=183

Beissner, K. L. (1992). Use of concept mapping to improve problem solving. *Journal of Physical Therapy, 6*(1), 22–27.

Belanoff, P., & Dickson, M. (1991). *Portfolios: Process and product.* Portsmouth, NH: Boynton/Cook & Heinemann.

Belbin, R. M. (2004). *Team roles at work.* Amsterdam, NL: Elsevier.

Bell, P., & Volckmann, D. (2011). Knowledge surveys in general chemistry: Confidence, overconfidence and performance. *Journal of Chemical Education, 88*(11), 1469–1476.

Benander, R., Denton, J., Page, D., & Skinner, C. (2000). Primary trait analysis: Anchoring assessment in the classroom. *Journal of General Education, 49*(4), 280–302.

Benford, R., & Lawson, A. E. (2001). *Relationships between effective inquiry use and the development of scientific reasoning skills in college biology labs.* Report to the National Science Foundation (Grant DUE 9453610).

Bergtrom, G. (2006). Clicker sets as learning objects. *Interdisciplinary Journal of Knowledge and Learning Objects, 2.* Retrieved from http://ijklo.org/Volume2/v2p105–110 Bergtrom.pdf

Berk, R. A. (2005). Survey of 12 strategies to measure teaching effectiveness. *International Journal of Teaching and Learning in Higher Education, 17*(1), 48–62.

Berke, A., & Kastberg, S. S. (1998, March). *Writing a teaching philosophy: The beginning of a teaching portfolio.* Paper presented at the 19th Annual Meeting of the Sharing Conference of the Southern Regional Faculty and Instructional Development Consortium, Kennesaw, GA.

Bernhardt, S. A. (1992). Teaching English: Portfolio evaluation. *Clearing House, 65*(6), 333–334.

Berry, M. J., & Westfall, A. (2015). Dial D for distraction: The making and breaking of cell phone policies in the college classroom. *College Teaching, 63*(2), 62–71.

Berry, P., Thornton, B., & Baker, R. (2006). Demographics of digital cheating: Who cheats, and what we can do about it. In M. Murray (Ed.), *Proceedings of the Ninth Annual Conference of the Southern Association for Information Systems* (pp. 82–87). Jacksonville, FL: Jacksonville University, Davis College of Business.

Berry, W. (2008). Surviving lecture: A pedagogical alternative. *College Teaching, 56*(3), 149–153.

Beyers, C. (2008). The hermeneutics of student evaluations. *College Teaching, 56*(2), 102–106.

Biggs, J. (2003). *Teaching for quality learning at university* (2nd ed.). Berkshire, UK: Society for Research into Higher Education and Open University Press.

Biktimirov, E. N., & Nilson, L. B. (2006). Show them the money: Using mind mapping in the introductory finance course. *Journal of Financial Education, 32,* 72–86.

Biktimirov, E. N., & Nilson, L. B. (2007). Adding animation and interactivity to finance courses with learning objects. *Journal of Financial Education, 33,* 35–47.

Bjork, E. L., & Bjork, R. A. (2011). Making things hard on yourself, but in a good way: Creating desirable difficulties to enhance learning. In M. A. Gernsbacher & J. Pomerantz (Eds.), *Psychology and the real world: Essays illustrating fundamental contributions to society* (2nd ed., pp. 56–64). New York, NY: Worth.

Bjork, R. A. (1994). Memory and metamemory considerations in the training of human beings. In J. Metcalfe & A. Shimamura (Eds.), *Metacognition: Knowing about knowing* (pp. 185–205). Cambridge, MA: MIT Press.

Bjork, R. A. (2013). Desirable difficulties perspective on learning. In H. Pashler (Ed.), *Encyclopedia of the mind.* Thousand Oaks, CA: Sage. Retrieved from http://bjork-lab.psych.ucla.edu/RABjorkPublications.php

Bligh, D. A. (2000). *What's the use of lectures?* San Francisco, CA: Jossey-Bass.

Bloom, B. (1956). *Taxonomy of educational objectives: The classification of educational goals. Vol. 1: Cognitive domain.* New York, NY: McKay.

Blue, T. (2003, March 14). "I don't know HOW to read this book!" *Irascible Professor.* Retrieved from http://irascibleprofessor.com/comments-03–14–03-epr.htm

Boice, R. (2000). *Advice for new faculty members: Nihil nimus.* Needham Heights, MA: Allyn & Bacon.

Bok, D. C. (2006). *Our underachieving colleges.* Princeton, NJ: Princeton University Press.

Bonwell, C. (2012). A disciplinary approach for teaching critical thinking. *National Teaching and Learning Forum, 21*(2), 1–7.

Bonwell, C. C., & Eison, J. A. (1991). *Active learning: Creating excitement in the classroom* (ASHE-ERIC Higher Education Report No. 1). Washington, DC: George Washington University, School of Education and Human Development.

Boud, D., Lawson, R., & Thompson, D. G. (2013). Does student engagement in self-assessment calibrate their judgment over time? *Assessment and Evaluation in Higher Education, 38*(8), 941–956.

Bourland, J. (1996, March). Hollywood hustle. *Parenting, 53,* 29.

Bowen, J. A. (2012). *Teaching naked: How moving technology out of your college classroom will improve student learning.* San Francisco, CA: Jossey-Bass.

Bowen, W. (2013). *Higher education in the digital age.* Princeton, NJ: Princeton University Press.

Bowman, N. A. (2011, April 11). *The validity of college seniors' self-reported gains as a proxy for longitudinal growth.* Paper presented at the Annual Meetings of the American Educational Research Association, New Orleans, LA.

Brabrand, C. (Co-producer/Writer/Director), & Andersen, J. (Co-producer). (2006). *Teaching teaching and understanding understanding* [DVD]. Denmark: University of Aarhus and Daimi Edutainment.

Bradley, K. (2007). Reading noncompliance: A case study and reflection. *MountainRise, 4*(1). Retrieved from http://mountainrise.wcu.edu/archive/vol4no1/html/bradley.pdf

Braga, M., Paccagnella, M., & Pellizzari, M. (2014). Evaluating students' evaluations of professors. *Economics of Education Review, 41,* 71–88.

Bransford, J. D., Brown, A. L., & Cocking, R. R. (1999). *How people learn: Brain, mind, experience, and school.* Washington, DC: National Academy Press.

Brauchle, K. C. (2000). Plagiarism and the Internet: Cut and paste your way to success. *National Teaching and Learning Forum, 10*(1), 10–11.

Braumoeller, B. F., & Gaines, B. J. (2001). Actions do speak louder than words: Deterring plagiarism with the use of plagiarism-detection software. *PS: Political Science and Politics, 34*(4), 835–839.

Braun, N. M. (2004). Critical thinking in the business curriculum. *Journal of Education for Business, 79*(4), 232–236.

Breslow, L. (2010, September/October). Wrestling with pedagogical change: The TEAL Initiative at MIT. *Change, 42,* 23–29.

Bridges, E. M. (1992). *Problem-based learning for administrators.* Eugene, OR: ERIC Clearinghouse on Educational Management.

Brinkmann, A. (2003). Mind mapping as a tool in mathematics education. *Mathematics Teacher, 96,* 96–101.

Briscoe, C., & LaMaster, S. U. (1991). Meaningful learning in college biology through concept mapping. *American Biology Teacher, 53*(4), 214–219.

Brookfield, S. D. (2012). *Teaching for critical thinking: Tools and techniques to help students question their assumptions.* San Francisco, CA: Jossey-Bass.

Brookfield, S. D., & Preskill, S. (2005). *Discussion as a way of teaching: Tools and techniques for democratic classrooms* (2nd ed.). San Francisco, CA: Jossey-Bass.

Brookhart, S. M. (1999). *The art and science of classroom assessment: The missing part of pedagogy* (ASHE-ERIC Higher Education Report, 27(1)). Washington, DC: George Washington University, Graduate School of Education and Human Development.

Brown, P. C., Roediger III, H. L., & McDaniel, M. A. (2014). *Making it stick: The science of successful learning.* Cambridge, MA: Belknap Press of Harvard University Press.

Brown, T., & Rose, B. (2008, November 19–21). *Use of meta-cognitive wrappers for field experiences.* Session presented at the National Association of Geoscience Teachers Workshops: The Role of Metacognition in Teaching Geoscience, Carleton College, Northfield, MN. Retrieved from http://serc.carleton.edu/NAGTWorkshops/metacognition/tactics/28926.html

Browne, M. N., & Keeley, S. M. (2010). *Asking the right questions: A guide to critical thinking* (9th ed.). Upper Saddle River, NJ: Prentice Hall, Pearson.

Bruff, D. (2007). Clickers: A classroom innovation. *Thriving in Academe, 25*(1), 5–8.

Bruff, D. (2009). *Teaching with classroom response systems: Creating active learning environments.* San Francisco, CA: Jossey-Bass.

Bruff, D. (2016). Clickers-Agile learning: Derek Bruff's blog on teaching and technology. Retrieved from http://derekbruff.org/?page_id=2

Budesheim, T. L., & Lundquist, A. R. (2000). Consider the opposite: Opening minds through in-class debates on course-related controversies. *Teaching of Psychology, 26,* 106–120.

Bugeja, M. J. (2007, January 26). Distractions in the wireless classroom. *Chronicle of Higher Education.* Retrieved from http://chronicle.com/jobs/news/2007/01/2007012601c.htm

Burchfield, C. M., & Sappington, J. (2000). Compliance with required reading assignments. *Teaching of Psychology, 27*(1), 58–60.

Burd, E. L., Smith, S. P., & Reisman, S. (2015). Exploring business models for MOOCs in higher education. *Innovative Higher Education, 40*(1), 37–49.

Bureau, D., & McRoberts C. (2001). Millennials: The corrective generation? *Perspectives,* 8–12.

Burrowes, P. A. (2003). A student-centered approach to teaching general biology that really works: Lord's constructivist model put to a test. *American Biology Teacher, 65*(7), 491–502.

Burt, D. (2010, December 1). Cheating confusion persists. *Yale Daily News.* Retrieved from http://yaledailynews.com/blog/2010/12/01/cheating-confusion-persists/

Butler, A. C., Marsh, E. J., Slavinsky, J. P., & Baraniuk, R. G. (2014). Integrating cognitive science and technology improves learning in a STEM classroom. *Educational Psychology Review.* doi:10.1007/s10648–014–9256–4

Buzan, T. (1974). *Use your head.* London, UK: BBC.

Cameron, J., & Pierce, W. D. (1994). Reinforcement, reward, and intrinsic motivation: A meta-analysis. *Review of Educational Research, 64,* 363–423.

Campus Compact. (2012). *Creating a culture of assessment: 2012 annual member survey.* Boston, MA: Author. Retrieved from http://www.compact.org/wp-content/uploads/2013/04/Campus-Compact-2012-Statistics.pdf

Campus Compact (2014). *Membership.* Retrieved from http://www.compact.org/membership/

Canfield, P. J. (2002). An interactive, student-centered approach to teaching large-group sessions in veterinary clinical pathology. *Journal of Veterinary Medical Education, 29*(2), 105–110.

Cardon, L. S. (2014). Diagnosing and treating millennial student disillusionment. *Change, 46*(6), 34–40.

Carey, B. (2014, September 4). Why flunking exams is actually a good thing. *New York Times Magazine.* Retrieved from http://www.nytimes.com/2014/09/07/magazine/why-flunking-exams-is-actually-a-good-thing.html?_r=0

Carlile, O., & Jordan, A. (2005). It works in practice but will it work in theory? The theoretical underpinnings of pedagogy. In G. O'Neill, S. Moore, & R. McMullan (Eds.), *Emerging issues in the practice of university teaching* (pp. 11–25). Dublin: All Ireland Society for Higher Education.

Carlson, S. (2005, October 7). The Net generation goes to college. *Chronicle of Higher Education,* p. A34.

Carnes, M. C. (2014). *Minds on fire: How role-immersion games transform college.* Cambridge, MA: Harvard University Press.

Carnevale, D. (1999, November 12). How to proctor from a distance: Experts say professors need savvy to prevent cheating in online courses. *Chronicle of Higher Education,* pp. A47–A48.

Carney, A. G., Fry, S. W., Gabriele, R. V., & Ballard, M. (2008). Reeling in the big fish: Changing pedagogy to encourage the completion of reading assignments. *College Teaching, 56*(4), 195–200.

Carrell, S. E., & West, J. E. (2010). Does professor quality matter? Evidence from random assignment of students to professors. *Journal of Political Economy, 118*(3), 409–432.

Carrier, C. A. (1983). Notetaking research implications for the classroom. *Journal of Instructional Development, 6*(3), 19–26.

Carroll, J. (2003a, May 2). Dealing with nasty students: The sequel. *Chronicle of Higher Education,* p. C5.

Carroll, J. (2003b, October 14). Constructing your in-class persona. *Chronicle of Higher Education.* Retrieved from http://chronicle.com/jobs/2003/10/2003101401c.html

Case, K., Bartsch, R., McEnery, L., Hall, S., Hermann, A., & Foster, D. (2008). Establishing a comfortable classroom from day one: Student perceptions of the reciprocal interview. *College Teaching, 56*(4), 210–214.

Cashin, W. E. (1995). *Student ratings of teaching: The research revisited* (IDEA Paper No. 32). Manhattan: Kansas State University, Center for Faculty Evaluation and Development.

Centra. J. A. (1993). *Reflective faculty evaluation: Enhancing teaching and determining faculty effectiveness.* San Francisco, CA: Jossey-Bass.

Cepeda, N. J., Pashler, H., Vul, E., Wixted, J. T., & Rohrer, D. (2006). Distributive practice in verbal recall tasks: A review and quantitative synthesis. *Psychological Bulletin, 132,* 354–380.

Cerbin, W. (1994). The course portfolio as a tool for continuous improvement of teaching and learning. *Journal of Excellence in College Teaching, 5,* 95–105.

Chambliss, D. F., & Takacs, C. G. (2014). *How college works.* Cambridge, MA: Harvard University Press.

Chi, M. T. H., Glaser, R., & Rees, E. (1982). Expertise in problem solving. In R. Steinberg (Ed.), *Advances in the psychology of human intelligence* (pp. 7–76). Mahwah, NJ: Erlbaum.

Chiaramonte, P. (1994). The agony and the ecstasy of case teaching. *Reaching through Teaching, 7*(2), 1–2.

Chickering, A. W., & Gamson, Z. F. (1987, March). Seven principles for good practice in undergraduate education. *AAHE Bulletin,* 3-7. Retrieved from http://files.eric.ed.gov/fulltext/ED282491.pdf

Chism, N. V. N. (1997–1998). Developing a philosophy of teaching statement. *Essays on Teaching Excellence, 9*(3), 1–2.

Chism, N. V. N. (2007). *Peer review of teaching: A sourcebook* (2nd ed.). San Francisco, CA: Jossey-Bass.

Chrisler, J. C. (2013). Teaching about gender: Rewards and challenges. *Psychology of Men and Masculinity, 14,* 264–267.

Chun, M. (2010). Taking teaching to (performance) task: Linking pedagogical and assessment practices. *Change, 42*(2), 22–29.

Clark, J. (2008). PowerPoint and pedagogy: Maintaining student interest in university lectures. *College Teaching, 56*(1), 39–45.

Clark, J. M., & Paivio, A. (1991). Dual coding theory and education. *Educational Psychology Review, 3*(3), 149–210.

Clark, R. E. (2001). *Learning from media: Arguments, analysis and evidence.* Charlotte, NC: Information Age Publishing.

Clayson, D. E. (2009). Student evaluations of teaching: Are they related to what students learn? A meta-analysis and review of the literature. *Journal of Marketing Education, 31*(1), 16–30. Retrieved from http://jmd.sagepub.com/content/31/1/16.full.pdf+html

Clayson, D. E. (2011). *A multi-disciplined review of the student teacher evaluation process.* Retrieved from http://business.uni.edu/clayson/Ext/SETSummary2011.doc

Clayson, D. E., Frost, T. E., & Sheffet, M. J. (2006). Grades and the student evaluation of instruction: A test of the reciprocity effect. *Academy of Management Learning and Education, 5*(1), 52–65.

Clayson, D. E., & Haley, D. A. (2011, Summer). Are students telling us the truth? A critical look at the student evaluation of teaching. *Marketing Education Review, 21,* 101–112.

Clayson, D. E., & Haley, D. A. (2013). An introduction to multitasking and texting: Prevalence and impact on grades and GPA in marketing classes. *Journal of Marketing Education, 35,* 26–40. Retrieved from http://jmd.sagepub.com/content/35/1/26.full.pdf+html

Clayton, P. H., Bringel, R. G., & Hatcher, J. A. (Eds.). (2013). *Research on service-learning: Conceptual frameworks and assessment, Vol. 2A. Students and faculty.* Sterling, VA: Stylus.

Cliburn, J. W. (1990). Concepts to promote meaningful learning. *Journal of College Science Teaching, 19*(4), 212–217.

Coffield, F., with Costa, C., Müller, W., & Webber, J. (2014). *Beyond bulimic learning: Improving teaching in further education.* London: Institute of Education Press.

Coffield, F., Moseley, D., Hall, E., & Ecclestone, K. (2004). *Learning styles and pedagogy in post-16 learning: A systematic and critical review.* London, UK: Learning and Skills Research Centre. Retrieved from http://www.lsda.org.uk/files/PDF/1543.pdf

Cohen, P. A. (1980). Effectiveness of student-rating feedback for improving college instruction: A meta-analysis of findings. *Research in Higher Education, 13*(4), 321–341.

Cohen, P. A. (1981). Student ratings of instruction and student achievement: A meta-analysis of multi-section validity studies. *Review of Educational Research, 51,* 281–309.

Collison, M. (1990a, January 17). Apparent rise in students' cheating has college officials worried. *Chronicle of Higher Education,* pp. A33–A34.

Collison, M. (1990b, October 24). Survey at Rutgers suggests that cheating may be on the rise at large universities. *Chronicle of Higher Education,* pp. A31–A32.

Colvin, K. F., Champaign, J., Liu, A., Zhou, Q., Fredericks, C., & Pritchard, D. E. (2014). Learning in an introductory physics MOOC: All cohorts learn equally, including an on-campus class. *International Review of Research in Open and Distance Learning, 15*(4). Retrieved from http://www.irrodl.org/index.php/irrodl/article/view/1902/3009

Connor-Greene, P. (2000). Assessing and promoting student learning: Blurring the line between teaching and learning. *Teaching of Psychology, 27*(2), 84–88.

Cornelius, T. L., & Owen-DeSchryver, J. (2008). Differential effects of full and partial notes on learning outcomes and attendance. *Teaching of Psychology, 35*(1), 6–12. Retrieved from http://www.unc.edu/~vsathy/fullorpartialnotes.pdf

Cornelius-White, J. (2007). Learner-centered teacher-student relationships are effective: A meta-analysis. *Review of Educational Research, 77*(1):113-143. doi: 10.3102/003465430298563

Cortright, R. N., Collins, H. L., & DiCarlo, S. E. (2005). Peer instruction enhanced meaningful learning: Ability to solve novel problems. *Advances in Physiology Education, 29*(2), 107–111.

Cortright, R. N., Collins, H. L., Rodenbaugh, D. W., & DiCarlo, S. E. (2003). Student retention of course content is improved by collaborative-group testing. *Advances in Physiology Education, 27*(3), 102–108.

Costa, C. (2014). Teaching and learning in context . . . with a little help from a web. In F. Coffield (Ed.), *Beyond bulimic learning: Improving teaching in further education* (pp. 117–134). London, UK: Institute of Education.

Cox, R. D. (2011). *The college fear factor: How students and professors misunderstand one another.* Cambridge, MA: Harvard University Press.

Crenshaw, D. (2008). *The myth of multitasking: How "doing it all" gets nothing done.* San Francisco, CA: Jossey-Bass.

Cross, K. P. (1988). In search of zippers. *AAHE Bulletin, 40*(10), 3–7.

Crouch, C. E., & Mazur, E. (2001). Peer instruction: Ten years of experience and results. *American Journal of Physics, 69,* 970–977.

Crowley, M. L. (1993). Student mathematics portfolio: More than a display case. *Mathematics Teacher, 86*(7), 544–547.

Crutchfield, T. N., & Klamon, K. (2014). Assessing the dimension and outcomes of an effective teammate. *Journal of Education for Business, 89*(6), 285–291.

Curren, J. M., & Rosen, D. E. (2006). Student attitudes toward college courses: An examination of influences and intentions. *Journal of Marketing Education, 28*(2), 135–148.

Cuseo, J. B. (2002). *Igniting student involvement, peer interactions, and teamwork.* Stillwater, OK: New Forums Press.

Dallimore, E. J., Hertenstein, J. H., & Platt, M. B. (2006). Non-voluntary class participation in graduate discussion courses: Effects of grading and cold-calling on student comfort. *Journal of Management Education, 30*(2), 354–377.

Dallimore, E. J., Hertenstein, J. H., & Platt, M. B. (2008). Using discussion pedagogy to enhance oral and written communication skills. *College Teaching, 56*(3), 163–170.

Daniel, D. B., & Willingham, D. T. (2012). Electronic textbooks: Why the rush? *Science, 333,* 156–1571. Retrieved from http://www.fas.harvard.edu/~bok_cen/sfn/2013/science30mar2012.pdf

Daniel, D. B., & Woody, W. D. (2013). E-textbooks at what cost? Performance and use of electronic v. print texts. *Computers and Education, 62,* 18–23. Retrieved from http://www.sciencedirect.com/science/article/pii/S0360131512002448

Daniels, A. C. (2000). *Bringing out the best in people: How to apply the astonishing power of positive reinforcement.* New York, NY: McGraw-Hill.

Daniels, A. C., & Daniels, J. E. (2004). *Performance management: Changing behavior that drives organizational effectiveness* (4th ed.). Atlanta, GA: Performance Management Publications.

Davidson, C. (2014, March 14). Changing higher education to change the world. *Chronicle of Higher Education.* Retrieved from http://chronicle.com/blogs/future/2014/03/14/changing-higher-education-to-change-the-world/

Davidson, H. (2008). *Welcome to Hall Davidson's site.* Retrieved from http://www.halldavidson.com/

Davidson, N., & Major, C. H. (2014). Boundary crossings: Cooperative learning, collaborative learning, and problem-based learning. *Journal of Excellence on College Teaching, 25*(3&4), 7–55.

Davis, B. G. (2009). *Tools for teaching* (2nd ed.). San Francisco, CA: Jossey-Bass.

Davis, G. R. (2015). *Syllabus for BIO 342: Human Physiology, Wofford University.* Retrieved from http://webs.wofford.edu/davisgr/bio342/index.htm

Davis, J. R., & Arend, B. D. (2013). *Facilitating seven ways of learning: A resource for more purposeful, effective, and enjoyable college teaching.* Sterling, VA: Stylus.

Dawisha, N., & Dawisha, K. (2014, September 3). How syllabi can help combat sexual assault. *Chronicle of Higher Education.* Retrieved from http://chronicle.com/blogs/conversation/2014/09/03/how-syllabi-can-help-combat-sexual-assault/?cid=at&utm_source=at&utm_medium=en

Deal, A. (2007, November). *Classroom response systems* (Teaching with Technology White Paper). Retrieved from http://www.cmu.edu/teaching/resources/Publications Archives/StudiesWhitepapers/ClassroomResponse_Nov07.pdf

Deci, E. L. (1971). Effects of externally mediated rewards on intrinsic motivation. *Journal of Personality and Social Psychology, 18*(1), 105–115.

Deci, E. L., Koestner, R., & Ryan, R. M. (1999). A meta-analytic view of experiments examining the effects of extrinsic rewards on intrinsic motivation. *Psychological Bulletin, 185,* 627–668.

Deci, E. L., & Ryan, R. M. (1985). *Intrinsic motivation and self-determination in human behavior.* New York, NY: Plenum.

Deci, E. L., & Ryan, R. M. (Eds.). (2002). *Handbook of self-determination research.* Rochester, NY: University of Rochester Press.

Dee, K. C. (2007). Student perceptions of high course workloads are not associated with poor student evaluations of instructor performance. *Journal of Engineering Education, 96*(1), 69–78.

Dee, T. S., & Jacob, B. A. (2012). Rational ignorance in education: A field experiment in student plagiarism. *Journal of Human Resources, 47*(2), 397–434.

DeJong, T., & Ferguson-Hessler, M. G. (1996). Types and quality of knowledge. *Educational Psychologist, 8*(2), 105–113.

Delaney, E. (1991). Applying geography to the classroom through structured discussions. *Journal of Geography, 90*(3), 129–133.

Dempster, F. N. (1996). Distributing and managing the conditions of encoding and practice. In E. L. Bork & R. A. Bork (Eds.), *Human memory* (pp. 197–236). Orlando, FL: Academic Press.

Dempster, F. N. (1997). Using tests to promote classroom learning. In R. F. Dillon (Ed.), *Handbook on testing* (pp. 332–346). Westport, CT: Greenwood Press.

Dennis, J. M., Phinney, J. S., & Chuateco, L. I. (2005). The role of motivation, parental support, and peer support in the academic success of ethnic minority first-generation college students. *Journal of College Student Development, 46,* 223–236.

Derek Bok Center for Teaching and Learning, Harvard University. (2006). *Tips for teachers: Teaching in racially diverse college classrooms.* Retrieved from http://isites. harvard.edu/fs/html/icb.topic58474/TFTrace.html

Derousseau, R. (2014, December 12). Professors grow weary of idea that technology can salvage higher education. *U.S. News & World Report,* Special Report. Retrieved from http://www.usnews.com/news/college-of-tomorrow/articles/2014/12/12/professors-grow-weary-of-idea-that-technology-can-salvage-higher-education

Derry, S. J. (1984). Effects of an organizer on memory for prose. *Journal of Educational Psychology, 76,* 98–107.

Deslauriers, L., Schelew, E., & Wieman, C. E. (2011). Improved learning in a large-enrollment physics class. *Science, 332,* 862–864. Retrieved from https://www.sciencemag.org/content/332/6031/862.full

Dimitrov, N. (2009). *Western guide to mentoring graduate students across cultures.* London, ON: Teaching Support Centre, University of Western Ontario, Canada. Retrieved from http://www.uwo.ca/tsc/resources/pdf/PG_3_MentoringAcrossCultures.pdf

Dinan, F. (2002). Chemistry by the case. *Journal of College Science Teaching, 32*(1), 36–41.

Dobrow, S. R., Smith, W. K., & Posner, M. A. (2011). Managing the grading paradox: Leveraging the power of choice in the classroom. *Academy of Management Learning and Education, 10*(2), 251–276.

Dochy, F., Segers, M., Van den Bossche, P., & Gijbels, D. (2003). Effects of problem-based learning: A meta-analysis. *Learning and Instruction, 13,* 533–568.

Doolittle, P. E., & Siudzinski, R. A. (2010). Recommended syllabus components: What do higher education faculty include in their syllabi? *Journal on Excellence in College Teaching, 21*(3), 29–61.

Doyle, T. (2008). *Helping students learn in a learner-centered environment: A guide to facilitating learning in higher education.* Sterling, VA: Stylus.

Doyle, T., & Zakrajsek, T. (2013). *The new science of learning: How to live in harmony with your brain.* Sterling, VA: Stylus.

Drake, R. (2009, February). *Essay preparedness and student success.* Poster session presented at the annual Lilly South Conference on College Teaching, Greensboro, NC.

Driver, M. (2001). Fostering creativity in business education: Developing creative classroom environments to provide students with critical workplace competencies. *Journal of Education for Business, 77,* 28–33.

Duch, B. J., & Allen D. E. (1996). Problems: A key factor in PBL. *About Teaching, 50,* 25–28.

Duch, B. J., Allen, D. E., & White, H. B., III. (1997–1998). Problem-based learning: Preparing students to succeed in the 21st century. *Essays on Teaching Excellence, 9*(7), 1–2.

Duch, B. J., Groh, S. E., & Allen, D. E. (2001). *The power of problem-based learning.* Sterling, VA: Stylus.

Duda, G. (2014). The road to a project-based classroom. *Change, 46*(6), 42-45.

Duncan, D. K., Hoekstra, A. R., & Wilcox, B. R. (2012). Digital devices, distraction, and student performance: Does in-class cell phone use reduce learning? *Astronomy Education Review, 11.* Retrieved from http://www.colorado.edu/physics/EducationIssues/papers/Wilcox/Duncan_2012_AER.pdf

Duncan, N. (2007). Feed-forward: Improving students' use of tutors' comments. *Assessment and Evaluation in Higher Education, 32*(2), 271–283.

Dunlosky, J., Rawson, K., Marsh, E., Nathan, M., & Willingham, D. (2013). Improving students' learning with effective learning techniques: Promising directions from cognitive and educational psychology. *Psychological Science in the Public Interest, 14*(1), 4–58.

Dweck, C. S. (2007). *Mindset: The new psychology of success.* New York, NY: Random House.

Dweck, C. S., & Leggett, E. (1988). A social-cognitive approach to motivation and personality. *Psychological Review, 95,* 256–273.

Eagan, M. K., Lozano, J. B., Hurtado, S., & Case, M. H. (2013). *The American freshman: National norms fall 2013.* Los Angeles: Higher Education Research Institute, UCLA. Retrieved from http://www.heri.ucla.edu/monographs/TheAmericanFreshman2013.pdf

Eagan, M. K., Stolzenberg, E. B., Lozano, J. B., Aragon, M. C., Suchard, M. R., & Hurtado, S. (2014). *Undergraduate teaching faculty: The 2013–2014 HERI Faculty Survey.* Los Angeles, CA: Higher Education Research Institute, UCLA. Retrieved from http://heri.ucla.edu/monographs/HERI-FAC2014-monograph.pdf

Ebel, R. L. (1978). The effectiveness of multiple true-false test items. *Educational and Psychological Measurement, 38*(1), 37–44.

Eddy, S. L., & Hogan, K. A. (2014). Getting under the hood: How and for whom does Increasing course structure work? *Life Science Education, 13*(3), 453–468. doi:10.1187/cbe.14–03–0050

Edens, K. M. (2000). Preparing problem solvers for the 21st century through problem-based learning. *College Teaching, 48*(2), 55–60.

Edwards, N. M. (2007). Student self-grading in social statistics. *College Teaching, 55*(2), 72–76.

Ehrlinger, J., Johnson, K., Banner, M., Dunning, D., & Kruger, J. (2008). Why the unskilled are unaware: Further explorations of (absent) self-insight among the incompetent. *Organizational Behavior and Human Decision Process, 105*(1), 98–121. Retrieved from http://www.ncbi.nlm.nih.gov/pmc/articles/PMC2702783/

Eisenberger, R., & Cameron, J. (1996). Detrimental effects of reward: Reality or myth? *American Psychologist, 51,* 1153–1166.

Ellis, D. (2006). *Becoming a master student* (11th ed.). Boston: Houghton Mifflin.

Eriksson, L. T., & Hauer, A. M. (2004). Mind map marketing: A creative approach in developing marketing skills. *Journal of Marketing Education, 26*(2), 174–187.

Ewens, W. (2000). Teaching using discussion. In R. Neff & M. Weimer (Eds.), *Classroom communication: Collected readings for effective discussion and questioning* (pp. 21–26). Madison, WI: Atwood.

Eyler J., & Giles, D. E., Jr. (1999). *Where's the learning in service-learning?* San Francisco, CA: Jossey-Bass.

Fabris, C. (2015, May 15). Want to make your course more "gameful"? A Michigan professor's tool could help. *Chronicle of Higher Education.* Retrieved from http://chronicle.com/blogs/wiredcampus/want-to-make-your-course-gameful-a-michigan-professors-tool-could-help/56649

Facione, P. A. (1990). *Critical thinking: A statement of expert consensus for purposes of educational assessment and instruction. Research findings and recommendations.* Retrieved from http://files.eric.ed.gov/fulltext/ED315423.pdf

Facione, P. A. (2011). *Think critically.* Upper Saddle River, NJ: Prentice Hall.

Facione, P. A. (2013). *Critical thinking: What it is and why it counts.* Retrieved from http://www.insightassessment.com/pdf_files/what&why2006.pdf

Facione, P. A., Facione, N. C., & Giancarlo, C. (2000). The disposition toward critical thinking: Its character, measurement, and relationship to critical thinking skills. *Journal of Informal Logic, 20*(1), 61–84.

Fadel, C. (2008). *Multimodal learning through media: What the research says.* Cisco Systems. Retrieved from http://www.cisco.com/web/strategy/docs/education/Multimodal-Learning-Through-Media.pdf

Fagen, A. P., Crouch, C. H., & Mazur, E. (2002). Peer instruction: Results from a range of classrooms. *Physics Teacher, 40*, 206–209.

Falchikov, N., & Boud, D. (1989). Student self-assessment in higher education: A meta-analysis. *Review of Educational Research, 59*(4), 395–430.

Falkenberg, S. (1996). *The feedback fallacy.* Retrieved from http://people.eku.edu/falkenbergs/feedback.htm

Farrand, P., Hussain, F., & Hennessy, E. (2002). The efficacy of the "mind map" study technique. *Medical Education, 36*, 426–431.

Fasko, D. (2003, April). *Case studies and method in teaching and learning.* Paper presented at the Annual Meeting of the Society of Educators and Scholars, Louisville, KY.

Featherly. K. (2014, September). The social club: Are Web 2.0 technologies the key to making distance learning truly effective? *Delta Sky*, 95–103.

Felder, R. M. (1993). Reaching the second tier: Learning and teaching styles in college science education. *Journal of College Science Teaching, 23*(5), 286–290. Retrieved from http://www4.ncsu.edu/unity/lockers/users/f/felder/public/Papers/Secondtier.html

Felder, R. M. (1996). Matters of style. *ASEE Prism, 6*(4), 18–23. Retrieved from http://www4.ncsu.edu/unity/lockers/users/f/felder/public/Papers/LS-Prism.htm

Felder, R. M. (1999). Memo to students who are disappointed with their last test grade. *Chemical Engineering Education, 33*(2), 136–137. Retrieved from http://www.ncsu.edu/felder-public/Colums/memo.pdf

Felder, R. M., & Brent, R. (2001). Effective strategies for cooperative learning. *Journal of Cooperation and Collaboration in College Teaching, 10*(2), 67–75.

Felder, R. M., & Brent, R. (2005). Understanding student differences. *Journal of Engineering Education, 94*(1), 57–72. Retrieved from http://www4.ncsu.edu/unity/lockers/users/f/felder/public/Papers/Understanding_Differences.pdf

Felder, R.M., & Silverman, L.K. (1988). Learning and teaching styles in engineering education. *Engineering Education, 78*(7), 674–681. Retrieved from http://www4.ncsu.edu/unity/lockers/users/f/felder/public/Papers/LS-1988.pdf

Felder, R. M., & Soloman, B. A. (n.d.a). *Index of learning styles (ILS).* Retrieved from http://www4.ncsu.edu/unity/lockers/users/f/felder/public/ILSpage.html

Felder, R. M., & Soloman, B.A. (n.d.b). *Learning styles and strategies.* Retrieved from http://www4.ncsu.edu/unity/lockers/users/f/felder/public/ILSdir/styles.htm

Felder, R. M., & Spurlin, J. (2005). Applications, reliability, and validity of the Index of Learning Styles. *International Journal of Engineering Education, 21*(1), 103–112. Retrieved from http://www4.ncsu.edu/unity/lockers/users/f/felder/public/ILSdir/ILS_Validation(IJEE).pdf

Feldman, K. A. (1989). The association between student ratings of specific instructional dimensions and student achievement: Refining and extending the synthesis of data from multisection validity studies. *Research in Higher Education, 30*(6), 583–645.

Feldmann, L. J. (2001). Classroom civility is another of our instructor responsibilities. *College Teaching, 49*(4), 137–141.

Feldon, D. F. (2010). Why magic bullets don't work. *Change, 42*(2), 15–21.

Felten, P. (2008). Visual literacy. *Change, 40*(6), 60–63.

Ferguson, M. (1989). The role of faculty in increasing student retention. *College and University, 69*, 127–134.

Fernald, P. S. (2004). The Monte Carlo quiz. *College Teaching, 52*(3), 95–99.

Ferris, M. E. (2015, April 20). With Twitter Statistics 101 takes flight. *Chronicle of Higher Education.* Retrieved from http://chronicle.com/article/With-Twitter-Statistics-101/229279

Ferris, W. P., & Hess, P. W. (1984). Peer evaluation of student interaction in organizational behavior and other courses. *Organizational Behavior Teaching Review, 9*(4), 74–82.

Finelli, C. J., Ott, M., Gottfried, A. C., Hershock, C., O'Heal, C., & Kaplan, M. (2008). Utilizing instructional consultations to enhance the teaching performance of engineering faculty. *Journal of Engineering Education, 97*(4), 397–411.

Fink, L. D. (2013). *Creating significant learning experiences: An integrated approach to designing college courses* (2nd ed.). San Francisco, CA: Jossey-Bass.

Fink, L. D., & Fink, A. K. (Eds.). (2009). *New directions for teaching and learning: No. 119. Designing courses for significant learning: Voices of experience.* San Francisco, CA: Jossey-Bass.

Fischman, G. E. (2001). Reflections about images, visual culture, and educational research. *Educational Researcher, 30*(8), 28–33.

Fischman, J. (2009, March 16). Students stop surfing after being shown how in-class laptop use lowers test scores. *Chronicle of Higher Education.* Retrieved from http://chronicle.com/blogs/wiredcampus/students-stop-surfing-after-being-shown-how-in-class-laptop-use-lowers-test-scores/4576

Flavell, J. H. (1976). Metacognitive aspects of problem solving. In L. B. Resnick (Ed.), *The nature of intelligence* (pp. 231–236). Mahwah, NJ: Erlbaum.

Foer, J. (2011). *Moonwalking with Einstein: The art and science of remembering everything.* New York, NY: Penguin. Retrieved from http://www.capitalessence.com/blog/wp-content/uploads/2011/12/Moonwalking_with_Einstein_-_Foer__Joshua.pdf

Foerde, K., Knowlton, B. J., & Poldrack, R. A. (2006). Modulation of competing memory systems by distraction. *Proceedings of the National Academy of Sciences USA, 103,* 11778–11783. Retrieved from http://www.pnas.org/content/103/31/11778.full

Forster, F., Hounsell, D., & Thompson, S. (1995). *Tutoring and demonstrating: A handbook.* Edinburgh, UK: University of Edinburgh, Center for Teaching, Learning, and Assessment.

Foster, A. (2008a, January 17). Despite skeptics, publishers tout new "fair use" agreements with universities. *Chronicle of Higher Education.* Retrieved from http://chronicle.com/daily/2008/01/1279n.htm

Foster, D. (2015). Private journals versus public blogs: The impact of peer readership on low-stakes reflective writing. *Teaching Sociology, 43*(2), 104–114.

Fox, H. (1994). (1994). *Listening to the world: Cultural issues in academic writing.* Urbana, IL: National Council of Teachers of English. Retrieved from http://www-personal.umich.edu/~hfox/listening.pdf

Freeman, S., Eddy, S. L., McDonough, M., Smith, M. K., Okoroafor, N., Jordt, H., & Wenderoth, M. P. (2014). Active learning increases student performance in science, engineering, and mathematics. *Proceedings of the National Academy of Sciences USA, 111,* 8410–8415. Retrieved from http://www.pnas.org/content/111/23/8410.full.pdf+html

Freeman, S., O'Connor, E., Parks, J. W., Cunningham, M., Hurley, D., Haak, D., Dirks, C., & Wenderoth, M. P. (2007). Prescribed active learning increases performance in introductory biology. *Cell Biology Education, 6,* 132–139.

Friedman, P., Rodriguez, F., & McComb, J. (2001). Why students do and do not attend classes: Myths and realities. *College Teaching, 49*(4), 124–133.

Frierson, H. T. (1986). Two intervention methods: Effects on groups of predominantly black nursing students' board scores. *Journal of Research and Development in Education, 19,* 18–23.

Frisby, B. N., & Martin, M. M. (2010). Instructor-student and student-student rapport in the classroom. *Communication Education, 59*(2), 146–164.

Frisby, D. A., & Sweeney, D. C. (1982). The relative merits of multiple true-false achievement tests. *Journal of Educational Measurement, 19*(1), 29–35.

Frymier, J. R. (1970). Motivation is what it's all about. *Motivation Quarterly, 1,* 1–3.

FTI Consulting. (2015). *U.S. postsecondary faculty in 2015: Diversity in people, goals, and methods, but focused on students.* Bill & Melinda Gates Foundation. Retrieved from http://postsecondary.gatesfoundation.org/wp-content/uploads/2015/02/US-Postsecondary-Faculty-in-2015.pdf

Gabel, C. (1999, March). *Using case studies to teach science.* Paper presented at the Annual Meeting of the National Association for Research in Science Teaching, Boston.

Gabriel, K. F. (2008). *Teaching unprepared students: Strategies for promoting success and retention in higher education.* Sterling, VA: Stylus.

Gauci, S. A., Dantas, A. M., Williams, D. A., & Kenn, R. E. (2009). Promoting student-centered active learning in lectures with a personal response system. *Advanced Physiological Education, 33*(1), 60–71. Retrieved from http://advan.physiology.org/content/33/1/60

Gedalof, A. J. (1998). *Green guide: No. 1. Teaching large classes.* Halifax, NS, Canada: Society for Teaching and Learning in Higher Education.

Geddes, L. (2014, May 23). How educators can get glowing course evaluations from students (even struggling students) in rigorous courses. The Learnwell Projects blog. Retrieved from http://www.thelearnwellprojects.com/how-educators-can-get-glowing-course-evaluations-from-students-even-struggling-students-in-rigorous-courses/

Gibbons, M. (2002). *The self-directed learning handbook: Challenging adolescent students to excel.* San Francisco, CA: Jossey-Bass.

Gilmore, T. N., & Schall, E. (1996). Staying alive to learning: Integrating enactments with case teaching to develop leaders. *Journal of Policy Analysis and Management, 15*(3), 444–457.

Ginns, P. (2005). Meta-analysis of the modality effect. *Learning and Instruction, 15,* 313–331.

Giuliodori, M. J., Lujan, H. L., & DiCarlo, S. E. (2006). Peer instruction enhanced student performance on qualitative problem-solving questions. *Advances in Physiology Education, 30,* 168–173.

Glaser, R. (1991). The maturing of the relationship between the science of learning and cognition and educational practice. *Learning and Instruction, 1*(1), 129–144.

Glazer, F. S. (2011). Baby steps to blended: Introduction of a blended unit to a conventional course. In F. S. Glazer (Ed.), *Blended learning: Across the disciplines, across the academy* (pp. 31–58). Sterling, VA: Stylus.

Glenn, D. (2009, December 15). Matching teaching style to learning style may not help students. *Chronicle of Higher Education.* Retrieved from http://chronicle.com/article/Matching-Teaching-Style-to/49497/

Glew, R. H. (2003). The problem with problem-based medical education: Promises not kept. *Biochemistry and Molecular Biology Education, 31*(1), 52–56.

Gobet, F., Lane, P.C.R., Croker, S., Cheng, P.C.H., Jones, G., Oliver, I., & Pine, J. M. (2001). Chunking mechanisms in human learning. *Trends in Cognitive Sciences, 5,* 236–243. doi:10.1016/S1364–6613(00)01662–4

Golding, T. L. (2008). Bonuses of a bonus assignment! *Teaching Professor, 22*(6), 5.

Gonsalves, L. M. (2002). Making connections: Addressing the pitfalls of white faculty/black male student communication. *College Composition and Communication Online, 53,* 435–465.

Gonzalez, V., & Lopez, E. (2001). The age of incivility: Countering disruptive behavior in the classroom. *AAHE Bulletin, 55*(8), 3–6.

Goodson, L. (2005, March). *Content, presentation and learning activities.* Paper presented at the 26th Annual Meeting of the Sharing Conference of the Southern Regional Faculty and Instructional Development Consortium, Lake Junaluska, NC.

Goodwin, B., & Miller, K. (2013). Evidence on flipped classroom still coming in. *Educational Leadership, 70*(6), 78–80.

Granitz, N. A., Koernig, S. K., & Harich, K. R. (2009). Now it's personal: Antecedents and outcomes of rapport between business faculty and their students. *Journal of Marketing Education, 31*(1), 52–65.

Grant-Thompson, S., & Atkinson, D. (1997). Cross-cultural mentor effectiveness and African American male students. *Journal of Black Psychology, 23,* 120–134.

Grasgreen, A. (2012, March 16). Who cheats, and how. *Inside Higher Education.* Retrieved from https://www.insidehighered.com/news/2012/03/16/arizona-survey-examines-student-cheating-faculty-responses

Gray, M. J., Ondaatje, E. H., Fricker, R. D., & Geschwind, S. A. (2000). Assessing service-learning: Results from a survey of "Learn and Service American Higher Education." *Change, 32*(2), 30–39.

Gray, M. J., Ondaatje, E. H., & Zakaras, L. (1999). *Combining service and learning in higher education: Summary report.* Santa Monica, CA: Rand Corporation.

Griffiths, E. (2010). Clearing the misty landscape: Teaching students what they didn't know then, but know now. *College Teaching, 58*, 32–37.

Gruhn, D., & Cheng, Y. (2014). A self-correcting approach to multiple-choice exams improves students' learning. *Teaching of Psychology, 41*(4), 335–339.

Grunert, J. (1997). *The course syllabus: A learning-centered approach*. San Francisco, CA: Jossey-Bass/Anker.

Guertin, L. (2011). Pre-recorded online audio review sessions. *College Teaching, 59*, 45. doi:10.1080/875675503252561

Guo, S., & Jamal, Z. (2007). *Green guide: No 8. Cultural diversity and inclusive teaching*. Ontario, Canada: Society for Teaching and Learning in Higher Education.

Haak, D. C., HilleRisLambers, J., Pitre, E., & Freeman, S. (2011). Increased structure and active learning reduce the achievement gap in introductory biology. *Science, 332*, 1213–1216. doi:10.1126/science.1204820

Habanek, D.V. (2005). An examination of the integrity of the syllabus. *College Teaching, 53*(2), 62–64.

Habron, G., & Dann, S. (2002). Breathing life into the case study approach: Active learning in an introductory natural resource management class. *Journal on Excellence in College Teaching, 13*(2/3), 41–58.

Hake, R. R. (1998). Interactive-engagement vs. traditional methods: A six thousand–student survey of mechanics test data for introductory physics courses. *American Journal of Physics, 66*, 64–74.

Halpern, D. F. (1998). Teaching critical thinking for transfer across domains: Dispositions, skills, structure training, and metacognitive monitoring. *American Psychologist, 53*(4), 449–455. Retrieved from http://projects.ict.usc.edu/itw/vtt/HalpernAmPsy98CritThink.pdf

Halpern, D. F. (1999). Teaching for critical thinking: Helping college students develop the skills and dispositions of a critical thinker. *New Directions for Teaching and Learning, 1999*(80), 69–74. Retrieved from http://onlinelibrary.wiley.com/doi/10.1002/tl.v1999:80/issueto.

Halpern, D. F. (2003). *Thought and knowledge: An introduction to critical thinking* (4th ed.). Mahwah, NJ: Erlbaum.

Halpern, D. F. (2004, December 1). *Teaching critical thinking skills across the curriculum*. Webinar produced by Starlink Training.

Halpern, D. F., & Associates. (1994). *Changing college classrooms*. San Francisco, CA: Jossey-Bass.

Halvorson, H. G. (2014). *The key to great feedback? Praise the process, not the person*. Retrieved from http://99u.com/articles/19442/the-key-to-great-feedback-praise-the-process-not-the-person

Haney, W., & Clarke, M. (2007). Cheating on tests: Prevalence, detection, and implications for on-line testing. In E. Anderman & T. Murdock (Eds.), *Psychology of academic cheating* (pp. 255–288). Burlington, MA: Elsevier.

Hansen, E. J. (2011). *Idea-based learning: A course design process to promote conceptual understanding*. Sterling, VA: Stylus.

Hanson, D. (2006). *Instructor's guide to process-oriented guided-inquiry learning*. Stony Brook, NY: Stony Brook University.

Hanson, D., & Wolfskill, T. (2000). Process workshops: A new model for instruction. *Journal of Chemical Education, 77*(1), 120–129.

Harding, T., Mayhew, M., Finelli, C., & Carpenter, D. (2007). The theory of planned behavior as a model of academic dishonesty in engineering and humanities undergraduates. *Ethics and Behavior, 17*(3), 255–279.

Hartley, J., & Davies, I. K. (1986). Note-taking: A critical review. *Programmed Learning and Educational Technology, 15*, 207–224. Retrieved from http://www.tandfonline.com/doi/abs/10.1080/0033039780150305?journalCode=riie19

Hartman, J. L. (2006, June). *Teaching and learning in the Net generation*. Plenary session presented at the annual meeting of the Association of American University Presses, New Orleans, LA.

Harvard University. (2008). *Instructional technology survey*. Cambridge, MA: Harvard University, Department of Romance Languages and Literatures.

Hattie, J. (2009). *Visible learning: A synthesis of over 800 meta-analyses relating to achievement*. New York, NY: Routledge.

Hattie, J., & Timperley, H. (2007). The power of feedback. *Review of Educational Research, 77*(1), 81–112. Retrieved from http://rer.sagepub.com/content/77/1/81.full

Heller, P., & Hollabaugh, M. (1992). Teaching problem solving through cooperative grouping. Part 2: Designing problems and structuring groups. *American Journal of Physics, 60*(7), 637–644.

Heller, P., Keith, R., & Anderson, S. (1992). Teaching problem solving through cooperative grouping. Part 1: Group vs. individual problem solving. *American Journal of Physics, 60*(7), 627–636.

Hertel, J. P., & Millis, B. J. (2002). *Using simulations to promote learning in higher education.* Sterling, VA: Stylus.

Higdon, J., & Topaz, C. (2009). Blogs and wikis as instructional tools: A social software adaptation of just-in-time-teaching. *College Teaching, 57*(2), 105–109.

Higher Education Research Institute. (2004, January 26). *Political interest on the rebound among the nation's freshmen, UCLA survey reveals.* Retrieved from www.gseis.ucla.edu/heri/03_press_release.pdf

Hintz, M. M. (2005). Can problem-based learning address content and process? *Biochemistry and Molecular Biology Education, 33,* 363–368.

Hmelo-Silver, C. E. (2004). Problem-based learning: What and how do students learn? *Educational Psychology Review, 16,* 235–266.

Hmelo-Silver, C. E., Duncan, R. G., & Chin, C. A. (2007). Scaffolding and achievement in problem-based and inquiry learning: A response to Kirschner, Sweller, and Clark (2006). *Educational Psychologist, 42*(2), 99–107.

Hobson, E. H. (2002). Assessing students' motivation to learn in large classes. *American Journal of Pharmaceutical Education, 56,* 82S.

Hobson, E. H. (2004). *Getting students to read: Fourteen tips* (IDEA Paper No. 40). Manhattan: Kansas State University, Center for Faculty Evaluation and Development.

Hodges, L. C. (2015). *Teaching undergraduate science: A guide to overcoming obstacles to student learning.* Sterling, VA: Stylus.

Hoeft, M. E. (2012). Why university students don't read: What professors can do to increase compliance. *International Journal for the Scholarship of Teaching and Learning, 6*(2). Retrieved from http://academics.georgiasouthern.edu/ijsotl/v6n2.html

Hoffman, E., Trott, J., & Neely, K. P. (2002). Concept mapping: A tool to bridge the disciplinary divide. *American Journal of Obstetrics and Gynecology, 187*(3), 41–43.

Holstead, C. E. (2015, March 4). The benefit of no-tech note-taking. *Chronicle of Higher Education.* Retrieved from http://chronicle.com/article/The-Benefits-of-No-Tech-Note/228089/

Hostetter, C., & Savion, L. (2013). Metacognitive skills— why bother (and how)? *National Teaching and Learning Forum, 23*(1), 4–7.

Hottell, D. L., Martinez-Aleman, A., & Rowan-Kenyon, H. T. (2014). Summer bridge program 2.0: Using social media to develop students' campus capital. *Change, 46*(5), 34–38.

Howard, D. R., & Miskowski, J. A. (2005). Using a module-based laboratory to incorporate inquiry into a large cell biology course. *Cell Biology Education, 4,* 249–260.

Howard, J. R. (2015). *Discussion in the college classroom: Getting your students engaged and participating in person and online.* San Francisco, CA: Jossey-Bass.

Howard, K. (2013–2014). *Community-based learning at Centre College: Faculty handbook.* Centre College Center for Teaching and Learning. Retrieved from http://ctl.centre.edu/assests/cblhandbook.pdf

Howard, M. G., Collins, H. L., & DiCarlo, S. E. (2002). "Survivor" torches "Who Wants to Be a Physician?" in the educational games ratings war. *Advances in Physiology Education, 26,* 30–36.

Howard-Rose, D., & Harrigan, K. (2003, August). *CLOE learning impact studies lite: Evaluating learning objects in nine Ontario university courses.* Paper presented at the MERLOT International Conference, Vancouver, BC, Canada.

Howe, N., & Strauss, W. (2000). *Millennials rising: The next great generation.* New York, NY: Vintage Books.

Hoyt, D. P., & Perera, S. (2000). *Teaching approach, instructional objectives, and learning* (IDEA Research Report No. 1). Manhattan, KS: IDEA Center.

Hu, S., Kuh, G., & Li, S. (2008). The effects of engagement in inquiry-oriented activities on student learning and personal development. *Innovative Higher Education, 33*(2), 71–81.

Huang, L.-S. (2014, September 29). Students riding on coattails during group work? Five simple ideas to try. *Faculty Focus.* Retrieved from http://www.facultyfocus.com/articles/effective-teaching-strategies/students-riding-coattails-group-work-five-simple-ideas-try/

Huang, S., Blacklock, P. J., & Capps, M. (2013, April 30). *Reading habits of college students in the United States.* Paper presented at the Annual Meeting of the American Educational Research Association, San Francisco.

Huang, Y-M., Trevisan, M., & Storfer, A. (2007). The impact of the "all-of-the-above" option and student ability on multiple choice tests. *International Journal for the Scholarship of Teaching and Learning, 1*(2). Retrieved from Available at: http://digitalcommons.georgiasouthern.edu/ij-sotl/vol1/iss2/11

Hudspith, B., & Jenkins, H. (2001). *Green guide: No. 3. Teaching the art of inquiry.* Halifax, NS, Canada: Society for Teaching and Learning in Higher Education.

Hufford, T. L. (1991). Increasing academic performance in an introductory biology course. *BioScience, 41,* 107–108.

Hung, W., Bailey, J. H., & Jonassen, D. H. (2003). Exploring the tensions of problem-based learning: Insights from research. In D. S. Knowlton & D. C. Sharp (Eds.), *New directions for teaching and learning: No. 95. Problem-based learning in the information age* (pp. 13–24). San Francisco, CA: Jossey-Bass.

Hunt, R. (2004). *What is inkshedding?* Retrieved from http://www.stthomasu.ca/~hunt/dialogic/whatshed.htm

Hutchings, P. (1998). Defining features and significant functions of the course portfolio. In P. Hutchings (Ed.), *The course portfolio: How faculty can examine their teaching to advance practice and student learning* (pp. 13–18). Washington, DC: American Association for Higher Education.

Hutton, P. A. (2006). Understanding student cheating and what educators can do about it. *College Teaching, 54*(1), 171–176.

Hyerle, D. (1996). *Visual tools for constructing knowledge.* Alexandria, VA: Association for Supervision and Curriculum Development.

Inside Higher Ed. (2014). *The 2014 Inside Higher Ed survey of faculty attitudes on technology.* Retrieved from https://www.insidehighered.com/system/files/media/IHE-FacTechSurvey2014%20final.pdf

Intrinsic motivation doesn't exist, researcher says. (2005, May 17). PhysOrg.com. Retrieved from http://www.physorg.com/news4126.html

Ip, A., Morrison, I., & Currie, M. (2001). *What is a learning object, technically?* Retrieved from http://users.tpg.com.au/adslfrcf/lo/learningObject(WebNet2001).pdf

Jackson, A. P., Smith, S. A., & Hill, C. L. (2003). Academic persistence among Native American college students. *Journal of College Student Development, 44,* 548–565.

Jacobs, L. C., & Chase, C. I. (1992). *Developing and using tests effectively: A guide for faculty.* San Francisco, CA: Jossey-Bass.

Jacobsen, M. (n.d.). *Multiple choice item construction.* Retrieved from http://people.ucalgary.ca/~dmjacobs/portage/

Jalajas, D. S., & Sutton, R. I. (1984). Feuds in student groups: Coping with whiners, martyrs, saboteurs, bullies, and deadbeats. *Journal of Management Education, 9*(4), 94–102.

Jassawalla, A. R., Malshe, A., & Sashittal, H. (2008). Student perceptions of social loafing in undergraduate business classroom teams. *Decision Sciences Journal of Innovative Education, 6*(2), 403–426.

Jensen, J. D. (2011). Promoting self-regulation and critical reflection through writing students' use of electronic portfolio. *International Journal of ePortfolio, 1*(1), 49–60.

Johnson, C., & Ury, C. (1998). Detecting Internet plagiarism. *National Teaching and Learning Forum, 7*(4), 7–8.

Johnson, C., & Ury, C. (1999). Preventing Internet plagiarism. *National Teaching and Learning Forum, 8*(5), 5–6.

Johnson, D. R. (2013). Technological change and professional control in the professoriate. *Science Technology Human Values 38*(1), 126–149. doi:10.1177/0162243911430236

Johnson, D. W., & Johnson, R. T. (1989). *Cooperation and competition: Theory and research.* Edina, MN: Interaction Books.

Johnson, D. W., Johnson, R. T., & Smith, K. A. (1991). *Active learning: Cooperation in the college classroom.* Edina, MN: Interaction Books.

Johnson, D. W., Johnson, R. T., & Smith, K. A. (2014). The power of cooperative learning or university classes: The interrelationships among theory, research, and practice. *Journal of Excellence in College Teaching, 25*(4). Available to subscribers at http://celt.muohio.edu/ject/archive.php

Johnson, R. T., & Johnson, D. W. (1994). An overview of cooperative learning. In J. Thousand, A. Villa, & A. Nevin (Eds.), *Creativity and collaborative learning* (pp. 31–44). Baltimore, MD: Brookes Press.

Johnson, V. E. (2003). *Grade inflation: A crisis in college education.* New York, NY: Springer-Verlag.

Johnston, K. M. (2003). *"Why do I have to change the way I learn just to fit the way you teach?" Steps to creating a teaching philosophy statement.* Workshop conducted in the Michigan State University Teaching Assistant Program, East Lansing.

Johnston, P. (2005, August 10). Dressing the part. *Chronicle of Higher Education.* Retrieved from http://chronicle.com/article/Dressing-the-Part/44918

Johnston, S., & Cooper, J. (1997). Quick-thinks: The interactive lecture. *Cooperative Learning and College Teaching, 8*(1), 2–6.

Johnstone, A. H., & Su, W. Y. (1994). Lectures—A learning experience? *Education in Chemistry, 35,* 76–79.

Jonas, H., Etzel, S., & Barzansky, B. (1989). Undergraduate medical education. *Journal of the American Medical Association, 262*(8), 1011–1019.

Jones, E. B. (2004). Culturally relevant strategies in the classroom. In A. M. Johns & M. K. Sipp (Eds.), *Diversity in the classroom: Practices for today's campuses* (pp. 51–72). Ann Arbor: University of Michigan Press.

Jones, J. B. (2010, November 29). Exam questions: Outsourcing vs. crowdsourcing. *Chronicle of Higher Education.* Retrieved from http://chronicle.com/blogs/profhacker/exam-questions-outsourcing-vs-crowdsourcing/28911

Jones, R. C. (2008). The "why" of class participation: A question worth asking. *College Teaching, 56*(1), 59–62.

Jones, S. K., Noyd, R. K., & Sagendorf, K. S. (2014). *Building a pathway for student learning: A how-to guide to course design.* Sterling, VA: Stylus.

Jones-Wilson, T. M. (2005). Teaching problem-solving skills without sacrificing course content: Marrying traditional lecture and active learning in an organic chemistry class. *Journal of College Science Teaching, 35*(1), 42–46.

Josephson Institute. (2012). *Report card on the ethics of American youth.* Retrieved from http://charactercounts.org/programs/reportcard/2012/index.html

Junco, R. (2012a). Too much face and not enough books: The relationship between multiple indices of Facebook use and academic performance. *Computers in Human Behavior, 28,* 187–198. Retrieved from http://www.sciencedirect.com/science/article/pii/S0747563211001932

Junco, R. (2012b). The relationship between frequency of Facebook use, participation in Facebook activities, and student engagement. *Computers and Education, 58*(1), 162–171. Retrieved from http://www.sciencedirect.com/science/article/pii/S0360131511001825

Junco, R. (2012c). In-class multitasking and academic performance. *Computers in Human Behavior, 28,* 2236–2243. Retrieved from http://www.sciencedirect.com/science/article/pii/S0747563212001926

Junco, R. (2015). Student class standing, Facebook use, and academic performance. *Journal of Applied Developmental Psychology, 36,* 18–29. doi:10.1016/j.appdev.2014.11.001. Retrieved from http://blog.reyjunco.com/pdf/JuncoClassStandingFBJADP.pdf

Junco, R., & Cotton, S. R. (2012). No A 4 U: The relationship between multitasking and academic performance. *Computers and Education, 59*(2), 505–514. Retrieved from http://www.sciencedirect.com/science/article/pii/S036013151100340X

Junco, R., Heiberger, G., & Loken, E. (2010). The effective of Twitter on college student engagement and grades. *Journal of Computer Assisted Learning, 27*(2). Retrieved from http://onlinelibrary.wiley.com/doi/10.1111/j.1365–2729.2010.00387.x/pdf

Justice, C., Rice, J., Warry, W., Inglis, S., Miller, S., & Sammon, S. (2007). Inquiry in higher education: Reflections and directions in course design and teaching methods. *Innovative Higher Education, 31*(4), 201–214.

Kaleta, R., & Joosten, T. (2007, May 8). Student response systems: A University of Wisconsin study of clickers. *EDUCAUSE Center for Applied Research, 10.* Retrieved from http://net.educause.edu/ir/library/pdf/ERB0710.pdf

Kalman, C. S. (2007). *Successful science and engineering teaching in colleges and universities.* San Francisco, CA: Jossey-Bass/Anker.

Kalman, J., & Kalman, C. (1996). Writing to learn. *American Journal of Physics, 64,* 954-955.

Kalyuga, S. (2000). When using sound with a text or picture is not beneficial for learning. *Australian Journal of Educational Technology, 16*(2), 161–172.

Karpicke, J., & Blunt, J. (2011). Retrieval practice produces more learning than elaborative studying with concept mapping. *Science, 331*(6018), 772–775. doi:10.1126/science.1199327

Katayama, A. D. (1997, November). *Getting students involved in note taking: Why partial notes benefit learners more than complete notes.* Paper presented at the Annual Meeting of the Mid-South Educational Research Association, Memphis, TN.

Kaufman, A. (1985). *Implementing problem-based medical education.* New York, NY: Springer.

Kaufman, A., Mennin, S., Waterman, R., Duban, S., Hansbarger, C., Silverblatt, H., Obenshain, S.S., Kantrowitz, M., Becker, T., & Samet J.. (1989). The New Mexico experiment: Educational innovation and institutional change. *Academic Medicine, 64,* 285–294.

Kaupins, G. (2005). Using popular game and reality show formats to review for exams. *Teaching Professor, 19*(1), 5–6.

Kelly, A. E., & O'Donnell, A. (1994). Hypertext and study strategies of pre-service teachers: Issues in instructional hypertext design. *Journal of Educational Computing Research, 10*(4), 373–387.

Kennedy, A., & Navey-David, S. (2004). Inquiry-guided learning and the foreign language classroom. In V. S. Lee (Ed.), *Teaching and learning through inquiry: A guidebook for institutions and instructors* (pp. 71–79). Sterling, VA: Stylus.

Kennedy, F., & Nilson, L. B. (2008). *Successful strategies for teams: Team member handbook.* Retrieved from http://www.clemson.edu/OTEI/documents/TeamworkHandbook.pdf

Kerkvliet, J. (1994). Cheating by economics students: A comparison of survey results. *Journal of Economic Education, 25*(2), 121–133.

Kerkvliet, J., & Sigmund, C. L. (1999). Can we control cheating in the classroom? *Journal of Economic Education, 30*(4), 331–334.

Kiernan, V. (2005, November 25). Students desire balance of technology and human contact, survey suggests. *Chronicle of Higher Education.* Retrieved from http://chronicle.com/article/Students-Desire-a-Balance-o/11687/

Kiewra, K. A. (1985). Providing the instructor's notes: An effective addition to student notetaking. *Educational Psychologist, 20,* 33–39.

Kiewra, K. A. (2005). *Learn how to study and SOAR to success.* Upper Saddle Creek, NJ: Pearson Prentice Hall.

Kimmel, R. M. (2002). Undergraduate labs in applied polymer science. In *Proceedings of the 2002 American Society for Engineering Education Annual Conference and Exposition* (Session 1526). Washington DC: American Society for Engineering Education.

Kinchin, I. M. (2000). Concept mapping in biology. *Journal of Biological Education, 34*(2), 61–68.

Kinchin, I. M. (2001). If concept mapping is so helpful to learning biology, why aren't we all using it? *International Journal of Science Education, 23*(12), 1257–1269.

Kinchin, I. M. (2006). Developing PowerPoint handouts to support meaningful learning. *British Journal of Educational Technology, 37,* 33–39.

King, M., & Shell, R. (2002). Teaching and evaluating critical thinking with concept maps. *Nurse Educator, 27*(5), 214–216.

Kirschner, P. A., & Karpinski, A. C. (2010). Facebook and academic performance. *Computers in Human Behavior, 26,* 1237–1245. Retrieved from http://www.sciencedirect.com/science/article/pii/S0747563210000646#

Kirschner, P. A., Sweller, J., & Clark, R. E. (2006). Why minimal guidance during instruction does not work: An analysis of the failure of constructivist, discovery, problem-based, experiential, and inquiry-based teaching. *Educational Psychologist, 41*(2), 75–86.

Klahr, D., & Nigam, M. (2004). The equivalence of learning paths in early science instruction: Effects of direct instruction and discovery learning. *Psychological Science, 15,* 661–667.

Kleiner, C., & Lord, M. (1999, November 22). The cheating game. *U.S. News and World Report,* 55–66.

Kloss, R. J. (1994). A nudge is best: Helping students through the Perry schema of intellectual development. *College Teaching, 42*(4), 151–158.

Knight, J. K., & Wood, W. B. (2005). Teaching more by lecturing less. *Cell Biology Education, 4,* 298–310.

Knowles, M. S. (1975). *Self-directed learning. A guide for learners and teachers,* Englewood Cliffs, NJ: Prentice Hall.

Kobrak, P. (1992). Black student retention in predominantly white regional universities: The politics of faculty involvement. *Journal of Negro Education, 61,* 509–530.

Kodani, C. H., & Wood, M. (2007). The benefits of music and stretching in maintaining student attention. *Teaching Professor, 21*(6), 5.

Koh, A. (2015, January 28). Live-tweeting assignments: To use or not to use? *Chronicle of Higher Education.* Retrieved from http://chronicle.com/blogs/profhacker/live-tweeting-assignments-to-use-or-not-to-use/

Kohn, A. (1993). *Punished by rewards.* Boston, MA: Houghton Mifflin.

Kolb, D. A. (1984). *Experiential learning: Experience as the source of learning and development.* Englewood Cliffs, NJ: Prentice Hall.

Kolowich, S. (2014, December 17). Five things we know about college students in 2014. *Chronicle of Higher Education.* Retrieved from http://chronicle.com/blogs/wiredcampus/5-things-we-know-about-college-students-in-2014/55313

Kosslyn, S. M. (1994). *Image and brain: The resolution of the imagery debate.* Cambridge, MA: MIT Press.

Kozma, R. B., Russell, J., Jones, T., Marx, N., & Davis, J. (1996). The use of multiple linked representations to facilitate science understanding. In S. Vosniadou, E. DeCorte, R. Glaser, & H. Mandl (Eds.), *International perspectives on the design of technology-supported learning environments* (pp. 41–60). Mahwah, NJ: Erlbaum.

Kraft, K. (2008, November 20). Using situated metacognition to enhance student understanding of the nature of science. Session presented at the National Association of Geoscience Teachers (NAGT) Workshops: The Role of Metacognition in Teaching Geoscience, Carleton College, Northfield, MN. Retrieved from http://serc.carleton.edu/NAGTWorkshops/metacognition/kraft.html

Kramer, J., & Arnold, A. (2004). Music 200: "Understanding Music": An inquiry-guided approach to music appreciation. In V. S. Lee (Ed.), *Teaching and learning through inquiry: A guidebook for institutions and instructors* (pp. 41–50). Sterling, VA: Stylus.

Krathwohl, D. R., Bloom, B. S., & Masia, B. B. (1999). *Taxonomy of educational objectives: Book 2. Affective domain.* Reading, MA: Addison-Wesley.

Kratzig, G. P., & Arbuthnott, K. D. (2006). Perceptual learning style and learning proficiency: A test of the hypothesis. *Journal of Educational Psychology, 98,* 238–246.

Kraushaar, J. M., & Novak, D. (2010). Examining the effects of student multitasking with laptops during the lecture. *Journal of Information Systems Education, 21*(2), 241–251. Retrieved from http://www.sjsu.edu/people/laura.jones/courses/psyc102sec03/s2/Kraushaar%20&%20Novak%202010%20multitasking%20during%20lecture.pdf

Kress, G., Jewitt, C., Ogborn, J., & Charalampos, T. (2006). *Multimodal teaching and learning: The rhetorics of the science classroom.* London: Continuum.

Kristensen, E. (2007). *Teaching at the University of Ottawa: A handbook for professors and TAs* (5th ed.). Ottawa, ON, Canada: University of Ottawa, Centre for University Teaching.

Kruger, J., & Dunning, D. (1999). Unskilled and unaware of it: How difficulties in recognizing one's own incompetence lead to inflated self-assessments. *Journal of Personality and Social Psychology, 77*(6), 1121–1134. Retrieved from http://dx.doi.org/10.1037/0022–3514.77.6.1121

Kubitz, K. A. (2014). The evidence, please. In J. Sibley & P. Ostafichuk (Eds.), *Getting started with team-based learning* (pp. 45–61). Sterling, VA: Stylus.

Kuh, G. D. (2008). *High-impact educational practices: What they are, who has access to them, and why they matter.* Washington, DC: Association of American Colleges and Universities.

Kuh, G. D., Kinzie, J., Schuh, J., Whitt, E., & Associates. (2005). *Student success in college: Creating conditions that matter.* San Francisco, CA: Jossey-Bass.

Kuhn, T. S. (1970). *The structure of scientific revolutions* (2nd ed.). Chicago, IL: University of Chicago Press.

Kusinitz, S. (2014, July 14). *Twelve reasons to integrate visual content into your marketing campaigns (infographic).* HubSpot Inbound Marketing. Retrieved from http://blog.hubspot.com/marketing/visual-content-marketing-infographic

Kustra, E.D.H., & Potter, M. K. (2008). *Green guide: No. 9. Leading effective discussions.* Ontario, Canada: Society for Teaching and Learning in Higher Education.

Kutner, M., Greenberg, E., Jin, Y., Boyle, B., Hsu, T., & Dunleavy, E. (2007). *Literacy in everyday life: Results from the 2003 National Assessment of Adult Literacy.* Washington, DC: U.S. Department of Education, National Center for Education Statistics.

Kuznekoff, J. H., & Titsworth, S. (2013). The impact of mobile phone usage on student learning. *Communication Education, 62*(3), 233–252. Retrieved from http://www.tandfonline.com/doi/full/10.1080/03634523.2013.767917

La Lopa, J. (2013). The difference between Bigfoot and learning styles: There may be better evidence to support the existence of Bigfoot. *Journal of Culinary Sciences and Technology, 11*(4), 356–376. doi:http://10.1080/15428052.2013.817861

Laird, R. (2004). Heuristic models/concept maps in neuroanatomy instruction. *Teacher, 6*(1&2), 17–25. Retrieved from http://apache.northgeorgia.edu/resource/otle/pubs/PDFnewsletters/Teacher_6–1and2.pdf

Lang, J. M. (2008). *On course: A week-by-week guide to your first semester of college teaching.* Cambridge, MA: Harvard University Press.

Lang, J. M. (2012, January 17). Metacognition and student learning. *Chronicle of Higher Education.* Retrieved from http://chronicle.com/article/MetacognitionStudent/130327/

Lang, J. M. (2013, October 13). *How can I use Twitter to improve teaching and learning?* Live broadcast of Magna Publications online seminar.

Lang, J. M. (2014). *Cheating lessons: Learning from academic dishonesty.* Cambridge, MA: Harvard University Press.

Langan, J. (2007). *Reading and student skills* (8th ed.). New York, NY: McGraw-Hill.

Larkin, J. H., & Simon, H. A. (1987). Why a diagram is (sometimes) worth ten thousand words. *Cognitive Science, 11*, 65–99.

Lasry, N. (2008). Clickers or flashcards: Is there really a difference? *Physics Teacher, 46*, 242–244.

Laws, P. (1991). Calculus-based physics without lectures. *Physics Today, 12,* 24–31.

Leamnson, R. (1999). *Thinking about teaching and learning: Developing habits of learning with first year college and university students.* Sterling, VA: Stylus.

Leamnson, R. (2000). Learning as biological brain change. *Change, 32*(6), 34–40.

Leamnson, R. (2002). Learning (your first job). Retrieved from http://www.udel.edu/CIS/106/iaydin/07F/misc/firstJob.pdf

Learning Sciences, University of Texas at Austin. (2015). Scenario-based approach. Retrieved from https://learningsciences.utexas.edu/content/scenario-based-approach

Leauby, B. A., & Brazina, P. (1998). Concept mapping: Potential uses in accounting education. *Journal of Accounting Education, 16*(1), 123–138.

Lee, V. S. (Ed.). (2004). *Teaching and learning through inquiry: A guidebook for institutions and instructors.* Sterling, VA: Stylus.

Lee, V. S. (2011). The power of inquiry as a way to learning. *Innovative Higher Education, 36*, 149–160. doi:10.1007/s10755–010–9166–4

Lee, V. S., Green, D. B., Odom, J., Schechter, E., & Slatta, R. W. (2004). What is inquiry-guided learning? In V. S. Lee (Ed.), *Teaching and learning through inquiry: A guidebook for institutions and instructors* (pp. 3–16). Sterling, VA: Stylus.

Leeming, F. C. (2002). The exam-a-day procedure improves performance in psychology classes. *Teaching of Psychology, 29*(3), 210–212.

Leichhardt, G. (1989). Development of an expert explanation: An analysis of a sequence of subtraction lessons. In L. Resnick (Ed.), *Knowing, learning, and instruction* (pp. 67–125). Mahwah, NJ: Erlbaum.

Lempert, D., Xavier, N., & DeSouza, B. (1995). *Escape from the ivory tower: Student adventures in democratic experiential education.* San Francisco, CA: Jossey-Bass.

Lepp, A., Barkley, J. E., & Karpinski, A. C. (2014). The relationship between cell phone use, academic performance, anxiety, and satisfaction with life in college students. *Computers in Human Behavior, 31*, 343–350. Retrieved from http://www.sciencedirect.com/science/article/pii/ S0747563213003993#

Levin, B. (1997, March). *The influence of context in case-based teaching: Personal dilemmas, moral issues or real change in teachers' thinking?* Paper presented at the Annual Meeting of the American Educational Research Association, Chicago, IL.

Levin, J. (2001, December). *Developing a learning environment where all students seek to excel.* Faculty workshop conducted at Clemson University, Clemson, SC.

Levine, A., & Cureton, J. S. (1998). *When hope and fear collide: A portrait of today's college student.* San Francisco, CA: Jossey-Bass.

Levine, A., & Dean, D. R. (2012). *Generation on a tightrope: A portrait of today's college student.* San Francisco, CA: Jossey-Bass.

Lewes, D., & Stiklus, B. (2007). *Portrait of a student as a young wolf: Motivating undergraduates* (3rd ed.). Pennsdale, PA: Folly Hill Press.

Lewis, R. J., & Wall, M. (1988). *Exploring obstacles to uses of technology in higher education: A discussion paper.* Washington, DC: Academy for Educational Development.

Lewis, S. E., & Lewis, J. E. (2005). Departing from lectures: An evaluation of a peer-led guided inquiry alternative. *Journal of Chemical Education, 82*(1), 135–139.

Li, M., Frieze, I. H., Nokes-Malach, T. J., & Cheong, J. (2013). Do friends always help your studies? Mediating processes between social relations and academic motivation. *Social Psychology of Education 16*(l), 129–149. doi:10.1007/s11218–012–9203–5

Lieux, E. M. (1996). Comparison study of learning in lecture vs. problem-based format. *About Teaching, 50*(1), 18–19.

Light, R. J. (1990). *The Harvard Assessment Seminar, first report: Explorations with students and faculty about teaching, learning, and student life.* Cambridge, MA: Harvard Graduate School of Education.

Light, R. J. (1992). *The Harvard Assessment Seminar, second report: Explorations with students and faculty about teaching, learning, and student life.* Cambridge, MA: Harvard Graduate School of Education.

Lin, T-C. (2014, December 4). Using quizzes to improve students' learning. *Teaching Professor.* Retrieved from http://www.magnapubs.com/newsletter/the-teaching-professor/108/Using-Quizzes-to-Improve-Students-Learning-13293-1.html

Lin, Y., McKeachie, W. J., & Kim, Y. C. (2001). College student intrinsic and/or extrinsic motivation and learning. *Learning and Individual Differences, 13*(3), 251–258.

Litzinger, T. A., Lee, S. H., Wise, J. C., & Felder, R. M. (2007). A psychometric study of the Index of Learning Styles. *Journal of Engineering Education, 96*(4), 309–319.

Locke, E. A., & Latham, G. P. (1990). *A theory of goal setting and task performance.* Upper Saddle River, NJ: Prentice Hall.

Lord, T. R. (1997). A comparison between traditional and constructivist teaching in college biology. *Innovative Higher Education, 21*(3), 197–216.

Lord, T. R. (1999). A comparison between traditional and constructivist teaching in environmental science. *Journal of Environmental Education, 30*(3), 22–28.

Lord, T., & Orkwiszewski, T. (2006). Didactic to inquiry-based instruction in a science laboratory. *American Biology Teacher, 68*(6), 342–345.

Loukopoulos, L. D., Dismukes, R. K., & Barshi, I. (2009). *The multitasking myth.* Burlington, VT: Ashgate.

Lovett, M. C. (2008, January). *Teaching metacognition.* Presented at the annual meeting of the Educause Learning Initiative. Retrieved from http://net.educause.edu/upload/presentations/ELI081/FS03/Metacognition-ELI.pdf

Lovett-Hooper, G., Komarraju, M., Western, R., & Dollinger, S. (2007). Is plagiarism a forerunner of other deviance? Imagined futures of academically dishonest students. *Ethics and Behavior, 17*(3), 323–336.

Lowery, J. W. (2001). The millennials come to campus. *About Campus, 6*(3), 6–12.

Luckie, D. B., Maleszewski, J. J., Loznak, S. D., & Krha, M. (2004). Infusion of collaborative inquiry throughout a biology curriculum increases student learning: A four-year study of "Teams and Streams." *Advances in Physiology Education, 28*(4), 199–209.

Lundberg, C. A., & Sheridan, D. (2015). Benefits of engagement with peers, faculty, and diversity for online learners. *College Teaching, 68*(1), 8–15.

Lundeberg, M. A., Levin, B., & Harrington, H. (1999). *Who learns what from cases and how? The research base for teaching and learning with cases.* Mahwah, NJ: Erlbaum.

Lundeberg, M. A., Mogen, K., Bergland, M., Klyczek, K., Johnson, D., & MacDonald, E. (2002). Fostering ethical awareness about human genetics through multimedia-based cases. *Journal of College Science Teaching, 32*(1), 64–69.

Lundeberg, M. A., & Yadav, A. (2006a). Assessment of case study teaching: Where do we go from here? Part I. *Journal of College Science Teaching, 35*(5), 10–13.

Lundeberg, M. A., & Yadav, A. (2006b). Assessment of case study teaching: Where do we go from here? Part II. *Journal of College Science Teaching, 35*(6), 8–13.

MacDonald, L. T. (2013). *Letter to next semester's students.* On Course Workshops. Retrieved from http://oncourseworkshop.com/staying-course/letter-next-semesters-students/

MacNell, L., Driscoll, A., & Hunt, A. N. (2014). What's in a name: Exposing gender bias in student evaluations of teaching. *Innovative Higher Education.* Retrieved from http://link.springer.com/article/10.1007%2Fs10755–014–9313–4

Major, C. H., & Palmer, B. (2001). Assessing the effectiveness of problem-based learning in higher education: Lessons from the literature. *Academic Exchange Quarterly, 5*(1), 4–9.

Mangen, A., Walgermo, B. R., & Brønnick, K. (2012). Reading linear texts on paper versus computer screen: Effects on reading comprehension. *International Journal of Education Research 58,* 61–68. doi:10.1016/ijer2012.12.002

Mangurian, L. P. (2005, February). *Learning and teaching practice: The power of the affective.* Paper presented at the Annual Lilly Conference on College Teaching South, Greensboro, NC.

Mann, S., & Robinson, A. (2009). Boredom in the lecture theatre: An investigation into the contributors, moderators and outcomes of boredom amongst university students. *British Educational Research Journal, 35*(2), 243–258. doi:10.1080/01411920802042911

Marks, M., Fairris, D., & Beleche, T. (2010). *Do course evaluations reflect student learning? Evidence from a pre-test/post-test setting.* Department of Economics, University of California, Riverside. Retrieved from http://faculty.ucr.edu/~mmarks/Papers/marks2010course.pdf

Marrs, K. A., & Novak, G. (2004). Just-in-time teaching in biology: Creating an active learner classroom using the Internet. *Cell Biology Education, 3,* 49–61.

Marsh, H. W. (1984). Students' evaluations of university teaching: Dimensionality, reliability, validity, potential biases, and utility. *Journal of Educational Psychology, 76,* 707–754.

Marshall, K. (2015, January 5). How to curate your digital identity as an academic. *Chronicle of Higher Education Vitae.* Retrieved from http://chronicle.com/article/How-to-Curate-Your-Digital/151001/

Martin, G. I. (2000). Peer carding. *College Teaching, 48*(1), 15–16.

Martin, H. H., Hands, K. B., Lancaster, S. M., Trytten, D. A., & Murphy, T. J. (2008). Hard but not too hard: Challenging courses and engineering students. *College Teaching, 56*(2), 107–113.

Marzano, R. J. (2003). *What works in schools: Translating research into action.* Alexandria, VA: Association for Supervision and Curriculum Development.

Maslow, A. H. (1966). *The psychology of science: A reconnaissance.* New York, NY: Joanna Cotler Books.

Mastascusa, E. J., Snyder, W. J., & Hoyt, B. S. (2011). *Effective instruction for STEM disciplines: From learning theory to college teaching.* San Francisco, CA: Jossey-Bass.

Maurer, T., & Longfield, J. (2013, October 4). *Improving reading compliance and quiz scores through the use of reading guides.* Panel presentation at the Annual Meetings of the International Society for the Scholarship of Teaching and Learning, Elon, NC.

Mayer, R. E. (2004). Should there be a three-strikes rule against pure discovery learning? The case for guided methods of instruction. *American Psychologist, 56,* 14–19.

Mayer, R. E. (2005). Introduction to multimedia learning. In R. E. Mayer (Ed.), *The Cambridge handbook of multimedia learning* (pp. 1–15). Cambridge, UK: Cambridge University Press.

Mayer, R. E. (2009). *Multimedia learning* (2nd ed.). Cambridge, UK: Cambridge University Press.

Mayer, R. E., & Gallini, J. K. (1990). When is an illustration worth ten thousand words? *Journal of Educational Psychology, 82*(4), 715–726.

Mayer, R. E., & Moreno, R. (2003). Nine ways to reduce cognitive load in multimedia learning. *Educational Psychologist, 38*(1), 43–52. Retrieved from http://www.uky.edu/~gmswan3/544/9_ways_to_reduce_CL.pdf

Mayer, R. E., & Sims, V. K. (1994). For whom is a picture worth ten thousand words? Extensions of a dual coding theory of multimedia learning. *Journal of Educational Psychology, 86*(3), 389–401.

Mazur, E. (1997). *Peer instruction: A user's manual.* Upper Saddle River, NJ: Prentice Hall.

Mazur Group. (2008). *Publications: Peer instruction.* Retrieved from http://mazur-www.harvard.edu/publications.php?function=search&topic=8.

McCabe, D. L. (2005). Cheating among college and university students: A North American perspective. *International Journal for Educational Integrity, 1*(1). Retrieved from http://www.ojs.unisa.edu.au/index.php/IJEI/article/viewFile/14/9

McCabe, D. L., Butterfield, K. D., & Treviño, L. K. (2012). *Cheating in college: Why students do it and what educators can do about it.* Baltimore, MD: John Hopkins University Press.

McCabe, D. L., & Pavela, G. (2000). Some good news about academic integrity. *Change, 32*(5), 32–38.

McCabe, D. L., & Pavela, G. (2005, March 11). New honor codes for a new generation. *Inside Higher Ed.* Retrieved from https://www.insidehighered.com/views/2005/03/11/pavela1

McCabe, D. L., & Treviño, L. K. (1996). What we know about cheating in college: Longitudinal trends and recent developments. *Change, 28*(1), 28–33.

McCabe, D. L., & Treviño, L. K. (1997). Individual and contextual influences on academic dishonesty: A multi-campus investigation. *Research in Higher Education, 38*(3), 379–396.

McCabe, D. L., Treviño, L. K., & Butterfield, K. D. (1999). Academic integrity in honor code and non-honor code environments: A qualitative investigation. *Journal of Higher Education, 70*(2), 211–234.

McClain, A. (1987). Improving lectures: Challenging both sides of the brain. *Journal of Optometric Education, 13,* 18–20.

McCoy, B. (2013). Digital distractions in the classroom: Student classroom use of digital devices for non-class related purposes. *Journal of Media Education, 4*(4), 5–14. Retrieved from http://en.calameo.com/read/000091789af53ca4e647f

McCreary, C. L., Golde, M. F., & Koeske, R. (2006). Peer instruction in the general chemistry laboratory: Assessment of student learning. *Journal of Chemical Education, 83*(5), 804–810.

McDaniel, M. A., & Butler, A. C. (2010). A contextual framework for understanding when difficulties are desirable. In A. S. Benjamin (Ed.), *Successful remembering and successful forgetting: Essays in Honor of Robert A. Bjork* (pp. 175–199). New York, NY: Psychology Press.

McDaniel, M. A., Howard, D. C., & Einstein, G. O. (2009). The read-recite-review study strategy: Effective and portable. *Psychological Science, 20*(4), 516–522.

McDermott, L. C., & Shaffer, P. S. (2002). *Tutorials in introductory physics.* Upper Saddle River, NJ: Prentice Hall.

McDermott, L. C., & Shaffer, P. S. (2011–2012). *Tutorials in introductory physics* (2nd ed.). New York, NY: Pearson.

McDermott, L. C., Shaffer, P. S., & Physics Education Group, University of Washington. (2012). *Tutorials in introductory physics homework.* New York, NY: Pearson.

McGaghie, W. C., McCrimmon, D. R., Mitchell, G., Thompson, J. A., & Ravitch, M. M. (2000). Quantitative concept mapping in pulmonary physiology: Comparison of student and faculty knowledge structures. *Advances in Physiology Education, 23*(1), 72–80.

McGuire, S. Y., with McGuire, S. (2015). *Teach students how to learn: Strategies you can incorporate in any course to improve student metacognition, study skills, and motivation.* Sterling, VA: Stylus.

McIntosh, M. (2010). Professors—Assign numbers to your students and return assignments quickly and easily. *Ezine Articles.* Retrieved from http://ezinearticles.com/?Professors--Assign-Numbers-to-Your-Students-and-Return-Assignments-Quickly-and-Easily&id=3799370

McKeachie, W. J. (1994). *Teaching tips: Strategies, research, and theory for college and university teachers* (9th ed.). Lexington, MA: D. C. Heath.

McKeachie, W. J. (2002). *Teaching tips: Strategies, research, and theory for college and university teachers* (11th ed.). Boston, MA: Houghton Mifflin.

McKeachie, W. B., Pintrich, P. R., Lin, Y-G., Smith, D. A., & Sharma, R. (1990). *Teaching and learning in the college classroom: A review of the literature* (2nd ed.). Ann Arbor, MI: National Center for Research to Improve Postsecondary Teaching and Learning, University of Michigan.

McKinney, K. (2001). *Responses from the POD Network discussion list on encouraging students to prepare for class.* Retrieved from http://www.cat.ilstu.edu/teaching_tips/handouts/pod.shtml

Mealy, D. L., & Host, T. R. (1993). Coping with test anxiety. *College Teaching, 40*(4), 147–150.

Mealy, D. L., & Nist, S. L. (1989). Postsecondary teacher directed comprehension strategies. *Journal of Reading, 32*(6), 484–493.

Medina, J. (2008). *Brain rules.* Seattle, WA: Pear Press.

Menges, R. J. (1988). Research on teaching and learning: The relevant and the redundant. *Review of Higher Education, 11,* 259–268.

Mento, A. J., Martinelli, P., & Jones, R. M. (1999). Mind mapping in executive education: Applications and outcomes. *Journal of Management Development, 18*(4), 390–407.

Metiri Group. (2008). *Multimodal learning through media: What the research says.* Cisco Systems. Retrieved from http://www.cisco.com/web/strategy/docs/education/Multimodal-Learning-Through-Media.pdf

Meyers, S., & Smith, B. C. (2011). The first day of class: How should instructors use class time? In J. E. Miller and J. E. Groccia (Eds.), *To improve the academy: Vol. 29. Resources for faculty, instructional, and organizational development* (pp. 147–159). San Francisco, CA: Jossey-Bass

Meyers, S. A. (2003). Strategies to prevent and reduce conflict in college classrooms. *College Teaching, 51*(3), 94–98.

Meyers, S. A. (2009). Do your students care whether you care about them? *College Teaching, 57*(4), 205–210.

Meyers, S. A., Bender, J., Hill, E. K., & Thomas, S. Y. (2006). How do faculty experience and respond to classroom conflict? *International Journal of Teaching and Learning in Higher Education, 18*(3), 180–187.

Mezeske, B. (2009). *The Graduate* revisited: Not "plastics" but "metacognition." *Teaching Professor, 23*(9), 1.

Michaelsen, L. K. (1997–1998). Keys to using learning groups effectively. *Essays on Teaching Excellence, 9*(5), 1–2.

Michaelsen, L. K., Knight, A. B., & Fink, L. D. (Eds.). (2004). *Team-based learning: A transformative use of small groups in college teaching.* Sterling, VA: Stylus.

Middendorf, J., & Kalish, A. (1996). The "change-up" in lectures. *National Teaching and Learning Forum, 5*(2), 1–4.

Mierson, S. (1998). A problem-based learning course in physiology for undergraduate and graduate basic science students. *Advances in Physiological Education, 20*(1), S16–S27.

Mierson, S., & Parikh, A. A. (2000). Stories from the field: Problem-based learning from a teacher's and a student's perspective. *Change, 32*(1), 20–27.

Miller, J. M., & Chamberlin, M. (2000). Women are teachers, men are professors: A study of student perceptions. *Teaching Sociology, 28,* 283–298.

Miller, T. M., & Geraci, L. (2011). Unskilled but aware: Reinterpreting overconfidence in low performing students. *Journal of Experimental Psychology: Learning, Memory, and Cognition, 37,* 502–506.

Milliron, V., & Sandoe, K. (2008). The Net generation cheating challenge. *Innovate: Journal of Online Education, 4*(6). Retrieved from http://www.innovateonline.info/index.php?view=article&id=499&action=article

Millis, B. J. (1990). Helping faculty build learning communities through cooperative groups. In L. Hilsen (Ed.), *To improve the academy: Vol. 9. Resources for faculty, instructional, and organizational development* (pp. 43–58). Stillwater, OK: New Forums Press.

Millis, B. J. (1992). Conducting effective peer classroom observations. In D. Wulff & J. Nyquist (Eds.), *To improve the academy: Vol. 11. Resources for faculty, instructional, and organizational development* (pp. 189–206). Stillwater, OK: New Forums Press.

Millis, B. J. (2004). A versatile interactive focus group protocol for qualitative assessments. In C. M. Wehlburg (Ed.), *To improve the academy: Vol. 22: Resources for faculty, instructional, and organizational development* (pp. 125–141). Bolton, MA: Anker.

Millis, B. J. (2005). *Question shuffle.* Retrieved from http://teaching.unr.edu/etp/teaching_tips/indexttips.html

Millis, B. J., & Cottell, P. G., Jr. (1998). *Cooperative learning for higher education faculty.* Phoenix, AZ: American Council on Education and Oryx Press.

Mills, J. E., & Treagust, D. F. (2003). Engineering education: Is problem-based or project-based learning the answer? *Australasian Journal of Engineering Education.* Retrieved from http://www.aaee.com.au/journal/2003/mills_treagust03.pdf

Montgomery, K. (2002). Authentic tasks and rubrics: Going beyond traditional assessments in college teaching. *College Teaching, 50*(1), 34–39.

Moore, A., Masterson, J. T., Christophel, D. M., & Shea, K. A. (1996). College teacher immediacy and student ratings of instruction. *Communication Education, 45*(1), 29–39.

Moore, A. H. (2003–2004). Great expectations and challenges for learning objects. *Essays on Teaching Excellence, 1*(4), 1–2.

Moore, E. (2013, January 7). Adapting PowerPoint lectures for online delivery: Best practices. *Faculty Focus.* Retrieved from http://www.facultyfocus.com/articles/online-education/adapting-powerpoint-lectures-for-online-delivery-best-practices/

Moore, S. (speaker). (2009). *Scott Moore: Using technology and collaboration to engage students* (Video). Center for Research on Learning and Teaching, University of Michigan. Retrieved from http://www.crlt.umich.edu/faculty/Thurnau/ThurnauVideos.php

Moore, V. A. (1996). Inappropriate challenges to professional authority. *Teaching Sociology, 24,* 202–206.

Moran, M., Seaman, J., & Tinti-Kane, H. (2011, April). Teaching, learning, and sharing: How today's higher education faculty use social media. Pearson Learning Solutions, Babson Survey Research Group, and Converseon. Retrieved from http://www.pearsonlearningsolutions.com/educators/pearson-social-media-survey-2011-bw.pdf

Moreno, R. (2004). Decreasing cognitive load in novice students: Effects of explanatory versus corrective feedback in discovery-based multimedia. *Instructional Science, 32,* 99–113.

Moreno, R., & Mayer, R. E. (1999). Cognitive principles of multimedia learning: The role of modality and contiguity. *Journal of Educational Psychology, 91*(2), 358–368.

Mowl, G., & Pain, R. (1995). Using self and peer assessment to improve students' essay writing: A case study from geography. *Innovations in Education and Training International, 32*(4), 324–335.

Moy, J. R., Rodenbaugh, D. W., Collins, H. L., & DiCarlo, S. E. (2000). Who wants to be a physician? An educational tool for reviewing pulmonary physiology. *Advances in Physiology Education, 24*(1), 30–37.

Mpofu, E. (2007). Service-learning effects on the academic learning of rehabilitation services students. *Michigan Journal of Community Service Learning, 14*(1), 46–52.

Mueller, P. A., & Oppenheimer, D. M. (2014). The pen is mightier than the keyboard: Advantages of longhand over laptop note taking. *Psychological Science, 25*(6), 1159–1168. doi:10.1177/0956797614524581.

Murrell, K. L. (1984). Peer performance evaluation: When peers do it, they do it better. *Journal of Management Education, 9*(4), 83–85.

Myers, C. B., & Myers, S. M. (2007). Assessing assessments: The effects of two exam formats on course achievement and evaluation. *Innovative Higher Education, 31,* 227–236.

Nadelson, S. (2007). Academic misconduct by university students: Faculty perceptions and responses. *Plagiary, 2*(2), 1–10.

Nadolski, R. J., Kirschner, P. A., & van Merriënboer, J. J. G. (2005). Optimizing the number of steps in learning tasks for complex skills. *British Journal of Educational Psychology, 84,* 429–434.

Najafi, F., Giovannucci, A., Wang, S. S.-H., & Medina, J. F. (2014). Coding of stimulus strength via analog calcium signals in Purkinje cell dendrites of awake mice. *eLife.* doi:http://dx.doi.org/10.7554/eLife.03663.

Nathan, R. (2005). *My freshman year: What a professor learned by becoming a student.* Ithaca, NY: Cornell University Press.

National Endowment for the Arts. (2007, November). *To read or not to read: A question of national consequence* (Research Report 47). Washington, DC: Author. Retrieved from http://www.nea.gov/research/ToRead.pdf

National Survey of Student Engagement. (2007). *Experiences that matter: Enhancing student learning and success.* Bloomington: Indiana University, Center for Postsecondary Research and Planning.

Nelson, C. E. (2000). How can students who are reasonably bright and who are trying hard to do the work still flunk? *National Teaching and Learning Forum, 9*(5), 7–8.

Nemire, R. E. (2007). Intellectual property development and use for distance education courses: A review of law, organizations, and resources for faculty. *College Teaching, 55*(1), 26–30.

Nettles, M. (1988). *Towards black undergraduate student equality in American higher education.* Westport, CT: Greenwood Press.

Nettleship, J. (1992). Active learning in economics: Mind maps and wall charts. *Economics, 28,* 69–71.

Nielsen, L. (2008, May 12). The value of using cell phones to enhance education and some concrete ways to do so [Web log post]. Retrieved from http://theinnovativeeducator.blogspot.com/2008/05/value-of-using-cell-phones-to-enhance.html

Nilson, L. B. (1992). Publishing research on teaching. In A. Allison & T. Frongia (Eds.), *The grad student's guide to getting published* (pp. 123–130). Upper Saddle River, NJ: Prentice Hall.

Nilson, L. B. (1997). Critical thinking as an exercise in courage. *National Teaching and Learning Forum, 6*(2), 1–4.

Nilson, L. B. (2002). The graphic syllabus: Shedding visual light on course organization. In D. Lieberman & C. Wehlburg (Eds.), *To improve the academy: Vol. 20. Resources for faculty, instructional, and organizational development* (pp. 238–259). Bolton, MA: Anker.

Nilson, L. B. (2002–2003). Helping students help each other: Making peer feedback more valuable. *Essays in Teaching Excellence, 14*(8), 1–2.

Nilson, L. B. (2003). Improving student peer feedback. *College Teaching, 51*(1), 34–38.

Nilson, L. B. (2007a). *The graphic syllabus and the outcomes map: Communicating your course.* San Francisco, CA: Jossey-Bass.

Nilson, L. B. (2007b). Best practices: Students will do the readings; Issues to consider: Holding students accountable: The options are endless, the results unexpectedly positive. *Thriving in Academe, 25*(3), 7.

Nilson, L. B. (2012). Time to raise questions about student ratings. In J. E. Groccia & L. Cruz (Eds.), *To improve the academy: Vol. 31. Resources for faculty, instructional, and organizational development* (pp. 213–227). San Francisco, CA: Jossey-Bass.

Nilson, L. B. (2013a). *Creating self-regulated learners: Strategies for strengthening students' self-awareness and learning skills.* Sterling, VA: Stylus.

Nilson, L. B. (2013b). Measuring student learning to document faculty teaching effectiveness. In J. E. Groccia & L. Cruz (Eds.), *To improve the academy: Vol. 32. Resources for faculty, instructional, and organizational development* (pp. 287–300). San Francisco, CA: Jossey-Bass.

Nilson, L. B. (2015). *Specifications grading: Restoring rigor, motivating students, and saving faculty time.* Sterling, VA: Stylus.

Nilson, L. B., & Jackson, N. S. (2004). Combating classroom misconduct (incivility) with bills of rights. *Proceedings of the Fourth Conference of the International Consortium for Educational Development.* Ottawa, ON, Canada.

Nilson, L. B., & Weaver, B. E. (Eds.). (2005). *New directions for teaching and learning: No. 101. Enhancing learning with laptops in the classroom.* San Francisco, CA: Jossey-Bass.

Nisbett, R. E. (1993). *Rules for reasoning.* Mahwah, NJ: Erlbaum.

Nixon-Cobb, E. (2005). Visualizing thinking: A strategy that improved thinking. *Teaching Professor, 19*(1), 3, 6.

Noppe, I., Achterberg, J., Duquaine, L., Huebbe, M., & Williams, C. (2007). PowerPoint presentation handouts and college student learning outcomes. *International Journal for the Scholarship of Teaching and Learning, 1*(1). Retrieved from http://academics.georgiasouthern.edu/ijsotl/v1n1/noppe/IJ_Noppe.pdf

North Carolina State University Physics Education R&D Lab (2015). About the SCALE-UP project. Retrieved from https://www.ncsu.edu/per/scaleup.html

Nosich, G. M. (2012). *Learning to think things through: A guide to critical thinking across the curriculum* (4th ed.). Upper Saddle River, NJ: Pearson/Prentice Hall.

Novak, G. M., Patterson, E. T., Gavrin, A. D., & Christian, W. (1999). *Just-in-time teaching: Blending active learning with Web technology.* Upper Saddle River, NJ: Prentice Hall.

Novak, J. D. (1977). An alternative to Piagetian psychology for sciences and mathematics education. *Science Education, 61*, 453–477.

Novak, J. D., & Gowin, B. D. (1984). *Learning how to learn.* Cambridge: Cambridge University Press.

Novak, J. M., Markey, V., & Allen, M. (2007). Evaluating cognitive outcomes of service-learning in higher education: A meta-analysis. *Communication Research Reports, 24*(2), 149–157.

Nuhfer, E. B. (2010). *A fractal thinker looks at student ratings.* Retrieved from http://sites.bio.indiana.edu/~bender/resources/Assessment/fractalevals10.pdf

Nuhfer, E., Harrington, R., Pasztor, S., & Whorf, S. (2014). Metadisciplinary awareness can illuminate the meaning, quality, and integrity of college degrees: Educating in fractal patterns XL. *National Teaching and Learning Forum, 23*(4), 9–11.

Nuhfer, E. B., & Knipp, D. (2003). The knowledge survey: A tool for all reasons. In C. Wehlburg & S. Chadwick-Blossey (Eds.), *To improve the academy: Vol. 21. Resources for faculty, instructional, and organizational development* (pp. 59–78). Bolton, MA: Anker.

Oakley, B., Brent, R., Felder, R. M., & Elhajj, I. (2004). Turning student groups into effective teams. *Journal of Student Centered Learning, 2*(1), 9–34. Retrieved from http://www4.ncsu.edu/unity/lockers/users/f/felder/public/Papers/Oakley-paper%28JSCL%29.pdf

Oblinger, D. (2003). Boomers, Gen-Xers, and millennials: Understanding the "new students." *EDUCAUSE Review, 38*(4), 36–40, 42, 44–45.

Odom, C. D. (2002, April). *Advances in instructional physics laboratories at Clemson University.* Colloquium presented at the College of Engineering and Sciences, Clemson University, Clemson, SC.

O'Donnell, A., & Dansereau, D. F. (1993). Learning from lecture: Effects of cooperative review. *Journal of Experimental Education, 61*(2), 116–125.

Okebukola, P. A. O. (1992). Can good concept mappers be good problem solvers in science? *Research in Science and Technological Education, 10*(2), 153–170.

Oliver-Hoyo, M., & Allen, D. (2005). Attitudinal effects of a student-centered active learning environment. *Journal of Chemical Education, 82*(6), 944–949.

Oliver-Hoyo, M., Allen, D., & Anderson, M. (2004). Inquiry-guided instruction. *Journal of College Science Teaching, 33*(6), 20–24.

Oliver-Hoyo, M., & Beichner, R. (2004). SCALE-UP: Bringing inquiry-guided methods to large enrollment courses. In V. S. Lee (Ed.), *Teaching and learning through inquiry: A guidebook for institutions and instructors* (pp. 51–69). Sterling, VA: Stylus.

Ophir, E., Nass, C., & Wagner, A. D. (2009). Cognitive control in media multitaskers. *Proceedings of the National Academy of Sciences of the United States of America, 106*, 15583–15587. Retrieved from http://www.pnas.org/content/early/2009/08/21/0903620106.full.pdf+html

Orlans, H. (1999). Scholarly fair use: Chaotic and shrinking. *Change, 31*(6), 53–60.

Orsmond, P., Merry, S., & Reiling, K. (1996). The importance of marking criteria in peer assessment. *Assessment and Evaluation in Higher Education, 21*(3), 239–249.

Ory, J. C., & Ryan, K. E. (1993). *Survival skills for college: Vol. 4. Tips for improving testing and grading.* Thousand Oaks, CA: Sage.

Paivio, A. (1971). *Imagery and verbal processes.* New York, NY: Holt.

Paivio, A. (1990). *Mental representations: A dual coding approach.* New York, NY: Oxford University Press.

Paivio, A., & Csapo, K. (1973). Picture superiority in free recall: Imagery and dual coding? *Cognitive Psychology, 5*, 176–206.

Paivio, A., Walsh, M., & Bons, T. (1994). Concreteness effects on memory: When and why? *Journal of Experimental Psychology: Learning, Memory, and Cognition, 20*(5), 1196–1204.

Palmer, M. S., Bach, D. J., & Streifer, A. C. (2014). Measuring the promise: A learning-focused syllabus rubric. *To Improve the Academy, 33*(1), 14–36.

Parish, B. (2013, May 2). 'Appropriate' technology. *Inside Higher Education.* Retrieved from http://www.insidehighered.207elmp01.blackmesh.com/views/2013/05/02/technology-innovation-should-focus-letting-teachers-teach-essay

Parry, M. (2013, March 24). You're distracted. This professor can help. *Chronicle of Higher Education.* Retrieved from http://chronicle.com/article/Youre-Distracted-This/138079/

Pascarella, E. T., & Terenzini, P. T. (2005). *How college affects students: A third decade of research.* San Francisco, CA: Jossey-Bass.

Pashler, H., McDaniel, M., Rohrer, D., & Bjork, R. (2009). Learning styles: Concepts and evidence. *Psychological Science in the Public Interest, 9*(3), 105–119. Retrieved from http://www3.interscience.wiley.com/journal/123216067/abstract?CRETRY=1&SRETRY=0

Patterson, R. W. (2015). *Can behavioral tools improve online student outcomes? Experimental evidence from a massive open online course.* Cornell Higher Education Research Institute. Retrieved from http://www.human.cornell.edu/pam/academics/phd/upload/PattersonJMP11_18.pdf

Pauk, W. (2001). *How to study in college.* Boston, MA: Houghton Mifflin.

Paul, R., & Elder, L. (2013a). *Critical thinking: Teaching students how to study and learn, Part III.* Retrieved from http://www.criticalthinking.org/pages/how-to-study-and-learn-part-three/515.

Paul, R., & Elder, L. (2013b). *The state of critical thinking today.* Retrieved from http://www.criticalthinking.org/pages/the-state-of-critical-thinking-today/523

Paul, R., & Elder, L. (2013c). *Universal intellectual standards.* Retrieved from http://www.criticalthinking.org/pages/universal-intellectual-standards/527

Paul, R., & Elder, L. (2013d). *Valuable intellectual traits.* Retrieved from http://www.criticalthinking.org/pages/valuable-intellectual-traits/528)

Paul, R., Elder, L., & Bartell, T. (2013). *Study of 38 public universities and 28 private universities to determine faculty emphasis on critical thinking in instruction.* Retrieved from http://www.criticalthinking.org/pages/study-of-38-public-universities-and-28-private-universities-to-determine-faculty-emphasis-on-critical-thinking-in-instruction/598

Paulsen, M. B., & Feldman, K. A. (1999). Student motivation and epistemological beliefs. In M. Theall (Ed.), *New directions for teaching and learning: No. 78. Motivation from within: Encouraging faculty and students to excel* (pp. 17–25). San Francisco, CA: Jossey-Bass.

Peirce, W. (2006). *Strategies for teaching critical reading.* Retrieved from http://academic.pg.cc.md.us/~wpeirce/MCCCTR/critread.html

Perry, W. G. (1968). *Forms of intellectual and ethical development in the college years: A scheme.* New York, NY: Holt.

Perry, W. G. (1985). Different worlds in the same classroom. *Journal of the Harvard-Danforth Center: On Teaching and Learning, 1,* 1–17.

Persellin, D. C., & Daniels, M. B. (2014). *A concise guide to improving student learning: Six evidence-based principles and how to apply them.* Sterling, VA: Stylus.

Plotnick, E. (1996). *Trends in educational psychology.* Syracuse, NY: ERIC Clearinghouse on Information and Technology. (ERIC Document Reproduction Service No. ED398861)

Plotnick, E. (2001). A graphical system for understanding the relationship between concepts. *Teacher Librarian, 2*(4), 42–44.

Posner, G. J., Strike, K. A., Hewson, P. W., & Gertzog, W. A. (1982). Accommodation of a scientific concept: Towards a theory of conceptual change. *Science Education, 66*(2), 211-227.

Potts, B. (1993). Improving the quality of student notes. *Practical Assessment, Research, and Evaluation, 3*(8). Retrieved from http://PAREonline.net/getvn.asp?v=3&n=8

Poythress, K. (2007, May 25). Cheating rampant on college campuses, survey reveals. *CNS News Culture.* Retrieved from http://www.cnsnews.com/public/content/article.aspx?RsrcID=7446

Prégent, R. (1994). *Charting your course: How to prepare to teach more effectively.* Madison, WI: Magna.

Preszler, R. W. (2009). Replacing lecture with peer-led workshops improves student learning. *Life Science*

Education, 8(3), 182–192. doi:10.1187/cbe.09–01–0002. Retrieved from http://www.ncbi.nlm.nih.gov/pmc/articles/PMC2736022/

Prince, M. (2004). Does active learning work? A review of the research. *Journal of Engineering Education, 93*(3), 223–231.

Prince, M., & Felder, R. M. (2006). Inductive teaching and learning methods: Definitions, comparisons, and research bases. *Journal of Engineering Education, 95*(2), 123–138.

Prince, M., & Felder, R. M. (2007). The many faces of inductive teaching and learning. *Journal of College Science Teaching, 36*(5), 14–20.

Profile of undergraduate students, 2003–04. (2007, August 31). *Chronicle of Higher Education Almanac Issue 2007–8*, p. 17.

Pryor, I. H., Hurtado, S., Saenz, V. B., Santos, J. L., & Korn, W. S. (2007). *The American freshman: Forty year trends.* Los Angeles: Higher Education Research Institute, UCLA. Retrieved from http://www.heri.ucla.edu/PDFs/pubs/TFS/Trends/Monographs/The AmericanFreshman40YearTrends.pdf

Qualters, D. M. (2001). Do students want to be active? *Journal of Scholarship of Teaching and Learning, 2*(1), 51–60.

Race, P., & Pickford, R. (2007). *Making teaching work: "Teaching smarter" in post-compulsory education.* London, UK: Sage.

Radosevich, D. J., Salomon, R., Radosevich, D. M., & Kahn, P. (2008). Using student response systems to increase motivation, learning, and knowledge retention. *Innovate, 5*(1). Retrieved from http://www.innovateonline.info/index.php?view=article&id=40&action=article

Raines, C. (2002). *Connecting generations: The sourcebook for a new workplace.* Menlo Park, CA: Crisp Publications.

Raymark, P., & Connor-Greene, P. (2002). The syllabus quiz. *Teaching of Psychology, 29*(4), 286–288.

Reay, N. W., Li, P., & Bao, L. (2008). Testing a new voting machine question methodology. *American Journal of Physics, 76*(2), 171–178.

Rebich, S., & Gauthier, C. (2005). Concept mapping to reveal prior knowledge and conceptual change in a mock summit course on global climate change. *Journal of Geoscience Education, 53*(4), 355–365.

Reddish, E. F. (2003). *Teaching physics with the physics suite.* Hoboken, NJ: Wiley.

Reddish, E. F., Saul, J. M., & Steinberg, R. N. (1997). On the effectiveness of active-engagement microcomputer-based laboratories. *American Journal of Physics, 65,* 45–54.

Reddish, E. F., Saul, J. M., & Steinberg, R. N. (1998). Students' expectations in introductory physics. *American Journal of Physics, 66*(3), 212–224.

Reddish, E. F., & Steinberg, R. N. (1999). Who will study physics, and why? *Physics Today, 52,* 24–30.

Redlawsk, D. P., Rice, T., & Associates. (2009). *Civic service: Service-learning with state and local government partners.* San Francisco, CA: Jossey-Bass.

Redmond, B. F., & Perrin, J. J. (2014). *Goal setting theory. PSYCH 484: Work Attitudes and Job Motivation,* Pennsylvania State University. Retrieved from https://wikispaces.psu.edu/display/PSYCH484/6.+Goal+Setting+Theory

Reed, D. (2013). *Is the syllabus a contract?* Retrieved from http://www.uri.edu/facsen/Curricular_Materials/Course_Proposals_2013–14/CAC_nov-25/Is_a_Syllabus_a_Contract.pdf

Regis, A., & Albertazzi, P. G. (1996). Concept maps in chemistry education. *Journal of Chemical Education, 73*(11), 1084–1088.

Rettinger, D., & Kramer, Y. (2009). Situational and personal causes of student cheating. *Research in Higher Education, 50,* 293–313. Retrieved from http://link.springer.com/article/10.1007/s11162–008–9116–5/fulltext.html

Rettinger, D. A., & Searcy, D. (2012). Student-led honor codes as a method for reducing university cheating. *Economic and Environmental Studies, 12*(3), 223–234. Retrieved from http://www.academia.edu/4265959/An_Honor_Code_Case_Study

Rhem, J. (2006). The high risks of improving teaching. *National Teaching and Learning Forum, 15*(6), 1–4.

Rhode Island Diploma System. (2005). *Exhibition toolkit: Support student self-management and reflection.* Retrieved from http://www.ride.ri.gov/highschoolreform/dslat/exhibit/exhact_1003.shtml#t

Rice, R. E., Sorcinelli, M. D., & Austin, A. E. (2000). *Heeding new voices: Academic careers for a new generation.* Washington, DC: American Association for Higher Education.

Reiner, C. M., Bothell, T. W., Sudweeks, R. R., & Wood. B. (2004). Preparing effective essay questions: A self-directed workbook for educators. Stillwater, OK: New Forums Press.

Riener, C., & Willingham, D. (2010). The myth of learning styles. *Change, 42*(5), 32–35.

Rigby, C. S., Deci, E. L., Patrick, B. C., & Ryan, R. M. (1992). Beyond the intrinsic-extrinsic dichotomy: Self-determination in motivation and learning. *Motivation and Emotion, 16*(3), 165–185.

Ripley, A. (2013). *The smartest kids in the world and how they got that way.* New York, NY: Simon & Schuster.

Roach, K. D. (1997). Effects of graduate teaching assistant attire on student learning, misbehaviors, and ratings of instruction. *Communication Quarterly.* Retrieved from http://zoology.wisc.edu/grad/attire.pdf

Robinson, B. D., & Schaible, R. (1993). Women and men teaching "Men, Women, and Work." *Teaching Sociology, 21,* 363–370.

Robinson, D. H., Katayama, A. D., DuBois, N. E., & Devaney, T. (1998). Interactive effects of graphic organizers and delayed review of concept application. *Journal of Experimental Education, 67*(1), 17–31.

Robinson, D. H., & Kiewra, K. A. (1995). Visual argument: Graphic organizers are superior to outlines in improving learning from text. *Journal of Educational Psychology, 87*(3), 455–467.

Robinson, D. H., & Molina, E. (2002). The relative involvement of visual and auditory working memory when studying adjunct displays. *Contemporary Educational Psychology, 27*(1), 118–131.

Robinson, D. H., & Schraw, G. (1994). Computational efficiency through visual argument: Do graphic organizers communicate relations in text too effectively? *Contemporary Educational Psychology, 19,* 399–414.

Robinson, D. H., & Skinner, C. H. (1996). Why graphic organizers facilitate search processes: Fewer words or computationally efficient indexing? *Contemporary Educational Psychology, 21,* 166–180.

Rodgers, M. L. (1995). How holistic scoring kept writing alive in chemistry. *College Teaching, 43*(1), 19–22.

Roediger, H. L. III, & Butler, A. C. (2010). The critical role of retrieval practice in long-term retention. *Trends in Cognitive Sciences, 15*(1), 20–27. doi:10.1016/j.tics.2010.09.003

Roediger, H. L., III, & Karpicke, J. D. (2006). The power of testing memory: Basic research and implications of the educational practice. *Perspective on Psychological Science, 1*(3), 181–210.

Rohrer, D., & Pashler, H. (2010). Recent research on human learning challenges conventional instructional strategies. *Educational Researcher, 39*(5), 406–412. doi:10.3102/0013189X10374770

Rohrer, D., Taylor, K., & Sholar, B. (2010). Tests enhance the transfer of learning. *Journal of Experimental Psychology: Learning, Memory, and Cognition, 36*(1), 233–239. Retrieved from http://uweb.cas.usf.edu/~drohrer/pdfs/Rohrer_et_al_2010JEPLMC.pdf

Romance, N. R., & Vitale, M. R. (1999). Concept mapping as a tool for learning. *College Teaching, 4*(2), 74–79.

Romero, C. C. (2009). *Cooperative learning instruction and science achievement for secondary and early postsecondary students: A systematic review.* Doctoral dissertation, Colorado State University.

Rosen, L. D., Carrier, L. M., & Cheever, N. A. (2013). Facebook and texting made me do it: Media-induced task-switching while studying. *Computers in Human Behavior, 29,* 948–958. Retrieved from http://dx.doi.org/10.1016/j.chb.2012.12.001

Ross, R. H., & Headley, E. L. (2002). Training new college professors to teach more effectively: What role does the case method play? *Journal of Excellence in College Teaching, 13*(2/3). Retrieved from http://celt.muohio.edu/ject/issue.php?v=13&n=2+and+3

Rowe, M. B. (1980). Pausing principles and their effects on reasoning in science. In F. B. Brawer (Ed.), *New directions for community colleges: No. 8. Teaching the science* (pp. 27–34). San Francisco, CA: Jossey-Bass.

Royce, A. P. (2000). *A survey of academic incivility at Indiana University: Preliminary report.* Bloomington: Indiana University, Center for Survey Research.

Royer, J., Cisero, C., & Carlo, M. S. (1993). Techniques and procedures for assessing cognitive skills. *Review of Educational Research 63*(2), 201-243.

Ruhl, K. L., Hughes, C. A., & Schloss, P. J. (1987). Using the pause procedure to enhance lecture recall. *Teacher Education and Special Education, 10,* 14–18.

Ruohoniemi, M., & Lindblom-Ylanne, S. (2009). Students' experiences concerning course workload and factors enhancing and impeding their learning: A useful resource for quality enhancement in teaching and curriculum planning. *International Journal for Academic Development, 14*(1), 69–81.

Ruscio, J. (2001). Administering quizzes at random to increase student reading. *Teaching of Psychology, 28*(3), 204–206.

Ryan, R. M., & Deci, E. L. (2000). Intrinsic and extrinsic motivations: Class definition and new directions. *Contemporary Education Psychology, 25*(1), 54–67.

Rybarczyk, B., Baines, A., McVey, M., Thompson, J., & Wilkins, H. (2007). A case-based approach increases student learning outcomes and comprehension of cellular respiration concepts. *Biochemistry and Molecular Biology Education, 35*, 181–186.

Sacks, D., Glazer, F., & Zhadko, O. (2014, November). *Creating a fulcrum: Empowering faculty to leverage educational technologies.* Session presented at the 39th Annual Conference of the Professional and Organizational Development Network in Higher Education, Dallas, TX.

Sanchez, C. A., & Wiley, J. (2009). To scroll or not to scroll: Scrolling, working memory capacity, and comprehending complex texts. *Human Factors, 51*(5), 730–738. Retrieved from http://people.oregonstate.edu/~sancchri/pubs/scroll.pdf

Sass, E. J. (1989). Motivation in the college classroom: What students tell us. *Teaching of Psychology, 16*(2), 86–88.

SCCtv, Boyer, M., & Harnish, J. (Coproducers/Writers/Directors). (2007). *Seminar: A skill everyone can learn.* Seattle, WA: University of North Seattle Community College.

Schau, C., & Mattern, N. (1997). Use of map techniques in teaching applied statistics courses. *American Statistician, 51*, 171–175.

Schell, J. (2012, September 4). How one professor motivated students to read before a flipped class, and measured their effort. Turn to Your Neighbor blog. Retrieved from http://blog.peerinstruction.net/2012/09/04/how-one-professor-motivated-students-to-read-before-a-flipped-class-and-measured-their-effort/

Schinske, J., & Tanner, K. (2014). Teaching more by grading less (or differently). *Cell Biology Education—Life Sciences Education, 13*, 159–166.

Schneider, A. (1999, January 22). Why professors don't do more to stop students who cheat. *Chronicle of Higher Education,* pp. A8–A10.

Schraw, G. (1998). Promoting general metacognitive awareness. *Instructional Science, 26,* 113–125. Retrieved from http://www.springerlink.com/content/w884l0214g78445h/

Schönwetter, D. J., Sokal, L., Friesen, M., & Taylor, L. L. (2002). Teaching philosophies reconsidered: A conceptual model for the development and evaluation of teaching philosophy statements. *International Journal for Academic Development, 7*(1), 83–97.

Schroeder, C. M., Scott, T. P., Tolson, H., Huang, T., & Lee, Y. (2007). A meta-analysis of national research: Effects of teaching strategies on student achievement in science in the United States. *Journal of Research in Science Teaching, 44*(10), 1436–1460.

Schuman, R. (2014, August 26). When—and why—did the college course syllabus get so insanely long? Syllabus Tyrannus. *Slate.* Retrieved from http://www.slate.com/articles/life/education/2014/08/college_course_syllabi_they_re_too_long_and_they_re_a_symbol_of_the_decline.html

Schuster, P. M. (2000). Concept mapping: Reducing clinical care plan paperwork and increasing learning. *Nurse Educator, 25*(2), 76–81.

Seesholtz, M., & Polk, B. (2009, October 10). Two professors, one valuable lesson: How to respectfully disagree. *Chronicle of Higher Education.* Retrieved from http://chronicle.com/article/Two-Professors-One-Valuable/48901/

Seldin, P., Miller, J. E., & Seldin, C. A. (2010). *The teaching portfolio: A practical guide to improved performance and promotion/tenure decisions.* San Francisco, CA: Jossey-Bass.

Semetko, H. A., & Scammell, M. (2012). *The Sage handbook of political communication.* Thousand Oaks, CA: Sage.

Seymour, E., & Hewitt, N. M. (1997). *Talking about leaving: Why undergraduates leave the sciences.* Boulder, CO: Westview Press.

Shaffer, L. (n.d.). *Texts and teaching.* Retrieved from http://faculty.plattsburgh.edu/lary.shaffer/texts%20and%20teaching.html

Shank, J. D. (2014). *Interactive open educational resources: A guide to finding, choosing, and using what's out there to transform college teaching.* San Francisco, CA: Jossey-Bass.

Sharkey, L., Overmann, J., & Flash, P. (2007). Evolution of a course in veterinary clinical pathology: The application of case-based writing assignments to focus on skill development and facilitation of learning. *Journal of Veterinary Medical Education, 34*(4), 423–430.

Shu, L. L., Gino, F., & Bazerman, M. H. (2011). Dishonest deed, clear conscience: When cheating leads to moral disengagement and motivated forgetting. *Personality and Social Psychology Bulletin, 37*(3), 330–349. doi: 10.1177/0146167211398138

Sibley, J. (2014, October 6). Seven mistakes to avoid when writing multiple-choice questions. *Faculty Focus.* Retrieved from http://www.facultyfocus.com/articles/educational-assessment/seven-mistakes-avoid-writing-multiple-choice-questions/

Sibley, J., & Ostafichuk, P. (Eds.), with Roberson, B., Franchini, B., & Kubitz, K. A. (2014). *Getting started with team-based learning.* Sterling, VA: Stylus.

Silberman, M. (1994). *Active learning: 101 strategies to teach any subject.* Needham Heights, MA: Allyn & Bacon.

Singham, M. (2007). Death to the syllabus. *Liberal Education, 93*(4). Retrieved from http://www.aacu.org/liberaleducation/le-fa07/le_fa07_myview.cfm

Singleton-Jackson, J. A., Jackson, D. L., & Reinhardt, J. (2010). Students as consumers of knowledge: Are they buying what we're selling? *Innovative Higher Education, 35*(4), 343–358.

Sirias, D. (2002). Using graphic organizers to improve the teaching of business statistics. *Journal of Education for Business, 78,* 33–37.

Slatta, R. W. (2004). Enhancing inquiry-guided learning with technology in history courses. In V. S. Lee (Ed.), *Teaching and learning through inquiry: A guidebook for institutions and instructors* (pp. 93–102). Sterling, VA: Stylus.

Slattery, J. M., & Carlson, J. F. (2005). Preparing an effective syllabus: Current best practices. *College Teaching, 53*(4), 159–164.

Slunt, K. M., & Giancarlo, L. C. (2004). Student-centered learning: A comparison of two different methods of instruction. *Journal of Chemical Education, 81*(7), 985–988.

Smit, D. (2010). *Strategies to improve students writing* (IDEA Paper No. 48). Manhattan, KS: IDEA Center. Retrieved from http://ideaedu.org/sites/default/files/IDEA_Paper_48.pdf

Smith, D. J., & Valentine, T. (2012). The use and perceived effectiveness of instructional practices in two-year technical colleges. *Journal of Excellence in College Teaching, 23*(1), 133-161. Retrieved from https://getd.libs.uga.edu/pdfs/smith_daniel_j_201005_edd/smith_daniel_j_201005_edd.pdf

Smith, M. K., Jones, F. H., Gilbert, S. L., & Wieman, C. E. (2013). The classroom observation protocol for undergraduate STEM (CIPUS): A new instrument to characterize university STEM classroom practices. *Life Sciences Education, 12,* 618–627.

Sokoloff, D., & Thornton, R. (1997). Using interactive lecture demonstrations to create an active learning environment. *Physics Teaching, 35,* 340–347.

Sokoloff, D., & Thornton, R. (2001). *Interactive lecture demonstrations.* Hoboken, NJ: Wiley.

Specht, L. B., & Sandlin, P. K. (1991). The differential effects of experiential learning activities and traditional lecture classes in accounting. *Simulation and Gaming, 22*(2), 196–210.

Spence, L. D. (2001). The case against teaching. *Change, 33*(6), 11–19.

Springer, L., Stanne, M. E., & Donovan, S. S. (1999). Effects of small-group learning on undergraduates in science, mathematics, engineering, and technology: A meta-analysis. *Review of Educational Research, 69*(1), 21–51.

Sproule, R. (2002). The underdetermination of instructor performance by data from the student evaluation of teaching. *Economics of Education Review, 21,* 287–295.

Squire, K. (2011). *Video games and learning: Teaching and participatory culture in the digital age.* New York, NY: Teachers College Press.

Staats, S., Hupp, J. M., Wallace, H., & Gresley, J. (2009). Heroes don't cheat: An examination of academic dishonesty and students' views on why professors don't report cheating. *Ethics and Behavior, 19*(3), 171–183.

Stage, F. K., Kinzie, J., Muller, P., & Simmons, A. (1999). *Creating learning centered classrooms: What does learning theory have to say?* Washington, DC: ERIC Clearinghouse on Higher Education.

Stahl, R. J. (1994). *Using "think time" and "wait time" skillfully in the classroom.* (ERIC Document Reproduction Service No. ED370885)

Stahl, S. A. (1999, Fall). Different strokes for different folks? A critique of learning styles. *American Educator.* Retrieved from http://www.aft.org/pubs-reports/american_educator/fall99/DiffStrokes.pdf

Stanfel, L. E. (1995). Measuring the accuracy of student evaluations of teaching. *Journal of Instructional Psychology, 22*(2), 117–125.

Steiner, S., Holley, L. C., Gerdes, K., & Campbell, H. E. (2006). Evaluating teaching: Listening to students while acknowledging bias. *Journal of Social Work Education, 42,* 355–376.

Steinkuehler, C. Squire, K., & Barab, S. (Eds.). (2012). *Games, learning, and society: Learning and meaning in the digital age.* New York, NY: Cambridge University Press.

Stenmark, J. K. (1989). *Assessment alternatives in mathematics: An overview of assessment techniques that promote learning.* Berkeley, CA: EQUALS, Lawrence Hall of Science and California Mathematics Council.

Stenmark, J. K. (1991). *Mathematics assessment: Myths, models, good questions, and practical suggestions.* Reston, VA: National Council of Teachers of Mathematics.

Stephan, E. A., Bowman, D. R., Park, W. J., Sill, B. L., & Ohland, M. W. (2014). *Thinking like an engineer: An active learning approach* (3rd ed.). Upper Saddle Creek, NJ: Prentice-Hall.

Stevens, D. D., & Cooper, J. E. (2009). *Journal keeping: How to use reflective writing for learning, teaching, professional insight and positive change.* Sterling, VA: Stylus.

Stevens, D. D., & Levi A. J. (2012). *Introduction to rubrics: An assessment tool to save grading time, convey effective feedback, and promote student learning* (2nd ed.). Sterling, VA: Stylus.

Strauss, W., & Howe, N. (2003). *Millennials go to college: Strategies for a new generation on campus.* Washington, DC: American Association of Collegiate Registrars and Admissions Officers.

Strobel, J., & van Barneveld, A. (2009). When is PBL more effective? A meta-synthesis of meta-analyses comparing PBL to conventional classrooms. *Interdisciplinary Journal of Problem-Based Learning, 3*(1), 44–58.

Student Assessment of Learning Gains (SALG) survey instrument. (n.d.). Retrieved from http://www.salgsite.org

Suarez, J., & Martin, A. (2001). Internet plagiarism: A teacher's combat guide. *Contemporary Issues in Technology and Teacher Education* [online serial], *1*(4). Retrieved from http://www.citejournal.org/vol1/iss4/currentpractice/article2.htm

Sullivan, C. S., Middendorf, J., & Camp, M. E. (2008). Engrained study habits and the challenge of warm-ups in just-in-time teaching. *National Teaching and Learning Forum, 17*(4), 5–8.

Supiano, B. (2014, November 17). Think students in your class might be cheating? Here's what to do. *Chronicle of Higher Education.* Retrieved from http://chronicle.com/article/Think-Students-in-Your-Class/150091/

Suskie, L. (2009). *Assessing student learning: A common sense guide* (2nd ed.). San Francisco, CA: Jossey-Bass.

Svinicki, M. (2004). *Learning and motivation in the postsecondary classroom.* Bolton, MA: Anker.

Svinicki, M. (2014). In note-taking, quantity and quality both count (or more is better but better is also better). *National Teaching and Learning Forum, 23*(5), 11–12.

Sweet, M., & Michaelsen, L. K. (2012). *Team-based learning in the social sciences and humanities: Group work that works to generate critical thinking and engagement.* Sterling, VA: Stylus.

Tai-Seale, T. (2001). Liberating service-learning and applying new practice. *College Teaching, 49*(1), 14–18.

Talbert, R. (2015, March 15). Three critical conversations started and sustained by flipping learning. *Faculty Focus.* Retrieved from http://www.facultyfocus.com/articles/effective-teaching-strategies/three-critical-conversations-started-sustained-flipped-learning/

Tallahassee Community College Library. (2013). *Cheating prevention in college classrooms.* Retrieved from http://tcc.fl.libguides.com/content.php?pid=281116&sid=2800329

Tanner, K. D. (2012). Promoting student metacognition. *Life Sciences Education, 11,* 113–120. Retrieved from http://www.lifescied.org/content/11/2/113.full

Tanner, M. J. (2014). Digital vs. print: Reading comprehension and the future of the book. *SJSU School of Information Student Research Journal, 4(*2). Retrieved from http://scholarworks.sjsu.edu/slissrj/vol4/iss2/6

Taricani, E. M., & Clariana, R. B. (2006). A technique for automatically scoring open-ended concept maps. *Educational Technology Research and Development, 54*(1), 65–82.

Taylor, A. K., & Kowalski, P. (2014). Student misconceptions: Where do they come from and what can we do? In V. A. Benassi, C. E. Overton, & C. M. Hakala (Eds.), *Applying science of learning in education: Infusing psychological science into the curriculum* (pp. 259–273). Division 2, American Psychological Association, Society for the Teaching of Psychology. Retrieved from http://teach-psych.org/ebooks/asle2014/index.php

Taylor, M. L. (2006). Generation NeXt comes to college: 2006 updates and emerging issues. In S. E. Van Kollenburg (Ed.), *A collection of papers on self-study and institutional improvement* (Vol. 2, pp. 48–55). Chicago, IL: Higher Learning Commission.

Teaching Assistant Program, Michigan State University. (n.d.). *MSU thoughts on teaching #10: What undergraduates say are the most irritating faculty behaviors.* Retrieved from http://tap.msu.edu/PDF/thoughts/tt10.pdf

Theall, M., & Franklin, J. (1999). What have we learned? A synthesis and some guidelines for effective motivation in higher education. In M. Theall (Ed.), *New directions for teaching and learning: No. 78. Motivation from within: Encouraging faculty and students to excel* (pp. 97–109). San Francisco, CA: Jossey-Bass.

Thomas, J. W. (2000). *A review of research on project-based learning.* San Rafael, CA: Autodesk Foundation.

Thompson, B. (2002, June 21). If I quiz them, they will come. *Chronicle of Higher Education,* p. B5.

Thorn, P. M. (2003). *Bridging the gap between what is praised and what is practiced: Supporting the work of change as anatomy and physiology instructors introduce active learning into their undergraduate classroom.* Doctoral dissertation, University of Texas, Austin.

Thorne, B. M. (2000). Extra credit exercises: A painless pop quiz. *Teaching of Psychology, 27*(3), 204–205.

Tigner, R. B. (1999). Putting memory research to good use: Hints from cognitive psychology. *College Teaching, 47*(4), 149–152.

Tindell, D. R., & Bohlander, R. W. (2012). The use and abuse of cell phones and text messaging in the classroom: A survey of college students. *College Teaching, 60*(1), 1–9. Retrieved from http://www.tandfonline.com/doi/full/10.1080/87567555.2011.604802

Tobias, S. (1990). *They're not dumb, they're different: Stalking the second tier.* Tucson, AZ: Research Corporation.

Thomason, A. (2014, September 3) Your 3 worst classroom distractions (and how to deal with them). *Chronicle of Higher Education.* Retrieved from http://chronicle.com/blogs/ticker/your-3-worst-classroom-distractions-and-how-to-deal-with-them/85255

Topping, K. (1998). Peer-assessment between students in colleges and universities. *Review of Educational Research, 68,* 249–276.

Toyama, K. (2015, May 19). Why technology will never fix education. *Chronicle of Higher Education.* Retrieved from http://chronicle.com/article/Why-Technology-Will-Never-Fix/230185/

Treisman, P. U. (1986). *A study of the mathematics performance of black students at the University of California, Berkeley.* Doctoral dissertation, University of California, Berkeley.

Tremblay, K. R., Jr., & Downey, E. P. (2004). Identifying and evaluating research-based publications: Enhancing undergraduate student critical thinking skills. *Education, 124*(4), 734–740.

Trujillo-Jenks, L., & Rosen, L. (2015, May 27). Fostering student learning through the use of debates. *Faculty Focus.* Retrieved from http://www.facultyfocus.com/articles/instructional-design/fostering-student-learning-through-the-use-of-debates/

Trumbore, A. (2014). Rules of engagement: Strategies to increase online engagement at scale. *Change, 46*(4), 38–45.

Tucker, P. (2006). Teaching the millennial generation. *Futurist, 40,* 1.

Tuckman, B. (1965). Developmental sequence in small groups. *Psychological Bulletin, 63*(6), 384–399.

Tulving, E. (1985). How many memory systems are there? *American Psychologist, 40,* 385–398.

Turner, C.S.V., & Myers, S. L., Jr. (2000). *Faculty of color in academe: Bittersweet success.* Needham Heights, MA: Allyn & Bacon.

Turnitin. (2014). Instructor feedback writ large: Student perceptions on effective feedback. White paper. Retrieved from http://www.turnitin.com/assets/en_us/media/201501-che.html

Tversky, B. (1995). Cognitive origins of conventions. In F. T. Marchese (Ed.), *Understanding images* (pp. 29–53). New York, NY: Springer-Verlag.

Tversky, B. (2001). Spatial schemas in depictions. In M. Gattis (Ed.), *Spatial schemas and abstract thought* (pp. 79–111). Cambridge, MA: MIT Press.

Tyner, K. (2010). *Media literacy: New agendas in communication.* New York, NY: Routledge.

Twenge, J. M. (2007). *Generation me: Why today's young Americans are more confident, assertive, entitled and more miserable than ever before.* New York, NY: Free Press.

Umbach, P. D., & Wawrzynski. M. R. (2005). Faculty do matter: The role of college faculty in student learning and engagement. *Research in Higher Education, 46*, 153–184.

University of Minnesota Libraries. (2015). *Copyright information and resources.* Retrieved from https://www.lib.umn.edu/copyright/

Urdan, T. (2003). Intrinsic motivation, extrinsic rewards, and divergent views of reality. Review of the book *Intrinsic and extrinsic motivation: The search for optimal motivation and performance. Educational Psychology Review, 15*(3), 311–325.

U.S. Department of Education, Institute for Education Sciences, National Center for Education Statistics (2013). *Digest of Education Statistics.* Washington, DC: Author. Retrieved from https://nces.ed.gov/programs/digest/d13/tables/dt13_306.10.asp

Vander Schee, B. A. (2009). Do students really know their academic strengths? *Teaching Professor, 23*(7). Retrieved from http://www.montana.edu/facultyexcellence/documents/dec1_academicstrengths.pdf

Vekiri, I. (2002). What is the value of graphical displays in learning? *Educational Psychology Review, 14*(3), 261–312.

Vella, J. (1994). *Learning to listen, learning to teach: The power of dialogue in educating adults.* San Francisco, CA: Jossey-Bass.

Vojtek, B., & Vojtek, R. (2000). Technology: Visual learning—This software helps organize ideas and concepts. *Journal of Staff Development, 21*(4). Retrieved

from http://www.nsdc.org/library/publications/jsd/vojtek214.cfm

Walker, V. L. (2009). 3D virtual learning in counselor education: Using Second Life in counselor skill development. *Journal of Virtual Worlds Research, 2*(1). Retrieved from http://journals.tdl.org/jvwr/article/view/423/463.

Wallace, J. D., & Mintzes, J. J. (1990). The concept map as a research tool: Exploring conceptual change in biology. *Journal of Research in Science Teaching, 27*(10), 1033–1052.

Waller, R. (1981, April). *Understanding network diagrams.* Paper presented at the Annual Meetings of the American Educational Research Association, Los Angeles. (ERIC Document Reproduction Service No. ED226695)

Wästlund, E., Reinikka, H., Norlander, T., & Archer, T. (2005). Effects of VDT and paper presentation on consumption and production of information: Psychological and physiological factors. *Computers in Human Behavior, 21*(2), 377–394. Retrieved from http://dx.doi.org/10.1016/j.chb.2004.02.007

Walvoord, B. E. (2014). *Assessing and improving student writing in college: A guide for institutions, general education, departments, and classrooms.* San Francisco, CA: Jossey-Bass.

Walvoord, B. E., & Anderson, V. J. (2010). *Effective grading: A tool for learning and assessment* (2nd ed.). San Francisco, CA: Jossey-Bass.

Wandersee, J. (2002a). Using concept circle diagramming as a knowledge mapping tool. In K. Fisher, J. Wandersee, & D. Moody (Eds.), *Mapping biology knowledge* (pp. 109–126). Dordrecht, NL: Springer Netherlands.

Wandersee, J. (2002b). Using concept mapping as a knowledge mapping tool. In K. Fisher, J. Wandersee, & D. Moody (Eds.), *Mapping biology knowledge* (pp. 127–142). Dordrecht, NL: Springer Netherlands.

Wasley, P. (2008, February 29). Antiplagiarism software takes on the honor code. *Chronicle of Higher Education,* p. A12.

Waterman, M. A., & Stanley, E. (2005). *Case format variations.* Retrieved from http://cstl-csm.semo.edu/waterman/cbl/caseformats.html

Waugh, C. K., & Gronlund, N. E. (2012). *Assessment of student achievement* (10th ed.). Upper Saddle River, NJ: Pearson.

Webb, N. G., & Barrett, L. O. (2014). Student views of instructor-student rapport in the college classroom. *Journal of the Scholarship of Teaching and Learning, 14*(2), 15–28.

Weimer, M. (2007). Helping students take stock of learning. *Teaching Professor, 21*(2), 4.

Weimer, M. (2013a). *Learner-centered teaching: Five key changes to practice* (2nd ed.). San Francisco, CA: Jossey-Bass.

Weimer, M. (2013b, January 9). First day of class activities that create a climate for learning. *Faculty Focus*: The Teaching Professor Blog. Retrieved from http://www.facultyfocus.com/articles/teaching-professor-blog/first-day-of-class-activities-that-create-a-climate-for-learning/

Weinberg, B. A., Fleisher, B. M., & Hashimoto, M. (2007). Evaluating methods of evaluating instruction: The case of higher education (NBER Working Paper No. 12844). Retrieved from http://www.nber.org/papers/w12844

Weinberg, B. A., Hashimoto, M., & Fleisher, B. M. (2009). Evaluating teaching in higher education. *Journal of Economic Education, 40*(3), 227–261.

Wergin, J. F. (1988). Basic issues and principles in classroom assessment. In J. H. McMillan (Ed.), *New directions for teaching and learning: No. 34. Assessing students' learning* (pp. 5-17). San Francisco, CA: Jossey-Bass.

West, D. C., Pomeroy, J. R., & Park, J. K. (2000). Critical thinking in graduate medical education: A role for concept mapping assessment? *Journal of the American Medical Association, 284*(9), 1105–1110.

Whimbey, A., & Lochhead, J. (1999). *Problem solving and comprehension*. Mahwah, NJ: Erlbaum.

Whitton, N. (2014). *Digital games and learning: Research and theory*. London: Routledge.

Wieman, C. E. (2007). Why not try a scientific approach to science education? *Change, 39*(5), 9–15.

Wieman, C. E. (2014). Large-scale comparison of science teaching methods send clear message. *Proceedings of the National Academy of Sciences USA, 111*(23), 8319–8320. Retrieved from http://www.pnas.org/content/111/23/8319.full.pdf+html

Wieman, C. (2015). A better way to evaluate undergraduate teaching. *Change, 47*(1), 6–15.

Wieman, C., & Gilbert, S. L. (2014). The Teaching Practices Inventory: A new tool for characterizing college and university teaching in mathematics and science. *Life Sciences Education, 13*, 552–569.

Wieman, C. E., Perkins, K., & Gilbert, S. (2010). Transforming science education at large research universities: A case study in progress. *Change, 42*(2), 7–14.

Wiesman, D. W. (2006). The effects of performance feedback and social reinforcement on up-selling at fast-food restaurants. *Journal of Organizational Behavior Management, 24*(6), 1–18.

Wiesman, D. W. (2007, April). *Achieving classroom civility through positive reinforcement: As easy as ABC*. Paper presented at the International Conference on College Teaching and Learning, Jacksonville, FL.

Wigfield, A., & Eccles, J. (2000). Expectancy-value theory of achievement motivation. *Contemporary Educational Psychology, 25*, 68–81.

Wiggins, G., & McTighe, J. (2005). *Understanding by design* (2nd ed.). New York, NY: Pearson.

Wilcox, K. R. (2014, November 7). The problem with learning technology. *Chronicle of Higher Education* Vitae. Retrieved from https://chroniclevitae.com/news/792-the-problem-with-learning-technology?cid=VTEVPMSED1

Wilke, R. R. (2003). The effect of active learning on student characteristics in a human physiology course for non-majors. *Advances in Physiology Education, 27*(4), 207–223.

Wilke, R. R., & Straits, W. J. (2001). The effects of discovery learning in a lower-division biology course. *Advances in Physiology Education, 25*(2), 62–69.

Wilkes, L., Cooper, K., Lewin, J., & Batts, J. (1999). Promoting science learning in BN learners in Australia. *Journal of Continuing Education in Nursing, 30*(1), 37–44.

Williams, W. M., & Ceci, S. J. (1997). "How am I doing?" Problems with student ratings of instructors and courses. *Change, 29*(5), 13–23.

Willingham, D. T. (2004, Summer). Reframing the mind: Howard Gardner and the theory of multiple intelligences. *Education Next, 4*(3). Retrieved from http://educationnext.org/reframing-the-mind/

Willingham, D. T.(2005a, Summer). Dovisual, auditory, and kinesthetic learners need visual, auditory, and kinesthetic instruction? *American Educator*. Retrieved from http://www.readingrockets.org/article/do-visual-auditory-and-kinesthetic-learners-need-visual-auditory-and-kinesthetic-instruction

Willingham, D. T. (2005b, Summer). Ask the cognitive scientist: How has the modality theory been tested? *American Educator*. Retrieved from http://www.aft.org/periodical/american-educator/summer-2005/how-has-modality-theory-been-tested

Willingham, D. T. (2007, Summer). Critical thinking: Why is it so hard to teach? *American Educator*, 8–19. Retrieved from http://www.aft.org/pubs-reports/xissues/summer07/Crit_Thinking.pdf

Wilson, J. H., & Ryan, R. G. (2013). Professor-student rapport scale: Six items predict student outcomes. *Teaching of Psychology, 40*(2), 130–133.

Wilson, J. H., & Taylor, K. W. (2001). Professor immediacy as behaviors associated with liking students. *Teaching of Psychology, 28,* 136–138.

Wilson, K., & Korn, J. H. (2007). Attention during lectures: Beyond ten minutes. *Teaching of Psychology, 34*(2), 85–89.

Wilson, M. A. (2008). *Syllabus for History of Life (Geology 100), Department of Geology, The College of Wooster.* Retrieved from http://www.wooster.edu/geology/HOL.html

Winn, W. (1987). Charts, graphs, and diagrams in educational materials. In D. M. Willows & H. A. Houghton (Eds.), *The psychology of illustration* (Vol. 1, pp. 152–198). New York, NY: Springer-Verlag.

Winn, W. (1991). Learning from maps and diagrams. *Educational Psychology Review, 3*(3), 211–247.

Winne, P. H., & Nesbit, J. C. (2010). The psychology of academic achievement. *Annual Review Psychology, 61,* 653–678. Retrieved from https://www.annualreviews.org/doi/full/10.1146/annurev.psych.093008.100348

Wirth, K. R. (n.d.). *Reading reflections. The Role of Metacognition in Teaching Geoscience: Topical Resources.* Retrieved from http://serc.carleton.edu/NAGTWorkshops/metacognition/activities/27560.html

Wirth, K. R., & Perkins, D. (2005). Knowledge surveys: The ultimate course design and assessment tool for faculty and students. In *Proceedings of the Innovations in the Scholarship of Teaching and Learning Conference*, Northfield, MN, April 2. Retrieved from http://www.macalester.edu/geology/wirth/WirthPerkinsKS.pdf

Wirth, K. R., & Perkins, D. (2008a, November 20). *Knowledge surveys.* Session presented at the National Association of Geoscience Teachers (NAGT) Workshops: The Role of Metacognition in Teaching Geoscience, Carleton College, Northfield, MN. Retrieved from http://serc.carleton.edu/NAGTWorkshops/assess/knowledgesurvey/

Wirth, K. R., & Perkins, D. (2008b). Learning to Learn. Retrieved from http://www.macalester.edu/academics/geology/wirth/learning.pdf

Wittmann, M. (2001). *Real-time physics dissemination project: Evaluation at test sites.* Retrieved from http://perlnet.umephy.maine.edu/research/RTPevaluation1.pdf

Wlodkowski, R. J. (1993). *Enhancing adult motivation to learn: A guide to improving instruction and increasing learner achievements.* San Francisco, CA: Jossey-Bass.

Wolcott, S. K. (2006). *Steps for better thinking; Steps for better thinking performance patterns; Templates for designing assignment questions.* Retrieved from http://www.wolcottlynch.com/EducatorResources.html

Wood, W. B., & Gentile, J. M. (2003). Teaching in a research context. *Science, 302*(5650), 1510. doi:10.1126/science.1091803

Woods, D. R. (2001). Issues in implementation of an otherwise conventional program. In D. Boud & G. Feletti (Eds.), *The challenge of problem-based learning* (2nd ed., pp. 173–179). London: Kogan Page.

Wright, W. A., Herteis, E. M., & Abernehy, B. (2001). *Learning through writing: A compendium of assignments and techniques.* Halifax, NS, Canada: Dalhousie University, Office of Instructional Development.

Wueste, D. E. (2008, August). *Ethics across the curriculum.* Faculty seminar conducted at Clemson University, SC.

Wurdinger, S., & Qureshi, M. (2015). Enhancing college students' life skills through project-based learning. *Innovative Higher Education, 40*(2), 297–286. Retrieved from http://link.springer.com/article/10.1007/s10755–014–9314–3

Wycoff, J. (1991). *Mind mapping: Your personal guide to exploring creativity and problem solving.* New York, NY: Berkley Books.

Yadav, A., Shaver, G. M., Meckl, P., & Firebaugh, S. (2014). Case-based instruction: Improving students' conceptual understanding through cases in a mechanical engineering course. *Journal of Research in Science Teaching, 51,* 659–677.

Yardley, J., Rodríguez, M. D., Bates, S. C., & Nelson, J. (2009). True confessions? Alumni's retrospective reports on undergraduate cheating behaviors. *Ethics and Behavior, 19*(1), 1–14. doi:10.1080/10508420802487096

Young, A. (2006). *Teaching writing across the curriculum* (4th ed.). Upper Saddle River, NJ: Pearson/Prentice Hall.

Young, J. R. (2003, August 8). Sssshhh. We're taking notes here. Colleges look for new ways to discourage disruptive behavior in the classroom. *Chronicle of Higher Education,* p. A29.

Young, J. R. (2004, November 12). When good technology means bad teaching. *Chronicle of Higher Education,* p. A31.

Young, J. R. (2009, November 22). Teaching with Twitter: Not for the faint of heart. *Chronicle of Higher Education.* Retrieved from http://chronicle.com/article/Teaching-With-Twitter-Not-/49230/

Young, J. R. (2010, March 28). High-tech cheating abounds, and professors bear some blame. *Chronicle of Higher Education.* Retrieved from http://chronicle.com/article/High-Tech-Cheating-on-Homework/64857/

Young, J. R. (2012, February 17). A tech-happy professor reboots after hearing his teaching advice isn't working. *Chronicle of Higher Education.* Retrieved from http://chronicle.com/article/A-Tech-Happy-Professor-Reboots/130741/

Zander, R. S., & Zander, B. (2000). *The art of possibility: Transforming professional and personal life.* Cambridge, MA: Harvard University Business Press.

Zax, D. (2009, October). Learning in 14-character bites. *ASEE Prism.* Retrieved from http://bit.ly/7bbPG5

Zeilik, M., Schau, C., Mattern, N., Hall, S., Teague, K. W., & Bisard, W. (1997). Conceptual astronomy: A novel model for teaching postsecondary science courses. *American Journal of Physics, 6*(10), 987–996.

Zhang, H., Yan, H.-M., Kendrick, K., & Li, C. (2012). Both lexical and non-lexical characters are processed during saccadic eye movements. *PLoS ONE* 7(9). doi:10.1371/journal.pone.0046

Zimmerman, B. J., Moylan, A., Hudesman, J., White, N., & Flugman, B. (2011). Enhancing self-reflection and mathematics achievement of at-risk students at an urban technical college. *Psychological Test and Assessment Modeling, 53*(1), 141–160. Retrieved from http://p16277.typo3server.info/fileadmin/download/ptam/1–2011_20110328/07_Zimmermann.pdf

Zlotkowski, E. (Ed.). (1998). *Successful service-learning programs: New models of excellence in higher education.* San Francisco, CA: Jossey-Bass.

Zubizarreta, J. (2004). *The learning portfolio: Reflective practice for improving student learning.* Bolton, MA: Anker.

Zubizarreta, J. (2009). *The learning portfolio: Reflective practice for improving student learning* (2nd ed.). San Francisco, CA: Jossey-Bass.

Zull, J. E. (2002). *The art of changing the brain: Enriching the practice of teaching by exploring the biology of learning.* Sterling, VA: Stylus.

Zull, J. E. (2011). *From brain to mind: Using neuroscience to guide change in education.* Sterling, VA: Stylus.

Zywno, M. S. (2003). A contribution to validation of score meaning for Felder-Soloman's Index of Learning Styles. In *Proceedings of the 2003 American Society for Engineering Education Annual Conference and Exposition* (Session 2351). Washington, DC: American Society for Engineering Education.